MORAL DILEMMAS
Readings in Ethics and Social Philosophy

Richard L. Purtill

Western Washington University

Wadsworth Publishing Company
Belmont, California
A Division of Wadsworth, Inc.

Philosophy Editor: Kenneth King

Production Editor: Jane Townsend

Managing Designer: Cynthia Bassett

Designer: Gary Head

Printed in the United States of America

1 2 3 4 5 6 7 8 9 10 — 89 88 87 86 85

ISBN 0-534-03366-0

Library of Congress Cataloging in Publication Data
Main entry under title:

Moral dilemmas.

   Includes index.
   1. Social ethics—Addresses, essays, lectures.
I. Purtill, Richard L., 1931–
HM216.M653   1984   170   84–3708
ISBN 0–534–03366–0

Contents

Preface

This is not the first book of readings of this kind, but I hope that it is the best. I wanted to improve on the strengths of previous books and learn from their mistakes. Some use selections that are too long to be manageable for class purposes; others cut selections to the bone so that more readings can be included. I have tried to choose selections that are long enough to make a point but short enough for students to read and comprehend before they are discussed in class.

Although all of these selections are fairly new, some of them have already become classics and must be included in any anthology claiming to do justice to certain topics. Other selections are unique to this book and represent points of view that might not otherwise be represented. Some of the articles have been recently published; others have been overlooked by anthologists. A few selections were written by men and women who are not professional philosophers but whose viewpoints should be recognized.

A special feature of this anthology is the large number of selections written by women and/or from a feminist perspective. Though only a small proportion of teachers of ethics and social philosophy are women, a large number of students will be especially interested in the work being done in these areas by women or from a feminist point of view.

I have tried, with every issue, to present ethical and social points of view based on religious beliefs or influenced by religious beliefs. Not all teachers of ethics and social philosophy will find such a point of view congenial, but they should realize that, in many cases, their students' views on moral and social issues are influenced by religious convictions, and they will appreciate topics discussed from this perspective.

The problems treated in this book are not the only topics of current debate, but they are issues that have been the subject of extensive discussion in philosophical books and journals in recent years. In each chapter I have tried to choose the presentations that best reflect every important position on the issues.

No teacher could hope to cover all of the material in this book in a one-quarter or one-semester course, but it seemed wise to include enough material to satisfy a wide range of interests. When I teach this course, I usually cover some topics of my own choice and then give the class a chance to choose some additional topics. Sections not covered in class can serve as the basis for term papers, so that students can work independently on topics of special interest to them.

I have tried to aid students and teachers by including chapter introductions, discussion questions, and suggestions for further reading. But the real importance of any book of readings lies in the quality of the readings themselves; the editor is mainly a master of ceremonies who introduces readers to the authors of the selections. I have included many authors with whose views I disagree, but none whose views I do not respect. I wish to thank the authors of these selections individually and collectively for their contributions and for their permission to present them in this book.

I would like to thank the manuscript reviewers: Karen Hanson, Indiana University; Christina Hoff, Clark University; Terrance McConnell, University of North Carolina at Greensboro; Louis P. Pojman, University of Texas; Kathy Squadrito, Indiana University–Purdue University at Fort Wayne; Steven W. White, East Tennessee State University. I wish to acknowledge the Bureau of Faculty Research at Western Washington University for its help in preparing the manuscript. Finally, my thanks to Dolores Sickles, who did the typing, to Ken King of Wadsworth Publishing Company, who encouraged me to undertake the project, and to Jane Townsend, my able and amiable production editor.

Introduction

Most systems of morality are in agreement on fundamental issues. They condemn murder, rape, and robbery, and praise fairness, promise keeping, and helping others. This is true of most philosophical theories about ethics as well as most moralities practiced by social groups or taught by religions. However, moral systems begin to disagree when fundamental values come into conflict. Is it legitimate to kill to avoid being killed? To kill to avoid rape? To kill to prevent robbery? Is it ever justifiable to break a promise in order to help someone or to avoid harming him or her? What if a fair distribution of some scarce good would leave each person too little of it to be of any use?

These cases of conflict of fundamental moral rules are what I call *moral dilemmas*. For an ethical theory to be workable in the real world it must have some reasonable way of resolving such moral dilemmas. By a *reasonable* way of resolving moral dilemmas, I mean one that can give reasons for deciding such problems one way rather than another, reasons that would have some weight with any impartial person.

Egoistic and subjectivistic theories do in a sense have a way of resolving moral dilemmas. The egoist decides on the basis of what is best for the egoist; the subjectivist in one way or another makes a decision on the basis of his or her own view of the situation. But egoistic or subjectivistic reasons are relative to the individual making the decision; they have no general application. One egoist will disagree with another: Egoist A wants what is best for A; Egoist B wants what is best for B. Two subjectivists may or may not find each other's view of or feelings about a given situation appealing, and by adopting a subjectivistic view they have ruled out the idea that there is some objective answer to the question of which point of view or set of feelings is better.

On the other hand, there are ethical theories that offer general principles for resolving moral dilemmas, principles that at least claim to offer consideration which would appeal to any impartial person. An act-utilitarian, for example, holds a basic principle that the best thing to do in any situation is what is for the greatest good of the greatest number. This principle offers a general way of resolving moral dilemmas, though its application to particular situations may be difficult or problematic.

Another ethical system that offers ways of resolving moral dilemmas is traditional Roman Catholic moral theology, which has a complex system of moral principles having an ultimate basis in religion. There is a whole field or subdivision of this traditional moral theology called *casuistry,* which is defined as that part of ethics which resolves cases of conscience, applying the general rules of religion and morality to particular instances which disclose special circumstances or conflicting duties.

This book is not concerned directly with the problem of justifying ethical theories. Rather, a number of efforts by contemporary philosophers to resolve particular moral dilemmas in a reasonable way are presented. Some of these philosophers would identify themselves with a particular ethical theory or a general religious or philosophical position. Others do not state their general ethical or philosophical commitments but simply address an ethical problem on the basis of principles that seem to them, for whatever reason, to recommend themselves to reasonable persons. However, in the introductions to these selections and in the discussion questions that follow them, questions are raised about just what ethical principles are invoked in these writings and how they might be justified.

One way of supporting an ethical theory is to show that the theory provides effective and reasonable solutions to a number of important moral dilemmas. The failure of an ethical theory to resolve moral dilemmas gives at least some evidence against that theory as a satisfactory system of ethics. Explicit conclusions about ethical theories are not drawn in this book, but the reader may very well come to the conclusion that certain theories give more satisfactory answers than others.

PART I

MATTERS OF LIFE AND DEATH

In almost every moral code a prohibition against killing other human beings is a basic principle. But it is a principle usually regarded as having some legitimate exceptions. The most frequently encountered exceptions are killing in war and execution of certain kinds of criminals. In the Old Testament, for instance, the Ten Commandments include "Thou shalt not kill," but within a few chapters of this commandment the death penalty is commanded for certain crimes and there are accounts of wars waged by the ancient Jewish people, which they regarded as having God's approval. A third exception regarded as legitimate in some but not all systems of morality is "last resort" killing of oneself or a loved one when further living would be intolerable—that is, suicide or euthanasia. The Judeo-Christian tradition regards suicide as wrong, but the classical Greek and Roman ethical tradition regarded it as legitimate and even in some cases as noble and praiseworthy.

In the modern age these matters of life and death have become even more problematic. Nuclear weapons make it possible to kill great numbers of people in a short time and make it almost impossible to separate the killing of combatants from the killing of innocent noncombatants. Modern advances in psychology and psychiatry have raised doubts about the responsibility of criminals. And contemporary medical technology has made it possible to keep people alive in situations in which at least some people would prefer not to be kept alive, adding new dimensions to the problems of suicide and euthanasia.

A problem closely related to the problems treated in this part is abortion. But since one of the key questions in the abortion debate is whether abortion is the killing of a human being, discussing it with the issues of life and death might prejudge the issue. Instead, it is considered at the beginning of Part II and can be discussed after or along with the problems of this part. Some philosophers would consider the killing of animals along with the killing of humans, but this problem is saved for Part III, where it is discussed in connection with other problems about our relation to the nonhuman environment.

The section on war and nuclear deterrence includes some selections on the problems raised by war in general as well as those raised specifically by nuclear war and the threat of nuclear war. Many of these issues assume greater or less importance from year to year and from country to country. I have tried to use reasonably timeless selections, but parts of some selections may refer to events and problems that are no longer in the forefront of public interest. A discussion of the issues that are currently most pressing would enhance the study of these topics.

The section on punishment and the death penalty includes selections on the general problems of punishment as well as selections specifically on the death penalty. In the section on suicide and euthanasia I have included selections that focus mainly on suicide and selections that focus mainly on euthanasia. In each case, as with the section on war and nuclear deterrence, it would be very difficult and not very useful to discuss one topic without bringing in the other. And a discussion of current topics of interest would be an excellent supplement.

1

War and Nuclear Deterrence

Hardly any reasonable person would take the view that it is perfectly acceptable for a nation to go to war any time it was in that nation's interest to do so, just as hardly any reasonable person would say that it is perfectly acceptable for an individual to use violence against other individuals whenever it was in his or her interest to do so. Even nations that start wars try to justify their actions by claiming they had no choice or by saying their opponents threatened or oppressed them. Similarly, once a war has begun, few would say that absolutely any action necessary to win the war is justified; most people would agree that some restrictions must be placed on what can be done in a war. One traditional list of the restrictions that must be placed on war are the so-called conditions for a just war. These grew out of centuries of discussions of what was allowable in war and represent at least a starting point for discussions of whether a given war can be justified. These conditions are as follows: Nation A is justified in waging war with Nation B if and only if:

1. Nation A has been attacked by Nation B or is going to the aid of Nation C, which has been attacked by Nation B.

2. The war has been legally declared by the properly constituted authorities of Nation A.

3. The intentions of Nation A in waging the war are confined to repelling the attack by Nation B and establishing a peace fair to all.

4. Nation A has a reasonable hope of success in repelling the attack and establishing a just peace.

5. Nation A cannot secure these ends without waging war; it has considered or tried all other means and wages war only as a last resort.

6. The good done by Nation A waging war against Nation B can reasonably be expected to outweigh the evil done by waging war.

7. Nation A does not use or anticipate using any means of waging war that are themselves immoral, such as the avoidable killing of innocent persons.

Many philosophers have held that it is justifiable to fight a war only if *all* of these conditions are satisfied.

Since the discovery and development of nuclear weapons people have begun to ask whether under modern conditions it is possible to satisfy all of these conditions and whether any war waged with nuclear weapons could possibly be a "just war." And if a war using nuclear weapons is unjust, can it be right to stockpile nuclear weapons and to threaten to use them, even if such a threat seems necessary to protect a country?

In the face of such problems some have taken the position of either total or limited *pacifism*. Total pacifism can be defined as the view that all wars are wrong under all circumstances. Limited pacifism is hard to distinguish from a just war view, since proponents of the just war view would agree that *some* wars are unjustified. But one popular form of limited pacifism is the view that under modern conditions every war is unjustified, since even a limited war fought with conventional weapons may spark a nuclear holocaust.

In the selections in this chapter none of the philosophers represented take a totally pro-war or a totally pacifistic view. In fact, Jan Narveson argues that pacifism is a view that cannot be consistently held, since if the use of violence is an evil we must be willing to use a lesser amount of violence to prevent a greater amount of violence. Elizabeth Anscombe takes a view of war less restrictive than the just war view, arguing, for example, that it can be justifiable to attack one's opponent first. However, she argues that the prohibition against taking innocent life is absolute, and if we cannot wage war under modern conditions without violating this prohibition we should renounce war.

The United States' policy of nuclear deterrence under Ronald Reagan's administration is presented in his two speeches, in which he explains his administration's justification for that policy. Douglas Lackey investigates the pros and cons of nuclear deterrence "to examine the extent to which we can rest content with the present strategic *détente*." The section closes with a portion of the 1983 pastoral letter by the Catholic Bishops of the United States, which deals with a number of the points raised in the earlier selections in the light of traditional and contemporary Catholic teaching. This pastoral letter has occasioned a great deal of discussion both inside and outside of the Catholic community.

Pacifism: A Philosophical Analysis

Jan Narveson

Several different doctrines have been called "pacifism," and it is impossible to say anything cogent about it without saying which of them one has in mind. I must begin by making it clear, then, that I am limiting the discussion of pacifism to a rather narrow band of doctrines, further distinctions among which will be brought out below. By "pacifism," I do *not* mean the theory that violence is evil. With appropriate restrictions, this is a view that every person with any pretensions to morality doubtless holds: Nobody thinks that we have a right to inflict pain wantonly on other people. The pacifist goes a very long step further. *His* belief is not only that violence is evil but also that it is morally wrong to use force to resist, punish, or prevent violence. This further step makes pacifism a radical moral doctrine. What I shall try to establish below is that it is in fact, more than merely radical—it is actually incoherent because self-contradictory in its fundamental intent. I shall also suggest that several moral attitudes and psychological views which have tended to be associated with pacifism as I have defined it do not have any necessary connection with that doctrine. Most proponents of pacifism, I shall argue, have tended to confuse these different things, and that confusion is probably what accounts for such popularity as pacifism has had.

It is next in order to point out that the pacifistic attitude is a matter of degree, and this in two respects. In the first place, there is the question: How much violence should not be resisted, and what degree of force is one not entitled to use in resisting, punishing, or preventing it? Answers to this question will make a lot of difference. For example, everyone would agree that there are limits to the kind and degree of force with which a particular degree of violence is to be met: we do not have a right to kill someone for rapping us on the ribs, for example, and yet there is no tendency toward pacifism in this. We might go further and maintain, for example, that capital punishment, even for the crime of murder, is unjustified without doing so on pacifist grounds. Again, the pacifist should say just what sort of a reaction constitutes a forcible or violent one. If somebody attacks me with his fists and I pin his arms to his body with wrestling holds which restrict him but cause him no pain, is that all right in the pacifist's book? And again, many non-pacifists could consistently maintain that we should avoid, to the extent that it is possible, inflicting a like pain on those who attempt to inflict pain on us. It is unnecessary to be a pacifist merely in order to deny the moral soundness of the principle, "an eye for an eye and a tooth for a tooth." We need a clarification, then, from the pacifist as to just how far he is and is not willing to go. But this need should already make us pause, for surely the pacifist cannot draw these lines in a merely arbitrary manner. It is his reasons for drawing the ones he does that count, and these are what I propose to discuss below.

The second matter of degree in respect of which the pacifist must specify his doctrine concerns the question: Who ought not to resist violence with force? For example, there are pacifists who would only claim that they themselves ought not to. Others would say that

From *Ethics*, vol. 75 (1965). Rewritten by the author, including the insertion of part of a subsequent article, "Is Pacifism Consistent?," from *Ethics*, vol. 78 (1968). Used by permission of the University of Chicago Press and the author.

only pacifists ought not to, or that all persons of a certain type, where the type is not specified in terms of belief or nonbelief in pacifism, ought not to resist violence with force. And finally, there are those who hold that everyone ought not to do so. We shall see that considerations about this second variable doom some forms of pacifism to contradiction.

My general program will be to show that (1) only the doctrine that everyone ought not to resist violence with force is of philosophical interest among those doctrines known as "pacifism"; (2) that doctrine, if advanced as a moral doctrine, is logically untenable; and (3) the reasons for the popularity of pacifism rest on failure to see exactly what the doctrine is. The things which pacifism wishes to accomplish, insofar as they are worth accomplishing, can be managed on the basis of quite ordinary and conservative moral principles.

Let us begin by being precise about the kind of moral force the principle of pacifism is intended to have. One good way to do this is to consider what it is intended to deny. What would nonpacifists, which I suppose includes most people, say of a man who followed Christ's suggestion and, when unaccountably slapped, simply turned the other cheek? They might say that such a man is either a fool or a saint. Or they might say, "It's all very well for him to do that, but it's not for me"; or they might simply shrug their shoulders and say, "Well, it takes all kinds, doesn't it?" But they would *not* say that a man who did that ought to be punished in some way; they would not even say that he had done anything wrong. In fact, as I have mentioned, they would more likely than not find something admirable about it. The point, then, is this: The non-pacifist does *not* say that it is your *duty* to resist violence with force. The non-pacifist is merely saying that there's nothing wrong with doing so, that one has every right to do so if he is so inclined. Whether we wish to add that a person would be foolish or silly to do so is quite another question, one on which the non-pacifist does not *need* to take any particular position.

Consequently, a genuine pacifist cannot merely say that we may, if we wish, prefer not to resist violence with force. Nor can he merely say that there is something admirable or saintly about not doing so, for, as pointed out above, the non-pacifist could perfectly well agree with that. He must say, instead, that, for whatever class of people he thinks it applies to, there is something positively wrong about meeting violence with force. He must say that, insofar as the people to whom his principle applies resort to force, they are committing a breach of moral duty—a very serious thing to say. Just how serious, we shall ere long see.

Next, we must understand what the implications of holding pacifism as a moral principle are, and the first such implication requiring our attention concerns the matter of the size of the class of people to which it is supposed to apply. It will be of interest to discuss two of the four possibilities previously listed, I think. The first is that in which the pacifist says that only pacifists have the duty of pacifism. Let us see what this amounts to.

If we say that the principle of pacifism is the principle that all and only pacifists have a duty of not opposing violence with force, we get into a very odd situation. For suppose we ask ourselves, "Very well, which people are the pacifists then?" The answer will have to be "All those people who believe that pacifists have the duty not to meet violence with force." But surely one could believe that a certain class of people, whom we shall call "pacifists," have the duty not to meet violence with force without believing that one ought not, oneself, to meet violence with force. That is to say, the "principle" that pacifists ought to avoid meeting violence with force, is circular: It presupposes that one already knows who the pacifists are. Yet this is precisely what that statement of the principle is supposed to answer! We are supposed to be able to say that anybody who believes that principle is a pacifist; yet, as we have seen, a person could very well believe that a certain class of people called "pacifists" ought not to meet violence with force without believing that he himself ought not to meet violence with force. Thus everyone could be a "pacifist" in the sense of believing that statement and yet no one believes that he *himself* (or anyone in particular) ought to avoid meeting violence with force. Consequently, pacifism cannot be specified in that way. A pacifist must be a person who believes either that he himself (at least) ought not to meet force with force or that some larger class of persons, perhaps everyone, ought not to meet force with force. He would then be believing something definite, and we are then in a position to ask why.

Incidentally, it is worth mentioning that when people say things such as "Only pacifists have the duty of pacifism," "Only Catholics have the duties of Catholicism," and, in general, "Only *X*-ists have the duties of *X*-ism" they probably are falling into a trap which catches a good many people. It is, namely, the mistake of supposing that what it *is* to have a certain duty is to *believe* that you have a certain duty. The untenability of this is parallel to the untenability of the previously mentioned attempt to say what pacifism is. For, if having a duty is believing that you have a certain duty, the question arises, "*What* does such a person believe?" The answer that must be given if we follow this analysis would then be, "He believes that he believes that he has a certain duty"; and so on, ad infinitum.

On the other hand, one might believe that having a duty does not consist in believing that one has and yet believe that only those people really have the duty who believe that they have it. But in that case, we would, being conscientious, perhaps want to ask the question, "Well, *ought* I to believe that I have that duty, or oughtn't I?" If you say that the answer is "Yes," the reason cannot be that you already do believe it, for you are asking whether you *should*. On the other hand, the answer "No" or "It doesn't make any difference—it's up to you," implies that there is really no reason for doing the thing in question at all. In short, asking whether I ought to believe that I have a duty to do *x*, is equivalent to asking whether I should *do x*. A person might very well believe that he ought to do *x* but be wrong. It might be the case that he really ought *not* to do *x*; in that case the fact that he believes he ought to do *x*, far from being a reason why he ought to do it, is a reason for us to point out his error. It also, of course, presupposes that he has some reason other than his belief for thinking it is his duty to do *x*.

Having cleared this red herring out of the way, we must consider the view of those who believe that they themselves have a duty of pacifism and ask ourselves the question: What general kind of reason must a person have for supposing a certain type of act to be *his* duty, in a moral sense? Now, one answer he might give is that pacifism as such is a duty, that is, that meeting violence with force is, as such, wrong. In that case, however, what he thinks is not merely that *he* has this duty, but that *everyone* has this duty.

Now he might object, "Well, but no; I don't mean that everyone has it. For instance, if a man is defending, not himself, but *other* people, such as his wife and children, then he has a right to meet violence with force." Now this, of course, would be a very important qualification to his principle and one of a kind which we will be discussing in a moment. Meanwhile, however, we may point out that he evidently still thinks that, if it weren't for certain more important duties, everyone would have a duty to avoid meeting violence with force. In other words, he then believes that, other things being equal, one ought not to meet violence with force. He believes, to put it yet another way, that if one does meet violence with force, one must have a special excuse or justification of a moral kind; then he may want to give some account of just which excuses and justifications would do. Nevertheless, he is now holding a general principle.

Suppose, however, he holds that no one *else* has this duty of pacifism, that only he himself ought not to meet force with force, although it is quite all right for others to do so. Now if this is what our man feels, we may continue to call him a "pacifist," in a somewhat attenuated sense, but he is then no longer holding pacifism as a *moral* principle or, indeed, as a principle at all.[1] For now his disinclination for violence is essentially just a matter of taste. I like pistachio ice cream, but I wouldn't dream of saying that other people have a duty to eat it; similarly, this man just doesn't *like* to meet force with force, although he wouldn't dream of insisting that others act as he does. And this is a secondary sense of "pacifism," first, because pacifism has always been advocated on moral grounds and, second, because non-pacifists can easily have this same feeling. A person might very well feel squeamish, for example, about using force, even in self-defense, or he might not be able to bring himself to use it even if he wants to. But none of these has anything to do with asserting pacifism to be a duty. Moreover, a mere attitude could hardly license a man to refuse military service if it were required of him, or to join ban-the-bomb crusades, and so forth. (I fear, however, that such attitudes have sometimes caused people to do those things.)

And, in turn, it is similarly impossible to claim that your support of pacifism is a moral one if your position is that a certain selection of people, but no one else, ought not to meet force with force, even though you are unprepared to offer any reason whatever for this selection. Suppose, for example, that you hold that only the Arapahoes, or only the Chinese, or only people more than six feet high have this "duty." If such were the case, and no reasons offered at all, we could only conclude that you had a very peculiar attitude toward the Arapahoes, or whatever, but we would hardly want to say that you had a moral principle. Your "principle" amounts to saying that these particular individuals happen to have the duty of pacifism just because they are the individuals they are, and this, as Bentham would say, is the "negation of all principle." Of course, if you meant that somehow the property of being over six feet tall *makes* it your duty not to use violence, then you have a principle, all right, but a very queer one indeed unless you can give some further reasons. Again, it would not be possible to distinguish this from a sheer attitude.

Pacifism, then, must be the principle that the use of force to meet force is wrong *as such*, that is, that nobody may do so unless he has a special justification.

There is another way in which one might advocate a sort of "pacifism," however, which we must also dispose of before getting to the main point. One might argue that pacifism is desirable as a tactic: that, as a matter of fact, some good end, such as the reduction of violence itself, is to be achieved by "turning the other cheek." For example, if it were the case that turning the other cheek caused the offender to break down and repent, then that would be a very good reason for behaving "pacifistically." If unilateral disarmament causes the other side to disarm, then certainly unilateral disarmament would be a desirable policy. But note that its desirability, if this is the argument, is due to the fact that peace is desirable, a moral position which anybody can take, pacifist or no, plus the purely contingent fact that this policy causes the other side to disarm, that is, it brings about peace.

And, of course, that's the catch. If one attempts to support pacifism, because of its probable effects, then one's position depends on what the effects are. Determining what they are is a purely empirical matter, and, consequently, one could not possibly be a pacifist as a matter of pure principle if his reasons for supporting pacifism are merely tactical. One must, in this case, submit one's opinions to the governance of fact.

It is not part of my intention to discuss matters of fact, as such, but it is worthwhile to point out that the general history of the human race certainly offers no support for the supposition that turning the other cheek always produces good effects on the aggressor. Some aggressors, such as the Nazis, were apparently just "egged on" by the "pacifist" attitude of their victims. Some of the S.S. men apparently became curious to see just how much torture the victim would put up with before he began to resist. Furthermore, there is the possibility that, while pacifism might work against some people (one might cite the British, against whom pacifism in India was apparently rather successful—but the British are comparatively nice people), it might fail against others (e.g., the Nazis).

A further point about holding pacifism to be desirable as a tactic is that this could not easily support the position that pacifism is a *duty*. The question whether we have no *right* to fight back can hardly be settled by noting that not to fight back might cause the aggressor to stop fighting. To prove that a policy is a desirable one because it works is not to prove that it is *obligatory* to follow it. We surely need considerations a good deal less tenuous than this to prove such a momentous contention as that we have no *right* to resist.

It appears, then, that to hold the pacifist position as a genuine, full-blooded moral principle is to hold that nobody has a right to fight back when attacked, that fighting back is inherently evil, as such. It means that we are all mistaken in supposing that we have a right of self-protection. And, of course, this is an extreme and extraordinary position in any case. It appears to mean, for instance, that we have no right to punish criminals, that all of our machinery of criminal justice is, in fact, unjust. Robbers, murderers, rapists, and miscellaneous delinquents ought, on this theory, to be let loose.

Now, the pacifist's first move, upon hearing this, will be to claim that he has been misrepresented. He might say that it is only one's *self* that one has no right to defend, and that one may legitimately fight in order to defend other people. This qualification cannot be made by those pacifists who qualify as conscientious objectors, of course, for the latter are refusing to defend their fellow citizens and not merely themselves. But this is comparatively trivial when we contemplate the next objection to this amended version of the theory. Let us now ask ourselves what it is about attacks on *other* people which could possibly justify *us* in defending them, while we are not justified in defending ourselves? It cannot be the mere fact that they are other people than ourselves, for, of course, everyone is a different person from everyone else, and if such a consideration could ever of itself justify anything at all it could also justify anything whatever. That mere difference of person, as such, is of no moral importance, is a presupposition of anything that can possibly pretend to be a moral theory.

Instead of such idle nonsense, then, the pacifist would have to mention some specific characteristic which every *other* person has which we lack and which justifies us in defending them. But this, alas, is impossible, for, while there may be some interesting difference between *me* on the one hand and everyone else on the other, the pacifist is not merely addressing himself to me. On the contrary, as we have seen, he has to address himself to everyone. He is claiming that each person has no right to defend himself, although he does have a right to defend other people. And, therefore, what is needed is a characteristic which distinguishes *each* person from everyone else, and not just *me* from everyone else—which is plainly self-contradictory.

Again, then, the pacifist must retreat in order to avoid talking nonsense. His next move might be to say that we have a right to defend all those who are not able to defend themselves. Big, grown-up men who are able to defend themselves ought not to do so, but they ought to defend mere helpless children who are unable to defend themselves.

This last, very queer theory could give rise to some amusing logical gymnastics. For instance, what about groups of people? If a group of people who cannot defend themselves singly can defend themselves together, then when it has grown to that size ought it to stop defending itself? If so, then every time a person *can* defend someone else, he would form with the person being defended a "defensive unit" which was able to defend itself, and thus would by this very presence debar himself from making the defense. At this rate, no one will ever get defended, it seems: The defenseless people by definition cannot defend themselves, while those who can defend them would enable the group consisting of the defenders and the defended to defend themselves, and hence they would be obliged not to do so.

Such reflections, however, are merely curious shadows of a much more fundamental and serious logical problem. This arises when we begin to ask: But why should even defenseless people be defended? If resisting violence is inherently evil, then how can it suddenly become permissible when we use it on behalf of other people? The fact that they are defenseless cannot possibly account for this, for it follows from the theory in question that everyone ought to put himself in the position of people who are defenseless by refusing to defend himself. This type of pacifist, in short, is using the very characteristic (namely, being in a state of not defending oneself) which he wishes to encourage in others as a reason for denying it in the case of those who already have it (namely, the defenseless). This is surely inconsistent.

To attempt to be consistent, at least, the pacifist is forced to accept the characterization of him at which we tentatively arrived. He must say that no one ought ever to be defended against attack. The right of self-defense can be denied coherently only if the right of defense, in general, is denied. This in itself is an important conclusion.

It must be borne in mind, by the way, that I have not said anything to take exception to the man who simply does not wish to defend himself. So long as he does not attempt to make his pacifism into a principle, one cannot accuse him of any inconsistency, however much one might wish to say that he is foolish or eccentric. It is solely with moral principles that I am concerned here.

We now come to the last and most fundamental problem of all. If we ask ourselves what the point of pacifism is, what gets it going, so to speak, the answer is, of course, obvious enough: opposition to violence. The pacifist is generally thought of as the man who is so much opposed to violence that he will not even use it to defend himself or anyone else. And it is precisely this characterization which I wish to show is morally inconsistent.

To begin with, we may note something which at first glance may seem merely to be a matter of fact, albeit one which should worry the pacifist, in our latest characterization of him. I refer to the commonplace observation that, generally speaking, we measure a man's degree of opposition to something by the amount of effort he is willing to put forth against it. A man could hardly be said to be dead set against something if he is not willing to lift a finger to keep it from going on. A person who claims to be completely opposed to something yet does nothing to prevent it would ordinarily be said to be a hypocrite.

As facts, however, we cannot make too much of these. The pacifist could claim to be willing to go to any length, short of violence, to prevent violence. He might, for instance, stand out in the cold all day long handing out leaflets (as I have known some to do), and this would surely argue for the sincerity of his beliefs.

But would it really?

Let us ask ourselves, one final time, what we are claiming when we claim that violence is morally wrong and unjust. We are, in the first place, claiming that a person *has no right* to indulge in it, as such (meaning that he has no right to indulge in it, *unless* he has an overriding justification). But what do we mean when we say that he has no right to indulge in it? Violence, of the type we are considering, is a two-termed affair; one does violence *to* somebody; one cannot simply "do violence." It might be oneself, of course, but we are not primarily interested in those cases, for what makes it wrong to commit violence is that it harms the people to whom it is done. To say that it is wrong is to say that those to whom it is done have a right *not* to have it done to them. (This must again be qualified by pointing out that this is so only if they have done nothing to merit having that right abridged.)

Yet what could that right to their own security, which people have, possibly consist in if not a right at least to be protected from whatever violence might be offered them? But lest the reader think that this is a gratuitous assumption, note carefully the reason why having a right involves having a right to be defended from breaches of that right. It is because the prevention of infractions of that right is precisely what one has a right to when one has a right at all. A right just *is* a status justifying preventive action. To say that you have a right to X but that no one has any justification whatever for preventing people from depriving you of it, is self-contradictory. If you claim a right to X, then to describe some action as an act of depriving you of X, is logically to imply that its absence is one of the things that you have a right to.

Thus far it does not follow logically that we have a right to use force in our own or anyone's defense. What does follow logically is that one has a right to whatever may be necessary to prevent infringements of his right. One might at first suppose that the universe *could* be so constructed that it is never necessary to use force to prevent people who are bent on getting something from getting it.

Yet even this is not so, for when we speak of "force" in the sense in which pacifism is concerned with it, we do not mean merely physical "force." To call an action a use of force is not merely to make a reference to the laws of mechanics. On the contrary, it is to describe whatever is being done as being a means to the infliction on somebody of something (ordinarily physical) which he does not want done to him; and the same is true for "force" in the sense in which it applies to war, assault and battery, and the like.

The proper contrary of "force" in this connection is "rational persuasion." Naturally, one way there *might* be of getting somebody not to do something he has no right to do is to convince him he ought not to do it or that it is not in his interest to do it. But it is inconsistent, I suggest, to argue that rational persuasion is the only morally permissible method of preventing violence. A pragmatic reason for this is easy enough to point to: Violent people are too busy being violent to be reasonable. We cannot engage in rational persuasion unless the enemy is willing to sit down and talk; but what if he isn't? One cannot contend that every human being can be persuaded to sit down and talk before he strikes, for this is not something we can determine just by reasoning; it is a question of observation. But these points are not strictly relevant anyway, for our question is not the empirical question of whether there is some handy way which can always be used to get a person to sit down and discuss moral philosophy when he is about to murder you. Our question is: *If* force is the only way to prevent violence in a given case, is its use justified *in that case?* This is a purely moral question which we can discuss without any special reference to matters of fact. And, moreover, it is precisely this question which we should have to discuss with the would-be violator. The point is that if a person can be rationally persuaded that he ought not to engage in violence, then precisely what he would be rationally persuaded of if we were to succeed would be the proposition that the use of force is justifiable to prevent him from doing so. For note that if we were to argue that only rational persuasion is permissible as a means of preventing him, we would have to face the question: Do we mean *attempted* rational persuasion, or *successful* rational persuasion, that is, rational persuasion which really does succeed in preventing him from acting? Attempted rational persuasion might fail (if only because the opponent is unreasonable), and then what? To argue that we have a right to use rational persuasion which also succeeds (i.e., we have a right to its success as well as to its use) is to imply that we have a right to prevent him from performing the act. But this, in turn, means that, if attempts at rational persuasion fail, we have a right to the use of force. Thus what we have a right to, if we ever have a *right* to anything, is not merely the use of rational persuasion to keep people from depriving you of the thing to which you have the right. We do indeed have a right to that, but we also have a right to anything else that might be necessary (other things being equal) to prevent the deprivation from occurring. And it is a logical truth, not merely a contingent one, that what *might* be necessary is *force*. (If merely saying something could miraculously deprive someone of the ability to carry through a course of action, then those speech-acts would be called a type of force, if a very mysterious one. And we could properly begin to oppose their use for precisely the same reasons as we now oppose violence.)

What this all adds up to, then, is that *if* we have any rights at all, we have a right to use force to prevent the deprivation of the thing to which we are said to have a right. But the pacifist, of *all* people, is the one most concerned to insist that we do have some rights, namely, the right not to have violence done to us. This is logically implied in asserting it to be a duty on everyone's part to avoid violence. And this is why the pacifist's position is self-contradictory. In saying that violence is wrong, one is at the same time saying that people have a right to its prevention, by force if necessary. Whether and to what extent it may be necessary is a question of fact, but, since it is a question of fact only, the moral right to use force on some possible occasions is established.[2]

We now have an answer to the question. How much force does a given threat of violence justify for preventive purposes? The answer, in a word, is "Enough." That the answer is this simple may at first sight seem implausible. One might suppose that some elaborate equation between the aggressive and the preventive force is needed: the punishment be proportionate to the crime. But this is a misunderstanding. In the first place, prevention and punishment are not the same, even if punishment is thought to be directed mainly toward prevention. The punishment of a particular crime logically cannot prevent *that* instance of the crime, since it presupposes that it has already been performed; and punishment need not involve the use of any violence at all, although law-enforcement officers in some places have a nasty tendency to assume the contrary. But preventive force is another matter. If a man threatens to kill me, it is desirable, of course, for me to try to prevent this by the use of the least amount of force sufficient to do the job. But I am justified even in killing him *if* necessary. This much, I suppose, is obvious to most people. But suppose his threat is much smaller: suppose that he is merely pestering me, which is a very mild form of aggression indeed. Would I be justified in killing him to prevent this, under any circumstances whatever?

Suppose that I call the police and they take out a warrant against him, and suppose that when the police come, he puts up a struggle. He pulls a knife or a gun, let us say, and the police shoot him in the ensuing battle. Has my right to the prevention of his annoying me extended to killing him? Well, not exactly, since the immediate threat in response to which he is killed is a threat to the lives of the policemen. Yet my annoyer may never have contemplated real violence. It is an unfortunate case of unpremeditated escalation. But this is precisely what makes the contention that one is justified in using enough force to do the job, whatever amount that may be, to prevent action which violates a right less alarming than at first sight it seems. For it is difficult to envisage a reason why extreme force is needed to prevent mild threats from realization except by way of escalation, and escalation automatically justifies increased use of preventive force.

The existence of laws, police, courts, and more or less civilized modes of behavior on the part of most of the populace naturally affects the answer to the question of how much force is necessary. One of the purposes of a legal system of justice is surely to make the use of force by individuals very much less necessary than it would otherwise be. If we try to think back to a "state of nature" situation, we shall have less difficulty envisaging the need for large amounts of force to prevent small threats of violence. Here Hobbes's contention that in such a state every man has a right to the life of every other becomes understandable. He was, I suggest, relying on the same principle as I have argued for here: that one has a right to use as much force as necessary to defend one's rights, which include the right of safety of person.

And needless to say, my arguments here do not give us any reason to modify the obviously vital principle that if force should be necessary, then one must use the least amount of it compatible with maintaining the rights of those being protected. There is, for example, no excuse for sending armed troops against unarmed students to contain protest marches and demonstrations.

I have said that the duty to avoid violence is only a duty, other things being equal. We might arrive at the same conclusion as we have above by asking the question: Which "other things" might count as being *un*equal? The answer to this is that whatever else they may be, the purpose of preventing violence from being done is necessarily one of these justifying conditions. That the use of force is never justified to prevent initial violence being done to one logically implies that there is nothing wrong with initial violence. We cannot characterize it as being wrong if preventive violence is not simultaneously being characterized as justifiable.

We often think of pacifists as being gentle and idealistic souls, which in its way is true enough. What I have been concerned to show is that they are also confused. If they attempt to formulate their position using our standard concepts of rights, their position involves a contradiction: Violence is wrong, *and* it is wrong to resist it. But the right to resist is precisely what having a right of person is, if it is anything at all.

Could the position be reformulated with a less "commital" concept of rights? I do not think so. It has been suggested[3] that the pacifist need not talk in terms of this "kind" of rights. He can affirm, according to this suggestion, simply that neither the aggressors nor the defenders "have" rights to what they do, that to affirm their not having them is simply to be against the use of force, without this entailing the readiness to use force if necessary to protect the said rights. But this will not do, I believe. For I have not maintained that having a right, or believing that one has a right, entails a *readiness* to defend that right. One has a perfect right not to resist violence to oneself if one is so inclined. But our question has been whether self-defense is justifiable, and not whether one's belief that violence is wrong entails a willingness or readiness to use it. My contention has been that such a belief does entail the justifiability of using it. If one came upon a community in which no sort of violence was ever resisted and it was claimed in that community that the non-resistance was a matter of conscience, we should have to conclude, I think, not that this was a community of saints, but rather that this community lacked the concept of justice—or perhaps that their nervous systems were oddly different from ours.

No position can ever be shown to contain a contradiction if we allow its upholder to interpret his language in any manner he chooses. Perhaps some pacifists have convinced themselves that to have a right is nothing more than to possess a certain peculiar non-natural property. I don't know. But what is this to the present subject? The language which the pacifist employs is not his private property, and his theories, if he should happen to have any, about the proper logical analysis of that language, are not entitled to any *special* hearing when we come to discuss what he is saying in it. What I want to know is: Is it anything but verbal hocus-pocus to affirm that we *have rights* but to deny that they ought ever to be defended? If a right isn't an entitlement to protection, then is it anything at all? This, I think, is the pacifist's dilemma. He would like to live in a world utterly at peace. So would most of us. But we do not, and so the question is, what to do about it? The pacifist's way is, as it were, to make Munich the cornerstone of our moral lives. We will act (or is that the right word here?) as if there were no violence anywhere, and then, hopefully, there will come a time when magic prevails and there is no more of it. By that time, the circle will no doubt also have been squared and infinity encompassed. But the rest of us, meanwhile, will wonder what has become of that supposed right to peace which we thought the pacifist was allowing us when we see him standing by, protesting at the top of his lungs, to be sure, but not *doing* anything about it, in the presence of violence by others.

It might be useful here to sum up the pacifist's problem, as I see it. To maintain the pacifist doctrine, I contend that one of the following three statements must be denied:

1. To will the end (as morally good) is to will the means to it (at least prima facie).

2. Other things being equal, the lesser evil is to be preferred to the greater.

3. There are no "privileged" moral persons: No person necessarily has a different status, counts for more or less than another as such, in matters of morals.

I claim what might be denied, that all of these may be defended on purely logical or "meta-ethical" grounds and that in any case the pacifist seems to be committed to them. He is committed to (1) because his objection to violence is that it produces suffering, unwanted pain, in the recipients. As far as I know, no pacifist objects to football or Indian leg-wrestling among consenting parties. He is committed to (2) because he holds that to inflict suffering is the greatest of evils and that *this* is why the claims of non-violence take precedence to those of, say, justice (if these are really different). And he is committed to (3) by virtue of his claiming to address this doctrine to everyone, on general moral grounds. But these three principles among them imply, as far as I can see, both the commitment to force when it is necessary to prevent more violence and also the conception of a right as an entitlement to defense. And they therefore leave pacifism, as a moral doctrine, in a logically untenable position.

Notes

[1] Compare, for example, K. Baier, *The Moral Point of View* (Ithaca: Cornell University Press, 1958), p. 191.

[2] This basic argument may be compared with a view of Kant's, to be found in the *Rechtslehre,* translated under the title *Metaphysical Elements of Justice* by J. Ladd, Library of Liberal Arts, pp. 35–36 (Introduction, D).

[3] I owe this suggestion to my colleague, Leslie Armour.

Discussion Questions

1. Narveson defines pacifism as the view that "it is morally wrong to use force to resist, punish, or prevent violence." How might people who would identify themselves as pacifists disagree with this definition? Is it a fair definition, or is it in some way loaded or unfair to the pacifist?

2. Narveson argues that as a matter of fact "the general history of the human certainly offers no support for the supposition that turning the other cheek always produces good effects on the aggressor." How might a believer in turning the other cheek reply to this? Is having a good effect on the aggressor the reason for turning the other cheek? What good effect might reasonably be expected?

3. Narveson argues that it is self-contradictory to hold that it is right to defend others but not right to defend yourself. What is his argument? How might it be criticized?

4. Many of Narveson's arguments seem to assume a certain view of moral principles. What is his view? What objections could be made to it?

5. Narveson says that if violence is wrong we have a right to be defended from violence by whatever means are effective. Does he argue for this key point in his article? If so, how? What counterarguments could be given on this point?

6. Criticize the use Narveson makes of his distinction between force and rational persuasion. How does he use this dichotomy to develop his argument?

7. What dangers might there be in Narveson's contention that we are justified in using whatever force is necessary to prevent violence?

8. How might a pacifist answer Narveson's rhetorical question "If a right isn't an entitlement to protection, then is it anything at all?"

9. Narveson lists three statements and argues that the pacifist must deny one of them. Could a pacifist maintain all three? If so, how? If not, which should a pacifist deny?

10. Try to construct a version of pacifism that escapes Narveson's criticisms. If you cannot do so, state why you find it impossible.

War and Murder

Elizabeth Anscombe

The Use of Violence by Rulers

Since there are always thieves and frauds and men who commit violent attacks on their neighbors and murderers, and since without law backed by adequate force there are usually gangs of bandits, and since there are in most places laws administered by people who command violence to enforce the laws against lawbreakers, the question arises: what is a just attitude to this exercise of violent coercive power on the part of rulers and their subordinate officers?

Two attitudes are possible: one, that the world is an absolute jungle and that the exercise of coercive power by rulers is only a manifestation of this; and the other, that it is both necessary and right that there should be this exercise of power, that through it the world is much less of a jungle than it could possibly be without it, so that one should in principle be glad of the existence of such power, and only take exception to its unjust exercise.

From *Nuclear Weapons: A Catholic Response*, edited by Walter Stein. Copyright © 1961 by the Merlin Press Ltd., published by Sheed & Ward, Inc., New York. Reprinted by permission of Andrews and McMeel, Inc.

It is so clear that the world is less of a jungle because of rulers and laws, and that the exercise of coercive power is essential to these institutions as they are now—all this is so obvious, that probably only Tennysonian conceptions of progress enable people who do not wish to separate themselves from the world to think that nevertheless such violence is objectionable, that some day, in this present dispensation, we shall do without it, and that the pacifist is the man who sees and tries to follow the ideal course, which future civilization must one day pursue. It is an illusion, which would be fantastic if it were not so familiar.

In a peaceful and law abiding country such as England, it may not be immediately obvious that the rulers need to command violence to the point of fighting to the death those that would oppose it; but brief reflection shows that this is so. For those who oppose the force that backs law will not always stop short of fighting to the death and cannot always be put down short of fighting to the death.

Then only if it is in itself evil violently to coerce resistant wills, can the exercise of coercive power by rulers be bad as such. Against such a conception, if it were true, the necessity and advantage of the exercise of such power would indeed be a useless plea. But that conception is one that makes no sense unless it is accompanied by a theory of withdrawal from the world as man's only salvation; and it is in any case a false one. We are taught that God retains the evil will of the devil within limits by violence: we are not given a picture of God permitting to the devil all that he is capable of. There is a current conception of Christianity as having revealed that the defeat of evil must always be by pure love without coercion; this at least is shown to be false by the foregoing consideration. And without the alleged revelation there could be no reason to believe such a thing.

To think that society's coercive authority is evil is akin to thinking the flesh evil and family life evil. These things belong to the present constitution of mankind; and if the exercise of coercive power is a manifestation of evil, and not the just means of restraining it, then human nature is totally depraved in a manner never taught by Christianity. For society is essential to human good; and society without coercive power is generally impossible.

The same authority which puts down internal dissension, which promulgates laws and restrains those who break them if it can, must equally oppose external enemies. These do not merely comprise those who attack the borders of the people ruled by the authority; but also, for example, pirates and desert bandits, and, generally, those beyond the confines of the country ruled whose activities are viciously harmful to it. The Romans, once their rule in Gaul was established, were eminently justified in attacking Britain, where were nurtured the Druids whose pupils infested northern Gaul and whose practices struck the Romans themselves as "dira immanitas." Further, there being such a thing as the common good of mankind, and visible criminality against it, how can we doubt the excellence of such a proceeding as that violent suppression of the man-stealing business[1] which the British government took it into its head to engage in under Palmerston? The present-day conception of "aggression," like so many strongly influential conceptions, is a bad one. Why *must* it be wrong to strike the first blow in a struggle? The only question is who is in the right.

Here, however, human pride, malice and cruelty are so usual that it is true to say that wars have mostly been mere wickedness on both sides. Just as an individual will constantly think himself in the right, whatever he does, and yet there is still such a thing as being in the right, so nations will constantly wrongly think themselves to be in the right—and yet there is still such a thing as their being in the right. Palmerston doubtless had no doubts in prosecuting the opium war against China, which was diabolical, just as he exulted in putting down the slavers. But there is no question but that he was a monster in the one thing, and a just man in the other.

The probability is that warfare is injustice, that a life of military service is a bad life, "militia or rather malitia," as St. Anselm called it. This probability is greater than the probability (which also exists) that membership of a police force will involve malice, because of the character of warfare: the extraordinary occasions it offers for viciously unjust proceedings on the part of military commanders and warring governments, which at the time attract praise and not blame from their people. It is equally the case that the life of a ruler is usually a vicious life: but that does not show that ruling is as such a vicious activity.

The principal wickedness which is a temptation to those engaged in warfare is the killing of the innocent, which may often be done with impunity and even to the glory of those who do it. In many places and times it has been taken for granted as a natural part of waging war: the commander, and especially the conqueror, massacres people by the thousand, either because this is part of his glory, or as a terrorizing measure, or as part of his tactics.

Innocence and the Right to Kill Intentionally

It is necessary to dwell on the notion of non-innocence here employed. Innocence is a legal notion; but here, the accused is not pronounced guilty under an existing code of law, under which he has been tried by an impartial judge, and therefore made the target of attack. There is hardly a possibility of this; for the administration of justice is something that takes place under the aegis of a sovereign authority; but in warfare—or the putting down by violence of civil disturbance—the sovereign authority is itself engaged as a party to the dispute and is not subject to a further earthly and temporal authority which can judge the issue and pronounce against the accused. The stabler the society, the rarer it will be for the sovereign authority to have to do anything but apprehend its internal enemy and have him tried; but even in the stablest society there are occasions when the authority has to fight its internal enemy to the point of killing, as happens in the struggle with external belligerent forces in international warfare, and then the characterization of its enemy as non-innocent has not been ratified by legal process.

This, however, does not mean that the notion of innocence fails in this situation. What is required, for the people attacked to be non-innocent in the relevant sense, is that they should themselves be engaged in an objectively unjust proceeding which the attacker has the right to make his concern, or—the commonest case—should be unjustly attacking him. Then he can attack them with a view to stopping them, and also their supply lines and armament factories. But people whose mere existence and activity supporting existence by growing crops, making clothes, etc. constitute an impediment to him—such people are innocent and it is murderous to attack them, or make them a target for an attack which he judges will help him towards victory. For murder is the deliberate killing of the innocent, whether for its own sake or as a means to some further end.

The right to attack with a view to killing is something that belongs only to rulers and those whom they command to do it. I have argued that it does belong to rulers precisely because of that threat of violent coercion exercised by those in authority which is essential to the existence of human societies. It ought not to be pretended that rulers and their subordinates do not choose[2] the killing of their enemies as a means, when it has come to fighting in which they are determined to win and their enemies resist to the point of killing; this holds even in internal disturbances.

When a private man struggles with an enemy he has no right to aim to kill him, unless in the circumstances of the attack on him he can be considered as endowed with the authority of the law and the struggle comes to that point. By a "private" man, I mean a man in a society; I am not speaking of men on their own, without government, in remote places; for such men are neither public servants nor "private." The plea of self-defense (or the defense of someone else) made by a private man who has killed someone else must in conscience—even if not in law—be a plea that the death of the other was not intended, but was a side effect of the measures taken to ward off the attack. To shoot to kill, to set lethal man-traps, or, say, to lay poison for someone from whom one's life is in danger, are forbidden. The deliberate choice of inflicting death in a struggle is the right only of ruling authorities and their subordinates.

In saying that a private man may not choose to kill, we are touching on the principle of "double effect." The denial of this has been the corruption of non-Catholic thought, and its abuse the corruption of Catholic thought. Both have disastrous consequences which we shall see. This principle is not accepted in English law: the law is said to allow no distinction between the foreseen and the intended consequences of an action. Thus, if I push a man over a cliff when he is menacing my life, his death is considered as intended by me, but the intention to be justifiable for the sake of self-defense. Yet the lawyers would hardly find the laying of poison tolerable as an act of self-defense, but only killing by a violent action in a moment of violence. Christian moral theologians have taught that even here one may not seek the death of the assailant, but may in default of other ways of self-defense use such violence as will in fact result in his death. The distinction is evidently a fine one in some cases: what, it may be asked, can the intention be, if it can be said to be absent in this case, except a mere wish or desire?

And yet in other cases the distinction is very clear. If I go to prison rather than perform some action, no reasonable person will call the incidental consequences of my refusal—the loss of my job, for example—intentional just because I knew they must happen. And in the case of the administration of a pain-relieving drug in mortal illness, where the doctor knows the drug may very well kill the patient if the illness does not do so first, the distinction is evident; the lack of it has led an English judge to talk nonsense about the administration of the drug's not having *really* been the cause of death in such a case, even though a post mortem shows it was. For everyone understands that it is a very different thing so to administer a drug, and to administer it with the intention of killing. However, the principle of double effect has more important applications in warfare, and I shall return to it later. . . .

Some Commonly Heard Arguments

There are a number of sophistical arguments, often or sometimes used on these topics, which need answering.

Where do you draw the line? As Dr. Johnson said, the fact of twilight does not mean you cannot tell day from night. There are borderline cases, where it is difficult to distinguish, in what is done, between means and what is incidental to, yet in the circumstances inseparable from, those means. The obliteration bombing of a city is not a borderline case.

The old "conditions for a just war" are irrelevant to the conditions of modern warfare, so that must be condemned out of hand. People who say this always envisage only major wars between the Great Powers, which Powers are indeed now "in blood stepp'd insofar" that it is unimaginable for there to be a war between them which is not a set of enormous massacres of civil populations. But these are not the only wars. Why is Finland so far free? At least partly because of the "posture of military preparedness" which, considering the character of the country, would have made subjugating the Finns a difficult and unreward- ing task. The offensive of the Israelis against the Egyptians in 1956 involved no plan of making civil populations the target of military attack.

In a modern war the distinction between combatants and non-combatants is meaningless, so an attack on anyone on the enemy side is justified. This is pure nonsense; even in war, a very large number of the enemy population are just engaged in maintaining the life of the country, or the sick, or aged, or children.

It must be legitimate to maintain an opinion—viz. that the destruction of cities by bombing is lawful—if this is argued by competent theologians and the Holy See has not pronounced. The argument from the silence of the Holy See has itself been condemned by the Holy See. . . . How could this be a sane doctrine in view of the endless twistiness of the human mind?

Whether a war is just or not is not for the private man to judge: he must obey his government. Sometimes this may be, especially as far as concerns causes of war. But the individual who joins in destroying a city, like a Nazi massacring the inhabitants of a village, is too obviously marked out as an enemy of the human race to shelter behind such a plea.

Finally, horrible as it is to have to notice this, we must notice that even the arguments about double effect—which at least show that a man is not willing openly to justify the killing of the innocent—are now beginning to look old-fashioned. Some Catholics are not scrupling to say that *anything* is justified in defense of the continued existence and liberty of the Church in the West. A terrible fear of communism drives people to say this sort of thing. "Our Lord told us to fear those who can destroy body and soul, not to fear the destruction of the body" was blasphemously said to a friend of mine; meaning: "so, we must fear Russian domination more than the destruction of people's bodies by obliteration bombing."

But whom did Our Lord tell us to fear, when he said: "I will tell you whom you shall fear" and "Fear not them that can destroy the body, but fear him who can destroy body and soul in hell"? He told us to fear God the Father, who can and will destroy the unrepentant disobedient, body and soul, in hell.

A Catholic who is tempted to think on the lines I have described should remember that the Church is the spiritual Israel: that is, that Catholics are what the ancient Jews were, salt for the earth and the people of God—and that what was true of some devout Jews of ancient times can equally well be true of us now: "You compass land and sea to make a convert, and when you have done so, you make him twice as much a child of hell as yourselves." Do Catholics sometimes think that they are immune from such a possibility? That the Pharisees—who sat in the seat of Moses and who were so zealous for the true religion—were bad in ways in which we cannot be bad if we are zealous? I believe they do. But our faith teaches no such immunity, it teaches the opposite. "We are in danger all our lives long." So we have to fear God and keep his commandments, and calculate what is for the best only within the limits of that obedience, knowing that the future is in God's power and that no one can snatch away those whom the Father has given to Christ.

It is not a vague faith in the triumph of "the spirit" over force (there is little enough warrant for that), but a definite faith in the divine promises, that makes us believe that the Church cannot fail. Those, therefore, who think they must be prepared to wage war with Russia involving the deliberate massacre of cities, must be prepared to say to God: "We had to break your law, lest your Church fail. We could not obey your commandments, for we did not believe your promises."

Notes

[1]It is ignorance to suppose that it takes modern liberalism to hate and condemn this. It is cursed and subject to the death penalty in the Mosaic law. Under that code, too, runaway slaves of all nations had asylum in Israel.

[2]The idea that they may lawfully do what they do, but should not *intend* the death of those they attack, has been put forward and, when suitably expressed, may seem high-minded. But someone who can fool himself into this twist of thought will fool himself into justifying anything, however atrocious, by means of it.

Discussion Questions

1. On what points would Anscombe and Narveson agree? On what points might they disagree?
2. What is the importance of Anscombe's distinction between those who do and those who do not wish to "separate themselves from the world"?
3. What is Anscombe's criticism of "the present-day conception of 'aggression' "? Does she give any argument? How might her view be criticized or supported?
4. What is the importance in Anscombe's argument of the principle that innocent persons must not be harmed? Is this principle argued for? How might it be criticized?
5. What points does Anscombe make about the doctrine of double effect? Criticize or support her view on this matter.
6. Are Anscombe's "commonly heard arguments" fairly stated? Develop a reply to Anscombe on behalf of the supporters of one of these arguments.
7. What is Anscombe's eventual conclusion about nuclear war? Do you agree or disagree? Give arguments for your position.

Peace and National Security: A New Defense

Ronald Reagan, *President of the United States*

Thank you for sharing your time with me tonight. The subject I want to discuss with you, peace and national security, is both timely and important—timely because I have reached a decision which offers a new hope for our children in the 21st century—a decision I will tell you about in a few minutes—and important because there is a very big decision that you

President Reagan's speech as made available by the White House. Delivered to the American people from the White House, Washington, D.C., March 23, 1983.

must make for yourselves. This subject involves the most basic duty that any President and any people share—the duty to protect and strengthen the peace.

At the beginning of this year, I submitted to the Congress a defense budget which reflects my best judgment, and the best understanding of the experts and specialists who advise me, about what we and our allies must do to protect our people in the years ahead.

That budget is much more than a long list of numbers, for behind all the numbers lies America's ability to prevent the greatest of human tragedies and preserve our free way of life in a sometimes dangerous world. It is part of a careful, long-term plan to make America strong again after too many years of neglect and mistakes. Our efforts to rebuild America's defenses and strengthen the peace began two years ago when we requested a major increase in the defense program. Since then the amount of those increases we first proposed has been reduced by half through improvements in management and procurement and other savings. The budget request that is now before the Congress has been trimmed to the limits of safety. Further deep cuts cannot be made without seriously endangering the security of the nation. The choice is up to the men and women you have elected to the Congress—and that means the choice is up to you.

Tonight I want to explain to you what this defense debate is all about, and why I am convinced that the budget now before the Congress is necessary, responsible and deserving of your support. And I want to offer hope for the future.

But first let me say what the defense debate is not about. It is not about spending arithmetic. I know that in the last few weeks you've been bombarded with numbers and percentages. Some say we need only a 5 percent increase in defense spending. The so-called alternate budget backed by liberals in the House of Representatives would lower the figure to 2 to 3 percent, cutting our defense spending by $163 billion over the next five years. The trouble with all these numbers is that they tell us little about the kind of defense program America needs or the benefits in security and freedom that our defense effort buys for us.

What seems to have been lost in all this debate is the simple truth of how a defense budget is arrived at. It isn't done by deciding to spend a certain number of dollars. Those loud voices that are occasionally heard charging that the Government is trying to solve a security problem by throwing money at it are nothing more than noise based on ignorance.

We start by considering what must be done to maintain peace and review all the possible threats against our security. Then a strategy for strengthening peace and defending against those threats must be agreed upon. And finally our defense establishment must be evaluated to see what is necessary to protect against any or all of the potential threats. The cost of achieving these ends is totaled up and the result is the budget for national defense.

There is no logical way you can say let's spend X billion dollars less. You can only say, which part of our defense measures do we believe we can do without and still have security against all contingencies? Anyone in the Congress who advocates a percentage or specific dollar cut in defense spending should be made to say what part of our defenses he would eliminate, and he should be candid enough to acknowledge that his cuts mean cutting our commitments to allies or inviting greater risk or both.

The defense policy of the United States is based on a simple premise: The United States does not start fights. We will never be an aggressor. We maintain our strength in order to deter and defend against aggression—to preserve freedom and peace.

Since the dawn of the atomic age, we have sought to reduce the risk of war by maintaining a strong deterrent and by seeking genuine arms control. Deterrence means simply this: Making sure any adversary who thinks about attacking the United States or our allies or our vital interests concludes that the risks to him outweigh any potential gains. Once he understands that, he won't attack. We maintain the peace through our strength; weakness only invites aggression.

This strategy of deterrence has not changed. It still works. But what it takes to maintain deterrence has changed. It took one kind of military force to deter an attack when we had far more nuclear weapons than any other power; it takes another kind now that the Soviets, for example, have enough accurate and powerful nuclear weapons to destroy virtually all of our missiles on the ground. Now this is not to say the Soviet Union is planning to make war on us. Nor do I believe a war is inevitable—quite the contrary. But what must be recognized is that our security is based on being prepared to meet all threats.

There was a time when we depended on coastal forts and artillery batteries because, with the weaponry of that day, any attack would have had to come by sea. This is a different world and our defenses must be based on recognition and awareness of the weaponry possessed by other nations in the nuclear age.

We can't afford to believe we will never be threatened. There have been two world wars in my lifetime. We didn't start them and, indeed, did everything we could to avoid being drawn into them. But we were ill-prepared for both—had we been better prepared, peace might have been preserved.

For 20 years, the Soviet Union has been accumulating enormous military might. They didn't stop when their forces exceeded all requirements of a legitimate defensive capability. And they haven't stopped now.

During the past decade and a half, the Soviets have built up a massive arsenal of new strategic nuclear weapons—weapons that can strike directly at the United States.

As an example, the United States introduced its last new intercontinental ballistic missile, the Minuteman III, in 1969, and we are now dismantling our even older Titan missiles. But what has the Soviet Union done in these intervening years? Well, since 1969, the Soviet Union has built five new classes of ICBM's, and upgraded these eight times. As a result, their missiles are much more powerful and accurate than they were several years ago and they continue to develop more, while ours are increasingly obsolete.

The same thing has happened in other areas. Over the same period, the Soviet Union built four new classes of submarine-launched ballistic missiles and over 60 new missile submarines. We built two new types of submarine missiles and actually withdrew 10 submarines from strategic missions. The Soviet Union built over 200 new Backfire bombers, and their brand new Blackjack bomber is now under development. We haven't built a new long-range bomber since our B-52's were deployed about a quarter of a century ago, and we've already retired several hundred of those because of old age. Indeed, despite what many people think, our strategic forces only cost about 15 percent of the defense budget.

Another example of what's happened: In 1978, the Soviets had 600 intermediate-range nuclear missiles based on land and were beginning to add the SS-20—a new, highly accurate mobile missile, with three warheads. We had none. Since then the Soviets have strengthened their lead. By the end of 1979, when Soviet leader Brezhnev declared "a balance now exists," the Soviets had over 800 warheads. We still had none. A year ago this month, Mr. Brezhnev pledged a moratorium, or freeze, on SS-20 deployment. But by last August, their 800 warheads had become more than 1,200. We still had none. Some freeze. At this time Soviet Defense Minister Ustinov announced "approximate parity of forces continues to exist." But the Soviets are still adding an average of three new warheads a week, and now have 1,300. These warheads can reach their targets in a matter of a few minutes. We still have none. So far, it seems that the Soviet definition of parity is a box score of 1,300 to nothing, in their favor.

So, together with our NATO allies, we decided in 1979 to deploy new weapons, beginning this year, as a deterrent to their SS-20's and as an incentive to the Soviet Union to meet us in serious arms control negotiations. We will begin that deployment late this year. At the same time, however, we are willing to cancel our program if the Soviets will dismantle theirs. This is what we have called a zero-zero plan. The Soviets are now at the negotiating table—and I think it's fair to say that without our planned deployments, they wouldn't be there.

Now let's consider conventional forces. Since 1974, the United States has produced 3,050 tactical combat aircraft. By contrast, the Soviet Union has produced twice as many. When we look at attack submarines, the United States has produced 27, while the Soviet Union has produced 61. For armored vehicles including tanks, we have produced 11,200. The Soviet Union has produced 54,000, a nearly 5-to-1 ratio in their favor. Finally, with artillery, we have produced 950 artillery and rocket launchers while the Soviets have produced more than 13,000, a staggering 14-to-1 ratio.

There was a time when we were able to offset superior Soviet numbers with higher quality. But today they are building weapons as sophisticated and modern as our own.

As the Soviets have increased their military power, they have been emboldened to extend that power. They are spreading their military influence in ways that can directly challenge our vital interests and those of our allies. . . .

This Soviet intelligence collection facility less than 100 miles from our coast is the largest of its kind in the world. The acres and acres of antenna fields and intelligence monitors are targeted on key U.S. military installations and sensitive activities. The installation, in Lourdes, Cuba, is manned by 1,500 Soviet technicians, and the satellite ground station allows instant communications with Moscow. This 28-square-mile facility has grown by more than 60 percent in size and capability during the past decade.

In western Cuba, we see [a] military airfield and its complement of modern Soviet-built MIG-23 aircraft. The Soviet Union uses this Cuban airfield for its own long-range reconnaissance missions, and earlier this month two modern Soviet antisubmarine warfare aircraft began operating from it. During the past two years, the level of Soviet arms exports to Cuba can only be compared to the levels reached during the Cuban missile crisis 20 years ago. . . .

Soviet military hardware . . . has made its way to Central America. [An] airfield with its MI-8 helicopters, antiaircraft guns and protected fighter sites is one of a number of military facilities in Nicaragua which has received Soviet equipment funneled through Cuba and reflects the massive military build-up going on in that country.

On the small island of Grenada, at the southern end of the Caribbean chain, the Cubans, with Soviet financing and backing, are in the process of building an airfield with a 10,000-foot runway. Grenada doesn't even have an air force. Who is it intended for? The Caribbean is a very important passageway for our international commerce and military lines of communication. More than half of all American oil imports now pass through the Caribbean. The rapid build-up of Grenada's military potential is unrelated to any conceivable threat to this island country of under 110,000 people, and totally at odds with the pattern of other eastern Caribbean States, most of which are unarmed. The Soviet-Cuban militarization of Grenada, in short, can only be seen as power projection into the region, and it is in this important economic and strategic area that we are trying to help the governments of El Salvador, Costa Rica, Honduras and others in their struggles for democracy against guerrillas supported through Cuba and Nicaragua. . . .

The Soviet Union is also supporting Cuban military forces in Angola and Ethiopia. They have bases in Ethiopia and South Yemen near the Persian Gulf oilfields. They have taken over the port we built at Cam Ranh Bay in Vietnam, and now, for the first time in history, the Soviet Navy is a force to be reckoned with in the South Pacific.

Some people may still ask: Would the Soviets ever use their formidable military power? Well, again, can we afford to believe they won't? There is Afghanistan, and in Poland, the Soviets denied the will of the people and, in so doing, demonstrated to the world how their military power could also be used to intimidate.

The final fact is that the Soviet Union is acquiring what can only be considered an offensive military force. They have continued to build far more intercontinental ballistic missiles than they could possibly need simply to deter an attack. Their conventional forces are trained and equipped not so much to defend against an attack as they are to permit sudden, surprise offensives of their own.

Our NATO allies have assumed a great defense burden, including the military draft in most countries. We are working with them and our other friends around the world to do more. Our defensive strategy means we need military forces that can move very quickly—forces that are trained and ready to respond to any emergency.

Every item in our defense program—our ships, our tanks, our planes, our funds for training and spare parts—is intended for one all-important purpose—to keep the peace. Unfortunately, a decade of neglecting our military forces had called into question our ability to do that.

When I took office in January 1981, I was appalled by what I found: American planes that could not fly and American ships that could not sail for lack of spare parts and trained personnel and insufficient fuel and ammunition for essential training. The inevitable result of all this was poor morale in our armed forces, difficulty in recruiting the brightest young Americans to wear the uniform and difficulty in convincing our most experienced military personnel to stay on.

There was a real question, then, about how well we could meet a crisis. And it was obvious that we had to begin a major modernization program to insure we could deter aggression and preserve the peace in the years ahead.

We had to move immediately to improve the basic readiness and staying power of our conventional forces, so they could meet—and therefore help deter—a crisis. We had to make up for lost years of investment by moving forward with a long-term plan to prepare our forces to counter the military capabilities our adversaries were developing for the future.

I know that all of you want peace and so do I. I know too that many of you seriously believe that a nuclear freeze would further the cause of peace. But a freeze now would make us less, not more, secure and would raise, not reduce, the risks of war. It would be largely unverifiable and would seriously undercut our negotiations on arms reduction. It would reward the Soviets for their massive military buildup while preventing us from modernizing our aging and increasingly vulnerable forces. With their present margin of superiority, why should they agree to arms reductions knowing that we were prohibited from catching up?

Believe me, it wasn't pleasant for someone who had come to Washington determined to reduce Government spending, but we had to move forward with the task of repairing our defenses or we would lose our ability to deter conflict now and in the future. We had to demonstrate to any adversary that aggression could not succeed and that the only real solution was substantial, equitable and effectively verifiable arms reduction—the kind we're working for right now in Geneva.

Thanks to your strong support, and bipartisan support from the Congress, we began to turn things around. Already we are seeing some very encouraging results. Quality recruitment and retention are up, dramatically—more high school graduates are choosing military careers and more experienced career personnel are choosing to stay. Our men and women in uniform at last are getting the tools and training they need to do their jobs.

Ask around today, especially among our young people, and I think you'll find a whole new attitude toward serving their country. This reflects more than just better pay, equipment and leadership. You the American people have sent a signal to these young people that it is once again an honor to wear the uniform. That's not something you measure in a budget, but it is a very real part of our nation's strength.

It will take us longer to build the kind of equipment we need to keep peace in the future, but we've made a good start.

We have not built a new long-range bomber for 21 years. Now we're building the B-1. We had not launched one new strategic submarine for 17 years. Now, we're building one Trident submarine a year. Our land-based missiles are increasingly threatened by the many huge, new Soviet ICBM's. We are determining how to solve that problem. At the same time, we are working in the Start and I.N.F. negotiations, with the goal of achieving deep reductions in the strategic and intermediate nuclear arsenals of both sides.

We have also begun the long-needed modernization of our conventional forces. The Army is getting its first new tank in 20 years. The Air Force is modernizing. We are rebuilding our Navy, which shrank from about 1,000 in the late 1960's to 453 ships during the 1970's. Our nation needs a superior Navy to support our military forces and vital interests overseas. We are now on the road to achieving a 600-ship Navy and increasing the amphibious capabilities of our marines, who are now serving the cause of peace in Lebanon. And we are building a real capability to assist our friends in the vitally important Indian Ocean and Persian Gulf region.

This adds up to a major effort, and it is not cheap. It comes at a time when there are many other pressures on our budget and when the American people have already had to make major sacrifices during the recession. But we must not be misled by those who would make defense once again the scapegoat of the Federal budget.

The fact is that in the past few decades we have seen a dramatic shift in how we spend the taxpayer's dollar. Back in 1955, payments to individuals took up only about 20 percent of the Federal budget. For nearly three decades, these payments steadily increased and this year will account for 49 percent of the budget. By contrast, in 1955, defense took up more than half of the Federal budget. By 1980, this spending had fallen to a low of 23 percent. Even with the increase I am requesting this year, defense will still amount to only 28 percent of the budget.

The calls for cutting back the defense budget come in nice simple arithmetic. They're the same kind of talk that led the democracies to neglect their defenses in the 1930's and invited the tragedy of World War II. We must not let that grim chapter of history repeat itself through apathy or neglect.

Yes, we pay a great deal for the weapons and equipment we give our military forces. And, yes, there has been some waste in the past. But we are now paying the delayed cost of our neglect in the 1970's. We would only be fooling ourselves, and endangering the future, if we let the bills pile up for the 1980's as well. Sooner or later these bills always come due, and the later they come due, the more they cost in treasure and in safety.

This is why I am speaking to you tonight—to urge you to tell your Senators and Congressmen that you know we must continue to restore our military strength.

If we stop in midstream, we will not only jeopardize the progress we have made to date—we will mortgage our ability to deter war and achieve genuine arms reductions. And we will send a signal of decline, of lessened will, to friends and adversaries alike.

One of the tragic ironies of history—and we've seen it happen more than once in this century—is the way that tyrannical systems, whose military strength is based on oppressing their people, grow strong while, through wishful thinking, free societies allow themselves to be lulled into a false sense of security.

Free people must voluntarily, through open debate and democratic means, meet the challenge that totalitarians pose by compulsion.

It is up to us, in our time, to choose, and choose wisely, between the hard but necessary task of preserving peace and freedom and the temptation to ignore our duty and blindly hope for the best while the enemies of freedom grow stronger day by day.

The solution is well within our grasp. But to reach it, there is simply no alternative but to continue this year, in this budget, to provide the resources we need to preserve the peace and guarantee our freedom.

Thus far tonight I have shared with you my thoughts on the problems of national security we must face together. My predecessors in the Oval Office have appeared before you on other occasions to describe the threat posed by Soviet power and have proposed steps to address that threat. But since the advent of nuclear weapons, those steps have been directed toward deterrence of aggression through the promise of retaliation—the notion that no rational nation would launch an attack that would inevitably result in unacceptable losses to themselves. This approach to stability through offensive threat has worked. We and our allies have succeeded in preventing nuclear war for three decades. In recent months, however, my advisers, including in particular the Joint Chiefs of Staff, have underscored the bleakness of the future before us.

Over the course of these discussions, I have become more and more deeply convinced that the human spirit must be capable of rising above dealing with other nations and human beings by threatening their existence. Feeling this way, I believe we must thoroughly examine every opportunity for reducing tensions and for introducing greater stability into the strategic calculus on both sides. One of the most important contributions we can make is, of course, to lower the level of all arms, and particularly nuclear arms. We are engaged right now in several negotiations with the Soviet Union to bring about a mutual reduction of weapons. I will report to you a week from tomorrow my thoughts on that score. But let me just say I am totally committed to this course.

If the Soviet Union will join with us in our effort to achieve major arms reduction we will have succeeded in stabilizing the nuclear balance. Nevertheless it will still be necessary to rely on the specter of retaliation—on mutual threat, and that is a sad commentary on the human condition.

Would it not be better to save lives than to avenge them? Are we not capable of demonstrating our peaceful intentions by applying all our abilities and our ingenuity to achieving a truly lasting stability? I think we are—indeed, we must!

After careful consultation with my advisers, including the Joint Chiefs of Staff, I believe there is a way. Let me share with you a vision of the future which offers hope. It is that we embark on a program to counter the awesome Soviet missile threat with measures that are defensive. Let us turn to the very strengths in technology that spawned our great industrial base and that have given us the quality of life we enjoy today.

Up until now we have increasingly based our strategy of deterrence upon the threat of retaliation. But what if free people could live secure in the knowledge that their security did not rest upon the threat of instant U.S. retaliation to deter a Soviet attack; that we could intercept and destroy strategic ballistic missiles before they reached our own soil or that of our allies?

I know this is a formidable technical task, one that may not be accomplished before the end of this century. Yet, current technology has attained a level of sophistication where it is reasonable for us to begin this effort. It will take years, probably decades, of effort on many fronts. There will be failures and setbacks just as there will be successes and breakthroughs. And as we proceed we must remain constant in preserving the nuclear deterrent and maintaining a solid capability for flexible response. But is it not worth every investment necessary to free the world from the threat of nuclear war? We know it is!

In the meantime, we will continue to pursue real reductions in nuclear arms, negotiating from a position of strength that can be insured only by modernizing our strategic forces. At the same time, we must take steps to reduce the risk of a conventional military conflict escalating to nuclear war by improving our nonnuclear capabilities. America does possess—now—the technologies to attain very significant improvements in the effectiveness of our conventional, nonnuclear forces. Proceeding boldly with these new technologies, we can significantly reduce any incentive that the Soviet Union may have to threaten attack against the United States or its allies.

As we pursue our goal of defensive technologies, we recognize that our allies rely upon our strategic offensive power to deter attacks against them. Their vital interests and ours are inextricably linked—their safety and ours are one. And no change in technology can or will alter that reality. We must and shall continue to honor our commitments.

I clearly recognize that defensive systems have limitations and raise certain problems and ambiguities. If paired with offensive systems, they can be viewed as fostering an aggressive policy and no one wants that.

But with these considerations firmly in mind, I call upon the scientific community who gave us nuclear weapons to turn their great talents to the cause of mankind and world peace: to give us the means of rendering these nuclear weapons impotent and obsolete.

Tonight, consistent with our obligations under the ABM Treaty and recognizing the need for close consultation with our allies, I am taking an important first step. I am directing a comprehensive and intensive effort to define a long-term research and development program to begin to achieve our ultimate goal of eliminating the threat posed by strategic nuclear missiles. This could pave the way for arms control measures to eliminate the weapons themselves. We seek neither military superiority nor political advantage. Our only purpose—one all people share—is to search for ways to reduce the danger of nuclear war.

My fellow Americans, tonight we are launching an effort which holds the purpose of changing the course of human history. There will be risks, and results take time. But with your support, I believe we can do it.

Arms Control Policy:
A Plea for Patience

Ronald Reagan, *President of the United States*

Last week I spoke to the American people about our plans for safeguarding this nation's security and that of our allies. And I announced a long-term effort in scientific research to counter, some day, the menace of offensive nuclear missiles. What I have proposed is that nations should turn their best energies to moving away from the nuclear nightmare. We must not resign ourselves to a future in which security on both sides depends on threatening the lives of millions of innocent men, women and children.

And today I would like to discuss another vital aspect of our national security—our efforts to limit and reduce the danger of modern weaponry.

We live in a world in which total war would mean catastrophe. We also live in a world that's torn by a great moral struggle—between democracy and its enemies, between the spirit of freedom and those who fear freedom.

In the last 15 years or more, the Soviet Union has engaged in a relentless military buildup, overtaking and surpassing the United States in major categories of military power, acquiring what can only be considered an offensive military capability. All the moral values which this country cherishes—freedom, democracy, the right of peoples and nations to determine their own destiny, to speak and write, to live and worship as they choose—all these basic rights are fundamentally challenged by a powerful adversary which does not wish these values to survive.

This is our dilemma, and it is a profound one: We must both defend freedom and preserve the peace. We must stand true to our principles and our friends while preventing a holocaust.

The Western commitment to peace through strength has given Europe its longest period of peace in a century. We cannot conduct ourselves as if the special danger of nuclear weapons did not exist. But we must not allow ourselves to be paralyzed by the problem—to abdicate our moral duty.

This is the challenge that history has left us. We of the 20th century, who so pride ourselves on mastering even the forces of nature. . . . We are forced to wrestle with one of the most complex moral challenges ever faced by any generation.

My views about the Soviet Union are well known, although sometimes I don't recognize them when they are played back to me, and our program for maintaining, strengthening and modernizing our national defense has been clearly stated. Today, let me tell you something of what we are doing to reduce the danger of nuclear war.

Since the end of World War II, the United States has been the leader in the international effort to negotiate nuclear arms limitations. In 1946, when the United States was the only country in the world possessing these awesome weapons, we did not blackmail others with threats to use them; nor did we use our enormous power to conquer

President Reagan's speech as made available by the White House. Delivered to the Los Angeles World Affairs Council, Beverly Hills, California, March 31, 1983.

territory, to advance our position or to seek domination. Doesn't our record alone refute the charge that we seek superiority, that we represent a threat to peace?

We proposed the Baruch plan for international control of all nuclear weapons and nuclear energy—for everything nuclear to be turned over to an international agency. This was rejected by the Soviet Union. Several years later, in 1955, President Eisenhower presented his "open skies" proposal: that the United States and the Soviet Union would exchange blueprints of military establishments and permit aerial reconnaissance to insure against the danger of surprise attack. This, too, was rejected by the Soviet Union.

Since then some progress has been made—largely at American initiative. The 1963 Limited Test Ban Treaty prohibited nuclear testing in the atmosphere, in outer space or under water. The creation of the hot line in 1963, upgraded in 1971, provides direct communication between Washington and Moscow to avoid miscalculation during a crisis. The Nuclear Nonproliferation Treaty of 1968 sought to prevent the spread of nuclear weapons.

In 1971 we reached an agreement on special communication procedures to safeguard against accidental or unauthorized use of nuclear weapons, and on a seabed arms control treaty which prohibits the placing of nuclear weapons on the seabed or the ocean floor. The Strategic Arms Limitation Agreements of 1972 imposed limits on antiballistic missile systems and on numbers of strategic offensive missiles. And the 1972 Biological Warfare Convention bans—or was supposed to ban—the development, production and stockpiling of biological and toxin weapons.

But while many agreements have been reached, we have also suffered many disappointments. The American people had hoped, by these measures, to reduce tensions and start to build a constructive relationship with the Soviet Union.

Instead we have seen Soviet military arsenals continue to grow in virtually every significant category. We have seen the Soviet Union project its power around the globe. We have seen Soviet resistance to significant reductions and measures of effective verification, especially the latter.

And, I am sorry to say, there have been increasingly serious grounds for questioning their compliance with the arms control agreements that have already been signed, and that we have both pledged to uphold. I may have more to say on this in the near future.

Coming into office, I made two promises to the American people about peace and security: I promised to restore our neglected defenses, in order to strengthen and preserve the peace, and I promised to pursue reliable agreements to reduce nuclear weapons. Both these promises are being kept.

Today, not only the peace but also the chances for real arms control depend on restoring the military balance. We know that the ideology of the Soviet leaders does not permit them to leave any Western weakness unprobed, any vacuum of power unfilled. It would seem that to them negotiation is only another form of struggle.

Yet I believe the Soviets can be persuaded to reduce their arsenals—but only if they see it's absolutely necessary. Only if they recognize the West's determination to modernize its own military forces will they see an incentive to negotiate a verifiable agreement establishing equal, lower levels. And, very simply, that is one of the main reasons why we must rebuild our defensive strength.

All of our strategic force modernization has been approved by the Congress except for the land-based leg of the Triad. We expect to get Congressional approval on this final program later this spring. A strategic forces modernization program depends on a national bipartisan consensus.

Over the last decade, four successive Administrations have made proposals for arms control and modernization that have become embroiled in political controversy. No one gained from this divisiveness; all of us are going to have to take a fresh look at our previous positions. I pledge to you my participation in such a fresh look and my determination to assist in forging a renewed bipartisan consensus.

My other national security priority on assuming office was to thoroughly re-examine the entire arms control agenda. Since then, in coordination with our allies, we have launched the most comprehensive program of arms control initiatives ever undertaken. Never before in history has a nation engaged in so many major simultaneous efforts to limit and reduce the instruments of war:

> Last month in Geneva the Vice President committed the United States to negotiate a total and verifiable ban on chemical weapons. Such inhumane weapons, as well as toxin weapons, are being used in violation of international law in Afghanistan, in Laos and Kampuchea.

> Together with our allies, we have offered a comprehensive new proposal for mutual and balanced reduction of conventional forces in Europe.

> We have recently proposed to the Soviet Union a series of further measures to reduce the risk of war from accident or miscalculation. And we are considering significant new measures resulting in part from consultations with several distinguished Senators.

> We have joined our allies in proposing a Conference on Disarmament in Europe. On the basis of a balanced outcome of the Madrid meeting, such a conference will discuss new ways to enhance European stability and security.

> We have proposed to the Soviet Union improving the verification provisions of two agreements to limit underground nuclear testing, but so far the response has been negative. We will continue to try.

> And, most importantly, we have made far-reaching proposals, which I will discuss further in a moment, for deep reductions in strategic weapons and for elimination of an entire class of intermediate-range weapons.

I am determined to achieve real arms control—reliable agreements that will stand the test of time, not cosmetic agreements that raise expectations only to have hopes cruelly dashed.

In all these negotiations certain basic principles guide our policy:

> First, our efforts to control arms should seek reductions on both sides—significant reductions.

> Second, we insist that arms control agreements be equal and balanced.

> Third, arms control agreements must be effectively verifiable. We cannot gamble with the safety of our people and the people of the world.

> Fourth, we recognize that arms control is not an end in itself but a vital part of a broad policy designed to strengthen peace and stability.

It is with these firm principles in mind that this Administration has approached negotiations on the most powerful weapons in the American and Soviet arsenals—strategic nuclear weapons.

In June of 1982, American and Soviet negotiators convened in Geneva to begin the Strategic Arms Reduction Talks, what we call Start. We have sought to work out an agreement reducing the levels of strategic weapons on both sides. I proposed reducing the number of ballistic missiles by one-half and the number of warheads by one-third. No more than half the remaining warheads could be on land-based missiles. This would leave both sides with greater security at equal and lower levels of forces.

Not only would this reduce numbers—it would also put specific limits on precisely those types of nuclear weapons that pose the most danger.

The Soviets have made a counter-proposal. We have raised a number of serious concerns about it—and this is important—they have accepted the concept of reductions. I expect this is because of the firm resolve that we've demonstrated. In the current round of negotiations, we have presented them with the basic elements of a treaty for comprehensive reductions in strategic arsenals. The United States also has, in Start, recently proposed a draft agreement on a number of significant measures to build confidence and reduce the risks of conflict.

This negotiation is proceeding under the able leadership of Ambassador Edward Rowny on our side.

We are also negotiating in Geneva to eliminate an entire class of new weapons from the face of the earth.

Since the end of the mid-1970's the Soviet Union has been deploying an intermediate-range nuclear missile, the SS-20, at a rate of one a week. There are now 351 of these missiles, each with three highly accurate warheads capable of destroying cities and military bases in Western Europe, Asia and the Middle East.

NATO has no comparable weapon. Nor did NATO in any way provoke this new, unprecedented escalation. In fact, while the Soviets were deploying their SS-20's, we were taking 1,000 nuclear warheads from shorter-range weapons out of Europe.

This major shift in the European military balance prompted our West European allies themselves to propose that NATO find a means of righting the balance. And in December of 1979, they announced a collective, two-track decision:

> First, to deploy in Western Europe 572 land-based cruise missiles and Pershing 2 ballistic missiles capable of reaching the Soviet Union—the purpose to offset and deter the Soviet SS-20's. The first of these NATO weapons are scheduled for deployment by the end of this year.
>
> Second, to seek negotiations with the Soviet Union for the mutual reduction of these intermediate-range missiles.

In November of 1981 the United States, in concert with our allies, made a sweeping new proposal. NATO would cancel its own deployment if the Soviets eliminated theirs. The Soviet Union refused and set out to intensify public pressures in the West to block the NATO deployment, which has not even started. Meanwhile, the Soviet weapons continue to grow in number.

Our proposal was not made on a take-it-or-leave-it basis. We are willing to consider any Soviet proposal that meets these standards of fairness:

> An agreement must establish equal numbers for both Soviet and American intermediate-range nuclear forces.
>
> Other countries' nuclear forces, such as the British and French, are independent and are not part of the bilateral U.S.-Soviet negotiations. They are, in

fact, strategic weapons and the Soviet strategic arsenal more than compensates for them.

Next, an agreement must not shift the threat from Europe to Asia. Given the range and mobility of the SS-20's, meaningful limits on these and comparable American systems must be global.

An agreement must be effectively verifiable.

And an agreement must not undermine NATO's ability to defend itself with conventional forces.

We have been consulting closely with our Atlantic allies and they strongly endorse these principles. Earlier this week I authorized our negotiator in Geneva, Ambassador Paul Nitze, to inform the Soviet delegation of a new American proposal which has the full support of our allies.

We are prepared to negotiate an interim agreement to reduce our planned deployment if the Soviet Union will reduce their corresponding warheads to an equal level. This would include all U.S. and Soviet weapons of this class, wherever they are located.

Our offer of zero on both sides will, of course, remain on the table as our ultimate goal. At the same time we remain open, as we have been from the very outset, to serious counter proposals.

The Soviet negotiators have now returned to Moscow, where we hope our new proposal will receive careful consideration during the recess.

Ambassador Nitze has proposed and the Soviets have agreed that negotiations resume in mid-May, several weeks earlier than scheduled.

I'm sorry that the Soviet Union, so far, has not been willing to accept the complete elimination of these systems on both sides. The question I now put to the Soviet Government is, if not elimination, to what equal level are you willing to reduce?

The new proposal is designed to promote early and genuine progress at Geneva. For arms control to be truly complete and world security strengthened, however, we must also increase our efforts to halt the spread of nuclear arms.

Every country that values a peaceful world order must play its part. Our allies, as important nuclear exporters, also have a very important responsibility to prevent the spread of nuclear arms. To advance this goal, we should all adopt comprehensive safeguards as a condition for nuclear supply commitments that we make in the future. In the days ahead, I will be talking to other world leaders about the need for urgent movement on this and other measures against nuclear proliferation.

Now that is the arms control agenda we have been pursuing. Our proposals are fair, they're far-reaching and comprehensive, but we still have a long way to go.

We Americans are sometimes an impatient people. I guess it's a symptom of our traditional optimism, energy and spirit. Often this is a source of strength. In a negotiation, however, impatience can be a real handicap. Any of you who have been involved in labor-management negotiations, or any kind of bargaining, know that patience strengthens your bargaining position. If one side seems too eager or desperate, the other side has no reason to offer a compromise and every reason to hold back, expecting that the more eager side will cave in first.

Well, this is a basic fact of life we can't afford to lose sight of when dealing with the Soviet Union. Generosity in negotiation has never been a trademark of theirs; it runs counter to the basic militancy of Marxist-Leninist ideology.

So it is vital that we show patience, determination and, above all, national unity. If we appear to be divided—if the Soviets suspect that domestic, political pressure will undercut our position—they will dig in their heels. And that can only delay an agreement and may destroy all hope for an agreement.

That's why I have been concerned about the nuclear freeze proposals, one of which is being considered at this time by the House of Representatives. Most of those who support the freeze, I'm sure, are well intentioned—concerned about the arms race and the danger of nuclear war. No one shares their concern more than I do. But however well intentioned they are, these freeze proposals would do more harm than good.

They may seem to offer a simple solution. But there are no simple solutions to complex problems. As H. L. Mencken once wryly remarked, he said for every problem there is one solution which is simple, neat and wrong.

The freeze concept is dangerous for many reasons:

It would preserve today's high, unequal and unstable levels of nuclear forces, and by so doing reduce Soviet incentives to negotiate for real reductions.

It would pull the rug out from under our negotiators in Geneva, as they have testified. After all, why should the Soviets negotiate if they have already achieved a freeze in a position of advantage to them?

Also, some think a freeze would be easy to agree on, but it raises enormously complicated problems of what is to be frozen, how it is to be achieved and, most of all, verified. Attempting to negotiate these critical details would only divert us from the goal of negotiating reductions, for who knows how long.

The freeze proposal would also make a lot more sense if a similar movement against nuclear weapons were putting similar pressures on Soviet leaders in Moscow. As former Secretary of Defense Harold Brown has pointed out, the effect of the freeze "is to put pressure on the United States, but not on the Soviet Union."

Finally, the freeze would reward the Soviets for their 15-year buildup while locking us into our existing equipment, which in many cases is obsolete and badly in need of modernization. Three-quarters of Soviet strategic warheads are on delivery systems five years old or less; three-quarters of the American strategic warheads are on delivery systems 15 years old or older. The time comes when everything wears out—the trouble is, it comes a lot sooner for us than for them. And, under a freeze, we couldn't do anything about it.

Our B-52 bombers are older than many of the pilots who fly them; if they were automobiles they would qualify as antiques. A freeze could lock us into obsolescence. It is asking too much to expect our service men and women to risk their lives in obsolete equipment. The two million patriotic Americans in the armed services deserve the best and most modern equipment to protect them—and us.

I'm sure every President has dreamt of leaving the world a safer place than he found it. I pledge to you, my goal—and I consider it a sacred trust—will be to make progress toward arms reductions in every one of the several negotiations now under way.

I call on all Americans, of both parties and all branches of government, to join in this effort. We must not let our disagreements or partisan politics keep us from strengthening the peace and reducing armaments.

I pledge to our allies and friends in Europe and Asia: We will continue to consult with you closely. We are conscious of our responsibility when we negotiate with our adversaries on conditions or issues of concern to you, and your safety and well-being.

To the leaders and people of the Soviet Union, I say: Join us in the path to a more peaceful, secure world. Let us vie in the realm of ideas, on the field of peaceful competition. Let history record that we tested our theories through human experience, not that we destroyed ourselves in the name of vindicating our way of life. And let us practice restraint in our international conduct, so that the present climate of mistrust can some day give way to mutual confidence and a secure peace.

What better time to rededicate ourselves to this undertaking than in the Easter season, when millions of the world's people pay homage to the one who taught us peace on earth, good will toward men?

This is the goal, my fellow Americans, of all the democratic nations—a goal that requires firmness, patience and understanding. If the Soviet Union responds in the same spirit, we are ready. And we can pass on to our posterity the gift of peace—that and freedom are the greatest gifts that one generation can bequeath to another. Thank you, and God bless you.

Discussion Questions

1. President Reagan has been called "The Great Communicator." Can you identify any rhetorical devices or persuasive techniques used by Mr. Reagan in the two preceding speeches? How effective do you think the speeches are in persuading their intended audiences?

2. In President Reagan's view what is the defense debate about? Do you agree? Why or why not?

3. On what principles does President Reagan say that United States defense policy is based? Support or criticize these principles.

4. What are President Reagan's objections to a nuclear freeze? Do you agree with his arguments? Why or why not?

5. In what ways has the international situation changed since these speeches were made? Do these changes support President Reagan's contentions in these speeches? Why or why not?

Ethics and Nuclear Deterrence

Douglas Lackey

The Strategic Arms Limitation Agreement signed by President Nixon in Moscow in May 1972 was universally and rightly hailed as a step toward peace. The principal clauses of the agreement limit the construction of antimissile systems, and these systems are the only devices within the scope of conceivable technology that can fend off a nuclear attack. In effect, the United States and the Soviet Union have agreed upon mutual defenselessness; each side has acknowledged, as practically a permanent condition, the ability of the other to attack and destroy it if it wishes. At the same time, this mutual guarantee of ability to attack carries with it a guarantee of the ability to *counterattack;* each side, if attacked first, can destroy the other with a counterstrike emanating from nuclear submarines surviving the initial attack.[1] Though this state of affairs is hardly utopian, it is a distinct improvement over the previous delicate balance of terror. If both sides are guaranteed the ability to counterattack, neither side, barring accidents and assuming the usual desire for self-preservation, will attack the other. For the first time since the introduction of intercontinental missiles in the early 1960s, the major powers have achieved stable deterrence.

Though the present strategic balance is an improvement over past uncertainties, this gives us no cause to believe that it is the best possible arrangement. For an indefinite period, to preserve this balance, the United States and the Soviet Union must spend large sums on armaments, endure the risk of nuclear accidents, face the possibility that any minor disagreement may escalate into a nuclear war, and maintain an attitude sufficiently bellicose to assure the other side that destruction will swiftly and surely follow upon attack. My purpose in this paper is to examine the extent to which we can rest content with the present strategic *détente.* There are two sorts of criticism possible: first, the utilitarian one that this policy will not produce the best consequences for the world over all the practical alternatives; second, the sterner criticism that our policy is intrinsically abhorrent and ought to be abandoned simply because of what it is. I shall take up each criticism in turn.

I. A Utilitarian Critique

Utilitarian critiques are always future-oriented; given the world as it is *now,* with the weapons that actually exist on both sides, which policy will produce the best future results? This prevents retroactive criticisms of past military decisions; and though they provide an interesting compendium of missed opportunities and mental lapses, the errors of the 1960s will not concern us here. The costs of the *present* policy (by present policy I mean the policy to maintain force levels at least as high as they now are, subject to the limitations of the SALT I agreement) have already been indicated. *First,* there is the enormous cost of maintaining and operating the present American weapons systems. (Notice that we cannot include present interest on loans taken to develop these systems; that is a critique of *past* action). *Second,* there is the enormous cost of the maintaining and operating of the corresponding arsenal in the Soviet Union. It is not unfair, I believe, to include costs of Soviet arms as part of the utilitarian cost of American policy, even though Americans do not decide whether Russia shall arm. "Cost" in a utilitarian calculation is cost to the human race, and each agent is responsible for such costs as can reasonably be predicted to follow from his policies. It is reasonable to predict, judging from what we know of the Soviet Union and its leadership, that if we maintain our present armament, the Russians will maintain theirs, and also reasonable to predict that if we acted differently as regards the level of arms, the Russians would also. Hence their expenditures should be charged against our policy. By parity of reasoning, the Russian policy must include among its costs the money that Americans, in all their rhetorical fury, can reasonably be predicted to spend in response to Russian armaments. But this would be relevant to a critique of Russian policy, and I am here concerned only with our own. *Third,* since the weapons of destruction exist and are very complex, there is a chance that systems will malfunction and some or all of the world be destroyed by accident. The malfunction may be due to mechanical failure, as is described in the book *Fail Safe,* or to human failure, as is depicted in the movie *Dr. Strangelove.* Though the chances of such accidents are considerably less than they were, say, in October of 1960, when an American nuclear attack was almost ordered against Russia in response to radar signals that had bounced off the moon, the possibility of either sort of failure is still quite real. For reasons quite analogous to those given above as regards the financial burden of armaments, the possibility of malfunction in Russian systems must be charged against our policy, just as much as the possibility of malfunction in American systems. Even though the Russian systems are not supervised by us, they exist in response to ours and their possible malfunctions are concomitants of our policies. Russian expenses and Russian risks are hidden costs of our policies usually ignored even by liberal critics.

The financial burden of armaments is certain; accidental nuclear war is just a possibility. In estimating the value of current defense policy one must subtract some factor for the possibility of accidental war. This factor will be, estimated by the usual methods, the product of the chance of war and the disutility of this result. Though the chance of accidental war is slight, it is not negligible when Russian malfunctions are also considered; and since the disutility of nuclear war is great, the total subtraction from the value of the present policy on this ground alone should be substantial. *Fourth,* since the weapons of destruction exist, there is always the possibility that they will be *deliberately* used, if the leaders of one nation deem some provocation sufficient. The subtraction for this factor, as with the third, is achieved by multiplying the chance that some conflict will escalate to nuclear war by the disutility of that war, which is considerable.

The "gains" that can be attributed to the present policy are said to be threefold. First, the certainty of an American counterattack deters the Russians from launching a nuclear attack on the United States in order to gain some end. To the extent that such attacks are deterred, the world gains and not just the United States. Second, the ability of the United States to launch a devastating counterattack vitiates all Russian attempts to use threats of attack as a regular instrument of policy. If the United States could not attack, the Soviet Union could blackmail the United States at every point, threatening destruction if concessions be not made. Third, if the United States retains its capacity to counterattack, then it has the option, in *extreme* situations, of threatening to attack even though attack is suicidal. Though the Soviet leaders know that any attack is unlikely, they cannot be *certain* that the American leaders will *not* go to war over the issue concerned; and accordingly such threats by the United States will not be totally without effect. President Kennedy used such threats, successfully, to secure the removal of Russian missiles from Cuba. In short, the maintenance of our present military capacity reduces the risk of attack and blackmail, and occasionally can be used to secure goals of policy.

Each of these three "gains" must be carefully analyzed. First, it is claimed that American armaments "reduce the threat of Russian attack." The superficial appeal of this claim disappears when we raise the question: Reduce the chances of attack *relative to what?* Certainly it reduces the chances of attack relative to some anti-Communist fantasy in which the leaders of the Soviet Union daily plot the conquest of the United States. But such fantasies are incredible and it is madness to praise a present policy because it is better than some imaginary evil. The fact is that with the present policy there is a certain chance of war, which can be calculated by combining the possibility of accidental war with the possibility of deliberate attack; and this is an evil of the policy which can only be justified on the grounds that all other policies on balance do even worse.

The same criticism applies to the second "plus" of our deterrence policy: it prevents nuclear blackmail. Our policy can "prevent" nuclear blackmail only if there *is* nuclear blackmail to be prevented. But there is little evidence that either side is prone to blackmail of this sort. On the Russian side, the military tradition is either to act or not to act: threatening to act is not a standard feature of Russian policy. The Soviets did not *threaten* to invade Hungary and Czechoslovakia; they simply invaded them. They did not threaten to attack us if we intercepted their ships steaming toward Cuba in 1962; they merely stopped them. As for the United States, the use of nuclear threats was eschewed in the Acheson era, when there was often something worth blackmailing; and in the Dulles era, though the nuclear sabers were often rattled as a general display, they remained preternaturally still during the Hungarian invasion, the most provocative Soviet act of the 1950s. During this period the United States could have attacked Russia at any time with relative impunity, yet it did not even threaten to attack. In short, the major powers are not given to nuclear blackmail.[2] If this blackmail problem ever does arise, it will arise in the context of nuclear *terrorists*—revolutionary kamikazes with nuclear devices—against whom the threat of counterattack is useless. The true situation is that with the present policy there is not a "reduction" in the chance of nuclear blackmail but rather a set chance of blackmail given present conditions, and no argument has yet been provided that this chance is less than the chance that one would have in all other alternative policies.

The third "plus" of present policy is that if we possess strength we can negotiate from strength—gaining ends we could not attain otherwise. (The latest variant on this theme is the reiterated argument of the present administration that we must first increase armaments in order to facilitate negotiations to decrease them.) This third plus may be a plus from the perspective of those who make American policy, but it can hardly be considered a plus for humanity in general. "To negotiate from strength" is a euphemism for the making of threats; the making of threats increases the chance of nuclear war. The great disutility of this result outweighs any gains that might result from "negotiating from strength," even if (as is unlikely) the negotiations are aimed at a moral result. In summary, then, even if the present policy results in more good than evil,[3] it is not demonstrated that it results in more good on balance than all alternative policies.

Of the alternative policies, the one that most clearly challenges the present policy of seeking bilateral arms reductions while maintaining the arms race is the policy of gradual unilateral disarmament. The most plausible unilateral disarmament policy at present would be this: first, to cease all nuclear testing; to declare a moratorium on armaments research; to deactivate the implementation of MIRV; to withdraw our stra- tegic air bases from Spain, Thailand, Formosa, etc.; and to phase out all Minuteman missiles and sites. All of this would be merely Stage I, since it would leave the strategic balance completely unimpaired, so long as the Soviet Union built no ABM and the United States retained its fleet of missile submarines. Each one of these steps should be accompanied by requests that similar steps be taken by the Soviet Union, but compliance by the Soviet Union should not be considered a precondition for any of the American initiatives.

Stage II of the disarmament procedure should be as follows: the United States should announce that it will not counterattack if attacked by the Soviet Union and shall progressively deactivate its nuclear submarines, down to a point in which the ability of the United States to reply to a Russian attack would be considerably reduced.[4] At the same time, the United States should undertake extensive steps to increase Soviet–American trade, in such areas as exploit the natural specializations of the respective countries.

The consequences of this alternative policy would be, at a minimum, a reduction of the chance of accidental and escalated nuclear war, relative to the present policy, and the diversion of American capital and intellect into enterprises more likely to increase the economic health of the nation.[5] In addition, it is highly likely that a reduction in the American level of armaments would lead to a reduction in Russian armaments, since one principal rationale for the Russian maintenance of these arms is the threat of American attack.

This leaves the question of "nuclear blackmail." If the United States enters into extensive economic arrangements with Russia, provided that these arrangements are not exploitative but based on a national specialization, the Soviet Union would have no cause to blackmail the United States, since an injury to a trading partner is an injury to oneself. Furthermore, the Soviet Union can ill-afford to alienate the United States, even if the United States lacks nuclear arms, since the United States holds the balance of power, both military and economic, between the Soviet Union and China, who are at present enemies by geography, by history, and by ideology. In short, though the possibility of nuclear blackmail exists if the United States abandons its armaments, there is little likelihood that there would be such blackmail; and, in my opinion, the small chance of this bad result is far outweighed by the decreased chance of accidental or deliberate nuclear war.

The policy that I recommend bears some resemblance to suggested policies of national pacifism in the 1930s. Since these policies were discredited by events, it is important to see that the problems of the 1970s are significantly different from those of the 1930s. The principal tension of the 1930s was between Germany and other states, and Germany possessed the most advanced military technology. The principal tension of the 1970s and 1980s will be between the advanced countries and the underdeveloped countries, within which the population bomb will explode. In short, tension in the 1930s was between strong and strong; in the 1980s it will be between strong and weak. The underdeveloped countries do not stand to the world on the same military basis that Germany stood to the rest of Europe. Furthermore, in the 1930s, Germany and Italy were infected with an ideology that contained self-fulfilling prophecies of the inevitability of war. There is no force in the contemporary scene that corresponds to fascism. Neither ideology of democracy nor the ideology of capitalism preach the inevitability of war, and in the ideology of communism, though there will be inevitable war between *classes,* there need be no inevitable war between *nations,* especially war by socialist states against capitalist states, who will be defeated not by external invasion but internal contradictions. There is no nation at present which simultaneously has the power, the desire, or the need to go to war.

Historical predictions are a risky business, and the policy of unilateral disarmament may appear unduly risky, even when its probable positive effects are considered. But if disarmament increases the risk of conquest, continued armament increases the risk of war; and of these two, the latter is the more serious, especially if the welfare of the entire world is considered and not the special national interests of the United States.

II. Prisoner's Dilemma Denied

A critic of the preceding section might argue that the whole proof hangs upon an overly generous interpretation of Russian intentions. "One can argue," a defender of armaments might retort, "that the United States has a moral obligation to disarm if the Soviet Union is also willing to disarm, since mutual disarmament benefits everyone. But if the Soviet Union does not disarm, no argument based on probabilities or expected values should compel us to disarm and open ourselves to conquest. Calculation of probabilities of historical events is mere guesswork, but no guesswork is involved in the judgment that Russian conquest of an armed United States is not possible but Russian conquest of a disarmed United States is a real possibility. The proper way to evaluate the strategic situation is to forget spurious probabilities and to use game-theoretic methods. In the strategic game, the disarming of the United States gives the Russians a move which simple logic compels them to take and which is disaster for us."

I would be willing, if pressed, to defend the probabilistic approach to deterrence theory, because I believe that the case for unilateral disarmament can be successfully made without spurious precision. In the preceding section, for example, I claimed that the chance of accidental war resulting from present policies is small but not negligible, and this degree of precision, which is not very great but all that the argument needs, can be supported by empirical evidence. But if a game-theoretic analysis is desired, I shall not shrink from providing one, since these analyses have their independent merits.

In a game-theoretic analysis of strategy, each opponent is viewed as having choices between various policies and payoffs are assigned to each opponent after all simultaneously make some choice of policy. In the deterrence situation as we now find it, in which each opponent knows that a first strike is suicidal, the main policy choices are "disarming unilaterally" or "remaining at an arms level equal to one's opponents." Symbolizing "retaining arms" as A and "disarming unilaterally" as D, the game matrix for deterrence looks like this:

Now, if both countries disarm, neither will attack the other, neither risks accidental war, and neither wastes resources on armaments; and if both countries maintain arms at present levels, neither will deliberately attack the other, but both risk accidental war, and both pay for armaments. Obviously the payoff figures for the D–D game should be higher than the payoff figures for the A–A game, and the payoff figures should be equal for each player in each case; for example:

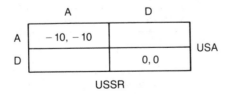

(Left-hand payoffs to USA, right-hand payoffs to USSR; scale of payoffs is arbitrary.)

This leaves us the difficulty of assigning the payoffs for the D–A games. A critic of disarmament might say that if one country is disarmed while the other remains armed, this is a tremendous advantage to the armed nation, which can do as it wills, and a tremendous disadvantage to the disarmed nation, which must suffer what it must. Accordingly, the disarmament critic sets the payoff for the armed country (against disarmed) very high, higher than the payoff for being armed (against armed); and he sets the payoff for the disarmed country (against armed) very low, lower than the payoff for being disarmed (against disarmed); for example:

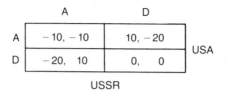

which is an instance of the game pattern known as the Prisoner's Dilemma. Having got this far, the critic of disarmament will argue: "The USSR will either arm or disarm. If the Soviet Union arms, it is preferable (−10 to −20) for the USA to arm; and if the Soviet Union disarms, then it is preferable (10 to 0) for the USA to arm. Therefore, whatever the Soviet Union does, it is preferable for the United States to remain armed."

This is the sort of reasoning that generates arms races, and arms races are admitted on all sides to be regrettable. The difficulty is to find a flaw in this reasoning that will allow one to escape from an arms race once one is caught up in it. There have been numerous attempts, by philosophers and peace-oriented game theoreticians, to demonstrate that the policy of disarmament is rational, or moral, in the Prisoner's Dilemma situation, but all these attempts have been unconvincing. My own feeling is that the main mistake is not in the disarmament critic's reasoning once the Prisoner's Dilemma is established, but in the reasoning that assigns the payoffs so as to create the Dilemma. If one considers nuclear arms only, then it is not a tremendous advantage to be armed when your so-called opponent is disarmed. Nuclear arms are expensive; they may blow up in your face; and they cannot be used for a war of aggrandizement, since when used against an enemy they destroy the spoils. The only serviceable use of nuclear arms is to destroy an opponent who threatens you; and if your opponent is disarmed, he is no threat. In short, I deny that the Prisoner's Dilemma is the correct model to use in analysis of the present deterrence situation; the real world, I believe, looks more like this:

	A	D
A	− 10, − 10	− 8, −2
D	− 2, −8	0, 0

If *this* matrix is the correct mirror of reality, then game-theoretic analysis shows that the strategy of disarmament is preferable whether one's "opponent" is disarmed or armed.

III. A Deontological Critique

Suppose that for some reason or lack of reason the Soviet Union launches a nuclear first strike against the United States. Even under these conditions it would be clearly immoral for the United States to retaliate in kind against the Soviet Union, since retaliation by the United States would result in the death of millions of innocent people, for no higher purpose than useless revenge. The present policy of deterrence requires preparations for such retaliation and threats and assurances by us that it will be forthcoming if the United States is attacked. Indeed, if our deterrent is to remain credible, the response of the United States to attack should be semiautomatic. Defenders of armaments justify all the preparations on the grounds that they will prevent an attack *on us;* if retaliation is ever needed, they say, the system has already failed. Now, a Russian attack against the United States would be at least as immoral as our retaliation against the Russians. So one aspect of the moral problem of deterrence is this: Is one justified in *threatening* to do something which is immoral, if the reasoned intention behind one's threat is to prevent something immoral from occurring?

Let us consider some analogous situations. (1) It would be immoral to [threaten to] kill a man in order to prevent default on a debt, even if one had no intention of killing the man at all, so long as he pays the debt. Indeed, it is immoral to threaten to kill a man in order to pay a debt, even if one has no intention of killing him under any circumstances, including nonpayment of the debt. In this case at least, threatening evil is not justified by good results or an increased chance of good results. Perhaps this lack of justification derives from the inherent wrongfulness of such threats of violence or from the bad results that would follow if everyone regularly made threats of this sort—whatever the cause, the good results that *actually* follow from the threat[6] do not justify it; even, I would say, in a state of nature containing no judicial system. (2) It might be objected that this example is unfair because the stakes in question are not high enough. Would it be equally immoral to threaten to kill Jones if the intention of the threat is to prevent Jones from doing murder himself, and if the threat will *be* carried out only when Jones actually does murder? This, perhaps, is the way deterrence theorists view the present strategic *détente*. It must be admitted that in this situation the threat to kill is not *obviously* immoral. Indeed, anyone who recommends capital punishment for convicted murderers is allowing that such threats, if tempered by due process of law, are *not* immoral.

The difficulty with this example is that it does not truly reflect the structure of our present nuclear policy. Our policy is not to threaten a potential *murderer* with death in order to prevent him from murdering, and to execute *him* when he actually does murder, but rather to threaten *someone else* with death in order to prevent a potential murderer from attacking and to execute *someone else* when the murderer actually strikes. An American counterattack would be directed against the Russian people, and it is not the Russian people who would be ordering an attack on the American people. Similarly, if leaders in the United States ordered an attack on Russia, the Russian counterattack would fall on the American people and not on the leaders who ordered the attack.[7] In the present *détente,* the leaders of each side hold the population of the other hostage and threaten to execute the hostages if the opposing *leaders* do not meet certain conditions. The proper moral examples, then, with which to analyze the *détente* should be examples of hostage-taking. (3) Suppose that the Hatfields and the McCoys live in an area sufficiently rural that disputes cannot be settled by appeal to a higher authority. For various reasons, the two families take a dislike to each other. Each family, let us assume, possesses hand grenades that could destroy the other family completely; and against these hand grenades there is no adequate defense. Each family, in what it considers to be a defensive move, kidnaps a child from the family of the other and holds it hostage. Each side wires its hostage to a device which will explode and kill the hostage if there is any loud noise nearby—such as the noise of a grenade attack or, what is not likely but still *possible,* the accidental explosion of the captors' own grenades or the sounding of a nearby clap of thunder. This example, I believe, fairly represents the present policies of deterrence.

A defender of Hatfield foreign policy might justify himself as follows: "We have no intention of killing the McCoy child, unless, of course, we are attacked. If we are attacked, we must kill him automatically (or else lose the credibility of this deterrent); but we feel that it is very unlikely that, under these conditions, any attack will occur. True, there is some small chance that the child will die by accident, but this is only a *small* chance, and so we have good reason to believe that this will not happen. At the same time, the presence of the hostage reduces the chance that the McCoys will attack, relative to the chances of attack if we had taken no hostage. If the child dies, we cannot be blamed, since we had good reason to believe that he would not, and if he lives, we are to be commended for adopting a policy which has in fact prevented an attack."

The moral reply here is obvious: the Hatfields have no *right* to seize the McCoy child, whatever dubious advantages they gain by seizing him. True they only *threaten* to kill him, but threatening to kill him increases the chance of his being killed, and they have no right to increase these chances. The moral repulsiveness of the Hatfield policy derives from its abuse of the innocent for dubious ends. Deterring the McCoys in this manner is like deterring one's neighbors from running into you on the road by seizing their children and tying them to the front bumper of your car.[8] If everyone did this, accidents might decrease and, on balance, more lives saved than lost. Perhaps it could be predicted that the chances of a single child dying on a car bumper are slight; perhaps, by a miracle, no child would die.[9] Whatever the chances and whatever the gains, no one could claim the right to use a single child in this way. Yet it seems that the present American policy uses the entire Russian population in just this manner. In the preceding section I argued that our deterrence policy does not produce the best results when all alternative policies are considered. These examples show that even if the policy *did* produce the best results, it still ought not to be adopted.

(4) The key step in the preceding criticism is that the Hatfields have no right to increase the chances of the McCoy child dying, and analogously the United States has no right to increase the chances of the Russian populations dying. The threat is illicit if the threat is real. This leads to the interesting possibility that the threat is licit if it is fraudulent. Suppose that the United States *says* that it will counterattack if the Soviet Union attacks and gives every indication that it will counterattack (missile silos are constructed, submarines cruise the oceans, etc.); but, in fact, unknown to anyone except the highest officials in the government, all the American warheads are disarmed and simply cannot go off. In this case the United States does not threaten, but merely *seems* to threaten to counterattack. If the chance of Russian attack is decreased, such a plan would have good results without the intrinsic repulsiveness of the present policy.

But this plan has practical and moral flaws. The practical flaw is that the bogus threat will not serve as a deterrent unless the Soviet Union *does* discover that, according to the usual analysis, the chances of war will be greatly increased. So, it is not obvious that this plan gives good results, since one must balance the decreased chance of war (if the Soviet Union respects the deterrent) against the increased chance of war (if the Soviet Union discovers that the deterrent is bogus). Furthermore, if this plan is successfully put into effect and the Soviet Union does not have a similar plan of its own, the bogus-warhead plan will result in high and wasteful Soviet expenditures and in an increased chance of accidental or deliberate attack from the Soviet side.

The chances of nuclear war have diminished considerably since the early 1960s;[10] our policies now are safer than they were then. But these improvements should not blind us to the inherent abhorrence of the present policies and the dangers that they pose. Mutual deterrence is neither rational, nor prudent, nor moral, compared to other policies that are not beyond the power of rational men.

Notes

[1]My opinion about the ability of nuclear submarines to survive a nuclear attack may seem akin to optimism about the Maginot Line. But I leave it to the reader to construct a plan to neutralize 30 cruising missile submarines. First, they must be located, which is technologically impossible at present. Then they must be destroyed, which is at present very difficult. And all this must be accomplished *simultaneously*, since, if just *one* submarine survives, it can annihilate any nation not protected by an antimissile system. Some plans have been suggested for seeding the oceans with mines, but it is very unlikely that magnetic mines could affix themselves to the 30th submarine before they were detected on the 1st. A slightly more plausible suggestion would be to interrupt the military communications system with dummy messages luring all the opponent's submarines into traps. But the small likelihood that such a scheme would succeed, coupled with the devastating effects of its probable failure, would prevent anyone but a madman from acting upon it. No military or strategic authority today questions the ability of nuclear submarines to survive nuclear attack, and this optimism stands in striking contrast to pessimistic critics in the 1930s who noted the impotence of the Maginot Line against air attacks. (See, for example, Bertrand Russell's *Which Way to Peace*, ch. 2.)

To test the solidity of the present stalemate, consider the strategic impact of the MIRVs (multiple, independently targeted, reentry vehicles) with which our Minuteman and Poseidon missiles are presently being equipped. This device enables up to ten warheads, each targeted to a different location, to be placed on a single ballistic missile! Under normal conditions, an offensive device like this would give immediate victory to the side that first developed it. But suppose, for example, that the United States develops the MIRV first, possesses no antimissile system, and decides to launch a devastating attack on the Soviet Union. However powerful this offensive thrust, *some* Russian submarines would survive, and the United States would be defenseless against their counterattack. Without an antimissile system, the MIRV is strategically worthless; yet construction of it in this country proceeds apace, lest the Russians get it first.

[2]Interestingly enough, one of the few persons who ever publicly advocated the use of nuclear blackmail was Bertrand Russell, who recommended in 1948 that the threat of nuclear attack be used to force the Russians to accept the Baruch-Lilienthal plan for the internationalization of atomic weapons. If a nuclear war ever does break out, Russell will have been proved right in his suggestion, but no one will remember it.

[3]Strictly speaking, "an increase in expected value."

[4]The reader may wonder why I consider it preferable to deactivate nuclear submarines rather than transfer them to an international agency. The reason I consider this undesirable is that American nuclear submarines are now ultimately responsible to civilian authority, and the tradition of military subservience to civilian authority is stronger in the United States than in most of the United Nations. Transfer of submarines to an international agency with no tradition of obedience would substantially increase chances of a nuclear *coup d'etat*.

[5]The argument that increased military expenditures are needed to preserve economic vitality is completely bogus. The world's two strongest and fastest developing economies—West Germany's and Japan's—are the economies of nations who have spent least for armaments, among major advanced nations, since 1945.

[6]This includes the actual increased chance that the debt will be paid.

[7]I am assuming that the Russian and American peoples cannot be held responsible for the decisions of their leaders. For the Russians, this is surely the case; for Americans, who live

in a relatively more democratic nation, the issue is more debatable. Still, whatever fraction of responsibility the American people would bear for an attack on Russia, it would hardly be sufficient to justify punishing millions of Americans with injury and death.

[8]This example is in Paul Ramsey, *Modern War and the Christian Conscience*.

[9]This miracle, in reference to nuclear weapons, we have seen since 1945.

[10]In the early 1960s, the American public overestimated the chance that nuclear war would occur. In the early 1970s, I believe that the public underestimates the chance that nuclear war will occur, and public interest in this issue is nil. But it is a good thing that this mistake is common, since lack of expectation that nuclear attacks will occur lessens the chance that nuclear accidents will be interpreted as hostile acts. In the strange world of nuclear deterrence, ignorance may bring bliss.

Discussion Questions

1. How does Lackey's discussion of nuclear deterrence connect up with some of the points about war made by Narveson, Anscombe, or President Reagan?
2. What initial assumptions does Lackey seem to be making? Are some of these open to criticism?
3. How does Lackey develop his utilitarian critique of nuclear deterrence? Which of his points are open to criticism? Develop one such criticism.
4. State and criticize Lackey's alternative policy.
5. Explain in your own words the Prisoner's Dilemma argument and Lackey's reasons for rejecting it. Is his rejection justified? Why or why not?
6. State and criticize the deontological critique proposed by Lackey.
7. What is Lackey's final conclusion? Do you agree or disagree? Support your position with arguments.

The Challenge of Peace

Catholic Bishops of the United States

The Second Vatican Council opened its treatment of modern warfare with the statement: "The whole human race faces a moment of supreme crisis in its advance toward maturity." We agree with the Council's assessment; the crisis of the moment is embodied in the threat which nuclear weapons pose for the world and much that we hold dear in the world. We have seen and felt the effects of the crisis of the nuclear age in the lives of people we serve. Nuclear weaponry has changed the nature of warfare, and the arms race poses a threat to human life and human civilization which is without precedent.

We write this letter from the perspective of Catholic faith. Faith does not insulate us from the daily challenges of life but intensifies our desire to address them precisely in light of the Gospel which has come to us in the person of the Risen Christ. Through the resources of reason and faith we desire in this letter to provide hope for people in our day and direction toward a world freed of the nuclear threat.

As Catholic bishops we write this letter as an exercise of our teaching ministry. The Catholic tradition on war and peace is a long and complex one; it stretches from the Sermon on the Mount to the statements of Pope John Paul II. We wish to explore and explain the resources of the moral-religious teaching and to apply it to specific questions of our day. In doing this we realize, and we want readers of this letter to recognize, that not all statements in this letter have the same moral authority. At times we state universally binding moral principles as well as formal church teaching; at other times we make specific applications, observations and recommendations which allow for diversity of opinion on the part of those who assess the factual data of a situation differently than we do. We expect, however, that our moral judgments will be given serious consideration by Catholics when they are forming their own views on specific problems.

The experience of preparing this letter has manifested to us the range of strongly held opinion in the Catholic community on questions of fact and judgment concerning issues of war and peace. We urge mutual respect among individuals and groups in the Church as this letter is analyzed and discussed. Obviously, as bishops, we believe that such differences should be expressed within the framework of Catholic moral teaching. We need not only conviction and commitment in the Church but also civility and charity.

While this letter is addressed principally to the Catholic community, we want it to make a contribution to the wider public debate in our country on the dangers and dilemmas of the nuclear age. Our contribution will not be primarily technical or political, but we are convinced that there is no satisfactory answer to the human problems of the nuclear age which fails to consider the moral and religious dimensions of the questions we face.

Although we speak in our own name, as Catholic bishops of the Church in the United States, we have been conscious in the preparation of this letter of the consequences our teaching will have not only for the United States but for other nations as well. One important expression of this awareness has been the consultation we have had, by correspondence and in an important meeting held at the Vatican (January 18–19, 1983), with representatives of European bishops' conferences. This consultation with bishops of other countries and, of course, with the Holy See, has been very helpful to us.

Catholic teaching has always understood peace in positive terms. In the words of Pope John Paul II: "Peace is not just the absence of war. . . . Like a cathedral peace must be constructed patiently and with unshakable faith." (Coventry, England, 1982.) Peace is the fruit of order. Order in human society must be shaped on the basis of respect for the transcendence of God and the unique dignity of each person, understood in terms of freedom, justice, truth and love. To avoid war in our day we must be intent on building peace in an increasingly interdependent world. In Part III of this letter we set forth a positive vision of peace and the demands such a vision makes on diplomacy, national policy, and personal choices.

While pursuing peace incessantly, it is also necessary to limit the use of force in a world comprised of nation states, faced with common problems but devoid of an adequate international political authority. Keeping the peace in the nuclear age is a moral and political imperative. In Parts I and II of this letter we set forth both the principles of Catholic teaching on war and a series of judgments, based on these principles, about concrete policies. In making these judgments we speak as moral teachers, not as technical experts.

I. Some Principles, Norms and Premises of Catholic Teaching:

A. On War:

1. Catholic teaching begins in every case with a presumption against war and for peaceful settlement of disputes. In exceptional cases, determined by the moral principles of the Just War tradition, some uses of force are permitted.

2. Every nation has a right to defend itself against unjust aggression.

3. Offensive war of any kind is not morally justifiable.

4. It is never permitted to direct nuclear or conventional weapons to "the indiscriminate destruction of whole cities or vast areas with their populations. . . . " (The Pastoral Constitution, #80.) The intentional killing of innocent civilians or non-combatants is always wrong.

5. Even defensive response to unjust attack can cause destruction which violates the principles of proportionality, going far beyond the limits of legitimate defense. This judgment is particularly important when assessing planned use of nuclear weapons. No defensive strategy, nuclear or conventional, which exceeds the limits of proportionality is morally permissible.

B. On Deterrence:

1. "In current conditions 'deterrence' based on balance, certainly not as an end in itself but as a step on the way toward a progressive disarmament, may still be judged morally acceptable. Nonetheless, in order to ensure peace, it is indispensable not to be satisfied with this minimum which is always susceptible to the real danger of explosion." (Pope John Paul II, Message to U.N. Special Session on Disarmament, #8, June 1982.)

2. No use of nuclear weapons which would violate the principles of discrimination or proportionality may be intended in a strategy of deterrence. The moral demands of Catholic teaching require resolute willingness not to intend or to do moral evil even to save our own lives or the lives of those we love.

3. Deterrence is not an adequate strategy as a long-term basis for peace; it is a transitional strategy justifiable only in conjunction with resolute deter-

mination to pursue arms control and disarmament. We are convinced that "the fundamental principle on which our present peace depends must be replaced by another, which declares that the true and solid peace of nations consists not in equality of arms but in mutual trust alone." (Pope John XXIII, Peace on Earth, #113.)

C. The Arms Race and Disarmament:

1. The arms race is one of the greatest curses on the human race; it is to be condemned as a danger, an act of aggression against the poor, and a folly which does not provide the security it promises. (Cf: The Pastoral Constitution, #81; Statement of the Holy See to the United Nations, 1976.)

2. Negotiations must be pursued in every reasonable form possible; they should be governed by the "demand that the arms race should cease; that the stockpiles which exist in various countries should be reduced equally and simultaneously by the parties concerned; that nuclear weapons should be banned; and that a general agreement should eventually be reached about progressive disarmament and an effective method of control." (Pope John XXIII, Peace on Earth, #112.)

D. On Personal Conscience:

1. Military Service: "All those who enter the military service in loyalty to their country should look upon themselves as the custodians of the security and freedom of their fellow countrymen; and when they carry out their duty properly, they are contributing to the maintenance of peace." (The Pastoral Constitution, #79.)

2. Conscientious Objection: "Moreover, it seems just that laws should make human provision for the case of conscientious objectors who refuse to carry arms, provided they accept some other form of community service." (The Pastoral Constitution, #79.)

3. Non-violence: "In this same spirit we cannot but express our admiration for all who forego the use of violence to vindicate their rights and resort to other means of defense which are available to weaker parties, provided it can be done without harm to the rights of others and of the community." (The Pastoral Constitution, #78.)

4. Citizens and Conscience: "Once again we deem it opportune to remind our children of their duty to take an active part in public life, and to contribute towards the attainment of the common good of the entire human family as well as to that of their own political community. . . . In other words, it is necessary that human beings, in the intimacy of their own consciences, should so live and act in their temporal lives as to create a synthesis between scientific, technical and professional elements on the one hand, and spiritual values on the other." (Pope John XXIII, Peace on Earth, #146; 150.)

II. Moral Principles and Policy Choices

As bishops in the United States, assessing the concrete circumstances of our society, we have made a number of observations and recommendations in the process of applying moral principles to specific policy choices.

A. On the Use of Nuclear Weapons:

1. Counter-Population Use: Under no circumstances may nuclear weapons or other instruments of mass slaughter be used for the purpose of destroying population centers or other predominantly civilian targets. Retaliatory action which would indiscriminately and disproportionately take many wholly innocent lives, lives of people who are in no way responsible for reckless actions of their government, must also be condemned.

2. The Initiation of Nuclear War: We do not perceive any situation in which the deliberate initiation of nuclear war, on however restricted a scale, can be morally justified. Non-nuclear attacks by another state must be resisted by other than nuclear means. Therefore, a serious moral obligation exists to develop non-nuclear defensive strategies as rapidly as possible. In this letter, we urge NATO to move rapidly toward the adoption of a "no first use" policy, but we recognize this will take time to implement and will require the development of an adequate alternative defense posture.

3. Limited Nuclear War: Our examination of the various arguments on this question makes us highly skeptical about the real meaning of "limited." One of the criteria of the Just-War teaching is that there must be a reasonable hope of success in bringing about justice and peace. We must ask whether such a reasonable hope can exist once nuclear weapons have been exchanged. The burden of proof remains on those who assert that meaningful limitation is possible. In our view the first imperative is to prevent any use of nuclear weapons and we hope that leaders will resist the notion that nuclear conflict can be limited, contained or won in any traditional sense.

B. On Deterrence:

In concert with the evaluation provided by Pope John Paul II, we have arrived at a strictly conditional moral acceptance of deterrence. In this letter we have outlined criteria and recommendations which indicate the meaning of conditional acceptance of deterrence policy. We cannot consider such a policy adequate as a long-term basis for peace.

C. On Promoting Peace:

1. We support immediate, bilateral verifiable agreements to halt the testing, production and deployment of new nuclear weapons systems. This recommendation is not to be identified with any specific political initiative.

2. We support efforts to achieve deep cuts in the arsenals of both superpowers; efforts should concentrate first on systems which threaten the retaliatory forces of either major power.

3. We support early and successful conclusion of negotiations of a comprehensive test ban treaty.

4. We urge new efforts to prevent the spread of nuclear weapons in the world, and to control the conventional arms race, particularly the conventional arms trade.

5. We support, in an increasingly interdependent world, political and economic policies designed to protect human dignity and to promote the human rights of every person, especially the least among us. In this regard, we call for the establishment of some form of global authority adequate to the needs of the international common good.

This letter includes many judgments from the perspective of ethics, politics and strategy needed to speak concretely and correctly to the "moment of supreme crisis" identified by Vatican II. We stress again that readers should be aware, as we have been, of the distinction between our statement of moral principles and official Church teaching and our application of these to concrete issues. We urge that special care be taken not to use passages out of context; nor should brief portions of this document be cited to support positions it does not intend to convey or which are not truly in accord with the spirit of its teaching.

In concluding this précis we respond to two key questions often asked about this pastoral letter:

Why do we address these matters fraught with such complexity, controversy and passion? We speak as pastors, not politicians. We are teachers, not technicians. We cannot avoid our responsibility to lift up the moral dimensions of the choices before our world and nation. The nuclear age is an era of moral as well as physical danger. We are the first generation since Genesis with the power to threaten the created order. We cannot remain silent in the face of such danger. Why do we address these issues? We are simply trying to live up to the call of Jesus to be peacemakers in our own time and situation.

What are we saying? Fundamentally, we are saying that the decisions about nuclear weapons are among the most pressing moral questions of our age. While these decisions have obvious military and political aspects, they involve fundamental moral choices. In simple terms, we are saying that good ends (defending one's country, protecting freedom, etc.) cannot justify immoral means (the use of weapons which kill indiscriminately and threaten whole societies). We fear that our world and nation are headed in the wrong direction. More weapons with greater destructive potential are produced every day. More and more nations are seeking to become nuclear powers. In our quest for more and more security we fear we are actually becoming less and less secure.

In the words of our Holy Father, we need a "moral about-face." The whole world must summon the moral courage and technical means to say no to nuclear conflict; no to weapons of mass destruction; no to an arms race which robs the poor and the vulnerable; and no to the moral danger of a nuclear age which places before humankind indefensible choices of constant terror or surrender. Peacemaking is not an optional commitment. It is a requirement of our faith. We are called to be peacemakers, not by some movement of the moment, but by our Lord Jesus. The content and context of our peacemaking is set not by some political agenda or ideological program, but by the teaching of his Church.

Ultimately, this letter is intended as an expression of Christian faith, affirming the confidence we have that the Risen Lord remains with us precisely in moments of crisis. It is our belief in his presence and power among us which sustains us in confronting the awesome challenge of the nuclear age. We speak from faith to provide hope for all who recognize the challenge and are working to confront it with the resources of faith and reason.

To approach the nuclear issue in faith is to recognize our absolute need for prayer: we urge and invite all to unceasing prayer for peace with justice for all people. In a spirit of prayerful hope we present this message of peace.

Discussion Questions

1. In your view is it appropriate for church leaders to make a statement of this kind? Why or why not?
2. With which of the principles, norms, and premises listed by the bishops would Narveson agree? With which might he disagree? Answer the same questions for Anscombe, President Reagan, and Lackey.
3. Which of the principles, norms, and premises do you agree with? Which do you disagree with? State your reasons.
4. The bishops justify their principles, norms, and premises by reference to Catholic teachings. Which of these principles could be justified on nonreligious grounds? How? Which could not? Why?
5. What is the general conclusion of the bishops' letter? Do you agree or disagree? Give arguments for your view.

Suggested Readings for Chapter One

Bennett, John C., ed. *Nuclear Weapons and the Conflict of Conscience*. New York: Charles Scribner's, 1962.

Ginsberg, Robert, ed. *The Critique of War*. Chicago: Henry Regnery, 1969.

Paskins, Barrie, and Michael Dockrill. *The Ethics of War*. Minneapolis: University of Minnesota Press, 1979.

Ramsey, Paul. *The Just War*. New York: Charles Scribner's, 1968.

Stein, Walter, ed. *Nuclear Weapons: A Catholic Response*. New York: Sheed and Ward, 1961.

Wasserstrom, Richard, ed. *War and Morality*. Belmont, Calif.: Wadsworth, 1970.

Walls, Donald. *The War Myth*. New York: Pegasus Books, 1967.

2

Punishment and the
Death Penalty

Aside from war, the situation in which even reasonable and merciful people are sometimes inclined to allow killing is that of legal execution for certain crimes. A number of questions are intertwined in this issue. For example, even if society has a right to sentence people to death for certain crimes, should society always, or ever, exercise this right? In order to make some headway in analyzing problems of capital punishment, we must first examine problems of punishment in general. If we have a theory as to when it is legitimate to punish in general, this theory should cast light on when, if ever, a punishment of death is appropriate.

There are several major theories of punishment; each to some extent depends on an analogy with other forms of human activity and each has consequences regarding when and how much punishment is legitimate.

The Reform Theory

This theory says that the purpose of punishment is to reform the offender. The analogy is to sickness and medicine; just as the purpose of medicine is to cure the patient, the purpose of punishment should be to cure the criminal. Some consequences of this view are that punishment should be applied for as long or short a time as is necessary to accomplish the cure and that if the criminal reforms without punishment there is no point at all to punishing him or her.

It might seem that a reform view would rule out death as a punishment, but this is not necessarily so. To those who hold the view that there is life after death and that our actions and choices in this life affect what happens to us in a future life, it may seem highly reasonable to execute certain kinds of criminals. Murderers, for example, who were convicted and sentenced to death might sincerely repent in the period between conviction and execution and save their souls even if they lost their lives.

The Deterrence Theory

In this theory the purpose of punishment is to deter or prevent crime—in other words, to frighten potential criminals out of committing crimes. The analogy is to using promises and threats as a means of controlling behavior. The purpose of a promise or threat is to affect behavior, and if it affects behavior in the desired way it is successful. Thus some consequences of the deterrence theory are that the punishment for a crime must be known and the punishment must ordinarily be carried out; just as when you promise or threaten you must do what you promise or threaten to do or lose credibility, the deterrence theory implies that punishments must be carried out or the law loses credibility.

The death penalty obviously deters the person executed from all future crimes, and there is a widespread feeling that executing a criminal for a given crime will deter others from committing it. The widespread feeling, however, seems to receive little support from scientific surveys that have been made.

The Retributive Theory

According to this theory, persons should be punished only if they deserve to be punished, and no more than they deserve to be punished. The relevant analogy is to monetary debts: Some individuals have claims to be paid certain amounts and others have claims against them to pay certain amounts. It would be unjust to demand money that is not owed or to demand more than is owed. Similarly, in the retributive view it is unjust to punish people unless they deserve to be punished or to punish them more than they deserve.

The retributive theory as it is usually held is not what I will call *strict retributivism*. Strict retributivism is the view that it is unjust to punish anyone more *or* less than he or she deserves or to reward anyone less *or* more than he or she deserves. Most retributivists are moderate retributivists; they hold that although it is unjust to punish more or reward less than deserved it is permissible and perhaps even admirable to punish less than deserved (mercy) or reward more (generosity).

Some consequences of the retributive theory are that once persons have been appropriately punished their debt is cancelled and they are "even" with society. On the other hand, someone who has been overpunished has a claim against society for some kind of compensation.

Since a retributive theory usually holds that there should be some balance between crime and punishment it may hold that the death penalty is appropriate for crimes such as murder. However, the moderate retributivist may maintain that even if it is just to execute a murderer it is not necessarily unjust to give a lesser punishment—in other words, to show mercy.

It is important to realize that all of these theories play some part in our ordinary thinking about punishment and the death penalty. We are reluctant to continue punishment if reform seems complete (as in the case of escaped criminals who have become good citizens and are then detected). We often feel that it is an important question whether various penalties, especially the death penalty, do deter criminals.

And we use expressions such as "criminals must pay their debt to society" that indicate retributivist presuppositions.

This chapter opens with an article by C. S. Lewis, who holds a moderate retributivist position with some elements of the other views. He argues that we may justly punish people only if they deserve punishment, but if they do deserve punishment we may take reformative or deterrent effects into consideration; he criticizes reform and deterrence theories. Next, J. R. Lucas argues for a sophisticated reason of a deterrence theory and criticizes both retributive and reform theories.

In the next three selections, Sidney Hook and Jacques Barzun argue in favor of the death penalty in some cases and Hugo Bedau criticizes their arguments. One interesting aspect of this exchange is the mixture of reform, deterrence, and retributive arguments in all three selections.

The Humanitarian Theory of Punishment

C. S. Lewis

In England we have lately had a controversy about Capital Punishment. I do not know whether a murderer is more likely to repent and make a good end on the gallows a few weeks after his trial or in the prison infirmary thirty years later. I do not know whether the fear of death is an indispensable deterrent. I need not, for the purpose of this article, decide whether it is a morally permissible deterrent. Those are questions which I propose to leave untouched. My subject is not Capital Punishment in particular, but that theory of punishment in general which the controversy showed to be almost universal among my fellow-countrymen. It may be called the Humanitarian theory. Those who hold it think that it is mild and merciful. In this I believe that they are seriously mistaken. I believe that the "Humanity" which it claims is a dangerous illusion and disguises the possibility of cruelty and injustice without end. I urge a return to the traditional or Retributive theory not solely, not even primarily, in the interests of society, but in the interests of the criminal.

According to the Humanitarian theory, to punish a man because he deserves it, and as much as he deserves, is mere revenge, and therefore, barbarous and immoral. It is maintained that the only legitimate motives for punishing are the desire to deter others by example or to mend the criminal. When this theory is combined, as frequently happens, with the belief that all crime is more or less pathological, the idea of mending tails off into that of healing or curing and punishment becomes therapeutic. Thus it appears at first

From *Res Judicatae,* 1953, by permission of the Melbourne University Law Review, Curtis Brown, London, and William Collins Son & Co. Ltd.

sight that we have passed from the harsh and self-righteous notion of giving the wicked their deserts to the charitable and enlightened one of tending the psychologically sick. What could be more amiable? One little point which is taken for granted in this theory needs, however, to be made explicit. The things done to the criminal, even if they are called cures, will be just as compulsory as they were in the old days when we called them punishments. If a tendency to steal can be cured by psychotherapy, the thief will no doubt be forced to undergo the treatment. Otherwise, society cannot continue.

My contention is that this doctrine, merciful though it appears, really means that each one of us, from the moment he breaks the law, is deprived of the rights of a human being.

The reason is this. The Humanitarian theory removes from Punishment the concept of Desert. But the concept of Desert is the only connecting link between punishment and justice. It is only as deserved or undeserved that a sentence can be just or unjust. I do not here contend that the question "Is it deserved?" is the only one we can reasonably ask about a punishment. We may very properly ask whether it is likely to deter others and to reform the criminal. But neither of these two last questions is a question about justice. There is no sense in talking about a "just deterrent" or a "just cure." We demand of a deterrent not whether it is just but whether it will deter. We demand of a cure not whether it is just but whether it succeeds. Thus when we cease to consider what the criminal deserves and consider only what will cure him or deter others, we have tacitly removed him from the sphere of justice altogether; instead of a person, a subject of rights, we now have a mere object, a patient, a "case."

The distinction will become clearer if we ask who will be qualified to determine sentences when sentences are no longer held to derive their propriety from the criminal's deservings. On the old view the problem of fixing the right sentence was a moral problem. Accordingly, the judge who did it was a person trained in jurisprudence; trained, that is, in a science which deals with rights and duties, and which, in origin at least, was consciously accepting guidance from the Law of Nature, and from Scripture. We must admit that in the actual penal code of most countries at most times these high originals were so much modified by local custom, class interests, and utilitarian concessions, as to be very imperfectly recognizable. But the code was never in principle, and not always in fact, beyond the control of the conscience of the society. And when (say, in eighteenth-century England) actual punishments conflicted too violently with the moral sense of the community, juries refused to convict and reform was finally brought about. This was possible because, so long as we are thinking in terms of Desert, the propriety of the penal code, being a moral question, is a question on which every man has the right to an opinion, not because he follows this or that profession, but because he is simply a man, a rational animal enjoying the Natural Light. But all this is changed when we drop the concept of Desert. The only two questions we may now ask about a punishment are whether it deters and whether it cures. But these are not questions on which anyone is entitled to have an opinion simply because he is a man. He is not entitled to an opinion even if, in addition to being a man, he should happen also to be a jurist, a Christian, and a moral theologian. For they are not questions about principle but about matter of fact; and for such *cuiquam in sua arte credendum*.[1] Only the expert "penologist" (let barbarous things have barbarous names), in the light of previous experiment, can tell us what is likely to deter: only the psychotherapist can tell us what is likely to cure. It will be in vain for the rest of us, speaking simply as men, to say, "but this punishment is hideously unjust, hideously disproportionate to the criminal's deserts." The experts with perfect logic will reply, "but nobody was talking about deserts. No one was talking about *punishment* in your archaic vindictive sense of the word. Here are the statistics proving that this treatment deters. Here are the statistics proving that this other treatment cures. What is your trouble?"

The Humanitarian theory, then, removes sentences from the hands of jurists whom the public conscience is entitled to criticize and places them in the hands of technical experts whose special sciences do not even employ such categories as rights or justice. It might be argued that since this transference results from an abandonment of the old idea of punishment, and, therefore, of all vindictive motives, it will be safe to leave our criminals in such hands. I will not pause to comment on the simple-minded view of fallen human nature which such a belief implies. Let us rather remember that the "cure" of criminals is to be compulsory; and let us then watch how the theory actually works in the mind of the Humanitarian. The immediate starting point of this article was a letter I read in one of our Leftist weeklies. The author was pleading that a certain sin, now treated by our laws as a crime, should henceforward be treated as a disease. And he complained that under the present system the offender, after a term in jail, was simply let out to return to his original environment where he would probably relapse. What he complained of was not the shutting up but the letting out. On his remedial view of punishment the offender should, of course, be detained until he was cured. And of course the official straighteners are the only people who can say when that is. The first result of the Humanitarian theory is, therefore, to substitute for a definite sentence (reflecting to some extent the community's moral judgment on the degree of ill-desert involved) an indefinite sentence terminable only by the word of those experts—and they are not experts in moral theology nor even in the Law of Nature —who inflict it. Which of us, if he stood in the dock, would not prefer to be tried by the old system?

It may be said that by the continued use of the word punishment and the use of the verb "inflict" I am misrepresenting Humanitarians. They are not punishing, not inflicting, only healing. But do not let us be deceived by a name. To be taken without consent from my home and friends; to lose my liberty; to undergo all those assaults on my personality which modern psychotherapy knows how to deliver; to be re-made after some pattern of "normality" hatched in a Viennese laboratory to which I never professed allegiance; to know that this process will never end until either my captors have succeeded or I grown wise enough to cheat them with apparent success—who cares whether this is called Punishment or not? That it includes most of the elements for which any punishment is feared—shame, exile, bondage, and years eaten by the locust—is obvious. Only enormous ill-desert could justify it; but ill-desert is the very conception which the Humanitarian theory has thrown overboard.

If we turn from the curative to the deterrent justification of punishment we shall find the new theory even more alarming. When you punish a man *in terrorem*,[2] make of him an "example" to others, you are admittedly using him as a means to an end; someone else's end. This, in itself, would be a very wicked thing to do. On the classical theory of Punishment it was of course justified on the ground that the man deserved it. That was assumed to be established before any question of "making him an example" arose. You then, as the saying is, killed two birds with one stone; in the process of giving him what he deserved you set an example to others. But take away desert and the whole morality of the punishment disappears. Why, in Heaven's name, am I to be sacrificed to the good of society in this way?—unless, of course, I deserve it.

But that is not the worst. If the justification of exemplary punishment is not to be based on desert but solely on its efficacy as a deterrent, it is not absolutely necessary that the man we punish should even have committed the crime. The deterrent effect demands that the public should draw the moral, "If we do such an act we shall suffer like that man." The punishment of a man actually guilty whom the public think innocent will not have the desired effect; the punishment of a man actually innocent will, provided the public think him guilty. But every modern State has powers which make it easy to fake a trial. When a victim is urgently needed for exemplary purposes and a guilty victim cannot be found, all the purposes of deterrence will be equally served by the punishment (call it "cure" if you prefer) of an innocent victim, provided that the public can be cheated into thinking him guilty. It is no use to ask me why I assume that our rulers will be so wicked. The punishment of an innocent, that is, an undeserving, man is wicked only if we grant the traditional view that righteous punishment means deserved punishment. Once we have abandoned that criterion, all punishments have to be justified, if at all, on other grounds that have nothing to do with desert. Where the punishment of the innocent can be justified on those grounds (and it could in some cases be justified as a deterrent) it will be no less moral than any other punishment. Any distaste for it on the part of a Humanitarian will be merely a hang-over from the Retributive theory.

It is, indeed, important to notice that my argument so far supposes no evil intentions on the part of the Humanitarian and considers only what is involved in the logic of his position. My contention is that good men (not bad men) consistently acting upon that position would act as cruelly and unjustly as the greatest tyrants. They might in some respects act even worse. Of all tyrannies a tyranny sincerely exercised for the good of its victims may be the most oppressive. It may be better to live under robber barons than under omnipotent moral busybodies. The robber baron's cruelty may sometimes sleep, his cupidity may at some point be satiated; but those who torment us for our own good will torment us without end for they do so with the approval of their own conscience. They may be more likely to go to Heaven yet at the same time likelier to make a Hell of earth. Their very kindness stings with intolerable insult. To be "cured" against one's will and cured of states which we may not regard as disease is to be put on a level with those who have not yet reached the age of reason or those who never will; to be classed with infants, imbeciles, and domestic animals. But to be punished, however severely, because we have deserved it, because we "ought to have known better," is to be treated as a human person made in God's image.

In reality, however, we must face the possibility of bad rulers armed with a Humanitarian theory of punishment. A great many popular blue prints for a Christian society are merely what the Elizabethans called "eggs in moonshine" because they assume that the whole society is Christian or that the Christians are in control. This is not so in most contemporary States. Even if it were, our rulers would still be fallen men, and, therefore, neither very wise nor very good. As it is, they will usually be unbelievers. And since wisdom and virtue are not the only or the commonest qualifications for a place in the government, they will not often be even the best unbelievers.

The practical problem of Christian politics is not that of drawing up schemes for a Christian society, but that of living as innocently as we can with unbelieving fellow-subjects under unbelieving rulers who will never be perfectly wise and good and who will sometimes be very wicked and very foolish. And when they are wicked the Humanitarian theory of punishment will put in their hands a finer instrument of tyranny than wickedness ever had before. For if crime and disease are to be regarded as the same thing, it follows that any state of mind which our masters choose to call "disease" can be treated as crime, and compulsorily cured. It will be vain to plead that states of mind which displease government need not always involve moral turpitude and do not therefore always deserve forfeiture of liberty. For our masters will not be using the concepts of Desert and Punishment but those of disease and cure. We know that one school of psychology already regards religion as a neurosis. When this particular neurosis becomes inconvenient to government, what is to hinder government from proceeding to "cure" it? Such "cure" will, of course, be compulsory; but under the Humanitarian theory it will not be called by the shocking name of Persecution. No one will blame us for being Christians, no one will hate us, no one will revile us. The new Nero will approach us with the silky manners of a doctor, and though all will be in fact as compulsory as the *tunica molesta* or Smithfield or Tyburn, all will go on within the unemotional therapeutic sphere where words like "right" and "wrong" or "free-dom" and "slavery" are never heard. And thus when the command is given, every prominent Christian in the land may vanish overnight into Institutions for the Treat-ment of the Ideologically Unsound, and it will rest with the expert jailers to say when (if ever) they are to re-emerge. But it will not be persecution. Even if the treat-ment is painful, even if it is life-long, even if it is fatal, that will be only a regrettable accident; the intention was purely therapeutic. In ordinary medicine there were painful operations and fatal operations; so in this. But because they are "treatment," not punish-ment, they can be criticized only by fellow-experts and on technical grounds, never by men as men and on grounds of justice.

This is why I think it essential to oppose the Humanitarian theory of punishment, root and branch, wherever we encounter it. It carries on its front a semblance of mercy which is wholly false. That is how it can deceive men of good will. The error began, perhaps, with Shelley's statement that the distinction between mercy and justice was invented in the courts of tyrants. It sounds noble, and was indeed the error of a noble mind. But the distinction is essential. The older view was that mercy "tempered" justice, or (on the highest level of all) that mercy and justice had met and kissed. The essential act of mercy was to pardon; and pardon in its very essence involves the recognition of guilt and ill-desert in the recipient. If crime is only a disease which needs cure, not sin which deserves punishment, it cannot be pardoned. How can you pardon a man for having a gumboil or a club foot? But the Humanitarian theory wants simply to abolish Justice and substitute Mercy for it. This means that you start being "kind" to people before you have considered their rights, and then force upon them supposed kindnesses which no one but you will recognize as kindnesses and which the recipient will feel as abominable cruelties. You have overshot the mark. Mercy, detached from Justice, grows unmerciful. That is the impor-tant paradox. As there are plants which will flourish only in mountain soil, so it appears that Mercy will flower only when it grows in the crannies of the rock of Justice: transplanted to the marshlands of mere Humanitarianism, it becomes a man-eating weed, all the more dangerous because it is still called by the same name as the mountain variety. But we ought long ago to have learned our lesson. We should be too old now to be deceived by those humane pretensions which have served to usher in every cruelty of the revolutionary period in which we live. These are the "precious balms" which will "break our heads."[3]

There is a fine sentence in Bunyan: "It came burning hot into my mind, whatever he said, and however he flattered, when he got me home to his House, he would sell me for a Slave."[4] There is a fine couplet, too, in John Ball:

> Be war or ye be wo;
> Knoweth your frend from your foo.[5]

Notes

[1]"We must believe the expert in his own field."

[2]"To cause terror."

[3]Psalm 141:6.

[4]*The Pilgrim's Progress,* ed. James Blanton Wharey, second edition revised by Roger Sharrock, Oxford English Texts (Oxford, 1960), Part I, p. 70.

[5]"John Ball's Letter to the Peasants of Essex, 1381," lines 11–12, found in *Fourteenth Century Verse and Prose,* ed. Kenneth Sisam (Oxford, 1921), p. 161.

Discussion Questions

1. Why does Lewis believe that a retributive theory of punishment is not only in the interests of society but also in the interests of the criminal? Do you agree? Why or why not?

2. Does Lewis give a fair statement of reform and deterrent views? How might a supporter of one of these views reply to Lewis?

3. In Lewis's view, is the retributive theory vindictive or revengeful? Why or why not? Do you agree with his arguments?

4. What are Lewis's arguments against a reform theory? A deterrent theory? What counterarguments could be given?

5. How does Lewis relate his views to Christianity? What criticisms could be made of the connection?

Or Else

J. R. Lucas

I

The quality of mercy is not to be restrained, and it is a decisive defect of both the pure retributivist and the pure utilitarian theories of punishment that they leave no room for the exercise of mercy. For the retributivist, mercy is logically possible but morally wrong. A man's crime calls for a certain penalty: we may choose not to inflict it, but if so, we are failing to do what is required. We are failing to "annul" the crime or to redress the balance, and although our action is describable it is not commendable. For the utilitarian, mercy is not even logically possible except as a foolish failure to do what is best for the criminal and

From the proceedings of the Aristotelian Society, 1968–1969. Copyright © 1969. Reprinted by permission of the Society.

for society as a whole. There is no independent tariff, based on the gravity of the crime, against which we can set pleas for mercy and promises of amendment. If ever it could be right to let somebody off, then it is mandatory to do so, and there is no argument for any heavier penalty at all. Punishment, on the utilitarian theory, is a matter of simple calculation—what course of action now will produce the best consequences in future—and there is no tension, no room for conflict between the competing ideals of mercy and justice. Both the theories are inadequate. The fundamental reason is that they operate too simple a tense logic, in which the only tenses are the past simple, present simple and future simple, whereas to account adequately for the concept of punishment, we need a schema more complicated both in tense and in mood, in which we can handle "past futures," and imperatives as well as indicatives. Both the backward-looking and the forward-looking theories make valid positive points, but deny or ignore other points equally valid. We cannot give an adequate account of a person's being punished without regard to what he has done: but equally essential, I shall argue, is the word "shall."

II

Punishments are unwelcome, to be avoided; what Aristotle termed φευκτα. They need not involve the infliction of pain nor of suffering in any but a highly metaphorical sense. One would have to love money very much indeed to regard a ten-shilling fine as an infliction of suffering: one can barely describe it even as a piece of unpleasantness. All that is essential is that given a free choice one would not have chosen to pay ten shillings to the Clerk of the Court. In a few cases where old lags commit crimes in order to be sent back to prison, we feel uneasy—it is because people in general do not want to go to prison that imprisonment is a punishment, and if a man does want to go to prison, then imprisonment ceases to be a punishment for him. More generally, it is absurd to punish somebody by letting him do what he would have chosen anyhow to do. I cannot punish you by giving you a ticket for the opera, or a thousand pounds in cash, or the opportunity of becoming a member of the MCC [a club]: for if you want to go to the opera or to be rich or to join the MCC, you will regard these opportunities as desirable, and if you do not want them, then you need not avail yourself to them, and are no worse off than you were before. Punishments may or may not be good for you, but they must be what you would not have chosen if left to yourself.

Not everything that befalls us against our will is to be construed as a punishment. Punishments not only must be against our will but must be brought about by the will of somebody else. They must be meted out by men or God, who can be asked "Why are you doing that to me?" and can answer "In order to punish you." Natural disasters and accidental damages are not, save on one peculiar theological view, punishments. Nor are the many hurts and frustrations that men inflict on one another in the pursuit of their several separate aims. I may cause a man great suffering by reviewing his book unfavorably, or by giving him the sack, or by awarding a fellowship to his rival or a contract to his competitor: but I am not punishing him. Nor am I punishing him if I quarantine him, certify him as a lunatic, or take him into protective custody. Nor even, as I shall argue later, if, as unsuccessful blackmailer, I carry out my threat to ruin him. We tend to philosophize about punishment in isolation from other ills that may beset us, and to think of the rest of life as a bed of roses into which the thorn of deliberately induced suffering is intermittently introduced by penologists. But life is full of crosses; and the exact nature of punishment is much better understood if it can be compared and contrasted with the other undesirables we are unable to avoid.

Many things are done against our will, but not in order to hurt or frustrate us. My neighbor who builds a piggery on his land is unmindful of my interests, but he does it for the sake of his profits, not my despite. Many actions are hurtful and known to be hurtful, and yet are done: but they are not done in order to be hurtful, and if there were an equally effective but less hurtful way of accomplishing the agent's purposes, he would be perfectly ready to adopt them. If we can, we inoculate people rather than confine them in quarantine, and give schizophrenics doses of nicotinamide instead of incarcerating them in a lunatic asylum, and it is a test of protective custody's being what it claims to be that the police will take the man to a place of safety and then enable him to resume the exercise of his liberty. Punishments, by contrast, not only are unwelcome but are intended to be, and would lose their point if they were not.

Punishment must not only be inflicted intentionally, but must be inflicted *for* something done. Quarantine, certification and protective custody are not punishments not only because they are not intended to be unwelcome but because to the question "Why are you doing this to me?" the answer is not "Because you did that" but "In order to protect other people (or yourself) from possible infection (or assault or harm)." In some spartan societies physical pain is intentionally inflicted in the course of initiation ceremonies: but although intentional, it is still not punishment, since the justification is not what the boy has done but what it will do for the boy or what it shows the boy to be. Quinton is right to argue that it is part of the concept of punishment that people can—logically can—be punished only *for* something done.[1] Although of course we may be mistaken, and although people other than the judge may think the accused man innocent, and although in some foreign country there may be a corrupt and cynical judge who knows the accused to have been framed on a trumped-up charge, there remains a logical impropriety in a judge saying "You did not do it, but I am punishing you nonetheless." No law of logic can prevent penalties from being exacted from men actually innocent; logic is concerned only with words, and forbids only that the innocent should be punished *under that description*. For what distinguishes punishment from other unwelcome attentions of agents is that when we ask "Why?," the answer begins "Because you have. . . . " Even in the difficult case of vicarious punishments, the person and the tense must remain the same. Although we may be prepared to stomach some members of a community or group being punished for actions done by the whole, or some other members of that community or group, our sense of justice is affronted. We are individualists, and believe that the courts, like lovers in France and Germany, should use the second person singular, not the second person plural. But the collective punishments, however wrong, do not destroy Quinton's thesis. I may, intelligibly if unjustly, be punished for what my children, my colleagues, my compatriots or my co-religionists have done, but not for what the flower children, the rotarians of Kansas City, the citizens of Peru or the ideologists of the Kremlin have done.

Punishments are intended to be unwelcome and are for something done by the person punished, or at least, either erroneously or vicariously, imputed to him. Moreover, what was done must be a *mis*deed. It may be morally wrong, or socially wrong, or wrong merely because prohibited by some law or convention or rule. But unless the person who is punishing me is prepared to say that what he is punishing me for is—in some sense—wrong, he is as incoherent as he would be if he said he was punishing me for nothing. He does not have to endorse its wrongfulness in any strong Harean sense. Mabbott cites the example of the Dean enforcing a College rule which he himself disagrees with,[2] and it is a common predicament. But although it may on occasion pose severe moral problems for the holders of office, it does not affect the logic of punishment, which is being imposed for an action which can, according to the relevant criteria, be described as wrong.

The fact that punishment must be for wrongdoing, helps us distinguish punishments from other unwelcome actions undertaken in respect of what has been done. In any free society, some decisions are left to the individual to take, and he may bargain with other individuals, offering to take some decision they want in return for their taking some decision he desires. And conversely, I may decide adversely unless the person concerned acts in the way I want or refrains from acting in the way I dislike. "Either you come down to seven and a half thousand," I may say to the vendor, "or I shall break off negotiations." If such a threat proves ineffective and I therefore carry it out and break off negotiations, my action cannot be correctly described as a punishment, although it is intended to be unwelcome to the vendor, and has been undertaken in respect of what he has done or has failed to do. Threats and punishments, although closely allied, are distinguished at least by this: that I can, with at least logical propriety, carry out a threat whenever the person concerned has failed to conform with my requirements, whereas it is logically impossible to punish except for wrongdoing. It is for this reason that the blackmailer cannot be said to be punishing his victim when he exposes him, since the victim's failure to pay up could not be described even by the blackmailer himself as wrong.

Punishment is not revenge. Punishment is disinterested, revenge self-regarding. I punish you for the wrong you have done, full stop, whereas I revenge myself on you for wrong you have done *me*. And whereas my logical credentials for taking revenge are unimpeachable—however unchristian it may be to take revenge upon those that do me wrong, it is quite intelligible—the position of the man who inflicts punishment is open to question: "Who made you judge over us? What business is it of yours?" The busybody cannot describe himself as such. Any man may feel righteous indignation, but one requires some *locus standi* [standing] to be able to inflict punishment. It need not be, as Hart maintains,[3] a legal authority. Parents can punish not because the law says so, but because they care for their children: and where we are prepared to talk of punishment non-metaphorically in the dim and difficult field of personal relations, it is on the basis of some community of value, some shared concern; the child can be said to punish his parents for having been away, because he sees their absence as a threat to family life, and inarticulately feels that they must be taught a lesson if family life is not to be disrupted. But personal relations are not susceptible of precise analysis, and the distinction between punishment and revenge becomes tenuous. In general, however, just as the wrong for which punishment is imposed is not personal, so the person imposing punishment must do so not in a purely personal capacity but as the representative of some society, some community of concern, some system of shared values.

III

Deeds speak louder than words. Punishments are intended, first and foremost, to underline the importance of some law, convention, custom, rule or moral principle, and to make manifest the imperative necessity of obedience. A plain, unvarnished injunction, with no sanctions attached, is, and will be regarded as, just a pious exhortation. For in a community of free agents, not all of whom are disposed to toe the line, there is a permanent possibility of disobedience, which we must be prepared to envisage and answer the question "Then what?" Mandatory injunctions are meant to be obeyed: if we are not prepared to take action to see that our injunctions are obeyed, then we cannot be said to mean that they shall be, but only to hope that they may be. And, *per contra*, if we want not merely to give advice "You ought to abstain from murder," but to give a commandment which is intended to be effective and can be seen to be intended to be effective, we have to say not simply "You shall abstain from murder," but "You shall abstain from murder, *or else.*" It is a threat, although not just a threat. Its prime function is to provide an added reason for acting in accordance with some law, convention, custom, rule or moral principle; and we use it to insist that laws, conventions, customs, rules or moral principles are obeyed, notwithstanding the fact that some people are not convinced of their validity or obligatoriness. Often it is rational to be more concerned with the avoidance of the action than with the autonomy of the agent. Better that potential murderers heteronomously refrain from killing their victims than that they authentically act upon their atavistic impulses. Rather than leaving the rule against murder to the rational approbation of each individual will, we add the additional consideration, if any be needed, that if one does murder, one's life will be nasty, solitary or short. In a world of partly rational but not highly moral agents it is the only way of securing compliance and showing everybody that we intend to secure compliance.

If there are occasions when we need to reinforce an "ought" with a threat to ensure a "shall," there may be occasions when we are faced with carrying out the threat, and have to punish. The sentence is the conclusion of *modus tollendo ponens* [an argument form] the major premise of which is, either explicitly or implicitly, an omnitemporal disjunction in the imperative mood,

> Either abstain from wrongdoing or be punished,

which is promulgated in order to be obeyed, while the minor premise is a dated statement of fact,

> You did not abstain from wrongdoing

from which we draw the conclusion

> Be punished.

Normal forward-looking theories of punishment confine their attention to the conclusion, and fail to see it as a conclusion, and it is a merit of Quinton's thesis that it insists that the conclusion can be justified only as such, as following upon the minor premise. But whereas we cannot justify the conclusion except by reference to the premises, we can justify the major premise by forward-looking considerations. So long as there may be at least one bad man about, if we attach great importance to some species of wrongdoing not being done, then it is rational to annex to that sort of wrongdoing the additional disincentive that is likely to be efficacious in persuading the bad man not to do it. Having done this, if the bad man still does it, his punishment follows as a matter of course, just as if we make a promise, we carry it out as a matter of course. In either case, there may be further considerations which invite mercy or justify us in breaking our promise; but in the absence of further considerations, we do not need to justify *de novo* [anew] either carrying out a threat or fulfilling a promise, for the whole practice would break down if we did not normally and as a matter of course act upon our word. Mercy is not impossible, in the way that it is impossible to "punish" an admittedly innocent man for something he did not do: but we could not make a practice of always being merciful, without ceasing to enforce the laws.

Punishment then should be viewed as playing an essential part in enforcing, inculcating or expressing a system of law, conventions, customs, rules or moral principles. It emphasizes that they are imperatives, and are meant to be obeyed. It is, indeed, intended to deter. But traditional deterrent theories have got their tense-logic wrong. They ask "What is the justification for being beastly to this man now?," and the answer "To deter— others from imitating, and himself from repeating, his offense" is open to all the standard objections. Instead, they should ask "What was the justification for saying to this man among others that, if he did not abstain from wrongdoing, he was going to face the consequences which are now befalling him?," and to this question forward-looking answers are in place. We are sometimes justified in threatening punishment in order the more emphatically to tell people that they shall not do what they ought not to do, because the consequences of their being thus addressed are good. If so, our complete justification for punishing this man now will be neither in the past simple tense nor in the future simple tense, but in the past future tense; and will be in the second person singular now, because in the second person plural earlier. It is for this reason that we are not led to the absurd consequences which seem to follow from any simple deterrent theory. It is not enough merely to pretend to punish, because, whatever the effect on the other people, the wrongdoer himself knows that he has not been punished, and that the laws *etc.* did not mean what they said, and were not, after all, to be taken seriously. Equally incoherent is the "punishing" of an innocent man: for although it may be an effective deterrent to third persons, it fails to make sense in the second person. We cannot tell the innocent man why we are punishing him, because the antecedent of the conditional threat has not been fulfilled.

The paradigm justification for using the threat of punishment is to secure the observance of laws, where their observance is very good or their non-observance very bad. We can also justify it not in order to secure uniform observance but in order to inculcate or instill them, and perhaps also merely to express the extreme importance we attach to them. In the paradigm case the argument is relatively simple: we need to have a rule, perhaps only as a convention, perhaps in order to secure some ulterior ends, and we need to be able to rely on everyone's keeping to the rule, whatever it is. We can ensure this in our society of frail and sometimes wicked men, only by annexing some penalty to law-breaking. And in deciding what laws to have and what penalties, we should be guided by more or less utilitarian considerations. Although the legislator is authorized to make certain sorts of action wrong and to prohibit them under penalty, and although it is primarily the law-breakers' own fault that they have brought unwelcome consequences upon themselves, yet the legislator cannot expect that nobody will contravene the law, and therefore needs to strike some sort of balance between the misdeeds we want not committed and the penalties we envisage imposing on those who do commit them. Parking offenses are not so bad that we could contemplate killing the miscreant who failed to abstain from them. Rather than put ourselves in the position where we might be committed to killing someone, we are prepared to put up with wrongdoing. Only if the evil to be avoided—e.g., somebody else's death—is comparable with that envisaged as a punishment, are we able to justify our having laid it down. So too with exemplary punishments, we justify them by balancing the exceptional evil of leaving unenforced a particular law at a particular time—e.g., a law against looting after an earthquake—against the exceptional severity of the punishment. It is also clear in cases of purely utilitarian legislation why the ancient tags *nullum crimen sine lege* [no crime unless there is a law], *nulla poena sine lege* [no penalty unless there is a law] apply, and why retrospective legislation is logically, as well as morally, repugnant. We cannot know, apart from there being a law against it, that the action is to be abstained from: only the law prohibiting it makes it wrong; only the law prohibiting it justifies the punishment. And if the major premise was not promulgated to me in time for me to act on it, I cannot reasonably be proceeded against for not having done so.

Where the wrongdoing forbidden under penalty is wrong independently of the prohibitions, or where the reason for threatening punishment is not simply that of enforcement, the argument becomes more complicated. Clearly the principle *nullum crimen sine lege* is no longer true analytically. No enactment is needed to tell us that murder is wrong. And even if we have not explicity promulgated a prohibition against murder with penalties specified, we need not feel debarred, as a matter of logic, from punishing offenders. For from the mere fact that the offender knew that it was very wrong, he could have inferred that its wrongfulness would be underlined by penalties. The principle *nulla poena sine lege* is thus not an analytic truth either, in the way that Quinton's principle, *no punishment except for having done wrong,* is. The point is often missed, because we often have it as a *legal* rule that no legal officer is to impose any legal punishment except in accordance with some antecedent law. There are good arguments for this principle of constitutional limitation: but if they are accepted, they establish the principle *nulla poena sine lege* as a constitutional principle, not an analytic truth. The argument over the Nüremberg trials was not over the intelligibility of describing war-crimes as crimes and inflicting punishments on their perpetrators, but over the morality of abrogating constitutional principles we normally and with good reason cherish. In undeveloped legal systems many laws have not been explicitly promulgated, and the principles *nullum crimen sine lege* and *nulla poena sine lege* do not apply; as equally in the informal setting of family, school or small community. Whereas a man accused of committing a *malum prohibitum* [something wrong because prohibited] can defend himself by the plea "I did not, and could not, know it was wrong," it would smack of legalism to argue, when accused of having committed a *malum in se* [something wrong in itself], "I knew it was wrong, but no penalties have been prescribed," and would invite the counter "If you knew it was wrong, you should have realized that you would not be allowed to get away with it." Sometimes the major premise of the syllogism does not need to have been explicitly promulgated, since when people know that the action is very wrong, they can infer, although not conclusively, the "or else," from the great wrongfulness of the action together with the further principle that crime does not—is not going to be allowed to—pay.

Although the paradigm reason for threatening punishment is to enforce, we also punish in order to teach; in particular, we punish children in order that they may realize what things are wrong, and learn not to do them. It is for their sakes that we insist upon their abstaining from wrongdoing, not because childish misdemeanors can cause harm to others. We punish children in order that they may learn to know what is wrong and avoid doing it on their own, autonomously and apart from the fear of consequences. When we seek to reform or educate our aim is forward-looking, and questions of cause and effect are relevant. Habits can be instilled, but moral principles need to be made one's own if they are not to degenerate into a legalistic pharisaism. We may be able to make people sober by Act of Parliament, and perhaps get them into good habits, but no Act of Parliament can make them autonomously good: and equally in education, punishment may be a useful pedagogic device, but is stringently limited in what it can achieve.

The major premise is in the second person plural. It is addressed to every one, not only to those who fail to comply and render themselves liable to punishment. And we annex penalties with an eye more to those who will comply and will not be punished, than to those who will actually undergo the punishment: and therefore sometimes we may annex penalties not so much in order to deter potential law-breakers as to express the importance felt by the law-abiding, and punishment then becomes, in Lord Denning's phrase, an emphatic denunciation of the crime. To this limited extent we need to qualify deterrence as the general justifying aim of punishment, and say simply that we threaten punishment in order to emphasize and make mandatory: but punishment would not serve either to educate or to express emphatic denunciation unless it were for most people also a deterrent.

Punishment, then, is part of the system whereby a code of law or set of moral principles is made mandatory in a society of partly rational and imperfectly well-intentioned agents. By annexing punishments to wrongdoing, we provide additional reasons for abstaining from wrongdoing, and show that we are in earnest in forbidding it, and intend our prohibitions to be taken seriously. We know, however, that sometimes we shall fail, and shall have to carry out the punishments we have threatened: and therefore ought not to purchase a minor good at the cost of inflicting great harm on those who fail to conform.

IV

It is difficult to praise punishment. Only a retributivist could make it out to be a good thing. But it can be defended, for the proffered alternative is far worse.

Contrary to their protestations, the enlightened reformers who would replace punishment by a form of treatment chosen scientifically by sociologists are more illiberal and more inhumane than their opponents. The traditionalists at least regard people as people to be addressed in the second person as rational agents, not discussed in the third and manipulated as experimental material. Laws, rules and moral precepts can be understood and can be rationally obeyed: and penalties, although essentially heteronomous, are also external. In order to secure obedience to the law, they do not take it upon themselves to alter a man's personality against his will, but only the factors he takes into account, and by bringing certain adventitious factors into his calculations, hope to tip the balance in favor of the right and against the wrong.

The traditionalists also respect freedom and privacy. Although they insist that laws should be obeyed, they give each man the benefit of a presumption in his favor, and assume that he will abstain from wrongdoing, and so long as he does so, they leave him alone; however much they suspect his motives and doubt whether he will continue along the straight and narrow, they respect the privacy of his motives and do not enquire into the purity of his heart. It is a great safeguard. The Quinton principle guarantees that provided we do no wrong, we shall suffer no ill by way of punishment; and provided insanity is strictly defined, we can be pretty sure of retaining our personal liberty by the simple expedient of keeping the law. Once we replace punishment, which looks backwards to the actual commission of an offense, by treatment which looks forward to the cure of potential offenders, there is nothing to prevent the authorities "treating" us all. We are all potential offenders. And while it is reasonably possible to clear oneself of a charge of having committed a particular crime in the past, it is quite impossible to prove that one is not going to misbehave in time to come. "I have done nothing wrong, you cannot touch me" is the other side of the punitive coin, which guarantees to the innocent security and freedom. But if the psychiatrists put me through a battery of tests and say that I am bound for a life of deviant behavior unless I come inside and have things injected into me, how can I gainsay them?

Even of offenders, the traditional concept of punishment is a much safer one to live with. True, a man may escape punishment by being deemed not to have been a rational agent—if a man was not capable of rational choice at the time of the offence, then the imperative major premise "Do not do it, or else" cannot have been properly addressed to him, and we cannot acquire any warrant for carrying out the "Or else." But it does not follow merely from his having done wrong, nor is it any kindness to him to argue, that he must have been mentally disturbed. Although it is bad to be blamed, it is even worse to be expelled from the community of rational agents. If we merely blame a man and punish him, we still are regarding him as rational and arguable with, and once his sentence is served he will be free to continue a normal independent life in the community, free to take his own decisions within the limits set by law, and choose his own course in life. If, however, we do not blame him, because he is not fully a person, then we no longer regard him as arguable with, but may restrain him as we would a wild animal. We do not punish him, but equally, if he is not reliably a rational agent, we are under no obligation to let him run loose among us.

We do not blame madmen, nor punish them: but we shut them up just the same, and without waiting for them to kill someone first. We have legal procedures under the Mental Health Act, 1960, for depriving people of their freedom for their own and other people's sake, but we hesitate to invoke them, and need many safeguards. Wrongdoing *may* by a sign of madness, and the Courts may in a number of different ways make an order for treatment, rather than punishment: but we are rightly reluctant to deprive a man of his status as a rational agent, and hand him over to the tender mercies of the psychiatrists. A rational agent who has done wrong, retains nevertheless many rights. Punishment, although unwelcome, is limited and external. It affords him and others a reason for not doing wrong, but does not impinge upon the inner citadels of his soul. We may hope that he will see the errors of his ways and repent, but we do not insist. We do not set about remolding his personality willy-nilly, although we may hope to influence him for the good. Once, however, we replace the punishment of a responsible agent by the treatment of an insane one, there are no limits set to what we may do: while, no doubt, we shall try to cure him, there is no limit on the time it may take or the methods we may use; nor are we in any way obliged to respect his actual desires and decisions, since these are *ex hypothesi* [by hypothesis] irrational and pathological. So long as we are convinced that our ends are for his good as we see it, we are free to adopt whatever means we like.

Lady Wootton claims that "the impact of psychiatric concepts upon the treatment of offenders and of other social deviants has been in overwhelming degree a humanizing influence" and concludes her argument, "Nor is it likely that pursuit of the patient's health will lead the doctor to prescribe the more brutal methods favoured by many penal codes."[4] But whereas mutilation is forbidden by the American Constitution and has long been absent from English Law, pre-frontal leucotomy and ECT are popular "treatments" perpetrated by psychiatrists on their patients. If I am sentenced to a term of imprisonment, grievous though the loss of liberty will be, I can at least expect to be released by the end of my sentence with my body and faculties more or less intact: but once the psychiatrists set about adjusting my personality to conform with what the sociologists say I should be like, I may never leave their hospital alive and still myself.

V

The institution of punishment is a reflection of human imperfection. If we were better, autonomous arguments alone would be effective: if we were worse, no arguments at all, not even heteronomous ones, would be adequate. But with human beings as they are, the institution of punishment enables somewhat selfish and somewhat unreasonable men to live together in communities, in reasonable confidence that certain rules will in fact be observed. It bridges the credibility gap between what we expect men to want to do and what we want to expect them to do. It is a pity to have to resort to such a stick to build a bridge; but utopian to think we can dispense with it, and inhuman to seek to replace emphatic imperatives by mere manipulations. Although it can be defeated, we ought to start with a presumption that a person is rational and able to answer for his actions, who may be influenced either by threats or by kindness and good treatment, but who remains an autonomous agent generally entitled to make up his mind for himself. And as long as we suspect that a person is merely bad and not mad, we should confine our attention to carrying out sanctions promulgated for badness, and not presume to refashion his personality altogether.

Notes

[1]A. M. Quinton, "On Punishment," *Analysis,* 15, 1954, pp. 133–142; reprinted in Peter Laslett, ed., *Philosophy, Politics and Society,* Oxford, 1956, pp. 83–91. See [Thomas] Hobbes, *Leviathan,* ch. 28.

[2]J. D. Mabbott, "Punishment," *Mind,* XLVIII, 1939, p. 155; reprinted in F. A. Olafson, ed., *Justice and Social Policy,* Englewood Cliffs, 1961, pp. 42–43; J. Feinberg, ed., *Reason and Responsibility,* Belmont, California, 1965, pp. 336–337; H. B. Acton, *The Philosophy of Punishment,* London, 1969.

[3]H. L. A. Hart, "Prolegomenon to Principles of Punishment," *Proceedings of the Aristotelian Society,* LX, 1959–60, p. 4; reprinted in Peter Laslett and W. G. Runciman, eds., *Philosophy, Politics and Society,* 2nd series, Oxford, 1962, p. 161; and in H. L. A. Hart, *Punishment and Responsibility,* Oxford, 1968, p. 5.

[4]Barbara Wootton, *Social Science and Social Pathology,* London, 1959, Ch. VIII, p. 206.

Discussion Questions

1. What is Lucas's criticism of a retributivist position? How might Lewis reply? What distinction made in the introduction to this section is relevant to Lucas's criticism?

2. What is Lucas's criticism of a pure utilitarian theory of punishment? How might a utilitarian reply?

3. What is Lucas's definition of punishment? Do you see any problems with it? Can you give any counterexamples to it?

4. How does Lucas distinguish between punishment and revenge? Does this answer the criticism that his theory (or the retributivist theory) is vengeful or vindictive? Why or why not?

5. What is Lucas's account of punishment? How is it like and unlike standard deterrence theories as defined in the introduction to this section? Argue for or against Lucas's theory.

6. What are Lucas's arguments for his theory? Are they successful?

The Death Sentence

Sidney Hook

Is there anything new that can be said for or against capital punishment? Anyone familiar with the subject knows that unless extraneous issues are introduced a large measure of agreement about it can be, and has been, won. For example, during the last 150 years the death penalty for criminal offenses has been abolished, or remains unenforced, in many countries; just as important, the number of crimes punishable by death has been sharply reduced in all countries. But while the progress has been encouraging, it still seems to me that greater clarity on the issues involved is desirable: Much of the continuing polemic still suffers from one or the other of the twin evils of vindictiveness and sentimentality.

Sentimentality, together with a great deal of confusion about determinism, is found in Clarence Darrow's speeches and writings on the subject. Darrow was an attractive and likeable human being, but a very confused thinker. He argued against capital punishment on the ground that the murderer was always a victim of heredity and environment—and therefore it was unjust to execute him. ("Back of every murder and back of every human act are sufficient causes that move the human machine beyond their control.") The crucifiers and the crucified, the lynch mob and its prey are equally moved by causes beyond their control and the relevant differences between them is therewith ignored. Although Darrow passionately asserted that no one knows what justice is and that no one can measure it, he nonetheless was passionately convinced that capital punishment was unjust.

It should be clear that if Darrow's argument were valid, it would be an argument not only against capital punishment but against all punishment. Very few of us would be prepared to accept this. But the argument is absurd. Even if we are all victims of our heredity and environment, it is still possible to alter the environment by meting out capital punishment to deter crimes of murder. If no one can help doing what he does, if no one is responsible for his actions, then surely this holds just as much for those who advocate and administer capital punishment as for the criminal. The denunciation of capital punishment as unjust, therefore, would be senseless. The question of universal determinism is irrelevant. If capital punishment actually were a deterrent to murder, and there existed no other more effective deterrent, and none as effective but more humane, a case could be made for it.

Nor am I impressed with the argument against capital punishment on the ground of its inhumanity. Of course it is inhumane. So is murder. If it could be shown that the inhumanity of murder can be decreased in no other way than by the inhumanity of capital punishment acting as a deterrent, this would be a valid argument for such punishment.

I have stressed the hypothetical character of these arguments because it makes apparent how crucially the wisdom of our policy depends upon the alleged facts. Does capital punishment serve as the most effective deterrent we have against murder? Most people who favor its retention believe that it does. But any sober examination of the facts

Reprinted from *The New Leader,* vol. 44 (1961). Copyright © The American Labor Conference on International Affairs, Inc. Reprinted by permission of the publisher.

will show that this has never been established. It seems plausible, but not everything which is plausible or intuitively credible is true.

The experience of countries and states which have abolished capital punishment shows that there has been no perceptible increase of murders after abolition—although it would be illegitimate to infer from this that the fear of capital punishment never deterred anybody. The fact that "the state with the very lowest murder rate is Maine, which abolished capital punishment in 1870," may be explained by the hypothesis that fishermen, like fish, tend to be cold-blooded, or by some less fanciful hypothesis. The relevant question is: what objective evidence exists which would justify the conclusion that if Maine had not abolished capital punishment, its death rate would have been higher? The answer is: no evidence exists.

The opinion of many jurists and law enforcement officers from Cesare Beccaria (the eighteenth century Italian criminologist) to the present is that swift and certain punishment of some degree of severity is a more effective deterrent of murder than the punishment of maximum severity when it is slow and uncertain. Although this opinion requires substantiation, too, it carries the weight which we normally extend to pronouncements by individuals who report on their life experience. And in the absence of convincing evidence that capital punishment is a more effective and/or humane form of punishment for murder than any other punishment, there remains no other reasonable ground for retaining it.

This is contested by those who speak of the necessity for capital punishment as an expression of the "community need of justice," or as the fulfillment of "an instinctive urge to punish injustice." Such views lie at the basis of some forms of the retributive theory. It has been alleged that the retributive theory is nothing more than a desire for revenge, but it is a great and arrogant error to assume that all who hold it are vindictive. The theory has been defended by secular saints like G. E. Moore and Immanuel Kant, whose dispassionate interest in justice cannot reasonably be challenged. Even if one accepted the retributive theory or believed in the desirability of meeting the community need of justice, it doesn't in the least follow that this justifies capital punishment. Other forms of punishment may be retributive, too.

I suppose that what one means by community need or feeling and the necessity of regarding it, is that not only must justice be done, it must be seen to be done. A requirement of good law is that it must be consonant with the feeling of the community, something which is sometimes called "the living law." Otherwise it is unenforceable and brings the whole system of law into disrepute. Meeting community feeling is a necessary condition for good law, but not a sufficient condition for good law. This is what Justice Holmes meant when he wrote in *The Common Law* that "The first requirement of a sound body of law is that it should correspond with the actual feelings and demands of the community, whether right or wrong." But I think he would admit that sound law is sounder still if in addition to being enforceable it is also just. Our moral obligation as citizens is to build a community feeling and demand which is right rather than wrong.

Those who wish to retain capital punishment on the ground that it fulfills a community need or feeling must believe either that community feeling *per se* is always justified, or that to disregard it in any particular situation is inexpedient because of the consequences, *viz.*, increase in murder. In either case they beg the question—in the first case, the question of justice, and in the second, the question of deterrence.

One thing is incontestable. From the standpoint of those who base the argument for retention of capital punishment on the necessity of satisfying community needs there could be no justification whatsoever for any *mandatory* death sentence. For a mandatory death sentence attempts to determine in advance what the community need and feeling will be, and closes the door to fresh inquiry about the justice as well as the deterrent consequences of any proposed punishment.

Community need and feeling are notoriously fickle. When a verdict of guilty necessarily entails a death sentence, the jury may not feel the sentence warranted and may bring in a verdict of not guilty even when some punishment seems to be legally and morally justified. Even when the death sentence is not mandatory, there is an argument, not decisive but still significant, against any death sentence. This is its incorrigibility. Our judgment of a convicted man's guilt may change. If he has been executed in the meantime, we can only do him "posthumous justice." But can justice ever really be posthumous to the victim? Rarely has evidence, even when it is beyond reasonable doubt, the same finality about its probative force as the awful finality of death. The weight of this argument against capital punishment is all the stronger if community need and feeling are taken as the prime criteria of what is just or fitting.

What about heinous political offenses? Usually when arguments fail to sustain the demand for capital punishment in ordinary murder cases, the names of Adolf Hitler, Adolf Eichmann, Joseph Stalin and Ilse Koch are introduced and flaunted before the audience to inflame their feelings. Certain distinctions are in order here. Justice, of course, requires severe punishment. But why is it assumed that capital punishment is, in these cases, the severest and most just of sentences? How can any equation be drawn between the punishment of one man and the sufferings of his numerous victims? After all, we cannot kill Eichmann six million times or Stalin twelve million times (a conservative estimate of the number of people who died by their order).

If we wish to keep alive the memory of political infamy, if we wish to use it as a political lesson to prevent its recurrence, it may be educationally far more effective to keep men like Eichmann in existence. Few people think of the dead. By the same token, it may be necessary to execute a politically monstrous figure to prevent him from becoming the object of allegiance of a restoration movement. Eichmann does not have to be executed. He is more useful alive if we wish to keep before mankind the enormity of his offense. But if Hitler had been taken alive, his death would have been required as a matter of political necessity, to prevent him from becoming a living symbol or rallying cry of Nazi die-hards and irreconcilables.

There is an enormous amount of historical evidence which shows that certain political tyrants, after they lose power, become the focus of restoration movements that are a chronic source of bloodshed and civil strife. No matter how infamous a tyrant's actions, there is usually some group which has profited by it, resents being deprived of its privileges, and schemes for a return to power. In difficult situations, the dethroned tyrant also becomes a symbol of legitimacy around which discontented elements rally who might otherwise have waited for the normal processes of government to relieve their lot. A *mystique* develops around the tyrant, appeals are made to the "good old days," when his bread and circuses were used to distract attention from the myriads of his tortured victims, plots seethe around him until they boil over into violence and bloodshed again. I did not approve of the way Mussolini was killed. Even he deserved due process. But I have no doubt whatsoever that had he been sentenced merely to life imprisonment, the Fascist movement in Italy today would be a much more formidable movement, and that sooner or later, many lives would have been lost in consequence of the actions of Fascist legitimists.

Where matters of ordinary crime are concerned these political considerations are irrelevant. I conclude, therefore, that no valid case has so far been made for the retention of capital punishment, that the argument from deterrence is inconclusive and inconsistent (in the sense that we do not do other things to reinforce its deterrent effect if we believe it has such an effect), and that the argument from community feeling is invalid.

However, since I am not a fanatic or absolutist, I do not wish to go on record as being categorically opposed to the death sentence in all circumstances. I should like to recognize two exceptions. A defendant convicted of murder and sentenced to life should be permitted to choose the death sentence instead. Not so long ago a defendant sentenced to life imprisonment made this request and was rebuked by the judge for his impertinence. I can see no valid grounds for denying such a request out of hand. It may sometimes be denied, particularly if a way can be found to make the defendant labor for the benefit of the dependents of his victim as is done in some European countries. Unless such considerations are present, I do not see on what reasonable ground the request can be denied, particularly by those who believe in capital punishment. Once they argue that life imprisonment is either a more effective deterrent or more justly punitive, they have abandoned their position.

In passing, I should state that I am in favor of permitting *any* criminal defendant, sentenced to life imprisonment, the right to choose death. I can understand why certain jurists, who believe that the defendant wants thereby to cheat the state out of its mode of punishment, should be indignant at the idea. They are usually the ones who believe that even the attempt at suicide should be deemed a crime—in effect saying to the unfortunate person that if he doesn't succeed in his act of suicide, the state will punish him for it. But I am baffled to understand why the absolute abolitionist, dripping with treacly humanitarianism, should oppose this proposal. I have heard some people actually oppose capital punishment in certain cases on the ground that: "Death is too good for the vile wretch! Let him live and suffer to the end of his days." But the absolute abolitionist should be the last person in the world to oppose the wish of the lifer, who regards this form of punishment as torture worse than death, to leave our world.

My second class of exceptions consists of those who having been sentenced once to prison for premeditated murder, murder again. In these particular cases we have evidence that imprisonment is not a sufficient deterrent for the individual in question. If the evidence shows that the prisoner is so psychologically constituted that, without being insane, the fact that he can kill again with impunity may lead to further murderous behavior, the court should have the discretionary power to pass the death sentence if the criminal is found guilty of a second murder.

In saying that the death sentence should be *discretionary* in cases where a man has killed more than once, I am *not* saying that a murderer who murders again is more deserving of death than the murderer who murders once. Bluebeard was not twelve times more deserving of death when he was finally caught. I am saying simply this: that in a sub-class of murderers, i.e., those who murder several times, there may be a special group of sane murderers who, knowing that they will not be executed, will not hesitate to kill again and again. For *them* the argument from deterrence is obviously valid. Those who say that there must be no exceptions to the abolition of capital punishment cannot rule out the existence of such cases on *a priori* grounds. If they admit that there is a reasonable probability that such murderers will murder again or attempt to murder again, a probability which usually grows with the number of repeated murders, and still insist they would *never* approve of capital punishment, I would conclude that they are indifferent to the lives of the human beings doomed, on their position, to be victims. What fancies itself as a humanitarian attitude is sometimes an expression of sentimentalism. The reverse coin of sentimentalism is often cruelty.

Our charity for all human beings must not deprive us of our common sense. Nor should our charity be less for the future or potential victims of the murderer than for the murderer himself. There are crimes in this world which are, like acts of nature, beyond the power of men to anticipate or control. But not all or most crimes are of this character. So long as human beings are responsible and educable, they will respond to praise and blame and punishment. It is hard to imagine it but even Hitler and Stalin were once infants. Once you *can* imagine them as infants, however, it is hard to believe that they were already monsters in their cradles. Every confirmed criminal was once an amateur. The existence of confirmed criminals testifies to the defects of our education—where they can be re-formed—and of our penology—where they cannot. That is why we are under the moral obligation to be intelligent about crime and punishment. Intelligence should teach us that the best educational and penological system is the one which prevents crimes rather than punishes them; the next best is one which punishes crime in such a way as to prevent it from happening again.

Discussion Questions

1. What is Hook's objection to Clarence Darrow's argument? Do you agree with Hook or Darrow? Give your reasons.
2. Hook argues that if capital punishment is inhumane, so is murder. What theory of punishment seems to support the point he is making? Do you agree or disagree?
3. What points does Hook make about the retributive theory? Would Lewis agree with Hook? Do you agree?
4. What points does Hook make about execution for political offenses? What theory of punishment seems implied? How could his argument be criticized?
5. In what circumstances would Hook allow a death sentence? Why? Do you agree or disagree? Give your reasons.

In Favor of Capital Punishment

Jacques Barzun

A passing remark of mine in the *Mid-Century* magazine has brought me a number of letters and a sheaf of pamphlets against capital punishment. The letters, sad and reproachful, offer me the choice of pleading ignorance or being proved insensitive. I am asked whether I know that there exists a worldwide movement for the abolition of capital punishment which has everywhere enlisted able men of every profession, including the law. I am told

From *The American Scholar*, vol. 31, no. 2 (Spring 1962), pp. 181–191. Copyright © 1962 by the United Chapters of Phi Beta Kappa. Reprinted by permission of the publisher and author.

that the death penalty is not only inhuman but also unscientific, for rapists and murderers are really sick people who should be cured, not killed. I am invited to use my imagination and acknowledge the unbearable horror of every form of execution.

I am indeed aware that the movement for abolition is widespread and articulate, especially in England. It is headed there by my old friend and publisher, Mr. Victor Gollancz, and it numbers such well-known writers as Arthur Koestler, C. H. Rolph, James Avery Joyce and Sir John Barry. Abroad as at home the profession of psychiatry tends to support the cure principle, and many liberal newspapers, such as the *Observer,* are committed to abolition. In the United States there are at least twenty-five state leagues working to the same end, plus a national league and several church councils, notably the Quaker and the Episcopal.

The assemblage of so much talent and enlightened good-will behind a single proposal must give pause to anyone who supports the other side, and in the attempt to make clear my views, which are now close to unpopular, I start out by granting that my conclusion is arguable; that is, I am still open to conviction, *provided* some fallacies and frivolities in the abolitionist argument are first disposed of and the difficulties not ignored but overcome. I should be glad to see this happen, not only because there is pleasure in the spectacle of an airtight case, but also because I am not more sanguinary than my neighbor and I should welcome the discovery of safeguards—for society *and* the criminal—other than killing. But I say it again, these safeguards must really meet, not evade or postpone, the difficulties I am about to describe. Let me add before I begin that I shall probably not answer any more letters on this arousing subject. If this printed exposition does not do justice to my cause, it is not likely that I can do better in the hurry of private correspondence.

I readily concede at the outset that present ways of dealing out capital punishment are as revolting as Mr. Koestler says in his harrowing volume, *Hanged by the Neck*. Like many of our prisons, our modes of execution should change. But this objection to barbarity does not mean that capital punishment—or rather, judicial homicide—should not go on. The illicit jump we find here, on the threshold of the inquiry, is characteristic of the abolitionist and must be disallowed at every point. Let us bear in mind the possibility of devising a painless, sudden and dignified death, and see whether its administration is justifiable.

The four main arguments advanced against the death penalty are: 1. punishment for crime is a primitive idea rooted in revenge; 2. capital punishment does not deter; 3. judicial error being possible, taking life is an appalling risk; 4. a civilized state, to deserve its name, must uphold, not violate, the sanctity of human life.

I entirely agree with the first pair of propositions, which is why, a moment ago, I replaced the term capital punishment with "judicial homicide." The uncontrollable brute whom I want put out of the way is not to be punished for his misdeeds, nor used as an example or a warning; he is to be killed for the protection of others, like the wolf that escaped not long ago in a Connecticut suburb. No anger, vindictiveness or moral conceit need preside over the removal of such dangers. But a man's inability to control his violent impulses or to imagine the fatal consequences of his acts should be a presumptive reason for his elimination from society. This generality covers drunken driving and teen-age racing on public highways, as well as incurable obsessive violence; it might be extended (as I shall suggest later) to other acts that destroy, precisely, the moral basis of civilization.

But why kill? I am ready to believe the statistics tending to show that the prospect of his own death does not stop the murderer. For one thing he is often a blind egotist, who cannot conceive the possibility of his own death. For another, detection would have to be infallible to deter the more imaginative who, although afraid, think they can escape discovery. Lastly, as Shaw long ago pointed out, hanging the wrong man will deter as effectively as hanging the right one. So, once again, why kill? If I agree that moral progress means an increasing respect for human life, how can I oppose abolition?

I do so because on this subject of human life, which is to me the heart of the controversy, I find the abolitionist inconsistent, narrow or blind. The propaganda for abolition speaks in hushed tones of the sanctity of human life, as if the mere statement of it as an absolute should silence all opponents who have any moral sense. But most of the abolitionists belong to nations that spend half their annual income on weapons of war and that honor research to perfect means of killing. These good people vote without a qualm for the political parties that quite sensibly arm their country to the teeth. The West today does not seem to be the time or place to invoke the absolute sanctity of human life. As for the clergymen in the movement, we may be sure from the experience of two previous world wars that they will bless our arms and pray for victory when called upon, the sixth commandment notwithstanding.

"Oh, but we mean the sanctity of life *within* the nation!" Very well: is the movement then campaigning also against the principle of self-defense? Absolute sanctity means letting the cutthroat have his sweet will of you, even if you have a poker handy to bash him with, for you might kill. And again, do we hear any protest against the police firing at criminals on the street—mere bank robbers usually—and doing this, often enough, with an excited marksmanship that misses the artist and hits the bystander? The absolute sanctity of human life is, for the abolitionists, a slogan rather than a considered proposition.

Yet it deserves examination, for upon our acceptance or rejection of it depend such other highly civilized possibilities as euthanasia and seemly suicide. The inquiring mind also wants to know, why the sanctity of *human* life alone? My tastes do not run to household pets, but I find something less than admirable in the uses to which we put animals—in zoos, laboratories and space machines—without the excuse of the ancient law, "Eat or be eaten."

It should moreover be borne in mind that this argument about sanctity applies—or would apply—to about ten persons a year in Great Britain and to between fifty and seventy-five in the United States. These are the average numbers of those executed in recent years. The count by itself should not, of course, affect our judgment of the principle: one life spared or forfeited is as important, morally, as a hundred thousand. But it should inspire a comparative judgment: there are hundreds and indeed thousands whom, in our concern with the horrors of execution, we forget: on the one hand, the victims of violence; on the other, the prisoners in our jails.

The victims are easy to forget. Social science tends steadily to mark a preference for the troubled, the abnormal, the problem case. Whether it is poverty, mental disorder, delinquency or crime, the "patient material" monopolizes the interest of increasing groups of people among the most generous and learned. Psychiatry and moral liberalism go together; the application of law as we have known it is thus coming to be regarded as an historic prelude to social work, which may replace it entirely. Modern literature makes the most of this same outlook, caring only for the disturbed spirit, scorning as bourgeois those who pay their way and do *not* stab their friends. All the while the determinism of natural science reinforces the assumption that society causes its own evils. A French jurist, for example, says that in order to understand crime we must first brush aside all ideas of Responsibility. He means the criminal's and takes for granted that of society. The murderer kills because reared in a broken home or, conversely, because at an early age he witnessed his parents making love. Out of such cases, which make pathetic reading in the literature of modern criminology, is born the abolitionist's state of mind: we dare not kill those we are beginning to understand so well.

If, moreover, we turn to the accounts of the crimes committed by these unfortunates, who are the victims? Only dull ordinary people going about their business. We are sorry, of course, but they do not interest science on its march. Balancing, for example, the sixty to seventy criminals executed annually in the United States, there were the seventy to eighty housewives whom George Cvek robbed, raped and usually killed during the months of a career devoted to proving his virility. "It is too bad." Cvek alone seems instructive, even though one of the law officers who helped track him down quietly remarks: "As to the extent that his villainies disturbed family relationships, or how many women are still haunted by the specter of an experience they have never disclosed to another living soul, these questions can only lend themselves to sterile conjecture."

The remote results are beyond our ken, but it is not idle to speculate about those whose death by violence fills the daily two inches at the back of respectable newspapers— the old man sunning himself on a park bench and beaten to death by four hoodlums, the small children abused and strangled, the middle-aged ladies on a hike assaulted and killed, the family terrorized by a released or escaped lunatic, the half-dozen working people massacred by the sudden maniac, the boatload of persons dispatched by the skipper, the mindless assaults upon schoolteachers and shopkeepers by the increasing horde of dedicated killers in our great cities. Where does the sanctity of life begin?

It is all very well to say that many of these killers are themselves "children," that is, minors. Doubtless, a nine-year-old mind is housed in that 150 pounds of unguided muscle. Grant, for argument's sake, that the misdeed is "the fault of society," trot out the broken home and the slum environment. The question then is, What shall we do, not in the Utopian city of tomorrow, but here and now? The "scientific" means of cure are more than uncertain. The apparatus of detention only increases the killer's antisocial animus. Reformatories and mental hospitals are full and have an understandable bias toward discharging their inmates. Some of these are indeed "cured"—so long as they stay under a rule. The stress of the social free-for-all throws them back on their violent modes of self-expression. At that point I agree that society has failed—twice: it has twice failed the victims, whatever may be its guilt toward the killer.

As in all great questions, the moralist must choose, and choosing has a price. I happen to think that if a person of adult body has not been endowed with adequate controls against irrationally taking the life of another, that person must be judicially, painlessly, regretfully killed before that mindless body's horrible automation repeats.

I say "irrationally" taking life, because it is often possible to feel great sympathy with a murderer. Certain *crimes passionnels* can be forgiven without being condoned. Blackmailers invite direct retribution. Long provocation can be an excuse, as in that engaging case of some years ago, in which a respectable carpenter of seventy found he could no longer stand the incessant nagging of his wife. While she excoriated him from her throne in the kitchen—a daily exercise for fifty years—the husband went to his bench and came back with a hammer in each hand to settle the score. The testimony to his character, coupled with the sincerity implied by the two hammers, was enough to have him sent into quiet and brief seclusion.

But what are we to say of the type of motive disclosed in a journal published by the inmates of one of our Federal penitentiaries? The author is a bank robber who confesses that money is not his object:

> My mania for power, socially, sexually, and otherwise can feel no degree of satisfaction until I feel sure I have struck the ultimate of submission and terror in the minds and bodies of my victims. . . . It's very difficult to explain all the queer fascinating sensations pounding and surging through me while I'm

holding a gun on a victim, watching his body tremble and sweat. . . . This is
the moment when all the rationalized hypocrisies of civilization are suddenly
swept away and two men stand there facing each other morally and ethically
naked, and right and wrong are the absolute commands of the man behind
the gun.

This confused echo of modern literature and modern science defines the choice
before us. Anything deserving the name of cure for such a man presupposes not only a
laborious individual psychoanalysis, with the means to conduct and to sustain it, socially
and economically, but also a re-education of the mind, so as to throw into correct
perspective the garbled ideas of Freud and Nietzsche, Gide and Dostoevski, which this
power-seeker and his fellows have derived from the culture and temper of our times. Ideas
are tenacious and give continuity to emotion. Failing a second birth of heart and mind, we
must ask: How soon will this sufferer sacrifice a bank clerk in the interests of making
civilization less hypocritical? And we must certainly question the wisdom of affording him
more than one chance. The abolitionists' advocacy of an unconditional "let live" is in truth
part of the same cultural tendency that animates the killer. The Western peoples' revulsion
from power in domestic and foreign policy has made of the state a sort of counterpart of
the bank robber: both having power and neither knowing how to use it. Both waste lives
because hypnotized by irrelevant ideas and crippled by contradictory emotions. If
psychiatry were sure of its ground in diagnosing the individual case, a philosopher might
consider whether such dangerous obsessions should not be guarded against by judicial
homicide *before* the shooting starts.

I raise the question not indeed to recommend the prophylactic execution of potential
murderers, but to introduce the last two perplexities that the abolitionists dwarf or obscure
by their concentration on changing an isolated penalty. One of these is the scale by which
to judge the offenses society wants to repress. I can for example imagine a truly democratic
state in which it would be deemed a form of treason punishable by death to create a
disturbance in any court or deliberative assembly. The aim would be to recognize the
sanctity of orderly discourse in arriving at justice, assessing criticism and defining policy.
Under such a law, a natural selection would operate to remove permanently from the
scene persons who, let us say, neglect argument in favor of banging on the desk with their
shoe. Similarly, a bullying minority in a diet, parliament or skupshtina would be prose-
cuted for treason to the most sacred institutions when fists or flying inkwells replace
rhetoric. That the mere suggestion of such a law sounds ludicrous shows how remote we
are from civilized institutions, and hence how gradual should be our departure from the
severity of judicial homicide.

I say gradual and I do not mean standing still. For there is one form of barbarity in
our law that I want to see mitigated before any other. I mean imprisonment. The enemies
of capital punishment—and liberals generally—seem to be satisfied with any legal outcome so long as they themselves avoid the vicarious guilt of shedding blood. They speak of
the sanctity of life, but have no concern with its quality. They give no impression of ever
having read what it is certain they have read, from Wilde's *De Profundis* to the latest
account of prison life by a convicted homosexual. Despite the infamy of concentration
camps, despite Mr. Charles Burney's remarkable work, *Solitary Confinement,* despite riots
in prisons, despite the round of escape, recapture and return in chains, the abolitionists'
imagination tells them nothing about the reality of being caged. They read without a
qualm, indeed they read with rejoicing, the hideous irony of "Killer Gets Life"; they sigh
with relief instead of horror. They do not see and suffer the cell, the drill, the clothes, the
stench, the food; they do not feel the sexual racking of young and old bodies, the hateful

promiscuity, the insane monotony, the mass degradation, the impotent hatred. They do not remember from Silvio Pellico that only a strong political faith, with a hope of final victory, can steel a man to endure long detention. They forget that Joan of Arc, when offered "life," preferred burning at the stake. Quite of another mind, the abolitionists point with pride to the "model prisoners" that murderers often turn out to be. As if a model prisoner were not, first, a contradiction in terms, and second, an exemplar of what a free society should not want.

I said a moment ago that the happy advocates of the life sentence appear not to have understood what we know they have read. No more do they appear to read what they themselves write. In the preface to his useful volume of cases, *Hanged in Error,* Mr. Leslie Hale, M.P., refers to the tardy recognition of a minor miscarriage of justice—one year in jail: "The prisoner emerged to find that his wife had died and that his children and his aged parents had been removed to the workhouse. By the time a small payment had been assessed as 'compensation' the victim was incurably insane." So far we are as indignant with the law as Mr. Hale. But what comes next? He cites the famous Evans case, in which it is very probable that the wrong man was hanged, and he exclaims: "While such mistakes are possible, should society impose an irrevocable sentence?" Does Mr. Hale really ask us to believe that the sentence passed on the first man, whose wife died and who went insane, was in any sense *revocable?* Would not any man rather be Evans dead than that other wretch "emerging" with his small compensation and his reasons for living gone?

Nothing is revocable here below, imprisonment least of all. The agony of a trial itself is punishment, and acquittal wipes out nothing. Read the heart-rending diary of William Wallace, accused quite implausibly of having murdered his wife and "saved" by the Court of Criminal Appeals—but saved for what? Brutish ostracism by everyone and a few years of solitary despair. The cases of Adolf Beck, of Oscar Slater, of the unhappy Brooklyn bank teller who vaguely resembled a forger and spent eight years in Sing Sing only to "emerge" a broken, friendless, useless, "compensated" man—all these, if the dignity of the individual has any meaning, had better have been dead before the prison door ever opened for them. This is what counsel always says to the jury in the course of a murder trial and counsel is right: far better hang this man than "give him life." For my part, I would choose death without hesitation. If that option is abolished, a demand will one day be heard to claim it as a privilege in the name of human dignity. I shall believe in the abolitionist's present views only after he has emerged from twelve months in a convict cell.

The detached observer may want to interrupt here and say that the argument has now passed from reasoning to emotional preference. Whereas the objector to capital punishment *feels* that death is the greatest of evils, I *feel* that imprisonment is worse than death. A moment's thought will show that feeling is the appropriate arbiter. All reasoning about what is right, civilized and moral rests upon sentiment, like mathematics. Only, in trying to persuade others, it is important to single out the fundamental feeling, the prime intuition, and from it to reason justly. In my view, to profess respect for human life and be willing to see it spent in a penitentiary is to entertain liberal feelings frivolously. To oppose the death penalty because, unlike a prison term, it is irrevocable is to argue fallaciously.

In the propaganda for abolishing the death sentence the recital of numerous miscarriages of justice commits the same error and implies the same callousness: what is at fault in our present system is not the sentence but the fallible procedure. Capital cases being one in a thousand or more, who can be cheerful at the thought of all the "revocable" errors? What the miscarriages point to is the need for reforming the jury system, the rules of evidence, the customs of prosecution, the machinery of appeal. The failure to see that this is the great task reflects the sentimentality I spoke of earlier, that which responds chiefly to the excitement of the unusual. A writer on Death and the Supreme Court is at pains to point out that when that tribunal reviews a capital case, the judges are particularly anxious and careful. What a left-handed compliment to the highest judicial conscience of the country! Fortunately, some of the champions of the misjudged see the issue more clearly. Many of those who are thought wrongly convicted now languish in jail because the jury was uncertain or because a doubting governor commuted the death sentence. Thus Dr. Samuel H. Sheppard, Jr., convicted of his wife's murder in the second degree is serving a sentence that is supposed to run for the term of his natural life. The story of his numerous trials, as told by Mr. Paul Holmes, suggests that police incompetence, newspaper demagogy, public envy of affluence and the mischances of legal procedure fashioned the result. But Dr. Sheppard's vindicator is under no illusion as to the conditions that this "lucky" evader of the electric chair will face if he is granted parole after ten years: "It will carry with it no right to resume his life as a physician. His privilege to practice medicine was blotted out with his conviction. He must all his life bear the stigma of a parolee, subject to unceremonious return to confinement for life for the slightest misstep. More than this, he must live out his life as a convicted murderer."

What does the moral conscience of today think it is doing? If such a man is a dangerous repeater of violent acts, what right has the state to let him loose after ten years? What is, in fact, the meaning of a "life sentence" that peters out long before life? Paroling looks suspiciously like an expression of social remorse for the pain of incarceration, coupled with a wish to avoid "unfavorable publicity" by freeing a suspect. The man is let out when the fuss has died down; which would mean that he was not under lock and key for our protection at all. He *was* being punished, just a little—for so prison seems in the abolitionist's distorted view, and in the jury's and the prosecutor's, whose "second degree" murder suggests killing someone "just a little."[1]

If, on the other hand, execution and life imprisonment are judged too severe and the accused is expected to be harmless hereafter—punishment being ruled out as illiberal—what has society gained by wrecking his life and damaging that of his family?

What we accept, and what the abolitionist will clamp upon us all the more firmly if he succeeds, is an incoherence which is not remedied by the belief that second degree murder merits a kind of second degree death; that a doubt as to the identity of a killer is resolved by commuting real death into intolerable life; and that our ignorance whether a maniac will strike again can be hedged against by measuring "good behavior" within the gates and then releasing the subject upon the public in the true spirit of experimentation.

These are some of the thoughts I find I cannot escape when I read and reflect upon this grave subject. If, as I think, they are relevant to any discussion of change and reform, resting as they do on the direct and concrete perception of what happens, then the simple meliorists who expect to breathe a purer air by abolishing the death penalty are deceiving themselves and us. The issue is for the public to judge; but I for one shall not sleep easier for knowing that in England and America and the West generally a hundred more human beings are kept alive in degrading conditions to face a hopeless future; while others—possibly less conscious, certainly less controlled—benefit from a premature freedom dangerous alike to themselves and society. In short, I derive no comfort from the illusion that in giving up one manifest protection of the law-abiding, we who might well be in any of these three roles—victim, prisoner, licensed killer—have struck a blow for the sanctity of human life.

Note

[1]The British Homicide Act of 1957, Section 2, implies the same reasoning in its definition of "diminished responsibility" for certain forms of mental abnormality. The whole question of irrationality and crime is in utter confusion, on both sides of the Atlantic.

Discussion Questions

1. What are the "fallacies and frivolities" Barzun finds in the abolitionist arguments? Could these arguments be strengthened? How?

2. What seems to be Barzun's theory of punishment? Does he argue for it? What criticisms could be made of his position?

3. Some of Barzun's arguments resemble those of Narveson on war. Compare the arguments, noting similarities and dissimilarities.

4. Barzun seems to argue that it is the badness of the criminal rather than the badness of the crime which determines whether execution is justified. Do you agree or disagree with his view? Give your arguments.

5. Barzun argues that life imprisonment is more barbarous than execution. Give arguments for or against this view.

6. What weight does Barzun give to the danger of executing an innocent person? How much weight should this have?

Death as a Punishment

Hugo Adam Bedau

I

Before turning to the main issues, one or two comments on the structure of the abolitionist's argument are in order. It is important for us to grant that the evidence supporting our position could be stronger and more complete than it is. But to admit this is not to confess that the evidence is weak or insufficient. Defenders of the death penalty frequently fail to realize that what evidence there is consistently favors abolition. More than that, too many retentionists complacently talk as if the burden of proof were not on them—as though somewhere it was once proved that the death penalty was a social, moral, or theological necessity, or as though the long history of executing our fellow-man was a sufficient

From *The Death Penalty in America*, Hugo A. Bedau, ed. Copyright © 1964 by the author. Reprinted by permission of Doubleday & Co., Inc. and the author.

justification for continuing the practice indefinitely, or as though compelling reasons for killing people no longer need to be given once this policy has become the law. Actually, the arguments offered today for retaining the death penalty, . . . are little more than dogmas, confusions and evasions. In particular, I know of very few instances where retentionists have earnestly tried to support their convictions by conducting an investigation into some area where the facts are in dispute, and none in which they have come up with convincing supporting evidence.

It also should be admitted that those who oppose the death penalty from a moral position of absolute non-violence and respect for human life have it somewhat easier when they justify their position as abolitionists than do those of us whose position is based on more complex considerations. Professor Barzun, however, is nothing if not misleading when he argues *ad hominem* (in his essay reprinted [earlier in this section]) that abolitionists betray their professed ideal of the "absolute" sanctity of human life by advocating the living death of life imprisonment and by failing to oppose with equal vigor various other forms of disrespect for human life: by nations in warfare, by private citizens in self-defense, by policemen in restraining or apprehending a felon. Abolitionists I have known who profess to believe in the "absolute" sanctity of human life do in fact oppose these other forms of legalized killing. But those who don't take this extreme view are still entitled to appeal to the sanctity of human life, and they suffer no inconsistency if they do, as I shall explain below.

Likewise, I find nothing inconsistent in those who disturb Professor Hook, because they oppose the death penalty on the ground that it isn't punishment enough (" 'Death is too good for the vile wretch!' "). The moral convictions from which they oppose the death penalty are not mine, any more than they are his. I am consoled by the knowledge that very few abolitionists hold such convictions. But what if the contrary were true? As a point of logic and as a matter of fact, opposition to the death penalty is consistent with a wide variety of moral and social (or even immoral and anti-social) principles. Here as elsewhere, politics makes strange bedfellows, among retentionists as well as abolitionists. It is only simpler, perhaps not wiser and certainly not necessary, to oppose the death penalty from a moral principle of absolute non-violence.

II

Let me now turn to the case for the death penalty that Professors Barzun and Hook have made out, for it deserves the closest attention. (I should say from the onset that I am quite aware of the several differences between Hook's and Barzun's arguments; and I know there is some risk of misrepresenting their views by allying them as closely as I have at several points. The reader will have to judge whether I have been unfair to one in the course of objecting to the other.)

It will not go unnoticed that, unlike many retentionists, they concede a great deal to the opposition. They understand that the question is not one of capital punishment or no punishment. They share our doubts about the social utility of the motives that usually animate the defenders of the death penalty. They admit that the doctrine of general deterrence cannot any longer be the lynch-pin of a reasonable man's defense of capital punishment in America. They implicitly recognize that the burden of proof is on them as advocates of killing certain types of persons, not on those who would let even the worst convicts live. As Professor Barzun rather wistfully comments, his concessions almost make him happier with the abolitionist than against him. Almost, but not quite. What remains of the case for the death penalty that he and Professor Hook are able to construct would crumble if several crucial distinctions were drawn, distinctions that would clarify their arguments and enable us to see the full consequences of the principles they espouse.

For example, one distinction of importance, neglected by Professor Barzun, is between a man's killing someone else when there is a clear and present danger that he will otherwise be the victim of some violent act, and the state's killing a man as a punishment, i.e., between a man's right to defend himself and society's right to punish criminals. It is because Barzun fails to make this distinction that he thinks abolitionists are inconsistent in appealing to the sanctity of human life. So far as law and the prevailing morality of Western civilization have been concerned, respect for human life has never been an obstacle to the use of force in self-defense; indeed, it has always been thought to be its justification. It has, however, obligated anyone who pleads self-defense in justification of a killing to satisfy society that the force he used really was necessary in the circumstances and was motivated solely by a desire to ward off imminent harm to himself. But to kill a person who in fact is not at the time dangerous (because he is in prison), on the possibility that he might at some later date be dangerous, would be to use unjustifiable force and thus to flout the respect human life is due. Were it to be shown that there is a threat to society, or to any of its members, in allowing a criminal in prison to remain there, comparable to the danger a man invites in a dark alley if he turns his back on a thug who has a weapon in his hand and violence on his mind, then—but *only* then—would it be inconsistent for the abolitionist to tolerate force sufficient to kill the thug in the alley but to refuse to kill the prisoner. It may be that the pacifist, with his commitment to the absolute sanctity of human life, would in theory and in practice have to tolerate the slaughter of innocent lives (including his own). But if such a disaster were a likely consequence of abolishing the death penalty, or of extending parole at least in principle to all capital offenders, few of us who favor both would advocate either. The facts here, in terms of which the degree of risk can alone be measured, happen to be on our side.

On the issue of whether abolition of the death penalty would improve the lot of persons unjustly convicted, I think both Professor Hook and Professor Barzun are misled and confusing. Barzun is unquestionably right when he points to cases where men have been exonerated after years in prison, only to find that their lives have been destroyed. Of course, abolishing the death penalty is no remedy for the injustice of convicting and punishing an innocent man. It is obviously as *wrong* to imprison an innocent man as it is to kill him. But I should have thought it is just as obviously *worse* for him to be killed than for him to be imprisoned. This point must not be blurred by speculating whether it is worse from the convict's point of view to be dead than to be imprisoned and perhaps never vindicated or released. If an innocent convict thinks he is better off dead than alive, this is for *him* to determine, not us. What we must decide is the less metaphysical question of what general penal policy the state should adopt, on the understanding that the policy will in practice be applied not only to the numerous guilty but also to a few who are innocent. No one can deny, even if Hook and Barzun neglect to stress it, that the *only* way the state is in a position to do something for the victim of a miscarriage of justice is if it has refused as a matter of principle to kill *any* of its convicts. Executing an innocent man is not impossible, and it is a great risk to run for the questionable advantage of executing a few guilty ones.

Nor am I impressed by the "humanitarian" concern for the agony of a man erroneously convicted which, in claiming to deliver him from the greater evil, would take not only his freedom but his life as well. I cannot believe in point of fact that Tom Mooney would have been better off had he been hanged in 1917 for a crime he did not commit, rather than pardoned as he was more than twenty years later. I know of no evidence that he came to the opposite conclusion. I leave it for anyone acquainted with the case of James Fulton Foster to judge whether he would have been better off dead than as he is: alive, exonerated, and free. Are these cases as exceptional as Professor Barzun evidently believes? Even if they were, how could putting a Mooney or a Foster to death ever be justified on *humanitarian* grounds?

These reflections suggest a general point. There is a fundamental distinction to be made between choosing the death penalty for yourself and choosing it for someone else. Both Hook and Barzun seem to believe that imprisonment, even for a guilty man (and certainly for themselves, were *they* in prison, innocent or guilty), may be a far worse punishment than execution, and that abolitionists deceive themselves in believing that they advocate the lesser penalty. I doubt that this is so: but even if it were, I am certain that their argument is a deception.

Just as most abolitionists would agree that if the death penalty must be kept then less gruesome modes of execution ought to be adopted than those currently in use, many of us would also agree that we ought to consider allowing our penal authorities, under proper judicial and medical supervision, to cooperate with any long-term prisoner who is too dangerous to be released and who would honestly and soberly prefer to be dead rather than endure further imprisonment. That there are such convicts I am willing to concede. The question here is this: is it wisest for the state to allow a convict to take his own life if he decides that it would be better for him to be dead than to suffer any more imprisonment? Can a person in good physical health, in a tolerable prison environment, and who professes to want to die be of sound mind? (Or isn't that important?) Does not civilized society always have a fundamental interest, if not an obligation, to try to provide even for its most incompetent members in that most oppressive of environments, a prison, some opportunity to make their lives worth living? Wouldn't a policy that amounts to euthanasia for certain convicts run counter to this interest and sap the motive to satisfy it?

These questions are not new, for they arise whenever "mercy killing" as a social policy is advocated. But they are instructive, for they indicate how the issue under discussion has subtly changed. No longer are we considering how we ought to punish crimes. Instead, we are asking whether we ought to allow a convict, if he so wishes, to be painlessly put to death for no other reason than so that his imprisonment and his despair may come to an end—as if there were no better alternatives! This question, and the other questions above, has little to do with the one posed by capital punishment: is it wisest for the state to impose death or imprisonment as the punishment for certain crimes, irrespective of what the convicts in question may prefer? To give an affirmative answer to the former is not to decide the latter at all. In arguing, as Hook and Barzun do, that convicts should have the right to obtain from their custodians the means for a decent suicide, they have not argued for capital punishment. They have not even shown that any convict who chooses death rather than imprisonment has made the wiser choice. It is a great misfortune, and shows the confusion I have imputed to him, that Professor Hook raises this whole issue as (in his words) one of several "exceptions" to his general disapproval of capital punishment. Supervised suicide for those convicts who want it, irrespective of their crime, is not an "exception" in which capital punishment would remain as part of a penal system; supervised suicide is an entirely different matter, as we have seen, with questions all its own.

It is essential in weighing their viewpoint to notice that Professors Hook and Barzun judge the crucial facts very differently than does Chief of Police Allen. . . . One reason why Hook and Barzun want to keep the death penalty is because they believe in mercy killings and the right of suicide even for the worst criminals, because they believe that a lifetime behind bars, with its endless humiliations, frustrations and utter wretchedness, is a far greater misery than a few moments of violent pain followed by eternal oblivion. But Allen wants the death penalty retained because he believes that a condemned man invariably prefers to have his sentence commuted to life imprisonment, which proves that the threat of the death penalty must be the greater terror and thus the better deterrent. It turns out that the death penalty cannot be replaced by imprisonment, as Arthur Koestler ironically remarked, because it is at once too cruel and not cruel enough.

Quite independently of the foregoing considerations Hook and Barzun advance what is by far their strongest argument for the death penalty, namely, that there is no other solution for the very worst criminals, those whose sole instinct is Kill, Kill, Kill. Having agreed on this, they disagree on everything else. Professor Hook plainly thinks these criminals are the *sane* unreformable twice-guilty murderers, for this is the class of criminals he expressly and repeatedly specifies. But it is just as clear that it is the "escaped lunatic," the "sudden maniac," the criminally *insane* killer (or rapist, or mugger), whether reformable or not, whom Professor Barzun is anxious to see executed. Moreover, whereas Hook insists that *mandatory* death penalties are unjustifiable, Barzun's preference must run the other way. For if our insistence on parole looks to him too much like "an expression of social remorse for the pain of incarceration," what must he think of a life sentence in the first place but that it is an expression of the jury's remorse for convicting the man at all? And it is just such sentimental nonsense, whether in a Parole Board or a jury, that is out of place when your safety and mine is at stake. Finally, whereas Professor Hook's argument presupposes that he regards the execution of a sane murderer as a *punishment,* it is very doubtful whether this is how Professor Barzun views the executions of those whom he would have put to death. Whether or not it was his intention, he makes it clear that it is "judicial homicide" he favors, and so far as he defends the death penalty it is mainly because it accomplishes much the same thing, namely, eugenic executions. I think Professor Hook has come to the defense of the death penalty on behalf of a small if not non-existent class of criminals. Whether or not we make the "exception" he advises, it appears that in practice it will make little difference (though, if my argument below is correct, this may not be so). Professor Barzun, however, has altogether ceased to defend the death penalty, and a great deal both in theory and practice depends on understanding why this is so.

What conception of insanity Professor Hook would accept, he does not indicate. Yet any defense of the death penalty for *sane* unreformable murderers turns on this point. He contends that there is no "*a priori* ground" to rule out the possibility of sane murderers murdering again after a term of imprisonment. He infers that the death penalty is necessary to prevent such criminals from repeating their crimes. But is there really no such *a priori* ground? Any murderer who murders again, after a term of imprisonment and under at least somewhat different circumstances—ought he not by definition to be classified as criminally irresponsible? Must he not be suffering from some mental or emotional defect, whether or not it has been identified by psychiatrists, which warrants the label, "insanity"? It is more than a mere possibility.

Of course, the classic Anglo-American definition of "insanity," in terms of the M'Naghten Rules of 1843, would never yield any such result. But these Rules are slowly giving way to others that might provide this.[1] For all that Professor Hook or I know, it may be that a careful study of the psychopathology of unreformed murderers would show a set of symptoms that would entitle them without exception to be treated as insane. If no such set of symptoms were located, or even hypothesized, I admit it would be arbitrary to stretch "insane" so as to describe every such murderer for no other reason than that he repeated his offense. But arbitrariness and the *a priori* with it lie all around us in this area. It must not be forgotten that the term "insane," unlike "paranoid," has never been a description of any set of symptoms. It has never been related to forms of mental illness via empirical hypotheses contributed by psychopathology. It is simply the term employed by the law when a court wishes to hold an accused not accountable for his criminal acts by reason of his "unsoundness of mind." The kinds and causes of his "unsoundness of mind" are not legal but medical questions. The legal questions concern how to frame and to apply a general rule that will specify as insane all and only those persons whose acts are traceable to their mental ill-health and who, on that account, are to be excused from criminal responsibility and its consequences.

Professor Hook's confidence that in theory at least there may be sane multiple murderers must derive from *his* definition of "insane"; and such a definition is itself an "*a priori* ground." Depending on where we want to come out, we can make assumptions in the form of a definition of "insane" which will have the result that all, or some, or no unreformed murderers are insane. The trouble is not, as Hook asserts, that there is no "*a priori* ground" for ruling out the possibility of such criminals, but that such a ground, being only an *a priori* one, in the sense that it consists of a definition, has other alternatives equally *a priori* but with very different consequences.

What this shows is that if one's purpose is really to execute unreformable murderers, it is best to ignore the incidental facts of their sanity. Otherwise, one's purpose may be frustrated by nothing more than a change in the legal definition of "insanity." Professor Barzun, who does not scruple on this question, has all the advantages, and hardcore retentionists would be well advised to ally themselves with his position rather than Hook's.

It is also necessary to argue with Professor Hook on empirical grounds. What is the probability that there are any "sane" persons knowledgeable and imaginative enough to know what might be in store for them if they commit another murder, vicious enough to kill with cool deliberation, and still stupid enough to risk years of imprisonment after having already experienced it (for we are hypothesizing that our murderers are repeaters)? The probability is apparently so slight that competent authorities agree it is negligible. But we do not need to settle for the educated guesses of the authorities. Five states (Michigan, Minnesota, Wisconsin, Rhode Island, Maine) have long been without capital punishment for murder. If they have suffered from the problem of the sane unreformable murderer (as their courts define "sanity"), there has been plenty of time to remedy it by adopting just such a statute as Professor Hook recommends. Is their failure merely proof of public apathy? Or is it perhaps proof that in these states, the most vindictive have become abolitionists, and that their vindictiveness has gone to their heads: they relish the knowledge, shared with Professor Barzun, that in their jurisdictions the murderer suffers the ultimate punishment, literal life imprisonment; and public satisfaction in this knowledge more than compensates for the risk that one of the unreformables might sometime be paroled?

I have yet to mention my strongest objection to Professor Hook's argument. It arises from what may be only a casual comment. Professor Barzun, it will be recalled, asks why society must wait until a man has killed several times before he may be executed, given that we are willing to have murderers executed at all. Elsewhere, Hook has said what amounts to his reply: because "the first time a man murders we are not sure that he is a mad dog." (Let us merely note the curious turn of phrase which has him eventually defending the execution of sane "mad dogs.") This is reasonable enough. But Hook now expresses the doctrine, in his essay, . . . that second-time murderers ought to be executed where there is "a reasonable probability" they "will murder again or attempt to murder again." This is a somewhat unsettling idea, and a revealing one as well. Would Hook consider allowing a court to sentence a person to death even if he had not yet committed a second murder, and had not even attempted one, so long as it was "reasonably probable" that he would? Suppose we had a delinquency diagnostic test which would tell us with "reasonable probability" that a given person would attempt to commit his *first* murder and that he would not respond to subsequent imprisonment. What would Professor Hook allow us to do with such knowledge? If he would allow us to execute a man after he has twice murdered, or after one murder and an attempted second murder, on the ground that there is no "reasonable probability" of rehabilitating him in prison, why should he not allow us to execute the man when he has killed but once? Or, indeed, before he has killed or attempted to kill at all? Is it the risk that even "reasonable probabilities" may in fact not lead to valid predictions? Then by the same token, executing a man no matter how many murders he has committed and no matter how often he has failed to respond to rehabilitation must also be rejected. Thus, the line Professor Hook attempts to draw between murderers deserving execution and those deserving imprisonment, which began by appearing firm and clear, turns out, thanks to the way one can manipulate the notion of "reasonable probabilities," to be no line at all.

Professor Barzun, unlike Professor Hook, directs his putative defense of the death penalty toward the class of criminals that, because of its number and danger, is of somewhat greater significance: the class inclined to violent and brutal acts, whether or not they are insane, whether or not they are reformable, and whether or not they have already committed any crimes. Barzun seems willing to embrace the "prophylactic execution of potential murderers," though only on the admittedly speculative assumption that the courts had a reliable test to predict future violence. Except for reservations about the sanity of those to be executed, Professor Hook's position, if I am right, leads to a similar conclusion. So this is the end of their line of argument purportedly advanced on behalf of the death penalty. The only way we can regard the desirability of such executions as relevant to the issue is if we ignore the fact that a system of capital punishment is, after all, a system of *punishment,* and that in such a system death can be inflicted on a person only for what he has done. A system of judicially sanctioned homicide, in which people are executed (at least in theory), *before* they have committed any crime at all, and thus are "punished" for what they will do and for the sort of person they will become, is not a system of punishment at all.

It is not a novel idea, either. In 1922, George Bernard Shaw, inspired both by genuine distress over the plight of men imprisoned for life and by pseudo-Darwinian eugenics, defended just such a system in his provocative essay, "The Crime of Imprisonment." But at least he recognized that in taking the position he did, he was *not* advancing an argument in favor of capital punishment or any other sort of punishment. Shaw defended the remarkable position that "we have no right to punish anybody." His conclusion that "persons who give more trouble than they are worth will run the risk of being . . . returned to the dust from which they sprung,"[2] was expressly offered as a reasonable man's alternative to every known system of punishment. On such a view the actual commission of a crime would be nothing but an incontrovertible symptom of a social disease which, whether or not it might be curable or might have been avoided, can be controlled only by exterminating the sick man. Were there some sure way of identifying the crime-prone before they break out with the fatal (to us) symptoms, there is every reason to put them out of the way. The medical analogy, to be sure, is not very apt. We are in effect advised to exterminate the sick and, if possible, the disease-prone, whereas analogy to public health measures suggests that we should bend every effort to immunize everyone with a suitable vaccine. Be that as it may, as Shaw well understood, to adopt such a system would certainly result in executions. But they would not be punishments, and the system would not be a system of capital punishment.

To take the line I have is not merely to quibble evasively. I do not want it thought that whereas I object to Barzun's defense of eugenic killings because he implies they are capital punishments, I would welcome them as readily as he and Shaw do if only they were called what they are. For I have serious reservations about the Shaw-Barzun position even when properly described and candidly defended for what it is. But each social question in its own time and place. One ought to be prepared to debate the merits of "judicial homicide" as a eugenic policy, for the very same reason one ought to be prepared to discuss euthanasia and abortion. These practices, like capital punishment itself, consist essentially in ending or preventing someone else's life, presumably for good reasons, and thus they pose variations on a theme of incomparable moral importance. But these issues are clearly independent of each other. Just as nothing has prevented us in the past from having capital punishment without also having euthanasia or eugenic killings, there is nothing to prevent us in the future from abolishing the death penalty and introducing executions in the name of mercy and social hygiene. It will be time enough to discuss these proposals when they are up for serious debate. Meanwhile, it does not take a philosopher to see that the death penalty can no more be defended by an argument for eugenic killings than it can be defended by an argument for suicide.

Yet the problem of the "incurables" does exist, and Professors Barzun and Hook have performed a service in forcing everyone to face this terrible fact. There is little doubt that some who have been executed fall into this category. One thinks of Albert Fish in New York, Gordon Northcott in California, and Charles Starkweather in Nebraska, to name only a few. In the light of our present knowledge about psychopathology and the actual methods of therapy and the personnel at our disposal, it would have been unreasonable to have hoped to cure and eventually release these men. But what does this prove? Not that it was theoretically impossible to cure them. Not that other men just as sick have never been known to get well. Not that such men cannot be safely incarcerated, for life if necessary. Apparently Professor Barzun is convinced that it is not worth our trouble to imprison such criminals possibly for life and that (as Professor Hook also believes) it is worse for them to be *made* to stay alive in prison rather than to be put to death; and that, regrettable as it may be, capital punishment ought to be preserved in America because it is a system that even now fairly well achieves the result he desires.

On the other hand, I am convinced that anyone who takes this view has thoroughly confused the possible merits of a utopian society, in which a hypothetically infallible system of "social defense" operates to eradicate all and only the unpreventable and incurable killers, with the very real evils of every known system of criminal justice which uses the death penalty. There is no doubt that a large number of the more than 7,000 persons capitally punished since 1900 in this nation were far from incurable. Fish, Northcott, and Starkweather are the much-publicized exceptions, not the rule. At the present time, no one has any idea how to work out a system of capital punishment that would be applied only to such persons, assuming for the sake of the argument that it would be desirable to execute them. In the end, there seems to me to be an enormous distance between Barzun's and Hook's implicit factual assumptions about society, crime, and the administration of justice, in terms of which they find their conclusions persuasive, and the actual circumstances in which the death penalty exists in this country. While they cannot be held responsible for what they have not defended, it is regrettable that the present system of capital punishment will reap the benefit of their argument.

III

In any serious discussion of the death penalty, those who are opposed to it should be ready to offer some alternative with detailed provisions that could be adopted with a minimum overhaul of the rest of the criminal code and penal system. In 1929, Lewis E. Lawes, then Warden of Sing Sing Prison and one of America's leading abolitionists, proposed the following model legislation for the punishment of murder:

> Upon conviction of murder in the first degree, the defendant shall be sentenced to life imprisonment.
>
> Prisoners serving life sentence shall receive no time allowance for commutation, or compensation until commuted to a definite term.
>
> No prisoner serving a life sentence shall be pardoned or commuted by the Governor until he has served at least twenty years actual time, unless the Court of Appeals shall make an order or decree, in which the majority of its members concur, to the effect that
>
> (a) Evidence which was not known at the time of the trial or which was not presented to the court or jury creates a probable doubt of the guilt of the accused; or,
>
> (b) Facts or circumstances exist which in the opinion of the court make a case for executive clemency consideration.
>
> After a prisoner shall have served twenty years actual time he shall be eligible for pardon or for commutation to a lesser term than life, and if commuted to a definite term of years, may thereafter earn commutation and compensation.
>
> A substantial percentage of the earnings of the prisoner shall be applied to the support of his dependents and to the support of the dependents of the person killed, to be apportioned in the discretion of the Superintendent of Prisons.[3]

This model statute, conservative though it may be at several points, is in fact much more radical than any abolition bill actively discussed in an American legislature during the past decade. Most contemporary abolitionists have compromised the principle of parole as a theoretical possibility for all murderers, and have supported bills that would replace the death penalty with a flat term of imprisonment for life. Other proposed bills have compromised by retaining the death penalty for the murder of a police officer or prison guard, and/or for any murder committed while on parole from a conviction for murder. Warden Lawes may have rejected these compromises, as I would, on the ground that optimum deterrence does not require them.

Nevertheless, to arrive at the wisest alternative to the death penalty, we should have to alter Warden Lawes's model statute in three major respects. The twenty-year minimum sentence which he would allow a court to impose should be reduced by half. Neither deterrence nor rehabilitation requires more. (The American Law Institute . . . has gone so far as to recommend a term of from one to ten years as the minimum court-imposed sentence. The Institute was able to do this, however, only because their proposal was part of a complete Model Penal Code.) The ten-year minimum I suggest could be adopted with few or no changes elsewhere in the system of punishments. Even ten years would be an unnecessarily long imprisonment in a few cases, but the widespread desire for Draconian punishments and the anxiety over premature release of murderers may require some such concession. The twenty-year minimum Warden Lawes proposed may have been tendered in a similar spirit of compromise.

Secondly, I think it best not to introduce the principle of compensation by the criminal as part of the punishment for murder. There is no doubt that compensatory punishments are more useful to the injured party (and to his dependents), to society, and even to the criminal than are retaliatory ones. But a convicted murderer could provide no more than a token compensation if it is to be obtained from his prison earnings, another portion of which may have to go to support his own dependents. The attractive idea that through deductions from his prison earnings the murderer may expiate his guilt at least to some degree (something that his rehabilitation alone could never accomplish) is probably an illusion, so long as the restitution is not of his own choice but is required by law. A cynical criminal might come to look upon the payments being exacted from him as nothing but part of the cost of his crime and without any moral significance. These are among the reasons why compensation by murderers is not to my knowledge practiced in any American abolition jurisdiction. A more practical proposal, if special indemnification for victims of criminal violence really seems desirable, would be for the government to offer assistance to the victim's dependents over and above their usual social security benefits.

Finally, Warden Lawes formulated his model statute in terms of the punishment for murder, thereby leaving it open whether other crimes should still be punished by death. In my view, his statute or something like it ought to be adopted as the punishment for *all* crimes that currently permit or require the punishment of death. Furthermore, whereas many states have written the death penalty for certain crimes (usually treason) into their constitutions, I should like to see a universal constitutional prohibition against capital punishment.

The formulation of an optimum alternative to the death penalty is a subject that few abolitionists ever thoroughly discuss. No doubt they would if they thought there was some hope of enacting such ideal legislation in the near future. As it is, however, abolitionists in America during the past decade have found themselves at one time or another defending almost every conceivable alternative. This has been confusing to the general public and has encouraged our opponents to view us as more desperate than we are. Whether the three revisions of Warden Lawes's model statute proposed here would command general assent among American abolitionists, I do not know. But I am convinced that if they became part of the criminal law throughout the country, we would have made a great step toward the ideal.

Notes

[1]See the essays collected by Richard Nice (ed.), *Crime and Insanity* (1958); and also the bibliography prepared by Dorothy Campbell Tompkins, *Insanity and the Criminal Law* (1960).

[2]*The Crime of Imprisonment* (1946), pp. 97–98.

[3]Lewis Lawes, *Man's Judgment of Death* (1924), pp. 28–29; reprinted in Julia Johnson (ed.), *Capital Punishment* (1939), p. 59.

Discussion Questions

1. Bedau feels that there is an important distinction between killing to avoid a clear and present danger and judicial execution. How does he use this distinction to criticize retributivists? How good is this argument?

2. What is Bedau's reply to Hook and Barzun on the issue of executing an innocent person? Is his reply successful?

3. How does Bedau deal with the issue of the convict who prefers death to a long prison term? Do you find his argument convincing? Why or why not?

4. How does Bedau reply to Hook and Barzun on the issue of the very worst criminals? How might Hook or Barzun reply?

5. Bedau suggests that Barzun's and Hook's position might lead to executing people likely to murder but who were not yet guilty of murder. Consider the pros and cons of this suggestion.

6. What are the advantages and disadvantages of Warden Lawes's proposal for an alternative to capital punishment?

Suggested Readings for Chapter Two

Bedau, Hugo Adam, ed. *The Death Penalty in America*. New York: Doubleday and Co., 1967.

Cedarblom, J. B., and William L. Blizek, eds. *Justice and Punishment*. Cambridge, Mass.: Ballinger, 1977.

Ewing, A. C. *The Morality of Punishment*. Montclair, N.J.: Patterson Smith, 1970.

Ezorsky, Gertrude, ed. *Philosophical Perspectives on Punishment*. Albany: State University of New York Press, 1972.

Gerber, Rudolph J., and Patrick D. McAnany, eds. *Contemporary Punishment: Views, Explanations and Justifications*. Notre Dame, Ind.: University of Notre Dame Press, 1972.

Grupp, Stanley E. *Theories of Punishment*. Bloomington, Ind.: Indiana University Press, 1971.

Honderick, Ted. *Punishment: The Supposed Justifications*. New York: Harcourt Brace Jovanovich, 1969.

Isonberg, Irwin, ed. *The Death Penalty*. New York: H. W. Wilson, 1977.

Madden, Edward, Rollo Handy, and Marvin Farzen. *Philosophical Perspectives on Punishment*. Springfield, Ill.: Charles C Thomas, 1968.

Moberly, Sir Walter. *The Ethics of Punishment*. Hamden, Conn.: Archer Books, 1968.

Murphy, Jeffrie, ed. *Punishment and Rehabilitation*. Belmont, Calif.: Wadsworth, 1973.

Van der Hoag, Ernest. *Punishing Criminals*. New York: Basic Books, 1975.

3

Suicide and Euthanasia

The situations of suicide and euthanasia are significantly different from war or capital punishment. The condemned criminal does not want to die; neither does the soldier killed in battle. But persons who take their own lives or wish to have their life taken by others are willing and sometimes even eager to die. Thus a good many of the principles applicable to war and capital punishment are not applicable to suicide and euthanasia. Instead, there are a variety of views that raise deep moral and ultimately religious questions. Some of the main positions may be briefly described as follows:

The Self-Ownership View

In this view, each of us has a sort of property right to his or her own life. Perhaps we can forfeit the right as we can forfeit other property rights, but unless we do, our life is our property. We can retain it if we choose or give it up if we choose. Just as I could if I like destroy my house, or employ someone else to destroy it, I can in this view take my own life or ask someone else to take it. If that person does kill me, he or she has done no wrong any more than a person would do wrong who destroyed my property at my request.

The Other-Ownership View

According to this view, which is in one sense the opposite or inverse of the self-ownership view, no one has the right to take his or her own life or ask others to take it because someone else has ownership. A great many religious believers hold that God is the "owner" of our lives and that we have no right to take our own lives or ask others to take it, any more than it would be right to destroy a house rented or loaned to us or ask someone else to do so. At various times certain people or societies have felt that a person's life belonged to the state or to the person's family, and suicide or euthanasia was therefore an offense against the state or family.

No-Ownership Views

Supporters of these views hold that it is a mistake to think of life in property terms and that suicide or euthanasia should be judged on the basis of other principles. Depending on the principles involved, a no-ownership view may or may not condone suicide or euthanasia. The principle that "suffering should always be minimized" might be used to justify suicide or euthanasia, while the principle "life should never be taken except to save other lives" might be used to condemn suicide or euthanasia.

In popular discussions of suicide, self-ownership or other-ownership arguments are very common but may be mixed up with other arguments, such as the desirability of minimizing suffering or the sanctity of life in general. Suicide may also be characterized as an instance of some form of behavior that is generally condemned—for example, "running away from your problems."

In the readings in this chapter, R. F. Holland spends a considerable amount of time distinguishing suicide from other seemingly similar acts. His position is to some extent an other-ownership one, though he also brings in related ideas of gratitude and loyalty. He concludes by arguing that some genuine suicides do not seem to violate this sense of gratitude and loyalty.

William F. May contrasts the attitudes found in the medical community and among people in general—the attitude that death is the greatest evil versus the attitude that pain is the greatest evil. He finds both attitudes overly simple and argues that an acceptable solution to the problems of suicide and euthanasia can only be found in a more complex and balanced view.

Both Holland and May assume in their discussions the workability of the distinction between killing someone and allowing that person to die. In his paper James Rachels challenges this distinction. Ernan Mc Mullin's article explores the religious dimension of the issue, as well as examining a number of connected life and death issues. Finally, Alistair MacIntyre's discussion can be regarded as a commentary on certain aspects of May's agruments. He discusses the question of whether we have a right to life and the question discussed by May of what it means to die "with dignity."

Suicide

R. F. Holland

I am concerned with the subject as an ethico-religious problem. Is suicide all right or isn't it; and if it isn't, why not?

The question should not be assumed to be susceptible of an answer in the way the question whether arsenic is poisonous is susceptible of an answer (which would be *the* answer to the question). Moreover in the case of arsenic the question what it is, and the question whether it is poisonous, are separable questions: you can know that arsenic is poisonous without having analyzed its nature. But to know or believe that suicide is objectionable *is* to have analyzed its nature or construed its significance in one way rather than another. So let us not ask at the outset whether suicide is objectionable as though we already knew perfectly well what it was (which we don't), but let us rather approach the problem by asking what it might *mean* to commit suicide— or simply, What *is* suicide? I do not think it is just one thing and I do not expect to get very far with the question.

Durkheim, whose book on suicide is one of the classics of sociology, seems to me not to have understood what suicide is. He believed that in order to avoid being prejudiced the inquirer into human behavior should never go by what people think ("the confused impressions of the crowd") but should make comparisons and look for the common properties of actions as a botanist or zoologist distinguishes objective common properties among flowers and fruits, fish and insects.[1] Durkheim thought it a condition of the possibility of investigation that systems of human behavior should be capable of being identified and classified as one thing or another quite independently of any reference to the agents' ideas. And since intentions involve ideas, he declined to allow that the question whether a man was a suicide could be settled in the negative by the discovery that he did not intend to take his life:

> . . . If the intention of self-destruction alone constituted suicide, the name suicide could not be given to facts which, despite apparent differences, are fundamentally identical with those always called suicide and which could not be otherwise described without discarding the term. The soldier facing certain death to save his regiment does not wish to die and yet is he not as much the author of his death as the manufacturer or merchant who kills himself to avoid bankruptcy? This holds true for the martyr dying for his faith, the mother sacrificing herself for her child, etc. Whether death is accepted merely as an unfortunate consequence, but inevitable given the purpose, or is actually itself sought and desired, in either case the person renounces existence, and the various methods of doing so can be only varieties of a single class.[2]

On this account of the matter it looks as if we have to say that a man who exposes himself to mortal danger, for whatever reason and whatever the circumstances, is exposing

From *Talk Of God,* Royal Institute of Philosophy Lectures, vol. 2, 1967–1968 (London: Macmillan, 1969). Reprinted by permission of St. Martin's Press and Macmillan Press, Ltd.

himself to suicide. Well, why not? Isn't it enough that the man should know what he is doing?

> The common quality of all these possible forms of supreme renunciation is that the determining act is performed advisedly; that at the moment of acting the victim knows the certain result of his conduct, no matter what reason may have led him to act thus. . . . We may say then conclusively: the term *suicide is applied to all cases of death resulting directly or indirectly from a positive or negative act of the victim himself which he knows will produce this result.*[3]

Durkheim here ignores the problem of how the investigator, especially one who is supposed to be collecting data in the spirit of a botanist, can judge whether or not a man knows what he is doing. And in trying to make the applicability of the term "suicide" to martyrdom turn upon this, he simply begs the question of *what* it is that the martyr is doing; for of this we are only entitled to say thus far that he goes to his death.

Though the martyr may go willingly to a death which he foresees, it is a death which has been decided upon for him first by someone else. Whether he now makes things easy or difficult for the decider is hardly to the point. He might accept the decision as justice and so in a way concur with it, assisting its implementation out of duty, as Socrates did. Socrates took the cup of hemlock and drank it, and thereby might be said strictly to have died by his own hand. Yet even this cannot make a man a suicide, given the fact that his death was not decreed by him. In the case of the mother who dies while rescuing her child from a blazing building, the death is not decided upon at all, inevitable though her action might cause it to be. Similarly with the soldier facing certain death to save his regiment, of whom Durkheim remarks that he does not wish to die. He would not necessarily be a suicide even if he did wish to die—to die well or just to die. For to wish that death might come, to hope that it will soon come, is still not to decree that one shall die. Socrates had a wish for death and thought it his business as a philosopher to "practice dying",[4] but not to practice suicide, which he said should be committed by no one.[5]

However I can imagine an objector insisting that there is a logical entailment which I have not got round between "Socrates knowingly and deliberately drank the poison" and "Socrates killed himself, i.e., was a suicide." One way of meeting this objection would be to accept the entailment and invoke the idea that in killing himself a man may be at the same time doing something else. Thus in killing himself by taking hemlock Socrates was also doing something else which belonged to the role of a state prisoner and formed part of the procedure for judicial execution in Athens. And the additional factor makes (so it might be said) a radical difference to the ethico–religious status of the self-slaughter. But although this has an illuminating sound the illumination is spurious because the alleged entailment between Socrates' taking of the hemlock and his committing suicide is non-existent. Taking hemlock does not, in the context of an Athenian judicial execution, amount to slaughtering oneself: in this circumstance it is no more an act of suicide than the condemned man's walk to the scaffold in our society.

If the suggestion be that Socrates was a man bent on self-destruction to whom the advent of his execution came in handy, then that is a different matter. But I should think the innuendo impossible to account for save as a misinterpretation of the fact that Socrates did in a certain sense wish to die. Hence he was able to take the poison gladly as the fulfillment of his wish. However, anyone construing that wish as a pointer towards suicide would be taking it for something other than it was through failing to relate it to its surrounds.

Though he did not go in for theology, Socrates thought it well said that mortals are the chattels of the Gods.[6] "Wouldn't you be angry," he went on, "if one of your chattels should kill itself when you had not indicated that you wanted it to die?" Socrates, then, did not wish to die before it was time for him to die. He did not wish to run away from anything. And it certainly cannot be said of him that he wished to die because he found no sense in living. On the contrary the sense he found in living was what on the one hand made him reject suicide and on the other hand enabled him to look on death, whenever it should come, as something to be welcomed rather than feared; hence it enabled him to die courageously. To put this another way, the sense he made of death and the sense he made of life were one and the same. A man who decides to commit suicide because he sees no sense in living cannot from this point of view be said to contemplate anything sensible in regard to his situation, for his death must be just as senseless to him as his life.

In contrast with the kind of objection that Socrates had against suicide, some of the objections to be heard against it are only of an external or accidental nature. For instance one reason, and it is a moral reason, which a man contemplating suicide might give for refraining is the fact that he has a wife and children who depend on him. However this consideration would be no more a reason against suicide than it would be a reason against his walking out on them and declining to return, so we do not learn from this example whether or not the suicide itself is especially objectionable. It would be likewise with the case of an army officer who cannot pay his gambling debts, so he wants to commit suicide, for which there are precedents anyway; but then he reflects that this would be a reprehensible thing to do because if he kills himself there will be no chance of the debts ever being repaid, whereas his duty is to try to work them off. The objection would be much the same if he were inclined to go off to live in Rhodesia under an assumed name.

I once read of an officer with gambling debts who confusedly thought he had a moral reason, not against, but in favor of shooting himself. The note he left behind contained a remark to the effect that he was choosing death rather than dishonor (at the time of writing he had not yet been found out). Now the great maxim of the military ethic, "death rather than dishonor," is exemplified by the conduct of the sentry who declines to leave his post when he could run away to safety but stays and carries out his duty although the consequence of doing so is death. Here the death and the dishonor are genuine alternatives—if he escapes the first he incurs the second, and if he embraces the first he avoids the second. But the case of the gambling officer is not like that at all. So far from being an alternative to the disgrace incurred by his inability to pay the debts, his death by suicide is rather a consequence of that disgrace. What he ends up with is both the death and the dishonor. There might or might not have been a way out of the dishonor had he stayed alive, but at least it is clear that killing himself is no way out of it. As Socrates observes in the *Phaedo*, death is not an escape from everything: if it were, it would indeed be a boon to the wicked.[7]

There are situations, though the gambling officer's is not one of them and neither is the sentry's, in which the only way of choosing death rather than dishonor would be to kill oneself—for instance if it is dishonorable to be taken captive and the only way of avoiding capture is to kill oneself. In just this situation Greek heroes fell upon their swords. However in regard to dishonor there is a distinction to be drawn between doing and suffering. The captured hero suffers his dishonor in being treated as a slave: he does not in his loss of freedom *do* anything dishonorable. He would therefore have been exhorted by Socrates not to commit suicide but to accept what comes, for Socrates believed that harm befell a man through his doing evil rather than through his suffering it.[8]

The choice before the hero on the eve of his capture is, one might say, between suicide and *indignity*. Opting for the former he chooses both nobly and rationally according to a thoroughly serious conception. For a man who is truly a hero cannot consent to live otherwise than as a hero; and above all the servile life is not open to him. Now if a Christian were to make that choice. . . . But then you see for a Christian it could not possibly be *that* choice. The status of the alternatives would not be the same although the Christian also might be described as choosing between suicide and indignity. However, in his case opting for the indignity would not be ignoble, while opting for the suicide would amount to consigning himself to damnation.

Let us now try to explore the idea of a choice between suicide and dishonor not in the sense of suffering but of doing something terrible. Compare the Greek hero with a modern spy who on his impending capture kills himself by swallowing a pill which has been supplied for use in this emergency. I am supposing that he swallows the pill not because of the possible consequences of the capture for himself but because he knows that under torture he will inevitably betray the secrets of his comrades and his country. Though I cannot imagine Socrates saying to a man in this predicament that he must not commit suicide, there is something he might have said to him earlier, namely that anyone who is concerned about his soul should beware of engaging in this sort of spying. For it is to enter into an institution the ethics of which require that in a certain eventuality you poison yourself; and the poisoning is not transformed into something other than suicide by the institutional role as it was in Socrates' own case by the role of being a condemned man in process of execution. Still, the fact that the spy's suicide is committed as an act of self-sacrifice gives it a very different flavor from the deed of the financier who does away with himself when his empire starts to totter. The financier "can't take it." This is also true, though on a much deeper level, of the Greek hero, who unlike the financier dies nobly. The hero commits suicide because there is something he cannot accept for himself, namely captivity. But the spy (in this particular variant out of many possible cases) is concerned solely with the good of others. Because of this one would like to deny that his is the spirit of a suicide. The difficulty is that he has supposedly entered the spying profession, which is a suicidal game, with his eyes open: he was not compelled to enter into it. But this consideration also means that his case fails to provide me with exactly the example I was looking for: I wanted an example of a completely forced choice between suicide and the doing of something morally terrible.

It might be held by a religious person that no man is ever forced to make such a choice; that it is something a good God would never inflict on a human being. But whether or not it be religiously imaginable, it is logically possible and I can depict a case where there will be no question of the agent's having voluntarily let himself in for the outcome by postulating that he suffers and knows that he suffers from a congenital form of mental instability, as a result of which he is overtaken from time to time by irresistible impulses towards something very horrible, such as raping children. Getting himself locked up is no solution, either because no one will listen to him or because no mental hospital is secure enough to contain him during one of his fits; and his fits come upon him without warning. So he decides to kill himself.

At first it may seem possible to argue that this man is not a suicide. For does he not belong to the category of those who are called upon to sacrifice their lives for the safety of others? Most often in such cases the order of events is: salvation of the imperiled followed by death of the saver, as in shipwrecks, when the men who have made possible the escape of others are trapped on board; or else the two events are concomitant, as at a grenade-throwing practice when one of the grenades is dropped and there is no time to throw it clear, whereupon an N.C.O. falls on the grenade and with his body shields the others from its effects. Either way, what the saver here decrees is another's salvation, with the unavoidable consequence of a death for himself which he does not decree. If, as with my imaginary maniac, the saver's own death has to take place first in order that the peril to others should be averted, the characterization of what is decreed can remain exactly the same as before. To put it another way, all the man really does is to preserve someone else and his death is encompassed as a consequence of this. The peculiarity of the case is that the death has to be encompassed first and is thus an instance of an effect preceding its cause.

But now I fear that the argument has overreached itself; not in positing an effect that precedes its cause, which I should accept here as a coherent conception, but in gliding over the fact that the man's death is not encompassed *for* him—he encompasses it directly himself. This is manifestly a doing and not a suffering; hence it was false to claim that "all he really does is to preserve someone else." That is not all, for he kills himself.

A comparable example, not this time from the imagination, is that of the explorer, Captain Oates. On the day before his death Oates had said that he could not go on and had proposed that the rest of the party should leave him in his sleeping bag. "That we could not do," says Scott, whose account of the upshot is as follows:

> He slept through the night before last, hoping not to wake; but he woke in the morning—yesterday. It was blowing a blizzard. He said, "I am just going outside and may be some time." He went out into the blizzard and we have not seen him since. . . . We knew that poor Oates was walking to his death, but although we tried to dissuade him, we knew it was the act of a brave man and an English gentleman.[9]

What Oates decreed was that his hard-pressed companions should be relieved of an encumbrance: of this there can be little doubt. He had borne intense suffering for weeks without complaint (Scott tells us) but remained cheerful right to the end. The sentiment that he was entitled to quit, or that anyway he was going to quit, never entered into it. Accordingly I want to deny he was a suicide, as I should have liked to do in the case of the maniac. And there is a feature of Oates's case that enables me to persist in my denial beyond the point to which I could take it in the other case. For if someone objects, "But he killed himself," in regard to the maniac there was no answer, but in Oates's case I can say, "No; the blizzard killed him." Had Oates taken out a revolver and shot himself I should have agreed he was a suicide.

We are back again at the distinction between doing and suffering, which here as elsewhere is fraught with difficulty. For if a man puts his head on a railway line and claims "I'm not going to kill myself, the train will do it," I shall reject that as a sophistical absurdity; yet I do not consider it absurd to claim that the blizzard killed Oates. But then of course neither is it absurd to claim that he killed himself by going out into the blizzard. And there is much to be said for a description that is midway between the two: "He let the blizzard kill him." To call one of these descriptions the right one is to say little more than "That's how I look at it."

Still I do not look at it arbitrarily when I say that Oates was killed by the blizzard. The indirectness of what he did in relation to the onset of his death and the entrance of time as a factor are features of the case which help to put it for me in this perspective. Yet do not time and a certain indirectness enter in as factors when a man puts his head on a railway line? They enter in, but not to the same effect because of the difference in the spirit and in the surroundings of what is done. That the blizzard is a natural phenomenon is something that makes a difference. To be sure, a man who out of sorrow drowns himself might also perhaps be said to expose himself to a natural phenomenon, but again the context and the spirit of it are different. Oates simply walks away from his companions—and in the act of doing so becomes exposed to the blizzard: he needs to put distance between himself and them and he cannot do so in any other way. He is concerned only with their relief. And he is well on the way towards death already. Such are the features of the case which in combination make it possible, though not obligatory, to say of him unsophistically what would naturally be said of a martyr, namely that he goes to his death.

The great divide among attitudes towards suicide lies between those in whose eyes this possibility is of special significance and those to whom it would not matter whether a man like Oates were held to be no suicide, or a suicide but an honorable one. The former are upholders of a religious ethics and I should call them that even though they might entertain no theological beliefs and never even mention a deity: the latter I should call humanists.

I am not suggesting that from the standpoint of an ethics untinged with religion it would have been exactly the same if Oates had shot himself. For it would have been ugly, unpleasant and messy, and hence a course to be rejected out of fastidiousness or consideration for the feelings of his companions. From the religiously ethical standpoint, however, the rejection of that course would be bound up with ideas of a different kind, about a man's relations to his life and destiny, or in other words about the soul.

Schopenhauer remarked that if there are any moral arguments against suicide they lie very deep and are not touched by ordinary ethics.[10] An ordinary ethics is for instance one in which the idea of prudence looms large, as it did for Aristotle, or which speaks, as Kant did, about the duty of self-preservation. Schopenhauer saw something vulgar in the idea of duties to oneself no matter what were deemed to be their foundation. But Kant spoke in a different vein when he called suicide the extreme point along the line of *crimina carnis* [crimes of the flesh] and when he drew attention to the element of disdain for the world in Stoicism ("leave the world as you might leave a smoky room").[11] Both of these latter considerations of Kant connect with the point which Schopenhauer took to be central about suicide, namely that it is a phenomenon of strong assertion of will.[12] The real reason why suicide must be condemned, Schopenhauer said, had to do with self-conquest. In this idea he was at one with Socrates and not far distant from the Christian religion. A Christian perhaps might speak, not so much of conquering, but rather of dying to the self, and the most spiritual expression of the idea for him would be in prayer—particularly in such a prayer as "Thy will, not mine, be done."

The sanctity of life is an idea that a religious person might want to introduce in connection with suicide, but if he left the matter there he would be representing suicide as objectionable in the same way and to the same degree as murder. It is only when he thinks of life as a gift that the difference starts to emerge. For the murderer does not destroy a gift that was given *to him*; he destroys something which was given to someone else but which happens to have got in his way. This argues his crime to be from the standpoint of ordinary ethics worse than that of the suicide, of whom at least it may be said that it was his own affair. On the other hand the suicide, unlike the murderer, is—religiously speaking— necessarily an ingrate; and the ingratitude here is of no ordinary kind, for it is towards his Creator, the giver of life, to whom everything is owed. That the destruction of a life should at the same time be the act of extreme ingratitude towards the giver of a life accounts for the special horror attaching to parricide, against which there is something like the same religious feeling as there is against suicide: as if these were two different ways of getting as close as possible to deicide. Or perhaps rather it is parricide which symbolizes the destruction of God and suicide the destruction of the universe. Thus G. K. Chesterton: "The man who kills a man, kills a man. The man who kills himself, kills all men; as far as he is concerned he wipes out the world."[13] Chesterton took himself there to be expressing the spirit of *all* suicides and in that he was mistaken. But there is no doubt that when a substitute for the end of the world is called for, suicide is the only possible one:

Dressed in flowing white robes, 26 people sat tense and silent in an upper room of a London house. Leader of the strange group was middle-aged solicitor Peter Shanning. He had given up practising law after experiencing what he called "an amazing series of dreams." He claimed it had been revealed to him that the world would come to an end on July 23rd, 1887, at 3 p.m. Shanning spent five years travelling the country and preaching. He gained 25 believers and they bought a house in north London. On the fatal day, they were gathered in a room, watching the clock ticking towards 3 p.m. Shanning sat quietly praying. Three o'clock came—and went. It wasn't the end of the world. But it was the end of Shanning. After his followers had left in bewilderment, he shot himself dead. (From a feature in a popular weekly paper.)

The fact that there is about suicide a kind of terribleness that ordinary, i.e., non-religious, ethics fails to touch is a weakness in ordinary ethics not only from the standpoint of religion but from the standpoint of philosophy. However, there is from the standpoint of philosophy a weakness to be discerned in the religious conception of suicide also. For according to the religious conception, all suicides are (unless their minds are unsound) guilty of an identical offense and separated from non-suicides by the same gulf; so that it does not really matter what kind of a suicide a man is so long as he is one.

Now this principle of equal disvalue, as it might be called, is manifestly objectionable to the non-religious conscience, which will either wish to remain silent in the face of suicide or else will wish to attribute to it an enormous range of disvalue, and also sometimes value, in a gamut that resists compression and runs from the squalid and mindless suicides of playboys or film starlets through the pitiful suicides of the oppressed and rejected, the anguished and maddened suicides of those goaded beyond endurance, the Stoic suicides and the heroic suicides, and thence to the self-sacrificial suicides, terminating with cases that religion would doubtless not classify as suicide at all. Ordinary ethics, however, will see no point in any alternative classification because it can descry variety in suicide where religion neglects it. And in this discrimination philosophy must side with ordinary ethics. For philosophy is a distinction-drawing business which emphasizes differences and focuses the mind on variant possibilities.

Consider for just a moment some of the alternative possibilities inherent in the case of the gambling officer I mentioned earlier, who thought he was choosing death rather than dishonor. The point was then that suicide could not be the kind of escape he thought it was. But suppose he realized that there were no possibility of escape from the dishonor anyway. If so, he could divide through by the dishonor and consider whether it might not be as well for him to commit suicide in order to put an end to his misery. If that were the idea, it could be objected on the one hand that the misery might pass and on the other hand that, even supposing it did not, the idea of being put out of one's misery is below human dignity and appropriate rather to dogs and horses.

However, it might not be simply a matter of his wanting to put himself out of his misery but rather that he has got himself into an impossible situation. And this is different, for it is now being supposed that the incurring of the dishonor means he can no longer carry on his life as a soldier. This possibility is closed to him, yet no other life is conceivable: soldiering *is* his life. The morality of the society, and the military ethic in particular, might well in all seriousness prescribe suicide for just this type of case.

On this interpretation, the suicide of the gambling officer has come to resemble that of an American journalist named Wertenbaker, who developed cancer in middle age and whose story has been told by his wife. Here too it was not, or not simply, a question of the man's inability to stand misery, but of his finding it impossible to carry on living as the kind of creature he had become. A difference between the two cases is that the officer's life, unlike the journalist's, becomes impossible as the result of something he himself did, and this consideration would be capable of affecting the outcome in more than one way. For on the one hand the knowledge that he has made a mess of his life through his own fault might drive a man to suicide out of sheer self-hatred ("he could murder himself"; and so he does). On the other hand he might be willing to abide by the consequences of his own folly out of a sense of equity which would not be there to sustain him if he thought he were the victim of a cruel and arbitrary fate. Not that Wertenbaker entertained this thought; he wrote as follows:

> Problem with death is to recognise the point at which you can die with all your faculties, take a healthy look at the world and people as you go out of it. Let them get you in bed, drug you or cut you, and you become sick and afraid and disgusting, and everybody will be glad to get rid of you. It shouldn't be such a problem if you can remember how it was when you were young. You wouldn't give up something for instance to add ten years to your life. All right, don't ask for them now. You wouldn't give up drinking and love-making and eating—and why should you have given them up? Nothing is ever lost that has been experienced and it can all be there at the moment of death—if you don't wait too long.[14]

What Wertenbaker saw no sense in was prolonging his life beyond a certain point, living on as something different from what he had been before, as a squalid pain-wracked thing, a dying man. It cannot be said that he found life meaningless. Rather, the meaning he found in life was such as to justify, to give him a reason for, doing away with himself in a certain circumstance.

In relation to the example of Wertenbaker, Chesterton's words about wiping out the world have little grip. Wertenbaker did not want to throw back the world in its creator's face—and not just because he had no belief in a creator either: if he had been offered his life over again he would have taken it gladly.

But all of it? No, not all of it: he was not prepared to accept *the whole* of the life that had been given him. Instead he despaired of it, despaired of the existence of any power to sustain him in his predicament. That he should have reviled what his life had become was understandable. The trouble was he did not love what he reviled; he had not "this primary and supernatural loyalty to things."

The last few words of that religiously ethical comment are Chesterton's again, and they help to make clear the point of the passage I quoted before.[15] But still I do not see how they could be expected to influence a man like Wertenbaker, who after all had his own kind of loyalty to things.

Notes

[1] *Suicide* (trans. Spaulding and Simpson) (London, 1952), pp. 41–42.
[2] Ibid., p. 43.
[3] Ibid., p. 44.
[4] *Phaedo*, 64A.
[5] *Phaedo*, 62A.
[6] *Phaedo*, 62B.

[7]*Phaedo,* 107C.

[8]*Gorgias,* 469B.

[9]*Scott's Last Expedition* (London, 1935), vol. i, p. 462.

[10]*Foundation of Morals.*

[11]*Lectures on Ethics: Suicide.*

[12]*World as Will and Idea,* § 69.

[13]*Orthodoxy* (New York: Dodd, Mead, 1909).

[14]Lael Tucker Wertenbaker, *Death of a Man* (New York, 1950), p. 10.

[15]His remark about the suicide wiping out of the world might otherwise seem to be no more than a solipsistic muddle.

Discussion Questions

1. Does Holland's attempt to distinguish suicide from other forms of death resulting from an action of the victim help to answer the question, "Is suicide all right or isn't it"? How does it help or fail to help?

2. What are Holland's objections to Durkheim's definition of suicide? On what are they based? Is Durkheim right or is Holland? Why?

3. In several cases Holland seems to argue that it is the *manner* in which a person takes his or her life rather than the intention that determines whether an act is suicide. Do you agree? Why or why not?

4. In Holland's view what is the relevance of religion to suicide? Argue for or against his view on this question.

5. What point is being made in the quotation from Chesterton? What use does Holland make of this point? How important is this point in deciding whether suicide is all right? Justify your answer.

The Right to Die and the Obligation to Care: Allowing to Die, Killing for Mercy, and Suicide

William F. May

When we assert human rights, we usually do so with some awareness of social, cultural, and political forces that would deny them. Thus our own bill of rights—including freedom of speech, assembly, and worship, and the right to bear arms—sprang from a healthy suspicion of those institutions—political and ecclesiastical—that threatened to deprive a citizenry of its due. When people, therefore, get concerned about the right to die, against what forces are they girding themselves when they assert the right?

In the view of some critics, the major cultural and social force opposed to the right to die is the ancient and continuing philosophical and theological tradition of the West. Commentators reach this conclusion citing the classical Christian opposition to suicide. For natural law theorists among the Christians, suicide was not only immoral but profoundly *unnatural*—literally, suicide violates our nature. One of the laws of nature, so the argument goes, is the law of self-preservation. This law is the first principle of nature within us and the precondition of all else. No one has the natural right to kill himself or to expect others to assist him in so doing.

Since God is the source and ground for the laws of nature, theologians called suicide not only immoral and unnatural, but sinful: a breach of divine command. Accomplices were thus guilty of the sin of murder. Successful suicides were not granted traditional funeral rites, i.e., Christian burial. Worse, popular reaction led to the abuse of the suicide's corpse and the persecution and humiliation of the unsuccessful suicide. The theologian defined suicide as sin and the population at large was disposed to punish the sinner.

The weight of the legal tradition of the West has similarly opposed the right to die. Self-destruction was not only immoral, unnatural, and sinful, but illegal. Suicide, to be sure, was a rather special crime; the successful perpetrator was able to remove himself permanently from the reach of social punishment. But only to a degree. The suicide knew beforehand, after all, that his family might be humiliated and his body degraded. Once again, any who assisted in this peculiar crime were considered murderers.

While the cumulative philosophical, theological, and legal tradition of the West has its consequences for the current discussion of the right to die, this ancient tradition is not the only, or even the most important, cultural force opposed to the right. In fact, as we shall see later, traditional society in the West was a great deal more hospitable to the right to die than its views on the single subject of suicide would suggest.

A third societal force that often denies the right to die is the medical profession. Whatever convictions about dying may prevail in society at large, the patient, after all, ends up in the hands of a specific profession, with its own particular ethos. While the

From *Death and Decision,* Ernan Mc Mullin, ed. Copyright © 1978 by the American Association for the Advancement of Science. Reprinted by permission of Westview Press, Inc.

physician in the ancient world was primarily a caretaker of the sick, increasingly the mission of the modern doctor has shifted from care to cure. Descriptions of caretaking tend to be pejorative; caretaking is fit work for handholders and those given to the bedside manner. Most of the money goes for cure and glamour follows money. The modern physician has been devoted to the fight against death. He or she is a member of a resistance movement. Even though other groups in the culture may deviate from an unconditional fight against death, the physician cannot. His or her patients rely on total dedication. Thus, the physician would break faith with himself and infect the professional relationship with distrust if he began to make decisions about whether to fight for life or hasten death.

A fourth pressure pushing against the right to die is the spectacular success of modern medical technology. Its achievements have led increasingly to the exclusive definition of the doctor as fighter. The success of medical technology creates a cultural momentum. It produces a moral scheme out of the technologist's impulse: what can be done, should be done. Success inspires the new piety—not toward nature, but toward the machine. In the Middle Ages, respect for the natural impulse to self-preservation led to the opposition to suicide; in recent times, piety toward the machine argues for the endless prolongation of life. The sheer existence of the machinery and a team that knows how to use it argues for its mechanical employment. The machine becomes *autonomous*. Instead of serving the life of the patient and assisting his recovery to permit him once again to serve others, the machine feeds on the patient. The patient becomes a demonstration of the potency of the machine and the virtuosity of the medical team. As one resident put it: "As a university teaching service, we tend to attempt resuscitation on all patients, particularly at the beginning of the semester."[1]

In the midst of all this enthusiasm, some people feel that they lose their autonomy and begin to talk much more passionately than in the past about the right to die. (Their passion distinguishes them from the Stoics' defense of self-destruction; Stoics were not supposed to get passionate about anything—even suicide.)

A final influence on the question of the right to die is people's perception of what might be called the metaphysical pressure in their lives. The destructiveness of disease, suffering, and death leads victims to enlist the physician as fighter and provokes in patients and families that terrified passivity with which they rely on both the physician and technology. Disease today seems not the absence of positive powers (sun, food, water, and sleep) but an invasion of forces that are negative and destructive. Modern people [have] interpreted disease as an invader with the identification of bacteria and cancers that wreak havoc in the body. This picture of some diseases dominates the interpretation of all disease, defines the role of the physician as fighter, and authorizes appropriations for weapons in the armory of drugs and procedures with which the professional can wage his war against disease and death.[2] The patient is like Poland lying helpless between two rival powers that fight out their battle across relatively defenseless terrain.

Sometimes suffering and death seem a single destructive experience; at others, the ordeal of suffering becomes distinct from the fear of death. When suffering and death are experienced as distinctive, the victim tends to develop different ethical responses. Professor Arthur C. McGill, in a plenary address before the American Academy of Religion, 1974, observed that many movements in ethics can be divided into those that define absolute evil as death and those that define it as suffering. If death is the *summum malum* [greatest evil], then one is likely to oppose abortion, euthanasia, and war. One would oppose the right to die. If suffering is the absolute evil, then one would be willing to pull the plug on an individual life to stop irremediable pain or to risk death in war rather than face an intolerable slavery.[3]

I suspect that each group has its own reflexive sense of preeminent good. When death is perceived as the absolute evil, life becomes sacred. When suffering is intolerable, then wealth, abundance, or quality of life seems more important than life itself. Thus the debate gets organized: on one side—those who hold to the sanctity of life; on the other—those who are more interested in the sanctity of comfort. One group abhors death and holds life sacred; the other abhors suffering, and prizes quality over life. Both revere a creature, not the creator.

My own position on these matters will become clearer as we proceed. Suffice it to say at this point that I cannot wholly side with either party to the debate. My reluctance is derived from theological grounds. These grounds can be laid out in two ways.

Conventional theological argument begins with a different conception of the sacred than that of either the pro-lifers or the quality-of-lifers. Monotheism permits one to recognize only God as sacred; creatures are good but are not God; they derive from God. For this reason the theist cannot subscribe to the slogan of that most famous of the pro-lifers—Albert Schweitzer—Reverence for Life. (To his credit, Schweitzer had the courage of his convictions. Because he was committed to life rather than to quality of life, he subordinated his dazzling careers as a musician, composer, philosopher, theologian, and scholar to his vocation as a physician in Lambarene, Africa.) But neither can the theist accept the other principle: a reverence for wealth, which prompts its devotees in the name of quality of life to deal ruthlessly with the impoverished or the helpless.

This conventional distinction between theism and contending views of the sacred is acceptable enough, but it does not get at the modern metaphysical problem. We have already observed that the absorbing modern issue is the problem of evil rather than the definition of good. The conflicting values of life and quality of life are reflexes from the deeper apprehensions about the evils of death and suffering. Hence the more decisive analysis theologically requires not the assertion that God transcends the perceived goods: life and quality of life, but rather that he ultimately encompasses the evils of disease, suffering, and death. These evils are real, but not ultimate. The Christian derives this conclusion from the event at the very center of Christian consciousness: an event in which suffering and death are not eliminated or repressed but fully exposed. In the cross, evil exposes itself in its ultimate impotence to separate man from God. For this reason, men and women need not cling fiercely to life or quality of life as though the only alternative to either is absolute nullity.

The Christian theist tradition recognizes that neither *life* nor *wealth* is an absolute good; neither death nor suffering is an absolute evil; that is, powerful enough to deprive human beings of that which is absolutely good. Therefore, the goods and ills we know in life are finally relative; we are free to enjoy goods, but not utterly and irrevocably desolate at their loss, commissioned to resist evil, but not as though in this resistance alone is our final resource.

This position would not establish in each case a third option alongside the other two or guidelines of its own. It would not always call for a different action, but would open up a somewhat brighter sky under which to act—a sky that has cleared from it the despair of those who believe that except for life, there is only death, or, except for quality of life, there is nothing but the final humiliation of poverty. The moral life, by the same token, is not a grim struggle of life against death or "quality of life" against poverty. Neither should our political life be a fierce conflict of pro-lifers against quality-of-lifers, each heaping epithets on the other, each charging the other with moral blindness. Both positions are ultimately too shrill to reject their advocate's own excesses: one group clamoring in panic for life at all costs; the other, proclaiming, give me quality of life or give me (or them) death. A theological perspective suggests that decisions should vary in different cases: sometimes to relieve suffering, other times to resist death. But in all cases, decisions should not reflect the pressure of that fear and despair from which absolutism is often derived.

This position has two general consequences for the medical profession and its use of technology. The profession, first, ought not to be defined wholly by a fight against death. When determined exclusively by that fight it presses for prolongation of life at any cost. The profession should be free to respond to patients' requests to cease and desist in the effort to prolong life when it can no longer serve the health of the host. "Thou shalt not kill, but needst not strive, officiously, to keep alive." Under some circumstances, the physician engaged in primary care may even be called upon to find ways (as Eric Cassell has put it) to assist some patients to consent to their own deaths. A physician is not always obligated to fight pneumonia if such death has become acceptable to the patient, in preference to death by extraordinarily painful, irreversible and protracted cancer. There is, after all, a time to live and a time to die. There is a right to die. Although the progressive impoverishment of the patient in dying is not in and of itself humiliating (the patient may respond to the ordeal with the dignity of humility rather than humiliation), this impoverishment becomes humiliating if it is gratuitously prolonged by the zeal of others.[4]

At the same time, however, neither physicians nor the society at large ought to prize so highly the quality of life that they solve the problem of suffering by eliminating the sufferer. This is often the solution to the problem of evil propounded by the advocates of active euthanasia. They deny the capacity to cope with life once terminal pain and suffering have appeared. They assume that life has peaked somewhere on a hill behind them and that all else ahead slopes downward toward oblivion. They doubt that end-time itself can be suffused with the human.

With this much in hand, we turn now to distinctions that are important to discussions of the right to die: 1) between maximal care and optimal care; 2) between allowing to die and mercy killing; 3) between euthanasia, passive or active, and suicide.

I

The basic assumption of an all-out war against death is that maximal treatment is optimal care. It is doubtful, however, that maximal medical assault by invasive diagnostic procedures, by aggressive and complicated drug management, by enthusiastic cutting and burning, is optimal care for patients. Often such treatment merely distracts from the use of precious time for what really matters. At worst, the end result can be somewhat like that Vietnam village that was destroyed by bombs in the course of being saved. It is salutary, therefore, that two teaching hospitals—precisely those institutions which by virtue of resources would be most tempted to wage all-out war—have pulled back recently from total war against death.

The Massachusetts General Hospital has adopted procedures recommended by its Critical Care Committee that would classify critically ill patients into four groups:

Class A   *Maximal therapeutic effort* without reservation.

Class B   *Maximal therapeutic effort without reservation but with daily evaluation.*

Class C   *Selective limitation of therapeutic measures.* . . . A Class C patient is not an appropriate candidate for admission to an Intensive Care Unit. . . .

Class D   *All therapy can be discontinued.* . . . though maximum comfort to the patient may be continued or instituted.[5]

The Massachusetts General Hospital (MGH) Report, by implication at least, dissolves two distinctions that previously established for some physicians and moralists clear-cut limits on therapeutic efforts; the distinctions between starting and stopping machines and between ordinary and heroic measures. In my judgment, the Report correctly abandons both distinctions for the more apt criterion of the patient's welfare.

A

Physicians commonly feel that they have discretion in a case only until they start the machines. Once machines are running, they lose the option of letting the patient die. This position is understandable psychologically. Once vital signs have been restored, it seems like killing to pull the plug. The distinction is misleading, however, in that it converts a machine from an instrument into a fatality. It assumes that once the machines are running, they are beyond the reach of decision-making. They are no longer anyone's human responsibility. This submissive attitude toward the equipment repeats the more general submissiveness that the patient (if competent) and his family feel toward the hospital staff. Once within the precincts of the hospital, the patient feels that he must comply with its routines and decisions. Like the visitor at the whorehouse, he tends to feel that he has to go along with what goes on there, once past the front door.

The MGH Report subordinates the operation of machines to the patient's welfare as it allows for the reclassification of patients and provides for daily evaluation of patients in Class B. The Report also establishes procedures for such acts as turning off mechanical ventilators at that point in therapy when the machine may offer maximal treatment but not optimal care.

B

Similarly the MGH Report implies rejection of the medical distinction between ordinary and heroic measures; with the help of this distinction, therapy to prolong life can be withheld but only if it can be characterized as heroic. While one may be basically sympathetic to the final intent of the distinction insofar as it allows some patients to die, the decision rests too heavily on the status of the means. If it can be said conscientiously in a given case that the patient's well-being is best served by the withdrawal of heroic measures, then his welfare may be just as aptly served by the withdrawal of something as ordinary today as penicillin.

The MGH Report, in effect, relaxes the distinction between ordinary and heroic when it provides for classification D, under which all therapy (but not all efforts to provide comfort) can be discontinued. This distinction could not be relaxed, of course, unless another criterion took its place in the light of which therapy is assessed. Professor Paul Ramsey in his important essay "On (Only) Caring for the Dying," proposed such a criterion: "The right medical practice will provide those who may get well with the assistance they need, and it will provide those who are dying with the care and assistance they need in their final passage. To fail to distinguish between these two sorts of medical practice would be to fail to act in accordance with the facts."[6] The crucial distinction does not fall between ordinary and heroic measures, but between two conditions of patients with two different sets of needs: those for whom efforts to cure are appropriate and those for whom efforts at remedy are in vain but for whom care remains imperative. A given procedure, whether ordinary or heroic, should be evaluated as to whether it offers optimal care or merely maximal treatment. The latter may, in fact, neglect the patient, gagging him with the irrelevant, while denying him what he truly needs.

It may overlook his real condition and wants: "Just as it would be negligence to the sick to treat them as if they were about to die, so it is another sort of 'negligence' to treat the dying as if they are going to get well or might get well."[7] The MGH Report, with its provision for daily evaluations, attempts to eliminate the negligence of misplaced treatment.

The MGH guidelines emphasize the needs and welfare of the patient but pay almost no attention, at least directly, to the further question of a patient in the process of decision-making. The guidelines assume that the staff will make most decisions *on behalf of patients.* Although the patient and family, along with many other parties, can initiate questions about treatment classification, the final decision rests with the attending physician. Neither the competent patient nor his or her family has an acknowledged or regularized place in making those decisions.[8] The Report does not evince that systematic and scrupulous respect for the competent patient and family that the Beth Israel Hospital of Boston demonstrates in its "Orders Not to Resuscitate."[9]

While declaring that the hospital's general policy is "to act affirmatively to preserve the life of all patients," the Beth Israel document acknowledges those situations in which heroic measures "might be both medically unsound and so contrary to the patient's wishes or expectations as not to be justified." The document then establishes procedures by which the competent patient (or family, in the case of an incompetent patient) can collaborate in a standing order not to resuscitate—specifically, in those cases that satisfy the conditions of irreversibility, irreparability, and imminence of death.

On the negative side, the Beth Israel document deals only with orders not to resuscitate. It thus operates too restrictively within the old distinctions between starting and stopping the machines and between ordinary and heroic measures. It does not deal with that more extended range of cases in which it may be appropriate for the patient's welfare to stop (and not just not start) procedures or even to stop procedures that are less than heroic.

On the positive side, the document tackles head-on the consent issue, the question of a patient's rights. This issue, however, is deeper than the formal question of patient freedom; that is, the question as to whether patients or physicians shall have the final decision as to when and for what reasons efforts to prolong life shall cease. To be sure, human dignity is at stake if patients are categorically denied the liberty to participate in decisions having to do with themselves, but dignity in this particular case, if it is actually to be exercised under the conditions of *informed* consent, rests on a deeper dignity; that is, the capacity of patients to cope with their own dying. Much well-intentioned medical practice is guided by the conviction that the liberty to cope with one's own dying is an unwanted liberty. The physician, for example, who brought the series of articles in *The New England Journal of Medicine* to my attention was skeptical about the readiness of patients to participate in decisions about their own dying. He commented candidly that he "liked" the Report of the Massachusetts General Hospital, but found the "other" policy statement that sought patient concurrence in such matters ghoulish. His judgment reflects a widely shared skepticism about the likelihood that patients will find it a favor to be confronted with the question of their courage in the face of death. Informed consent remains "pro forma" if the patient is unwilling to face his own dying. He signs the papers quickly because he is disinclined to entertain the prospect of a medical failure. The issue of informed consent poses at the deepest level the question of the human possibility for dignity, humility, and courage in facing death; the problem, ultimately, of consent to one's own dying. At its deepest level, the question of the right to die springs from the duty to die well.

II

Some moralists, like Joseph Fletcher, believe that the distinction between allowing to die and mercy killing is hypocritical quibbling over technique. They are disposed to call "allowing to die" passive euthanasia and mercy killing active euthanasia and collapse the distinction between the two. Since the consequences are the same—whether the patient dies by acts of omission or commission—what matters the route the patient took there? By either procedure he ends up dead.

Other moralists, opposed to active euthanasia, believe that the distinction between allowing to die and mercy killing is worth preserving and in favor of the former. This position can be defended in two ways, either by exploring the obligations of the community to the dying or by examining the rights (and, for some religious traditions, the duties) of the dying. Most opponents of active euthanasia begin with the obligations of the community, particularly those of medical professionals. Professor Ramsey, as we have seen, has defined that professional obligation as the mandate to give care. This imperative sets a limit on the efforts to prolong the process of dying. It justifies allowing to die. There comes a time when physicians, family, and friends must cease and desist, not in order to abandon the patient, but to provide for care and only care. Otherwise treatment is misdirected and ultimately negligent. Professor Ramsey, however, would not extend the mandate of care to mercy killing. To care in the form of killing is to defect from the obligation by eliminating the patient to whom care is directed. While the irreversibly dying live, they claim from us care and not something else—neither officious efforts to prolong their lives nor short cuts to end them. Mercy killing is impatient with the patient. In its own inverted way it abandons him.

Since Professor Ramsey bases his rejection of active euthanasia on the imperative to care, rather than on the absolute sacredness of life, he must concede, at least theoretically, two special circumstances under which mercy killing might be permissible: when the patient is in a permanent comatose state so profound as to be totally inaccessible to human care or when the dying patient experiences extreme and unendurable pain for which no relief can be offered. (Whether in fact any patients satisfy either of these conditions is a determination which only the competent physician [and not the moralist] can make; and even physicians, if the reports of the staff at St. Christopher's Hospice can be credited, have failed to explore fully the degree to which pain can be held at bay.) Under these very limited conditions, active euthanasia may be allowable to, but never obligatory upon, the professional. The right to die, therefore, reaches its acceptable limit in the negative right, as Professor James Childress has put it, of "not having one's dying process extended or interfered with." The proponents of active euthanasia push on to the more positive claim "to have others help one to become dead." The right to die passes over into the right to be killed with serious negative consequences (argues Professor Childress in an unpublished paper on "To Kill or Let Die") for the trust between doctor and patient upon which the professional relationship depends.

The so-called "death with dignity" movement attempts to specify contractually those conditions under which a patient may be allowed to die without compromising the obligation of the community to care. This group proposes that a patient reach an agreement with his or her physician concerning those circumstances (terminal and irreversible) under which one would want life-supporting systems withdrawn.

So far so good. I do, however, have a caveat to offer on the subject. The term "death with dignity" should not be restricted to the contractual freedom to choose the time of one's own dying. While it may include that, it needs to include much more than that if this freedom is to be protected.

The decision of a patient to instruct his or her physician to pull the plug is not a *dignified* decision if it is humanly or financially *coerced*. The decision becomes forced when the society devotes too much money to glamourous techniques for the prolongation of life at the expense of *humane care* for the dying. Under these circumstances, an individual may have only a forced choice between inhuman prolongation versus a rapid termination of his life. He needs also the third option of an environment of dignified care.

Put another way, dying with dignity (in the sense of the rapid termination of life) requires, if it is to be an uncoerced decision, protecting the dignity of dying itself. This, in turn, requires caring for the dying with dignity and this will not occur unless we respect the dignity of caring for the dying. Adequate social support is required for systems and professions concerned with care, if there is to be real freedom in the choice not to avail oneself further of the opportunity for care.

To put it bluntly—if a member of the middle class instructs his doctor under certain conditions to withdraw procedures the result of which is to bring about death, we can be reasonably sure of the uncoerced nature of his decision. By virtue of finances he has available resources to secure a level of care beyond minimal standards. But others less fortunate than he may be driven to a decision to terminate because the care of the dying is so poor. Their only available solution is to terminate life as quickly as possible. The poor should not be made an offer which they cannot afford to decline because the current alternative for living is unacceptable.

Very practically, then, the right to die must be protected from abuse but its placement within the larger context of the right to equal access to life and health care. Death with dignity is too narrowly defined if it simply places within my reach the chance to get out of a miserable life. The movement may even be pernicious if it decreases within the society the motivation to provide humane care.

In a large city in another country, there is a road called "The Street of the Good Death." The street is so called because of an exceptionally fine hospital located there. The hospital, however, is noted neither for its life-prolonging equipment nor for its readiness to put to sleep its inmates but for its provision of good care for the dying. Euthanasia happens to be the name of that street.

A somewhat less conventional way of approaching the distinction between allowing to die and mercy killing is to focus on the obligations not of the community but of the dying. With the exception of the Roman Catholic tradition in moral theology, modern teachers in the field of medical ethics are almost mute on the subject. The reason for this silence lies in the somewhat selective appropriation today of the ancient religious tradition of the West. In a secular age, we are disposed to retain a remnant of the ethic of love (translated into medical ethics as the obligation of the community to care) but we know little of the ancient ethic of humility and patience, virtues which the patient may need when care has done all it can. Modern Western Protestant Christianity and secular humanism which has been its offshoot has been almost exclusively committed to the virtue of love rather than the virtue of humility, to the dynamics of giving rather than the more difficult art of receiving. The sick are distressed. What is more natural than to respond to their distress with the works of charity? Give them what they need, and since they can apparently be given more in a hospital, put them there and put them in the hands of professionals who are expert givers.

Well and good, but we are almost totally silent on the subject of the virtues of the patient. Medical ethics concentrates exclusively on the ethics of the expert, the master giver. The subtlest dehumanization of the patient may occur in that we do not take seriously the question of his virtues and vices, the nobility or the meanness of his responses to his condition. We act and reflect as though the patient does not have a moral life. The virtues of patience and courage may be as important to death with dignity as an environment of care. Sometimes the strongest response to the humiliation of illness is not loving care, but the patient's own humility. Moreover, as we take seriously the moral role of the patient, we may begin to see that the physician receives from, as well as gives to, his patients and that humility may be an unexpected ingredient in professional life.

It is impossible to discuss today the question of the patient and his responsibilities without reckoning with the concept of a good death. To its credit, the euthanasia movement has reintroduced the patient into the discussion of medical ethics because it poses the question of a good death. This question, however, will have to be discussed in historical perspective because Western society appears to have experienced a major change in its conception of a good death.

Most modern people equate a good death with a sudden death. They want to go quickly in an accident; they prefer a heart attack to cancer. To the best of my knowledge, Soren Kierkegaard of the nineteenth century was the first to draw attention to the modern preference for a sudden death.[10] (Ironically, the modern world has produced simultaneously a desire for a sudden death and the incredibly expensive C-T Scanner, a half million dollar early warning system about diseases largely irremediable!) The preference has become so widespread today that almost any other choice seems incomprehensible. If, of course, any other choice is truly unintelligible, then one would be more inclined to collapse the distinction between active and passive euthanasia and go the quickest route possible.

Yet historically, it would appear, another preference is possible. We know, for example, that people in the Middle Ages preferred some advance warning about their death. They listed a sudden death among the many evils from which devout folk should pray for deliverance. Clearly, a warning is desirable if people feel that they have some way of preparing for an event. The housewife deems it unfortunate when a guest catches her in hair curlers without something in the pantry. She prefers a little warning so that she can rise to the occasion. The traditional prayers of the church concerning death acknowledged a link between warning and preparation. The Rogation Day list of evils from which the believer prayed for deliverance included the evil of a *sudden* and *unprovided for* death. Conversely, a good death included warning and very specific preparations.

Medieval literature was filled with premonitions of death.[11] The customary phrase was "his time has come." After forewarning, the dying man or woman made preparations. First, the dying person might adopt prescribed gestures or postures: sometimes the head oriented to the East, the hands crossed, or the face turned up to heaven. Preparations included, second, the important business of going through the experiences of grief and reconciliation with relatives, companions, and helpers. Grief occurred on both sides. Those about to be bereaved needed to express their grief over imminent loss, and the dying man needed to grieve over the loss of his world. Such mourning was short-lived but not to be denied or obscured. Some measure of suffering was an acceptable part of human dying. The further work of preparation included the reconciliation of the dying man or woman with companions and friends. Finally, the dying person uttered prayers of confession and petition, followed by the only specifically ecclesiastical part of the occasion, the prayers of absolution by the priest.

Where did all this work of preparation take place? In the bedchamber of the dying. We must remember, moreover, that the bedroom was not on this occasion a *private* room. "The dying man's bedchamber became a public place to be entered freely" by relatives, friends, servants, and children. Only in the eighteenth century, with medical concern for hygiene, did doctors begin to isolate the dying person in his bedroom. Thenceforward dying became a secret act.

Until the last two hundred years dying was a public ceremony; but who organized this ceremony? As Ariés points out: The dying person himself functioned as the master of ceremonies.

How did he learn to do it? Very simply. As a child he had seen others accept responsibility for their own dying. He had not been excluded from the room. He knew the protocol. He would do it in turn when his own time had come. "Thus, death was familiar and near, evoking no great awe or fear." That is why Ariés characterizes this whole period as living and dying with a sense of "tamed death."

The contrast today is striking. Instead of dying at home in one's own bedchamber, 80% of Americans die in a hospital or in a nursing home. Earlier, dying was a public ceremony witnessed by a company including relatives, helpers, friends, and children. But today, death often comes, even for those who have families, secretly in the hospital, unwatched except at a technical level by the all-monitoring eye of a cardiac machine. If the patient were to meet death heroically, only the machine would know it.

> A visitor to a hospital can often spot a room where a terminally ill patient is being treated. It's usually, if not invariably, dark. The shades are always pulled down, the draperies are closed, the people speak softly—if at all. There's often a physical withdrawal from the dying patient's bed.[12]

Finally, in earlier centuries, the person dying organized himself for the event with some sense of protocol. Today, however, others manage dying. We call it *management* of the *terminally* ill. A new specialist has been added to interpret and handle the event: the thanatologist. "So live that when thy thanatologist comes. . . ." Still another specialist looms on the horizon, the dolorist. Generally, though, machines take charge; relatives and friends must give them berth; and hospital attendants are their acolytes. Death has become a mechanical process. The person has been robbed of his own dying; and if you add to theft the ignorance in which he is often kept, he loses what earlier cultures felt to be important to a good death—the forewarning that invited one not simply to participate in medical decisions but to prepare and to take over one's own dying.

Perhaps it is clear now why one must be hesitant about judging earlier Western culture, on the question of its attitude toward the right to die, entirely on the basis of its opposition to suicide: it may have been opposed to *suicide,* but it was *not* opposed to the *right to die.* In fact, it fully expected a person to reckon with, and to govern his own dying. The age acknowledged that not all suffering is utterly inhuman; dependency, abhorrent. Although it is wrong to sentimentalize suffering or to romanticize death and dying, it is equally wrong to assume that men and women cannot be human in the midst of suffering and death, that they have no role to play in the face of dependency, no virtues to evince.

Modern culture, to the contrary, not only denies the right to die by its often mindless prolongation of life, but, just as seriously, denies with the same heedlessness the right of the person to do his own dying. Since modern procedures, moreover, have made dying at the hands of the experts and the machines a prolonged and painful business, emotionally and financially as well as physically, they have built up pressure behind the euthanasia movement which asserts, not the right to die, but the right to be killed.

The basic thrust of the euthanasia movement is to engineer death rather than to face dying. Euthanasia would bypass dying to get one dead as quickly as possible. It proposes to relieve suffering by knocking out the interval between the two states, living and dead. The emotional impulse behind the movement is understandable in an age when dying is made such an inhumanly endless business. The movement opposes the horrors of a purely technical death by using technique to eliminate the victim. The alternative I have outlined argues, at least in principle, that warning can provoke good; that with forewarning and time for preparation, reconciliation can take place; and that advance grieving by those about to be bereaved may ease their pain. Some psychiatrists have observed that those bereaved who lost someone accidentally have a more difficult time recovering from the loss than those who have suffered through a period of illness before the death. Those who have lost a close relative by accident are more likely to experience what Geoffrey Gorer has called limitless grief. The community, moreover, needs its aged and dependent, its sick and its dying, and the virtues which they sometimes evince—the virtues of humility, courage, and patience—just as much as the community needs the virtues of justice and love manifest in the agents of its care. Thus, on the whole, I am in favor of social policy that would take seriously the notion of allowing to die, rather than killing for mercy, that is, which would recognize that moment in illness when it is no longer meaningful to bend every effort to cure or to prolong life and when it is fitting to allow patients to do their own dying. This policy seems most consonant with the obligations of the community to care and the patient to finish his course.

III

Does the right to die extend to the right to suicide? Clearly not without a distinction. Allowing to die and mercy killing normally cover cases in which the patient is manifestly and imminently dying from a disease the course of which is physically irreversible. The suicide is not necessarily, or even usually, dying. Further, the responses of allowing to die and mercy killing usually apply to patients who move toward a state into which care cannot reach. The suicide may suffer; and his isolation is often such that he does not receive or accept care. But, physically at least and psychologically perhaps, his pain and suffering could be relieved; he is accessible to care. Do professionals, friends, and relatives therefore have an obligation, protestations to the contrary, to preserve life? A concluding comment on this limited aspect of suicide is in order.

Several considerations argue for intervention. a) Although life is not an absolute, it is a fundamental good. b) The impulse to suicide is often transient yet the act has irreversible consequences. A given intervention may not always prevent a future successful attempt at suicide but it will assure at least that the eventual deed is deliberate or compulsive (rather than merely impulsive). c) The fact that suicide usually has destructive consequences for survivors argues against it. d) Since the ratio of attempted to successful suicides is 8:1 or 10:1, the act must be interpreted at the least as ambivalent. Occasionally an unsuccessful suicide may result from incompetence; usually, however, it is, in the common parlance, a "cry for help." If this is so, then the medical profession, friends, and relatives fail in their duties if they refuse to respond.

One exception and one qualification need to be considered: so-called rational suicide is the exception. It results neither from biological/emotional problems or from fateful circumstances but rather from a philosophical conviction—debatable, to be sure, with respect to the status of the right, but nevertheless rationalized and determined. One might want to argue with such a person, but one should not forcibly prevent him from committing the act or punish him should, through some fluke, it be unsuccessful in its outcome.

The "cry for help" argument needs interpretation and leads to a qualification. I would prefer to substitute the phrase, "a cry for a change." A "cry for help" signals that the would-be suicide basically wants to be relieved of his suicide impulse and get a little attention. Suicide prevention operating at this level does not go deep enough. It merely resists suicide but seems to have no better plan than to put the suicide back into the same old box, this time relieved of his impulse to get out of the box because he has gotten the attention he wants.

Why, however, has the suicide cried for help in the peculiar way that he has? Because he is crying for a peculiar kind of help, that is, help that will bring an utterly radical change in his life. Attempted suicide is a violent statement of the wish for a change, a declaration that describes the change in the most radical of terms—a change from life to death.

The suicide wishes for, in James Hillman's phrase,[13] the experience of death—the death of his old life. He has no appetite for a return to his former existence, superficially divested of the impulse to die. He wants to die, he needs to die to his former life and come into a new life. He needs to go through a death experience, that is, a total and radical transformation of himself. He wishes for a sea-change in the very depths of his being. Thus mere suicide prevention is not enough help for those whose will to die is a haunted expression of the will to live abundantly.

Notes

[1] See Diana Crane, *The Sanctity of Social Life: Physicians' Treatment of Critically Ill Patients* (New York: Russell Sage Foundation, 1975).

[2] For this more demonic and melodramatic interpretation of disease, see René Dubos, *The Mirage of Health,* ch. on "Aesculapius and Hygeia" (New York: Harper & Row, 1971); Arthur C. McGill, *Suffering: A Test of Theological Method,* ch. 2, "Demonism: the Spiritual Reality of Our Age" (Philadelphia: Geneva Press, 1966); and Ivan Illych, *Medical Nemesis* (New York: Pantheon Books, 1976).

[3] It is doubtful whether the perception of death or suffering as absolute evil controls ethical decisions consistently and deductively in all areas. I would be surprised, e.g., if pro-lifers were invariably opponents of the Vietnam War.

[4] Recall, for instance, Chevy Chase's news bulletins on the struggle to keep Generalissimo Franco alive. Life-prolongation extended beyond the humiliating to the ridiculous.

[5] "Optimum Care for Hopelessly Ill Patients; A Report of the Clinical Care Committee of the Massachusetts General Hospital," *The New England Journal of Medicine* 295:7 (Aug. 12, 1976), 362–64.

[6] Paul Ramsey, *The Patient as Person* (New Haven: Yale University Press, 1970), p. 133.

[7] *Ibid.,* p. 133. Professor Ramsey exercises care to show how some Roman Catholic moralists (e.g., Fr. Gerald Kelly, S.J.) have taken steps, albeit cautious, in the direction of his views. Physicians tend to distinguish between ordinary and heroic measures, on the basis of the status of the means used. Recent interpreters of the Roman Catholic distinction between ordinary and extraordinary means are more inclined to include the condition of the patient and not just the status of the means as factors in decision-making. Although his remarks are carefully hedged, Fr. Kelly recognizes circumstances under which a means as ordinary as water may be inappropriate. For this reason, my criticisms in this section have been chiefly directed against the distinction made by the medical community.

[8] The single exception is the requirement that the physician consult with and secure the concurrence of the family in the decision to perform certain acts of commission (such as turning off a mechanical ventilator on a patient) that will lead to death.

[9]Mitchell T. Rabkin, M.D., Gerald Gillerman, J.D., and Nancy R. Rice, J.D., "Orders Not to Resuscitate," *The New England Journal of Medicine, op. cit.,* pp. 364–66.

[10]See his *Thoughts on Crucial Situations in Life* (Minneapolis: Augsburg Publishing House, 1941).

[11]For what follows, see Philippe Ariés, *Western Attitudes Towards Death* (Baltimore: Johns Hopkins Press, 1974).

[12]Donald Kimetz, M.D., *Louisville Courier Journal,* Feb. 10, 1976.

[13]James Hillman, *Suicide and the Soul* (New York: Harper & Row, 1964), ch. 4.

Discussion Questions

1. May mentions five forces that threaten the alleged right to die. Which of these forces is strongest in your opinion? Which is most justified in the attitude it takes? Why?

2. May makes a contrast between those who regard death as the greatest evil and those who regard pain and loss as the greatest evil. Which do you regard as the greater evil? Why?

3. If you were terminally ill what would you want done with regard to your treatment? How is your answer connected to your ethical or religious principles?

4. In May's view what constitutes "death with dignity?" Do you agree? Why or why not?

5. What are May's criticisms of the euthanasia movement? How might a supporter of this movement reply to May?

Active and Passive Euthanasia

James Rachels

The distinction between active and passive euthanasia is thought to be crucial for medical ethics. The idea is that it is permissible, at least in some cases, to withhold treatment and allow a patient to die, but it is never permissible to take any direct action designed to kill the patient. This doctrine seems to be accepted by most doctors, and it is endorsed in a statement adopted by the House of Delegates of the American Medical Association on December 4, 1973:

> The intentional termination of the life of one human being by another—mercy killing—is contrary to that for which the medical profession stands and is contrary to the policy of the American Medical Association.

From *The New England Journal of Medicine,* vol. 292, no. 2 (Jan. 9, 1975), pp. 78–80. Reprinted by permission.

> The cessation of the employment of extraordinary means to prolong the life of the body when there is irrefutable evidence that biological death is imminent is the decision of the patient and/or his immediate family. The advice and judgment of the physician should be freely available to the patient and/or his immediate family.

However, a strong case can be made against this doctrine. In what follows I will set out some of the relevant arguments, and urge doctors to reconsider their views on this matter.

To begin with a familiar type of situation, a patient who is dying of incurable cancer of the throat is in terrible pain, which can no longer be satisfactorily alleviated. He is certain to die within a few days, even if present treatment is continued, but he does not want to go on living for those days since the pain is unbearable. So he asks the doctor for an end to it, and his family joins in the request.

Suppose the doctor agrees to withhold treatment, as the conventional doctrine says he may. The justification for his doing so is that the patient is in terrible agony, and since he is going to die anyway, it would be wrong to prolong his suffering needlessly. But now notice this. If one simply withholds treatment, it may take the patient longer to die, and so he may suffer more than he would if more direct action were taken and a lethal injection given. This fact provides strong reason for thinking that, once the initial decision not to prolong his agony has been made, active euthanasia is actually preferable to passive euthanasia, rather than the reverse. To say otherwise is to endorse the option that leads to more suffering rather than less, and is contrary to the humanitarian impulse that prompts the decision not to prolong his life in the first place.

Part of my point is that the process of being "allowed to die" can be relatively slow and painful, whereas being given a lethal injection is relatively quick and painless. Let me give a different sort of example. In the United States about one in 600 babies is born with Down's syndrome. Most of these babies are otherwise healthy—that is, with only the usual pediatric care, they will proceed to an otherwise normal infancy. Some, however, are born with congenital defects such as intestinal obstructions that require operations if they are to live. Sometimes, the parents and the doctor will decide not to operate, and let the infant die. Anthony Shaw describes what happens then:

> . . . When surgery is denied [the doctor] must try to keep the infant from suffering while natural forces sap the baby's life away. As a surgeon whose natural inclination is to use the scalpel to fight off death, standing by and watching a salvageable baby die is the most emotionally exhausting experience I know. It is easy at a conference, in a theoretical discussion, to decide that such infants should be allowed to die. It is altogether different to stand by in the nursery and watch as dehydration and infection wither a tiny being over hours and days. This is a terrible ordeal for me and the hospital staff—much more so than for the parents who never set foot in the nursery.[1]

I can understand why some people are opposed to all euthanasia, and insist that such infants must be allowed to live. I think I can also understand why other people favor destroying these babies quickly and painlessly. But why should anyone favor letting "dehydration and infection wither a tiny being over hours and days?" The doctrine that says that a baby may be allowed to dehydrate and wither, but may not be given an injection that would end its life without suffering, seems so patently cruel as to require no further refutation. The strong language is not intended to offend, but only to put the point in the clearest possible way.

My second argument is that the conventional doctrine leads to decisions concerning life and death made on irrelevant grounds.

Consider again the case of the infants with Down's syndrome who need operations for congenital defects unrelated to the syndrome to live. Sometimes, there is no operation, and the baby dies, but when there is no such defect, the baby lives on. Now, an operation such as that to remove an intestinal obstruction is not prohibitively difficult. The reason why such operations are not performed in these cases is, clearly, that the child has Down's syndrome and the parents and doctor judge that because of that fact it is better for the child to die.

But notice that this situation is absurd, no matter what view one takes of the lives and potentials of such babies. If the life of such an infant is worth preserving, what does it matter if it needs a simple operation? Or, if one thinks it better that such a baby should not live on, what difference does it make that it happens to have an unobstructed intestinal tract? In either case, the matter of life and death is being decided on irrelevant grounds. It is the Down's syndrome, and not the intestines, that is the issue. The matter should be decided, if at all, on that basis, and not be allowed to depend on the essentially irrelevant question of whether the intestinal tract is blocked.

What makes this situation possible, of course, is the idea that when there is an intestinal blockage, one can "let the baby die," but when there is no such defect there is nothing that can be done, for one must not "kill" it. The fact that this idea leads to such results as deciding life or death on irrelevant grounds is another good reason why the doctrine should be rejected.

One reason why so many people think that there is an important moral difference between active and passive euthanasia is that they think killing someone is morally worse than letting someone die. But is it? Is killing, in itself, worse than letting die? To investigate this issue, two cases may be considered that are exactly alike except that one involves killing whereas the other involves letting someone die. Then, it can be asked whether this difference makes any difference to the moral assessments. It is important that the cases be exactly alike, except for this one difference, since otherwise one cannot be confident that it is this difference and not some other that accounts for any variation in the assessments of the two cases. So, let us consider this pair of cases:

In the first, Smith stands to gain a large inheritance if anything should happen to his six-year-old cousin. One evening while the child is taking his bath, Smith sneaks into the bathroom and drowns the child, and then arranges things so that it will look like an accident.

In the second, Jones also stands to gain if anything should happen to his six-year-old cousin. Like Smith, Jones sneaks in planning to drown the child in his bath. However, just as he enters the bathroom Jones sees the child slip and hit his head, and fall face down in the water. Jones is delighted; he stands by, ready to push the child's head back under if it is necessary, but it is not necessary. With only a little thrashing about the child drowns all by himself, "accidentally," as Jones watches and does nothing.

Now Smith killed the child, whereas Jones "merely" let the child die. That is the only difference between them. Did either man behave better, from a moral point of view? If the difference between killing and letting die were in itself a morally important matter, one should say that Jones's behavior was less reprehensible than Smith's. But does one really want to say that? I think not. In the first place, both men acted from the same motive, personal gain, and both had exactly the same end in view when they acted. It may be inferred from Smith's conduct that he is a bad man, although that judgment may be withdrawn or modified if certain further facts are learned about him—for example, that he is mentally deranged. But would not the very same thing be inferred about Jones from his conduct? And would not the same further considerations also be relevant to any modification of this judgment? Moreover, suppose Jones pleaded, in his own defense, "After all, I didn't do anything except just stand there and watch the child drown. I didn't kill him; I only let him die." Again, if letting die were in itself less bad than killing, this defense should have at least some weight. But it does not. Such a "defense" can only be regarded as a grotesque perversion of moral reasoning. Morally speaking, it is no defense at all.

Now, it may be pointed out, quite properly, that the cases of euthanasia with which doctors are concerned are not like this at all. They do not involve personal gain or the destruction of normal healthy children. Doctors are concerned only with cases in which the patient's life is of no further use to him, or in which the patient's life has become or will soon become a terrible burden. However, the point is the same in these cases: the bare difference between killing and letting die does not, in itself, make a moral difference. If a doctor lets a patient die, for humane reasons, he is in the same moral position as if he had given the patient a lethal injection for humane reasons. If his decision was wrong—if, for example, the patient's illness was in fact curable—the decision would be equally regrettable no matter which method was used to carry it out. And if the doctor's decision was the right one, the method used is not in itself important.

The AMA policy statement isolates the crucial issue very well; the crucial issue is "the intentional termination of the life of one human being by another." But after identifying this issue, and forbidding "mercy killing," the statement goes on to deny that the cessation of treatment is the intentional termination of a life. This is where the mistake comes in, for what is the cessation of treatment, in these circumstances, if it is not "the intentional termination of the life of one human being by another?" Of course it is exactly that, and if it were not, there would be no point to it.

Many people will find this judgment hard to accept. One reason, I think, is that it is very easy to conflate the question of whether killing is, in itself, worse than letting die, with the very different question of whether most actual cases of killing are more reprehensible than most actual cases of letting die. Most actual cases of killing are clearly terrible (think, for example, of all the murders reported in the newspapers), and one hears of such cases every day. On the other hand, one hardly ever hears of a case of letting die, except for the actions of doctors who are motivated by humanitarian reasons. So one learns to think of killing in a much worse light than of letting die. But this does not mean that there is something about killing that makes it in itself worse than letting die, for it is not the bare difference between killing and letting die that makes the difference in these cases. Rather, the other factors—the murderer's motive of personal gain, for example, contrasted with the doctor's humanitarian motivation—account for different reactions to the different cases.

I have argued that killing is not in itself any worse than letting die; if my contention is right, it follows that active euthanasia is not any worse than passive euthanasia. What arguments can be given on the other side? The most common, I believe, is the following:

"The important difference between active and passive euthanasia is that, in passive euthanasia, the doctor does not do anything to bring about the patient's death. The doctor does nothing, and the patient dies of whatever ills already afflict him. In active euthanasia, however, the doctor does something to bring about the patient's death: he kills him. The doctor who gives the patient with cancer a lethal injection has himself caused his patient's death; whereas if he merely ceases treatment, the cancer is the cause of the death."

A number of points need to be made here. The first is that it is not exactly correct to say that in passive euthanasia the doctor does nothing, for he does do one thing that is very important: he lets the patient die. "Letting someone die" is certainly different, in some respects, from other types of action—mainly in that it is a kind of action that one may perform by way of not performing certain other actions. For example, one may let a patient die by way of not giving medication, just as one may insult someone by way of not shaking his hand. But for any purpose of moral assessment, it is a type of action nonetheless. The decision to let a patient die is subject to moral appraisal in the same way that a decision to kill him would be subject to moral appraisal: it may be assessed as wise or unwise, compassionate or sadistic, right or wrong. If a doctor deliberately let a patient die who was suffering from a routinely curable illness, the doctor would certainly be to blame for what he had done, just as he would be to blame if he had needlessly killed the patient. Charges against him would then be appropriate. If so, it would be no defense at all for him to insist that he didn't "do anything." He would have done something very serious indeed, for he let his patient die.

Fixing the cause of death may be very important from a legal point of view, for it may determine whether criminal charges are brought against the doctor. But I do not think that this notion can be used to show a moral difference between active and passive euthanasia. The reason why it is considered bad to be the cause of someone's death is that death is regarded as a great evil—and so it is. However, if it has been decided that euthanasia—even passive euthanasia—is desirable in a given case, it has also been decided that in this instance death is no greater an evil than the patient's continued existence. And if this is true, the usual reason for not wanting to be the cause of someone's death simply does not apply.

Finally, doctors may think that all of this is only of academic interest—the sort of thing that philosophers may worry about but that has no practical bearing on their own work. After all, doctors must be concerned about the legal consequences of what they do, and active euthanasia is clearly forbidden by the law. But even so, doctors should also be concerned with the fact that the law is forcing upon them a moral doctrine that may well be indefensible, and has a considerable effect on their practices. Of course, most doctors are not now in the position of being coerced in this matter, for they do not regard themselves as merely going along with what the law requires. Rather, in statements such as the AMA policy statement that I have quoted, they are endorsing this doctrine as a central point of medical ethics. In that statement, active euthanasia is condemned not merely as illegal but as "contrary to that for which the medical profession stands," whereas passive euthanasia is approved. However, the preceding considerations suggest that there is really no moral difference between the two, considered in themselves (there may be important moral differences in some cases in their *consequences,* but, as I pointed out, these differences may make active euthanasia, and not passive euthanasia, the morally preferable option). So, whereas doctors may have to discriminate between active and passive euthanasia to satisfy the law, they should not do any more than that. In particular, they should not give the distinction any added authority and weight by writing it into official statements of medical ethics.

Note

[1] A. Shaw: "Doctor, Do We Have a Choice?" *The New York Times Magazine,* Jan. 30, 1972, p. 54.

Discussion Questions

1. Both Holland and May assume that there is a difference between killing and letting die. If Rachels is right, how would this affect their arguments?

2. Are you convinced by Rachels's examples that the distinction between killing and letting die is unworkable in those cases? Does this show that the distinction is unworkable in general? Why or why not?

3. Does Rachels give a fair statement of the counterarguments to his position? How could a supporter of the view he criticizes reply to Rachels?

4. Attempt to define the difference between active and passive euthanasia in a way that is not open to Rachels's objections. Can this be done? Why or why not?

Death and Decision

Ernan Mc Mullin

Death has never quite seemed to lie within the bounds of human decision, as other episodes do. Of course, killing has always gone on, and under certain circumstances has been thought proper. The exacting of death as a punishment for serious crime may be as old as man himself. Human sacrifice and the exposing of unwanted children have been recurrent features of the human story. And in our unending wars, soldiers and civilians die by the hand of others; it is regretted but nonetheless praised. But these are special circumstances; in the normal course, man may not deprive another of life, nor may he take responsibility for furthering his own death. Murder and suicide are wrong; even carelessness that may hasten the death of another or of oneself is seriously culpable.

In the Western tradition, our attitudes on these issues have been shaped to a large extent by Christian theology, and specifically by the doctrines of creation, resurrection, and redemption. God is not merely a shaper of recalcitrant matter; human life is not a punishment, nor an unending sequence of unwanted recurrences. God is creator of all; matter serves Him, and time is his first creature, since it is within time that His plan is to be realized. Life is His making, and human life is the unique once-only-given opportunity to become as like to Him as material restrictions allow. Death marks the end of becoming for the individual; at the moment of death, his life is irrevocably what he has made it. But it is not the end in the sense of cessation of being. It is the beginning of a new existence with God, no longer bound by the limitations of time, decision, and change. Life is thus God's first and greatest gift; one owes it the reverence proper to such a gift. And death is not a loss of this gift so much as its fulfillment, the moment of self-gathering when all the strands of a life fall finally into pattern and take on a definitive and permanent reality.

Man's freedom is shadowed by man's weakness, his ability to turn from God. It is also shadowed by suffering, which is inescapably the lot of a finite creature of human

From *Death and Decision,* Ernan Mc Mullin, ed. Copyright © 1978 by the American Association for the Advancement of Science. Reprinted by permission of Westview Press, Inc.

aspirations and human sensibilities. The Judaeo-Christian tradition has always linked sin and suffering, has seen them as somehow derivative from a genuine freedom on the part of a creature to reject its Creator. The agonized death of Christ on a cross led Christians further to see in his sacrifice a form of redemption, a buying-back of fallen man, a restoration to man of the possibilities meant for him. Christ could have avoided suffering; that he did not, and that his suffering took on the meaning it did, made of pain and deprivation borne in the service of others a holy thing, something from which even the most virtuous could not be exempt.

It is important to recall the details of the Christian story of life and death, if one is to understand the depth of the present perplexities in regard to the proper limits of our power to decide when a particular life should terminate. There are two quite different sorts of reason why these perplexities have multiplied in recent decades. Medical science has advanced enormously in its ability to extend life. It has also altered the conditions under which the seriously ill are cared for, removing them almost entirely from ordinary human contact. Questions of a new sort arise as to how it should employ its powers, as to what its precise goals ought to be, as to whom its decision-making should involve. Medical science cannot of itself develop answers to such questions. And the resources of the Christian moral tradition are not sufficient to provide the kind of straightforward guidance that people seek in matters of such urgency. Distinctions that have helped in the past (such as that between extraordinary and ordinary means, or between killing and allowing to die) do not seem to meet the new situations that arise in everyday hospital practice.

If developments in medical science and therapeutic techniques were all that had to be considered, the problems would not appear quite as intractable as they do. There is another sort of change whose implications for complex new moral issues of this kind are much more far-reaching. This is the growing pluralism in Western society in regard to moral and social norms generally. The Christian tradition no longer commands universal adherence, and no other source of moral authority (of the kind the Party claims to be in the Second World) has taken its place. Liberal democracy has often been alleged to rest on a utilitarian ethic; yet a wide diversity of metaethical principles quite evidently informs moral controversy in Western countries. And the notion of "utility" is in any event so broad as not to be of much help in decisions about termination of life. When moral problems arise, of a kind that the conventional wisdom of our society does not seem able to handle, there are no longer agreed principles to which one can turn; there is no authority that can propose courses of action with the likelihood of their general acceptance.

What makes this sort of uncertainty all the more serious is that the decision to end a life on medico-moral grounds almost always involves groups of people: a hospital staff, a family. . . . A single doctor, or the patient, or a guardian may take primary responsibility, but others are almost inevitably implicated too. If agreement on the relevant values is lacking, the further difficulty arises of devising a plan of action that will be acceptable to all concerned, and of deciding on the hierarchy of responsibilities among those involved.

It may be helpful to separate five different medical contexts in which the question of deliberately terminating a life may arise. There are important differences between the moral issues raised in each case.

Case A

Abortion is probably the commonest sort of deliberate life-termination. It is still an illegal act in a great many countries, but is quite commonplace in others, like Japan. The law will often specify restrictions (e.g., the fetus must be no more than six months old; the grounds must be the physical health of the mother, or that the conception followed rape, or that the fetus is known to have a serious defect . . .). Few defenders of abortion would allow the killing of newborn infants. So that the controversy tends to focus around two sorts of issue. First, is the fetus fully "human"? Does it have the same rights as it would have once it leaves the womb? If not, why not? It is difficult to see why separation from the womb should make a basic difference to the "humanness" or the "personhood" of the infant organism. Is there perhaps an earlier stage at which this transition to "humanness" occurs, at the point when separate existence is in principle possible, for example? Or when the nervous system first begins to form? Efforts to define and defend such points of transition have not been notably successful. Once the fertilized ovum is implanted, its development to biological maturity is continuous. Discontinuity occurs only in its relationship to its mother, when it ceases (or could cease) to be dependent on her.

A second set of problems centers around the question of appropriate grounds. The strongest justifying reason would be that the presence of the fetus endangers the life of the mother. In such a case, can the fetus be treated as an "aggressor"? Or is it rather that the mother's "personhood" balanced against that of the fetus, justifies the preference given her? Suppose it is not the life of the mother but only her convenience that is at stake? She may not wish a child at this time for economic or social or personal reasons, and did not intend one to be conceived. How strong a reason ought she have to be morally justified in deciding on abortion? Does it make a difference if the conception was against her will? If the fetus is not the fruit of a fully free affirmative act on both sides, does it forfeit its right to life?

There are two morally simple and consistent positions here: one, that abortion under any circumstances is wrong; the other that abortion for any non-frivolous reason is permissible. The "in-between" range of positions is morally complex because relative weight is being given to the various reasons for aborting a fetus on the one hand, as well as to its degree of development on the other. A balance is reached between the gravity of the reason and the loss caused, somewhat as in wartime decisions to bomb areas where civilian casualties are inevitable. The assessment of relative weight of the factors concerned is extremely difficult, and dangerously subject to rationalization. The moral issues here are the more indefinite but no less important ones of selfishness, of reverence for life, of taking responsibility for the consequences of action. They do not admit of hard-and-fast norms, but depend on the maturity of an informed faculty of moral judgement, on the ability to make a just balance.

Case B

Suppose the fetus has grave physical defects. Can it be killed for its own good? This raises rather different issues, ones that can be more readily stated for the newborn. If a newborn baby is so deformed that it cannot live long anyway, may its life be shortened, say by not feeding it? If it suffers from some handicap (Down's syndrome, thalidomide induced limb-loss . . .) that will notably lessen the quality of life later open to it, may efforts to keep it alive be less energetic than for a normal child?

From a utilitarian standpoint, the answer to such questions is relatively simple to state. Since such children are usually a heavy burden on their family, on hospital resources, on society generally, the greatest good of the greatest number would seem to require their rapid and painless termination. And, of course, the same might be said for the insane, for habitual criminals, and for other groups of socially unwanted citizens. But the traditions of Western society have never condoned this kind of answer. Reverence for life as the unique gift of God, respect and care for the weak, have been (and still remain) deeply ingrained, and have led to a very different response.

This response would begin by rejecting utilitarian norms, specifically the notion that the convenience of a group (family, hospital, society) can serve as sufficient warrant for the death of an individual. That a newborn *spina bifida* is difficult and expensive to care for, that a mongoloid child can be an emotionally disastrous burden for its parents, are not accepted as proper reasons for depriving a child of life. Rather one must ask: what is good for the child itself? How is its welfare to be safeguarded?

If the child is not (so far as one can tell) in serious pain, its welfare would seem to demand that ordinary care be given to it, just as to a normal child. If it is seriously handicapped, so that it is already clear that it cannot live a full human life, it should still be cared for and helped to the fullest enjoyment of whatever level of life *is* possible to it. That this imposes burdens on family and society is undeniable, but (according to this second view) such burdens are an inescapable part of what it is to be human. A full-hearted acceptance of them is thus a sign of true maturity.

If the child is in great pain, the case is not much different from that of an adult (Case E below). Causing the child additional pain (by not feeding it, for example) seems particularly hard to justify. Distinctions between active and passive euthanasia, between extraordinary and ordinary therapeutic means, are often cited in such cases but seem inadequate to justify the actual causing of pain. If a decision has been made to hasten the child's death, whatever its merits, it is at least arguable that it should be carried out painlessly.

There are thus two quite different general sorts of response to Case B, one utilitarian and community-oriented, the other Christian in its Western roots and oriented to the welfare of the individual and the protection of life. And there are various modifications of both; one might, for example, attach considerable weight to the "utility," understood as happiness, of the child in arriving at a utilitarian assessment. Or one might note that the acceptance of responsibility for the weak has very great value ("utility") for a family or a community. But such considerations do not disguise the fact that Case B can mark a parting of the moral ways, as the history of Nazi Germany unforgettably showed.

Case C

The kind of case which has had most notoriety lately is that of the comatose patient being kept alive by means of a sophisticated technology. The enormous publicity given the Quinlan case in the U.S. made it appear more or less the paradigm, despite the fact that it did have some rather special features. What is distinctive about Case C is, first, that the patient himself or herself cannot be directly consulted; second, that the quality of even minimal human living has been irreparably lost; and finally, that biological life is being sustained only by the use of special means (machines, drugs . . .). Each of these clauses raises a host of difficulties.

If the patient cannot be consulted, who *is* to bear the responsibility for life—termination in such a case? The doctor or the patient's family? Or both in consultation? Where there is disagreement, which should prevail? If the patient has signified in advance what his or her wishes would be in such an outcome, ought this be given primary weight? This last has become a matter of much concern since the notion of a "living will" became popular some years ago.

A disturbing recent development in the U.S. is the transfer of decision-making in such cases to the law courts. The threat (sometimes real, sometimes imagined) of malpractice suits has transformed the practice of American medicine in the past decade; hardly anyone would say that this has been for the overall benefit of either patient or doctor. It has made doctors unwilling to take responsibility for decisive action in grey areas, where a lawyer may later be able to argue that sufficient grounds for the action cannot be shown. The termination of life-support for a permanently comatose patient is a grey area, not so much for the usual reason that the family might afterwards choose to sue, as for the reason that under U.S. law such an action can plausibly be construed as a criminal offense, i.e., murder. In practice, doctors are far less willing now to take responsibility for discontinuance of life-support than they were, because of the publicity given such cases and the real uncertainty (which state legislatures and the Congress have done nothing to remove) about the legal situation.

The second feature of Case C is that it should be known that normal human functioning cannot be restored. But how is this to be known? Sometimes there is such a destruction of brain tissue, for example, that doctors can be "morally certain" that restoration is impossible, i.e., no cases are known where restoration of function followed such destruction, and there are theoretical reasons for arguing in this case that mental functioning would be impossible in the absence of the needed organic support. But quite often, no such conviction can be reached. It is a matter of probability only, with the likelihood of disagreement between the medical experts. If there is *any* reasonable chance that mental function may be restored, is one entitled to terminate? Suppose there is a high likelihood of permanent brain damage, ought this alter one's treatment of the comatose patient? In particular, would it justify the termination of life-support specifically to prevent such an outcome, i.e., recovery from the coma with highly impaired brain-functioning?

This last question is not typical of Case C; what is peculiar to this sort of case is that one cannot call upon the good of the patient as a factor in the decision, as one ordinarily can elsewhere. If the patient is permanently comatose, he is not suffering, is not unhappy. The termination no longer matters, one way or the other, to the patient. It matters now only to the community. One can argue that the patient would not have wanted to survive in this attenuated, and no longer fully human, way. The patient may, in fact, have indicated this in advance; if he did not, it is not (experience has shown) so easy to prove a presumptive intention. In any event, the decision will usually hinge on the relative weight given in the community to such factors as reverence for life (and the consequent unwillingness to take steps to end life even where the minimal possibility of properly human living no longer exists), pain caused to family, economic cost, allocation of scarce medical resources, and so on.

There is a similarity between Case A and Case C in that the fetus has not yet attained full human functioning, and the permanently comatose patient cannot have it restored; in both cases, this has been held to justify relaxation of the normal prohibition on killing of humans. There is, of course, an important difference between the two cases. The fetus is "potentially" human, in the sense that, given normal environment and nurture, it will become fully human. The comatose patient has been but is no longer fully human. The respect and care given him are a testimony not of his present humanity, but of the physical continuity of this organism with a person who was in the fullest sense to be esteemed and protected.

Christians will want to ask: but has the soul left the body? Is this organism we see in the hospital bed still a son of God, not yet returned to the Father? This is a peculiarly intractable question. If one adopts a soul-body dualism of the Platonic kind often favored in the Christian tradition, involving a natural immortality of spirit or soul, then the question becomes: does soul remain in an organism which no longer can sustain any of the higher functioning characteristic of soul? The answer would seem to be: no, but there would be no unanimity about this in the Greek philosophical tradition. On the other hand, if one returns to the Jewish beliefs that underlay the Christian doctrine of resurrection, immortality is not an inevitable consequence of a spirit-constituent of man, rather it is a gift or covenant involving the whole person. What goes back to God is not the spirit (to which the body would be rather awkwardly joined later) but the *person,* in his life and achievement as a free and responsible being. This would suggest that if this conscious life and achievement is definitively ended, the human being is no longer there; he has (according to the Christian hope) returned to God who first set him out on his voyage.

The third feature of Case C is that biological life is being sustained only by special means, so that if one were to discontinue these, it is presumed the patient would die. Once again, the first difficulty is how to be sure of this as the Quinlan case dramatically demonstrated. When after the long legal battle the patient was disconnected from the support-machinery, she survived, to the great surprise of most of the physicians who had been consulted about her state. The emphasis given this aspect of Case C is due in the main to the distinction between "extraordinary" and "ordinary" therapy, the traditional principle being that one is not compelled to resort to the former.

It is difficult, however, to draw this distinction in practice. On which side does penicillin lie? Is it a question of the expense or of the complexity or of the novelty of the proposed therapy? One could make the case that virtually all therapy in the modern hospital is "extraordinary"; conversely, one could argue that, given our resources, it is "ordinary." But leaving aside the difficulties in making this distinction work, it may be asked whether it has the importance in Case C it has been assumed to have. It would be fairly generally agreed that complex life-support may be withdrawn from a permanently comatose patient at the discretion of medical staff and family. But the central feature of Case C is not the "extraordinary" therapy, it is the permanence of the cessation of conscious functioning. Even if the patient is able to live without the aid of expensive and unevenly available technology, the substantive question still remains: what sort of efforts ought to be made to keep him or her alive?

There is a natural repugnance to the denial of food to an organism needing it for survival. But there are always drugs needed to ward off the diseases such a patient is prone to. The doctor would seem to have some discretion about whether or not to administer these drugs, not because they are "extraordinary," but because it might be said that continuance of biological life is not obligatory. How would this differ from administering a painless lethal drug?

There has been a great deal of debate about the distinction between killing and allowing to die, active and passive euthanasia. Without rehearsing the details of this debate, it may at least be noted that the moral responsibility for the outcome in such cases as we have been discussing may well be the same whether the intervention of the doctor be "active" or "passive." What differs is rather a matter of appropriateness, none the less important for being described by this weaker term. The doctor is understood to have the discretion whether or not to administer a healing drug. But the administering of what would be, in effect, a poison is not only not something he can be required by others to do, it is not even seemly for someone whose function in the community is to restore health. There is no reason why the *doctor* should be the one to intervene actively in this manner. Assuming that it were moral to terminate the life of a comatose patient in this way, one might better ask a representative of the family (or, for that matter, a judge, if one were involved) to be the agent.

Would the use of a poison ever in fact be allowable in such a case? In terms of effectiveness, it might be no more lethal in its action than the withholding of penicillin from a comatose patient with pneumonia. Why is it, then, that most people would reject one course and not the other? Of the reasons that might be cited, perhaps the most convincing is that we have a clear duty not to kill our fellow humans, except in very special circumstances such as self-defense. We do not have so clear a duty to provide them with the necessities of life; this would ordinarily be a matter of charity rather than justice. When faced with a comatose patient, we are inclined to transfer the same principles, even though the case is now a quite special one.

Furthermore, the reverence for life so basic to Western culture would make killing a more serious infringement than allowing to die, even though the responsibility for the outcome may be the same. The choice of means makes a difference in terms of the attitude signified. Any weakening in the inviolability accorded human life, any opening to a new callousness, could have profoundly harmful effects elsewhere. This argument (like so many others we have seen) is not a coercive one, but it is one that gives the prudent person pause as he contemplates the predicament of the comatose patient, and guards against a too-easy conclusion that the survival of such an organism is *wholly* without value.

Case D

Modern medicine has discovered a great many ways of prolonging the period of dying. Chemotherapy for certain sorts of cancer is perhaps the best known, and there are many surgical procedures which delay onset of death but cannot restore health. Our fourth case is that of an incurably ill person whose life may be lengthened by a particular therapy. There are variations on the case. For example, there may be a small chance that the therapy may in fact cure the person. Or the therapy may itself be painful or disfiguring or enormously expensive or still in an experimental stage. But the "basic" Case D is that of a person whose life may be prolonged but not saved.

Of all the cases we have considered, it is this one perhaps which most clearly typifies the ambiguous results of medical technology, especially of the up-to-date highly specialized hospital. The aim of such hospitals is to cure. But failing that, prolonging life can easily seem the next best goal. If there is a technique that can keep a patient alive, there will be a natural tendency to try it. But, of course, trying it may *not* be in the best interests of the patient. How are these interests to be determined?

First, the wishes of the patient himself or herself must have primary force. It is perfectly proper for someone to refuse to make use of a life-prolonging maneuver. It is also proper for him to request that every effort be made to extend his life as long as possible. There can obviously be a great many reasons that could justify either decision. In order that the decision may be a good one, the physician has an obligation to clarify the alternatives as best he can for the patient. He has to be especially careful to leave no doubt that the therapy *is* merely one of prolongation and to specify the negative effects that may follow from its use.

But what if the patient is impaired in judgement, as is so very often the case with people so gravely ill? Or what if he simply leaves it up to the expert to decide, as patients so often will? Here the physician has to balance all the relevant factors: the quality of the life that the therapy would, if successful, make possible; the possible side-effects of its use; the importance (if it can be assessed) to the patient of extra time; and above all, the patient's temperament. The family will ordinarily be involved in such a decision; it is especially important that this be so nowadays if the malpractice threat is not to become a separate and distorting influence.

There are no clear-cut norms for such a decision; experience and wisdom are needed to assess the various factors and to try to balance them against one another. Case D is of itself relatively uncontroversial: hardly anyone would hold that life ought to be prolonged at all costs. But there are many complicating features that may make decisions extremely difficult to reach. Notable among these is the sheer momentum of medical technology itself, and the tendency on the part of the dying to grasp at straws that in their earlier more rational existence would have been unhesitatingly rejected. Can their wishes in such a case be overruled? This is one of the most delicate and painful questions a physician can have to face.

Case E

The previous two types of case are to a large extent the product of the rapid advances in medicine of our own century. But what of the case as old as man himself, of someone who is dying in very great pain: is he entitled to shorten his life? Are others permitted to help him in such an endeavor? It is understood that he is clear-headed enough to know the significance of what he is doing and that there is no way to alleviate his pain medically. (The "pain" might, by extension, be the bitter indignity of a physical situation that is destroying self-respect). May such a person act to end his life directly, by the use of poison, for example?

If one were to rely on simple utilitarian norms, the answer would be quick and easy: yes. Even if one takes the happiness of the individual agent as guide, it would still seem that such an action would be sanctioned. Yet in the Western tradition, it would be generally regarded as suicide and those who cooperated in it would be thought culpable. This is a case which has always troubled Christian moralists but on which Christian teaching has in the past been unequivocal. The writers of the Old Testament repeat over and over that the moment of death is in God's hand, not ours. Our life is His giving, and it is His to determine the manner of its taking away. The example of Christ in the New Testament who suffered so terribly in his dying, conveyed very strongly the notion that suffering has a redemptive value, not only for the individual himself but for the community generally. Those who surround the dying person will be ennobled and strengthened by his acceptance of the pain that, in the Providence of God, is his in his last moments. His pain thus takes on a value in the order of salvation and is not to be regarded simply as an evil.

Needless to say, these ideas encounter strenuous opposition today. For those for whom death marks an absolute termination and not the transition to a fuller life with God, and for whom the notions of Providence and redemption make no sense, a refusal to consider active euthanasia on such grounds would carry no weight. Even outside the Christian context, however, there would not be agreement about the propriety of euthanasia in these circumstances. Resignation in the face of suffering is not characteristic of our activist age; virtue is found in the struggle to overcome the given, rather than its patient acceptance.

Yet it would be hard to deny the wisdom that is born of suffering and the contribution such wisdom can make to others. In the U.S., death is concealed to such an extent behind the walls of hospitals and funeral parlors that encounter with death is simply not part of the culture. There is an immaturity, a refusal to face the human condition, that observers from other cultures have often noted. Dying people, suffering people, have an important social role to play, one that is now almost entirely denied them in our culture. This is not to say that suffering should not be shortened, when possible. But the fact that it has become such a private and unrecognized affair makes the lot of the dying person far harder to bear.

Case E is simple to state, but on an existential level it is the most harrowing of the five we have described. So much will depend on the patient's earlier experience of suffering, on his attitude towards death, on his readiness for death. We have been discussing the kinds of decision about termination of life that have to be made in the context of medical science. But there is one far more basic sort of decision that faces every dying person; it is the decision to accept death, to close the books peacefully and in confidence. In a symposium about "Death and decision" it is well to recall that *this* is the crucial decision, and the one hardest to reach.

It will be noted in all five cases outlined above, there are no simple and easily applicable principles that would enable a moralist looking at the type of case to say *a priori:* this is wrong, or this is right. In each, there are many factors to balance, many intangibles to grope for. A person's decision about death in the last analysis will be guided by what he, and the others around him, believe the significance of life, and therefore of death, to be. And this is not something easily set down, nor readily universalizable.

Discussion Questions

1. How does Mc Mullin's discussion of problems about death make use of religious principles? Could someone who was opposed to religion still agree with these principles? Why or why not?

2. Mc Mullin says that medical science cannot itself develop answers to questions about when to terminate life and that the Christian moral tradition cannot provide straightforward guidance on these problems. Do you agree? Why or why not?

3. What problem does Mc Mullin see in the growing pluralism of our society? How do you think that this problem might be solved?

4. Mc Mullin considers abortion among issues as to whether to terminate a human life. Some pro-abortionists would argue that abortion is not terminating a human life. Argue for this position against Mc Mullin's view or argue for Mc Mullin's view against this position.

5. What common principles seem to be employed in Mc Mullin's discussions of his cases A through E? Argue for or against one or more of these principles.

The Right to Die Garrulously

Alasdair MacIntyre

I want in this paper to make two central points: one, rather more briefly, about rights and one, at somewhat greater length, about death and dying. On rights I want to distinguish three classes of claim to the possession of a right. There are first of all claims to rights where the right in question has been, or is alleged to have been, *created* (rather than merely recognized) by positive law, and secondly where the right in question has been, or is alleged to have been, created by a promise. With these types of claim I shall not be concerned further. The third type of claim is to a type of right alleged to belong to human beings *as such,* independently of what any positive law may say. Examples of such alleged rights are those cited in the *Declaration of Independence* and in the *U.N. Declaration of Human Rights* and those defended by Professor Ronald Dworkin in his recent book *Taking Rights Seriously*,[1] including an alleged right of every human being to "equal concern and respect."[2]

It is presumably rights of this third kind that are invoked in most discussions of death and dying. The question: "Do individuals have a right in certain circumstances—for example, extreme and unrelievable pain or the occurrence of such brain damage that there can be no possibility of recovery except as an idiot—to be deprived of further life-support or to have their life taken, provided that at the relevant time they do consent or have consented to this?" is invariably discussed as a question about an alleged natural or human right which individuals as such do or do not possess. This is perhaps unfortunate, because it seems clear that the answer to all such questions must be "No."

This is not because of the merits or demerits of any of the particular arguments advanced about suicide or about brain damage or about medical technology. It is because there are no such rights. The ground for asserting this is the second best of all possible grounds for making universal negative existential assertions: nobody has ever given us the slightest reason for believing that there are. (The best of all possible grounds for making such an assertion is that the concept in question necessarily has no embodiment, as, e.g., that of the greatest integer).

In the eighteenth century the existence of such natural rights was defended on the grounds that the statements asserting them were self-evident truths; but the required concept of self-evidence could not be sustained. In the United Nations declaration of 1949 what has since become the normal U.N. practice of not giving reasons for *any* assertions whatsoever is followed with great rigor. And Professor Dworkin's retort to the charge that the existence of such rights cannot be proved is only that from the fact that a statement cannot be demonstrated to be true, it does not follow that that statement is not true.[3] Which is true, but could be used equally in vindication of every unprovable statement whatsoever. Some other recent philosophers have tended to speak here of their and our moral "intuitions"; but one of the things that we learn from the history of philosophy is that the occurrence of the word "intuition" in philosophy is usually a sign that something has gone badly wrong.

I conclude that there are no valid claims to rights of this third kind. Such rights are at one with unicorns, witches and Meinong's glass mountain. Jeremy Bentham said the last word about them, philosophically if not chronologically, when he declared that "natural rights" are "nonsense" and "imprescriptible, inalienable natural rights" "nonsense on stilts." But this radical conclusion does not terminate, it only opens my present inquiry. For there are a fourth class of claims to rights to the discussion of which we must now turn.

In the game of chess each player has a right to move in turn, the player who is White having the right to move first. In natural science scientists have the right to use the findings of other scientists, provided they acknowledge priority of publication. At the coronation of the O'Neill, the O'Cathain had the right to place the crown on the O'Neill's head.[4] In each of these cases the possession of the right is only intelligible in the context of a developed and complex form of human practice. The exercise of such rights is a necessary part of such practices and their violation is to varying degrees destructive of such practice. The justification of the claim to possess such a right must initially refer us to the rules of the practice and thereafter to the possible justifications of the practice. Notice that such rights do not belong to individuals as such, but only to individuals in virtue of their filling certain roles, roles the effective discharge of which is essential to the practice. Positive law may on occasion recognize certain of these rights or even prescribe that they shall be enforced. But such rights are not created by positive law in the way, for example, that the right of a Massachusetts resident to challenge what he or she takes to be an incorrect billing within sixty days is created by positive law.

In order to discover whether a given claim of this fourth type is or is not valid, it is obvious that we must first determine whether there is or is not a practice in the relevant area of human life, understanding by a practice some form of rule-governed behavior which has its own goods, in the way in which games, scientific inquiry and Irish tribal rituals do. To say this is to suggest strongly to the contemporary American mind that rights of this fourth type could have nothing to do with any alleged right to die. For we characteristically take it for granted that death and dying are episodes in or terminating the lives of individuals which are not and could not be a part of any coherent practice in the required sense. That is, our dominant culture lacks any coherent concept, and perhaps any concept at all, of a right way to die or a wrong way to die, of a good death or a bad death.

Yet in lacking such concepts and correspondingly lacking any shared practice of death and dying, modern American culture is at odds with many other cultures, including a number of its own predecessors: American Indian, some African, Irish, some Asian, much of the European middle ages and some of the ancient world. I am not going to argue in this paper for the superiority of the perspective on death and dying of such cultures to our contemporary American standpoint; all that I shall be able to do is to give some account of what this alternative perspective is.

It was Robert Herz,[5] Durkheim's pupil, who first drew the attention of anthropologists to the fact that in certain societies—his own studies were in Indonesia—death is not only or primarily the terminating episode in the life of an individual, but an event in the life of that society of which the individual formed a part and from which he drew his identity. The funeral rites are an occasion in which the social group confronts the loss of part of itself and summons up the resources to reconstitute itself. The dead individual is not wholly lost to the group; as spirit or as ancestor or both he is still part of that continuity which links the living both to the dead and to the as yet unborn. Death and the ceremonies of death are thus a moment of transition for both the individual and the group.

From the point of view which Herz describes, a society or a group—a tribe, a family, a local community, a nation—is not a collection of individuals, each with his or her own independent identity, who merely happen to be united in social relationships. Rather the group is primary and the individual's identity is partly, but crucially constituted by his or her membership of and place in the group. The individual who lacks any such membership and place, who has no identity but his own, is that marginal man "the stranger." And when a stranger dies, there is nobody to mourn that trivial passing. With the stranger we may make agreements or temporary arrangements for one transient purpose or another; but contractual arrangements—those very arrangements which the theorists who celebrated the birth of modern individualist society, such as Hobbes and Locke, thought to underlie all social relationships—constitute no fundamental social bond.

From the standpoint of the communities which Herz describes, modern America would appear for the most part as merely a collectivity of strangers, of only accidentally related individuals; and the predominant individualist attitudes to death and dying would confirm them in their view. Yet it is not merely from the standpoint of the Malay archipelago in the early twentieth century that America would look like this. In a quite different culture, one in which our own is rooted, Sophocles' Philoctetes describes himself as "friendless, solitary, without a city, a corpse among the living"[6] and the last characterization follows from the first three. To lack the identity conferred by a city and by friendship (in the Greek understanding of that concept) is to be an unburied corpse. And to be an unburied corpse is to lack that relationship to the community which is conferred by funeral rites.

What unites these very different cultures then is a conception of death as a distinctively social event and of the dying man and those around him as fulfilling social roles. These roles have both a backward looking and a prospective character. The backward-looking aspect of the role of the dying man concerns the fact that death is the completion of life. "Call no man happy until he is dead" said the prudent Greek proverb; but what follows is that death is precisely the point at which a man may be called happy. The death of such a man is in no way to be regretted, and mourning for such a man is not a species of regret. What then is the connection between death, the completion of life and happiness?

The conception of death and dying in at least some of such societies is inseparable from a conception of life as divided into determinate stages each of which specifies a type of role. To have passed through the stages is to have reached the right time to die, and it is a fundamental conviction of such societies that there is a time when it is right to die. To die before one's time is a terrible misfortune, unless one gave one's life as a sacrifice for the social group, in battle, for instance, and so completed an honorable life in another way. The right time to die may be conventionally fixed at some particular age, that of seventy, for example. But no individual is free to make a choice in this matter. The right time for him to die will come sooner or later, and he must wait for it. Philippe Ariés[7] has presented convincing evidence that in such societies men possess an ability to recognize the approach of that moment, an ability that has disappeared together with the concept of there being such a moment. That there should be such an ability must seem to us in some ways strange; but it will perhaps appear less strange if we realize that the whole of life is in this perspective an approach to one's death. It is in the period before death that one becomes one of the old, that is of those who have assimilated the moral and social knowledge that has been handed down. The old preserve and enrich the tradition; their stories and sayings are the collective inherited memory of the society. Hence the young cannot afford not to listen to the old. Nor is becoming old in any way a misfortune; every period of life has its own advantages and disadvantages. One of the disadvantages of being young is that one necessarily lacks what only the old can teach. This is why, as Aristotle noted, the young cannot excel in moral philosophy.

Once again the contrast with contemporary America is almost too obvious. Here death is often feared and old age, if anything, is feared more. The old have no assigned respected role in the community. Their stories are treated not as inherited wisdom, but as boring anecdotes. A whole mythology about the declining powers of the old has been constructed. The old have become functionless, just as the dying have no socially recognized role.

This deprivation of role and function is clearly connected to another difference between America and the type of traditional society which I am trying to characterize. The old in that type of society are those who make the present one with the past. But the past in America is the object of ambiguity and suspicion. History has for some considerable time been the least popular subject in American high schools. Apart from a few patriotic episodes, there is little or no shared social memory. This does not of course mean that the past, American European and African, is not as omnipresent in America as elsewhere. Fragmented traditions and mythologies draw all the more power from the fact that their very existence, let alone their power, goes so largely unrecognized. But the power of the past in the present has in our culture been divorced from explicit social function; and so unsurprisingly any conception of death as the moment at which we become one with the past has been lost too.

The role of the dying man is therefore twofold in the relevant type of traditional society. On the one hand he has to make that reckoning with his own past life which is required, if life is to be completed satisfactorily, if his life is to be called happy: debts must be paid, sins must be confessed, farewells must be made, each with the appropriate ceremony. If we owe a cock to Aesculapius, we must pay it. But at the same time the dying man has to hand on to the next generation or generations the tasks and the possessions that have hitherto been his. He must tell them now what he will never be able to tell them again. Hence the symbolic importance of the deathbed scene. The dying man has both a duty and a right to speak at that point at whatever length he chooses. He has the right to die garrulously.

This role and function can like any other be discharged well or badly. The dying man owes it to others to perform it and to perform it well. It is in the context of these observations that the question of a right to die can be raised once more. What from the perspective of this kind of alien culture would have to be said about such a right? Part of the answer is clear. If there is a right time to die and a time which it is not open to one to choose, then one can have no right to bring about one's own death prematurely. If one owes participation in the ceremonies of death to others, then once again one can have no right to deprive them or indeed oneself of those ceremonies. Hence there can be no general right to suicide.

It is a good deal more difficult to pose the question of how in the perspective afforded by such cultures one would have to argue about the type of case in which *either* consciousness has been disintegrated or shortly will be by extremes of pain perhaps combined with the effects of certain drugs *or* consciousness has been lost altogether because of brain-damage, but life can still be maintained by the expensive resources of modern medical technology *or* consciousness, but only idiot consciousness, can be restored after such brain-damage. For it is characteristic of such traditional societies that they tend to disappear early under the impact of just those technologies and economic forms which in the end produce the contemporary dilemmas of medical ethics. Hence any discussion of how they might have responded is bound to be speculative.

One thing however is clear. In all these conditions physical death has been disjoined from any possible role for the dying man. The tasks which such traditional cultures assigned to the role of the dying man cannot be discharged well or badly for they cannot be discharged. Hence in such cases all those reasons which led us to conclude that there could be no general right to suicide have no application. Hence there is no reason to conclude that the patient has not in such circumstances a right to die. Anyone therefore whose premises derived from this cultural tradition would perhaps have to reach conclusions at odds *both* with those contemporary conservative moralists, often though not always Roman Catholic, who argue that because suicide is wrong there can be no such right to die *and* with those contemporary liberal moralists, often though not always Protestants or secularists, who argue for the existence of such a right on the basis of a view that suicide is a permissible type of act.

I said earlier that I was not going to argue for or against the superiority of the traditional perspective which I have described to our contemporary American point of view. To do so we should have to explore the rival metaphysical presuppositions of these two alien and antagonistic forms of human culture; for such radically different and incompatible views of death and dying presuppose rival views of human nature, rival accounts of the nature of morality, indeed rival ontologies. The argument therefore would have to extend far beyond the scope of this paper. Nonetheless it will not have escaped notice that my very mode of description presupposes a sympathetic identification with the traditional and a certain hostility to modernity. So that one response even to my method of posing the questions about the right to die may be to suggest I am raising considerations interesting enough to the antiquarian, but now socially irrelevant. After all the cultures of which I speak have each and every one, when they confronted modernity, been substantially defeated by the modernization process. So that to look for the restoration of their standpoint in our own culture will seem to many hopelessly romantic and anachronistic. The gap between them and us seems too wide; and their standpoint, it might be noted, is as much at odds with our humanity at its best as it is with our inhumanity at its worst. From the standpoint of the cultures in which a dying man's dignity derives from his and others' sense of the tasks which he has to perform, policies of kindness towards the dying are as irrelevant as policies of neglect. Is then the metaphysical argument between the two types of culture not even worth joining because history has already decided the issue? Is my own standpoint nothing but a fragment of irrelevant medievalism?

There are at least two reasons for not assenting to these suggestions too hastily. The first is that there have been growing signs lately of an American ability to recognize the rootlessness of our social condition and to look for some means of remedying that rootlessness. But I doubt if a socially shared recovery of roots is possible without altering our socially shared attitudes to death. For a central thesis of this paper has been that our attitudes to death and to aging on the one hand and our attitudes to history and the past on the other are at key points inseparable.

A second reason for those who share my point of view not to accept so dismissive a response too easily is rather different. Our attitudes do indeed derive from the European middle ages; but the civilization of the middle ages was itself a response to a constellation of problems not unfamiliar in the contemporary sense. First a period in which a high culture became the victim of a loss of literacy, of inflation and of the growth of new forms of large-scale property; and then an ensuing collapse into the barbarism of the Dark Ages. Out of which the medieval world grew, relying on the strength of that in the culture which had enabled it to survive barbarism. If then "the middle ages" is a name which we give to one possible outcome of barbarism, a realistic analysis of the contemporary American scene may suggest that the middle ages may turn out to lie in our future as well as in our past, and not necessarily in too distant a future; for consider another way of viewing the implications of my argument. In the first part of the paper I rejected any concept of natural or human rights attaching to individuals as such as intellectually untenable. But if the case against such rights is as overwhelming as I think it is, why have they been so widely appealed to? One central answer is that appeal to such rights has seemed to give us a ground, a sufficient reason, for treating with respect and care those whom we could find no good reason for treating with respect and care in the context of our ordinary social relationships. In traditional societies it is not hard to find such good reasons. Why should I treat this dying person with respect and care? Because he or she is a member of my family, my community, my tribe. What if he or she is not? Then I must treat this stranger as a member of my family, my community, my tribe, as my neighbor. But what happens when those of my family, community, tribe or whatever are weakened and attenuated as they are in the modernization process? When there is no set of social relationships which define what it is to be a neighbor? Then the only resort is to appeal to me to show respect and care for the suffering or dying stranger *because he is a human being*. But if his claim to consideration arises only from his being a man, then it must be because some set of rights attaches to *being a human being*. And in this case everybody must have rights. Or so I reconstruct an argument implicit in modern appeals to rights, functioning to fill a social void, and relying on its kinship to unacknowledged older notions, both religious and legal, for part of its power.

Abstract humanity, however, turns out to be a relatively impotent moral notion and appeals to human rights as such have in the past only functioned effectively in their negative form. "You have no right to do this to us . . . " addressed by the spokesmen of suffering communities to their oppressors—whether by Massachusetts colonists to King George III or by Robespierre to those who would limit the suffrage in revolutionary France or by black people in Alabama and Mississippi to the post-Reconstruction South— can be a crucial form of political expression which does not suffer from any of the intellectual defects of the positive argument for natural rights; indeed it is precisely because of the fatal defects in the positive argument that it is able to make its case. If there are no human rights as such, then no human being can have a natural right to oppress another. So it is easy to understand why the appeal to natural rights has been historically powerful as protest or as revolution, but not as a ground for individual caring and concern for other individuals, such as the dying and the incurable.

I am suggesting, then, that in a society dominated by the concepts of abstract individualism the problems of the dying and the incurable may to some large extent be insoluble; but from this it does not follow that there is no ground for hope. It is rather to suggest that, to the extent that we do grapple socially and morally with the problems of the dying and intellectually with the problem of the right to die, we may gradually mount at the level of local communities—those of the home and the hospital—one of the most effective challenges that modern individualism has so far had to meet.

Notes

[1] Ronald Dworkin, *Taking Rights Seriously*. London: Duckworth, 1976.

[2] *Op. cit.,* p. 180.

[3] *Op. cit.,* p. 81.

[4] Francis John Burne, *Irish Kings and High-Kings*. London: Batsford, 1973.

[5] Robert Herz, *The Collective Representation of Death* in *Death and the Right Hand*. Trans. Robert & Claudia Needham. London: Cohen and West, 1960.

[6] L. 1018.

[7] Philippe Ariés, *Western Attitudes Towards Death*. Baltimore and London: Johns Hopkins University Press, 1974.

Discussion Questions

1. What point does MacIntyre make about rights? Do you agree or disagree? Why?
2. What does MacIntyre think is the importance of death as a social and personal event? What consequences does he draw from this? Argue for or against his position on this point.
3. What criticisms does MacIntyre make of our society in relation to dying? Do you agree or disagree? Why?
4. How might local communities meet the challenge mentioned in the last paragraph of MacIntyre's paper?
5. What does MacIntyre mean by the right to die garrulously? Is this a right you would want for yourself? Why or why not?

Suggested Readings for Chapter Three

Abernathy, Virginia, ed. *Frontiers in Medical Ethics.* Cambridge, Mass.: Ballinger, 1980.

Behnke, John A., and Sissela Bok, eds. *The Dilemmas of Euthanasia.* New York: Anchor Books, 1975.

Hunt, Robert, and John Arras, eds. *Ethical Issues in Modern Medicine.* Section 33, Euthanasia. Palo Alto, Calif.: Mayfield, 1977.

Lobby, Daniel H., ed. *Life or Death, Ethics and Options.* Seattle: University of Washington Press, 1968.

Mc Mullin, Ernan, ed. *Death and Discussion.* AAAS Selected Symposia Series. Boulder, Colo.: Westview Press, 1978.

Weir, Robert F., ed. *Ethical Issues in Death and Dying.* New York: Columbia University Press, 1977.

A TWO-SEXED SPECIES

The moral problems considered in Part II—abortion, sexual ethics, and sexual equality—are connected by the fact that they would not exist, at least in their present form, if the human species did not have two sexes with different biological functions. At least some of the problems abortion presents are created by the fact that while both a man and a woman are necessary to conceive a child, it is the woman who must bear the inconvenience, discomfort, and occasional danger of bearing the child. Even when the child is wanted by both parents this creates some friction; if one or the other parent does not want the child the problems are a great deal worse.

In addition to the problems raised by abortion there are many other moral dilemmas raised by sex. The biological function of sex is procreation, and in many animal species sexual intercourse is infrequent, is of short duration, and seems to be directed only to ensuring the continuance of the species. But because sexual intercourse in humans can be, though it is not always, both intensely pleasurable and associated with strong emotional attachment, sex in humans can be a great force for either good or evil.

Social inequality between men and women has probably resulted from biological differences, at least to the extent that pregnant women are handicapped in some kinds of competitive activities. Human beings have, in fact, seized on differences much less basic than sexual differences as an excuse to exploit or discriminate against other groups of human beings. Whatever the reasons, it is a historical fact that it has usually been men who have exploited and discriminated against women.

In all three areas—abortion, sexual relations, and sex-based discrimination—there are complex moral dilemmas complicated by intense emotions. No simple solutions to these problems are likely to be satisfactory and even the best solutions are likely to meet with strong emotional resistance. Religious beliefs also have a strong influence on people's thinking and practice in all of these areas.

In all three problem areas there is a complex interplay among different views of the ideal relationship between men and women. The unisex view holds that in every possible respect the rights, responsibilities, and privileges of both men and women should be the same. In extreme unisex view sexual differences should be no more important in our society than differences in height or eye color. But even less extreme unisex views hold that the very fact that one sex has a given right or responsibility is an argument for giving the other sex the same right or responsibility.

The view of sexual pluralism holds that sexual differences can legitimately be used as the basis for differences in rights and responsibilities. Extreme sexual pluralism can take the form of male (or female) chauvinism—maintaining that one sex is superior and should rule the other. But more moderate forms of sexual pluralism are much more defensible. The majority still feel, rightly or wrongly, that it is legitimate to give one sex and not the other the right to use certain toilet facilities, to give males the right to marry females and vice versa but to deny people of the same sex the right to marry each other, and so forth.

The ways in which the unisex and sexual pluralism views enter into a particular moral problem can be quite complex. Consider abortion, for instance. The concept of the right to abortion on demand can be regarded as a unisex view in that it can be used to free women from an unwanted responsibility that men do not share. However, leaving the choice solely to the pregnant woman is a form of sexual pluralism in that it gives the choice to the mother and removes it from the father. Of course there are reasons, perhaps good or even decisive reasons, for this, but it does treat people differently because of a sex-based difference.

In the area of sexual intercourse, an extreme unisex view, to be consistent, would have to regard homosexual intercourse as no better or worse than heterosexual intercourse. At the other extreme some sexual pluralists might defend the traditional double standard of sexual ethics whereby women are obliged to be faithful to their spouses but men are not so obliged.

In the area of sexual discrimination, the sexual pluralist view would seem by definition to support at least some forms of sexual inequality. But this is not necessarily so. If certain functions and responsibilities are assigned to one sex and other functions and responsibilities to the other sex, the two sexes might be different but still equal. For instance, in our system of government the legislature and judicial branches of government have different functions and responsibilities, but one is not superior to the other.

Probably most people hold neither a pure unisex view nor a pure pluralist view. Even an extreme political liberal will probably regard it as reasonable to make some discriminations on the basis of sex. And for traditional Christian believers the statement in one of St. Paul's epistles that "in Jesus Christ is neither slave or free, Jew or Gentile, male or female" indicates a unisex view on a certain level (all souls equal before God), even though Paul recommended certain practices that many people today regard as discriminatory (e.g., women were not to speak in church).

Obviously the problems in this part can be classified in many different ways, and some of them might arise in other forms even in a unisex society. But as they exist in our society all of them are affected by the fact that human beings as they are today create not only biologically but in many other ways a two-sexed society.

4

Abortion

Of all the moral dilemmas discussed in this book, perhaps abortion generates the most heat and the least light. On one side of the question are those to whom abortion represents the killing of innocent and defenseless persons; on the other side are those who consider abortion simply a minor operation, of no concern except to the woman having the abortion. The great majority are somewhere between these extremes, willing to grant that abortion is sometimes allowable, unwilling to force an unwanted pregnancy on an unwilling woman, but also seeing abortion as an unfortunate and even extreme solution to a genuine problem.

Reasoned arguments about abortion do occur, though they are not much listened to by many of the people most involved in pro- or antiabortion activities. Two key issues are whether the fetus is or is not a person and whether the pregnant woman's rights override those of the fetus, even if it is a person. It is not enough to say that these are private or religious questions that each person must settle for herself or himself. A slaveholder in the Old South or a contemporary slave-owning society might say, "You think these slaves are persons and have rights; I don't. It is a matter of religious belief or personal philosophy. You are free to treat them as persons with rights. I am free not to. I won't interfere with you; don't you interfere with me." The alleged solution does not solve anything. If you believe the slaves are persons you may feel that you are obliged to free them or shield them from abuse or death; leaving the slaveholder alone is just what your beliefs forbid you to do.

On the other hand the proabortionist might regard the antiabortionist the way most people would regard someone who argued that animals are persons and have rights. If animal-rights supporters tried to prevent the killing of animals or other uses of animals that are currently regarded as legitimate, they would be interfering with what many people regard as appropriate and desirable activities. (The views of people who regard animals as having rights are discussed later.)

Thus there is no neutral solution to this problem: If society forbids or regulates abortions it is favoring one side, but if it does not forbid or regulate abortions it is favoring the other side. Furthermore, almost all of the emotional arguments on either side fail to reach the people on the other side. Pictures of aborted fetuses may be disturbing, but pictures of the slaughtering of animals for meat would be disturbing to most nonvegetarians. There are heartrending cases of women whose sufferings could be relieved by an abortion, but there are heartrending cases of people who could be released from their suffering only by killing some adult human, such as a senile and demanding parent.

People with strong connections on one side or the other of this issue are not too likely to be moved by reasoned arguments for the other side, and it is not at all clear that there is any acceptable middle ground. Nevertheless, it is the philosopher's job to look at reasonable arguments and to try to reach a rationally based conclusion on the basis of those arguments. Clear thinking does not always lead to right action but confused and muddled thinking hardly ever does. And even if agreement cannot be reached at present, a better understanding of the pros and cons may give the two sides more respect for each other, which is valuable in itself and may lead to greater agreement in the long run.

This chapter presents a variety of arguments covering a wide range of positions on the issue. Germain Grisez presents the traditional arguments against abortion, writing from a Roman Catholic point of view but arguing philosophically rather than on the basis of theology. Judith Jarvis Thomson agrees for the sake of argument that the fetus is a person and then gives a widely discussed argument that even so abortion is permissible, though not having an abortion may be admirable. Underlying her argument is an important thesis in ethics: Not every action is either obligatory or forbidden. Some actions are permissible even though it might be admirable or heroic to refrain from them, and it is permissible to refrain from doing some things even though it might be admirable or heroic to do them.

Mary Anne Warren argues that the fetus is not a person and, therefore, that no one's rights are violated by abortion, whereas women's rights would be violated by forbidding or even regulating abortion. Jane English takes the position that we cannot satisfactorily solve the problem of whether the fetus is a person and must resolve the issue of abortion while leaving this question open. Finally, James P. Sterba tries to step back from the issue and view it in a larger perspective, arguing that the principles used to resolve certain other ethical problems can be applied to the abortion issue.

So many contributions of very high quality have been made on this issue by philosophers in recent years that it is hard to represent every view adequately. However, the papers in this chapter exhibit a wide range of views and a high quality of discussion; they provide a good first word, though certainly not the last word, on this issue.

Abortion: Ethical Arguments

Germain Grisez

Utilitarianism—The New Morality

If we set aside the personhood of the unborn, arguments against abortion are arguments against contraception. Since I have treated this point at length elsewhere, I will not deal with it here.

However, if we accept the position that the aborted *are* persons, the ethical issues are far from settled. What is excluded is any extreme position that would in effect equate abortion with contraception.

Thus the view that abortion is justified whenever the woman wants it, because she has a right to control her own reproductive capacity, is ruled out as soon as one grants that the fetus also is a person with rights. For if this is true, the fetus's right to life obviously is more important than the woman's right to dispose of her own reproductive capacity. Clearly, an obligation on a pregnant woman to forego abortion no more infringes on her rights than an obligation to forego infanticide infringes on parental rights.

We have responsibilities to those who are dependent on us, and we can hardly claim a right to kill merely to free ourselves of the burden of putting up with and caring for our dependents. If they are *ours,* they are not ours to dispose of as we will; that is the difference between our property and our relatives. The former is an extension of ourselves, but the latter, being other persons, have some importance in themselves.

Arguments that no unwanted child should be permitted to be born and that we must value quality of life more than mere quantity of life also have been introduced into the abortion controversy after having been used to defend the morality of contraception. However, a utilitarian theory of morality can use these arguments even on the supposition that the unborn are persons. And a utilitarian theory would be even more likely to argue the justifiability of abortion in particularly difficult cases—for example, when the mother's health is seriously endangered, when the child will be seriously defective, when the circumstances of the child's conception render its prospects very dim, or when the birth of the child would seriously lessen the chances of several brothers and sisters for a good life.

How would a utilitarian ethics defend abortion in such cases?

Utilitarianism holds that the moral good or evil of human acts is determined by the results of the acts. If an act has good consequences then that act will be good; if it has bad consequences, it will be bad. Of course, most acts have consequences that are partly good and partly bad. Therefore, utilitarianism holds that the morally good act will be the one that on the whole gives the best results. Whenever we act there are alternatives, including not acting or delaying action. If we can add up the good results expected from each alternative and subtract in each case the expected bad results from the good, then according

Reprinted, with notes omitted, from Germain Grisez, *Abortion: The Myths, the Realities, and the Arguments* (New York: Corpus Books, 1970), pp. 287–290, 304–307, 315–321, 333–334, 340–346. Used by permission of the author.

to utilitarian ethics we should choose the act that carries the prospect of the *greatest net good*. Only that act will be a morally good and right one to choose. Other possibilities will be more or less immoral depending upon how far their net value falls short of the single morally good act.

Of course, this theory of morality immediately raises two questions. One question is whether the person acting must consider the good of others, or only his own good, or both. The other question is what will count as good consequences.

The answer of classical utilitarianism to the first of these questions is that one should consider the good of all indiscriminately when counting up good and bad results. We should seek "the greatest good of the greatest number"—so the maxim goes. Thus the agent himself, his friends and family, his enemies and those he has never met would all deserve equal consideration. This position is somewhat unclear, since it does not settle what to do if greater total good can be done to fewer persons by one act and a somewhat lesser total good to a much larger number of persons by the alternative. I think that this and other like ambiguities must be settled on the side of greatest net value, if the simple theory is to be maintained.

The other question—what will count as good consequences?—also has a classic answer. The good is pleasure and the absence of pain. Utilitarians have been criticized for the narrowness of this conception of good, but what they mean by "pleasure" includes every sort of enjoyment, felt satisfaction, and desirable experience. On this theory, the only thing good for its own sake is that conscious experience be as one would wish: rich, intense, and without pain, anguish, or boredom.

An issue often debated among those who espouse utilitarianism is whether each individual act must be judged immediately by the standard of good consequences or whether particular acts should be judged by moral norms which, in turn, would be submitted to the utilitarian test. The first position is called "act-utilitarianism" and the second "rule-utilitarianism." Rule-utilitarianism may seem more plausible, because it leaves room for the ordinary belief that there are some moral norms that should be respected.

However, the two positions actually amount to the same thing. For act-utilitarianism admits that the judgment that is right in any given case should be followed by anyone who faces a similar set of alternatives having a like balance of good and bad consequences. Thus the judgment of the individual act really is universal, and amounts to a rule. And rule-utilitarians, for their part, do not hold that the rules should be maintained even if on the whole and in the long run a change would be for the better. Thus the rules are subject to revisions which admit all reasonable exceptions, and reasonableness is judged by the criterion of utility.

Rule-utilitarians often argue that their position takes account of situations in which it is harmless to the community and advantageous for each individual to act in a certain way but disastrous for all if everyone acts in that way—e.g., the contamination of a public waterway by private sewage systems. However, act-utilitarianism can justify making and enforcing rules to restrain everyone from contributing to a situation when cumulative action would result in common disadvantage. Among the bad consequences of an individual act are the implications it has for the action of others and together with the action of others. Thus if utilitarianism were a usable method of moral judgment, act- and rule-utilitarianism would yield the same results.

Utilitarianism is a secular ethic in the sense that it has developed as a "new morality" in conscious reaction to traditional religious ethics. The origins of the theory are in modern humanism, which especially in the nineteenth century sought to reform society and to change established customs, many of which rationalized grievous inequalities on the ground that the advantages of the upper classes were theirs by rights founded in "traditional" morality. Since religious morality had been perverted to defend social injustices, humanistic reformers sought a non-religious ethics to serve as the ideology of needed reform. The utilitarian theory was one candidate for this function; Marxism was another. But utilitarianism was compatible with the political outlook of Britain and America, while Marxism was not.

Utilitarianism and Marxism are both this-worldly. Both locate the good in people themselves. Both consider any act good if it has sufficiently good consequences. But Marxism locates the good in an ideal society—a kind of Kingdom of God without God—while utilitarianism locates the good in the experience of individuals—a kind of heavenly bliss without heaven.

Not surprisingly, therefore, utilitarian and Marxist ethics agree in justifying the killing of some people when such killing has sufficiently good consequences. The Marxist will justify killing if it promotes the revolution and the coming into being of the communist society. The utilitarian does not expect any such ideal society, and he does not subordinate individual happiness to the community. But the utilitarian can justify killing some to save more, killing those whose lives are more miserable than satisfying, and the like.

Thus we can understand most common arguments in favor of abortion, for most of these arguments simply assume without proof (or even question) a utilitarian type of ethics. Surely, the argument will begin, it is right to induce abortion if it is necessary to save the mother's life, since otherwise both she and the baby would die together, and it is better to save one than to lose both lives. Then, of course, even if it is a case of *either/or*, it usually will be better to kill the baby, since the mother's life will normally mean more to herself and others than the unborn's life means to it and to others. Next, the lack of advanced awareness and susceptibility to mental anguish in the unborn (or even in the young child) will justify killing it if its continued existence will spoil someone else's life (the mother's health; the well being of existing children; the protection of society from the population explosion). Then too, if the child's own life will likely be more a misery than a joy, it may be killed (defects of a serious sort; perhaps the burden of being illegitimate; perhaps even the sad condition of being unwanted).

Everyone is familiar by now with the utilitarian sort of argument. It is usually, and most effectively, presented by detailing some actual, horrible case which appeals strongly to humane sensibility. We identify with the mother and feel acutely the weight of net value for and in her on the side of abortion. We neglect the embryo, even if we admit it to be human, because we have no memory of being in its condition, because it looks odd (perhaps, even, repulsive), because we do not know it, because it has no role in our society.

Those who argue for abortion on utilitarian grounds have adopted an effective rhetoric that does little justice to their opponents. The two chief elements in this rhetoric are an appeal to contemporary prejudice against the authority of traditional religion and an appeal to humane sympathy for the plight of persons in the face of objective, "impersonal" moral standards. Proponents of abortion may be fully sincere in this rhetoric. The prevailing rejection of abortion as immoral undoubtedly arose from the religious tradition, and many opponents argue on the basis of religious faith rather than develop a rational alternative to utilitarianism. Also the depersonalization of modern life in technological and bureaucratic society often pits the person against cold, "objective" requirements, and opponents of utilitarianism have not shown sufficiently that utilitarianism itself reflects modern depersonalization. Most important of all, opponents of utilitarianism have not effectively shown why mere good consequences cannot be an adequate criterion of moral goodness.

A Reformulation of the Ethical Issue

In denying that there is any kind of act so evil that good consequences might not sometimes justify it, utilitarianism excluded the notion that we have any duties that we must always fulfill, regardless of consequences. But if we have no such duties, then neither do we have any unexceptionable rights. Rights and duties are correlative. If I have an unalienable right to life, then it is always wrong for others to kill me. If it is sometimes justified for them to kill me, then my right to life is not unalienable—rather, it all depends on circumstances.

In general, we tend to believe that all men are equal in their right to life and that all men have an equal duty to respect the lives of others. We make exceptions in regard to capital punishment and justified killing in war. But in such cases we think that the criminal or the enemy has somehow surrendered the common, equal right to respect for life.

Obviously, our belief in equality in the right to life is incompatible with utilitarianism. Also, though less obviously, any approach that tries to justify any killing of one human being by another on the basis of factual differences between the two is slipping into a utilitarian attitude toward the good of human life. For, in fact, it is of course true that all of us differ from one another in many ways and all of us are unequal on the basis of each and every difference. No one is superior in every respect; there is some way in which each of us is definitely inferior to others.

To decide that some of these differences, some of these inequalities, some of these ways of being inferior can so detract from the basic worth of a person as to warrant his destruction by another is essentially to decide that all persons have a certain definite and limited worth and that certain facts characterizing persons can lessen that worth in a definite and calculable way. Now, this is precisely the mistake of utilitarianism. It understands human worth not in terms of what is intrinsic to the person and his life—dignity—but in terms of what is extrinsic—value *for something*. Human goods can then be appraised and weighed, and the right to kill will depend upon computation.

In effect, utilitarianism puts a price on every man's head. Every person is transformed into an object. On the model of technological reasoning, the price of one is compared with the price of another. Those whose lives, if continued, would detract from rather than add to the sum total of human value must be eliminated, just as an employer gets rid of an unproductive employee by firing him.

We may feel safe enough, personally, in using the factual inequality and inferiority of the embryo as a ground for treating its life as expendable. After all, we are not now and never again will be unequal and inferior in just the way that the embryo is. But in reasoning thus we are being arbitrary, for we are selecting as decisive the characteristics we prefer among all the differences of human beings. And we must always remember that there is no common denominator of the importance of these differences.

Thus, we may suppose that the embryo's right to life must give way because it is undeveloped, because its specifically human abilities are latent in potentiality. If the embryo could argue with us, however, he might contend that the life of an adult is of less worth than his. After all, the adult has less time left to live, and all that he has gained in actualization he has lost in possibility. Most of what he could have been has been sacrificed in his becoming what he is, and much that he has been can never be recaptured.

"Isn't it part of the *wonder* you feel when you hold an infant," the embryo might ask us, "that he can still be anything, that all of life lies open before him? And isn't it part of the *sadness* you feel as you grow older that possibilities are closing off for you, like so many gates slamming shut in the maze of life, until there remains only one gate open—the one that leads into the darkness of death? If death is not better than life," the embryo might conclude his case against the mature adult, "then my life is far better than yours, for my life is a process of development and ever increasing vitality, while yours is a process of deterioration and waning vitality as you decline toward death."

I do not suggest that the embryo's argument would be sound; obviously it is fallacious to suppose that the dignity of a person is measured by his degree of vitality. But the embryo's argument would be no more fallacious than ours, if we measure his worth by his degree of development. And our argument would certainly sound fallacious to him, if he were able to hear and comprehend it.

The ethical issue regarding abortion, therefore, is not precisely stated when it is put in terms of whether it is ever morally right to kill the unborn and, if so, under what conditions. Rather, the question is whether it is ever morally right for any human person to kill another one and, if so, under what conditions. To question the absoluteness of the right to life of the unborn is to question the absoluteness of everyone's right to life. Since, as persons, we are incomparable with one another in dignity and equal in our right to life, the principle that protects the lives of all of us also protects the lives of those unborn, while any reasonable ground for morally approving the killing of those unborn also is a reasonable ground for morally approving the killing of persons in any other period or condition of their lives.

Since, in fact, we do believe that on the whole it is wrong to kill human beings but that in certain cases such killing is justifiable, our problem is reduced to investigating whether this belief is correct and, if so, why. Then we must apply to the special case of the unborn any ground that justifies killing, to see which justifications for abortion, if any, are valid.

It might be objected that our examination of the question whether the aborted are human beings did not demonstrate absolutely that they are, in fact, persons. But this objection would miss the point of that consideration in two ways.

In the first place, we saw that beyond doubt the *facts* show the embryo at every stage to be a *living, human individual*. To go beyond this is not a question of fact but a question of metaphysics. We should not expect and will never get a factual answer to the ulterior question. What our arguments revealed is that there is no compelling reason to deny that the embryo is a person. As the Anglican committee frankly stated, to deny personality to the embryo is merely a postulate necessary to leave room for killing it. If ethics is to be anything better than rationalization, such an approach will not do. We must admit, at the very least, that the embryo can as well be considered a person as not.

And therefore, in the second place, ethics must proceed on the supposition that abortion does kill a person. For ethics is concerned with moral responsibility for doing what is right and wrong, and right and wrong are in one's willingness, not in what is beyond our knowledge, actual or even possible. We do not consider ourselves immoral if we discover that some action of ours seriously harmed another, though we did not know and could not have known it would have that effect. Similarly, we cannot consider ourselves blameless if we are willing to kill what may or may not be a person, even if it is not.

In being willing to kill the embryo, we accept responsibility for killing what we must admit *may* be a person. There is some reason to believe it is—namely the *fact* that it is a living, human individual and the inconclusiveness of arguments that try to exclude it from the protected circle of personhood.

To be willing to kill what for all we know could be a person is to be willing to kill it if it is a person. And since we cannot absolutely settle if it is a person except by a metaphysical postulate, for all practical purposes we must hold that to be willing to kill the embryo is to be willing to kill a person.

Consequently, we may not evade moral responsibility for killing a person if we take responsibility for an abortion. This is not yet to say that the responsibility is always *guilt*, that will be true only if killing such persons is always *wrong*.

The important point to realize is that ethical consideration of abortion must not treat it as an isolated case, as if it had nothing to do with the whole question of the ethics of killing human beings. Certainly, the literature we have reviewed also shows that abortion is connected with other forms of killing such as infanticide, and euthanasia. If a utilitarian theory is accepted, not only the personhood of the unborn, but the personhood of all of us is put in jeopardy. Anyone with sufficient ingenuity in metaphysical argument should be able to construct some sort of plausible theory of personality according to which any one of us will turn out to be a non-person.

It is also important to notice that in locating the ethical issue in the way I do, the following discussion does not become completely separated from serious ethical reflection with which I do not wholly agree. The Protestant situationists (as distinguished from those who hold a form of utilitarianism) examine the issue of abortion in the context of a firm conviction that the real issue is the justifiability of taking the lives of persons. Moreover, not only theological moral reflection but also secular medical and jurisprudential consideration, until the last few years, proceeded generally on the same basis. . . .

One need neither confuse the moral reality of the act with its behavioral aspect nor divide the *meaningfulness* of the behavior from the *enactment* of the purpose to observe that human acts sometimes are means to ends extrinsic to themselves: for example, the work of a person who is only interested in pay. If the work is that of a gunman who will kill anyone for a price, then the psychological intention by which he sets himself directly against human life is morally significant, for this intention orients the self in a manner that is incompatible with openness to the basic good of human life and respect for it. Whatever his ulterior purpose might be, his acts are morally evil, for one basic human good is treated as expendable for the sake of another (or of the same in another realization). . . .

Nevertheless, it seems to me that the principle of double effect in its modern formulation is too restrictive insofar as it demands that even in the order of physical causality the evil aspect of the act not precede the good. The critics are right, I believe, in their insistence that the behavioral aspect of the act is not morally determinate apart from the meaning that shapes the human act. In this respect, Aquinas's formulation seems to me to have been more accurate, for he did not make an issue of which effect (aspect of the act) is prior in physical causality, but he did insist that when a single human act has a good and a bad aspect the latter could not rightly fall within the scope of intention, even as a means to a good end.

From the point of view of human moral activity, the initiation of an indivisible process through one's own causality renders all that is involved in that process equally immediate. So long as no other human act intervenes or could intervene, the meaning (intention) of the behavior which initiates such a process is no less immediate to what is, from the point of view of physical causality, a proximate effect or a secondary or remote consequence. For on the hypothesis that no other human act intervenes or could intervene, the moral agent who posits a natural cause *simultaneously* (morally speaking) posits its foreseen effects. The fact that not everything in the behavior which is relevant to basic human goods equally affects the agent's moral standing arises not from the diverse physical dispositions of the elements of the behavioral aspect of the act, but from the diverse dispositions of the agent's intention with regard to the intelligible aspects of the act.

But it is the intelligible aspects of the indivisible human act that count, not purposes sought and values hoped for in ulterior human acts, whether of the agent himself or of another. For otherwise the end will justify the means, and some sort of utilitarianism or inadequate consistency-criterion will replace the true standard of moral value.

Moreover, even if the particular process initiated by one's behavior is in fact indivisible, he obviously does not escape full moral responsibility for significant aspects of it that could have been avoided by the choice of an alternative behavior having the same determining intention but a diverse mode of accomplishment. Then too, if the unity of the process is merely *de facto,* arising from the agent's failure to divide and limit his behavior, then the act is not truly indivisible and the determining intention will not exclude moral responsibility for aspects of the act that could have been excluded, but were not.

This theoretical formulation will be considerably clarified by application to some examples. Obviously, cases generally approved by application of the principle of double effect as it is conventionally formulated also will be approved if the modification I am suggesting is correct, since the modification broadens the strict condition about the order of the effects as it is usually expressed. For this reason, we need not review many examples usually used to illustrate the principle, but we must consider some where the proposed modification leads to a result different from the usual formulation. Also, it will be worth noting how the proposed modification would deal more restrictively with some of the types of cases mentioned by critics of the traditional principle.

According to the present theory, then, in which cases would it be permissible to do the deadly deed involving the unborn? We must bear in mind from the previous argument that they must be treated as persons whose lives are inviolable to any direct attack. The question therefore becomes a matter of trying to apply the revised version of the principle of double effect to these cases.

. . . There are relatively few cases in which the life or physical health of the mother seems to require abortion. Two types of cases of this sort are those involving ectopic pregnancy (implantation of the embryo outside the uterus) and certain cases involving impaired heart and/or kidney function.

Ectopic pregnancy, we have seen in dealing with religious aspects, has been dealt with by Catholic moralists by the argument that the condition itself is pathological, and that the pathology, even apart from the developing embryo, presents a threat to the mother. It must be removed, and in the process the embryo is incidentally removed.

Assuming the soundness of the position, I think a simpler justification is possible. This justification will also apply to abortions previously considered direct having strict medical indications such as those mentioned involving impaired heart and/or kidney function.

The justification is simply that the very same act, indivisible as to its behavioral process, has both the good effect of protecting human life and the bad effect of destroying it. The fact that the good effect is subsequent in time and in physical process to the evil one is irrelevant, because the entire process is indivisible by human choice and hence all aspects of it are equally present to the agent at the moment he makes his choice.

It will be helpful, perhaps, in gaining acceptance for this view—although it is not theoretically essential to the argument—if we note that it is not precisely the infant's death that benefits the mother but its removal from her. From this point of view, even if the abortion were intended (which I do not think it has to be), the killing of the infant would not have to be intended. The distinction is clearly illustrated if we imagine a probable future development—an artificial womb. Embryos aborted in such cases could conceivably be saved and brought to birth by such a device. Thus, the very meaning of *abortion* need not be *feticide,* for even if the two cannot now be separated in fact, they could be, and what could be separate in fact obviously cannot be identical in meaning.

If the threat to the mother's life or health can be obviated without the removal of the unborn child, then the aspects of the human act which involves abortion are, in fact, separable. In such a case one cannot argue that the alternative to abortion is difficult, inconvenient, and costly. For that is to make these factors of cost equal in value to the dignity of human life. If one does not take an alternative in which the good effect is achieved without the deadly deed, then killing falls within the scope of one's intention.

What if there is no alternative to abortion, in some sort of case, if the mother's health is to be protected, although the risk to her does not involve the probability of accelerated death? In principle, if the good effect is attained in and through the same indivisible process which is initiated by the abortifacient procedure, then the abortion need not be intended. However, one does not sacrifice life for health, since the latter is only a partial aspect of the former.

To subordinate life to health is something I could not do in my own case—I would never be healthier dead. Nor can one reasonably prefer health to life, the part of life (health) to the whole of life. To act on such a preference involving another's life and my health indicates that it is not the basic human good itself, but a particular realization of it, that concerns me. This is a limiting attitude, not compatible with moral uprightness.

This conclusion that abortion is not morally permitted when only health is at stake also applies to the entire area of the psychiatric indication. Moreover, the good effects presumably justifying such cases of abortion are not achieved through a physical process that is unified and morally indivisible, but rather in ulterior effects of distinct human acts.

For this reason, even if a threat of suicide is serious and abortion would prevent it (something hardly likely . . .), abortion would not be justified in such a case. The good effect would be achieved only by preventing another act, and the abortion itself would be a means, intentionally chosen, to this ulterior end.

In times past complications of delivery raised serious problems. Now where medical facilities are available such difficulties are rare, most difficult cases being prevented by timely surgery. However, if it were impossible to prevent the mother's death (or, worse, the death of both) except by cutting up and removing the child piecemeal, it seems to me that this death-dealing deed could be done without the killing itself coming within the scope of intention. The very deed which deals death also (by hypothesis) initiates a unified and humanly indivisible physical process which saves life. But if it is possible to save the mother without the death-dealing deed, then the intent to kill would enter the agent's act as its determining meaning.

The attempt to justify abortion in cases involving prospective birth defects obviously is unsatisfactory. If the goods sought are in others, then the deadly deed does not itself achieve them, and it becomes an intended means to an ulterior end. On the other hand, if life is a human good, even a defective life is better than no life at all—some value is better than no value. In any case, defects cannot touch many central values of the human person. . . . The real reasons underlying this "indication" are utilitarian—the supposition that an infant is like a product, and that imperfect specimens should be scrapped.

A sound appraisal of the moral significance of abortion as a method of eliminating the defective was given by Martin Ginsberg, a New York State Assemblyman, in the 1969 New York legislative debate. The proposed bill would have permitted abortion

> when there is medical evidence of substantial risk that the foetus, if born, would be so grossly malformed, or would have such serious physical or mental abnormalities, as to be permanently incapable of caring for himself.

Mr. Ginsberg, a thirty-eight-year-old lawyer who was crippled by polio at the age of thirteen months, walks only with difficulty, using metal crutches and leg braces.

He began his speech by mentioning a number of persons who achieved greatness despite handicaps—Toulouse Lautrec, Alec Templeton, Charles Steinmetz, Lord Byron, and Helen Keller. Then he went on:

> What this bill says is that those who are malformed or abnormal have no reason to be part of our society. If we are prepared to say that a life should not come into this world malformed or abnormal, then tomorrow we should be prepared to say that a life already in this world which becomes malformed or abnormal should not be permitted to live.

Ginsberg, who did not oppose abortion law relaxation in general, was given a standing ovation by the Assembly.

The bill's sponsor, Albert H. Blumenthal, attacked Ginsberg, accusing him of telling women they could not protect themselves from harm:

> That's what you're telling my wife, Marty. You're telling her she has no right to protect herself from harm. You don't have that right, Marty. Nobody gave you that right. Not God. Not man.

However, Blumenthal did not explain how eliminating possible defective children would protect mothers from harm. Although before the debate there were six votes more than the number needed for passage pledged in favor of the bill, the *New York Times,* which has promoted abortion law relaxation for years, was forced to headline: "Assembly Blocks Abortion Reform in Sudden Switch—14 Legislators Pledged to Bill Defect After Polio Victim Urges Defeat."

Abortion used as a form of birth prevention—whether in cases of illegitimate children, or in cases of economic hardship, or in cases of simple reluctance to have a child—clearly cannot be justified. Here the whole point of the operation is to get rid of the baby, to end its life, because its continued existence is simply rejected. This is not to say that in some such cases there is not a genuinely good ulterior motive—e.g., avoiding future hardship for already existing children in an impoverished family. However, these good motives—while they may well win our sympathy and deserve our compassion—do not ethically justify the abortifacient procedure, for it achieves none of these goods. They are present only in future human actions.

Moreover, the goods sought in all such cases are achievable otherwise. The unmarried girl should be helped and arrangements made for the child's care, whether or not she wishes to bring it up. The problems of poverty and social stress would yield to our compassion if it were real and active enough, not merely a weak sympathy. Those who do not want children need not conceive them; they do so by their own free acts.

But what about the rare case in which a woman is raped and conceives a child of her attacker? She has not had a choice; the child has come to be through no act of hers. Moreover, it is not clear that her precise concern is to kill the child. She simply does not wish to bear it. If the artificial uterus were available she might be happy to have the baby removed and placed in such a device, later to be born and cared for as any infant that becomes a social charge. Now, clearly, one could not object if that were done. May the death of the child that is in fact brought about by aborting it actually be unintended in this case? I believe that the answer must be yes.

But this answer does not mean that abortion in such a case would be ethically right. I fail to see what basic human good is achieved if the developing baby is aborted. The victim of rape has been violated and has a good reason to resent it. Yet the unborn infant is not the attacker. It is hers as much as his. She does not wish to bear it—an understandable emotional reaction. But really at stake is only such trouble, risk and inconvenience as is attendant on any pregnancy. To kill the baby for the sake of such goods reveals an attitude toward human life that is not in keeping with its inherently immeasurable dignity. One of the simpler modes of obligation is violated—that which requires us to do good to another when we can and there is no serious reason not to do it.

Even psychologically, I doubt the wisdom of a woman who has been raped disposing of a child conceived of the attack. Her problem is largely to accept herself, to realize that she is not inherently tainted and damaged by her unfortunate experience. The unborn child is partly hers, and she must accept herself in it if she is really to overcome her sense of self-rejection. To get rid of the child is to evade this issue, not to solve it. A woman who uses such an evasion may feel temporary relief but may be permanently blocked from achieving the peace with herself she seeks.

Incest presents no special problem. Clearly here abortion is a method of disposing of an unwanted baby. I see no reason why incest often is coupled with rape in discussions of abortion, except for the fact that both arouse in most people an emotion of revulsion which proponents of abortion seek to divert from parties who are guilty to individuals who are innocent—the nameless unborn.

If abortion is justified, then it should be performed in a way that gives the child a chance of survival, if there is any chance at all. The effort to save the aborted child and to find ways of saving all who are justifiably aborted would be a token of sincerity that the death of the child really was not in the scope of the intention.

If abortion is intended, how it is done is ethically irrelevant except to the extent that some methods might unnecessarily endanger the mother as well. Certainly, abortion is no less immoral if it is done with an abortion pill near the beginning of pregnancy than if it is done with a curette later on, or by delivering the child at or after viability and putting it down an incinerator, as has happened in England under the new abortion law.

One might wonder about the moral status of birth control methods that are probably or possibly abortifacient, as . . . is the case with the IUD and the "pill." If one recognizes that human life is at stake if these methods do indeed work in an abortifacient manner, then it is clear that the willingness to use them is a willingness to kill human beings directly. The effect of killing the already conceived individual, if it occurs, is no accident, but the precise thing sought in committing oneself to birth prevention. *If one is willing to get a desired result by killing, and does not know whether he is killing or not, he might as well know that he is killing,* for he is willing to accept that as the meaning of his act: Everyone who knows the facts and who prescribes or uses birth control methods that might be abortifacient is an abortionist at heart.

The judgment may be seen more clearly by considering it from the point of view of someone who sincerely believes conception-prevention to be legitimate and any interference after conception to be unjustifiably killing a person. On these assumptions, it clearly is insufficient to know that a given method prevents *births,* such a person would be willing to prevent conception but absolutely unwilling to interfere once conception had occurred. The abortifacient character of a technique, even if certainly known to occur in only a small percentage of cases, could not be viewed as incidental to the intended conception-prevention, since in those cases there would be no conception-prevention. Nor could the abortions which might occur be outside the scope of the intention defined as *birth prevention,* since if conception were not prevented, the only meaning of "birth prevention" would be *abortion*. Uncertainty about a method's mode of action would perhaps be tolerable if the uncertainty regarded side effects. However, here the uncertainty is concerned with the very meaning of the *intended* birth prevention: whether it is conception-prevention or abortion.

It is often said that one should not becloud the ethical issues regarding abortion by referring to it as *murder*. Certainly the word has a legal sense, and it would prejudice the jurisprudential discussion of abortion . . . to classify abortion with the crime of murder. On the other hand, "murder" also has an ethical sense: it is the wrongful and purposeful taking of human life. It would be question-begging to call abortion "murder" before examining its morality. Now that we have completed such an examination, however, it is accurate and appropriate to say that abortion, whenever it involves the direct attack on human life (which is almost always) is *murder*. To reject this classification of the act is itself a merely emotional reaction, an attempt to sanctify evil by removing its bad name.

To say this, however, is not to assert that everyone who has an abortion or who performs an abortion incurs the full moral responsibility for murder. Many who do the evil deed do not know, or do not fully appreciate, what they do—this is true of all murder, not only of abortion. Some act through fear, through anxiety, through shame. They are less guilty than those who act through cool and brutal calculation, such as a utilitarian, if he were true to his principles, should applaud. Still, if one's lack of appreciation of what the deadly deed really means or if one's weakness to resist is a product of one's own habit of treating the good of life lightly or of one's unwillingness to see and feel the wrong one does, then responsibility is not lessened, but increased.

Granting that someone has done his best to see what is right and to be ready to do the right as he sees it, he is of course free of moral guilt. In this sense, one who follows steadfastly the direction of a firm and honest conscience is doing as he ought. Still, conscience must be shaped according to ethical truth. A sincere conscience can be mistaken, and such a mistake does not make the deed good, although it does not make the doer guilty.

Roman Catholic readers may notice that my conclusions about abortion diverge from common theological teachings and also diverge from the official teaching of the Church as it was laid down by the Holy Office in the nineteenth century. I am aware of the divergence, but would point out that my theory is consonant with the more important and more formally definite teaching that direct killing of the unborn is wrong. I reach conclusions that are not traditional by broadening the meaning of "unintended" in a revision of the principle of double effect, not by accepting the rightness of direct killing or the violability of unborn life because of any ulterior purpose or indication.

Most important, I cannot as a philosopher limit my conclusions by theological principles. However, I can as a Catholic propose my philosophic conclusions as suggestions for consideration in the light of faith, while not proposing anything contrary to the Church's teaching as a practical norm of conduct for my fellow believers. Those who really believe that there exists on this earth a community whose leaders are appointed and continuously assisted by God to guide those who accept their authority safely through time to eternity would be foolish to direct their lives by some frail fabrication of mere reason instead of by conforming to a guidance system designed and maintained by divine wisdom.

I do not doubt that the survivors of a nuclear holocaust, when they look back upon our time, will clearly discern a common thread uniting our deterrent strategy, our increasing resort to violence in place of orderly civil process, and our relaxed attitude toward the killing of the unborn. If we want freedom and progress together with law and order, we must begin by recommitting ourselves to the basic good of human life, a good that is fundamental to all the others. If we do not respect human life, what human good will we any longer respect?

Discussion Questions

1. According to Grisez, what consequences would follow from admitting that the fetus is a person? What consequences would *not* follow? Do you agree? Why or why not?

2. Grisez raises the issue of quality of life with regard to abortion. Compare his discussion with some of the discussions of quality of life with regard to suicide and euthanasia (e.g., May and Mc Mullin in Chapter 3).

3. Grisez argues against a utilitarian defense of abortion. Does he state this defense in a satisfactory way? How might a utilitarian reply to Grisez?

4. Compare Grisez's treatment of right to life in abortion with discussions of the same issue with regard to euthanasia. Does the comparison support or damage Grisez's argument?

5. Does Grisez beg the question as to whether the embryo is a person? Why or why not?

6. How does Grisez relate abortion to a general ethical position? Argue for or against his position on this issue.

A Defense of Abortion

Judith Jarvis Thomson

Most opposition to abortion relies on the premise that the fetus is a human being, a person, from the moment of conception. The premise is argued for, but, as I think, not well. Take, for example, the most common argument. We are asked to notice that the development of a human being from conception through birth into childhood is continuous; then it is said that to draw a line, to choose a point in this development and say "before this point the thing is not a person, after this point it is a person" is to make an arbitrary choice, a choice for which in the nature of things no good reason can be given. It is concluded that the fetus is, or anyway that we had better say it is, a person from the moment of conception. But this conclusion does not follow. Similar things might be said about the development of an acorn into an oak tree, and it does not follow that acorns are oak trees, or that we had better say they are. Arguments of this form are sometimes called "slippery slope arguments"—the phrase is perhaps self-explanatory—and it is dismaying that opponents of abortion rely on them so heavily and uncritically.

From Judith Jarvis Thomson, "A Defense of Abortion," *Philosophy and Public Affairs,* vol. 1, no. 1 (copyright © 1971 by Princeton University Press), pp. 47–66. Reprinted by permission of the publisher.

I am inclined to agree, however, that the prospects for "drawing a line" in the development of the fetus look dim. I am inclined to think also that we shall probably have to agree that the fetus has already become a human person well before birth. Indeed, it comes as a surprise when one first learns how early in its life it begins to acquire human characteristics. By the tenth week, for example, it already has a face, arms and legs, fingers and toes; it has internal organs, and brain activity is detectable.[1] On the other hand, I think that the premise is false, that the fetus is not a person from the moment of conception. A newly fertilized ovum, a newly implanted clump of cells, is no more a person than an acorn is an oak tree. But I shall not discuss any of this. For it seems to me to be of great interest to ask what happens if, for the sake of argument, we allow the premise. How, precisely, are we supposed to get from there to the conclusion that abortion is morally impermissible? Opponents of abortion commonly spend most of their time establishing that the fetus is a person, and hardly any time explaining the step from there to the impermissibility of abortion. Perhaps they think the step too simple and obvious to require much comment. Or perhaps instead they are simply being economical in argument. Many of those who defend abortion rely on the premise that the fetus is not a person, but only a bit of tissue that will become a person at birth; and why pay out more arguments than you have to? Whatever the explanation, I suggest that the step they take is neither easy nor obvious, that it calls for closer examination than it is commonly given, and that when we do give it this closer examination we shall feel inclined to reject it.

I propose, then, that we grant that the fetus is a person from the moment of conception. How does the argument go from here? Something like this, I take it. Every person has a right to life. So the fetus has a right to life. No doubt the mother has a right to decide what shall happen in and to her body; everyone would grant that. But surely a person's right to life is stronger and more stringent than the mother's right to decide what happens in and to her body, and so outweighs it. So the fetus may not be killed; an abortion may not be performed.

It sounds plausible. But now let me ask you to imagine this. You wake up in the morning and find yourself back to back in bed with an unconscious violinist. A famous unconscious violinist. He has been found to have a fatal kidney ailment, and the Society of Music Lovers has canvassed all the available medical records and found that you alone have the right blood type to help. They have therefore kidnapped you, and last night the violinist's circulatory system was plugged into yours, so that your kidneys can be used to extract poisons from his blood as well as your own. The director of the hospital now tells you, "Look, we're sorry the Society of Music Lovers did this to you—we would never have permitted it if we had known. But still, they did it, and the violinist now is plugged into you. To unplug you would be to kill him. But never mind, it's only for nine months. By then he will have recovered from his ailment and can safely be unplugged from you." Is it morally incumbent on you to accede to this situation? No doubt it would be very nice of you if you did, a great kindness. But do you *have* to accede to it? What if it were not nine months, but nine years? Or longer still? What if the director of the hospital says, "Tough luck, I agree, but you've now got to stay in bed, with the violinist plugged into you, for the rest of your life. Because remember this. All persons have a right to life, and violinists are persons. Granted you have a right to decide what happens in and to your body, but a person's right to life outweighs your right to decide what happens in and to your body. So you cannot ever be unplugged from him." I imagine you would regard this as outrageous, which suggests that something really is wrong with that plausible-sounding argument I mentioned a moment ago.

In this case, of course, you were kidnapped; you didn't volunteer for the operation that plugged the violinist into your kidneys. Can those who oppose abortion on the ground I mentioned make an exception for a pregnancy due to rape? Certainly. They can say that persons have a right to life only if they didn't come into existence because of rape; or they can say that all persons have a right to life, but that some have less of a right to life than others, in particular, that those who came into existence because of rape have less. But these statements have a rather unpleasant sound. Surely the question of whether you have a right to life at all, or how much of it you have, shouldn't turn on the question of whether or not you are the product of a rape. And in fact the people who oppose abortion on the ground I mentioned do not make this distinction, and hence do not make an exception in case of rape.

Nor do they make an exception for a case in which the mother has to spend the nine months of her pregnancy in bed. They would agree that would be a great pity, and hard on the mother; but all the same, all persons have a right to life, the fetus is a person, and so on. I suspect, in fact, that they would not make an exception for a case in which, miraculously enough, the pregnancy went on for nine years, or even the rest of the mother's life.

Some won't even make an exception for a case in which continuation of the pregnancy is likely to shorten the mother's life; they regard abortion as impermissible even to save the mother's life. Such cases are nowadays very rare, and many opponents of abortion do not accept this extreme view. All the same, it is a good place to begin: a number of points of interest come out in respect to it.

I

Let us call the view that abortion is impermissible even to save the mother's life "the extreme view." I want to suggest first that it does not issue from the argument I mentioned earlier without the addition of some fairly powerful premises. Suppose a woman has become pregnant and now learns that she has a cardiac condition such that she will die if she carries the baby to term. What may be done for her? The fetus, being a person, has a right to life, but as the mother is a person too, so has she a right to life. Presumably they have an equal right to life. How is it supposed to come out that an abortion may not be performed? If mother and child have an equal right to life, shouldn't we perhaps flip a coin? Or should we add to the mother's right to life her right to decide what happens in and to her body, which everybody seems to be ready to grant—the sum of her rights now outweighing the fetus's right to life?

The most familiar argument here is the following. We are told that performing the abortion would be directly killing[2] the child, whereas doing nothing would not be killing the mother, but only letting her die. Moreover, in killing the child, one would be killing an innocent person, for the child has committed no crime, and is not aiming at his mother's death. And then there are a variety of ways in which this might be continued. (1) But as directly killing an innocent person is always and absolutely impermissible, an abortion may not be performed. Or, (2) as directly killing an innocent person is murder, and murder is always and absolutely impermissible, an abortion may not be performed.[3] Or, (3) as one's duty to refrain from directly killing an innocent person is more stringent than one's duty to keep a person from dying, an abortion may not be performed. Or, (4) if one's only options are directly killing an innocent person or letting a person die, one must prefer letting the person die, and thus an abortion may not be performed.[4]

Some people seem to have thought that these are not further premises which must be added if the conclusion is to be reached, but that they follow from the very fact that an innocent person has a right to life.[5] But this seems to me to be a mistake, and perhaps the simplest way to show this is to bring out that while we must certainly grant that innocent persons have a right to life, the theses in (1) through (4) are all false. Take (2), for example. If directly killing an innocent person is murder, and thus is impermissible, then the mother's directly killing the innocent person inside her is murder, and thus is impermissible. But it cannot seriously be thought to be murder if the mother performs an abortion on herself to save her life. It cannot seriously be said that she *must* refrain, that she *must* sit passively by and wait for her death. Let us look again at the case of you and the violinist. There you are, in bed with the violinist, and the director of the hospital says to you, "It's all most distressing, and I deeply sympathize, but you see this is putting an additional strain on your kidneys, and you'll be dead within the month. But you *have* to stay where you are all the same. Because unplugging you would be directly killing an innocent violinist, and that's murder, and that's impermissible." If anything in the world is true, it is that you do not commit murder, you do not do what is impermissible, if you reach around to your back and unplug yourself from that violinist to save your life.

The main focus of attention in writings on abortion has been on what a third party may or may not do in answer to a request from a woman for an abortion. This is in a way understandable. Things being as they are, there isn't much a woman can safely do to abort herself. So the question asked is what a third party may do, and what the mother may do, if it is mentioned at all, is deduced, almost as an afterthought, from what it is concluded that third parties may do. But it seems to me that to treat the matter in this way is to refuse to grant to the mother that very status of person which is so firmly insisted on for the fetus. For we cannot simply read off what a person may do from what a third party may do. Suppose you find yourself trapped in a tiny house with a growing child. I mean a very tiny house, and a rapidly growing child—you are already up against the wall of the house and in a few minutes you'll be crushed to death. The child on the other hand won't be crushed to death; if nothing is done to stop him from growing he'll be hurt, but in the end he'll simply burst open the house and walk out a free man. Now I could well understand it if a bystander were to say, "There's nothing we can do for you. We cannot choose between your life and his, we cannot be the ones to decide who is to live, we cannot intervene." But it cannot be concluded that you too can do nothing, that you cannot attack it to save your life. However innocent the child may be, you do not have to wait passively while it crushes you to death. Perhaps a pregnant woman is vaguely felt to have the status of house, to which we don't allow the right of self-defense. But if the woman houses the child, it should be remembered that she is a person who houses it.

I should perhaps stop to say explicitly that I am not claiming that people have a right to do anything whatever to save their lives. I think, rather, that there are drastic limits to the right of self-defense. If someone threatens you with death unless you torture someone else to death, I think you have not the right, even to save your life, to do so. But the case under consideration here is very different. In our case there are only two people involved, one whose life is threatened, and one who threatens it. Both are innocent: the one who is threatened is not threatened because of any fault, the one who threatens does not threaten because of any fault. For this reason we may feel that we bystanders cannot intervene. But the person threatened can.

In sum, a woman surely can defend her life against the threat to it posed by the unborn child, even if doing so involves its death. And this shows not merely that the theses in (1) through (4) are false; it shows also that the extreme view of abortion is false, and so we need not canvass any other possible ways of arriving at it from the argument I mentioned at the outset.

II

The extreme view could of course be weakened to say that while abortion is permissible to save the mother's life, it may not be performed by a third party, but only by the mother herself. But this cannot be right either. For what we have to keep in mind is that the mother and the unborn child are not like two tenants in a small house which has, by an unfortunate mistake, been rented to both: the mother *owns* the house. The fact that she does adds to the offensiveness of deducing that the mother can do nothing from the supposition that third parties can do nothing. But it does more than this: it casts a bright light on the supposition that third parties can do nothing. Certainly it lets us see that a third party who says "I cannot choose between you" is fooling himself if he thinks this is impartiality. If Jones has found and fastened on a certain coat, which he needs to keep him from freezing, but which Smith also needs to keep him from freezing, then it is not impartiality that says "I cannot choose between you" when Smith owns the coat. Women have said again and again "This body is *my* body!" and they have reason to feel angry, reason to feel that it has been like shouting into the wind. Smith, after all, is hardly likely to bless us if we say to him, "Of course it's your coat, anybody would grant that it is. But no one may choose between you and Jones who is to have it."

We should really ask what it is that says "no one may choose" in the face of the fact that the body that houses the child is the mother's body. It may be simply a failure to appreciate this fact. But it may be something more interesting, namely the sense that one has a right to refuse to lay hands on people, even where it would be just and fair to do so, even where justice seems to require that somebody do so. Thus justice might call for somebody to get Smith's coat back from Jones, and yet you have a right to refuse to be the one to lay hands on Jones, a right to refuse to do physical violence to him. This, I think, must be granted. But then what should be said is not "no one may choose," but only "*I* cannot choose," and indeed not even this, but "*I* will not *act*," leaving it open that somebody else can or should, and in particular that anyone in a position of authority, with the job of securing people's rights, both can and should. So this is no difficulty. I have not been arguing that any given third party must accede to the mother's request that he perform an abortion to save her life, but only that he may.

I suppose that in some views of human life the mother's body is only on loan to her, the loan not being one which gives her any prior claim to it. One who held this view might well think it impartiality to say "I cannot choose." But I shall simply ignore this possibility. My own view is that if a human being has any just, prior claim to anything at all, he has a just, prior claim to his own body. And perhaps this needn't be argued for here anyway, since, as I mentioned, the arguments against abortion we are looking at do grant that the woman has a right to decide what happens in and to her body.

But although they do grant it, I have tried to show that they do not take seriously what is done in granting it. I suggest the same thing will reappear even more clearly when we turn away from cases in which the mother's life is at stake, and attend, as I propose we now do, to the vastly more common cases in which a woman wants an abortion for some less weighty reason than preserving her own life.

III

Where the mother's life is not at stake, the argument I mentioned at the outset seems to have a much stronger pull. "Everyone has a right to life, so the unborn person has a right to life." And isn't the child's right to life weightier than anything other than the mother's own right to life, which she might put forward as ground for an abortion?

This argument treats the right to life as if it were unproblematic. It is not, and this seems to me to be precisely the source of the mistake.

For we should now, at long last, ask what it comes to, to have a right to life. In some views having a right to life includes having a right to be given at least the bare minimum one needs for continued life. But suppose that what in fact *is* the bare minimum a man needs for continued life is something he has no right at all to be given? If I am sick unto death, and the only thing that will save my life is the touch of Henry Fonda's cool hand on my fevered brow, then all the same, I have no right to be given the touch of Henry Fonda's cool hand on my fevered brow. It would be frightfully nice of him to fly in from the West Coast to provide it. It would be less nice, though no doubt well meant, if my friends flew out to the West Coast and carried Henry Fonda back with them. But I have no right at all against anybody that he should do this for me. Or again, to return to the story I told earlier, the fact that for continued life that violinist needs the continued use of your kidneys does not establish that he has a right to be given the continued use of your kidneys. He certainly has no right against you that *you* should give him continued use of your kidneys. For nobody has any right to use your kidneys unless you give him such a right; and nobody has the right against you that you shall give him this right—if you do allow him to go on using your kidneys, this is a kindness on your part, and not something he can claim from you as his due. Nor has he any right against anybody else that *they* should give him continued use of your kidneys. Certainly he had no right against the Society of Music Lovers that they should plug him into you in the first place. And if you now start to unplug yourself, having learned that you will otherwise have to spend nine years in bed with him, there is nobody in the world who must try to prevent you, in order to see to it that he is given something he has a right to be given.

Some people are rather stricter about the right to life. In their view, it does not include the right to be given anything, but amounts to, and only to, the right not to be killed by anybody. But here a related difficulty arises. If everybody is to refrain from killing that violinist, then everybody must refrain from doing a great many different sorts of things. Everybody must refrain from slitting his throat, everybody must refrain from shooting him—and everybody must refrain from unplugging you from him. But does he have a right against everybody that they shall refrain from unplugging you from him? To refrain from doing this is to allow him to continue to use your kidneys. It could be argued that he has a right against us that *we* should allow him to continue to use your kidneys. That is, while he had no right against us that we should give him the use of your kidneys, it might be argued that he anyway has a right against us that we shall not now intervene and deprive him of the use of your kidneys. I shall come back to third-party interventions later. But certainly the violinist has no right against you that *you* shall allow him to continue to use your kidneys. As I said, if you do allow him to use them, it is a kindness on your part, and not something you owe him.

The difficulty I point to here is not peculiar to the right of life. It reappears in connection with all the other natural rights; and it is something which an adequate account of rights must deal with. For present purposes it is enough just to draw attention to it. But I would stress that I am not arguing that people do not have a right to life—quite to the contrary, it seems to me that the primary control we must place on the acceptability of an account of rights is that it should turn out in that account to be a truth that all persons have a right to life. I am arguing only that having a right to life does not guarantee having either a right to be given the use of or a right to be allowed continued use of another person's body—even if one needs it for life itself. So the right to life will not serve the opponents of abortion in the very simple and clear way in which they seem to have thought it would.

IV

There is another way to bring out the difficulty. In the most ordinary sort of case, to deprive someone of what he has a right to is to treat him unjustly. Suppose a boy and his small brother are jointly given a box of chocolates for Christmas. If the older boy takes the box and refuses to give his brother any of the chocolates, he is unjust to him, for the brother has been given a right to half of them. But suppose that, having learned that otherwise it means nine years in bed with that violinist, you unplug yourself from him. You surely are not being unjust to him, for you gave him no right to use your kidneys, and no one else can have given him any such right. But we have to notice that in unplugging yourself, you are killing him; and violinists, like everybody else, have a right to life, and thus in the view we were considering just now, the right not to be killed. So here you do what he supposedly has a right you shall not do, but you do not act unjustly to him in doing it.

The emendation which may be made at this point is this: the right to life consists not in the right not to be killed, but rather in the right not to be killed unjustly. This runs a risk of circularity, but never mind: it would enable us to square the fact that the violinist has a right to life with the fact that you do not act unjustly toward him in unplugging yourself, thereby killing him. For if you do not kill him unjustly, you do not violate his right to life, and so it is no wonder you do him no injustice.

But if this emendation is accepted, the gap in the argument against abortion stares us plainly in the face: it is by no means enough to show that the fetus is a person, and to remind us that all persons have a right to life—we need to be shown also that killing the fetus violates its right to life, i.e., that abortion is unjust killing. And is it?

I suppose we may take it as a datum that in a case of pregnancy due to rape the mother has not given the unborn person a right to the use of her body for food and shelter. Indeed, in what pregnancy could it be supposed that the mother has given the unborn person such a right? It is not as if there were unborn persons drifting about the world, to whom a woman who wants a child says "I invite you in."

But it might be argued that there are other ways one can have acquired a right to the use of another person's body than by having been invited to use it by that person. Suppose a woman voluntarily indulges in intercourse, knowing of the chance it will issue in pregnancy, and then she does become pregnant; is she not in part responsible for the presence, in fact the very existence, of the unborn person inside? No doubt she did not invite it in. But doesn't her partial responsibility for its being there itself give it a right to the use of her body?[6] If so, then her aborting it would be more like the boy's taking away the chocolates, and less like your unplugging yourself from the violinist— doing so would be depriving it of what it does have a right to, and thus would be doing it an injustice.

And then, too, it might be asked whether or not she can kill it even to save her own life: If she voluntarily called it into existence, how can she now kill it, even in self-defense?

The first thing to be said about this is that it is something new. Opponents of abortion have been so concerned to make out the independence of the fetus, in order to establish that it has a right to life, just as its mother does, that they have tended to overlook the possible support they might gain from making out that the fetus is *dependent* on the mother, in order to establish that she has a special kind of responsibility for it, a responsibility that gives it rights against her which are not possessed by any independent person—such as an ailing violinist who is a stranger to her.

On the other hand, this argument would give the unborn person a right to its mother's body only if her pregnancy resulted from a voluntary act, undertaken in full knowledge of the chance a pregnancy might result from it. It would leave out entirely the unborn person whose existence is due to rape. Pending the availability of some further argument, then, we would be left with the conclusion that unborn persons whose existence is due to rape have no right to the use of their mothers' bodies, and thus that aborting them is not depriving them of anything they have a right to and hence is not unjust killing.

And we should also notice that it is not at all plain that this argument really does go even as far as it purports to. For there are cases and cases, and the details make a difference. If the room is stuffy, and I therefore open a window to air it, and a burglar climbs in, it would be absurd to say, "Ah, now he can stay, she's given him a right to the use of her house—for she is partially responsible for his presence there, having voluntarily done what enabled him to get in, in full knowledge that there are such things as burglars, and that burglars burgle." It would be still more absurd to say this if I had had bars installed outside my windows, precisely to prevent burglars from getting in, and a burglar got in only because of a defect in the bars. It remains equally absurd if we imagine it is not a burglar who climbs in, but an innocent person who blunders or falls in. Again, suppose it were like this: people-seeds drift about in the air like pollen, and if you open your windows, one may drift in and take root in your carpets or upholstery. You don't want children, so you fix up your windows with fine mesh screens, the very best you can buy. As can happen, however, and on very, very rare occasions does happen, one of the screens was defective; and a seed drifts in and takes root. Does the person-plant who now develops have a right to the use of your house? Surely not—despite the fact that you voluntarily opened your windows, you knowingly kept carpets and upholstered furniture and you knew that screens were sometimes defective. Someone may argue that you are responsible for its rooting, that it does have a right to your house, because after all you *could* have lived out your life with bare floors and furniture, or with sealed windows and doors. But this won't do—for by the same token anyone can avoid a pregnancy due to rape by having a hysterectomy, or anyway by never leaving home without a (reliable!) army.

It seems to me that the argument we are looking at can establish at most that there are *some* cases in which the unborn person has a right to the use of its mother's body, and therefore *some* cases in which abortion is unjust killing. There is room for much discussion and argument as to precisely which, if any. But I think we should sidestep this issue and leave it open, for at any rate the argument certainly does not establish that all abortion is unjust killing.

V

There is room for yet another argument here, however. We surely must all grant that there may be cases in which it would be morally indecent to detach a person from your body at the cost of his life. Suppose you learn that what the violinist needs is not nine years of your life, but only one hour: all you need do to save his life is to spend one hour in that bed with him. Suppose also that letting him use your kidneys for that one hour would not affect your health in the slightest. Admittedly you were kidnapped. Admittedly you did not give anyone permission to plug him into you. Nevertheless it seems to me plain you *ought* to allow him to use your kidneys for that hour—it would be indecent to refuse.

Again, suppose pregnancy lasted only an hour, and constituted no threat to life or health. And suppose that a woman becomes pregnant as a result of rape. Admittedly she did not voluntarily do anything to bring about the existence of a child. Admittedly she did nothing at all which would give the unborn person a right to the use of her body. All the same it might well be said, as in the newly emended violinist story, that she *ought* to allow it to remain for that hour—that it would be indecent in her to refuse.

Now some people are inclined to use the term "right" in such a way that it follows from the fact that you ought to allow a person to use your body for the hour he needs, that he has a right to use your body for the hour he needs, even though he has not been given that right by any person or act. They may say that it follows also that if you refuse, you act unjustly toward him. This use of the term is perhaps so common that it cannot be called wrong; nevertheless it seems to me to be an unfortunate loosening of what we would do better to keep a tight rein on. Suppose that box of chocolates I mentioned earlier had not been given to both boys jointly, but was given only to the older boy. There he sits, stolidly eating his way through the box, his small brother watching enviously. Here we are likely to say "You ought not to be so mean. You ought to give your brother some of those chocolates." My own view is that it just does not follow from the truth of this that the brother has any right to any of the chocolates. If the boy refuses to give his brother any, he is greedy, stingy, callous—but not unjust. I suppose that the people I have in mind will say it does follow that the brother has a right to some of the chocolates, and thus that the boy does act unjustly if he refuses to give his brother any. But the effect of saying this is to obscure what we should keep distinct, namely the difference between the boy's refusal in this case and the boy's refusal in the earlier case, in which the box was given to both boys jointly, and in which the small brother thus had what was from any point of view clear title to half.

A further objection to so using the term "right" that from the fact that A ought to do a thing for B, it follows that B has a right against A that A do it for him, is that it is going to make the question of whether or not a man has a right to a thing turn on how easy it is to provide him with it; and this seems not merely unfortunate, but morally unacceptable. Take the case of Henry Fonda again. I said earlier that I had no right to the touch of his cool hand on my fevered brow, even though I needed it to save my life. I said it would be frightfully nice of him to fly in from the West Coast to provide me with it, but that I had no right against him that he should do so. But suppose he isn't on the West Coast. Suppose he has only to walk across the room, place a hand briefly on my brow—and lo, my life is saved. Then surely he ought to do it, it would be indecent to refuse. Is it to be said "Ah, well, it follows that in this case she has a right to the touch of his hand on her brow, and so it would be an injustice in him to refuse"? So that I have a right to it when it is easy for him to provide it, though no right when it's hard? It's rather a shocking idea that any-one's rights should fade away and disappear as it gets harder and harder to accord them to him.

So my own view is that even though you ought to let the violinist use your kidneys for the one hour he needs, we should not conclude that he has a right to do so—we should say that if you refuse, you are, like the boy who owns all the chocolates and will give none away, self-centered and callous, indecent in fact, but not unjust. And similarly, that even supposing a case in which a woman pregnant due to rape ought to allow the unborn person to use her body for the hour he needs, we should not conclude that he has a right to do so; we should conclude that she is self-centered callous, indecent, but not unjust, if she refuses.

The complaints are no less grave; they are just different. However, there is no need to insist on this point. If anyone does wish to deduce "he has a right" from "you ought," then all the same he must surely grant that there are cases in which it is not morally required of you that you allow that violinist to use your kidneys, and in which he does not have a right to use them, and in which you do not do him an injustice if you refuse. And so also for mother and unborn child. Except in such cases as the unborn person has a right to demand it—and we were leaving open the possibility that there may be such cases—nobody is morally *required* to make large sacrifices, of health, of all other interests and concerns, of all other duties and commitments, for nine years, or even for nine months, in order to keep another person alive.

VI

We have in fact to distinguish between two kinds of Samaritan: the Good Samaritan and what we might call the Minimally Decent Samaritan. The story of the Good Samaritan, you will remember, goes like this:

> A certain man went down from Jerusalem to Jericho, and fell among thieves, which stripped him of his raiment, and wounded him, and departed, leaving him half dead.
>
> And by chance there came down a certain priest that way; and when he saw him, he passed by on the other side.
>
> And likewise a Levite, when he was at the place, came and looked on him, and passed by on the other side.
>
> But a certain Samaritan, as he journeyed, came where he was; and when he saw him he had compassion on him.
>
> And went to him, and bound up his wounds, pouring in oil and wine, and set him on his own beast, and brought him to an inn, and took care of him.
>
> And on the morrow, when he departed, he took out two pence, and gave them to the host, and said unto him, "Take care of him; and whatsoever thou spendest more, when I come again, I will repay thee."   (Luke 10:30–35)

The Good Samaritan went out of his way, at some cost to himself, to help one in need of it. We are not told what the options were, that is, whether or not the priest and the Levite could have helped by doing less than the Good Samaritan did, but assuming they could have, then the fact they did nothing at all shows they were not even Minimally Decent Samaritans, not because they were not Samaritans, but because they were not even minimally decent.

These things are a matter of degree, of course, but there is a difference, and it comes out perhaps most clearly in the story of Kitty Genovese, who, as you will remember, was murdered while thirty-eight people watched or listened, and did nothing at all to help her. A Good Samaritan would have rushed out to give direct assistance against the murderer. Or perhaps we had better allow that it would have been a Splendid Samaritan who did this, on the ground that it would have involved a risk of death for himself. But the thirty-eight not only did not do this, they did not even trouble to pick up a phone to call the police. Minimally Decent Samaritanism would call for doing at least that, and their not having done it was monstrous.

After telling the story of the Good Samaritan, Jesus said "Go, and do thou likewise." Perhaps he meant that we are morally required to act as the Good Samaritan did. Perhaps he was urging people to do more than is morally required of them. At all events it seems plain that it was not morally required of any of the thirty-eight that he rush out to give direct assistance at the risk of his own life, and that it is not morally required of anyone that he give long stretches of his life—nine years or nine months—to sustaining the life of a person who has no special right (we were leaving open the possibility of this) to demand it.

Indeed, with one rather striking class of exceptions, no one in any country in the world is *legally* required to do anywhere near as much as this for anyone else. The class of exceptions is obvious. My main concern here is not the state of the law in respect to abortion, but it is worth drawing attention to the fact that in no state in this country is any man compelled by law to be even a Minimally Decent Samaritan to any person; there is no law under which charges could be brought against the thirty-eight who stood by while Kitty Genovese died. By contrast, in most states in this country women are compelled by law to be not merely Minimally Decent Samaritans, but Good Samaritans to unborn persons inside them. This doesn't by itself settle anything one way or the other, because it may well be argued that there should be laws in this country—as there are in many European countries—compelling at least Minimally Decent Samaritanism.[7] But it does show that there is a gross injustice in the existing state of the law. And it shows also that the groups currently working against liberalization of abortion laws, in fact working toward having it declared unconstitutional for a state to permit abortion, had better start working for the adoption of Good Samaritan laws generally, or earn the charge that they are acting in bad faith.

I should think, myself, that Minimally Decent Samaritan laws would be one thing, Good Samaritan laws quite another, and in fact highly improper. But we are not here concerned with the law. What we should ask is not whether anybody should be compelled by law to be a Good Samaritan, but whether we must accede to a situation in which somebody is being compelled—by nature, perhaps—to be a Good Samaritan. We have, in other words, to look now at third-party interventions. I have been arguing that no person is morally required to make large sacrifices to sustain the life of another who has no right to demand them, and this even where the sacrifices do not include life itself; we are not morally required to be Good Samaritans or anyway Very Good Samaritans to one another. But what if a man cannot extricate himself from such a situation? What if he appeals to us to extricate him? It seems to me plain that there are cases in which we can, cases in which a Good Samaritan would extricate him. There you are, you were kidnapped, and nine years in bed with that violinist lie ahead of you. You have your own life to lead. You are sorry, but you simply cannot see giving up so much of your life to the sustaining of his. You cannot extricate yourself, and ask us to do so. I should have thought that—in light of his having no right to the use of your body—it was obvious that we do not have to accede to your being forced to give up so much. We can do what you ask. There is no injustice to the violinist in our doing so.

VII

Following the lead of the opponents of abortion, I have throughout been speaking of the fetus merely as a person, and what I have been asking is whether or not the argument we began with, which proceeds only from the fetus's being a person, really does establish its conclusion. I have argued that it does not.

But of course there are arguments and arguments, and it may be said that I have simply fastened on the wrong one. It may be said that what is important is not merely the fact that the fetus is a person, but that it is a person for whom the woman has a special kind of responsibility issuing from the fact that she is its mother. And it might be argued that all my analogies are therefore irrelevant—for you do not have that special kind of responsibility for that violinist, Henry Fonda does not have that special kind of responsibility for me. And our attention might be drawn to the fact that men and women both *are* compelled by law to provide support for their children.

I have in effect dealt (briefly) with this argument in section 4 above; but a (still briefer) recapitulation now may be in order. Surely we do not have any such "special responsibility" for a person unless we have assumed it, explicitly or implicitly. If a set of parents do not try to prevent pregnancy, do not obtain an abortion, but rather take it home with them, then they have assumed responsibility for it, they have given it rights, and they cannot *now* withdraw support from it at the cost of its life because they now find it difficult to go on providing for it. But if they have taken all reasonable precautions against having a child, they do not simply by virtue of their biological relationship to the child who comes into existence have a special responsibility for it. They may wish to assume responsibility for it, or they may not wish to. And I am suggesting that if assuming responsibility for it would require large sacrifices, then they may refuse. A Good Samaritan would not refuse—or anyway, a Splendid Samaritan, if the sacrifices that had to be made were enormous. But then so would a Good Samaritan assume responsibility for that violinist; so would Henry Fonda, if he is a Good Samaritan, fly in from the West Coast and assume responsibility for me.

VIII

My argument will be found unsatisfactory on two counts by many of those who want to regard abortion as morally permissible. First, while I do argue that abortion is not impermissible, I do not argue that it is always permissible. There may well be cases in which carrying the child to term requires only Minimally Decent Samaritanism of the mother, and this is a standard we must not fall below. I am inclined to think it a merit of my account precisely that it does *not* give a general yes or a general no. It allows for and supports our sense that, for example, a sick and desperately frightened fourteen-year-old schoolgirl, pregnant due to rape, may of *course* choose abortion, and that any law which rules this out is an insane law. And it also allows for and supports our sense that in other cases resort to abortion is even positively indecent. It would be indecent in the woman to request an abortion, and indecent in a doctor to perform it, if she is in her seventh month, and wants the abortion just to avoid the nuisance of postponing a trip abroad. The very fact that the arguments I have been drawing attention to treat all cases of abortion, or even all cases of abortion in which the mother's life is not at stake, as morally on a par ought to have made them suspect at the outset.

Secondly, while I am arguing for the permissibility of abortion in some cases, I am not arguing for the right to secure the death of the unborn child. It is easy to confuse these two things in that up to a certain point in the life of the fetus it is not able to survive outside the mother's body; hence removing it from her body guarantees its death. But they are importantly different. I have argued that you are not morally required to spend nine months in bed, sustaining the life of that violinist; but to say this is by no means to say that if, when you unplug yourself, there is a miracle and he survives, you then have a right to turn round and slit his throat. You may detach yourself even if this costs him his life; you have no right to be guaranteed his death, by some other means, if unplugging yourself does not kill him. There are some people who will feel dissatisfied by this feature of my argument. A woman may be utterly devastated by the thought of a child, a bit of herself, put out for adoption and never seen or heard of again. She may therefore want not merely that the child be detached from her, but more, that it die. Some opponents of abortion are inclined to regard this as beneath contempt—thereby showing insensitivity to what is surely a powerful source of despair. All the same, I agree that the desire for the child's death is not one which anybody may gratify, should it turn out to be possible to detach the child alive.

At this place, however, it should be remembered that we have only been pretending throughout that the fetus is a human being from the moment of conception. A very early abortion is surely not the killing of a person, and so is not dealt with by anything I have said here.[8]

Notes

[1]Daniel Callahan, *Abortion: Law, Choice and Morality* (New York, 1970), p. 373. This book gives a fascinating survey of the available information on abortion. The Jewish tradition is surveyed in David M. Feldman, *Birth Control in Jewish Law* (New York, 1968), part 5, the Catholic tradition in John T. Noonan, Jr., "An Almost Absolute Value in History," in *The Morality of Abortion,* ed. John T. Noonan, Jr. (Cambridge, Mass., 1970).

[2]The term "direct" in the arguments I refer to is a technical one. Roughly, what is meant by "direct killing" is either killing as an end in itself, or killing as a means to some end, for example, the end of saving someone else's life. See note 6, below, for an example of its use.

[3]Cf. *Encyclical Letter of Pope Pius XI on Christian Marriage,* St. Paul Editions (Boston, n.d.), p. 32: "however much we may pity the mother whose health and even life is gravely imperiled in the performance of the duty allotted to her by nature, nevertheless what could ever be a sufficient reason for excusing in any way the direct murder of the innocent? This is precisely what we are dealing with here." Noonan (*The Morality of Abortion,* p. 43) reads this as follows: "What cause can ever avail to excuse in any way the direct killing of the innocent? For it is a question of that."

[4]The thesis in (4) is in an interesting way weaker than those in (1), (2), and (3): they rule out abortion even in cases in which both mother *and* child will die if the abortion is not performed. By contrast, one who held the view expressed in (4) could consistently say that one needn't prefer letting two persons die to killing one.

[5]Cf. the following passage from Pius XII, *Address to the Italian Catholic Society of Midwives:* "The baby in the maternal breast has the right to life immediately from God. —Hence there is no man, no human authority, no science, no medical, eugenic, social, economic or moral 'indication' which can establish or grant a valid juridical ground for a direct deliberate disposition of an innocent human life, that is a disposition which looks to its destruction either as an end or as a means to another end perhaps in itself not illicit. —The baby, still not born, is a man in the same degree and for the same reason as the mother" (quoted in Noonan, *The Morality of Abortion,* p. 45).

[6]The need for a discussion of this argument was brought home to me by members of the Society for Ethical and Legal Philosophy, to whom this paper was originally presented.

[7]For a discussion of the difficulties involved, and a survey of the European experience with such laws, see *The Good Samaritan and the Law,* ed. James M. Ratcliffe (New York, 1966).

[8]I am very much indebted to James Thomson for discussion, criticism, and many helpful suggestions.

Discussion Questions

1. Thomson assumes for the sake of argument that the fetus is a person, but argues in passing against this assumption. What are her arguments? How might Grisez reply to them?

2. Do you agree with Thomson's conclusion in the violinist case? Why or why not? Do you agree that the violinist case is analogous to abortion? Why or why not?

3. What are Thomson's arguments against the "extreme view"? Are they successful? Why or why not?

4. How does Thomson argue in cases where the mother's life is not at stake? Support or criticize her arguments.

5. What point is Thomson making in her discussion of the Good Samaritan and the Minimally Decent Samaritan? How does this relate to ethical theory in general? Does this strengthen or weaken her argument?

6. Is Thomson arguing in a utilitarian way? Why or why not? How might Grisez reply to Thomson?

On the Moral and Legal Status of Abortion

Mary Anne Warren

The question which we must answer in order to produce a satisfactory solution to the problem of the moral status of abortion is this: How are we to define the moral community, the set of beings with full and equal moral rights, such that we can decide whether a human fetus is a member of this community or not? What sort of entity, exactly, has the inalienable rights to life, liberty, and the pursuit of happiness? Jefferson attributed these rights to all *men,* and it may or may not be fair to suggest that he intended to attribute them *only* to men. Perhaps he ought to have attributed them to all human beings. If so, then we arrive, first, at [the] problem of defining what makes a being human, and, second, at the equally vital question, . . . What reason is there for identifying the moral community with the set of all human beings, in whatever way we have chosen to define that term?

1. On the Definition of "Human"

One reason why this vital second question is so frequently overlooked in the debate over the moral status of abortion is that the term "human" has two distinct, but not often

From *The Monist,* vol. 57, no. 1 (January 1973). Reprinted by permission of the publisher and the author. Postscript on infanticide reprinted by permission of the author.

distinguished, senses. This fact results in a slide of meaning, which serves to conceal the fallaciousness of the traditional argument that since (1) it is wrong to kill innocent human beings, and (2) fetuses are innocent human beings, then (3) it is wrong to kill fetuses. For if "human" is used in the same sense in both (1) and (2) then, whichever of the two senses is meant, one of these premises is question-begging. And if it is used in two different senses then of course the conclusion doesn't follow.

Thus, (1) is a self-evident moral truth,[1] and avoids begging the question about abortion, only if "human being" is used to mean something like "a full-fledged member of the moral community." (It may or may not also be meant to refer exclusively to members of the species *Homo sapiens*.) We may call this the *moral* sense of "human." It is not to be confused with what we will call the *genetic* sense, i.e., the sense in which *any* member of the species is a human being, and no member of any other species could be. If (1) is acceptable only if the moral sense is intended, (2) is non-question-begging only if what is intended is the genetic sense.

In "Deciding Who Is Human," Noonan argues for the classification of fetuses with human beings by pointing to the presence of the full genetic code, and the potential capacity for rational thought.[2] It is clear that what he needs to show, for his version of the traditional argument to be valid, is that fetuses are human in the moral sense, the sense in which it is analytically true that all human beings have full moral rights. But, in the absence of any argument showing that whatever is genetically human is also morally human, and he gives none, nothing more than genetic humanity can be demonstrated by the presence of the human genetic code. And, as we will see, the *potential* capacity for rational thought can at most show that an entity has the potential for *becoming* human in the moral sense.

2. Defining the Moral Community

Can it be established that genetic humanity is sufficient for moral humanity? I think that there are very good reasons for not defining the moral community in this way. I would like to suggest an alternative way of defining the moral community, which I will argue for only to the extent of explaining why it is, or should be, self-evident. The suggestion is simply that the moral community consists of all and only *people*, rather than all and only human beings;[3] and probably the best way of demonstrating its self-evidence is by considering the concept of personhood, to see what sorts of entity are and are not persons, and what the decision that a being is or is not a person implies about its moral rights.

What characteristics entitle an entity to be considered a person? This is obviously not the place to attempt a complete analysis of the concept of personhood, but we do not need such a fully adequate analysis just to determine whether and why a fetus is or isn't a person. All we need is a rough and approximate list of the most basic criteria of personhood, and some idea of which, or how many, of these an entity must satisfy in order to properly be considered a person.

In searching for such criteria, it is useful to look beyond the set of people with whom we are acquainted, and ask how we would decide whether a totally alien being was a person or not. (For we have no right to assume that genetic humanity is necessary for personhood.) Imagine a space traveler who lands on an unknown planet and encounters a race of beings utterly unlike any he has ever seen or heard of. If he wants to be sure of behaving morally toward these beings, he has to somehow decide whether they are people, and hence have full moral rights, or whether they are the sort of thing which he need not feel guilty about treating as, for example, a source of food.

How should he go about making this decision? If he has some anthropological background, he might look for such things as religion, art, and the manufacturing of tools, weapons, or shelters, since these factors have been used to distinguish our human from our prehuman ancestors, in what seems to be closer to the moral than the genetic sense of "human." And no doubt he would be right to consider the presence of such factors as good evidence that the alien beings were people, and morally human. It would, however, be overly anthropocentric of him to take the absence of these things as adequate evidence that they were not, since we can imagine people who have progressed beyond, or evolved without ever developing, these cultural characteristics.

I suggest that the traits which are most central to the concept of personhood, or humanity in the moral sense, are, very roughly, the following:

1. consciousness (of objects and events external and/or internal to the being), and in particular the capacity to feel pain;

2. reasoning (the *developed* capacity to solve new and relatively complex problems);

3. self-motivated activity (activity which is relatively independent of either genetic or direct external control);

4. the capacity to communicate, by whatever means, messages of an indefinite variety of types, that is, not just with an indefinite number of possible contents, but on indefinitely many possible topics;

5. the presence of self-concepts, and self-awareness, either individual or racial, or both.

Admittedly, there are apt to be a great many problems involved in formulating precise definitions of these criteria, let alone in developing universally valid behavioral criteria for deciding when they apply. But I will assume that both we and our explorer know approximately what (1)–(5) mean, and that he is also able to determine whether or not they apply. How, then, should he use his findings to decide whether or not the alien beings are people? We needn't suppose that an entity must have *all* of these attributes to be properly considered a person; (1) and (2) alone may well be sufficient for personhood, and quite probably (1)–(3) are sufficient. Neither do we need to insist that any one of these criteria is *necessary* for personhood, although once again (1) and (2) look like fairly good candidates for necessary conditions, as does (3), if "activity" is construed so as to include the activity of reasoning.

All we need to claim, to demonstrate that a fetus is not a person, is that any being which satisfies *none* of (1)–(5) is certainly not a person. I consider this claim to be so obvious that I think anyone who denied it, and claimed that a being which satisfied none of (1)–(5) was a person all the same, would thereby demonstrate that he had no notion at all of what a person is—perhaps because he had confused the concept of a person with that of genetic humanity. If the opponents of abortion were to deny the appropriateness of these five criteria, I do not know what further arguments would convince them. We would probably have to admit that our conceptual schemes were indeed irreconcilably different, and that our dispute could not be settled objectively.

I do not expect this to happen, however, since I think that the concept of a person is one which is very nearly universal (to people), and that it is common to both proabortionists and antiabortionists, even though neither group has fully realized the relevance of this concept to the resolution of their dispute. Furthermore, I think that on reflection even the antiabortionists ought to agree not only that (1)–(5) are central to the concept of personhood, but also that it is a part of this concept that all and only people have full moral rights. The concept of a person is in part a moral concept; once we have admitted that *x* is a person we have recognized, even if we have not agreed to respect, *x*'s right to be treated as a member of the moral community. It is true that the claim that *x* is a *human being* is more commonly voiced as part of an appeal to treat *x* decently than is the claim that *x* is a person, but this is either because "human being" is here used in the sense which implies personhood, or because the genetic and moral senses of "human" have been confused.

Now if (1)–(5) are indeed the primary criteria of personhood, then it is clear that genetic humanity is neither necessary nor sufficient for establishing that an entity is a person. Some human beings are not people, and there may well be people who are not human beings. A man or woman whose consciousness has been permanently obliterated but who remains alive is a human being which is no longer a person; defective human beings, with no appreciable mental capacity, are not and presumably never will be people; and a fetus is a human being which is not yet a person, and which therefore cannot coherently be said to have full moral rights. Citizens of the next century should be prepared to recognize highly advanced, self-aware robots or computers, should such be developed, and intelligent inhabitants of other worlds, should such be found, as people in the fullest sense, and to respect their moral rights. But to ascribe full moral rights to an entity which is not a person is as absurd as to ascribe moral obligations and responsibilities to such an entity.

3. Fetal Development and the Right to Life

Two problems arise in the application of these suggestions for the definition of the moral community to the determination of the precise moral status of a human fetus. Given that the paradigm example of a person is a normal adult human being, then (1) How like this paradigm, in particular how far advanced since conception, does a human being need to be before it begins to have a right to life by virtue, not of being fully a person as of yet, but of being *like* a person? and (2) To what extent, if any, does the fact that a fetus has the *potential* for becoming a person endow it with some of the same rights? Each of these questions requires some comment.

In answering the first question, we need not attempt a detailed consideration of the moral rights of organisms which are not developed enough, aware enough, intelligent enough, etc., to be considered people, but which resemble people in some respects. It does seem reasonable to suggest that the more like a person, in the relevant respects, a being is, the stronger is the case for regarding it as having a right to life, and indeed the stronger its right to life is. Thus we ought to take seriously the suggestion that, insofar as "the human individual develops biologically in a continuous fashion . . . the rights of a human person might develop in the same way."[4] But we must keep in mind that the attributes which are relevant in determining whether or not an entity is enough like a person to be regarded as having some of the same moral rights are no different from those which are relevant to determining whether or not it is fully a person—i.e., are no different from (1)–(5)—and that being genetically human, or having recognizably human facial and other physical features, or detectable brain activity, or the capacity to survive outside the uterus, are simply not among these relevant attributes.

Thus it is clear that even though a seven- or eight-month fetus has features which make it apt to arouse in us almost the same powerful protective instinct as is commonly aroused by a small infant, nevertheless it is not significantly more personlike than is a very small embryo. It is *somewhat* more personlike; it can apparently feel and respond to pain, and it may even have a rudimentary form of consciousness, insofar as its brain is quite active. Nevertheless, it seems safe to say that it is not fully conscious, in the way that an infant of a few months is, and that it cannot reason, or communicate messages of indefinitely many sorts, does not engage in self-motivated activity, and has no self-awareness. Thus, in the *relevant* respects, a fetus, even a fully developed one, is considerably less personlike than is the average mature mammal, indeed the average fish. And I think that a rational person must conclude that if the right to life of a fetus is to be based upon its resemblance to a person, then it cannot be said to have any more right to life than, let us say, a newborn guppy (which also seems to be capable of feeling pain), and that a right of that magnitude could never override a woman's right to obtain an abortion, at any stage of her pregnancy.

There may, of course, be other arguments in favor of placing legal limits upon the stage of pregnancy in which an abortion may be performed. Given the relative safety of the new techniques of artificially inducing labor during the third trimester, the danger to the woman's life or health is no longer such an argument. Neither is the fact that people tend to respond to the thought of abortion in the later stages of pregnancy with emotional repulsion, since mere emotional responses cannot take the place of moral reasoning in determining what ought to be permitted. Nor, finally, is the frequently heard argument that legalizing abortion, especially late in the pregnancy, may erode the level of respect for human life, leading, perhaps, to an increase in unjustified euthanasia and other crimes. For this threat, if it is a threat, can be better met by educating people to the kinds of moral distinctions which we are making here than by limiting access to abortion (which limitation may, in its disregard for the rights of women, be just as damaging to the level of respect for human rights).

Thus, since the fact that even a fully developed fetus is not personlike enough to have any significant right to life on the basis of its personlikeness shows that no legal restrictions upon the stage of pregnancy in which an abortion may be performed can be justified on the grounds that we should protect the rights of the older fetus, and since there is no other apparent justification for such restrictions, we may conclude that they are entirely unjustified. Whether or not it would be *indecent* (whatever that means) for a woman in her seventh month to obtain an abortion just to avoid having to postpone a trip to Europe, it would not, in itself, be *immoral,* and therefore it ought to be permitted.

4. Potential Personhood and the Right to Life

We have seen that a fetus does not resemble a person in any way which can support the claim that it has even some of the same rights. But what about its *potential,* the fact that if nurtured and allowed to develop naturally it will very probably become a person? Doesn't that alone give it at least some right to life? It is hard to deny that the fact that an entity is a potential person is a strong prima facie reason for not destroying it; but we need not conclude from this that a potential person has a right to life, by virtue of that potential. It may be that our feeling that it is better, other things being equal, not to destroy a potential person is better explained by the fact that potential people are still (felt to be) an invaluable resource, not to be lightly squandered. Surely, if every speck of dust were a potential person, we would be much less apt to conclude that every potential person has a right to become actual.

Still, we do not need to insist that a potential person has no right to life whatever. There may well be something immoral, and not just imprudent, about wantonly destroying potential people, when doing so isn't necessary to protect anyone's rights. But even if a potential person does have some prima facie right to life, such a right could not possibly outweigh the right of a woman to obtain an abortion, since the rights of any actual person invariably outweigh those of any potential person, whenever the two conflict. Since this may not be immediately obvious in the case of a human fetus, let us look at another case.

Suppose that our space explorer falls into the hands of an alien culture, whose scientists decide to create a few hundred thousand or more human beings, by breaking his body into its component cells, and using these to create fully developed human beings, with, of course, his genetic code. We may imagine that each of these newly created men will have all of the original man's abilities, skills, knowledge, and so on, and also have an individual self-concept, in short that each of them will be a bona fide (though hardly unique) person. Imagine that the whole project will take only seconds, and that its chances of success are extremely high, and that our explorer knows all of this, and also knows that these people will be treated fairly. I maintain that in such a situation he would have every right to escape if he could, and thus to deprive all of these potential people of their potential lives; for his right to life outweighs all of theirs together, in spite of the fact that they are all genetically human, all innocent, and all have a very high probability of becoming people very soon, if only he refrains from acting.

Indeed, I think he would have a right to escape even if it were not his life which the alien scientists planned to take, but only a year of his freedom, or, indeed, only a day. Nor would he be obligated to stay if he had gotten captured (thus bringing all these people-potentials into existence) because of his own carelessness, or even if he had done so deliberately, knowing the consequences. Regardless of how he got captured, he is not morally obligated to remain in captivity for *any* period of time for the sake of permitting any number of potential people to come into actuality, so great is the margin by which one actual person's right to liberty outweighs whatever right to life even a hundred thousand potential people have. And it seems reasonable to conclude that the rights of a woman will outweigh by a similar margin whatever right to life a fetus may have by virtue of its potential personhood.

Thus, neither a fetus's resemblance to a person, nor its potential for becoming a person provides any basis whatever for the claim that it has any significant right to life. Consequently, a woman's right to protect her health, happiness, freedom, and even her life,[5] by terminating an unwanted pregnancy, will always override whatever right to life it may be appropriate to ascribe to a fetus, even a fully developed one. And thus, in the absence of any overwhelming social need for every possible child, the laws which restrict the right to obtain an abortion, or limit the period of pregnancy during which an abortion may be performed, are a wholly unjustified violation of a woman's most basic moral and constitutional rights.[6]

Postscript on Infanticide

Since the publication of this article, many people have written to point out that my argument appears to justify not only abortion, but infanticide as well. For a newborn infant is not significantly more personlike than an advanced fetus, and consequently it would seem that if the destruction of the latter is permissible so too must be that of the former. Inasmuch as most people, regardless of how they feel about the morality of abortion, consider infanticide a form of murder, this might appear to represent a serious flaw in my argument.

Now, if I am right in holding that it is only people who have a full-fledged right to life, and who can be murdered, and if the criteria of personhood are as I have described them, then it obviously follows that killing a new-born infant isn't murder. It does *not* follow, however, that infanticide is permissible, for two reasons. In the first place, it would be wrong, at least in this country and in this period of history, and other things being equal, to kill a new-born infant, because even if its parents do not want it and would not suffer from its destruction, there are other people who would like to have it, and would, in all probability, be deprived of a great deal of pleasure by its destruction. Thus, infanticide is wrong for reasons analogous to those which make it wrong to wantonly destroy natural resources, or great works of art.

Secondly, most people, at least in this country, value infants and would much prefer that they be preserved, even if foster parents are not immediately available. Most of us would rather be taxed to support orphanages than allow unwanted infants to be destroyed. So long as there are people who want an infant preserved, and who are willing and able to provide the means of caring for it, under reasonably humane conditions, it is *ceteris paribus,* wrong to destroy it.

But, it might be replied, if this argument shows that infanticide is wrong, at least at this time and in this country, doesn't it also show that abortion is wrong? After all, many people value fetuses, are disturbed by their destruction, and would much prefer that they be preserved, even at some cost to themselves. Furthermore, as a potential source of pleasure to some foster family, a fetus is just as valuable as an infant. There is, however, a crucial difference between the two cases: so long as the fetus is unborn, its preservation, contrary to the wishes of the pregnant woman, violates her rights to freedom, happiness, and self-determination. Her rights override the rights of those who would like the fetus preserved, just as if someone's life or limb is threatened by a wild animal, his right to protect himself by destroying the animal overrides the rights of those who would prefer that the animal not be harmed.

The minute the infant is born, however, its preservation no longer violates any of its mother's rights, even if she wants it destroyed, because she is free to put it up for adoption. Consequently, while the moment of birth does not mark any sharp discontinuity in the degree to which an infant possesses the right to life, it does mark the end of its mother's right to determine its fate. Indeed, if abortion could be performed without killing the fetus, she would never possess the right to have the fetus destroyed, for the same reasons that she has no right to have an infant destroyed.

On the other hand, it follows from my argument that when an unwanted or defective infant is born into a society which cannot afford and/or is not willing to care for it, then its destruction is permissible. This conclusion will, no doubt, strike many people as heartless and immoral; but remember that the very existence of people who feel this way, and who are willing and able to provide care for unwanted infants, is reason enough to conclude that they should be preserved.

Notes

[1]Of course, the principle that it is (always) wrong to kill innocent human beings is in need of many other modifications, e.g., that it may be permissible to do so to save a greater number of other innocent human beings, but we may safely ignore these complications here.

[2]John Noonan, "Deciding Who is Human," *Natural Law Forum,* 13 (1968), 135.

[3]From here on, we will use "human" to mean genetically human, since the moral sense seems closely connected to, and perhaps derived from, the assumption that genetic humanity is sufficient for membership in the moral community.

[4]Thomas L. Hayes, "A Biological View," *Commonweal,* 85 (March 17, 1967), 677–78; quoted by Daniel Callahan, in *Abortion: Law, Choice and Morality* (London: Macmillan & Co., 1970).

[5]That is, insofar as the death rate, for the woman, is higher for childbirth than for early abortion.

[6]My thanks to the following people, who were kind enough to read and criticize an earlier version of this paper: Herbert Gold, Gene Glass, Anne Lauterbach, Judith Thomson, Mary Mothersill, and Timothy Binkley.

Discussion Questions

1. How reasonable are Warren's criteria for personhood? Try to find counterexamples to Warren's concept of a person, such as something not a person that meets the criteria or a person who does not meet the criteria.

2. Do some of Warren's criteria beg the question (e.g., "the *developed* capacity to solve . . . relatively complex problems")? Would a set of criteria like Thomson's but including the idea of *potential* possession of each capability be satisfactory? Why or why not?

3. Does it follow from Warren's criteria that I am not a person when I am in a deep and dreamless sleep? Why or why not?

4. Both sides in the abortion debate sometimes use "slippery slope" arguments. Are some of Warren's arguments on fetal development and the right to life slippery slope arguments? Why or why not?

5. Argue for or against Warren's or Thomson's position on the right to life of potential persons.

6. Does Warren adequately answer the objection that her position would allow infanticide? Why or why not?

7. Apply Thomson's criteria of personhood to cases of euthanasia. What conclusions would you reach? What does this show about Warren's argument?

Abortion and the Concept of a Person

Jane English

The abortion debate rages on. Yet the two most popular positions seem to be clearly mistaken. Conservatives maintain that a human life begins at conception and that therefore abortion must be wrong because it is murder. But not all killings of humans are murders. Most notably, self defense may justify even the killing of an innocent person.

Liberals, on the other hand, are just as mistaken in their argument that since a fetus does not become a person until birth, a woman may do whatever she pleases in and to her own body. First, you cannot do as you please with your own body if it affects other people adversely.[1] Second, if a fetus is not a person, that does not imply that you can do to it anything you wish. Animals, for example, are not persons, yet to kill or torture them for no reason at all is wrong.

At the center of the storm has been the issue of just when it is between ovulation and adulthood that a person appears on the scene. Conservatives draw the line at conception, liberals at birth. In this paper I first examine our concept of a person and conclude that no single criterion can capture the concept of a person and no sharp line can be drawn. Next I argue that if a fetus is a person, abortion is still justifiable in many cases; and if a fetus is not a person, killing it is still wrong in many cases. To a large extent, these two solutions are in agreement. I conclude that our concept of a person cannot and need not bear the weight that the abortion controversy has thrust upon it.

I

The several factions in the abortion argument have drawn battle lines around various proposed criteria for determining what is and what is not a person. For example, Mary Anne Warren[2] lists five features (capacities for reasoning, self-awareness, complex communication, etc.) as her criteria for personhood and argues for the permissibility of abortion because a fetus falls outside this concept. Baruch Brody[3] uses brain waves. Michael Tooley[4] picks having-a-concept-of-self as his criterion and concludes that infanticide and abortion are justifiable, while the killing of adult animals is not. On the other side, Paul Ramsey[5] claims a certain gene structure is the defining characteristic. John Noonan[6] prefers conceived-of-humans and presents counterexamples to various other candidate criteria. For instance, he argues against viability as the criterion because the newborn and infirm would then be non-persons, since they cannot live without the aid of others. He rejects any criterion that calls upon the sorts of sentiments a being can evoke in adults on the grounds that this would allow us to exclude other races as non-persons if we could just view them sufficiently unsentimentally.

These approaches are typical: foes of abortion propose sufficient conditions for personhood which fetuses satisfy, while friends of abortion counter with necessary

From *Canadian Journal of Philosophy*, vol. 5, no. 2 (October 1975), pp. 233–243. Reprinted by permission.

conditions for personhood which fetuses lack. But these both presuppose that the concept of a person can be captured in a strait jacket of necessary and/or sufficient conditions.[7] Rather, "person" is a cluster of features, of which rationality, having a self concept and being conceived of humans are only part.

What is typical of persons? Within our concept of a person we include, first, certain biological factors: descended from humans, having a certain genetic makeup, having a head, hands, arms, eyes, capable of locomotion, breathing, eating, sleeping. There are psychological factors: sentience, perception, having a concept of self and of one's own interests and desires, the ability to use tools, the ability to use language or symbol systems, the ability to joke, to be angry, to doubt. There are rationality factors: the ability to reason and draw conclusions, the ability to generalize and to learn from past experience, the ability to sacrifice present interests for greater gains in the future. There are social factors: the ability to work in groups and respond to peer pressures, the ability to recognize and consider as valuable the interests of others, seeing oneself as one among "other minds," the ability to sympathize, encourage, love, the ability to evoke from others the responses of sympathy, encouragement, love, the ability to work with others for mutual advantage. Then there are legal factors: being subject to the law and protected by it, having the ability to sue and enter contracts, being counted in the census, having a name and citizenship, the ability to own property, inherit, and so forth.

Now the point is not that this list is incomplete, or that you can find counterinstances to each of its points. People typically exhibit rationality, for instance, but someone who was irrational would not thereby fail to qualify as a person. On the other hand, something could exhibit the majority of these features and still fail to be a person, as an advanced robot might. There is no single core of necessary and sufficient features which we can draw upon with the assurance that they constitute what really makes a person; there are only features that are more or less typical.

This is not to say that no necessary or sufficient conditions can be given. Being alive is a necessary condition for being a person, and being a U.S. Senator is sufficient. But rather than falling inside a sufficient condition or outside a necessary one, a fetus lies in the penumbra region where our concept of a person is not so simple. For this reason I think a conclusive answer to the question whether a fetus is a person is unattainable.

Here we might note a family of simple fallacies that proceed by stating a necessary condition for personhood and showing that a fetus has that characteristic. This is a form of the fallacy of affirming the consequent. For example, some have mistakenly reasoned from the premise that a fetus is human (after all, it is a human fetus rather than, say, a canine fetus), to the conclusion that it is *a* human. Adding an equivocation on "being," we get the fallacious argument that since a fetus is something both living and human, it is a human being.

Nonetheless, it does seem clear that a fetus has very few of the above family of characteristics, whereas a newborn baby exhibits a much larger proportion of them—and a two-year-old has even more. Note that one traditional anti-abortion argument has centered on pointing out the many ways in which a fetus resembles a baby. They emphasize its development ("It already has ten fingers . . . ") without mentioning its dissimilarities to adults (it still has gills and a tail). They also try to evoke the sort of sympathy on our part that we only feel toward other persons ("Never to laugh . . . or feel the sunshine?"). This all seems to be a relevant way to argue, since its purpose is to persuade us that a fetus satisfies so many of the important features on the list that it ought to be treated as a person. Also note that a fetus near the time of birth satisfies many more of these factors than a fetus in the early months of development. This could provide reason for making distinctions among the different stages of pregnancy, as the U.S. Supreme Court has done.[8]

Historically, the time at which a person has been said to come into existence has varied widely. Muslims date personhood from fourteen days after conception. Some medievals followed Aristotle in placing ensoulment at forty days after conception for a male fetus and eighty days for a female fetus.[9] In European common law since the Seventeenth Century, abortion was considered the killing of a person only after quickening, the time when a pregnant woman first feels the fetus move on its own. Nor is this variety of opinions surprising. Biologically, a human being develops gradually. We shouldn't expect there to be any specific time or sharp dividing point when a person appears on the scene.

For these reasons I believe our concept of a person is not sharp or decisive enough to bear the weight of a solution to the abortion controversy. To use it to solve that problem is to clarify *obscurum per obscurius* [the obscure by the obscure].

II

Next let us consider what follows if a fetus is a person after all. Judith Jarvis Thomson's landmark article, "A Defense of Abortion"[10] [reprinted earlier in this chapter] correctly points out that some additional argumentation is needed at this point in the conservative argument to bridge the gap between the premise that a fetus is an innocent person and the conclusion that killing it is always wrong. To arrive at this conclusion, we would need the additional premise that killing an innocent person is always wrong. But killing an innocent person is sometimes permissible, most notably in self defense. Some examples may help draw out our intuitions or ordinary judgments about self defense.

Suppose a mad scientist, for instance, hypnotized innocent people to jump out of the bushes and attack innocent passers-by with knives. If you are so attacked, we agree you have a right to kill the attacker in self defense, if killing him is the only way to protect your life or to save yourself from serious injury. It does not seem to matter here that the attacker is not malicious but himself an innocent pawn, for your killing of him is not done in a spirit of retribution but only in self defense.

How severe an injury may you inflict in self defense? In part this depends upon the severity of the injury to be avoided: you may not shoot someone merely to avoid having your clothes torn. This might lead one to the mistaken conclusion that the defense may only equal the threatened injury in severity; that to avoid death you may kill, but to avoid a black eye you may only inflict a black eye or the equivalent. Rather, our laws and customs seem to say that you may create an injury somewhat, but not enormously, greater than the injury to be avoided. To fend off an attack whose outcome would be as serious as rape, a severe beating or the loss of a finger, you may shoot; to avoid having your clothes torn, you may blacken an eye.

Aside from this, the injury you may inflict should only be the minimum necessary to deter or incapacitate the attacker. Even if you know he intends to kill you, you are not justified in shooting him if you could equally well save yourself by the simple expedient of running away. Self defense is for the purpose of avoiding harms rather than equalizing harms.

Some cases of pregnancy present a parallel situation. Though the fetus is itself innocent, it may pose a threat to the pregnant woman's well-being, life prospects or health, mental or physical. If the pregnancy presents a slight threat to her interests, it seems self defense cannot justify abortion. But if the threat is on a par with a serious beating or the loss of a finger, she may kill the fetus that poses such a threat, even if it is an innocent person. If a lesser harm to the fetus could have the same defensive effect, killing it would not be justified. It is unfortunate that the only way to free the woman from the pregnancy entails the death of the fetus (except in very late stages of pregnancy). Thus a self defense model supports Thomson's point that the woman has a right only to be freed from the fetus, not a right to demand its death.[11]

The self defense model is most helpful when we take the pregnant woman's point of view. In the pre-Thomson literature, abortion is often framed as a question for a third party: do you, a doctor, have a right to choose between the life of the woman and that of the fetus? Some have claimed that if you were a passer-by who witnessed a struggle between the innocent hypnotized attacker and his equally innocent victim, you would have no reason to kill either in defense of the other. They have concluded that the self defense model implies that a woman may attempt to abort herself, but that a doctor should not assist her. I think the position of the third party is somewhat more complex. We do feel some inclination to intervene on behalf of the victim rather than the attacker, other things equal. But if both parties are innocent, other factors come into consideration. You would rush to the aid of your husband whether he was attacker or attackee. If a hypnotized famous violinist were attacking a skid row bum, we would try to save the individual who is of more value to society. These considerations would tend to support abortion in some cases.

But suppose you are a frail senior citizen who wishes to avoid being knifed by one of these innocent hypnotics, so you have hired a bodyguard to accompany you. If you are attacked, it is clear we believe that the bodyguard, acting as your agent, has a right to kill the attacker to save you from a serious beating. Your rights of self defense are transferred to your agent. I suggest that we should similarly view the doctor as the pregnant woman's agent in carrying out a defense she is physically incapable of accomplishing herself.

Thanks to modern technology, the cases are rare in which pregnancy poses as clear a threat to a woman's bodily health as an attacker brandishing a switchblade. How does self defense fare when more subtle, complex and long-range harms are involved?

To consider a somewhat fanciful example, suppose you are a highly trained surgeon when you are kidnapped by the hypnotic attacker. He says he does not intend to harm you but to take you back to the mad scientist who, it turns out, plans to hypnotize you to have a permanent mental block against all your knowledge of medicine. This would automatically destroy your career which would in turn have a serious adverse impact on your family, your personal relationships and your happiness. It seems to me that if the only way you can avoid this outcome is to shoot the innocent attacker, you are justified in so doing. You are defending yourself from a drastic injury to your life prospects. I think it is no exaggeration to claim that unwanted pregnancies (most obviously among teenagers) often have such adverse life-long consequences as the surgeon's loss of livelihood.

Several parallels arise between various views on abortion and the self defense model. Let's suppose further that these hypnotized attackers only operate at night, so that it is well known that they can be avoided completely by the considerable inconvenience of never leaving your house after dark. One view is that since you could stay home at night, therefore if you go out and are selected by one of these hypnotized people, you have no right to defend yourself. This parallels the view that abstinence is the only acceptable way to avoid pregnancy. Others might hold that you ought to take along some defense such as Mace which will deter the hypnotized person without killing him, but that if this defense fails, you are obliged to submit to the resulting injury, no matter how severe it is. This parallels the view that contraception is all right but abortion is always wrong, even in cases of contraceptive failure.

A third view is that you may kill the hypnotized person only if he will actually kill you, but not if he will only injure you. This is like the position that abortion is permissible only if it is required to save a woman's life. Finally we have the view that it is all right to kill the attacker, even if only to avoid a very slight inconvenience to yourself and even if you knowingly walked down the very street where all these incidents have been taking place without taking along any Mace or protective escort. If we assume that a fetus is a person, this is the analogue of the view that abortion is always justifiable, "on demand."

The self defense model allows us to see an important difference that exists between abortion and infanticide, even if a fetus is a person from conception. Many have argued that the only way to justify abortion without justifying infanticide would be to find some characteristic of personhood that is acquired at birth. Michael Tooley, for one, claims infanticide is justifiable because the really significant characteristics of person are acquired some time after birth. But all such approaches look to characteristics of the developing human and ignore the relation between the fetus and the woman. What if, after birth, the presence of an infant or the need to support it posed a grave threat to the woman's sanity or life prospects? She could escape this threat by the simple expedient of running away. So a solution that does not entail the death of the infant is available. Before birth, such solutions are not available because of the biological dependence of the fetus on the woman. Birth is the crucial point not because of any characteristics the fetus gains, but because after birth the woman can defend herself by a means less drastic than killing the infant. Hence self defense can be used to justify abortion without necessarily thereby justifying infanticide.

III

On the other hand, supposing a fetus is not after all a person, would abortion always be morally permissible? Some opponents of abortion seem worried that if a fetus is not a full-fledged person, then we are justified in treating it in any way at all. However, this does not follow. Non-persons do get some consideration in our moral code, though of course they do not have the same rights as persons have (and in general they do not have moral responsibilities), and though their interests may be overridden by the interests of persons. Still, we cannot just treat them in any way at all.

Treatment of animals is a case in point. It is wrong to torture dogs for fun or to kill wild birds for no reason at all. It is wrong Period, even though dogs and birds do not have the same rights persons do. However, few people think it is wrong to use dogs as experimental animals, causing them considerable suffering in some cases, provided that the resulting research will probably bring discoveries of great benefit to people. And most of us think it all right to kill birds for food or to protect our crops. People's rights are different from the consideration we give to animals, then, for it is wrong to experiment on people, even if others might later benefit a great deal as a result of their suffering. You might volunteer to be a subject, but this would be supererogatory; you certainly have a right to refuse to be a medical guinea pig.

But how do we decide what you may or may not do to non-persons? This is a difficult problem, one for which I believe no adequate account exists. You do not want to say, for instance, that torturing dogs is all right whenever the sum of its effects on people is good—when it doesn't warp the sensibilities of the torturer so much that he mistreats people. If that were the case, it would be all right to torture dogs if you did it in private, or if the torturer lived on a desert island or died soon afterward, so that his actions had no effect on people. This is an inadequate account, because whatever moral consideration animals get, it has to be indefeasible, too. It will have to be a general proscription of certain actions, not merely a weighing of the impact on people on a case-by-case basis.

Rather, we need to distinguish two levels on which consequences of actions can be taken into account in moral reasoning. The traditional objections to Utilitarianism focus on the fact that it operates solely on the first level, taking all the consequences into account in particular cases only. Thus Utilitarianism is open to "desert island" and "lifeboat" counterexamples because these cases are rigged to make the consequences of actions severely limited.

Rawls' theory could be described as a teleological sort of theory, but with teleology operating on a higher level.[12] In choosing the principles to regulate society from the original position, his hypothetical choosers make their decision on the basis of the total consequences of various systems. Furthermore, they are constrained to choose a general set of rules which people can readily learn and apply. An ethical theory must operate by generating a set of sympathies and attitudes toward others which reinforces the functioning of that set of moral principles. Our prohibition against killing people operates by means of certain moral sentiments including sympathy, compassion and guilt. But if these attitudes are to form a coherent set, they carry us further: we tend to perform supererogatory actions, and we tend to feel similar compassion toward person-like non-persons.

It is crucial that psychological facts play a role here. Our psychological constitution makes it the case that for our ethical theory to work, it must prohibit certain treatment of non-persons which are significantly person-like. If our moral rules allowed people to treat some person-like non-persons in ways we do not want people to be treated, this would undermine the system of sympathies and attitudes that makes the ethical system work. For this reason, we would choose in the original position to make mistreatment of some sorts of animals wrong in general (not just wrong in the cases with public impact), even though animals are not themselves parties in the original position. Thus it makes sense that it is those animals whose appearance and behavior are most like those of people that get the most consideration in our moral scheme.

It is because of "coherence of attitudes," I think, that the similarity of a fetus to a baby is very significant. A fetus one week before birth is so much like a newborn baby in our psychological space that we cannot allow any cavalier treatment of the former while expecting full sympathy and nurturative support for the latter. Thus, I think that anti-abortion forces are indeed giving their strongest arguments when they point to the similarities between a fetus and a baby, and when they try to evoke our emotional attachment to and sympathy for the fetus. An early horror story from New York about nurses who were expected to alternate between caring for six-week premature infants and disposing of viable 24-week aborted fetuses is just that—a horror story. These beings are so much alike that no one can be asked to draw a distinction and treat them so very differently.

Remember, however, that in the early weeks after conception, a fetus is very much unlike a person. It is hard to develop these feelings for a set of genes which doesn't yet have a head, hands, beating heart, response to touch or the ability to move by itself. Thus it seems to me that the alleged "slippery slope" between conception and birth is not so very slippery. In the early stages of pregnancy, abortion can hardly be compared to murder for psychological reasons, but in the latest stages it is psychologically akin to murder.

Another source of similarity is the bodily continuity between fetus and adult. Bodies play a surprisingly central role in our attitudes toward persons. One has only to think of the philosophical literature on how far physical identity suffices for personal identity or Wittgenstein's remark that the best picture of the human soul is the human body. Even after death, when all agree the body is no longer a person, we still observe elaborate customs of respect for the human body; like people who torture dogs, necrophiliacs are not to be trusted with people.[13] So it is appropriate that we show respect to a fetus as the body continuous with the body of a person. This is a degree of resemblance to persons that animals cannot rival.

Michael Tooley also utilizes a parallel with animals. He claims that it is always permissible to drown newborn kittens and draws conclusions about infanticide.[14] But it is only permissible to drown kittens when their survival would cause some hardship. Perhaps it would be a burden to feed and house six more cats or to find other homes for them. The alternative of letting them starve produces even more suffering than the drowning. Since the kittens get their rights second-hand, so to speak, *via* the need for coherence in our attitudes, their interests are often overridden by the interests of full-fledged persons. But if their survival would be no inconvenience to people at all, then it is wrong to drown them, *contra* Tooley.

Tooley's conclusions about abortion are wrong for the same reason. Even if a fetus is not a person, abortion is not always permissible, because of the resemblance of a fetus to a person. I agree with Thomson that it would be wrong for a woman who is seven months pregnant to have an abortion just to avoid having to postpone a trip to Europe. In the early months of pregnancy when the fetus hardly resembles a baby at all, then, abortion is permissible whenever it is in the interests of the pregnant woman or her family. The reasons would only need to outweigh the pain and inconvenience of the abortion itself. In the middle months, when the fetus comes to resemble a person, abortion would be justifiable only when the continuation of the pregnancy or the birth of the child would cause harms—physical, psychological, economic or social—to the woman. In the late months of pregnancy, even on our current assumption that a fetus is not a person, abortion seems to be wrong except to save a woman from significant injury or death.

The Supreme Court has recognized similar gradations in the alleged slippery slope stretching between conception and birth. To this point, the present paper has been a discussion of the moral status of abortion only, not its legal status. In view of the great physical, financial and sometimes psychological costs of abortion, perhaps the legal arrangement most compatible with the proposed moral solution would be the absence of restrictions, that is, so-called abortion "on demand."

So I conclude, first, that application of our concept of a person will not suffice to settle the abortion issue. After all, the biological development of a human being is gradual. Second, whether a fetus is a person or not, abortion is justifiable early in pregnancy to avoid modest harms and seldom justifiable late in pregnancy except to avoid significant injury or death.[15]

Notes

[1] We also have paternalistic laws which keep us from harming our own bodies even when no one else is affected. Ironically, anti-abortion laws were originally designed to protect pregnant women from a dangerous but tempting procedure.

[2] Mary Anne Warren, "On the Moral and Legal Status of Abortion," *Monist* 57 (1973), p. 55.

[3] Baruch Brody, "Fetal Humanity and the Theory of Essentialism," in Robert Baker and Frederick Elliston, eds., *Philosophy and Sex* (Buffalo, N.Y., 1975).

[4] Michael Tooley, "Abortion and Infanticide," *Philosophy and Public Affairs* 2 (1971).

[5] Paul Ramsey, "The Morality of Abortion," in James Rachels, ed., *Moral Problems* (New York, 1971).

[6]John Noonan, "Abortion and the Catholic Church: A Summary History," *Natural Law Forum* 12 (1967), pp. 125–131.

[7]Wittgenstein has argued against the possibility of so capturing the concept of a game, *Philosophical Investigations* (New York, 1958), §66–71.

[8]Not because the fetus is partly a person and so has some of the rights of persons, but rather because of the rights of person-like non-persons. This I discuss in part III below.

[9]Aristotle himself was concerned, however, with the different question of when the soul takes form. For historical data, see Jimmye Kimmey, "How the Abortion Laws Happened," *Ms* 1 (April, 1973), pp. 48ff, and John Noonan, *loc. cit.*

[10]J. J. Thomson, "A Defense of Abortion," *Philosophy and Public Affairs* 1 (19, 1).

[11]*Ibid.*, p. 52.

[12]John Rawls, *A Theory of Justice* (Cambridge, Mass., 1971), §3–4.

[13]On the other hand, if they can be trusted with people, then our moral customs are mistaken. It all depends on the facts of psychology.

[14]*Op. cit.*, pp. 40, 60–61.

[15]I am deeply indebted to Larry Crocker and Arthur Kuflik for their constructive comments.

Discussion Questions

1. Why does English conclude that the concept of a person cannot be decisive for the abortion question? Do you agree? Why or why not?

2. What is English's argument from the self-defense model? Argue for or against her conclusions.

3. English argues that there are some things we ought not to do to nonpersons such as animals. How does she apply this to abortion? Is her argument successful? Why or why not?

4. How might Grisez argue against English's view that abortion may be justified even if the fetus is a person?

5. How might Warren argue against English's view that abortion may not be justified even if the fetus is not a person?

Abortion, Distant Peoples, and Future Generations

James P. Sterba

Those who favor a liberal view on abortion and thus tend to support abortion on demand are just as likely to support the rights of distant peoples to basic economic assistance and the rights of future generations to a fair share of the world's resources.[1] Yet, as I shall argue, many of the arguments offered in support of abortion on demand by those who favor a liberal view on abortion are actually inconsistent with a workable defense of these other social goals. If I am right, many of those who favor a liberal view on abortion (whom I shall henceforth refer to as "liberals") will have to make an unwelcome choice: either moderate their support for abortion or moderate their commitment to the rights of distant peoples and future generations. I shall argue that the most promising way for liberals to make this choice is to moderate their support for abortion.

The Welfare Rights of Distant Peoples

It used to be argued that the welfare rights of distant peoples would eventually be met, as a by-product of the continued economic growth of the technologically developed nations of the world. It was believed that the transfer of investment and technology to the less developed nations of the world would eventually, if not make everyone well off, at least satisfy everyone's basic needs. Now we are not so sure. Presently more and more evidence points to the conclusion that without some substantial sacrifice on the part of the technologically developed nations of the world, many of the less developed nations will never be able to provide their members with even the basic necessities for survival. For example, it has been projected that in order to reduce the income gap between the technologically developed nations and the underdeveloped nations to 5 to 1 and the income gap between the technologically developed nations and the developing nations to 3 to 1 would require a total investment of 7200 billion (in 1963 dollars) over the next fifty years.[2] [For comparison, the Gross National Product of the United States for 1973 was about 922 billion (in 1963 dollars).] Even those who argue that an almost utopian world situation will obtain in the distant future still would have to admit that, unless the technologically developed nations adopt some policy of redistribution, malnutrition and starvation will continue in the less developed nations for many years to come.[3] Thus a recognition of the welfare rights of distant peoples would appear to have significant consequences for developed and underdeveloped nations alike.

Of course, there are various senses in which distant peoples can be said to have welfare rights and various moral grounds on which those rights can be justified. First of all, the welfare rights of distant peoples can be understood to be either "action" rights

From *The Journal of Philosophy*, vol. LXXVII, no. 7, pp. 424–440. Reprinted by permission of the publisher and author.

or "recipient" rights. An *action right* is a right to act in some specified manner. For example, a constitutional right to liberty is usually understood to be an action right; it guarantees each citizen the right to act in any manner that does not unjustifiably interfere with any other citizen's constitutional rights. On the other hand, a *recipient right* is a right to receive some specific goods or services. Typical recipient rights are the right to have a loan repaid and the right to receive one's just earnings. Secondly, the welfare rights of distant peoples can be understood to be either *in personam* rights or *in rem* rights. In personam rights are rights that hold against some specific namable person or persons, whereas in rem rights hold against "the world at large," that is, against everyone who will ever be in a position to act upon the rights in question. The constitutional right to liberty is usually understood to be an in rem right; the right to have a loan repaid or the right to receive one's just earnings are typical in personam rights. Finally, the rights of distant peoples can be understood to be either legal rights, that is, rights that *are enforced* by legal sanctions, or moral rights, that is, rights that *ought to be enforced* either simply by moral sanctions or by both moral and legal sanctions. Accordingly, what distinguishes the moral rights of distant peoples from the requirements of super-erogation (the nonfulfillment of which is never blameworthy) is that the former but not the latter can be justifiably enforced either by moral sanctions or by moral and legal sanctions. Since we will be primarily concerned with the moral rights of distant peoples to a certain minimum of welfare, hereafter "right(s)" should be understood as short for "moral right(s)."

Of the various moral grounds for justifying the welfare rights of distant peoples, quite possibly the most evident are those which appeal either to a right to life or a right to fair treatment.[4] Indeed, whether one interprets a person's right to life as an action right (as political conservatives tend to do) or as a recipient right (as political liberals tend to do), it is possible to show that the right justifies welfare rights that would amply provide for a person's basic needs.[5] Alternatively, it is possible to justify those same welfare rights on the basis of a person's recipient right to fair treatment. In what follows, however, I do not propose to work out these moral justifications for the welfare rights of distant peoples.[6] Rather I wish to show that if one affirms welfare rights of distant peoples, as liberals tend to do, then there are certain arguments for abortion that one in consistency should reject. These arguments for abortion all begin with the assumption that the fetus is a person and then attempt to show that abortion can still be justified in many cases.

Distant Peoples and Abortion

One such argument is based on a distinction between what a person can demand as a right and what is required by moral decency. Abortion, it is said, may offend against the requirements of moral decency, but it rarely, if ever, violates anyone's rights. Judith Jarvis Thomson[7] [see selection earlier in this chapter] illustrates this view as follows:

> . . . even supposing a case in which a woman pregnant due to rape ought to allow the unborn person to use her body for the hour he needs, we should not conclude that he has a right to do so; we should conclude that she is self-centered, callous, indecent, but not unjust if she refuses.

In Thomson's example, the sacrifice the pregnant woman would have to make to save the innocent fetus-person's life is certainly quite minimal.[8] Yet Thomson and other defenders of abortion contend that this minimal sacrifice is simply a requirement of moral decency and that neither justice nor the rights of the fetus-person requires the woman to contribute the use of her womb even for one hour! But if such a minimal life-sustaining sacrifice is required neither by justice nor by the rights of the fetusperson, then how could one maintain that distant peoples have a right to have their basic needs satisfied? Obviously to satisfy the basic needs of distant peoples would require a considerable sacrifice from many people in the technologically developed nations of the world. Taken individually, such sacrifices would be far greater than the sacrifice of Thomson's pregnant woman. Consequently, if the sacrifice of Thomson's pregnant woman is merely a requirement of moral decency, then the far greater sacrifices necessary to meet the basic needs of distant peoples, if required at all, could only be requirements of moral decency. Thus liberals who want to support the welfare rights of distant peoples would in consistency have to reject this first argument for abortion.

Another argument for abortion that is also inconsistent with the welfare rights of distant peoples grants that the fetus-person has a right to life and then attempts to show that his right to life often does not entitle him to the means of survival. Thomson again illustrates this view:

> If I am sick unto death, and the only thing that will save my life is the touch of Henry Fonda's cool hand on my fevered brow, then all the same, I have no right to be given the touch of Henry Fonda's cool hand on my fevered brow. It would be frightfully nice of him to fly in from the West Coast to provide it. It would be less nice, though no doubt well meant, if my friends flew out to the West Coast and carried Henry Fonda back with them. But I have no right at all against anybody that he should do this for me.

According to Thomson, what a person's right to life explicitly entitles him to is not the right to receive or acquire the means of survival, but only the right not to be killed or let die unjustly.

To understand what this right not to be killed or let die unjustly amounts to, consider the following example:

> Tom, Dick, and Gertrude are adrift on a lifeboat. Dick managed to bring aboard provisions that are just sufficient for his own survival. Gertrude managed to do the same. But Tom brought no provisions at all. So Gertrude, who is by far the strongest, is faced with a choice. She can either kill Dick to provide Tom with the provisions he needs or she can refrain from killing Dick, thus letting Tom die.

Now, as Thomson understands the right not to be killed or let die unjustly, Gertrude's killing Dick would be unjust, but her letting Tom die would not be unjust because Dick has a greater right to his life and provisions than either Tom or Gertrude.[9] Thus killing or letting die unjustly always involves depriving a person of something to which he has a greater right—typically either his functioning body or property the person has which he needs to maintain his life. Consequently, a person's right to life would entitle him to his functioning body and whatever property he has which he needs to maintain his life.

Yet Thomson's view allows that some persons may not have property rights to goods that are necessary to meet their own basic needs whereas others may have property rights to more than enough goods to meet their own basic needs. It follows that if persons with property rights to surplus goods choose not to share their surplus with anyone else, then, according to Thomson's account, they would still not be violating anyone's right to life. For although, by their decision not to share, they would be killing or letting die those who lack the means of survival, they would not be doing so unjustly, because they would not be depriving anyone of his property.

Unfortunately, Thomson never explains how some persons could justifiably acquire property rights to surplus goods that would restrict others from acquiring or receiving the goods necessary to satisfy their basic needs. And Thomson's argument for abortion crucially depends on the justification of just such restrictive property rights. For otherwise the fetus-person's right to life would presumably entail a right to receive the means of survival.

It is also unclear how such restrictive property rights would be compatible with each person's right to fair treatment. Apparently, one would have to reinterpret the right to fair treatment so that it had nothing to do with receiving the necessary means of survival. A difficult task indeed.

But most importantly, accepting this defense of abortion with its unsupported assumption of restrictive property rights would undermine the justification for the welfare rights of distant peoples. For the same sort of rights that would restrict the fetus-person from receiving what he needs for survival would also restrict distant people from receiving or acquiring what they need for survival. Thus liberals who support the welfare rights of distant peoples would have an additional reason to reject this argument for abortion.[10]

Of course, many liberals cannot but be unhappy with the rejection of the two arguments for abortion which we have considered. For although they would not want to give up their support for the welfare rights of distant peoples, they are still inclined to support abortion on demand.

Searching for an acceptable resolution of this conflict, liberals might claim that what is wrong with the preceding arguments for abortion is that they both make the generous assumption that the fetus is a person. Once that assumption is dropped, liberals might claim, arguments for abortion on demand can be constructed which are perfectly consistent with the welfare rights of distant peoples. Although this line of argument initially seems quite promising, on closer examination it turns out that even accepting arguments for abortion on demand that do not assume that the fetus is a person raises a problem of consistency for the liberal. This is most clearly brought out in connection with the liberal's support for the welfare rights of future generations.

The Welfare Rights of Future Generations

At first glance the welfare rights of future generations appear to be on a par with the welfare rights of distant peoples. For, assuming that there will be future generations, then, they, like generations presently existing, will have their basic needs that must be satisfied. And, just as we are now able to take action to provide for the basic needs of distant peoples, so likewise we are now able to take action to provide for the basic needs of future generations (e.g., through capital investment and the conservation of resources). Consequently, it would seem that there are just as good grounds for providing for the basic needs of future generations as there are for providing for the basic needs of distant peoples.

But there is a problem. How can we claim that future generations *now* have rights that provision be made for their basic needs when they don't presently exist? How is it possible for persons who don't yet exist to have rights against those who do? For example, suppose we continue to use up the earth's resources at present or even greater rates, and, as a result, it turns out that the most pessimistic forecasts for the twenty-second century are realized.[11] This means that future generations will face widespread famine, depleted resources, insufficient new technology to handle the crisis, and a drastic decline in the quality of life for nearly everyone. If this were to happen, could persons living in the twenty-second century legitimately claim that we in the twentieth century violated their rights by not restraining our consumption of the world's resources? Surely it would be odd to say that we violated their rights over a hundred years before they existed. But what exactly is the oddness?

Is it that future generations generally have no way of claiming their rights against existing generations? Although this does make the recognition and enforcement of rights much more difficult (future generations would need strong advocates in the existing generations), it does not make it impossible for there to be such rights. After all, it is quite obvious that the recognition and enforcement of the rights of distant peoples is a difficult task as well.

Or is it that we don't believe that rights can legitimately exercise their influence over long durations of time? But, if we can foresee and control the effects our actions will have on the ability of future generations to satisfy their basic needs, then why should we not be responsible for those same effects? And if we are responsible for them, then why should not future generations have a right that we take them into account?

Perhaps what really bothers us is that future generations don't exist when their rights are said to demand action. But how else could persons have a right to benefit from the effects our actions will have in the distant future if they did not exist just when those effects would be felt? Those who exist contemporaneously with us could not legitimately make the same demand upon us, for they will not be around to experience those effects. Only future generations could have a right that the effects our actions will have in the distant future contribute to satisfying their basic needs. Nor need we assume that, in order for persons to have rights, they must exist when their rights demand action. Thus, to say that future generations have rights against existing generations we can simply mean that there are enforceable requirements upon existing generations that would benefit or prevent harm to future generations. Using this interpretation of the rights of future generations, it is possible to justify welfare rights for future generations by appealing either to a right to life or a right to fair treatment, but here again, as in the case of the welfare rights of distant peoples, I shall simply assume that such justifications can be worked out.[12]

The welfare rights of future generations are also closely connected with the population policy of existing generations. For example, under a population policy that places restrictions on the size of families and requires genetic screening, some persons will not be brought into existence who otherwise would come into existence under a less restrictive population policy. Thus, the membership of future generations will surely be affected by whatever population policy existing generations adopt. Given that the size and genetic health of future generations will obviously affect their ability to provide for their basic needs, the welfare rights of future generations would require existing generations to adopt a population policy that takes these factors into account.

But what population policy should existing generations adopt? There are two policies that many philosophers have found attractive.[13] Each policy represents a version of utilitarianism, and each has its own difficulties. One policy requires population to increase or decrease so as to produce the largest total net utility possible. The other policy requires population to increase or decrease so as to produce the highest average net utility possible. The main difficulty with the policy of total unity is that it would justify any increase in population—even if, as a result, the lives of most people were not very happy—so long as some increase in total utility were produced. On the other hand, the main difficulty with the policy of average utility is that it would not allow persons to be brought into existence—even if they would be quite happy—unless the utility of their lives were equal or greater than the average. Clearly what is needed is a policy that avoids both these difficulties.

Peter Singer has recently proposed a population policy designed to do just that—a policy designed to restrict the increase of population more than the policy of total utility but less than the policy of average utility.[14] Singer's policy justifies increasing a population of M members to a population of $M + N$ members only if M of the $M + N$ members would have at least as much utility as the population of M members had initially.

At first it might seem that Singer's population policy provides the desired compromise. For his policy does not seem to justify every increase in population that increases total net utility but rather justifies only those increases which do not provide less utility to members equal in number to the original population. Nor does his policy require increases in population to meet or surpass the average utility of the original population. But the success of Singer's compromise is only apparent. As Derek Parfit has shown,[15] Singer's policy shares with the policy of total utility the same tendency to increase population in the face of continually declining average utility.

For consider a population with just two members: Abe and Edna. Imagine that Abe and Edna were deliberating whether to have a child and they calculated that, if they had a child, (1) the utility of the child's life would be somewhat lower than the average utility of their own lives, and (2) the child would have no net effect on the total utility of their own lives taken together. Applied to these circumstances, Singer's population policy would clearly justify bringing the child into existence. But suppose further that, after the birth of Clyde, their first child, Abe and Edna were deliberating whether to have a second child and they calculated that, if they had a second child, (1) the utility of the child's life would be somewhat lower than the utility of Clyde's life, and (2) the child would have no net effect on the total utility of their own lives and Clyde's taken together. Given these circumstances, Singer's policy would again justify bringing this second child into existence. And, if analogous circumstances obtained on each of the next ten occasions that Abe and Edna consider the question of whether to bring additional children into existence, Singer's population policy would continue to justify adding new children irrespective of the general decline in average utility resulting from each new addition to Abe and Edna's family. Thus Singer's policy has the same undesirable result as the policy of total utility. It avoids the severe restriction on population increase of the policy of average utility but fails to restrict existing generations from bringing into existence persons who would not be able to enjoy even a certain minimum level of well-being.

Fortunately, a policy with the desired restrictions can be grounded on the welfare rights of future generations. Given that the welfare rights of future generations require existing generations to make provision for the basic needs of future generations, existing generations would have to evaluate their ability to provide both for their own basic needs and for the basic needs of future generations. Since existing generations by bringing persons into existence would be determining the membership of future generations, they would have to evaluate whether they are able to provide for that membership. And if existing generations discover that, were population to increase beyond a certain point, they would lack sufficient resources to make the necessary provision for each person's basic needs, then it would be incumbent upon them to restrict the membership of future generations so as not exceed their ability to provide for each person's basic needs. Thus, if the rights of future generations are respected, the membership of future generations would never increase beyond the ability of existing generations to make the necessary provision for the basic needs of future generations. Consequently, not only can the welfare rights of future generations be justified on the basis of each person's right to life and each person's right to fair treatment, they also can be used to justify a population policy that provides the desired compromise between the policies of average and total utility.

Future Generations and Abortion

Now the population policy that the welfare rights of future generations justify suggest an argument for abortion that liberals would be inclined to accept. The argument assumes that the fetus is not a person and then attempts to show that aborting the fetus is either justified or required if the fetus will develop into a person who lacks a reasonable opportunity to lead a good life. Most versions of the argument even go so far as to maintain that the person who would otherwise be brought into existence in these unfavorable circumstances has in fact a right not to be born, i.e., a right to be aborted. Joel Feinberg puts the argument as follows:

> . . . if, before the child has been born, we know that the conditions for the fulfillment of his most basic interests have already been destroyed, and we permit him nevertheless to be born, we become a party to the violation of his rights.
>   In such circumstances, therefore, a proxy for the fetus might plausibly claim on its behalf, *a right not to be born*. That right is based on his future rather than his present interests (he has no actual present interests); but of course it is not contingent on his birth because he has it before birth, from the very moment that satisfaction of his most basic future interests is rendered impossible. . . .[16]

The argument is obviously analogous to arguments for euthanasia. For, as in arguments for euthanasia, it is the nonfulfillment of a person's basic interests which is said to provide the legitimate basis for the person's right to have his life terminated.

However, in order for this argument to function as part of a defense for abortion on demand, it is necessary to show that no similar justification can be given for a right to be born. And it is here that the assumption that the fetus is not a person becomes important. For if the fetus were a person and if, moreover, this fetus-person had a reasonable opportunity to lead a good life, then, it could be argued, this fetus-person would have a right to be born. Thus, proceeding from the assumption that the fetus is not a person, various arguments have been offered to show that a similar justification cannot be given for a right to be born.[17]

One such argument bases the asymmetry on a failure of reference in the case of the fetus that would develop into a person with a reasonable opportunity for a good life. The argument can be summarized as follows:

> If I bring into existence a person who lacks a reasonable opportunity to lead a good life, there will be a person who can reproach me that I did not prevent his leading an unfortunate existence. But if I do not bring into existence a person who would have a reasonable opportunity to lead a good life, there will be no person who can reproach me for preventing his leading a fortunate existence. Hence, only the person who lacks a reasonable opportunity to lead a good life can claim a right not to be born.

But notice that, if I do not bring into existence a person who would lack a reasonable opportunity to lead a good life, there will be no person who can thank me for preventing his leading an unfortunate existence. And, if I do bring into existence a person who had a reasonable opportunity to lead a good life, there will be a person who can thank me for not preventing his leading a fortunate existence. Thus, whatever failure of reference there is, it occurs in both cases, and therefore, cannot be the basis for any asymmetry between them.[18]

A second argument designed to establish the asymmetry between the two cases begins with the assumption that a person's life cannot be compared with his nonexistence unless the person already exists. This means that, if one allows a fetus to develop into a person who has a reasonable opportunity to lead a good life, one does not make that person better off than if he never existed. And it also means that if one allows a fetus to develop into a person who lacks a reasonable opportunity to lead a good life one does not make that person worse off than if he never existed. But what then justifies a right not to be born in the latter case? According to the argument, it is simply the fact that unless the fetus is aborted a person will come into existence who lacks a reasonable opportunity to lead a good life. But if this fact justifies a right not to be born, why, in the former case, would not the fact that unless the fetus is aborted a person will come into existence who has a reasonable opportunity to lead a good life suffice to justify a right to be born? Clearly, no reason has been given to distinguish the cases.

Furthermore, consider the grounds for aborting a fetus that would develop into a person who lacks a reasonable opportunity to lead a good life. It is not simply that the person is sure to experience some unhappiness in his life because in every person's life there is some unhappiness. Rather it is because the amount of expected unhappiness in this person's life would render his life not worth living. This implies that the justification for aborting in this case is based on a comparison of the value of the person's life with the value of his nonexistence. For how else can we say that the fact that a fetus would develop into a person who lacks a reasonable opportunity to lead a good life justifies our preventing the person's very existence? Consequently, this argument depends upon a denial of the very assumption with which it began, namely that the person's life cannot be compared with his nonexistence unless that person already exists.

Nevertheless, it might still be argued that an analogous justification cannot be given for a right to be born on the grounds that there is a difference in strength between one's duty to prevent a fetus from developing into a person who lacks a reasonable opportunity to lead a good life and one's duty not to prevent a fetus from developing into a person who has a reasonable opportunity to lead a good life. For example, it might be argued that the former duty is a relatively strong duty to prevent harm, whereas the latter duty is a relatively weak duty to promote well-being, and that only the relatively strong duty justifies a correlative right—in this case, a right not to be born. But, even granting that our duty to prevent harm is stronger than our duty to promote well-being, in the case at issue we are dealing not just with a duty to promote well-being but with a duty to promote *basic* well-being. And, as liberals who are committed to the welfare rights of future generations would be the first to admit, our duty to prevent basic harm and our duty to promote basic well-being are not that distinct from a moral point of view. From which it follows that, if our duty to prevent basic harm justifies a right not to be born in the one case, then our duty to promote basic well-being would justify a right to be born in the other.

Nor will it do to reject the notion of a right to be born on the grounds that if the fetus is not a person then the bearer of such a right, especially when we violate that right by performing an abortion, would *seem* to be a potential or possible person. For the same would hold true of the right not to be born which is endorsed by liberals such as Feinberg and Narveson: the bearer of such a right, especially when we respect that right by performing an abortion, would also *seem* to be a potential or possible person. In fact, however, neither notion necessarily entails any metaphysical commitment to possible persons who "are" whether they exist or not. For to say that a person into whom a particular fetus would develop has a right not to be born is to say that there is an enforceable requirement upon certain persons the violation of which would fundamentally harm the person who would thereby come into existence. Similarly, to say that a person into whom a particular fetus would develop has a right to be born is to say that there is an enforceable requirement upon certain persons the respecting of which would fundamentally benefit the person who would thereby come into existence. So understood, neither the notion of a right to be born nor that of a right not to be born entails any metaphysical commitment to possible persons as bearers of rights.

Of course, recognizing a right to be born may require considerable personal sacrifice, and some people may want to reject any morality that requires such sacrifice. This option, however, is not open to liberals who are committed to the welfare rights of future generations. For such liberals are already committed to making whatever personal sacrifice is necessary to provide for the basic needs of future generations. Consequently, liberals committed to the welfare rights of future generations cannot consistently reject a prohibition of abortion in cases involving a right to be born simply on the grounds that it would require considerable personal sacrifice.

But there is an even more basic inconsistency in being committed both to the welfare rights of future generations and to abortion on demand. For, as we have seen, commitment to the welfare rights of future generations requires the acceptance of a population policy according to which existing generations must ensure that the membership of future generations does not exceed the ability of existing generations to provide for the basic needs of future generations. Thus for liberals who assume that the fetus is not a person, this population policy would have the same implications as the argument we considered which justifies abortion in certain cases on the basis of a person's right not to be born. For if existing generations violate this population policy by bringing into existence persons whose basic needs they cannot fulfill, they would also thereby be violating the right not to be born of those same persons, since such persons would not have a reasonable opportunity to lead a good life. But, as we have also seen, accepting this argument which justifies abortion in certain cases on the basis of a person's right not to be born commits one to accepting also a parallel argument for prohibiting abortion in certain other cases on the basis of a person's right to be born. Consequently, commitment to the population policy demanded by the welfare rights of future generations will likewise commit liberals to accepting this parallel argument for prohibiting abortion in certain cases. Therefore, even assuming that the fetus is not a person, liberals cannot consistently uphold the welfare rights of future generations while endorsing abortion on demand.

There remains the further question of whether liberals who are committed to the welfare rights of distant peoples and future generations can make a moral distinction between contraception and abortion—assuming, that is, that the fetus is not a person. In support of such a distinction, it might be argued that, in cases where abortion is at issue, we can roughly identify the particular person into whom a fetus would develop and ask whether that person would be fundamentally benefited or fundamentally harmed by being brought into existence, whereas we cannot do anything comparable in cases where contraception is at issue. Yet, though this difference does exist, it does not suffice for morally distinguishing abortion from contraception. For notice that if persons do not practice contraception when conditions are known to be suitable for bringing persons into existence who would have a reasonable opportunity to lead a good life, then there will normally come into existence persons who have thereby benefited. Similarly, if persons do not practice contraception when conditions are known to be unsuitable for bringing persons into existence who would have a reasonable opportunity to lead a good life (e.g., when persons who would be brought into existence would very likely have seriously debilitating and ultimately fatal genetic defects), then there will normally come into existence persons who have thereby been harmed. On grounds such as these, therefore, we could certainly defend a "right not to be conceived" and a "right to be conceived" which are analogous to our previously defended "right not to be born" and "right to be born." Hence, it would follow that liberals who are committed to the welfare rights of distant peoples and future generations can no more consistently support "contraception on demand" than they can consistently support abortion on demand.

Needless to say, considerably more sacrifice would normally be required of existing generations in order to fulfill a person's right to be born or right to be conceived than would be required to fulfill a person's right not to be born or right not to be conceived. For example, fulfilling a person's right to be born may ultimately require caring for the needs of a child for many years whereas fulfilling a person's right not to be born may require only an early abortion. Therefore, because of the greater sacrifice that would normally be required to fulfill a person's right to be born, that right might often be overridden in particular circumstances by the rights of existing persons to have their own basic needs satisfied. The existing persons whose welfare would have priority over a person's right to be born are not only those who would be directly involved in bringing the person into existence but also those distant persons whose welfare rights would otherwise be neglected if goods and resources were diverted to bringing additional persons into existence. This would, of course, place severe restrictions on any population increase in technologically developed nations so long as persons in technologically underdeveloped nations still fail to have their basic needs satisfied. But for persons committed to the welfare rights of distant peoples as well as to the welfare rights of future generations, no other policy would be acceptable.

Obviously these results cannot but be embarrassing for many liberals. For what has been shown is that, with or without the assumption that the fetus is a person, liberals who are committed to the welfare rights of distant peoples and future generations cannot consistently endorse abortion on demand. Thus, assuming that the welfare rights of distant peoples and future generations can be firmly grounded on a right to life and a right to fair treatment, the only morally acceptable way for liberals to avoid this inconsistency is to moderate their support for abortion on demand.[19]

Notes

[1]It is not difficult to find philosophers who not only favor a liberal view on abortion and thus tend to support abortion on demand, but also favor these other social goals as well. See Jan Narveson, "Moral Problems of Population," *Monist,* LVII, 1 (January 1973): 62–86, and "Aesthetics, Charity, Utility and Distributive Justice," *ibid.,* LVI, 4 (October 1972): 527–551; Joel Feinberg, "Is There a Right to Be Born?" in James Rachels, ed., *Understanding Moral Philosophy* (Encino, Calif.: Dickenson, 1976), pp. 346–357, and "The Rights of Animals and Future Generations," in William Blackstone, *Philosophy and Environmental Crisis* (Athens: Univ. of Georgia Press, 1972), pp. 41–68; Michael Tooley, "Abortion and Infanticide," *Philosophy & Public Affairs,* II, 1 (Fall 1972): 37–65, and "Michael Tooley Replies," *ibid.,* II, 4 (Summer 1973): 419–432; Mary Anne Warren, "Do

Potential People Have Moral Rights?", *Canadian Journal of Philosophy*, VII, 2 (June 1977): 275–289.

[2]Mihajlo Mesarovic and Eduard Pestel, *Mankind at the Turning Point* (New York: New American Library, 1975), ch. 5.

[3]Herman Kahn, William Brown, and Leon Martel, *The Next 200 Years* (New York: William Morrow, 1976), ch. 2.

[4]For other possibilities, see Onora Nell, "Lifeboat Earth," *Philosophy & Public Affairs*, IV, 3 (Spring 1975): 273–292; Peter Singer, "Famine, Affluence and Morality," *ibid.*, I, 3 (Spring 1972): 229–243.

[5]A person's basic needs are those which must be satisfied if the person's health and sanity are not to be seriously endangered.

[6]For an attempt to work out these justifications, see ch. VI of my book, *The Demands of Justice* (Notre Dame, Ind.: University Press, 1980).

[7]"A Defense of Abortion," *Philosophy & Public Affairs*, I, 1 (Fall 1971): 47–66.

[8]Hereafter the term "fetus-person" will be used to indicate the assumption that the fetus is a person. The term "fetus" is also understood to refer to any human organism from conception to birth.

[9]See her "Killing, Letting Die, and the Trolley Problem," *Monist*, LIX, 2 (April 1976): 204–217.

[10]Notice that my critique of Thomson's arguments for abortion on demand differs from critiques that attempt to find an *internal* defect in Thomson's arguments. [For example, see Richard Werner's "Abortion: The Moral Status of the Unborn," *Social Theory and Practice*, III, 2 (Fall 1974): 210–216.] My approach has been to show that Thomson's arguments are *externally* defective in that a liberal who is committed to the welfare rights of distant peoples cannot consistently accept those arguments. Thus, Jan Narveson's telling objections to Werner's internalist critique of Thomson's arguments [see his "Semantics, Future Generations and the Abortion Problem," *ibid.*, III, 4 (Fall 1975): 464–466] happily do not apply to my own critique.

[11]Donella H. Meadows, Dennis L. Meadows, Jorgen Randers, and William W. Behrens III, *The Limits to Growth* (New York: New American Library, 2d ed., 1974), chs. 3 and 4.

[12]For an attempt to work out these justifications, see *The Demands of Justice*, ch. VI.

[13]See Henry Sidgwick, *The Methods of Ethics* (London: Macmillan, 7th ed., 1907; Chicago: University Press, 1962), pp. 414–416; Narveson, "Moral Problems of Population," pp. 62–86.

[14]"A Utilitarian Population Principle," in Michael Bayles, ed., *Ethics and Population* (Cambridge, Mass.: Schenkman, 1976), pp. 81–99.

[15]"On Doing the Best for Our Children," in Michael Bayles, ed., *op. cit.*, pp. 100–115. For additional problems with Singer's population policy, see R. I. Sikora, "Is It Wrong to Prevent the Existence of Future Generations?" in Sikora and Brian Barry, eds., *Obligations to Future Generations* (Philadelphia: Temple UP, 1978), pp. 128–132.

[16]Feinberg, op. cit.

[17]See Narveson, "Utilitarianism and New Generations," *Mind*, LXXVI, 301 (January 1967): 62–72, and "Moral Problems of Population," *op. cit.*

[18]For a similar argument, see Timothy Sprigge, "Professor Narveson's Utilitarianism," *Inquiry*, XI, 3 (Autumn 1968: 332–346), p. 338.

[19]Earlier versions of this paper were presented at a Symposium on Potentiality and Human Values sponsored by the American Society for Value Inquiry in 1978, at the Pacific Division Meeting of the American Philosophical Association in 1979, and at the Conference on Life Sciences and Human Values held at Geneseo, New York, in 1979. In the course of working through various versions of this paper, I have benefited from the comments of many different people, in particular, Janet Kourany, David Solomon, Jan Narveson, Gregory Kavka, Mary Ann Warren, and Ernest Partridge.

Discussion Questions

1. Suppose that Sterba is right in saying that liberal views on abortion are inconsistent with liberal views on other issues. What would this show? What options are open to the liberal if Sterba is correct?

2. What basis does Sterba suggest for the welfare rights of distant persons? How might these arguments be criticized?

3. Does the analogy Sterba suggests between distant people's rights and the rights of the fetus beg some key questions? Why or why not?

4. How might Thomson reply to Sterba's arguments that her position is inconsistent?

5. How are future generations analogous or not analogous to the fetus? How would Warren's position on rights of potential persons apply to unborn generations? Is this a good criticism of Warren's view? How might she reply?

Suggested Readings for Chapter Four

Burtchaell, James T., ed. *Abortion Parley*. Kansas City: Andrew & McMeel, 1980.

Callahan, Daniel. *Abortion: Law, Choice and Morality*. New York: Macmillan, 1970.

Feinberg, Joel, ed. *The Problem of Abortion*. Belmont, Calif.: Wadsworth, 1973.

Grisez, Germain. *Abortion: The Myths, the Realities and the Arguments*. New York: Corpus Books, 1970.

Noonan, John T. *The Morality of Abortion: Legal and Historical Perspectives*. Cambridge, Mass.: Harvard University Press, 1970.

5

Sexual Ethics

Ethical problems having to do with sexual intercourse and related matters are disputable in more than one sense. For some people these problems seem almost the whole of morality: An "immoral" person is one who is immoral in his or her sexual life. Others, however, question the whole idea of a specifically sexual ethics. They agree that it is possible to lie about or be deceitful about our sexual activities or to harm others in ways involving sexual activities. However, they deny that an act of sexual intercourse can be in or of itself moral or immoral.

The division between those who do and those who do not think there is a specifically sexual morality does not *necessarily* coincide with the division between conservative and liberal sexual morality. In a brief, oversimple definition, a conservative view of sexual morality is the view that sexual intercourse is morally right if it occurs only between people married to each other. Fornication—that is, sexual intercourse between people who are not married—and adultery—that is, sexual intercourse between people at least one of whom is married to someone else—are both regarded as wrong. So also are masturbation, homosexual activity, and a number of other sexual activities that are regarded as perversions. At the other extreme, one liberal view of sexual morality is that any sexual activity engaged in by one or two (or more) consenting adults is morally unobjectionable.

Some holders of a conservative view of sexual morality agree that there is no specifically sexual morality but try to show that each item of the conservative view can be justified by generally applicable moral principles. Adultery, for example, is wrong because it is the breaking of a promise or commitment, seduction wrong because it involves deceit or exploitation, and so on. However, many people question whether this justification project can be adequately carried out, and in practice those who deny that there is a specifically sexual morality tend to hold a more liberal view of sexual ethics.

Whether or not they attempt to reduce sexual ethics to general moral principles that do not specifically mention sex (such as "keep your promises"), peoples' views of ethics on sexual matters are presumably closely connected with their general ethical theory. For example, a holder of the conservative view who is a rule-utilitarian might regard marriage as an institutions that contributes to the greatest good of the greatest number and regard activities such as homosexuality as wrong because they damage this institution. Religious views also usually have a major effect on views of sexual morality; a great deal of the support for conservative views of morality comes from those who are traditional Jewish or Christian believers.

Because this point of view has been so influential historically, the selections in this chapter begin with a statement of a biblically based Protestant Christian view of sexual ethics by Norman L. Geisler. Although the appeal to the Bible is theology, not philosophy, Geisler also attempts to give a philosophical justification of the biblical view.

The papers by J. Gosling, Thomas Nagel, and Robert Solomon all explore in various ways the question of what is distinctive about sexual activity and what consequences this has for sexual morality. Nagel and Solomon draw, broadly speaking, liberal conclusions, while Gosling draws more conservative conclusions, but they are all trying to explore the idea of sexual activity as a form of expression or communication.

Gosling is mainly concerned with sexual activity as it relates to marriage. Both Nagel and Solomon examine the idea of sexual perversion partly because they regard the topic as the source of important insights into sexual morality in general. As Nagel says, "There is something to be learned about sex from the fact that we possess a concept of sexual perversion." But, of course, homosexual activity and other activities regarded by some as perversions are the subject of much heated debate.

Since much condemnation of and campaigning against homosexual activity is religiously motivated, the final selection provides an interesting contrast. It is a statement made by the Washington State Catholic Conference. While taking a traditional, conservative position on the morality of homosexual acts, the commission reaches interesting conclusions about some kinds of opposition to such activities.

The selections in this chapter were chosen because each of them says something new or especially interesting about this area of ethics rather than merely reiterating liberal or conservative views. This area of behavior is so important to most people and so involved with our deepest convictions about ourselves and our world that greater understanding is well worth seeking, even though the prospects for agreement are not good.

The Christian and Sex

Norman L. Geisler

Sex is one of the most important interpersonal relations in which individuals engage. It is one of the most powerful and yet most perverted forces in the world. Perhaps one of the reasons for its perversion is its power. If power tends to corrupt, then great power tends to corrupt greatly. On the other hand much of the misuse of sex may result from a misunderstanding of it. What is a Christian view of sex? What do the Scriptures really teach about sexual activity?

The Biblical Basis for Sex

Basically, the Bible says three things about sex: (1) sex is good, (2) sex is powerful, and therefore, (3) sex needs to be controlled. In fact, the very first references to sex in Scripture imply all three of these factors.

The Nature of Sex

Sex is intrinsically good; it is not evil. The Scriptures declare that "God created man in his own image . . . ; male and female [that is sex!] he created them" (Gen. 1:27). And when He had finished, "God saw everything that he had made, and behold, it was very good" (v. 31). Sex is good. God made it and it somehow reflects His own goodness. Perhaps it is because of the creative power of sex that it resembles an aspect of the being of God. Or, maybe it is in its force to bring about the strongest bond of unity and oneness. In whatever other way we are supposed to understand that sex is good like God, it is plain that fundamentally sex is good because God made it and declared it good.

Sex is essentially good   Sex is good in and of itself because it is part of the creation of God. Unlike many non-Christian philosophies (of Gnostic and Platonic varieties), the Bible declares matter and the physical universe (including man's body and bodily organs) to be good. After each day's creation it is written again and again, "And God saw that it was *good*" (Gen. 1:10, 12, 18, 21, 25). After the final day it reads, " . . . and behold, it was *very good*" (v. 31). Sex was an integral part of this very good creation. The Bible confirms this view elsewhere saying, "Everything created by God is good . . ." (1 Tim. 4:4). If sex seems impure to some, we are reminded that "to the pure all things are pure, but to the corrupt and unbelieving nothing is pure" (Titus 1:15).
   Speaking specifically of sex, the writer of the epistle to the Hebrews declared, "Let marriage be held in honor among all, and let the marriage bed be undefiled" (Heb. 13:4). Marriage is an honorable state. Marriage could hardly be considered honorable unless

sex is good, since sex is an integral part of marriage. So holy is sex that it is used in Scripture to illustrate the most intimate union one can have with God. Paul wrote, "For this reason a man shall leave his father and mother and be joined to his wife, and the two shall become one. This is a great mystery, and I take it to mean Christ and the church" (Eph. 5:31, 32).

The intrinsic goodness of sex may be deduced, as well, from the fact that God has commanded sexual union. God said to the first pair, "Be fruitful and multiply, and fill the earth . . . " (Gen. 1:28)—a command which the race is fulfilling very well! When Eve had her first child she declared, "I have gotten a man with the help of the Lord" (Gen. 4:1), thus acknowledging God's approval of the sexual process. Surely, judging by the numerous references throughout the Scripture to the blessing of children (cf. Ps. 127:4, 5; Prov. 17:6), God judges sex to be good.

Sex is powerful   Not only is sex essentially good but it is very powerful. This was implied in the fact that it could be used to "multiply" people and "fill" the earth (Gen. 1:28). The power of sex is not only dramatically demonstrated by its ability to reproduce in abundance but by the kind of creature it is producing. The children of human parents are generated in the image of God. Adam was made in God's image, and "he became the father of a son in his own likeness, after his image . . . " (Gen. 9:6; James 3:9). Hence, by the process of human sexuality are produced not only many beings but many little "gods." Jesus quoted Psalm 82:6 which says, "I say, 'You are gods, sons of the Most High, all of you.' " (John 10:35). When the nature of the human creature produced through sex is fully appreciated, it is probably no exaggeration to consider sex one of the most significant powers on earth.

When a human male sperm and a female ovum unite, a little "god" is in the making. All things being equal, the result of that conception will be a creature which both resembles and represents God on earth. Without deciding here the question about whether the unborn embryo or fetus is truly human, it is an indisputable fact that, given the proper circumstances, it definitely will become an immortal creature. Humans are immortal, never-dying persons. They will live forever. Surely, this is no ordinary power given to the sons of men that is capable of conveying into the world a never-dying person, made in the likeness of God Himself. Therefore, human sex is not only good by nature but great in power. It is great both by virtue of how much it can produce and also by virtue of what kind of creature is the product, viz., a never-dying person.

Sex needs to be controlled   It goes without saying that anything as powerful as sex needs to be controlled. No one in his right mind would let immature children play with dynamite. Nor would any responsible agents make atomic weapons available to the general public. And yet sex is in many ways more potent than either dynamite or atomic power. The only reasonable position to take with regard to any force as potent as sex is that it must be controlled or regulated. There must be means of channeling and directing the power of sex for the good of men. For, like atomic power, if sex power is not harnessed for good purposes, then its abuse may threaten to destroy mankind.

According to the Bible, the God-ordained means of directing and regulating the good and great power of sex is known as *marriage*. From the very beginning God declared, "Therefore a man leaves his father and his mother and *cleaves* to his wife, and they become one flesh" (Gen. 2:24). Jesus added, "So they are no longer two but *one*. What therefore God has *joined together,* let no man put asunder" (Matt. 19:6). That is to say, marriage which joins male and female in a unique and abiding relationship is the channel established by God in order to regulate the power of sex.

Of course, sex is not only a power to procreate; it is also a power for pleasure. But whatever kind of power sex is, it needs to be controlled. No passion should go unbridled.[1] Rape and sadistic sexual crimes cannot be justified on the mere grounds that they bring pleasure to the abuser. Even if it were true that only pleasures are intrinsically good, it does not follow that *all* pleasures are good. Some pleasures are harmful to oneself and/or others. For example, the pleasures some get from being cruel or unjust or hateful are not good pleasures. Further, not all pleasures are equally good; some are higher than others. Hence, one cannot justify an uncontrolled exercise of sex merely on the grounds that it is pleasureful. All pleasures must be controlled, and there are higher spiritual satisfactions than the mere physical pleasures of sex. According to the Scriptures, the channel for controlling the pleasure power of sexual intercourse (as well as its procreative power) is marriage. This conclusion is amply supported by a study of the function of sex within the Scriptures.

The Function of Sex

The function of sex may be viewed from several different vantage points: (1) before marriage, (2) within monogamous marriage, (3) outside of marriage, (4) within polygamous marriage, (5) and for divorcees.

The role of sex before marriage   So far as the Bible is concerned, there is no role for premarital sexual intercourse. Intercourse *is* a marriage. Any conjugal relationship is a marriage in God's eyes. It is not necessarily a lawful or rightful union, but it is a union. The first reference to marriage declares that man and woman become "one flesh" (Gen. 2:24), implying that marriage occurs when two bodies are joined. That sexual intercourse is marriage is even clearer from the common way of describing the act as a man "lying" with a woman. Moses commanded, "If a man is found lying with the wife of another man, both of them shall die . . . " (Deut. 22:22).

The New Testament further confirms this by using the words "marriage" and "marriage bed" in parallel (Heb. 13:4). In fact, there are no explicit condemnations of premarital sex in the Old Testament. For if an unbetrothed couple engaged in intercourse, the fellow was obliged to pay the marriage fee to the father and to assume the girl as his wife (Deut. 22:28). And when a man goes in to a harlot the Bible considers this a "marriage." Paul wrote, "Do you not know that he who joins himself to a prostitute becomes one body with her," quoting as his proof that the Scriptures say, "The two shall become one" (1 Cor. 6:16). In brief, there is no such thing as premarital intercourse in the Bible. If the couple were not married, then intercourse made them married. If they were already married, then intercourse with another person constituted a second, adulterous marriage for them. Harlotry is considered an illegitimate marriage.

An engaged couple who have intercourse have thereby consummated their marriage before God and ought to legalize it before the state as soon as possible, because God commands citizens to be obedient to governmental regulations (Rom. 13:1; 1 Peter 2:13). Engaged couples, according to Paul, should either control their sexual drives or else marry. He wrote, "If any one thinks that he is not behaving properly toward his betrothed, if his passions are strong, and it has to be, let him do as he wishes: let them marry—it is no sin" (1 Cor. 7:36). On the other hand, "whoever is firmly established in his heart, being under no necessity but having his desire under control, and has determined this in his heart, to keep her as his betrothed, he will do well" (v. 37). That is, intercourse is not proper for engaged couples. They should either keep their emotions in check or marry. And when they do engage in intercourse, then they are married in God's eyes and should legalize it before the state, if it is the law of the land to do so.

As to premarital sex relations among those who are not ready to marry the answer is no. If one is not ready to assume the responsibilities of a wife and family then he should not play with sex. The exhortation of Solomon is applicable here: " . . . an adulteress stalks a man's very life. Can a man carry fire in his bosom and his clothes not be burned" (Prov. 6:26, 27). One should not "make out" unless he is prepared to go all the way. And he should not go all the way until he is married, for intercourse is marriage in God's eyes.

As far as autosexuality is concerned (i.e., masturbation), it is generally wrong. Sublimation (draining sexual energy through exercises) and natural nocturnal emissions are considered to be legitimate ways to burn up excess sexual energy. Masturbation is sinful (1) when its only motive is sheer biological pleasure, (2) when it is allowed to become a compulsive habit, and/or (3) when the habit results from inferior feelings and causes guilt feelings. Masturbation is sinful when it is performed in connection with pornographic images, for as Jesus said, lust is a matter of the interests of the heart (Matt. 5:28). On the other hand, masturbation can be right when it is used as a limited, temporary program of self-control to avoid lust before marriage. If one is fully committed to leading a pure life until marriage, it may be permissible on occasion to use autosexual stimulation to relieve one's tension. As long as it does not become a habit nor a means of gratifying one's lust, masturbation is not necessarily immoral. In fact, when the motive is not *lust* but *self-control,* masturbation can be a moral act (cf. 1 Cor. 7:5; 9:25). The biblical rule is that whatever can be done to the glory of God, whatever does not enslave the doer (1 Cor. 10:31; 6:12) is to that extent moral. Masturbation used in moderation without lust for the purpose of retaining one's purity is not immoral.[2]

The role of sex in marriage   There are several basic functions of sex in marriage, and all of them indicate why marriage is the God-ordained way to regulate these functions. Three positive roles of sex within marriage are: (1) to bring about a unique, intimate *unity* of two persons; (2) to provide *ecstasy* or pleasure for the persons involved in this unique relationship; (3) to bring about a *multiplicity* of persons in the world by having children. Respectively, the three basic functions of sex in marriage are unification, recreation, and procreation.

First, marriage is aimed at bringing two human beings into the closest possible human relationship. "The two shall become *one*" is repeated over and over in Scripture (Gen. 2:24; Matt. 19:5; 1 Cor. 6:16; Eph. 5:31). So unique is this marital union brought about by sex that the Bible uses it to illustrate the mystical union a believer has with Christ (Eph. 5:32). And it is the unique one-of-a-kind nature of the sex relation which calls for a man to sustain it with only one woman. It is not really possible to have two one-of-a-kind relations at once. Marriage—in fact, monogamous marriage—is the only controlled way to maintain a continuously unique relationship between husband and wife. In polygamy there is the ever-present threat of jealousy and the question of who is the "favorite" wife. Indeed, it is not possible to have two "favorite" wives in the same sense. Therefore, it is possible for a man to have a unique relation with one wife only. Monogamous marriage is God's ideal of attaining this ideal relationship between two persons.

The second function of marriage is recreational. Sexual intercourse is literally a re-creation of the bliss of the native nuptial unity. It is a sacramental reminder of the joy of one's first love. Sexual union is the happy reunion of those who were made one by marriage. The satisfaction sex provides is the pleasure gained from reaffirming the original pledge of mutual love. In this regard, the re-creational and reunificational functions of marriage are inseparable. For the real pleasure of sex is that gained from the reaffirmation and re-enforcement of the unique union marriage brought about at the beginning. So the attempt to have the pleasure of sex without the unique and abiding relationship of marriage is illusory. The real joy comes only with the real union, and the real union comes only if there is a unique and abiding relation between two persons of the opposite sex.

The third role of marriage is procreation. The fruit of unity in matrimony is multiplicity of offspring. Of course, children are the natural but not necessary fruit of marriage. Although marriage is the natural thing to do, it is not necessary to marry. One single person may choose not to marry, without sinning (cf. Matt. 19:12; 1 Cor. 7:7, 8). Likewise, a married couple may decide not to have children, without sinning (cf. 1 Cor. 7:5), even though it is natural to have them. When children do result from marriage they are a further reason for maintaining marriage as a unique and abiding relation between parents. Children need loving discipline (Prov. 22:15; Eph. 6:4; Col. 3:21). They need the unity and security provided by a happy marriage of their parents. Neither polygamy nor divorce nor anonymity nor community of parents have proven to be strengthening factors in the personalities of children. Scarcely anything is superior to an abiding unity between mother and father for the rearing of healthy, happy children.

A word of summary is now necessary. The function of sex within marriage is threefold: unification, recreation, and procreation. All of these roles demonstrate the need for marital fidelity. Whenever the unique relationship of marriage is broken by extra-marital intercourse one has both destroyed the unique unity of marriage and lessened the true pleasure possible, to say nothing of weakening the basis of stability for any offspring from this union.

From these three positive functions of sex in marriage one negative role may be deduced. Sex within marriage is the way to satisfy what would be lust and lead to promiscuity outside marriage. "Because of the temptation to immorality, each man should have his own wife and each woman her own husband," wrote the apostle (1 Cor. 7:2). All single persons should keep themselves under sexual self-control, "but if they cannot exercise self-control, they should marry. For it is better to marry than to be aflame with passion" (1 Cor. 7:9). Likewise, to the young Thessalonian Christians Paul wrote, "For this is the will of God, your sanctification: that you abstain from immorality; that each one of you know how to take a wife for himself in holiness and honor, not in the passion of lust like heathen . . . " (1 Thess. 4:3–5). In a word, along with the three positive purposes of sex within marriage is one negative reason, viz., that marriage will provide a preventive channel for the sexual drive so that one can avoid immorality.

The role of sex outside marriage With the purposes of marriage in mind one can more easily understand the strong prohibitions in Scripture about illicit extra-marital relations. Adultery, fornication, harlotry, and sodomy (homosexuality) all come under strong condemnation. Each one of these sins in its own way violates a divinely ordained inter-personal relationship.

Adultery and harlotry are wrong for two basic reasons, viz., they are multiple marriages. First, they are attempts to carry on *many* most-intimate relationships at once. In each case one is cheating on the one he really loves the most and probably lying to the one(s) he does not love the most. The second reason fornication is wrong is that it is intended to be only a temporary union whereas God desires a sexual union to be abiding and permanent (Matt. 19:6). There is no way to assure the highest pleasure in a marital union unless it is found within the context of a mutual life-long commitment of love.

The Bible is emphatic: "You shall not commit adultery" (Ex. 20:14). In the Old Testament the adulterers were to be put to death (Lev. 20:10). The New Testament is also emphatically against adultery. Jesus pronounced it wrong even in its basic motives (Matt. 5:27, 28). Paul called it an evil work of the flesh (Gal. 5:19), and John envisioned in the lake of fire some of those who practiced it (Rev. 21:8).

The word "fornication" is often used in Scripture of illicit sexual relations outside of marriage, although the general understanding is that it implies that at least one member of the relationship was not married. The Jerusalem apostles urged all Christians to abstain from fornication (also called unchastity) (Acts 15:20). Paul said that the body is not for fornication and that a man should flee it (1 Cor. 6:13, 18). The Ephesians were told that fornication should not be even once named (or spoken of) among them (5:3). Fornication is evil because it, too, is a "marriage" outside of marriage, because it joins persons in an illicit way without their intending to carry through the abiding and unique implications of their relationship.

Homosexuality is not in the same class with the heterosexual sins of adultery, harlotry, and fornication. Homosexuality is unlike these three in that no intercourse in the strict sense of the word occurs and no births can result from it. However, homosexuality in the sense of sexually stimulating and manipulating a person of the same sex is definitely forbidden in Scripture. In the Old Testament this sin was called sodomy, after Sodom, that wicked city which was destroyed on account of this perversity (Gen. 19:5–8, 24). Later, the law of Moses forbade any "sodomite" (A.V.)[3] from being part of the community of Israel (Deut. 23:17). Later, during the reforms of King Asa, "he put away the male cult prostitutes out of the land . . . " (1 Kings 15:12). There are many references to the sins of Sodom (cf. Isa. 3:9; Ezek. 16:46). The New Testament is equally clear on the subject. Romans chapter one speaks of homosexuality as that which "exchanged natural relations for unnatural . . . " (v. 26). It is a "shameless act" which results from vile passions (v. 27). In another passage Paul wrote, "Do not be deceived; neither the immoral, nor idolaters, nor adulterers, nor homosexuals . . . will inherit the kingdom of God" (1 Cor. 6:9). These are all a perversion of the proper use of sex. Heterosexual acts are wrong outside marriage because they set up a husband-wife relation between those who are not husband and wife. Homosexual acts are wrong because they set up a unique husband-wife relation between those who cannot be husband and wife, since they are both of the same sex.

Of course, the biblical prohibitions on homosexuality do not refer to close friendships (with physical affection) between those of the same sex. Such friendships are both normal and beautiful. David and Jonathan are a classic example. The Scriptures say, "The soul of Jonathan was knit to the soul of David, and Jonathan loved him as his own soul" (1 Sam. 18:1). Intimate friendship is one thing; illegitimate and unnatural sexual encounters are quite another thing. . . .

Hierarchical Basis for a Christian View of Sex

. . . Does not the justifiable case of divorce (viz., when one's partner has been unfaithful) mentioned by Jesus (Matt. 19:9) provide an exception to the morality of the marital bond? From a biblical and hierarchical point of view the answer . . . is no. . . . There are no legitimate exceptions to the permanence of the marriage bond (divorce as such is wrong); there are only some transcendent obligations which may intervene. That is, some duties are higher than others. There are some circumstances where even the monogamous marital relation is overshadowed by a higher responsibility. . . .

Divorce and a Hierarchy of Duty

Divorce is not an exception to the biblical ethic, "What therefore God has joined together, let no man put asunder" (Matt. 19:6). However, the biblical rule is not: "Divorce is always wrong." The rule is this: "A permanent, abiding, and unique relation is always right." In other words, the Scriptures are concerned with the *permanence* of marriage. The rule is to keep a unique love relation going at all costs as long as it does not mean the perpetuation of an evil or lesser good in favor of a greater good.

The question, then, is not really of "divorce" (separation) but one of whether there really is still a "marriage" (union) of two persons. That is, of course, man should not divide what God has united; the question is: Has God united this couple? If God has not united them in a unique and abiding love, then it can be just as wrong to try to unite what God has not united. Jesus' reference to fornication or unchastity as a ground for separation is a case in point. If one partner has broken the unique marital relation by sexually joining himself (or herself) to another, then both the permanence and uniqueness of the bond has been broken. In such a case, where there is no chance of restoring and perpetuating a permanently meaningful relation, then separation is better.

In 1 Corinthians 7 Paul seems to develop further the legitimate grounds for terminating a marriage to include the unwillingness of the unbelieving partner to keep the contract going after the other has become a Christian. "But if the unbelieving partner desires to separate, let it be so; in such a case the brother or sister is not bound [to their marriage vows]" (v. 15).[4] If this is the correct interpretation of the passage, then Paul is supporting the point that God is primarily concerned with making permanent those relations where there is a willingness or consent among the partners. Of course, this does not mean that mere incompatibility is a ground for divorce. Love demands effort to overcome differences. But if there cannot be a unique and abiding union, there is no reason to force a permanent impersonalism out of it. God is interested in permanently joining persons in a personal relationship. If this is not possible between persons A and B, then we may assume that separating them will be more helpful to more persons (children included) than solidifying this bad relationship.

Under what higher responsibilities, then, are divorce or separation justified? (1) When God never joined them in a unique love relation to begin with and when there is no hope that it will occur in the future (Matt. 19:6). (2) When the unique relation is irreparably broken by unfaithfulness (Matt. 19:9). (3) When one partner "dies," i.e., when a permanent physical separation occurs. This may be an actual physical death or its equivalent. A soldier "lost in action" may in time be pronounced legally "dead" and his wife released to remarry. Even a spaceman's being lost in space could qualify his wife to remarry. These are not exceptions to the permanence of marriage. For a permanent marriage partnership depends on there being two persons willing to carry on this unique relation.

Fornication and a Hierarchy of Duty

If polygamy and divorce or separation may sometimes be justified in view of a higher responsibility, can fornication or sexual intercourse outside of marriage ever be morally right? Again the answer is no, not as such. However, there may be some overriding responsibilities which could exempt one from his normal responsibilities. For example, one may be obliged to engage in sexual intercourse outside of his own marriage in order to save a life. Such would be the greatest good in that situation. Surely the refusal to save a life (or lives) by way of sex would not be right. Of course, one would want to explore all other possible alternatives before he assumed there was really no other way to save the life.

Sexual encounters for purely therapeutic reasons would be morally unjustifiable. There are other ways to release tension and to heal. Besides, sexual fidelity is a higher value than the achievement of one's psychic balance. Indeed, sexual infidelity may very well contribute to psychic imbalance. Fletcher is wrong in implying that the harlot was right in teaching the young sailor self-confidence.[5] There are other ways of teaching self-confidence without sinning sexually. Lower ethic responsibilities like sexual fidelity are to be suspended only in view of higher ones like saving a life and then only if there is no other way to save the life.

There may be times when the lives of many people depend on the information that can be obtained only by the sacrifice of one's sexual purity. If so, then the patriotic "prostitute" is a moral possibility. Esther put her sex as well as her life on the line for her people, being urged that she was called to the kingdom for such a purpose as this (Esth. 4:14). In a similar manner it is conceivable that sex could be used to save lives if that was the *only* way to get the needed information or whatever.

Summary and Conclusion

Sexual fidelity is based in the highly personal, unique, and abiding relationship which sexual intercourse establishes between two persons of the opposite sex. God made sex good and gave the good channel through which it is to be exercised, viz., the life-long commitment called marriage. Only the monogamous relation perfectly exemplifies this unique (one-of-a-kind) relation. No man can have two one-of-a-kind marital relations at once. Polygamy is thus eliminated from the morally normative. Only if there is some higher, transcending duty can one be morally exempt from his monogamous relation.

In like manner, the marriage commitment is life-long. Marriage is not only a unique relationship but a permanent one. What God has joined men should not separate. This does not mean that God has joined everyone who have joined themselves. Then, too, there are cases when the lower duty to one's wife is transcended by a higher duty to human life. On such occasions intercourse outside marriage might possibly be morally justified. However, the higher obligation does not break the lower one; it merely suspends it temporarily. There are no exceptions to the rule of sexual fidelity; there are only some exemptions in view of higher values. Sexual fidelity is a high moral value, but human life and direct duty to God are even higher. The Christian ought always to do the highest good possible.

Notes

[1] As Plato observed long ago, uncontrolled passions have a despotic effect on the individual as well as on his society. Cf. *Republic* IX, 576–579.

[2] The discussion here is summarized from a recent book by Herbert J. Miles, *Sexual Understanding Before Marriage,* Grand Rapids, Zondervan Publishing House, 1971, pp. 137f.

[3] The Revised Standard Version renders "sodomite" by the words "cult prostitute."

⁴Others interpret this to mean that they are not bound to continue to live together. That is, the verse is approving separation but not divorce.

⁵Joseph Fletcher, *Situation Ethics,* pp. 126–127.

Discussion Questions

1. If you did not accept the Bible as authorative would Geisler's arguments have any weight? Why or why not?

2. Is Geisler's position in any way unlike what you see as the usual Christian view of sexual morality? What in Geisler's position do you agree or disagree with? Why?

3. Geisler argues that because sex is powerful it needs to be controlled. Do you agree that it needs to be controlled in the way that Geisler states? Why or why not?

4. Argue for or against all or part of Geisler's view of the function of sex.

5. What hierarchy of values does Geisler's position imply? Give arguments for or against this hierarchy of values.

Sexual Perversion

Thomas Nagel

There is something to be learned about sex from the fact that we possess a concept of sexual perversion. I wish to examine the concept, defending it against the charge of unintelligibility and trying to say exactly what about human sexuality qualifies it to admit of perversions. Let me make some preliminary comments about the problem before embarking on its solution.

Some people do not believe that the notion of sexual perversion makes sense, and even those who do disagree over its application. Nevertheless I think it will be widely conceded that, if the concept is viable at all, it must meet certain general conditions. First, if there are any sexual perversions, they will have to be sexual desires or practices that can be plausibly described as in some sense unnatural, though the explanation of this natural/unnatural distinction is of course the main problem. Second, certain practices will be perversions if anything is, such as shoe fetishism, bestiality, and sadism; other practices, such as unadorned sexual intercourse, will not be; about still others there is controversy. Third, if there are perversions, they will be unnatural sexual *inclinations* rather than merely unnatural practices adopted not from inclination but for other reasons. I realize that this is at variance with the view, maintained by some Roman Catholics, that contraception is a sexual perversion. But although contraception may qualify

From the *Journal of Philosophy,* vol. 66 (1969). Reprinted by permission of the author and the publisher.

as a deliberate perversion of the sexual and reproductive functions, it cannot be significantly described as a *sexual* perversion. A sexual perversion must reveal itself in conduct that expresses an unnatural *sexual* preference. And although there might be a form of fetishism focused on the employment of contraceptive devices, that is not the usual explanation for their use.

I wish to declare at the outset my belief that the connection between sex and reproduction has no bearing on sexual perversion. The latter is a concept of psychological, not physiological interest, and it is a concept that we do not apply to the lower animals, let alone to plants, all of which have reproductive functions that can go astray in various ways. (Think of seedless oranges.) Insofar as we are prepared to regard higher animals as perverted, it is because of their psychological, not their anatomical similarity to humans. Furthermore, we do not regard as a perversion every deviation from the reproductive function of sex in humans: sterility, miscarriage, contraception, abortion.

Another matter that I believe has no bearing on the concept of sexual perversion is social disapprobation or custom. Anyone inclined to think that in each society the perversions are those sexual practices of which the community disapproves, should consider all the societies that have frowned upon adultery and fornication. These have not been regarded as unnatural practices, but have been thought objectionable in other ways. What is regarded as unnatural admittedly varies from culture to culture, but the classification is not a pure expression of disapproval or distaste. In fact it is often regarded as a *ground* for disapproval, and that suggests that the classification has an independent content.

I am going to attempt a psychological account of sexual perversion, which will depend on a specific psychological theory of sexual desire and human sexual interactions. To approach this solution I wish first to consider a contrary position, one which provides a basis for skepticism about the existence of any sexual perversions at all, and perhaps about the very significance of the term. The skeptical argument runs as follows:

"Sexual desire is simply one of the appetites, like hunger and thirst. As such it may have various objects, some more common than others perhaps, but none in any sense 'natural.' An appetite is identified as sexual by means of the organs and erogenous zones in which its satisfaction can be to some extent localized, and the special sensory pleasures which form the core of that satisfaction. This enables us to recognize widely divergent goals, activities, and desires as sexual, since it is conceivable in principle that anything should produce sexual pleasure and that a nondeliberate, sexually charged desire for it should arise (as a result of conditioning, if nothing else). We may fail to empathize with some of these desires, and some of them, like sadism, may be objectionable on extraneous grounds, but once we have observed that they meet the criteria for being sexual, there is nothing more to be said on *that* score. Either they are sexual or they are not: sexuality does not admit of imperfection, or perversion, or any other such qualification—it is not that sort of affection."

This is probably the received radical position. It suggests that the cost of defending a psychological account may be to deny that sexual desire is an appetite. But insofar as that line of defense is plausible, it should make us suspicious of the simple picture of appetites on which the skepticism depends. Perhaps the standard appetites, like hunger, cannot be classed as pure appetites, in that sense either, at least in their human versions.

Let us approach the matter by asking whether we can imagine anything that would qualify as a gastronomical perversion. Hunger and eating are importantly like sex in that they serve a biological function and also play a significant role in our inner lives. It is noteworthy that there is little temptation to describe as perverted an appetite for substances that are not nourishing. We should probably not consider someone's appetites as *perverted* if he liked to eat paper, sand, wood, or cotton. Those are merely rather odd and very unhealthy tastes: they lack the psychological complexity that we expect of perversions. (Coprophilia, being already a sexual perversion, may be disregarded.) If on the other hand someone liked to eat cookbooks, or magazines with pictures of food in them, and preferred these to ordinary food—or if when hungry he sought satisfaction by fondling a napkin or ashtray from his favorite restaurant—then the concept of perversion might seem appropriate (in fact it would be natural to describe this as a case of gastronomical fetishism). It would be natural to describe as gastronomically perverted someone who could eat only by having food forced down his throat through a funnel, or only if the meal were a living animal. What helps in such cases is the peculiarity of the desire itself, rather than the inappropriateness of its object to the biological function that the desire serves. Even an appetite, it would seem, can have perversions if in addition to its biological function it has a significant psychological structure.

In the case of hunger, psychological complexity is provided by the activities that give it expression. Hunger is not merely a disturbing sensation that can be quelled by eating; it is an attitude toward edible portions of the external world, a desire to relate to them in rather special ways. The method of ingestion: chewing, savoring, swallowing, appreciating the texture and smell, all are important components of the relation, as it is the passivity and controllability of the food (the only animals we eat live are helpless mollusks). Our relation to food depends also on our size: we do not live upon it or burrow into it like aphids or worms. Some of these features are more central than others, but any adequate phenomenology of eating would have to treat it as a relation to the external world and a way of appropriating bits of that world, with characteristic affection. Displacements or serious restrictions of the desire to eat could then be described as perversions, if they undermined that direct relation between man and food which is the natural expression of hunger. This explains why it is easy to imagine gastronomical fetishism, voyeurism, exhibitionism, or even gastronomical sadism and masochism. Indeed some of these perversions are fairly common.

If we can imagine perversions of an appetite like hunger, it should be possible to make sense of the concept of sexual perversion. I do not wish to imply that sexual desire is an appetite—only that being an appetite is no bar to admitting of perversions. Like hunger, sexual desire has as its characteristic object a certain relation with something in the external world; only in this case it is usually a person rather than an omelet, and the relation is considerably more complicated. This added complication allows scope for correspondingly complicated perversions.

The fact that sexual desire is a feeling about other persons may tempt us to take a pious view of its psychological content. There are those who believe that sexual desire is properly the expression of some other attitude, like love, and that when it occurs by itself it is incomplete and unhealthy—or at any rate subhuman. (The extreme Platonic version of such a view is that sexual practices are all vain attempts to express something they cannot in principle achieve: this makes them all perversions, in a sense.) I do not believe that any such view is correct. Sexual desire is complicated enough without having to be linked to anything else as a condition for phenomenological analysis. It cannot be denied that sex may serve various functions—economic, social, altruistic—but it also has its own content as a relation between persons, and it is only by analyzing that relation that we can understand the conditions of sexual perversion.

I believe it is very important that the object of sexual attraction is a particular individual, who transcends the properties that make him attractive. When different persons are attracted to a single person for different reasons: eyes, hair, figure, laugh, intelligence—we feel that the object of their desire is nevertheless the same, namely that person. There is even an inclination to feel that this is so if the lovers have different sexual aims, if they include both men and women, for example. Different specific attractive characteristics seem to provide enabling conditions for the operation of a single basic feeling, and the different aims all provide expressions of it. We approach the sexual attitude toward the person through the features that we find attractive, but these features are not the objects of that attitude.

This is very different from the case of an omelet. Various people may desire it for different reasons, one for its fluffiness, another for its mushrooms, another for its unique combination of aroma and visual aspect; yet we do not enshrine the transcendental omelet as the true common object of their affections. Instead we might say that several desires have accidentally converged on the same object: any omelet with the crucial characteristics would do as well. It is not similarly true that any person with the same flesh distribution and way of smoking can be substituted as object for a particular sexual desire that has been elicited by those characteristics. It may be that they will arouse attraction whenever they recur, but it will be a new sexual attraction with a new particular object, not merely a transfer of the old desire to someone else. (I believe this is true even in cases where the new object is unconsciously identified with a former one.)

The importance of this point will emerge when we see how complex a psychological interchange constitutes the natural development of sexual attraction. This would be incomprehensible if its object were not a particular person, but rather a person of a certain *kind*. Attraction is only the beginning, and fulfillment does not consist merely of behavior and contact expressing this attraction, but involves much more.

The best discussion of these matters that I have seen appears in part III of Sartre's *Being and Nothingness*.[1] Since it has influenced my own views, I shall say a few things about it now. Sartre's treatment of sexual desire and of love, hate, sadism, masochism, and further attitudes toward others, depends on a general theory of consciousness and the body which we can neither expound nor assume here. He does not discuss perversion, and this is partly because he regards sexual desire as one form of the perpetual attempt of an embodied consciousness to come to terms with the existence of others, an attempt that is as doomed to fail in this form as it is in any of the others, which include sadism and masochism (if not certain of the more impersonal deviations) as well as several nonsexual attitudes. According to Sartre, all attempts to incorporate the other into my world as another subject, i.e., to apprehend him at once as an object for me and as a subject for whom I am an object, are unstable and doomed to collapse into one or other of the two aspects. Either I reduce him entirely to an object, in which case his subjectivity escapes the possession or appropriation I can extend to that object; or I become merely an object for him, in which case I am no longer in a position to appropriate his subjectivity. Moreover, neither of these aspects is stable; each is continually in danger of giving way to the other. This has the consequence that there can be no such thing as a *successful* sexual relation, since the deep aim of sexual desire cannot in principle be accomplished. It seems likely, therefore, that the view will not permit a basic distinction between successful or complete and unsuccessful or incomplete sex, and therefore cannot admit the concept of perversion.

I do not adopt this aspect of the theory, nor many of its metaphysical underpinnings. What interests me is Sartre's picture of the attempt. He says that the type of possession that is the object of sexual desire is carried out by "a double reciprocal incarnation" and that this is accomplished, typically in the form of a caress, in the following way: "I make myself flesh in order to impel the Other to realize *for herself* and *for me* her own flesh, and my caresses cause my flesh to be born for me in so far as it is for the Other *flesh causing her to be born as flesh*" (391; italics Sartre's). The incarnation in question is described variously as a clogging or troubling of consciousness which is inundated by the flesh in which it is embodied.

The view I am going to suggest, I hope in less obscure language, is related to this one, but it differs from Sartre's in allowing sexuality to achieve its goal on occasion and thus in providing the concept of perversion with a foothold.

Sexual desire involves a kind of perception, but not merely a single perception of its object, for in the paradigm case of mutual desire there is a complex system of superimposed mutual perceptions—not only perceptions of the sexual object, but perceptions of oneself. Moreover, sexual awareness of another involves considerable self-awareness to begin with—more than is involved in ordinary sensory perception. The experience is felt as an assault on oneself by the view (or touch, or whatever) of the sexual object.

Let us consider a case in which the elements can be separated. For clarity we will restrict ourselves initially to the somewhat artificial case of desire at a distance. Suppose a man and a woman, whom we may call Romeo and Juliet, are at opposite ends of a cocktail lounge, with many mirrors on the walls which permit unobserved observation, and even mutual unobserved observation. Each of them is sipping a martini and studying other people in the mirrors. At some point Romeo notices Juliet. He is moved, somehow, by the softness of her hair and the diffidence with which she sips her martini, and this arouses him sexually. Let us say that X *senses* Y whenever X regards Y with sexual desire. (Y need not be a person, and $X's$ apprehension of Y can be visual, tactile, olfactory, etc., or purely imaginary; in the present example we shall concentrate on vision.) So Romeo senses Juliet, rather than merely noticing her. At this stage he is aroused by an unaroused object, so he is more in the sexual grip of his body than she of hers.

Let us suppose, however, that Juliet now senses Romeo in another mirror on the opposite wall, though neither of them yet knows that he is seen by the other (the mirror angles provide three-quarter views). Romeo then begins to notice in Juliet the subtle signs of sexual arousal: heavy-lidded stare, dilating pupils, faint flush, et cetera. This of course renders her much more bodily, and he not only notices but senses this as well. His arousal is nevertheless still solitary. But now, cleverly calculating the line of her stare without actually looking her in the eyes, he realizes that it is directed at him through the mirror on the opposite wall. That is, he notices, and moreover senses, Juliet sensing him. This is definitely a new development, for it gives him a sense of embodiment not only through his own reactions but through the eyes and reactions of another. Moreover, it is separable from the initial sensing of Juliet; for sexual arousal might begin with a person's sensing that he is sensed and being assailed by the perception of the other person's desire rather than merely by the perception of the person.

But there is a further step. Let us suppose that Juliet, who is a little slower than Romeo, now senses that he senses her. This puts Romeo in a position to notice, and be aroused by, her arousal at being sensed by him. He senses that she senses that he senses her. This is still another level of arousal, for he becomes conscious of his sexuality through his awareness of its effect on her and of her awareness that this effect is due to him. Once she takes the same step and senses that he senses her sensing him, it becomes difficult to state, let alone imagine, further iterations, though they may be logically distinct. If both are alone, they will presumably turn to look at each other directly, and the proceedings will continue on another plane. Physical contact and intercourse are perfectly natural extensions of this complicated visual exchange, and mutual touch can involve all the complexities of awareness present in the visual case, but with a far greater range of subtlety and acuteness.

Ordinarily, of course, things happen in a less orderly fashion—sometimes in a great rush—but I believe that some version of this overlapping system of distinct sexual perceptions and interactions is the basic framework of any full-fledged sexual relation and that relations involving only part of the complex are significantly incomplete. The account is only schematic, as it must be to achieve generality. Every real sexual act will be psychologically far more specific and detailed, in ways that depend not only on the physical techniques employed and on anatomical details, but also on countless features of the participants' conceptions of themselves and of each other, which become embodied in the act. (It is a familiar enough fact, for example, that people often take their social roles and the social roles of their partners to bed with them.)

The general schema is important, however, and the proliferation of levels of mutual awareness it involves is an example of a type of complexity that typifies human interactions. Consider aggression, for example. If I am angry with someone, I want to make him feel it, either to produce self-reproach by getting him to see himself through the eyes of my anger, and to dislike what he sees—or else to produce reciprocal anger or fear, by getting him to perceive my anger as a threat or attack. What I want will depend on the details of my anger, but in either case it will involve a desire that the object of that anger be aroused. This accomplishment constitutes the fulfillment of my emotion, through domination of the object's feelings.

Another example of such reflexive mutual recognition is to be found in the phenomenon of meaning, which appears to involve an intention to produce a belief or other effect in another by bringing about his recognition of one's intention to produce that effect. (That result is due to H. P. Grice,[2] whose position I shall not attempt to reproduce in detail.) Sex has a related structure: it involves a desire that one's partner be aroused by the recognition of one's desire that he or she be aroused.

It is not easy to define the basic types of awareness and arousal of which these complexes are composed, and that remains a lacuna in this discussion. I believe that the object of awareness is the same in one's own case as it is in one's sexual awareness of another, although the two awarenesses will not be the same, the difference being as great as that between feeling angry and experiencing the anger of another. All stages of sexual perception are varieties of identification of a person with his body. What is perceived is one's own or another's *subjection* to or *immersion* in his body, a phenomenon which has been recognized with loathing by St. Paul and St. Augustine, both of whom regarded "the law of sin which is in my members" as a grave threat to the dominion of the holy will.[3] In sexual desire and its expression the blending of involuntary response with deliberate control is extremely important. For Augustine, the revolution launched against him by his body is symbolized by erection and the other involuntary physical components of arousal. Sartre too stresses the fact that the penis is not a prehensile organ. But mere involuntariness characterizes other bodily processes as well. In sexual desire the involuntary responses are combined with submission to spontaneous impulses: not only one's pulse and secretions but one's actions are taken over by the body; ideally, deliberate control is needed only to guide the expression of those impulses. This is to some extent also true of an appetite like hunger, but the takeover there is more localized, less pervasive, less extreme. One's whole body does not become saturated with hunger as it can with desire. But the most characteristic feature of a specifically sexual immersion in the body is its ability to fit into the complex of mutual perceptions that we have described. Hunger leads to spontaneous interactions with food; sexual desire leads to spontaneous interactions with other persons, whose bodies are asserting their sovereignty in the same way, producing involuntary reactions and spontaneous impulses in *them*. These reactions are perceived, and the perception of them is perceived, and that perception is in turn perceived, at each step the domination of the person by his body is reinforced, and the sexual partner becomes more possessible by physical contact, penetration, and envelopment.

Desire is therefore not merely the perception of a preexisting embodiment of the other, but ideally a contribution to his further embodiment which in turn enhances the original subject's sense of himself. This explains why it is important that the partner be aroused, and not merely aroused, but aroused by the awareness of one's desire. It also explains the sense in which desire has unity and possession as its object: physical possession must eventuate in creation of the sexual object in the image of one's desire, and not merely in the object's recognition of that desire, or in his or her own private arousal. (This may reveal a male bias: I shall say something about that later.)

To return, finally, to the topic of perversion: I believe that various familiar deviations constitute truncated or incomplete versions of the complete configuration, and may therefore be regarded as perversions of the central impulse.

In particular, narcissistic practices and intercourse with animals, infants, and inanimate objects seem to be stuck at some primitive version of the first stage. If the object is not alive, the experience is reduced entirely to an awareness of one's own sexual embodiment. Small children and animals permit awareness of the embodiment of the other, but present obstacles to reciprocity, to the recognition by the sexual object of the subject's desire as the source of his (the object's) sexual self-awareness.

Sadism concentrates on the evocation of passive self-awareness in others, but the sadist's engagement is itself active and requires a retention of deliberate control which impedes awareness of himself as a bodily subject of passion in the required sense. The victim must recognize him as the source of his own sexual passivity, but only as the active source. De Sade claimed that the object of sexual desire was to evoke involuntary responses from one's partner, especially audible ones. The infliction of pain is no doubt the most efficient way to accomplish this, but it requires a certain abrogation of one's own exposed spontaneity. All this, incidentally, helps to explain why it is tempting to regard as sadistic an excessive preoccupation with sexual technique, which does not permit one to abandon the role of agent at any stage of the sexual act. Ideally one should be able to surmount one's technique at some point.

A masochist on the other hand imposes the same disability on his partner as the sadist imposes on himself. The masochist cannot find a satisfactory embodiment as the object of another's sexual desire, but only as the object of his control. He is passive not in relation to his partner's passion but in relation to his nonpassive agency. In addition, the subjection to one's body characteristic of pain and physical restraint is of a very different kind from that of sexual excitement: pain causes people to contract rather than dissolve.

Both of these disorders have to do with the second stage, which involves the awareness of oneself as an object of desire. In straightforward sadism and masochism other attentions are substituted for desire as a source of the object's self-awareness. But it is also possible for nothing of that sort to be substituted, as in the case of a masochist who is satisfied with self-inflicted pain or of a sadist who does not insist on playing a role in the suffering that arouses him. Greater difficulties of classification are presented by three other categories of sexual activity: elaborations of the sexual act; intercourse of more than two persons; and homosexuality.

If we apply our model to the various forms that may be taken by two-party heterosexual intercourse, none of them seem clearly to qualify as perversions. Hardly anyone can be found these days to inveigh against oral-genital contact, and the merits of buggery are urged by such respectable figures as D. H. Lawrence and Norman Mailer. There may be something vaguely sadistic about the latter technique (in Mailer's writings it seems to be a method of introducing an element of rape), but it is not obvious that this has to be so. In general, it would appear that any bodily contact between a man and a woman that gives them sexual pleasure, is a possible vehicle for the system of multi-level interpersonal awareness that I have claimed is the basic psychological content of sexual interaction. Thus a liberal platitude about sex is upheld.

About multiple combinations, the least that can be said is that they are bound to be complicated. If one considers how difficult it is to carry on two conversations simultaneously, one may appreciate the problems of multiple simultaneous interpersonal perception that can arise in even a small-scale orgy. It may be inevitable that some of the component relations should degenerate into mutual epidermal stimulation by participants otherwise isolated from each other. There may also be a tendency toward voyeurism and exhibitionism, both of which are incomplete relations. The exhibitionist wishes to display his desire without needing to be desired in return; he may even fear the sexual attentions of others. A voyeur, on the other hand, need not require any recognition by his object at all: certainly not a recognition of the voyeur's arousal.

It is not clear whether homosexuality is a perversion if that is measured by the standard of the described configuration, but it seems unlikely. For such a classification would have to depend on the possibility of extracting from the system a distinction between male and female sexuality; and much that has been said so far applies equally to men and women. Moreover, it would have to be maintained that there was a natural tie between the type of sexuality and the sex of the body, and also that two sexualities of the same type could not interact properly.

Certainly there is much support for an aggressive-passive distinction between male and female sexuality. In our culture the male's arousal tends to initiate the perceptual exchange, he usually makes the sexual approach, largely controls the course of the act, and of course penetrates whereas the woman receives. When two men or women engage in intercourse they cannot both adhere to these sexual roles. The question is how essential the roles are to an adequate sexual relation. One relevant observation is that a good deal of deviation from these roles occurs in heterosexual intercourse. Women can be sexually aggressive and men passive, and temporary reversals of role are not uncommon in heterosexual exchanges of reasonable length. If such conditions are set aside, it may be urged that there is something irreducibly perverted in attraction to a body anatomically like one's own. But alarming as some people in our culture may find such attraction, it remains psychologically unilluminating to class it as perverted. Certainly if homosexuality is a perversion, it is so in a very different sense from that in which shoe-fetishism is a perversion, for some version of the full range of interpersonal perceptions seems perfectly possible between two persons of the same sex.

In any case, even if the proposed model is correct, it remains implausible to describe as perverted every deviation from it. For example, if the partners in heterosexual intercourse indulge in private heterosexual fantasies, that obscures the recognition of the real partner and so, on the theory, constitutes a defective sexual relation. It is not, however, generally regarded as a perversion. Such examples suggest that a simple dichotomy between perverted and unperverted sex is too crude to organize the phenomena adequately.

I should like to close with some remarks about the relation of perversion to good, bad, and morality. The concept of perversion can hardly fail to be evaluative in some sense, for it appears to involve the notion of an ideal or at least adequate sexuality which the perversions in some way fail to achieve. So, if the concept is viable, the judgment that a person or practice or desire is perverted will constitute a sexual evaluation, implying that better sex, or a better specimen of sex, is possible. This in itself is a very weak claim, since the evaluation might be in a dimension that is of little interest to us. (Though, if my account is correct, that will not be true.)

Whether it is a moral evaluation, however, is another question entirely—one whose answer would require more understanding of both morality and perversion than can be deployed here. Moral evaluation of acts and of persons is a rather special and very complicated matter, and by no means all our evaluations of persons and their activities are moral evaluations. We make judgments about people's beauty or health or intelligence which are evaluative without being moral. Assessments of their sexuality may be similar in that respect.

Furthermore, moral issues aside, it is not clear that unperverted sex is necessarily *preferable* to the perversions. It may be that sex which receives the highest marks for perfection *as sex* is less enjoyable than certain perversions; and if enjoyment is considered very important, that might outweigh considerations of sexual perfection in determining rational preference.

That raises the question of the relation between the evaluative content of judgments of perversions and the rather common *general* distinction between good and bad sex. The latter distinction is usually confined to sexual acts, and it would seem, within limits, to cut across the other: even someone who believed, for example, that homosexuality was a perversion could admit a distinction between better and worse homosexual sex, and might even allow that good homosexual sex could be better *sex* than not very good unperverted sex. If this is correct, it supports the position that, if judgments of perversion are viable at all, they represent only one aspect of the possible evaluation of sex, even *qua sex*. Moreover it is not the only important aspect: certainly sexual deficiencies that evidently do not constitute perversions can be the object of great concern.

Finally, even if perverted sex is to that extent not so good as it might be, bad sex is generally better than none at all. This should not be controversial: it seems to hold for other important matters, like food, music, literature, and society. In the end, one must choose from among the available alternatives, whether their availability depends on the environment or on one's own constitution. And the alternatives have to be fairly grim before it becomes rational to opt for nothing.[4]

Notes

[1] Translated by Hazel E. Barnes (New York: Philosophical Library, 1956).
[2] "Meaning," *Philosophical Review*, LXVI, 3 (July 1957): 377–388.
[3] See Romans, VII, 23; and the *Confessions*, Book 8, V.
[4] My research was supported in part by the National Science Foundation.

Discussion Questions

1. On what points would Nagel agree with Geisler? On what points would they disagree? Where they disagree, who is right? Why?
2. How does Nagel define sexual perversion? What objections could be raised against this definition?
3. According to Nagel, what is the importance of Sartre's theories for understanding sex? Where does Nagel disagree with Sartre? Who is right? Why?
4. What is Nagel's theory of sex as a human interaction? Argue for or against his theory.
5. Nagel concludes that "bad sex is generally better than none at all." Do you agree or disagree? Why?

Sex and Perversion

Robert Solomon

Sexuality is often said to be one of the appetites, like thirst and hunger—an instinctual drive, the animal lust that invades the ego from the subconscious "it" and that is without logic, morality, scruples, and often without taste. But if sexuality were merely an appetite, it would be inexplicable that our lives should be so complicated, so threatened, so secretive and repressed, so ritualized and obsessed by a desire that has so little survival value and such dangers. Like the appetites, sexuality admits of failures of both deficiency and excess, although it is understandably only the former that is common cause for grievance. Sexuality also admits of infinite variations for the sake of sociability, elegance, taste, and diversion, once its most primitive demands have been met, and here again it resembles thirst and hunger. But sexuality, at least in this and many other societies, is thought to have a dimension that hunger and thirst surely lack, a moral and interpersonal dimension that is essential to our very conception of sexuality. . . .

. . . It was Freud, primarily in his "Three Contributions to the Theory of Sex," who changed our conception of sexuality from reproduction to sex-for-its-own-sake, to personal satisfaction. (Although it is necessary to stress that Freud took the new concept, as well as the old one, to be a *biological,* and thereby a "natural," conception.) It was Freud who argued that sexual activity is aimed at release of tension or "discharge" (which he called, misleadingly, "pleasure") and as such aims at no further goals. So conceived, the paradigm sexual activity might be thought of not in terms of heterosexual intercourse but in terms of scratching an itch. Of course the activity that releases tension also serves to increase the tension to be released (the greater the "pleasure"). So conceived, genital sex is but a single possibility for sexual activity, based on the *contingency* that the genitals of an adult generally provide the most prominent erogenous zone; that is, it itches or can be made to itch more than any other place on the body and thus feels better when appropriately scratched. Freud's theory, although based on painstaking empirical observations, clearly marks a conceptual or philosophical revolution as well as a scientific one. According to this conception of sex, heterosexual intercourse loses both its logically and its biologically privileged position in the repertoire of human sexual response. It is no longer *logically* privileged because sex is now conceived in terms of discharge (or "pleasure"), and it is at most a contingent fact (and probably not even that) that most people gain the greatest release of tension (or "pleasure") from intercourse alone. It is no longer biologically privileged because sex as sex is no longer conceived in terms of the further purposes it serves but rather in its own terms. It should be noted that sexuality, so conceived, is no longer "an aspect of," but is the contrary of, reproductive sex: it is defined as an activity that, as sex, has no further aims. Accordingly, intercourse with the explicit intention to conceive children is no longer pure sex, but sex plus something else. . . .

[But] If sexuality were merely release of tension for its own sake, the paradigm of sexuality would remain, as I suggested, the scratching of an itch, and if that itch happened to involve the genitals, sexuality would take as its paradigm masturbation. But this concept of sexuality, which agrees with the traditional conceptions in accepting as its

From the *Journal of Philosophy,* vol. 71, no. 11 (1974). Reprinted by permission of the author and publisher.

paradigm the sexual "union" of two people, surely is not our concept. And, given Freud's account, the appropriate question is why we bother, given the enormous amount of effort and the continuous threats to our egos and our health, to attempt to engage in sex mutually instead of in solitude and in the safety and convenience of our own rooms. On this account it would seem that our sexual paradigm ought to be masturbation, and sexual release with other people an unnecessary complication. And before he backslides into heterosexual evacuation lust, Freud appears to hold just this view, insofar as sexual release to bodily tension remains for him the "primary process." But clearly our sexual paradigms are to be found elsewhere, in our attraction for and enjoyment of other people, in what Freud calls the "secondary processes." According to Freud it is not just the body that seeks release, but the "psychic apparatus," and the tension from which it suffers is not due to "inner" tensions alone, but to relations and identifications with sexual "objects," that is, other people.

In insisting that the paradigm of sexuality involves a relationship with other people, let me quickly point out that this is as far as can be from the pious linkage of sex and love. One may love another person with whom he or she is sexually involved, but there are any number of attitudes he or she might take toward the person to whom he or she is sexually attracted, among which, unfortunately, hate, fear, resentment, anger, jealousy, insecurity, mastery, and competition are probably far more common and more powerful than the rare and delicate threads of love and respect.

Freud's revolutionary breakthrough, though incomplete, was also too radical. In focusing our attention on the autonomous tension-releasing function of sexuality he freed sexuality from its former religious and moral restrictions, but at the expense of completely cutting it off from all other human activities. This new-found autonomy of sexuality, the source of our sexual freedom, has now become our main sexual problem. As more of us enjoy more sexual activity, sex itself has become less satisfying and more "meaningless." We now have to see once again that sexual tension and its release is not the whole of sex, nor even its major aspect. Rather it is Freud's "secondary" aspect of sexuality, the "psychical" aspect, that explains its nature and its overwhelming importance in our affairs. For sex is primarily for us a way of relating to other people and only secondarily and in a primitive way a matter of release of "sexual tension."

The belief that sexuality is primarily a matter of enjoyment has become commonplace since Freud; in fact it is often suggested that sexual activity is the closest we can come to "pure pleasure." But this emphasis on pleasure, like Freud's stress on release of tension (these were equivalent for him), fails to explain the enormous stress we put on these activities. (Man is basically *not* a pleasure-seeking animal.) It fails to explain why sex for us is *essentially* with other people, why our own enjoyment in sex is so bound up with the pleasure of someone else. Aristotle, in his attack on the hedonists of his day, insisted that pleasure was not an activity itself but rather an accompaniment of gratifying activity. In sex, we are not satisfied by our enjoyment, but rather we enjoy ourselves because we are satisfied. But then, once again, what is the activity that we satisfy in sexuality?

The problem still with us is the predominantly male paradigm of "evacuation lust," once rationalized as the "natural" means to reproduction, now justified by appeal to the "natural" enjoyment it involves. Sexuality typically involves discharge of tension (both physical and psychological), but Freud's "primary process" is not the essence of sexuality, and evacuation lust is not its paradigm. One might say that evacuation lust plays a role in sex similar to swallowing in wine tasting. It is typically the "end" of the activity, but surely neither its goal nor its essence (it is even frowned upon in professional circles). I take our obsession with evacuation lust, in the post-Freudian as well as pre-Freudian mentality, to be a symptom of our sensual and aesthetic deprivation, like the lusty and excessive need of a "wino" who swallows without tasting a glass of delicate white Burgundy. If there is a category of sexual perversion, of abusive and demeaning sex, what often passes for "normal" or "straight" sex surely deserves a place on the list. And what is essential to sex will remain hidden from us so long as we remain fixated on the wonders of the genital orgasm.

One might suggest that what properly characterizes sexuality is not the narrow conception of pleasure entailed by the evacuation-lust model but rather the broader conception of pleasure as sensuousness. And, of course, this would be reasonable enough. It reinstates Freud's important demand that sexuality may involve any part of or the whole body, as well as the genitals. And sexuality, whatever else it may be, is surely a bodily conception. (One may be forced to stretch this demand slightly to include purely verbal or visual sexual activities—for example: telephone sex, anonymous or not; and pornography, where the body is only referred to or represented rather than actually touched. But I think it is somewhat of a tautology that no desire or activity can be sexual if it does not involve the body as a center of focus. I take it that this is what Sartre intends by his awkward phrase, "incarnation of oneself as flesh.") Which parts of the body are paradigmatically sexual varies considerably, of course, from society to society, and so do the roles of the various nontactile senses in sexual activities. In our society female breasts have acquired a somewhat bizarrely exaggerated sexual role; the sense of smell, a mysteriously diminished and even taboo sexual sense. Because of this variation it is not easy to distinguish those bodily activities that are essentially sexual from those that are not. Wrestling and dancing, acrobatics and athletics, for example, involve considerable bodily contact; yet we would not want to say that they are in every instance sexual. Teen-age petting and dancing may differ from these other activities only in minute details, yet be clearly sexual. And the wrestling scene from *Women in Love,* for example, is surely more than "symbolically" sexual. A furtive glance across the room may be highly sexual in spite of the fact that it involves the most minute movements. We may agree without controversy that sexuality is essentially physical. Yet bodily focus is not sufficient to distinguish sexuality. What else would be sufficient?

An additional component of sexuality, also to be found in Freud, is tension and the expectation of its release. "Arousal," on this account, is not merely a preliminary to sexuality but part of its essence. (Even boring sex is exciting, insofar as it is sex at all.) The fact that excitement is essential to sexuality explains how it is that many people find danger "highly sexual" and why many sexual relations can be improved if they are made a bit more daring or dangerous (short of terror, which understandably kills sexual enthusiasm). The same equation allows us to understand the confused medley of reactions we find to cinematic violence. It also allows us to understand one of the apparent anomalies of our sexual behavior, the fact that our most satisfying sexual encounters are often with strangers, where there are strong elements of tension—fear, insecurity, guilt, anticipation. Conversely, sex may be least satisfying with those whom we love and know well and whose habits and reactions are extremely well known to us. It ought to strike us as odd that we can be upsettingly attracted to a stranger who is not particularly attractive, who shares little in common with us, and who presents us with an evident set of personal and perhaps moral and medical threats. At the same time, married couples who find each other most attractive, compatible, nonthreatening, and comfortable often find intercourse more of a routine or a repetitive ritual, or as evacuation lust, to be completed efficiently and without fanfare, or perhaps as a battleground, with only a minimum of sexual desire or excitement.

But tension, arousal, and excitement, together with bodily sensuality, still add up to something much less than sexuality. Enthusiastic acrobatics or dancing is still less than sexual, and a gentle touch on a finger or cheek cannot be understood simply in the above terms. Moreover, the concepts of "tension," "arousal," and "excitement" tell us far less than they might at first appear to. We might think that such tension is uniquely sexual, but it is not. Arousal is arousal, whether it is found in reactions of fear, anger, hatred, anxiety, love, or desire. As far as excitement itself is concerned, making love, dancing, a cold shower, a Librium, a fistfight, or a two-mile jog might be equally effective. What makes tension, arousal, and excitement sexual is the nature of its object, what the tension is *about*. And it is not mere sensuality that is aroused, and it is not merely a human body (one's own or someone else's) that excites us. But to understand this "something more" that is essential to sexuality we shall have to leave the safe and well-explored confines of sensuousness and the variety of bodily activities and modes of coupling. We need a new theory in which sensuality and bodily activities and excitement might be mentioned in passing, but only as "but of course. . . . "

Sex as Language

Sexuality is primarily a means of communicating with other people, a way of talking to them, of expressing our feelings about ourselves and them. It is essentially a language, a body language, in which one can express gentleness and affection, anger and resentment, superiority and dependence far more succinctly than would be possible verbally, where expressions are unavoidably abstract and often clumsy. If sexuality is a means of communication, it is not surprising that it is *essentially* an activity performed with other people. And, if it is our best means to express what are often our dominant and difficult-to-verbalize feelings and relationships, it is not surprising that sexuality is one of the most powerful forces in our lives.

It is also evident, though not obvious, that any bodily contact and any human activity, including genital contact and the physical activity of intercourse, both might and might not be sexual. (It is difficult, but not impossible, for gentle genital contact and intercourse not to be sexual, just as it is difficult, as Wittgenstein said, to say "It is cold" in English and not mean by that that it is cold. But in a suitable context, for example, speaking in code, one might mean almost anything by "It is cold." Similarly, in suitably asexual contexts, for example, on a movie set or in a Masters and Johnson experiment, genital contact and intercourse may not be sexual, for then they would not be plausible instances of body language.)

There are other body languages, of course, and most of them can be more or less distinguished from sexual body language. Aggression, for example, while often sharing a body vocabulary with sexuality, is surely distinct. Fear is also expressed in body language, sharing some of its vocabulary with sexuality, but its bodily expression is not sexual as such. Defense, insecurity, domination, and self-confidence, and any number of various desires (including particular sensuous pleasures) are also expressed in body language. Sex is basically a nonverbal language that takes bodily movements, postures, and sensations as its form, whatever content it expresses. Now, in a sense there is but one body language, since we have but one body; but there can be different body languages, much as there are different verbal languages, in different societies. Edgar Rice Burroughs imagines a people who laugh to express sadness and cry to express amusement. More within reality, Chinese open their eyes to express anger, whereas we narrow them; so we can imagine, and find, peoples whose sexual expressions vary considerably from ours. Body languages must be publicly learned and will vary between different groups, although there are obviously biological restrictions that supply the depth grammar of all human body languages. Not all body language is sexual, and not all people need have a sexual language. (There are societies in which intercourse serves a purely reproductive or ritualistic function, or even a la Freud, the pure function of providing pleasure. Such a society, however, ours is not.

The basic vocabulary of body language is the gesture, which might be an activity but is usually an expression or a stance. The gesture is the bodily equivalent of a sentence. Particular movements (for example, the lifting of an arm) and touches have meaning only as part of a gesture. Body languages, like verbal languages, are born and grow in a societal context, as means of communication. They are, to use J. L. Austin's term, "performances" (the notion of "constative" or "descriptive" makes only minimal sense here), and they are learned and have meaning only in context. Of course, once one learns the body language, one can employ it, so to speak, alone. But in body language, as in verbal language, there can be no strictly private language. (Autoeroticism, far from being our sexual paradigm, is at best considered a borderline case.) Having learned the body language, one who travels for the sake of "adventure" to a paradisical island or to a radically different society will be grossly misunderstood. Or one can conscientiously, as does a dancer, learn new expressions and new forms of expressive elegance. But one first needs a language to vary, a given language in order to learn another. Body language, again like verbal language, is the realization of a capacity that is not equally shared by everyone. Some people are inarticulate, even retarded, others brilliant and creative. Sexual "losers" are often people who suffer more from bodily inarticulateness than verbal inability, and impotence is more often a matter of aphasia than physical damage. There are those whose body language is forceful without being either articulate or graceful. And there are those who, perhaps forceful, perhaps not, are elegant and even creative in their use of body language. An athlete might be forceful, but not articulate, and in spite of his skills of physical enunciation and projection and his large bodily vocabulary, have nothing to say. A dancer might be highly elegant, but ultimately be a solipsist. Most people, needless to say, here as in speech, know only those features of the language that are most common, most easily articulated, least committal, and least personal. Some people, including dancers by profession, articulate their body language with such perfection that every gesture is an exact and perfect expression.

Whatever else sexuality might be and for whatever purposes it might be used or abused, it is first of all language. When spoken it tends to result in pregnancy, in scandal, in jealousy and divorce (the "perlocutionary" effects of language, in Austin's terminology). It is a language that, like verbal language, but sometimes more effectively, can be used to manipulate people, to offend and to ingratiate oneself with them. It can be enjoyable, not just on account of its phonetics, which are neither enjoyable nor meaningful in themselves, but because of *what* is said. One enjoys not just the tender caress but the message it carries; and one welcomes a painful thrust or bite not because of masochism but because of the meaning, in context, that it conveys. Most sexologists, one might add, commit the McLuhanesque fallacy of confusing the medium with the message.

Sexuality, while having a certain structure that confines it, can take any number of forms. It is a language we first learn on the borderlines of sex, in shaking hands, standing with our hands on our hips, letting a cigarette droop from our lips in Junior High School, scratching our forehead or our thighs in public, looking at each other, kissing, smiling, walking, and eventually, petting and making love. Like dancing, sexuality is an extension and fine development of everyday movements, capable of open-ended refinement and individual variation, as poetry of the body. But where dancing takes its audience to be anonymous and its message impersonal, sexuality is always personal and deeply revealing. One might argue that sexuality is much less refined, much less self-consciously an "art" than dancing; but this, I would counter, is a mark of our general vulgarity and lack of self-consciousness in all things important. Nothing can or ought to be more human an art form than intimate communication.

We can now see what is wrong with "pansexualism," the idea that all human activities are sexual. Not all human activities are linguistic activities, for not all activities are intended to communicate or express either desire or interpersonal feelings. Athletic activity, acrobatics, and much dancing, for example, may be concerned with the precise performance of the body, but those activities themselves are not intended to communicate or express personal desire or feelings. And of course there are many activities that are communicative and expressive that are not essentially sexual, for example, writing poetry or philosophy, signaling a right-hand turn, or sending a telegram. But any human activity *can* be sexual insofar as it involves the use of the body as an expression of interpersonal desire. (Stances and postures need not involve touching. Consider, for example, a "provocative" appearance.) But unlike verbal language, body language is not well adapted to addressing large audiences and consequently can only appear vulgar when removed from a more intimate setting. Similarly, sex, as language, is predominantly reciprocal. And that is why mutual touch and intercourse must remain our paradigm.

Sexual Perversion Reinterpreted

If sexuality is a form of language that can be used to express almost anything, it follows that the use of sexuality admits of any number of creative as well as forced variations. As a language it also admits of breaches in comprehension, and it is here that we can locate what little is left of our conception of "sexual perversion." It should now be clear that this is not a moral term but more a logical category, a breach of comprehensibility. Accordingly, it would be advisable to drop the notion of perversion altogether and content ourselves with "sexual incompatibility" or "sexual misunderstanding." It is not always easy to distinguish abuses of the language from abuses expressed by the language, or to separate nonsense from sophistry, sexual fanaticism from sexual "politics." It is not always clear what is to count as a literal expression, a metaphorical usage, an imaginative expression, a pun, a solecism, or a bad joke. And so what might be taken as incomprehensibility and perversion by a sexual conservative would be taken as poetry or pun by someone else. Perversion, then, is a communication breakdown; it may have general guidelines but ultimately rests in the context of the bodily mutual understanding of the people involved. Quite the contrary of a moral or quasi-moral category, "sexual incompatibility" is strictly relativized, within the language, to the particular people involved.

If sexuality is essentially a language, it follows that masturbation, while not a perversion, is a deviation and not, as Freud thought, the primary case. Masturbation is essentially speaking to oneself. But not only children, lunatics, and hermits speak to themselves; so do poets and philosophers. And so masturbation might, in different contexts, count as wholly different extensions of language. With Freud, we would have to distinguish masturbation as autoeroticism from masturbation as narcissism—the first being more like muttering to oneself, the latter more like self-praise; the first being innocent and childlike, the latter potentially either pathetic or selfish and self-indulgent. Masturbation is not "self-abuse," as we were once taught, but it is, in an important sense, self-denial. It represents an inability or a refusal to say what one wants to say, going through the effort of expression without an audience, like writing to someone and then putting the letter in a drawer. If sexuality is a language, then it is primarily communicative. Autoeroticism, therefore, along with Freud's primary processes, is not primary at all, but conceptually secondary or derivative, similar to a young child's early attempts at language, which can be interpreted as phonemes only within the context of the language his parents already speak. But any language, once learned, can be spoken privately. Masturbation is this secondary, private use of sexual language—minimal rather than primary, the Archimedean standpoint of sex, essential as an ultimate retreat, but empty and without content. Masturbation is the sexual equivalent of a Cartesian soliloquy.

It is clear that between two people almost any activity *can* be fully sexual when it is an attempt to communicate mutual feelings through bodily gestures, touches, and movements. But this requires serious qualification. Expressions of domination and dependence are among the most primitive vocabulary items in our body language. But these may go beyond mere expressions and gestures to become a kind of "acting out"; and there is a difference, if only of degree, between gestures and full-blooded actions. When expressions of domination and dependence turn into actions, they become sadism and masochism, respectively. If these feelings are not complementary, they can only be interpreted as a communication breakdown, as sexual incompatibility. When sadistic actions are not expected, they are to sexuality as real bullets in a supposedly prop gun are to the stage. Again, the possible extension of sexual language depends mutually upon the participants. The subtlety and explicitness of a language depend upon the perceptivity of the conversationalists. For the articulate and the quick, sadism and masochism may consist of an apparently minor change in sexual positions, a slight but degrading change of posture that is ample expression of mutually negative or hostile feelings or of complementary dominance and submission. For the more dense or uninitiated, such expression may require outright infliction of pain or discomfort, a painful pinch or punch. In many cases we might want to say that, as Billy Budd was inarticulate, and violent as a result, sadism and masochism may be matters of inarticulateness and lack of interpersonal perception as well as products of the hostile feelings to be expressed.

There is no reason, apart from traditional squeamishness, to suppose that the employment of parts of the body other than the genitals in sexuality is perverse or need result in a breakdown of communication. Not only are these not perversions in themselves, but it may well be that those who would call them perversions are somewhat perverse themselves. The cry of perversion with regard to body language is very much like that of censorship with regard to the written word. To judge something tasteless is often itself a sign of bad taste, as in the case of the judges who banned *Ulysses* or *Lady Chatterley's Lover*. They did not prove abuses of language by the authors they condemned but rather, by attempting to castrate the language and expel some of its finest moments, displayed themselves as illiterates. Similarly, sexuality conceived as a language of intimacy and feeling that calls for ever new variation and inventiveness has as its worst violators those who, unimaginative and illiterate themselves, attempt to force others to accept their limited and impoverished vocabulary. But it might also be admitted, though it rarely is, that the common sexual variations are not for the sake of variety and pleasure alone. Oral sex and anal sex, for example, carry unavoidable expressions of domination and subservience, though these surely need not be considered degrading (as they are treated in some of Norman Mailer's writings) and may be exceptionally expressive of tenderness and trust.

Vulgarity, in this as in any art form, can be a charm in small doses but an offense when overdone. It is because sex is a language that demands subtlety and artfulness that over-frankness and vulgarity are, if not perversions, at least gross abuses of the language, as very bad poetry might still be considered poetry. This explains, for example, why overt propositions and subway exhibitionism are generally offensive, which is a mystery if one considers sex, as most people do, one of the "appetites." There are, for example, no acceptable sexual expressions that are parallel to the straightforward expression of hunger in "Let's eat" or "When is dinner?" or "Dinner is ready." Eating, of course, can be much more than the satisfaction of hunger; it can become an elegant social (and thereby also, sometimes, sexual) activity as well. But sexuality, far from being the "animal" instinct in us, appears only in those human activities where considerable refinement is possible. Sexuality permits of vulgarity only because it is itself a matter of refinement. It is therefore not at all one of those physiological functions that well-meaning sexual pedants often describe. Thus blatant sexual propositions and subway exhibitionism are offensive, not because they deviate from some "normal sexual aim" (the former, at least, being an unusually direct approach to the "normal sexual aim"), but because they are vulgar, the equivalent of an antipoetry poet who writes an entire poem consisting of a single vulgar word, or a comedian who, unable to handle condensation and understatement, has to spell out his obscene jokes explicitly. Similarly, sexuality lies in subtlety. There is sometimes nothing less appealing or satisfying, even when one is in a fully sexual mood, than a too-straightforward sexual encounter, "unadorned" by preliminary conversation—both verbal and bodily.

To other so-called perversions the same considerations apply, and the degree of the breakdown in communication is not always clear. Sexual activities themselves are not perverted; people are perverted. Fetishism in general might be a product of stupidity, poor vocabulary, or fear of communicating, but it might be extreme ingenuity in the face of an impoverished sexual field. A voyeur might be someone with nothing to say, but the voyeur might count as a good listener in those cases in which he makes himself known. Sexual *inversions*, as Freud calls them, are not deviations of *sex* (according to the theory developed here, homosexuality is not such an inversion), but relations with children or animals would be like carrying on an adult conversation with a child who does not have the vocabulary to understand or a dog who nods dumb agreement to every proposal. Multiple sexual encounters are surely not in themselves perversions; quite the contrary, languages are not designated for exclusive two-party use. But it is clear that such multiple relationships, like trying to hold several conversations at once or working on several books at the same time, can be distracting, confusing, and ultimately disastrous. There is some difference—but only in manageability—between Don Juanism, or serial multiplicity, on one hand, and group sex, on the other. In the first case one risks carrying over from one conversation gestures that are appropriate to another, but such relationships offer the compensation and reward of being always fresh and novel, without the immediate danger of falling into the bodily equivalent of a Harold Pinter conversational rut. (Here, too, we can appreciate the attractiveness of strangers over those whom we already know well.) Group sex, on the other hand, makes the matter of gesture and response immensely complicated, and while it creates the serious danger of simultaneous incoherent polylogues, it offers the rare possibility of linguistic forms unavailable with fewer voices, much as a larger group of musicians, after protracted training, can create movements impossible for smaller groups and soloists. Therefore, whether or not Don Juanism and group sex are satisfying depends, as before, not on the nature of the activity but on the skill and performance of the participants.

There is, however, still room for a concept of sexual perversion. It does not involve any deviation of "sexual aim or object," as Freud insisted, nor does it involve any special deviation in sexual activity, peculiar parts of the body, special techniques, or personality quirks. As a language, sex has at least one possible perversion: the nonverbal equivalent of lying, or *insincerity*. And, as an art, sex has a possible perversion in *vulgarity*. Given the conception of sexuality as the art of body language that I have defended, we are forced to see the brutal perverseness of our conception of sexuality, in which insincerity and vulgarity, artificial sexual "roles" and "how-to" technology still play such an essential and generally accepted part.

Discussion Questions

1. What does Solomon mean by "sexual paradigm"? How does he employ this concept in his discussion?

2. Give counterarguments for at least one of Solomon's arguments against the sexual paradigm that he rejects.

3. How is Solomon's view like Nagel's? How is it unlike? Where they disagree, with which do you agree? Why?

4. In Solomon's view, what is Freud's major contribution to understanding sex? Would Freud agree? Why or why not?

5. What analogies does Solomon see between sex and language? How useful is this analogy? Defend your answer.

6. How does Solomon apply his theory of sex to sexual perversion? Argue for or against this application.

Love and Sexual Intercourse

J. Gosling

As has been said, attraction between members of different sexes may take many forms. It may vary from one or other kind of love. In fact, of course, any given person may not find himself attracted by the other sex at all, but find himself drawn predominantly to take sexual pleasure either by himself or with a member of the same sex. It is not the purpose of this chapter to discuss such cases except by implication, but it is worth remembering that few people if any of a marriageable age can be dubbed simply heterosexual, homosexual or auto-erotic. Rather they are to some extent indeterminate, with a bias in one direction. The purpose of this chapter, however, is to make a few remarks about the place of sexual relations in marriage, and here it is important to recognize that the form that the attraction between the partners takes may vary from couple to couple, and from one period to another in the lives of any particular couple. This is an important factor because just as it is impossible to say without qualification whether love is a good thing, so is it impossible to say without qualification whether sexual intercourse is a good thing. For this will express the sort of relationship that holds between the partners, and so will change in character as that changes. Considered as an action between persons there is no such thing as a sheer act of intercourse, which is just that and nothing else. There is, of course, a general physical description which fits on all occasions, but it is always also either a case of seeking pleasure, wanting to dominate, wanting to give pleasure, to dedicate oneself, to comfort or whatever it may be. It is always, that is to say, an expression of the one person's attitude to

From J. Gosling, *Marriage and the Love of God* (Sheed & Ward, Inc.). Reprinted by permission of Andrews and McMeel, Inc.

the other. Consequently, whether it is good or bad, and in what way, is a question that admits of as many possible answers as in the general case of love, for it all depends on the attitude expressed.

The statement that intercourse is an expression of love, though common, is not, unfortunately, as clear as it is common, and many people find difficulty in the whole idea of an action expressing love at all. This is especially true of those who tend to look upon sexual intercourse as primarily either a matter of pleasure-seeking, or a means to children. The act is then seen as mainly productive in one way or another, and then people become puzzled as to why it is said to express anything. Surely, anyway, the best expression of love is in generosity and consideration, in charitable action, and how can copulation be considered to be any of these? The more one concentrates on the physical act, thinking just in terms of physical union and thinking of it in isolation, the more puzzling talk of expression becomes. Yet I suppose that to those who are married this is far and away the most obvious aspect of it. . . .

Now sexual relations certainly tend to mean something to most people as a sign of love, more or less so according to temperament and upbringing. However strong the desire just to release tension, or the curiosity as to what the experience is like, most people have some feeling that not just anyone will do, that they are not prepared to let just anyone fondle them. To allow sexual intimacy is felt, more or less dimly, to open the way for a more general intimacy, to be committing oneself to more than just a passing frolic. This sense may, of course, become overlaid; curiosity or a desire to keep up with one's contemporaries may lead to its being ignored; but even so such things as jealousy, a sense of let-down at one's partner's fickleness, or discontent with not very deep relationships, tend to show a certain discomfort with sexual intimacies that mean nothing. It is, however, only one among many elements in most people's experience of sexual desire. Along with it goes a strong urge for the physical sensations associated with intercourse, or a desire for conquest, to see the other person yield, or for one or other of a number of more or less obvious perversions. Any one of these elements may become dominant, so that intercourse ceases to mean anything in the way of love-making, and merely manifests a person's desire to subjugate or be titillated or whatever it may be. I take it that these latter attitudes are not ones for a Christian to encourage, but if they are not to develop then intercourse should be encouraged to mean something. For this to happen it is necessary, as it is with every significant action, for people to reflect from time to time on its significance, so that it comes to play more the role of a meaningful act.

It is here worth noting a point about action of this general sort: if a person, to whom such an action means something, starts indulging in it without meaning anything by it, this tends to develop an attitude contrary to that which the action usually signifies. Suppose, for instance, that shaking hands is to me a sign of friendship and reconciliation, and as such means a good deal to me. I now start developing a habit of performing it without meaning anything by it, and without putting any other gesture in its place. In doing this I am either developing an attitude of deceit, or else am to some extent substituting an indiscriminate and non-committal geniality for my former more definite ways. My changed habits in this respect show a changed attitude. In general the meaning-less use of such actions has its effect on the user. The same is true with sexual relations. A person may get into the way of kissing or having intercourse without meaning anything much by it, but in doing so he develops a relatively insensitive attitude to others, which is liable to show in the manner of his advances, and be quickly felt. There is, however, this important difference between sexual intercourse and other cases so far mentioned, in that it has what might be called a natural rather than a conventional significance. By this I mean that its being a way of showing love is not just a matter of custom, so that we might expect to find a society where this is the way of sealing contracts, while hand-shaking is the prime expression of sexual affection. That shaking hands should mean what it does is quite fortuitous, and relative to a certain form of society. Not so sexual intercourse. There is a universal tendency to feel that to enter on some form of sexual relations is to make some committal of oneself. This can, as I have said, become overlaid, but in that case the sort of sexual activity a person goes in for will tend to develop an attitude at odds with that it usually signified. In this way, any sexual activity will manifest and reinforce a certain attitude to others.

To draw the threads of this together so far: when sexual intercourse is said to express the love between the partners, three related things are being said. First, that to most people intercourse means something as an act of love and so, secondly, that they can and do tend to mean something by it.

It is not always true, however, that it does mean something nor that something is meant by it, and so those who call it an expression of love are usually in effect advocating that this possibility should be developed. Further, even when intercourse means nothing to a person as an act of love, and hence he means nothing at all by it, this in itself *manifests* something of his attitude to others, and this also is covered by the phrase "expression of . . . ." I have tended, with regard to the first two points, to use the word signify rather than express, in order to reserve the latter word for later.

The point that I wish to bring out is that intercourse between married people usually signifies their love for one another, their general devotion in all aspects of their lives. This becomes increasingly the case with time, so that intercourse becomes something they are unwilling to have if there is anything in their attitude or intentions that works against the spirit of their marriage and something also which commits them further in their devotion.

When one talks of intercourse as expressing or symbolizing or signifying there is a danger of sounding too high-flown. People sometimes worry that to them it is a more comfortable and homely matter: they do not have their minds full of thoughts of lifelong devotion at the time, and such thoughts would be a distraction. This worry is intensified if remarks are made about the religious significance of intercourse. It should be clear that the main requirements for a person to mean something by his action is not that he or she should at the time of his performance be thinking of what it signifies—though there is no harm in that—but that it should in fact play the requisite role in their lives. The best time for considering its significance and so ensuring that it does play this role, is at a time when one is not performing it. Many people, during their wedding ceremonies, find their minds distracted from the meaning of what they are doing. Their thoughts are anxiously on the organ-playing, the whereabouts of the wedding-ring; and the exact purpose of "Till death do us part" is not attended to. None of this shows that they meant nothing by their part in the ceremony. The important point is that they should know what they are doing, and intend to follow through what they undertake. Similarly, for intercourse to have significance it is not necessary that it should be made an occasion for meditation on its significance.

One final point in this section: in speaking of intercourse I have been referring to the whole process of love-making leading up to final union, this last being, not so much the goal which earlier caresses are devices for bringing on, as something which is wanted as a culmination because of the love aroused earlier. Seen in this way, it becomes clear why intercourse is an obviously appropriate way of signifying what it does. Each partner has to make himself available to the other, to go to some trouble to bring the other pleasure, and all this done in the context of an intimacy leading to the final union and embrace.

The necessary absence of barriers and inhibitions is an apt sign of a willingness to give oneself to the other in respects that go beyond the immediate activity.

The significance of intercourse, however, is not all that is referred to by calling it an expression of love. For almost all that has been said so far could be applied with minor adaptations to such cases as shaking hands; but this is not an activity about which anyone becomes either enthusiastic or anxious as people do about intercourse. It has not the emotional aura. People do not go to bed together from time to time as a means of giving a more or less statutory pledge. They want intercourse in a way in which they never want to shake hands. Contact and association with the other arouse physical and emotional reactions leading to a desire for final union. Usually such feelings are aroused in the context of other feelings. It may be that those concerned have just had some good news, or a success, or that they have been remembering the circumstances of their first meeting, or that one or both are upset and require comforting. In some such circumstances sexual desire is liable to be aroused, and because certain feelings are then the occasion of intercourse it is said to express their joy, gratitude, sympathy or whatever it may be. These in turn are feelings which typically form part of the pattern of a loving relationship, and so as they are in this case manifestations of love, the intercourse that "expresses" them is said to be an expression of love.

Some such points as these are often, I think, part of what people mean when they talk of intercourse as an expression of love, and while it needs treating with some care, it is a point worth making. For in part, at least, it constitutes a protest against talking of sexual relations in a purely purposive way, as though they should normally be entered into only for some further reason, such as getting a child, and without regard to the feelings of the partners. Against this people want rightly to insist that they are and should be an expression of the feelings between the partners. Why they should be I will consider in a moment. That in fact intercourse is normally something which occurs in one or other of a great variety of emotional contexts seems plainly true, and is part of what gives it its great variety, as its mood is rarely the same on any two occasions.

It is worth asking why intercourse is at all an appropriate way of expressing sympathy or gratitude or joy. It is not, after all, most people's usual way. And here the answer surely is that it is just because it signifies what it does that it becomes an appropriate expression. It is because it signifies the one person's devotion to the other that it becomes a natural way of offering comfort; and it is just because old memories make one glad to be married that they form a natural occasion of intercourse. In other words, it is because intercourse means what it does, and because there exists a loving relationship, that it becomes an appropriate expression of the partners' feelings on these occasions. This may seem a very obvious point, but sometimes people who wax enthusiastic about intercourse as an expression of love seem not to distinguish between talking of it as arising out of a certain emotion and talking of it as signifying devotion. In consequence they give the impression of recommending sexual relations so long as the people concerned are in the mood for it. This is hardly consistent with recommending that people should mean something by it, in the sense outlined above, for one may get in the mood with any passing acquaintance. As failure to distinguish is liable to bring the whole talk of expression into disrepute, it is worth marking the difference.

In a loving marriage, then, intercourse may be said to signify the love of the partners for each other, and to be an expression of their feelings. It also has another function, not strictly of an expressive kind, which it shares with other activities, that of bringing warmth and life to the relationship. This it does in part simply by being meant, but also by being enjoyable. This it has in common with many other things such as wedding anniversaries, birthday parties, outings to celebrate some turn in one's fortunes. With all these it is important that they should be enjoyable. The point of a birthday party, for instance, is to produce an atmosphere of well-being, enabling people to think kindly of the person whose birthday it is. A party where the food is cold and the guests quarrel fails in its object. It is not enough, either, that someone should get some enjoyment. One guest may get great pleasure from baiting another, but that does not make the party a success. For this the pleasure must be sociable. Good food and drink are important because they usually make people sociable, and so make the party lively. If they do not, they defeat their purpose, however much individuals may enjoy them. Enjoyable occasions of this sort are important in life. They enable us to relax, and sharpen our appreciation of those around us and of our good fortune. They send us back to the normal routine refreshed, and more prepared and able to take it in our stride, give more color to life and result in more friendly feelings towards those associated with them.

This is a fairly obvious fact about many human pleasures, but it needs insisting on in connection with sexual relations. For sexual urges are early seen as an interest in and desire for certain physical sensations and a certain release of tension. This idea is extended to marriage also, and then a problem arises, for clearly pleasure is a strong element in sexual attraction, and how can it avoid being selfish? This does not, however, cover the typical situation in marriage. I do not mean to suggest that desire for pleasurable physical sensations is suddenly absent. It is not, and it can ruin a marriage if it becomes dominant. But usually the desire for intercourse has a wider object. It is a desire to share intimacy, to give pleasure, to express joy, to show vividly the love one bears one's partner. It is important that this should be an enjoyable activity, and an important part of the enjoyment is the accompanying physical sensations. For while it is possible for a person to become engrossed in the pursuit of these to the neglect of his partner, their normal effect is to increase the sense of intimacy, awaken and brighten the partners' sense of each other's worth, make it easier to be considerate. It may, of course, be that on occasion intercourse may not be all that enjoyable for one or other partner, and that it is best for one to put aside his feelings for the sake of the other. But this should not be the rule, for intercourse should serve for the recurrent refreshment of their love. Indeed, the background confidence as to what it means itself adds to the enjoyment.

When people become suspicious about the element of pleasure in intercourse, it seems that they are concerned that an interest in physical titillation may become a prime motive. Usually in marriage, the partners are more interested in making love to one another: this is what they enjoy. If you ask a married man why he has intercourse with his wife, he is likely to be a little surprised, and may well answer "Because I enjoy it, of course." It would be a mistake, however, to take this answer as meaning that his sole or dominant motive was his own gratification. To understand his answer we need to know how he thinks of intercourse. As was said earlier, there is no such thing as a sheer act of intercourse: it is always also seeking sexual release, making love or whatever it may be. When we know how this man would describe his action, we shall know what he enjoys. If he thinks of intercourse as showing his love in this way the answer "because I enjoy it" is not necessarily giving a selfish motive: it may be the answer of a man puzzled by the question. For the question suggests that there is some special reason needed to induce a person to have intercourse. Viewing intercourse as making love, and so good, he takes the question as suggesting that still some extra inducement is needed; he is declaring that he needs no special persuasion to declare his love, he enjoys doing it. When it comes to motive, he does it because it is showing his love, not from interest in his own pleasure.

It is important, then, that intercourse should be enjoyed and that it should mean something to the partners as a sign of their mutual devotion. It usually occurs, as I said earlier, in the context of some shared emotion or some emotional response. An essential element in coming to know another person and being able to help him is coming to understand and become sensitive to his feelings, moods, attitudes and responses, and learning to enter into them, respond to them, cope with them. As has been said, many emotional situations are very natural occasions for intercourse, and it in turn helps to increase the partners' knowledge of each other. Suppose, for instance, that one of the partners is upset, has undergone a disappointment or is feeling unable to cope with life. The distress arouses the other's sympathy and a desire to console. This may lead to the reassurance of love-making. Now clearly it tells the one a good deal of the extent of the other's sympathy, that his or her distress should call forth this measure of reassurance; and the tenderness and consideration of love-making, its whole manner, will be a revelation of the other's character. In this way, intercourse increases one's knowledge of one's partner, as its form manifests his or her varied reactions to different occasions.

Sexual intercourse, in short, plays a variety of important roles, and they are not, of course, unrelated. It is because it takes the form of showing tenderness, giving pleasure and making oneself available to the other that it is an apt sign of devotion. It is in part because it does signify devotion that it gives pleasure and is a natural expression of certain feelings. That it should mean something, should be enjoyable and should express the partners' feelings are all-important in married life, and are all, I think, being insisted upon together by those who say that it is an expression of love. I have distinguished them in order to see what of weight is contained in this insistence. I shall now relapse into the simple language of "expressing" to include all these things, unless it is important to specify.

It will be clear that whether intercourse is a force for good or evil will depend on whether it is an expression of love between the partners and what form that love takes. When, however, it is expressive, and the relationship is one of love then it shows and strengthens that love. It is therefore of some importance that it should come to play this role in the lives of Christians. . . .

. . . The love two people have for one another is neither black nor white. Consequently intercourse is quite likely at first to be not altogether satisfactory, and to lead to strains in the relationship, to disappointments and impatience. Everyone has some urge to enjoy it and is liable to approach it with this purpose very much in mind. It needs, therefore, to be thought about and seen as an expression of love; insofar as it tends to be anything else it is a hindrance rather than a help to the relationship. Insofar as it succeeds in being that, it cements and enriches the relationship. It does, however, need to be thought about in these terms apart from the times when it is actually practiced. To some extent it is almost instinctive to see intercourse as an expression of love; but then the desire for the pleasure of intercourse, whether with someone loved or not, is also instinctive. One has to *learn* to reinforce the first of these ways, and intercourse only becomes established as an unselfish expression of love with time and thought.

So far I have treated of sexual relations as, I think, they naturally appear to most married people unless previous instruction and upbringing have given a strong bias in another direction. The only way in which anything specifically Christian has been brought in has been by way of saying that if it is a Christian love which holds between the partners, then it will be a Christian love which is expressed and increased by intercourse. There are, however, further points to be made about sexual intercourse in a Christian context. . . . The experience of falling in love should sharpen one's appreciation of what God has created, at least in one respect. It is the beginnings of loving someone as God does, and this is the way in which it has been most startlingly revealed, in the love of Christ. Intercourse, which naturally signifies the total devotion of each partner to the other, now comes to signify a total devotion to one whom God loves, a devotion similar to that which God himself shows. The person to whom one makes love is made in God's image and likeness, and remade in the likeness of Christ. This is why, in the marriage service, we have the words "With my body I thee worship": intercourse is seen as doing honor to one whom God loves and has died for, one who has been incorporated into Christ. Intercourse signifies and points to a love like that of our Lord himself, leading even, if need be, to giving up of life for the person loved. . . .

Discussion Questions

1. Compare Gosling's view of sexual intercourse with Nagel's or Solomon's. With which do you more nearly agree? Why?
2. How is Gosling's view like or unlike Geisler's? With which do you more nearly agree? Why?
3. Could Gosling's theory be used to defend homosexual activity? Why or why not?
4. Gosling writes from a Roman Catholic point of view. Does this seem to you to have an important effect on his theory? Why or why not?

The Prejudice Against Homosexuals and the Ministry of the Church

The Washington State Catholic Conference

The Washington State Catholic Conference's Theological Commission developed [this] statement on the morality involved in this issue based on Catholic theological principles.

The WSCC Theological Commission is composed of representatives from the fields of systematic theology, ethics and moral theology. The statement developed by the commission was reviewed and approved by the WSCC board of directors, which is composed of the bishops of the three dioceses of Washington State and their appointed delegates.

Introduction

This paper deals with the obligation of authorities in church and state towards homosexuals. In particular, it focuses upon the nature and the reprehensibleness of the prejudice against such persons in our society and the need to combat such prejudice by policy measures in both church and state. However, since this paper has been commissioned by church authorities to represent an official church position, it does not attempt to rethink or

From *Catholic Northwest Progress*, 1983. Reprinted by permission of the Washington State Catholic Conference.

to develop substantially the Catholic position on the morality of homosexuality—however much such rethinking and development is needed in this and all other areas of the church's tradition. Rather, it presents the current official position as a given for its limited purposes.

At the outset we need to define briefly a few terms. *Orientation* refers to a habitual state of being which inclines one toward certain attitudes and actions. A *homosexual orientation* (some female homosexuals speak of "preference" rather than "orientation") inclines one to prefer as a sexual partner a person of one's own sex. Thus, one is attracted to persons of the same sex and is more desirous of having genital sex with such persons than with persons of the opposite sex. If such a person engages in genital activity with a person of the same sex, he or she is said to be *acting out homosexually*. This *acting out* is perhaps better called *homogenital activity*. Finally, a *homosexual* (or *homosexual person*) is one who is homosexually oriented, whether he or she acts out or not. A *gay* is a male homosexual; a *lesbian* is a female homosexual; a *straight person* is one who is heterosexual.

Background Elements of the Situation We Face

Two elements constitute the background against which we take up the Catholic principles regulating the obligations of the church and the state to combat by public measures conditions prejudicial to homosexual persons: (1) the *de facto* conditions of prejudice against gays and lesbians; and (2) the teaching of the church on homosexuality and prejudice against homosexual persons.

1. Prejudice Against Homosexuals

There is considerable evidence that homosexuals are victims of prejudice. Many in the general population "prejudice" homosexuals in that without evidence they intellectually impute evils such as child molesting to gays and lesbians. Further, because of such prejudgments they often manifest hostile attitudes to homosexuals and act toward them in such a way as to inflict harm upon them, even grave physical harm, simply because they are identified as being homosexual.

The causes of such prejudice are partially known. Some persons fear an orientation and a style of living that differ in important respects from their own. They are gripped by fear of the unknown. Others have received misinformation and prejudicial attitudes from parents and the surrounding environment. In addition, many Christians have based irrational opposition to homosexuals upon a false or fundamentalistic reading of the scriptures. Within the Catholic Church magisterial teaching has been incorrectly used as a basis for acts against gays and lesbians, and the teaching itself, at times, has been expressed in a way that has occasioned prejudicial attitudes and activity on the part of some church members.

2. Church Teaching on Homosexuality and Prejudice Against Homosexual Persons

a. Church teaching on the morality of homosexual orientation and acts   First of all, church teaching is positive with regard to homosexual persons considered in the totality of their beings. It should be quite obvious that homosexuality is an abstraction. No one is only a homosexual just as no one is only a mother, only a president, or only an artists with no other constituents in her/his makeup. Hence, a homosexual person may manifest virtues and qualities that are admirable by any standard. In fact, there is some evidence that many homosexuals possess important attributes that are often, unfortunately, lacking in their straight counterparts. Thus, it appears that sensitivity to the needs of persons and the ability to express warm feelings towards both men and women are frequently present in gays. Hence, the church, which considers a person as a whole, can find much good to be praised and affirmed in any homosexual person. Although one's sexuality affects to some extent all that one is and does, just as does every basic quality, homosexual orientation and homosexual acting out constitute but one aspect, and not the most important aspect, of concrete gay and lesbian persons. Accordingly, no matter what one thinks about their homosexuality, one is never justified in labeling such persons as homosexual and then condemning them under that category. No person is merely a category. He or she is composed of many good attributes that outstrip any single category.

Second, church teaching does not morally condemn homosexual orientation. It is true that it views such an orientation as not fully appropriate since in the person so oriented there is lacking an integration of the psychic side with the procreative possibilities of the physical side. The more a person is integrated, the more he or she unites the physical, the psychological, the intellectual, the volitional and the social. A specific capacity of the physical sex act is to generate a child. An integration of the person implies that the tendency of that person moves him or her toward expressing that physical power in a manner that respects its procreative abilities. Because this integrating tendency is lacking in one homosexually oriented, the church has traditionally seen such orientation as falling short of the norm of total integration implied in the two great commandments.

However, this inappropriateness of homosexual orientation does not imply that it is sinful in itself or that it is caused by the person's own sin. Although it is apparently true that a small number of lesbians have made a positive choice of their orientation, the evidence seems to indicate that in the vast number of cases homosexuality is not caused by the person but by factors yet unknown; since the condition is not the result of an individual's free choice, it cannot possibly be the result of personal sin. Instead, it is one of the many results of the human condition that leaves each of us lacking some part of the full integration to which we are called. An older theology spoke of concupiscence and the remains of original sin. Other examples of such remains of original sin are a tendency to anger, inability to commit oneself, inability to communicate with those to whom one is bound, etc. To the degree that such orientations are not caused by the individuals involved, they may not be called sinful. Moral criticism, reproach and blame—if ever they have validity—have validity only with regard to orientations that are freely caused, thoughts and desires that are consented to, and deeds that are freely performed.

Nor are homosexual persons to be blamed for not changing their orientation. It is true that one is obliged to change a habitual orientation which falls short of the ideal insofar as one is able to do so. This is a certain but often forgotten corollary of the two greatest commandments of the law. However, the best evidence seems to indicate that we have no known way of altering a definite homosexual orientation. To the extent that this continues to be the case, it is unfair and cruel to reproach such persons for not altering or trying to alter their basic condition.

Third, church teaching is positive about most activities of gays and lesbians. Only homogenital activity and the foreplay to it is disapproved by the church since it sees these acts as attaining their full significance only in the context of marriage. However, the ordinary acts of life, the expressions of concern and tenderness, the virtues of charity and magnanimity, in short, all that is praised in straight persons is just as much to be accepted, affirmed and praised in homosexual persons. Every other person we know does some kind of activity with which we disagree. Yet, because we recognize that much of their activity is acceptable, we do not condemn globally the actions of such persons. Gays and lesbians have just as much right to our approval and acceptance of their overall activity.

Fourth, church teaching indicates that even with regard to homogenital activity no one except Almighty God can make certain judgments about the personal sinfulness of acts. This is so because of the conjunction of two factors. On the one hand, each person has unique qualities, unique strengths, and a unique set of weaknesses. Thus, some find it easy to control their tempers and passions; but they are dull, uncreative and little concerned about what is going on about them. Others are inclined to anger and sensuality but they are intensely and creatively interested in the world about them. Each person has a unique starting point for moral living—himself or herself as concretely existing. On the other hand, each person is held to move ever more closely *toward* the ultimate norm of total and integrated love for God, for self, and for every other human person *from where that person happens to be with the strengths and weaknesses that person has.* All specific commandments express aspects of the ideal norm that all are called to—the norm of total love of God and persons. The combination of these two factors indicates that morality has to do with each person's taking the next step toward fulfilling the norm of the two great commandments. A person is guilty of sin only when she or he does not do what she or he is capable of doing in progress toward that norm. Because we cannot know just how hard that person is trying to live up to the total norm of the two great commandments from where the person is in a given act, we are unable to judge the degree to responsibility the individual bears for the act that in some aspects his or her act falls short of the moral norm. Thus, we cannot judge the degree of sin involved in a man's failure to grow in his ability to communicate with or show tenderness toward his wife because we do not know just how much he is able to change the present orientation that makes it so difficult for him to share his ideas and tender feelings. In a similar fashion, we cannot judge that a homosexual who engages in homogenital activity is committing subjective sin. What we can say is that this activity falls short of the ultimate norm of Christian morality in the area of genital expression.

b. Church teaching and prejudice against homosexuals   First of all, prejudice in all its forms falls short of the norm of Christian morality. One can be prejudiced in orientation and attitude, in thought, or in activity. One is prejudiced in orientation and attitude against another person when one's instinctive emotions and interior reactions reject that person or significant aspects of her/his activity with little or no justifying evidence. Thus, to be fearful of some minority person merely because he or she is a minority person or to have a mistrustful attitude toward the teaching ability of all gays or lesbians merely because they are homosexual is to be prejudiced in orientation and attitude. One is prejudiced in thought when without evidence one explicitly thinks evil of another person. Finally, one is prejudiced in activity when one implements in external activity one's prejudicial attitude or thought. *All such forms of prejudice fall short of the Christian norm and must be combatted to the extent possible.* This teaching applies in a special way to gays and lesbians because they have been subjected to prejudice in a gross form.

Second, *the prejudice against homosexuals is a greater infringement of the norm of Christian morality than is homosexual orientation or activity.* A parallel example may illustrate why this is so. Suppose persons who are unable or unwilling to commit themselves, who are incapable of expressing affection toward their spouses, or who are completely insensitive to the needs of others—qualities, by the way, which are frequently destructive of marriage—are labelled "the uncommitted," "those lacking affection," and "the insensitive."

Suppose, further, that they are so labelled despite fine qualities they otherwise possess and that they are subjected to indignities solely because of the negative qualities which furnish the basis for the labels they bear. The vast majority of persons would consider such treatment of the uncommitted, the insensitive and the non-affective as grossly prejudicial and immoral. And they would be right. Yet homosexuals are subject to such treatment merely because they are homosexuals.

Such prejudice hampers homosexual persons in their efforts to grow, makes it easy for them to become embittered at the unfair treatment they experience, and at times leads to their being inflicted with severe bodily injury and even death. Further, such prejudice distorts the personality of the persons who manifest the prejudice, warps their judgment, and leads them to treat other human beings made in the image and likeness of God in a manner that ignores their dignity. The enormity of the moral evil of such prejudice should be obvious.

Third, while the church's teaching with regard to homosexuality (as outlined above) does not by itself cause prejudice (no more than does its teaching against pre-marital sex cause, by itself, prejudice against unmarried couples who live together), it seems true to say that the manner in which church teaching has been concretely conveyed has contributed to the prejudice against gays and lesbians. The tendency of some Catholic teachers to speak about homosexual orientation and activity as if these were *the* supreme evils or as if they constituted a dangerous attack on marital values illustrates the point. Further, there have been persons in the church who have contributed to the general prejudice against homosexuals by the derogatory language and tone they use in referring to gays and lesbians. Finally, many Catholics have heard the church's teaching against the background furnished by a society whose actions and attitudes are permeated with prejudice against homosexuals. As a result they have given to the church's teaching a nuance which is prejudicial to homosexual persons.

All this brings out that the church has a serious obligation with regard to homosexual persons. Because all forms of prejudice are affronts to the dignity of persons, because the prejudice against homosexuals is such a great moral evil, and because church persons have contributed to the constitution of an environment that is prejudicial to homosexuals, the church is seriously obliged to work toward the uprooting of such prejudice.

Roles of Church and State in Rectifying this Prejudicial Situation

1. General Considerations

The church and the state have partially overlapping and partially different functions in promoting the common good. The state is an agent of public order and it deals only with external situations and activities which affect public peace, public moral existence and justice amidst its citizens. In principle, the state should recognize liberty of thought and should regulate external activity only to the extent that public peace, justice and moral existence would be violated by its failure to act. Hence, the state does not enjoy the role of making judgments on private thoughts or private actions of citizens; nor does it have the function of enjoining its own value system upon its citizens.

The church also functions in the promotion of the common good of society. Like the state it has a role in the fostering of public order. Thus, the church has the right and duty to promote laws and situations within the state that foster external order and justice. In addition, the church is also obligated to care for the public order in its own domain—the parishes, hospitals, and other institutions which it conducts in the carrying out of its mission—by appropriate legislation. In short, both church and state have a part to play in the regulation of public order. Thus, both have obligations to meet the evil of prejudice insofar as that evil affects the public peace, public moral existence, and justice among those whom they serve.

However, the church has a further function which it does not share with the state—that of promoting the internalization of the value system inherent in its tradition. This means that it has the right and the duty to inculcate principles of personal and private living and to foster structures that will help enroot these principles in the feelings, attitudes, and activities of its members. Hence, the church is concerned with more than exterior and public activity; it is concerned with the development of the whole person.

2. Specific Applications to the Prejudice Against Homosexuals

a. Applications pertaining to church and state First, the orientation or inclination of any person of itself and apart from any overt activity may not be the basis for depriving him/her of ordinary rights to courtesy, employment, advancement, equal benefits, etc., in either church or state. Hence, the mere fact that a person has a homosexual orientation is *never* sufficient reason for public discrimination. State and church authorities have duties to protect these rights of homosexuals. Further, insofar as orientations and inclinations do not of themselves affect the public order, efforts to uncover homosexual tendencies by questionnaires and other investigative techniques are reprehensible.

Second, church and state authority should see to it that external behavior which is not a matter of public knowledge should not of itself be the basis for discriminating against employees. Should an employer learn of private external behaviors, he/she may not use such information as the basis for terminating or otherwise discriminating against an employee. Only if the behavior in question seriously affects the ability of the person to fulfill the duties of his/her position may a superior discharge him/her. Thus, one may remove an airplane pilot upon discovering that he is frequently drunk on the grounds that he may endanger the lives of passengers. Similarly, if it be true that homosexual intelligence agents are easily subject to blackmail, one may remove them from their posts. The same would hold true for agents involved in any other activities which target them for blackmail.

Third, a person may be disciplined or even discharged from a position if his/her conduct disturbs the just public order. Hence, two homosexuals who make a public display of affection which seriously disrupts a school lunchroom may be dismissed. Two heterosexuals who do the same thing may also be dismissed, and for the same reason— serious disturbance of public order. However, if the disturbance of order stems more from prejudicial attitudes of the public than from the activity of the homosexual persons, authorities are obligated to do all that is possible to combat such attitudes.

Fourth, all persons are entitled to humane public treatment. Therefore, public authority in church and state should not allow gays and lesbians, no matter how manifest their lifestyles may be, to be subjected to violence, public insult or scorn, or other public indignities.

In general, individuals have the right to act freely in society as long as they do no harm to others. Public authority should not restrict freedom when such harm does not occur. In fact, it should safeguard such freedom. This is so even if individuals perform acts

which others in the society consider immoral. Hence, Catholic theologians have steadfastly opposed laws which punish or restrict private pre-marital sex. To attempt to control
such activity by preventative or punitive legislation would lead to invasion of privacy,
snooping, and a host of other evils. Similar reasoning applies to homosexual activity of a
private nature.

b. Applications which differ from church to state   The mission of the church differs from that of
the state. Both are obligated to foster the public order, but the church must also promote
the value system that is integral to its mission. To the degree that its value system goes
beyond the public order which defines the limits of the state's competence, to that degree
will the principles of operation of the church differ from those of the state.

This means, in the first place, that the church is obligated to combat, as far as
possible, not just manifest prejudice against gays and lesbians but also the underlying
prejudicial understandings and attitudes. Jesus came not just to change the activity of
persons but to bring about a conversion of heart, mind, and soul as well—in short, a
turning of the whole person toward complete love and acceptance of God and every
human being, especially the victims of injustice and discrimination. It is not a coincidence
that he was found amidst the poor, the despised, the publicans, and the prostitutes.
Though we have no explicit record of Jesus' attitude toward homosexuals, we do
know that he championed those who were subjected to prejudiced attitudes and behavior in his time.

Secondly, and more concretely, the church can combat the evil of prejudice against
homosexuals by strongly proclaiming the gross evil of prejudicial attitudes toward lesbians and gays; by fostering legislation at all levels in the state and in the ecclesiastical arena
to remove systemic prejudice; by making efforts to purify of all prejudice the manner in
which it conveys its moral teaching on homosexuality; by encouraging empirical research
on homosexuality and the ways to combat prejudice against lesbians and gays; and by
fostering ongoing theological research and criticism, with regard to its own theological
tradition on homosexuality, none of which is infallibly taught.

Thirdly, the church needs to be sensitive to the danger of occasioning prejudice by its
manner of implementing its moral position on homosexuality. As we have indicated . . .
the church sees such an orientation and such acts as falling short of the norm. Accordingly,
the church is obliged to reflect this in its explicit teaching, in its hiring practices, and in the
overall way it projects values.

Hence, the church has a right to set certain standards of conduct for those who
participate in its mission. It has a right and a duty to require that the persons it employs, if
they are active homosexuals, neither publicize their lifestyles nor advocate homogenital
activity as perfectly acceptable. In other words, it has a right to ask that those who
participate in its mission project publicly by word and action its own traditional moral
principles. Accordingly, the church also has a right to dismiss persons who speak against
its principles or who so conduct themselves in the public arena that their example gives
scandal with regard to these principles. Of course, this in no way means that the church
should not employ homosexuals. Such persons can and should be employed as long as
they do nothing to negate the church's moral position in a serious way. The same can be
said for persons who do not live up to the church's moral norms in other areas. There are
no special principles for homosexuals. The church is obligated to see that they are treated
just like other human beings.

By contrast, on the principles we have stated, the state has no business demanding
that gays or lesbians project publicly its given set of moral values. Hence, homosexuals

who make public their lifestyle or who advocate homosexual orientation and acting out as completely moral should not be excluded from employment as long as their activity does not disrupt the public order. The state should protect them against discrimination occasioned by their lifestyle.

Fourthly, there are a few sensitive issues regarding employment of homosexuals in church institutions. Thus, a number of Catholics are concerned about the role of homosexuals in professions which have care of their children. There are those who think that gays and lesbians inevitably impart a homosexual value system to children or that they will molest children. This is a prejudice and must be unmasked as such. There is no evidence that exposure to homosexuals, of itself, harms a child, just as there is no evidence that exposure to couples who live in nonmarital unions, of itself, corrupts the young. Accordingly, there is no need to make efforts to screen out all homosexually oriented persons from our educational system. What is to be required is that all those who participate should impart by word and action the Catholic value system. Those who seek employment within the church can be asked directly if they intend to impart Catholic doctrine and the broad Catholic value system. That is all.

Another problem arises in cases where a Catholic community is rent by deep-seated prejudices against lesbians and gays. In such circumstances it may be impossible to hire homosexuals, even those who do not act out, without having Catholic institutions wrecked or severely hampered in their operation by prejudiced individuals. In such cases those in authority have to balance the harm to the community caused by the destructive activities of these prejudiced persons against the injustice resulting from being pressured not to hire homosexuals or to terminate those already hired. In certain circumstances, those in authority may judge prudentially that they will have to give in to the pressure. In other circumstances, they will prudentially judge that the common good is better fostered by taking a firm stand and braving the wrath of persons blinded by prejudice. Thus prudence in this matter is not to be identified with "playing it safe." Rather, it is to be identified with selecting the best means in ambiguous circumstances of moving toward a greater realization of the common good. No matter what decision is taken, solid efforts must be made to root out such prejudicial attitudes and activities from the community.

Ultimately all people need to be reminded that homosexuals are persons, and, as such, that they have rights and feelings that must be respected. In particular, lesbians and gays have the right and the duty to contribute to society, and they should be encouraged to live up to that right and duty. They are children of God, and they should be treated with all the respect and dignity that children of God deserve. They should be helped by the rest of society to grow toward the wholeness of life revealed in the words and deeds of Jesus.

Discussion Questions

1. How does the view of homosexuality in this statement differ from those of the previous authors in this section? How is it like some of those views? Which view do you most nearly agree with? Why?

2. Is the view of prejudice against homosexuals in this statement inconsistent with the strictures against homosexuality in the earlier part of the statement? Why or why not?

3. The statement alleges that "prejudice against homosexuals is a greater infringement of the norm of Christian morality than is homosexual orientation or activity." Do you agree? Why or why not?

4. How might Geisler agree or disagree with this statement of the Washington State Catholic Conference? What arguments for or against the statement might he give?

5. Do you agree or disagree with the recommendations at the end of the statement? Why?

Suggested Readings for Chapter Five

Atkinson, Ronald. *Sexual Morality*. New York: Harcourt Brace Jovanovich, 1965.

Baker, Robert, and Frederick Elliston, eds. *Philosophy and Sex*. Buffalo, N.Y.: Prometheus, 1975.

Bertucci, Peter A. *Sex, Love and the Person*. New York: Sheed and Ward, 1967.

Capon, Robert Farrar. *Bed and Board*. New York: Sheed and Ward, 1965.

Gosling, J. H. *Marriage and the Love of God*. New York: Sheed and Ward, 1965.

Whiteley, C. H., and W. N. Whiteley. *Sex and Morals*. New York: Basic Books, 1967.

6

Sexual Equality

One important aspect of sexual equality has been touched on in the general introduction to this section: the question of whether a unisex society or a sexually pluralistic society is better. In a unisex society, the ideal is that sexual differences should make no more difference in treatment of persons than, for example, differences in eye color. In a sexually pluralistic society the ideal is "difference in role, parity of esteem." This would allow some activities or occupations to be reserved largely or entirely for one sex or the other, so long as occupations or activities characteristic of one sex are not given greater esteem or importance than those characteristic of the other sex.

In practice our society is neither unisex nor sexually pluralistic. The sex of a person does make many differences in the way that person is treated, and although some occupations are largely reserved for one sex it is often the case that an occupation characteristic of one sex receives significantly less esteem than one characteristic of another sex, even if the occupations are quite similar.

Furthermore, in occupations or activities in which both sexes are represented it is often the case that members of one sex receive less esteem and less compensation than members of the other sex.

In our society, as in most societies, women are the members of the disadvantaged sex. Of course, there are minor exceptions, but by and large it is more advantageous from many points of view—financial, among others—to be male than to be female in our culture. If women and men do similar jobs the men are likely to be better paid and have more authority. Occupations seen as "women's work" are significantly worse paid than occupations seen as "men's work," and the "women's" occupations usually receive less respect.

Increasingly, people are coming to realize that this state of affairs is obviously unjust and that none of the alleged justifications for this situation comes anywhere near giving an adequate defense of it. More and more individuals are seeing that things must be changed, and government and other institutions of society have begun to work for change. However, little progress has been made, at least compared to the progress that might be expected from the amount of talk about the problem. The selection in this chapter by Dorothy L. Sayers was written about fifty years ago; depressingly, very few of Sayers's complaints are out of date.

Whereas it is fairly easy to find able and intelligent representatives of all points of view on such issues as abortion or suicide, it is difficult to find a respectable defense of sexual inequality. Arguably, the paper in this chapter by J. R. Lucas is a defense of sexual pluralism rather than sexual inequality. In her vigorous criticism of Lucas's paper, Susan Haack argues that Lucas's position is in fact a defense of sexual inequality. A defender of Lucas might argue that Haack sometimes equates sexual pluralism and sexual inequality. One issue at stake here is whether a sexually equal society must be a unisex society.

In the next two papers Alison Jaggar and Elizabeth Wolgast address this issue. Jaggar argues that only a unisex society can be a sexually equal society, while Wolgast finds that "the idea that sex differences are or should be negligible is curious."

In the course of their discussions Sayers, Lucas, Haack, Jaggar, and Wolgast explore many other issues. Sayers discusses the relation of this issue to Christianity and to the attitude of Christ himself. Lucas discusses alleged biological differences between the sexes which are the subject of current controversies. Jaggar considers a variety of arguments for differential treatment of men and women, and Wolgast cites a wide range of anthropological and biological evidence.

The practice of preferential hiring or affirmative action is mentioned in a number of the readings in this chapter as a device to secure some degree of sexual equality. This practice is discussed along with other new problems and challenges, in Part III.

The Human-Not-Quite-Human

Dorothy L. Sayers

The first task, when undertaking the study of any phenomenon, is to observe its most obvious feature; and it is here that most students fail. It is here that most students of the "Woman Question" have failed, and the Church more lamentably than most, and with less excuse. That is why it is necessary, from time to time, to speak plainly, and perhaps even brutally, to the Church.

The first thing that strikes the careless observer is that women are unlike men. They are "the opposite sex"—(though why "opposite" I do not know; what is the "neighboring sex"?). But the fundamental thing is that women are more like men than anything else in

From Dorothy L. Sayers, *Are Women Human?* (William B. Eerdmans Publishing Co., 1981). Reprinted by permission of the publisher.

the world. They are human beings. *Vir* is male and *Femina* is female: but *Homo* is male and female.

This is the equality claimed and the fact that is persistently evaded and denied. No matter what arguments are used, the discussion is vitiated from the start, because Man is always dealt with as both *Homo* and *Vir,* but Woman only as *Femina.*

I have seen it solemnly stated in a newspaper that the seats on the near side of a bus are always filled before those on the off side, because, "men find them more comfortable on account of the camber of the road, and women find they get a better view of the shop windows." As though the camber of the road did not affect male and female bodies equally. Men, you observe, are given a *Homo* reason; but Women, a *Femina* reason, because they are not fully human.

Or take the sniggering dishonesty that accompanies every mention of trousers. The fact is that, for *Homo,* the garment is warm, convenient and decent. But in the West (though not in Mohammedan countries or in China) *Vir* has made the trouser his prerogative, and has invested it and the skirt with a sexual significance for physiological reasons which are a little too plain for gentility to admit. (Note: that the objection is always to the closed knicker or trouser; never to open drawers, which have a music-hall significance of a different kind.) It is this obscure male resentment against interference with function that complicates the simple *Homo* issue of whether warmth, safety, and freedom of movement are desirable qualities in a garment for any creature with two legs. Naturally, under the circumstances, the trouser is *also* taken up into the whole *Femina* business of attraction, since *Vir* demands that a woman shall be *Femina* all the time, whether she is engaged in *Homo* activities or not. If, of course, *Vir* should take a fancy to the skirt, he will appropriate it without a scruple; he will wear the houppelande or the cassock if it suits him; he will stake out his claim to the kilt in Scotland or in Greece. If he chooses (as he once chose) to deck himself like a peacock in the mating season, that is *Vir's* right; if he prefers (as he does today) to affront the eye with drab color and ridiculous outline, that is *Homo's* convenience. Man dresses as he chooses, and Woman to please him; and if Woman says she ever does otherwise, he knows better, for she is not human, and may not give evidence on her own behalf.

Probably no man has ever troubled to imagine how strange his life would appear to himself if it were unrelentingly assessed in terms of his maleness; if everything he wore, said, or did had to be justified by reference to female approval; if he were compelled to regard himself, day in day out, not as a member of society, but merely *(salvâ reverentiâ)* as a virile member of society. If the center of his dress-consciousness were the cod-piece, his education directed to making him a spirited lover and meek paterfamilias; his interests held to be natural only insofar as they were sexual. If from school and lecture-room, Press and pulpit, he heard the persistent outpouring of a shrill and scolding voice, bidding him remember his biological function. If he were vexed by continual advice how to add a rough male touch to his typing, how to be learned without losing his masculine appeal, how to combine chemical research with seduction, how to play bridge without incurring the suspicion of impotence. If, instead of allowing with a smile that "women prefer cave-men," he felt the unrelenting pressure of a whole social structure forcing him to order all his goings in conformity with that pronouncement.

He would hear (and would he like hearing?) the female counterpart of Dr. Peck[1] informing him: "I am no supporter of the Horseback Hall doctrine of 'gun-tail, plough-tail and stud' as the only spheres for masculine action; but we do need a more definite conception of the nature and scope of man's life." In any book on sociology he would find, after the main portion dealing with human needs and rights, a supplementary chapter devoted to "The Position of the Male in the Perfect State." His newspaper would assist him with a "Men's Corner," telling him how, by the expenditure of a good deal of money and a couple of hours a day, he could attract the girls and retain his wife's affection; and when he had succeeded in capturing a mate, his name would be taken from him, and society would present him with a special title to proclaim his achievement. People would write books called, "History of the Male," or "Males of the Bible," or "The Psychology of the Male," and he would be regaled daily with headlines, such as "Gentleman-Doctor's Discovery," "Male-Secretary Wins Calcutta Sweep," "Men-Artists at the Academy." If he gave an interview to a reporter, or performed any unusual exploit, he would find it recorded in such terms as these: "Professor Bract, although a distinguished botanist, is not in any way an unmanly man. He has, in fact, a wife and seven children. Tall and burly, the hands with which he handles his delicate specimens are as gnarled and powerful as those of a Canadian lumberjack, and when I swilled beer with him in his laboratory, he bawled his conclusions at me in a strong, gruff voice that implemented the promise of his swaggering moustache." Or: "There is nothing in the least feminine about the home surroundings of Mr. Focus, the famous children's photographer. His 'den' is panelled in teak and decorated with rude sculptures from Easter Island; over his austere iron bedstead hangs a fine reproduction of the Rape of the Sabines." Or: "I asked M. Sapristi, the renowned chef, whether kitchen-cult was not a rather unusual occupation for a man. 'Not a bit of it!' he replied, bluffly. 'It is the genius that counts, not the sex. As they say in *la belle Ecosse,* a man's a man for a' that'—and his gusty, manly guffaw blew three small patty pans from the dresser."

He would be edified by solemn discussions about "Should Men Serve in Drapery Establishments?" and acrimonious ones about "Tea-Drinking Men"; by cross-shots of public affairs "from the masculine angle," and by irritable correspondence about men who expose their anatomy on beaches (so masculine of them), conceal it in dressing-gowns (too feminine of them), think about nothing but women, pretend an unnatural indifference to women, exploit their sex to get jobs, lower the tone of the office by their sexless appearance, and generally fail to please a public opinion which demands the incompatible. And at dinner-parties he would hear the wheedling, unctuous, predatory female voice demand: "And why should you trouble your handsome little head about politics?"

If, after a few centuries of this kind of treatment, the male was a little self-conscious, a little on the defensive, and a little bewildered about what was required of him, I should not blame him. If he traded a little upon his sex, I could forgive him. If he presented the world with a major social problem, I should scarcely be surprised. It would be more surprising if he retained any rag of sanity and self-respect.

"The rights of woman," says Dr. Peck, "considered in the economic sphere, seem to involve her in competition with men in the struggle for jobs." It does seem so indeed, and this is hardly to be wondered at; for the competition began to appear when the men took over the women's jobs by transferring them from the home to the factory. The medieval woman had effective power and a measure of real (though not political) equality, for she had control of many industries—spinning, weaving, baking, brewing, distilling, perfumery, preserving, pickling—in which she worked with head as well as hands, in command of her own domestic staff. But now the control and direction—all the intelligent part—of those industries have gone to the men, and the women have been left, not with their "proper" *work* but with *employment* in those occupations. And at the same time, they are exhorted to be feminine and return to the home from which all intelligent occupation has been steadily removed.

There has never been any question but that the women of the poor should toil alongside their men. No angry, and no compassionate, voice has been raised to say that women should not break their backs with harvest work, or soil their hands with blacking grates and peeling potatoes. The objection is only to work that is pleasant, exciting or profitable—the work that any human being might think it worth while to do. The boast, "My wife doesn't need to soil her hands with work," first became general when the commercial middle classes acquired the plutocratic and aristocratic notion that the keeping of an idle woman was a badge of superior social status. Man must work, and woman must exploit his labor. What else are they there for? And if the woman submits, she can be cursed for her exploitation; and if she rebels, she can be cursed for competing with the male: whatever she does will be wrong, and that is a great satisfaction.

The men who attribute all the ills of *Homo* to the industrial age, yet accept it as the norm for the relations of the sexes. But the brain, that great and sole true Androgyne, that can mate indifferently with male or female and beget offspring upon itself, the cold brain laughs at their perversions of history. The period from which we are emerging was like no other: a period when empty head and idle hands were qualities for which a man prized his woman and despised her. When, by an odd, sadistic twist of morality, sexual intercourse was deemed to be a marital right to be religiously enforced upon a meek reluctance—as though the insatiable appetite of wives were not one of the oldest jokes in the world, older than mothers-in-law, and far more venerable than kippers. When to think about sex was considered indelicate in a woman, and to think about anything else unfeminine. When to "manage" a husband by lying and the exploitation of sex was held to be honesty and virtue. When the education that Thomas More gave his daughters was denounced as a devilish indulgence, and could only be wrung from the outraged holder of the purse-strings by tears and martyrdom and desperate revolt, in the teeth of the world's mockery and the reprobation of a scandalized Church.

What is all this tenderness about women herded into factories? Is it much more than an excuse for acquiescing in the profitable herding of men? The wrong is inflicted upon *Homo*. There are temperaments suited to herding and temperaments that are not; but the dividing lines do not lie exactly along the sexual boundary. The Russians, it seems, have begun to realize this; but are revolution and blood the sole educational means for getting this plain fact into our heads? Is it only under stress of war that we are ready to admit that the person who does the job best is the person best fitted to do it? Must we always treat women like Kipling's common soldier?

> It's vamp and slut and gold-digger, and "Polly, you're a liar!" But it's "Thankyou, Mary Atkins" when the guns begin to fire.

We will use women's work in wartime (though we will pay less for it, and take it away from them when the war is over). But it is an unnatural business, undertaken for no admissible feminine reason—such as to ape the men, to sublimate a sexual repression, to provide a hobby for leisure, or to make the worker more bedworthy—but simply because, without it all *Homo* (including *Vir*) will be in the soup. But to find satisfaction in doing good work and knowing that it is wanted is human nature; therefore it cannot be feminine nature, for women are not human. It is true that they die in bombardments, much like real human beings: but that we will forgive, since they clearly cannot enjoy it; and we can salve our consciences by rating their battered carcasses at less than a man's compensation.[2]

Women are not human. They lie when they say they have human needs: warm and decent clothing; comfort in the bus; interests directed immediately to God and His universe, not intermediately through any child of man. They are far above man to inspire him, far beneath him to corrupt him; they have feminine minds and feminine natures, but their mind is not one with their nature like the minds of men; they have no human mind and no human nature. "Blessed be God," says the Jew, "that hath not made me a woman."

God, of course, may have His own opinion, but the Church is reluctant to endorse it. I think I have never heard a sermon preached on the story of Martha and Mary that did not attempt, somehow, somewhere, to explain away its text. Mary's, of course, was the better part—the Lord said so, and we must not precisely contradict Him. But we will be careful not to despise Martha. No doubt, He approved of her too. We could not get on without her, and indeed (having paid lip-service to God's opinion) we must admit that we greatly prefer her. For Martha was doing a really feminine job, whereas Mary was just behaving like any other disciple, male or female; and that is a hard pill to swallow.

Perhaps it is no wonder that the women were first at the Cradle and last at the Cross. They had never known a man like this Man—there never has been such another. A prophet and teacher who never nagged at them, never flattered or coaxed or patronized; who never made arch jokes about them, never treated them either as "The women, God help us!" or "The ladies, God bless them!"; who rebuked without querulousness and praised without condescension; who took their questions and arguments seriously; who never mapped out their sphere for them, never urged them to be feminine or jeered at them for being female; who had no axe to grind and no uneasy male dignity to defend; who took them as he found them and was completely unself-conscious. There is no act, no sermon, no parable in the whole Gospel that borrows its pungency from female perversity; nobody could possibly guess from the words and deeds of Jesus that there was anything "funny" about woman's nature.

But we might easily deduce it from His contemporaries, and from His prophets before Him, and from His Church to this day. Women are not human; nobody shall persuade that they are human; let them say what they like, we will not believe it, though One rose from the dead.

Notes

[1]Dr. Peck had disclaimed adherence to the *Kinder, Kirche, Küche* school of thought.

[2]This last scandal did in the end outrage public opinion and was abolished.

Discussion Questions

1. Which attitudes and practices described by Sayers have changed since the date of this article (1926)? Which have not changed? What explanations can you find for the changes and lack of change?

2. Does Sayers's argument show that it is as absurd to judge women constantly in terms of their femaleness as it would be to judge men constantly in terms of their maleness? Why or why not?

3. What does Sayers's argument from history show? Is the fact that occupations formerly controlled by women are now controlled by men an argument for or against sexual equality? Give reasons to support your answer.

4. What is Sayers's complaint against "the Church"? Does it apply to some churches more than others? Is her complaint justified? Why or why not?

5. How does Sayers characterize Christ's attitude to women? What part does the characterization play in her argument? What is the importance of the attitude of Christ on this matter?

Because You Are a Woman

J. R. Lucas

Plato was the first feminist. In the *Republic* he puts forward the view that women are just the same as men, only not quite so good. It is a view which has often been expressed in recent years, and generates strong passions. Some of these have deep biological origins, which a philosopher can only hope to recognize and not to assuage. But much of the heat engendered is due to unnecessary friction between views which are certainly compatible and probably correct. And here a philosopher can help. If we can divide the issues neatly, at the joints, then we need not quarrel with one another for saying something, probably true, because what is being maintained is misconstrued and taken to mean something else, probably false.

The feminist debate turns on the application of certain concepts of justice, equality and humanity. Should the fact—"the mere fact"—of a person's being a woman disqualify her from being a member of the Stock Exchange, the Bench of Bishops or the House of Lords, or from obtaining a mortgage, owning property, having a vote or going to heaven? Is it not, say the feminists, just as irrational and inequitable as disqualifying a man on the grounds of the color of his hair? Is it not, counter the anti-feminists, just as rational as drawing a distinction between men on the one hand and children, animals, lunatics, Martians and computers on the other? Whereupon we come to enunciate the formal platitude that women are the same as men in some respects, different from them in others, just as men are the same in some respects as children, animals, lunatics, Martians and computers, and different in others. And then we have to embark on more substantial questions of the respects in which men and women are the same, and those in which they are different; and of whether any such differences could be relevant to the activity or institution in question, or could be comparable to the differences, generally acknowledged to exist, between *homo sapiens* and the rest of creation. Even if women are different from men, a feminist might argue, why should this be enough to debar them from the floor of the Stock Exchange, when, apparently, there is no objection to the presence of computers?

We are faced with two questions. We need to know first what exactly are the ways in which women differ from men, and this in turn raises issues of the methods whereby such questions may be answered. Only when these methodological issues have been discussed can we turn to the more substantial ones of morals and politics concerned with whether it can ever be right to treat a woman differently from a man on account of her sex, or whether that is a factor which must always be regarded as in itself irrelevant.

I

The facts of femininity are much in dispute. The development of genetic theory is some help, but not a decisive one. We know that men differ from women in having one Y-chromosome and only one X-chromosome whereas women have two X-

From J. R. Lucas, " 'Because You Are a Woman,' " *Philosophy*, 48 (1973) 161–171. Reprinted by permission of The Royal Institute of Philosophy and the author.

chromosomes. Apart from the X- and Y-chromosomes, exactly the same sort of chromosomes turn up in men and women indifferently. The genetic make-up of each human being is constituted by his chromosomes, which occur in pairs, one of each pair coming from the father, the other from the mother. Men and women share the same gene pool. So far as chromosomes, other than the X- and Y-ones, are concerned, men and women of the same breeding community are far more alike than members of different species, or even men of different races. This constitutes a powerful argument against the doctrine, attributed by some to the Mahometans, that women have no souls; contrary to the view of many young males, they are not just birds; or, in more modern parlance, it gives empirical support to arguments based on the principle of Universal Humanity. Women are worthy of respect, for the same reasons as men are. If it is wrong to hurt a man, to harm him, humiliate him or frustrate him, then it is wrong to hurt, harm, humiliate or frustrate a woman; for she is of the same stock as he, and they share the same inheritance and have almost all their chromosome types in common.

Early genetic theory assumed a one–one correlation between pairs of hereditary genetic factors and their manifested effects in the individual. Whether I had brown eyes or blue eyes depended on whether I had the pair of factors BB, Bb or bB, in all of which cases I should have brown eyes, or whether I had bb, in which case I should have blue eyes. No other genetic factor was supposed to be relevant to the color of my eyes, nor was the possession of a B or a b gene relevant to anything else about me. If this theory represented the whole truth, the feminist case would be simple. Sex is irrelevant to everything except sex. The fact of a man's being male or a woman's being female would be a "mere fact" with no bearing on anything except sexual intercourse and the procreation of children. It would be rational to hold that only a male could be guilty of rape, and it might be permissible to have marriage laws which countenanced only heterosexual unions, and to look for proofs of paternity as well as of maternity. Perhaps we might go a very little further, and on the same grounds as we admit that negroes are not really eligible for the part of Iago, admit that males could not really expect to be employed as models for female fashions, and *vice versa*. Beyond these few and essentially unimportant exceptions, it would be as wrong for the law to discriminate between the sexes as it would be if it were to prefer blondes.

Simple genetic theory is, however, too simple. It needs to be complicated in two ways. First, although chromosomes occur in pairs, each single one being inherited more or less independently of every other one, each chromosome contains not just one, but many, many genetic factors, and these are not all independently inherited, and some, indeed, like the one responsible for hemophilia, are sex-linked. There are, so far as we know, relatively few effects—and those mostly bad—which are caused by factors contained in the Y-chromosome, and there is a slight *a priori* argument against many features being thus transmitted (because the Y-chromosome is much smaller than the others, and so, presumably, carries less genetic information): but there could well be more complicated effects due to a relatively rare recessive gene not being marked in the male as it probably would have been in the female. Mathematical talent might be like hemophilia or color-blindness: it is consonant with what we know of genetic theory that only one in a thousand inherit the genetic factor, which if it is inherited by a boy then becomes manifest, but which if it is inherited by a girl, still in 999 cases out of a thousand is masked by a dominant unmathematicality. The second complication is more fundamental than the first. Genetic factors not only are not inherited independently of the others, but do not operate independently of the others. What is important is not simply whether I have BB, Bb, or bb, but whether I have one of these pairs in conjunction with some set of other pairs of factors. In particular, whether a person is male or female may affect whether or not some other hereditary factor manifests itself or not. Only men go bald. There are many physical features and physiological processes which are affected by whether a person is male or female. So far as our bodies are concerned, the fact of a person's being a man or a woman is not a "mere fact" but a fundamental one. Although there are many similarities between men and women, the differences are pervasive, systematic and of great biological significance. Almost the first question a hospital needs to ask is "M or F?"

Many feminists are dualists, and while conceding certain bodily differences between men and women, deny that there is any inheritance of intellectual ability or traits of character at all. Genetic theory, as far as it goes, is against them. There is reasonable evidence for the inheritance of skills and patterns of behavior in other animals, and in particular of those patterns of behavior we should normally ascribe to the maternal instinct. Human beings are far too complicated to manifest many abilities or traits of character that are simple enough to be susceptible of scientific test; and although we often detect family resemblances in ways of walking and talking, as well as in temperament and emotion, it is not clear how far these are due to inherited factors and how far they have been acquired by imitation or learning. It is, however, a common experience to note resemblances between different members of the same family who have never seen each other and have had no opportunity of imitating one another. Such instances, when cited, are often dismissed as mere anecdotes, belonging to mythology rather than science, and unworthy of the attention of modern-minded thinkers in this day and age. It is difficult to stand one's ground in the face of the charge of being unscientific, for the word "scientific" has strong evaluative overtones, and to be "unscientific" smacks of quackery and prejudice. But it remains the case that all discussions about political and social issues must be "unscientific" in that they are not exclusively based on the measurable results of repeatable experiments. For what we are concerned with is what people feel, decide, and ought to do about these things, and people are different, and feel differently and decide to do different things. If we refuse to admit to the argument any evidence other than the measurable results of reputable experiments, we may still be able to discuss questions of public health, but cannot even entertain those of justice or the political good. And if the feminist rejects all anecdotal evidence on principle, then she is making good her dualism by stipulation, because she is not prepared to recognize intellectual abilities or traits of character in the way in which they normally are recognized. This, of course, is not to urge that every story a boozy buffer cares to tell should be accepted as true or relevant; but only that the word "scientific" needs to be handled with caution, and not used to rule out of court whole ranges of evidence and whole realms of experience. The canons of scientific evidence are, very properly, strictly drawn; and scientists accept the corollary that the topics amenable to scientific research are correspondingly limited. There are many discussions which cannot be evaluated within the canon of scientific argument upon the basis of scientific observations alone, among them discussions about what is right and good for individuals and societies. But they need not be any the worse for that, although they will be if the participants do not show the same fairness and reasonableness in their discussions as scientists do in their researches.

Another methodological issue is raised by those who acknowledge that there have been and are differences in the intellectual achievements and the typical behavior of women as compared with men, but attribute all of them exclusively to the social pressures brought to bear upon women which have prevented them from exercising their talents to the full or giving rein to their natural inclinations. When the advocate of male supremacy marshals his masses of major poets against a solitary Sappho, the feminist explains that women have been so confined by domestic pressures and so inhibited by convention that those few with real poetic talent have never had opportunity to bring it to flower. Poets might be poor, but at least they could listen to the Muse undistracted by baby's cries:

whereas potential poetesses, unless their lot were cast in Lesbos, were married off and made to think of clothes and nappies to the exclusion of all higher thoughts.

It is difficult to find hard evidence either for or against this thesis. In this it is like many rival explanations or interpretations in history or literature. What moves us to adopt one rather than another is that it seems to us more explanatory or more illuminating than the alternative; and what seems to us more explanatory or illuminating depends largely on our own experience and understanding—and our own prejudices. But although we are very liable to be swayed by prejudice, it does not follow that we inevitably are, and although we are often guided by subjective considerations in deciding between various hypotheses, it does not follow that there is nothing, really, to choose between them. We can envisage evidence, even if we cannot obtain it, which would decide between the two alternatives. The feminist claim would be established if totally unisex societies sprang up and flourished; or if there were as many societies in which the roles of men and women were reversed as there were traditional ones. Indeed, the existence of any successful and stable society in which the roles of the sexes are reversed is evidence in favor of the claim. Evidence against is more difficult to come by. Few people deny that social pressures have a very considerable bearing on our behavior and capacities. Some people argue from the analogy with other animals, whose behavior is indubitably determined genetically and differs according to their sex; or argue, as I have done, by extrapolation from purely physical features. Both arguments are respectable, neither conclusive. Man is an animal, but very unlike other animals, particularly in respect of the extreme plasticity of human behavior, nearly all of which is learned. Very few of our responses are purely instinctive; and it is unsafe to claim confidently that maternal feelings must be. What would constitute evidence against the feminist claim would be some intellectual ability or character trait which seemed to be both relatively independent of social circumstance and distributed unevenly between the sexes. Mathematical talent might be a case in point. It seems to be much more randomly distributed in the population than other forms of intellectual ability. If Ramanujan could triumph over his circumstances, then surely numerate sisters to Sappho should abound. But this is far from being a conclusive argument.

There are no conclusive arguments about feminine abilities and attitudes. But the discoveries of the scientists, so far as they go, lend some support to traditional views. It could well be the case that intellectual and psychological characteristics are, like physical ones, influenced by genetic factors. If this is so, the way in which a particular pair of genes in an individual genotype will be manifested in the phenotype will depend on the other genes in the genotype, and may depend greatly on whether there are two X-chromosomes or one X and one Y. It could be that the masculine mind is typically more vigorous and combative, and the feminine mind typically more intuitive and responsive, with correspondingly different ranges of interests and inclinations. It would make evolutionary sense if it were, and would fit in with what else we know about the nature of man: but it is still possible to maintain the contrary view; and even if there are in fact differences between men and women, it does not follow that their treatment should be different too.

II

If it could be established that there were no innate intellectual or emotional differences between men and women, the feminists' case would be pretty well made; but it does not follow that to admit that there are differences carries with it an adequate justification for every sort of discrimination, and it is useful to consider what sort of bearing various types of difference might have. Suppose, for example, that mathematical ability were distributed unevenly and according to the same pattern as hemophilia, so that only one in n males have it and only one in n^2 females. This would be a highly relevant factor in framing our educational policy. It would justify the provision of far more opportunities for boys to study higher mathematics than for girls. But it would not justify the total exclusion of girls. Most girls prefer nursing to numeracy, but those few who would rather solve differential equations ought not to be prevented from doing so on the grounds that they are female. Two principles underlie this judgment. First that the connection between sex and mathematical ability is purely contingent; and secondly that we are in a position in which considerations of the individual's interests and deserts are paramount. Even if there are very few female mathematicians, there is no reason why any particular woman should not be a mathematician. And if any particular woman is, then her being a woman is irrelevant to her actual performance in mathematics. Her being a woman created a presumption, a purely contingent although usually reliable presumption, that she was no good at mathematics. It is like presumptive evidence in a court of law, which could be rebutted, and in this case was, and having been rebutted is of no more relevance in this individual situation, which is all we are concerned with.

Female mathematicians are rare. Few disciplines are so pure as mathematics. In most human activities—even in most academic pursuits—the whole personality is much more involved, and the irrelevance of a person's sex far more dubious. Differences between the sexes are likely to come into play most in ordinary human relations where one person tells another what to do, or persuades, or cajoles or encourages or warns or threatens or acquiesces. Insofar as most positions in society are concerned with social relations, it cannot be argued that the differences between the sexes are, of necessity, irrelevant. Although it might be the case that working men would as readily take orders from a fore-woman as a foreman, or that customers would be as pleased to find a handsome boy receptionist as a pretty girl, there is no reason to suppose that it must be so. Moreover, life is not normally either an examination or a trial. It is one of the disadvantages of our meritocratic age that we too readily assume that all social transactions are exclusively concerned with the individual, who needs to be given every opportunity and whose rights must be zealously safeguarded. But examinations and trials are artificial and cumbersome exceptions to the general rule, in which no one individual is the center of concern. To deny people the fruits of their examination success or to deprive them of their liberty on any grounds irrelevant to their own desert is wrong: but it is not so evidently wrong to frustrate Miss Amazon's hopes of a military career in the Grenadier Guards on the grounds not that she would make a bad soldier but that she would be a disturbing influence in the mess room. Laws and institutions are characteristically two-faced. They set norms for the behavior of different parties, and need to take into consideration the interests and claims of more than one person. They also need to apply generally and cannot be tailor-made to each particular situation: they define roles rather than fit actual personalities, and roles need to fit the typical rather than the special case. Even if Miss Amazon is sure not to attract sidelong glances from the licentious soldiery, her sisters may not be; and it may be easier to operate an absolute bar than leave it to the recruiting officer to decide whether a particular woman is sufficiently unattractive to be safe. This type of case turns up in many other laws and public regulations. We lay down rigid speed limits because they are easier to apply. There are many towns in which to drive at 30 mph would be dangerous, and many suburbs in which to drive at 45 mph would sometimes be safe. Some boys of ten are better informed about public affairs than other voters of thirty. But the advantage of having a fixed speed limit or a fixed voting age outweighs its admitted unfairness.

We can now see what sort of facts would bring what sort of principles to bear upon our individual decisions and the general structure of our laws and institutions. We need to know not only whether there are differences, but whether these differences are integrally or only contingently connected with a person's sex, and whether they apply in all cases or only as a rule. The more integrally and the more invariably a difference is connected with a person's sex, the more we are entitled to insist that the mere fact of being male or female can constitute a conclusive reason against being allowed to do something. The less integral a difference is, the more the arguments from Formal Equality (or Universalizability) and from Justice will come into play, requiring us to base our decisions only on the features relevant to the case in hand. The less invariable a difference is, the more the arguments from Humanity and again from Justice will come into play, requiring us to pay respect to the interests and inclinations of each individual person, and to weigh her actual interests, as against those of the community at large, on the basis of her actual situation and actual and reasonable desires.

However much I, a male, want to be a mother, a wife or a girl-friend, I am disqualified from those roles on account of my sex, and I cannot reasonably complain. Not only can I not complain if individuals refuse to regard me as suitable in those roles, but I have to acknowledge that it is reasonable for society generally to do so, and for the state to legislate accordingly. The state is justified in not countenancing homosexual "marriages," because of our general understanding of what marriage really is, and the importance we attach to family life. For exactly the same reasons, women are debarred from being regarded in a fatherly or husbandly light; and hence also in those parts of the Christian Church that regard priests as being essentially fathers in God from being clergymen or bishops. How far roles should be regarded as being integrally dependent on sex is a matter of dispute. In very intimate and personal relationships it is evident that the whole personality is involved, and that since a man—or at least many, non-Platonic men— responds to a woman in a different way from that in which he responds to a man or a woman to a woman, it is natural that these roles should be essentially dependent on sex. But as the roles become more limited, so the dependence becomes less. I could hardly complain if I was not given the part of Desdemona or a job as an *au pair* boy on account of my sex: but if I had very feminine features and had grown my hair long and golden, or if I were particularly deft at changing nappies, I might feel a little aggrieved, and certainly I could call in question any law that forbade a man to play the part of a woman or be a nursemaid. Some substantial public good would need to be shown to justify a legal decision enforceable by penal sanctions being uniformly based not on my actual inability to fill the role required but only my supposed unsuitability on account of my sex. We demand a higher standard of cogency in arguments justifying what laws there should be than in those concerned only with individual decisions; and although this standard can be satisfied, often by admitting considerations of the public good, yet the arguments need to be adduced, because, in framing laws, we need to be sensitive to individual rights and careful about our criteria of relevance. Although it may be the case that a nurse is a better nurse for having the feminine touch, we hesitate to deem it absolutely essential; and although many more women than men have been good nurses, we do not believe that it must invariably be so. There are male nurses. We reckon it reasonable to prefer a woman in individual cases, but do not insist upon it in all cases by law. We are reluctant to impose severe legal disqualifications, but equally would hesitate to impose upon employers an obligation not to prefer women to play female parts or to be nurses or to join a family in an *au pair* capacity. For we recognize that a person's sex can reasonably be regarded as relevant to his or her suitability for particular posts, and that many institutions will operate on this basis, and are entitled to. I am justified in refusing to employ a male *au pair* girl or a female foreman, although if there are many males anxious to be looking after young children or many women anxious to supervise the work of others, it may be desirable on grounds of Humanity to establish special institutions in which they can fulfil their vocations. If we will not let Miss Amazon join the Grenadier Guards, let there be [women's military groups] for her to join instead.

Although we are rightly reluctant to impose legal disqualifications on individuals on grounds extraneous to their individual circumstances, it is inherent in all political thinking that we may find considerations of the general case overriding those of the individual one; and often we frame our laws with an eye to what men and women are generally like rather than what they invariably are. A man may not adopt an infant girl unless she is more than twenty-five years younger than he; for some men might otherwise use adoption to acquire not so much a daughter as a wife. In many societies women have less freedom in disposing of their property than men; for else, things being as they are, some women would be prevailed upon to divest themselves of it to their long-term disadvantage. Ardent feminists have chafed at the shackles of marriage, and demand freedom from this degrading institution for their sisters as well as themselves. But if this freedom were established it would be the libertine males who would enjoy the benefits of liberation, being then free to leave the women to bear the burdens of parenthood all on their own. If most mothers care more for their children and their homes than most fathers do, then in the absence of institutions that recognize the fact they will in fact be disadvantaged. Some discrimination is needed to redress the balance. But discrimination, even positive discrimination, can work to the disadvantage of individuals, however much it may benefit most people on the whole.

The would-be female Stakhanovite is penalized by the law forbidding firms to employ female labor for sixty hours a week, just as the youthful entrepreneur is handicapped by his legal incapacity, as a minor, to pledge his credit except for the necessities of life, and the skilled racing motorist by the law forbidding him to drive, however safely, at more than 70 miles per hour. In each case the justification is the same: the restriction imposed on the individual, although real and burdensome, is not so severe as to outweigh the benefits that are likely to accrue in the long run to women in general, or to minors, or to motorists. It is in the nature of political society that we forgo some freedoms in order that either we ourselves or other people can secure some good. All we can in general demand is that our sacrifices should not be fruitless, and that if we give up some liberty or immunity it is at least arguable that it will be on balance for the best.

Arguments in politics are nearly always mixed, and involve appeals to different principles, according to how the question is construed. We can elucidate some canons of relevance for some of the principles which may be invoked. Where the principle is that of Universal Humanity, the reason "Because you are a woman" is always irrelevant to its general applicability, though it may affect the way it is specified: perhaps women feel more strongly about their homes than men do, so that although we ought not, on grounds of humanity, to hurt either men or women, deprivation of her home would constitute a greater hurt to a woman than to a man. The principle of Universal Humanity is pervasive in its applications, but is conclusive only over a much more limited range. It is always wrong to torture; but often we cannot help hurting people's feelings or harming their interests if other values—justice, liberty, the public good—are to be preserved. And therefore arguments based on the principle of universal humanity may be overridden by ones based on other principles, also valuable. When the principle invoked is that of Formal Equality (or Universalizability) the reason "Because you are a woman" cannot be dismissed out of hand as necessarily irrelevant. A person's sex is not a "mere fact," evidently and necessarily separate from all other facts, and such that it is immediately obvious that no serious argument can be founded upon it. Particularly with those roles that involve relationships with other people, and especially where those relationships are fairly personal ones, it is likely to matter whether it is a man or a woman that is chosen. When some principle of Justice is at stake, the criteria of relevance become fairly stringent. We are concerned only with the individual's actions, attitudes and abilities, and the reason "Because you are a woman" must either be integrally connected with matter in issue (as in "Why cannot I marry the girl I love?") or be reliably, although only contingently, connected with it (as in "Why cannot I get myself employed for 60 hours a week?"); and in the latter case we feel that Justice has been compromised, although perhaps acceptably so, if there is no way whereby an individual can prove she is an exception to the rule and be treated as such. As the interests of the individual become more peripheral, or can be satisfied in alternative ways that are available, the principle of justice recedes, and we are more ready to accept rules and institutions based on general principles of social utility or tradition, and designed only to fit the general case. It is legitimate to base public feeling on such differences as seem to be relevant, but the more a law or an institution is based on merely a contingent, and not an integral, concomitance, the more ready we should be to cater for exceptions.

With sufficient care we may be able to disentangle what is true in the feminists' contention from what is false. At least we should be able to avoid the dilemma, which seems to be taken for granted by most participants in the debate, that we must say that women either are in all respects exactly the same as men or else are in all respects different from, and inferior to, them, and not members of the same universe of discourse at all. I do not share Plato's feelings about sex. I think the sexes are different, and incomparable. No doubt, women are not quite as good as men, *in some respects*: but since men are not nearly as good as women in others, this carries with it no derogatory implication of uniform inferiority. Exactly what these differences are, and, indeed, what sort of differences they are, is a matter of further research; and exactly what bearing they should have in the application of the various principles we value in making up our mind about social matters is a matter for further philosophical thought. But without any further thought we can align our emotions with the proponents of Women's Lib on the most important issue of all. What angers them most is the depersonalization of women in the Admass society: and one cannot but sympathize with their protest against women being treated as mere objects of sexual gratification by men; but cannot avoid the conclusion that their arguments and activities in fact lead towards just that result which they deplore. If we are insensitive to the essential femininity of the female sex, we shall adopt an easy egalitarianism which, while denying that there are any genetic differences, allows us to conclude in most individual cases that women, judged by male standards of excellence, are less good than their male rivals. Egalitarianism ends by depersonalizing women and men alike.

Discussion Questions

1. What issue is Lucas addressing? What does he try to show? Do you agree or disagree? Why?

2. According to Lucas, what are the ways in which women differ from men? What relevance does this have to his argument?

3. How does Lucas answer the "feminist" claim that any differences between the sexes in character and intellect is due to social pressures? Is his answer satisfactory? Why or why not?

4. Lucas concedes that "if it could be established that there were no innate intellectual or emotional differences between men and women, the feminists' case would be pretty well made." What does this show about Lucas's own position?

5. What is Lucas's argument against homosexual marriages? How would Nagel, Solomon, or the Washington State Catholic Conference agree or disagree with Lucas? Who is right? Why?

6. What is Lucas's basic argument for treating men and women differently? Argue for or against his position.

On the Moral Relevance of Sex

Susan Haack

Mr. Lucas expresses the hope that the philosopher may, by removing misunderstandings which cause unnecessary friction, take some of the heat out of the feminist debate ["Because You Are a Woman," previous selection in this chapter]. But it is doubtful, since he begins by attributing to the feminist the view that "women are just the same as men, only not quite so good," whether he has understood what that debate is about. And his contribution to this debate is so confused, and so prejudiced, that it is likely to have anything but the moderating effect for which he professedly hopes.

It is notable that much of what is most exceptionable in Mr. Lucas's paper is not explicitly asserted, but more indirectly conveyed. In consequence, an adequate criticism must examine his rhetoric at least as closely as his logic; and since his logic and his rhetoric are almost inextricably intertwined, will have to proceed via close textual study. I propose, therefore, to take two particularly pernicious paragraphs, and to expose their deficiencies in detail; then to indicate briefly the frequency of similar deficiencies in the rest of the paper; and finally to show that, once what is insinuated has been discounted, what, of genuine argument, remains, is unexceptionable only because almost without substance.

Mr. Lucas proposes to examine two questions: in what ways women differ from men? and whether it can ever be right to treat a woman differently from a man on account of her sex? His attempt [section I] on the first of these questions is marred by inattention to relevant information—for example, he considers briefly the possibility that genetic differences may give rise to behavioral differences between men and women, but never the possibility that hormonal differences may do so; and, indeed, by plain falsehood—he claims, for example . . . that only men go bald. I shall therefore devote my detailed attention rather to his attempt [section II] on the second question, beginning with a paragraph where Lucas is discussing whether possible differences between men and women might justify exclusion of women from certain occupations.

Reprinted from *Philosophy* 49, 1974, by permission of The Royal Institute of Philosophy and the author.

Section II, Paragraph 2

Mr. Lucas has remarked several times in the course of [section] I that it is possible that women are less mathematically talented than men. Now he observes that female mathematicians are, in fact, rare. He leaves it conveniently vague whether by "mathematician" he means "professional mathematician" or "person with mathematical ability." He goes on to comment that few disciplines are so "pure" as mathematics. The impression is thus most economically conveyed that women are so woolly-minded and emotional that they are unable to cope with so abstract a subject. However, Lucas next contrasts the purity of mathematics with the "involvement of the whole personality" in other disciplines and pursuits, and concludes that in these other disciplines and pursuits, therefore, sex is not wholly irrelevant. At this point he seems to have fallen victim to his own rhetoric; previously mathematical ability had been his most highly stressed example of a possibly sex-linked characteristic, whereas now he is committed to the thesis that the "purer" a pursuit is, the less relevant to it a person's sex is likely to be. This confusion is, however, essential to the next step of the argument. Lucas has previously envisaged the exclusion of women from various pursuits, but only on the basis of their incapacity: although innumerate females were to be excluded, the "exceptional" female mathematician (the phrase has, incidentally, a splendid ambiguity) was to be permitted to pursue her profession. But now Lucas allows other, far more questionable, grounds of discrimination, viz. the adverse reactions of other people. This argument applies to those pursuits where "the whole personality is involved." It rests, however, on a rather serious equivocation. There are importantly different ways in which the whole personality may be involved in a discipline or a job: it might be argued, for instance, that the study of literature requires *personal involvement* in a way the study of mathematics does not; quite differently, it might be argued that the job of foreman or public relations officer requires *involvement with other people* in a way production line jobs do not. It is the first kind of "personal involvement" which is suggested by the contrast with the "purity" of mathematics and might, *if* personality were shown to be sex-dependent, be relevant to a person's ability in, say, literature. It is the second kind of "personal involvement" which is relevant to Lucas's claim that the adverse reactions of other people would justify discrimination. Lucas's examples include (1) that it might be proper to refuse to employ a woman as foreman, because other (i.e., male) employees would be unwilling to take orders from her, and (2) that it might not be improper "to frustrate Miss Amazon's hopes of a military career in the Grenadier Guards on the grounds not that she would make a bad soldier but that she would be a disturbing influence in the mess room." . . . The first of these examples allows discrimination on grounds, not of the incompetence of an applicant for a job, but purely of the prejudice of other employees. This is certainly unacceptable in the case of racial discrimination; employers refusing to employ black workers on the ground that white employees would object are, quite rightly, liable to the attentions of the Race Relations Board. It is no less unacceptable where discrimination is on the basis of sex rather than race. The second example is, if possible, more alarming. For one thing, the assumption that men are so licentious that women cannot be allowed to work with them for fear of the resulting havoc clearly betrays that view of women as sexual objects which Lucas subsequently . . . claims, less than convincingly, to deplore. For another, the principles employed in this case rapidly lead, if taken seriously, to absurdity—for presumably they would equally well justify the exclusion of *men* from the Grenadier Guards for fear that male recruits might provoke licentious behavior on the part of their homosexual colleagues.

It is bad enough that Lucas is prepared to support discrimination on the strength of other people's reactions even when those reactions are the result of sheer prejudice; worse, that his argument entails that this kind can be more pervasive than discrimination on grounds of incapacity. But this turns out to be the case, since to the objection that a particular woman may be so unattractive as to pose no threat to the Guards' peace of mind, Lucas replies that all women ought, nevertheless, to be excluded, apparently because of the simplicity of such an inclusive rule. He supports this claim by an analogy with other cases where, he claims, considerations of generality outweigh considerations of fairness, e.g., the imposition of a uniform speed limit or voting age. The analogy is used in a misleading way. In the first place, it is not made as clear as it should be that the analogy is not relevant to the claim that women sufficiently attractive to disturb the Guards should be excluded, but only to the claim that even women not sufficiently attractive to be disturbing should also be excluded. One suspects, however, one is intended to suppose that Lucas has shown that considerations of the public good support the exclusion of attractive women. The analogy used is in any case dubious, since the prohibitions on driving over a certain speed, or on voting under a certain age, are based on the presumed *incapacity* of motorists to drive safely above a certain speed, or of minors to vote sensibly, whereas the case with which these are compared is of a prohibition based on something other than incapacity.

It is important to notice how Lucas's apparent moderation, in allowing competent women to pursue careers for which they are suited, is now entirely nullified. For Lucas must allow that a competent woman may properly be excluded from any profession on the grounds of the prejudice or boorishness of her (male?) colleagues.

Section II, Paragraph 4

The point of this paragraph is to argue that the more "integrally" some trait is connected with a person's sex, the more justification it provides for discrimination. Lucas begins with an example of the kind of discrimination against men which he thinks such a principle would allow: however much a man wishes to be a mother, a wife, or a girl-friend, he is, Lucas comments, disqualified in virtue of his sex, and cannot complain. In fact, Lucas argues, it would be reasonable for the state to "legislate accordingly." . . . On the face of it, this is plainly ridiculous; it would be wholly *un*reasonable for the state to legislate against men being mothers; not, of course, because men are entitled to be mothers if they wish, but because it is worse than pointless to legislate against something which is anyway impossible. But it turns out to be no accident that Lucas employs the vague phrase "legislate accordingly." For the kind of discrimination which he thinks he has shown to be reasonable is not this absurd kind, but quite another: the refusal, for instance, to countenance homosexual marriages. It becomes apparent that Lucas is using "integral" in two ways: a connection may be "integral" because analytic, or because contingent but highly correlated. This enables Lucas to move from the no doubt correct statement that a man can hardly complain because he cannot be a mother (where the connection is integral in the first sense), to the much more doubtful proposition that the state is justified in refusing to allow homosexuals to marry each other (where any relevant connection is presumably integral, if at all, only in the second sense). Interestingly, the equivocation is marked by the comment that legislation against homosexual marriage is justified "because of our general understanding of what marriage is." This equivocation enables Lucas to by-pass entirely the substantial question, whether there are good reasons why the state should not recognize contracts which are in all respects like marriage, except for the sex of the parties concerned.

Lucas then attempts to mitigate the effects of the kinds of sexual discrimination he has supported, by suggesting that, to compensate for any unfairness involved, there should be special institutions in which men who wish to be nurses or nannies, or women who wish to be foremen or soldiers, can work. This suggests that Lucas would favor a sort of sexual apartheid, which is surely even more absurd than the racial kind. And in any case the proposal is totally inappropriate to discrimination on the basis of ability. If it were agreed that Miss Amazon should be excluded from the Grenadier Guards because she would be a disturbing influence, then there would be *some* point in allowing her to pursue a military career in another institution where this danger was avoided. But if Mr. Nightingale is excluded from the nursing profession because he is clumsy and unsympathetic, then there is absolutely *no* reason to allow him to pursue a nursing career in some segregated institution. One wonders whom Mr. Lucas would assign as *patients?*

The standard of argument of the rest of the paper is not better than that of the paragraphs I have examined in detail. Similar rhetorical tricks are used throughout. For instance: vocabulary is employed which carries unwarranted, but one suspects not unwelcome, connotations. One example is "pure" in the first paragraph discussed; another is Lucas's use of the emotively laden word "feminine" as if it were equivalent to "female" (as in "the facts of femininity are much in dispute" . . .). The interpretation of key words, such as "discrimination," is left wholly vague. There is heavy use of, frequently misleading, analogy; as with the supposed analogy between legal restrictions on the hours for which women may be employed, and legal restrictions on the capacity of minors to pledge their credit, and between legal restrictions on the age of female child whom a man may adopt, and legal restrictions on the freedom women have to dispose of their own property. . . . Sometimes the effect of the rhetoric is not just to convey a false impression, but almost irremediably to confuse the argument. This is for instance the case with the equivocation on "personal involvement" and "integral" discussed previously. It also occurs when, anxious to convey an appearance of moderation, Lucas makes a concession, e.g., that it is wrong to deny people the results of their examination success, only to nullify it by a subsequent claim, e.g., that the prejudice of other people justifies discrimination even against the competent. This procedure occurs on an even grander scale when Lucas magnanimously concedes that the principle of universal humanity applies to women as well as men, only to go on to observe that the principle of formal equality does not; which, since he stresses that the latter principle overrides the former, entirely nullifies the apparent concession.

One could perhaps have ignored Mr. Lucas's evident prejudice, had his paper, its rhetorical embellishments aside, contributed seriously to the debate. Unfortunately, remarkably little of substance survives when the rhetoric is disregarded. [Section] I of the paper addresses the question, what the differences are between men and women; but offers only the disappointing answer, that it is possible that women differ from men in respect of intellectual and emotional traits, but also possible that they do not. There is a considerable volume of relevant research (*how* considerable is indicated by the fact that in even so summary a book as Hutt's *Males and Females* (Penguin, 1972), there are references to something like 150 items), but Lucas resolutely ignores it. This is especially remarkable in view of the clear relevance of some empirical studies, e.g., Tyler's of men's and women's performances in mathematical and verbal tests, to possible differences which Lucas explicitly mentions. To be fair, Lucas professes scepticism about the competence of scientific methods to answer this question; but it is not easy to take this seriously when he offers no specific criticism of any relevant piece of research. [Section] II addresses itself to the question: what differences between men and women would warrant treating them differently, but contributes little by way of an answer except (1) that it is *possible* that sex is sometimes relevant, and (2) that unfairness to individuals may sometimes be outweighed by public good. True, Lucas offers the more substantial principle, that the more integrally a trait is connected with sex, the more likely it is that it will warrant sexual discrimination; but the usefulness of this principle is vitiated by his equivocation on "integral." And he suggests that sex is relevant to "Formal Equality" rather than "Universal Humanity," but the usefulness of this cannot be assessed while the content of these principles remains unspecified.

Lucas thinks that "with sufficient care we may be able to disentangle what is true in the feminists' contention from what is false." . . . This task will require more care than he has given it.[1]

Note

[1] I have benefited from discussions of Mr. Lucas's paper with Dr. J. Robertson, of the University of Cape Town, and Miss C. Battersby, of the University of Warwick.

Discussion Questions

1. Does Haack represent Lucas's position fairly? If not, where does she distort what he says? How might Lucas object to Haack's *statement* of his views?

2. What facts about differences between the sexes are at issue between Lucas and Haack? What is the importance of these facts to the argument?

3. Where do Lucas and Haack seem to differ on principles? Which principles are at issue? Are the principles used by Lucas?

4. Haack claims that Lucas would "support discrimination on the strength of other people's reactions even when those reactions are the result of sheer prejudice." How might Lucas reply?

5. Haack states that Lucas "would favor a sort of sexual apartheid, which is surely even more absurd than the racial kind." How might Lucas describe his proposal? To what extent is the issue between Lucas and Haack really the issue of a unisex versus a sexually pluralistic society? Which position do you prefer? Why?

On Sexual Equality

Alison Jaggar

Oh Ma, what is a feminist?
A feminist, my daughter,
Is any woman now who cares
To organize her own affairs
As men don't think she oughter.

I. Sexual Equality: Integration or Separation?

A more conventional, though not more apt, definition of a feminist is one who believes that justice requires equality between women and men. Not that equality is a sufficient condition of human or of women's liberation, but it is at least a necessary one. For this reason, and since the concept of equality is already notoriously elusive, it seems worthwhile to spend a little time reflecting on what it would mean for the sexes to be equal.

Equality, in the sense with which social philosophers are concerned, is a social ideal. Therefore, sexual equality does not mean that individuals of different sexes should be physically indistinguishable from each other (as misogynists sometimes pretend is the goal of women's liberation). It means rather that those of one sex, in virtue of their sex, should not be in a socially advantageous position vis-à-vis those of the other sex. A society in which this condition obtained would be a nonsexist society. Although all feminists, by definition, agree that sexism should be eliminated, disagreement arises among us over how this should be done and how our common goal of sexual equality should be achieved.

The traditional feminist answer to this question has been that a sexually egalitarian society is one in which virtually no public recognition is given to the fact that there is a physiological sex difference between persons. This is not to say that the different reproductive functions of each sex should be unacknowledged in such a society nor that there should be no physicians specializing in female and male complaints, etc. But it is to say that, except in this sort of context, the question whether someone is female or male should have no significance.

It is easy to see why both traditional feminism and much of the contemporary women's liberation movement take this view of sexual equality. Since the distinction between the sexes is embedded in our most basic institutions (employment, marriage, the draft, even our language),[1] and since the societal disadvantages of being female are well known, it is natural to suppose that the one is the cause of the other and hence that equality requires the de-institutionalization of sexual differences. For this reason, feminists have always fought hard against the notion that an individual's sex should be an acceptable test for ter[2] fitness to do such things as fill a certain job, borrow money, etc. Much of their effort has been expended in trying to provide legal guarantees to protect women from

From *Ethics,* 84 (1974), 275–92, ©1974 by The University of Chicago Press. Reprinted with permission of the publisher and author.

differential treatment in so-called public life. Recently, and in accord with the contemporary rejection of the old public/private dichotomy on which classical liberalism laid so much stress, some radical feminists have extended the principle that equality requires the minimization of sexual differences even into what used to be called private life. Thus, Shulamith Firestone believes that a sexually egalitarian society requires that an individual may freely express ter "natural" "polymorphous perversity" by sexual encounters with other people of any age and of either sex,[3] and Ti-Grace Atkinson advocates the total abolition of what she calls "the institution of sexual intercourse."[4]

In order to understand more clearly what is meant by this call for the deinstitutionalization of sexual differences, let me pause for a moment to consider what it is for an activity to be institutionalized. Some of the radical feminists' proposals may be confusing if they are thought to suggest that *every* cooperative activity constitutes a social institution. One unfortunate consequence of taking this suggestion seriously would be to undermine the distinction between individual and institutional prejudice, a distinction which is very useful in the analysis of discriminatory behavior.[5] At least for present purposes, then, I shall take a social institution to be a relatively stable way of organizing a significant social activity. To institutionalize activity streamlines social intercourse by defining socially recognized roles and thus enables prediction of what those participating in the practice are likely to do. It also, and perhaps more importantly, provides a standard of correctness by reference to which the propriety of certain kinds of behavior may be judged. It is clear from this definition why even such an apparently individual matter as sexual intercourse, to the extent that it is governed by community norms and even regulated by law, should be acknowledged as a social institution. This definition also makes it clear that some forms of activity may be institutionalized in one society and not in another; it depends on the extent of social regulation and control.

Institutional sexism is a social disadvantage which attaches to individuals of one sex or the other as the result of a certain way of institutionalizing activity. In this, it differs from individual sexism which occurs when a certain individual or group of individuals express hatred or contempt for an individual or group of (usually) the other sex by an act of hostility which may or may not be violent but which is not part of a socially stabilized pattern of discrimination. As social philosophers, we must obviously be concerned primarily with the former type of discrimination, for our first task is to articulate a social ideal.

Let us now return to what I see as my central question, namely, does equality between the sexes require that there should be no institutional recognition of sexual differences, that is, no institutions which differentiate systematically between women and men? I have already remarked that the mainstream of feminist thought has held almost continuously that the answer to this question is yes. In the mainstream tradition, the nonsexist society is one which is totally integrated sexually, one in which sexual differences have ceased to be a matter of public concern. That this should be the ultimate goal of the women's liberation movement follows logically from one very natural interpretation of such familiar slogans as "Women want to be treated as human beings" or "as persons" or "as individuals." On this interpretation, to treat someone as a person is to ignore ter sex.[6]

Recently, however, the traditional feminist goal of sexual integration has been challenged—and challenged by those who, on the criterion of their belief in sexual equality, are undeniably feminists. Just as there is a faction within the black liberation movement which rejects the ideals of "color blindness" and racial integration in favor of black pride and racial separatism, so there are now some feminists who argue that a person's sex is an inescapable and important fact about tem which ought to be socially recognized rather than ignored.

The issue between these two groups of feminists is not entirely clear. In some cases, it seems to be merely a matter of tactics or strategy: what is the best way of improving the position of women in this society? But the disagreement is also a philosophical one, philosophical in two senses. On the one hand, it involves certain more or less familiar conceptual problems: what constitutes justice or equality? what constitutes a person? even, what constitutes a sexual difference? And, on the other hand, it involves a normative disagreement over the kind of society for which we should aim.

In this paper, I shall explore the philosophical differences between these two groups of feminists and try to establish that sexual separation, or the institutionalization of sexual differences, is neither necessary nor desirable. I shall begin by attempting to refute various philosophical arguments to the conclusion that it is impossible, logically and practically, to ignore a person's sex. I shall then deal with other arguments which purport to present good reasons for the institutionalization of sexual differences. Thus, I shall move from the more clearly conceptual to the more explicitly normative claims. My overriding aim will be to defend the traditional feminist conception of sexual equality as the de-institutionalization of sexual differences. . . .

III. The Distinction Between the Sexes

The traditional feminist claim that sexual equality is to be achieved by ignoring sexual differences obviously presupposes a certain view of what a sexual difference is. As a matter of historical fact (though not conceptual necessity), sexual integrationists have regarded an individual's sex as being an entirely physiological characteristic.[7] It is assumed that the physiological differences are not accompanied by any significant differences between the sexes in such apparently nonphysical functions as sensitivity, reasoning, moral delibera-tion, etc. This makes it plausible to claim that sexual differences can be ignored in most social contexts except those directly concerned with reproduction.

The picture might change, however, if this view about what constitutes a sexual difference were shown to be inadequate, if it could be argued successfully that the concept of sex should include not only a difference in reproductive organs but also certain nonphysical differences. Empirical research in this area is still inconclusive, to say the least, but if a philosophical argument could demonstrate that sexual differences necessarily stretch beyond the physical, this should force us to rethink the claim that such differences are socially irrelevant. And if sexual differences were shown to be much more far-reaching than we had hitherto supposed, we might come to believe that it was practically if not logically impossible to ignore a person's sex.

There are, of course, a number of arguments by misogynists purporting to show that women are intellectually and morally inferior to men. But I shall take these as already refuted by other writers and turn instead to the one author I have been able to discover who deals with the question in a manner which is both philosophical and feminist. This is Professor Christine Garside, who first takes up the issue in a paper entitled "Women and Persons":[8]

> . . . women will always be different from men as the result of self-determination, because we differ in physical structure, we differ in our present social experience, we differ in our inherited past and so on.
>
> I suspect that it was in some part the fear of loss of polarity between the sexes which led to the traditional denial of self-determination for women. This fear,

however, is groundless for a true polarity will emerge when women and men press forward in active self-determination.[9]

The concluding paragraph of her paper runs thus:

> Finally, I would like to reiterate my belief that there is no need to fear loss of polarity when women do achieve liberation on the level of self-determination. . . . There is no way that women can ever become identical to men. Nor is there any reason why they should desire to do so. The heritage and experience of women is as rich as the heritage and experience as [of?] men; and once women recognize their right to self-determination and release their creative energies into the world this will be obvious.[10]

Now, in its narrowest interpretation, the claim that women can never be identical to men is simply tautologous, trivially true, just like the claim that people with big feet can never be identical to people with small ones. But of course Garside is saying more than this, and her most recent paper, "True Sex-Polarity,"[11] gives a fuller exposition of her views. In this account, she utilizes Scriven's notion of "normical" properties, properties which do not belong analytically to an object but whose presence is not purely accidental or, as she says, "arbitrary." "A normical property is one which is needed in a thorough explanation of the thing which has the property."[12] An object may lack any one of its normical properties, but it could not lack them all and still be an object of that type.

Garside claims that there is only one property which belongs analytically to women, namely, that of being a person, but she believes that this one property is supplemented by a number of normical properties. "What it is to be a woman includes having a particular kind of body, having a recent history of being brought up in a patriarchal society, having an inherited history of female archetypes, having present experiences which occur because one is female, and having a future which calls for a revolution from being oppressed. There are other things as well, but these are most central."[13]

In elaborating this definition, Garside gives a rich and evocative account of what it is to be female. The alternative account, which I wish to espouse, is much starker. For me, to be a woman is no more and no less than to be a female human being. All and only female human beings are women. To be female and to be human are the necessary and sufficient conditions for being a woman. . . .

Neither Garside nor I dispute the empirical facts regarding women's history, socialization, etc. But we do differ, apparently, in the significance that we attach to those facts. Garside seems to believe that they are of great importance, that they result in distinct and permanent differences between male and female nature, if that is an acceptable gloss for her term "sex-polarity." I'm less sure about this. I simply don't know how important these factors are. I suppose the importance of at least some of them might be investigated empirically—although I don't know how one could investigate empirically her claim that "it feels different to be a woman than to be a man."[14] At the moment, given the oppressive conditions of the present and the past, those factors may be very important. But one may hope that, as conditions improve, as women experience less discrimination, for example, those factors may weigh less heavily. So not only is it not conceptually true, it may not even be empirically true that, in a more than trivial philosophical sense, there will always be a sexual polarity.

Garside's presumption that there are certain necessary features of personal experience seems to be philosophically sound. I would accept that it is indeed a conceptual truth that persons must have physical experiences, social experiences, and some kind of cultural heritage. But what does not seem to be conceptually true is that these features have an inescapably sexual character. I am not, of course, asserting, *a priori,* that the differences between women and men have been shown conclusively to be limited to the purely reproductive and that, therefore, complete sexual integration is possible in all social contexts except those directly involving reproduction. What I am claiming, however, is that we have as yet no good reason, either *a priori* or empirical, for denying the possibility of sexual integration. So, since I believe that integration is a desirable ideal, I claim that we should work on the assumption that it is possible. Only if empirical research or new philosophical arguments demonstrate other differences between the sexes shall we need to question again the possibility of this ideal.

IV. The Rights of Women

Even in the absence of reason to believe in a sexual polarity which transcends the physiological distinction, it might be argued that the simple physiological differences between women and men were alone sufficient to justify the institutionalization of sexual differences. The facts that women are, in general, smaller and (in some ways) weaker than men, that we give birth to children, and so on, may be thought to constitute in themselves inequalities which require social remedy. In the past, such arguments have been used by male supremacists as justification for forcing on women a kind of "protection" which guarantees to us an inferior social position, but the biological facts may also be used by feminists as grounds for arguing that women should receive special treatment in order to offset our biological inequality. Such a feminist is Shulamith Firestone, who believes that the goal of social equality between the sexes requires a technological advance which will allow for the extrauterine reproduction of children, thus freeing women from what Firestone calls "the fundamental inequality of the bearing and rais-ing of children."[15]

This claim apparently takes for granted the conclusion of [the] argument . . . that one's sex should be essentially determined by the shape of ter reproductive organs. Its novelty seems to lie in its view of equality. For it presupposes that equality is not merely equality of opportunity, that is, not merely the absence of social impediments based on sex to any individual's attaining whatever position in society tey chooses to aim for. Instead, equality is viewed in a more positive sense, as a certain level of physical and economic security which society ought to provide for each of its members. In order that each individual should reach this level, it may be necessary to grant special social rights to certain disadvantaged groups, and it is claimed that women constitute a group which requires such rights in order to achieve social equality with men.

In order to qualify as a genuine female right, any proposal must be envisioned as a permanent feature of a nonsexist society. It cannot be viewed simply as a temporary measure, like alimony or the preferential hiring of women, which are usually advocated as necessary only to correct an unequal situation but which should be discontinued as soon as the imbalance is remedied. To be a genuine "female right," the alleged right must be seen as belonging permanently to all women simply in virtue of our sex and not, for example, in virtue of our social status or in virtue simply of our being human. When the sexual distinction is seen primarily as a difference in reproductive organs, it follows that the kind of special rights which women are said to need in a sexually egalitarian society should be connected with our reproductive function. They include the right to protection from assault and rape, the right to abortion, the right to maternity leave, and the right to guaranteed care and/or financial support for our children.

In my opinion, the trouble with this position lies not in its vision of social equality as a positive condition but, rather, in its view of the sexual distinction. Despite its apparent acceptance of the view that sex is merely physiological, I think that those who claim the need for special female rights are surreptitiously extending the sexual distinction to cover more than a physiological difference. For example, it may well be true that society in general should take on the responsibility of providing and caring for children, but this proposal should not be presented as a *female* right. To do so is to make the obviously false assumption that the sexual difference consists not only in women's capacity to give birth to children but also in our having an obligation to raise them. Even on the dubious presumption that the welfare of children is the total responsibility of whoever produced them, it is clear that this measure would provide relief to *both* parents of the children, the father as well as the mother. But perhaps a preferable way of seeing this proposal is not as a right of parents at all but rather as a right of children.

Similarly, to suggest that the right to freedom from assault and rape is a specifically female right is to presuppose that women alone are desirable sexual objects or that women alone are incapable of defending themselves. Such suggested female rights are far better viewed as applications of general human rights, so that adequate protection may be afforded to any individual, male or female, who needs it. Thus, the right to maternity leave should be covered by the statement that those who are temporarily incapable of contributing to material production should not be expected to do so. The stress on the special nature of maternity leave does indeed emphasize that pregnancy and childbirth are not sicknesses, but it also suggests that women need special privileges which men don't require. This suggestion is misleading. We do not, after all, elevate "prostate leave" into a special right of men.

The proposed female right to abortion is more complicated. It is certainly something which does not apply to men, but it is often defended either as a way of allowing women to enjoy the general human right of "control over one's own body" or, perhaps more plausibly, as a way of allowing women the general human right of sexual freedom.[16] The former right, however, is extremely ill-determined and controversial; how much control over ter own body should a typhoid carrier have, for example? And the latter right, of sexual freedom, may well be thought to be limited by a consideration of the rights of the fetus. If this is so, however, then a feminist could argue that, in the absence of foolproof contraceptive methods, the right to sexual freedom should be limited for men as well as for women. The complexity of this special case makes it impossible to discuss adequately here, but it certainly does not seem to me to present a clear case of a special female right which ought to be guaranteed by a sexually egalitarian society.

In general, I would argue that, so long as we view the difference between the sexes as a simple physiological difference—and we have no conclusive grounds for doing more—then there is no reason to draw up a special bill of rights for women in order to ensure our equality. The rights of women can be protected quite adequately in a society which recognizes basic human rights.

V. The Preservation of Female "Culture"

Another challenge to the belief that sexual equality requires complete sexual integration is rooted in the rejection of the classical liberal model of a society as composed of a multitude of isolated individuals, each intent on pursuing ter own private advantage to the best of ter ability. It is now frequently argued that this model is inadequate to account for the complexities of modern society and that it should be superseded by a different picture of society as composed of a series of groups organized on a variety of different bases. It is this latter model which underlies the arguments of some feminists who argue for a kind of sexual separation. These feminists claim that women, like it or not, form a series of special-interest groups and that in order to gain social equality we ought to seek power for our groups as a whole in order to rival the power of the groups presently formed by men. Such feminists often deny that integration on an individual level is a realistic goal. This pluralist model of equality contrasts sharply with that view which sees equality in terms of assimilation and integration by individuals. It is generally associated with the type of conservatism and reaction which is perhaps most clearly typified by the South African system of apartheid, so it is interesting to see that the motto of "separate but equal" can also be adopted by genuine feminists.[17]

The pluralistic model of equality is supported by arguments which are sometimes strikingly similar to those used by the factions of the U.S. black liberation movement which advocate racial separatism. One such argument is that women have a distinctive culture which would be lost if complete sexual integration were to occur. It is also contended that individual women will not be recognized by men as genuine equals in any sphere so long as we belong to an inferior "caste." For this reason, it is claimed, the assimilation of individuals is impossible until the prestige of women as a group has been raised through the establishment of strong female institutions capable of challenging the power of the present male-dominated institutions. The institutions most generally regarded as crucial to feminism are education, health, and the media, but there are some advocates of separate female financial institutions and even a female military force. Persuaded by such arguments, a number of women even deny that a genuine heterosexual love relationship is possible in the present conditions of male/female inequality and they therefore recommend exclusively lesbian sexual arrangements. Finally, it is claimed that women need to have strong supportive female groups behind them before they can "get it together" as individuals sufficiently to face integration with men. For this reason, too, therefore, sexual separation is seen as a more appropriate goal for the women's liberation movement than complete sexual integration on an individual level.

The trouble with most of these arguments is that they rest on empirical premises about the psychology of oppressed groups whose truth is, to say the least, controversial. But in any case, they do not directly attack the notion of individual sexual integration as an ideal; they claim merely that sexual separation is a necessary step on the way to this ultimate goal. The only argument which challenges the *ultimate* desirability of complete sexual integration is the one which advocates the preservation of a distinctive female "culture" and sees separation as the only way of achieving this.

For the sake of evaluating this argument, let us assume that there does indeed exist a worldwide split between female and male "culture."[18] "Male culture" consists of the art, philosophy, and science which are identified with national culture and from which, it is claimed, women have been excluded almost totally. "Female culture," on the other hand, is less visible and less closely tied to national boundaries. In the past, it has included many invaluable contributions to civilization, such as folk medicine, the preparation and preservation of food, spinning, weaving, pottery, and so on. Nowadays, however, it has been reduced to a number of relatively simple domestic skills, mainly involving such tasks as cooking, cleaning, and child care, in a few unprestigious skills such as typing which are used in work outside the home, and in the subtle skills which women use to make themselves attractive to men. "Female culture" is said to embody values which are contrary, antipathetic, to those embodied in the institutions of "male culture," such as the government, army, religion, and economy. In particular, it is claimed that "female culture" demands and fosters such values as empathy, intuition, love, responsibility, endurance, practicality, and humanization.

It is certainly true that the above-mentioned characteristics are highly valued in few, if any, national or "male" cultures. Instead, these cultures often emphasize such qualities as discipline, self-control, efficiency, etc. But there are other aspects of "female culture," especially in its debased modern aspect, which are perhaps less admirable. They include lack of initiative, dependence, timidity, narcissism, cunning, manipulativeness, etc. Nor can the existence of these features be written off entirely as propagandist examples of sexual stereotyping. On the contrary, they are the necessary concomitants of the culture of an economically dependent group; they typify a slave culture. And this being so, it seems obvious that they represent aspects of "female culture" which liberated women will not want to preserve.

It is doubtful, indeed, whether those aspects even could be preserved in a society where women were organizing their own institutions in competition with those of men. The necessity of competition would entail that women would have to adopt the "male" values of discipline, efficiency, etc., simply in order to face the male challenge. This is, of course, the same problem that faces utopian socialist or anarchist groups who wish to institute values different from those which prevail at present but who have to survive in a world where their values are at a practical disadvantage, at least with respect to quantity of production.

Whatever may be the solution to this dilemma in other spheres, it seems clear that the problem as it arises for women cannot be solved by sexual separation. Not only is it extremely unlikely that female institutions could ever challenge successfully the dominant male ones, but they would be corrupted if they did so. They would have to abandon those values we have designated as characteristically female ones, and thus women would be forced to become imitations of men.

What we now call female culture could not survive if it were placed in competition with, instead of in subordination to, the male culture. Nor, I would argue, should we want it to. We should recognize that our culture is to a large extent the culture of an oppressed group, and while we may not wish to let it be forgotten entirely, at the same time we should distinguish those elements which we want to keep alive. Obviously we do not really want to perpetuate the supposedly feminine skills of hair curling or straightening, makeup, and the "arts" of seduction. What we must do instead is to create a new androgynous culture which incorporates the best elements of both the present male and the present female cultures, which values both personal relationships and efficiency, both emotion and rationality.

This result cannot be achieved through sexual separation. Our ideal of sexual equality must go beyond the achievement of a balance of economic and political power for contending female and male groups. Ultimately, I believe that we must seek total integration on a personal level, so that an individual's sex is viewed as a fact which is irrelevant to ter place in society.

VI. Sexual Differentiation as Intrinsically Valuable

I want to consider one more argument against sexual integration. The proponents of this argument may well accept the simple physiological view of the sexual distinction, but they still propose, on what seem to be semiaesthetic grounds, that it is desirable to preserve a social distinction between the sexes. Freud seems to be taking this position when he suggests that, if women leave "the calm uncompetitive activity of home" and join "the struggle for existence exactly as men," we should mourn "the passing away of the most delightful thing the world can offer us—our ideal of womanhood."[19]

I call arguments on these lines *vive la différence* arguments. They recur with predictable regularity whenever women's liberation is being discussed. They claim that the basic physiological differences between the sexes should be the grounds of social differentiation because in this way we can add a spice of pleasurable variety to life. They argue that sexual equality in the sense that one sex should not have more social advantages than the other does not entail that the sexes should have identical social roles. They ask, rhetorically, "Wouldn't it be unfortunate if we were all alike?" These arguments are persuasive because of their suggestion that those who do not recognize the pleasures of institutionalizing sexual differences are gloomy puritans. They suggest that their proponents are advocating not sexual inequality but merely a kind of healthy hedonism.

Simone de Beauvoir's response to Freud's argument is to point out what both women and men invariably lose as well as what we gain when a sexual role system is established. She agrees "that he would be a barbarian indeed who failed to appreciate exquisite flowers, rare lace, the crystal-clear voice of the eunuch, and feminine charm."[20] But then she asks, "Does a fugitive miracle—and one so rare—justify us in perpetuating a situation that is baneful for both sexes? One can appreciate the beauty of flowers, the charm of women, and appreciate them at their true value; if these treasures cost blood or misery, they must be sacrificed."[21]

De Beauvoir's point is well taken. The forcing of women into a socially shaped mold of femininity may indeed have its compensations, but, as contemporary women's liberation literature never tires of reminding us, those advantages have been more than offset in practice by their corresponding disadvantages. Such disadvantages include not only female frustration, the wasting of female potential and talent, loss of female initiative, and so on, but also a corresponding denial of self-realization to men. Insofar as sexual discrimination exists in contexts other than the reproductive, and hence is based on a difference which is irrelevant in those contexts, it is bound to limit arbitrarily the options of both women and men.

There is, however, a more far-reaching argument against sexual separation. This is hinted at by some radical feminists, such as Ti-Grace Atkinson, when they claim that the sexual role system should be abolished not just because the goal of "separate but equal" seems to be unrealizable in fact but because it is one aspect of a role system which ideally should be abolished in its entirety. I take such talk about the desirability of a "role system" to be a way of talking about the desirability of institutionalizing human activity. This claim is sometimes thought to be involved in the political theory of anarchism, and since many of the radical feminist writings, especially those of Firestone and Atkinson, pay homage to some fundamental anarchist ideals, I shall draw on the anarchist tradition in an attempt to reconstruct the kind of considerations which may well have influenced Atkinson in rejecting a role system.[22]

One general objection to a role system is that it might tempt us to define a person by ter relation to a social institution. Thus, a person comes to be seen simply as a tinker, a tailor, a soldier, or a sailor. Not only is such stereotyping an obvious disfigurement of an individual's humanity, but it seems to conflict with the anarchist ideal of a person able to do many different kinds of work in a society where specialization of human function has been minimized if not eliminated.

The institutionalization of human activity might also be thought inimical to the anarchist ideal of social freedom. To the extent that social institutions embody norms of behavior and impose sanctions, even if only as mild as social disapproval, on individuals who depart from those norms, the freedom of the individual might be thought to be compromised. Indeed, it is a conceptual truth that, in order to be playing a role at all, the behavior of the player must be circumscribed by the requirements of that role.

Finally, the existence of a role system might appear to be incompatible with the moral autonomy of the individual.[23] If the obligations of a person's role are taken as defining the whole of ter moral obligations, then it becomes impossible for that individual to rise above the conventional morality of professional ethics. Insofar as one conforms to ter role, one may be forced to do what is morally wrong or be unable to do what is morally right. A soldier may have to kill and a salaried employee may be unable to avoid contributing to the war effort. In order to act morally, therefore, it seems to be necessary to transcend one's role, to examine critically the obligations which define it. Thus, a morally autonomous person must, despite the functionalist theory of contemporary sociologists, be more than the sum of ter roles.

These arguments are very persuasive, and in my original draft of this paper I accepted them. However, I now believe that they can be answered, that human freedom and equality do not require the de-institutionalization of all human activity.[24] I doubt, in fact, whether the very concept of a society without some kind of "role system" is coherent. It seems to me now that a society necessarily includes social institutions which define social roles, in fact, that it is precisely the norms embodied in those institutions which provide the criteria for the identification of that society.

Not only are norms logically necessary to a society; by ensuring a certain degree of social predictability, they are also practically necessary. However, in order that social institutions should not be oppressive, certain conditions must be fulfilled. The norms which we endorse should be determined rationally by all concerned. Such norms should help rather than hinder justice and personal self-determination; to use a couple of obvious examples, such things as exploitation and rape should not be permissible. And the norms which define a social role should not be viewed as absolutely binding on the one who is performing that role: roles should be seen, rather, as imposing *prima facie* duties which may, in certain circumstances, be overridden. In this case, to adopt a role will not per se limit one's moral autonomy.[25] Finally, a person should not be assigned any role involuntarily; instead, tey should be able to choose from a variety of roles.

These requirements necessitate the abolition of a role system based on sex. Sex roles are not determined by those concerned. They are irrational whenever they regulate our behavior in contexts other than the reproductive, for in doing so they unwarrantably presuppose that the difference between the sexes is more than a simple physiological distinction. Sex roles are restrictive and oppressive, in fact if not in principle. And, necessarily, they are ascribed by others rather than assumed voluntarily. Hence, while I cannot agree that personal liberation and equality require the total de-institutionalization of all human activity, I do believe that women's and men's liberation and sexual equality require that the distinction between the sexes should ultimately be de-institutionalized. I am not, of course, advocating that a genuine feminist should refuse to recognize physiological sexual differences. To do this would suggest that feminism involves a reversion to the kind of Victorian hypocrisy which preferred to call a woman's legs her "limbs." But I do claim that a sexually egalitarian society must be integrated in the sense that sexual differences should not be institutionally recognized.

VII. Conclusion

This account of sexual equality is obviously not purely analytic, nor is it intended to be. It is designed to persuade. And if it is accepted, various practical conclusions follow from it.

If sexual equality requires integration, then a feminist should seek to modify our language by the use of neuter proper names and the elimination of gender in order to undermine the sexist consciousness which presently permeates it.[26] Tey must, of course, continue the long and tedious struggle against institutionalized sexual discrimination. And when people complain that you can't tell the boys from the girls nowadays, the feminist response must be to point out that it should make no difference. As Florynce Kennedy demanded, "Why do they want to know anyway? So that they can discriminate?"

Notes

[1] The sexism implicit in our language is documented by Robert Baker in "'Pricks' and 'Chicks': A Plea for 'Persons,'" in *Philosophy and Sex,* R. Baker and F. Elliston, eds. (Buffalo, New York: Prometheus Books, 1975). It is also shown by Kate Miller and Casey Swift in an article called "De-Sexing the English Language," *Ms.* (Spring 1972).

[2] In this paper I adopt the suggestions of Miller and Swift for a new form of the generic singular pronoun. Instead of using "he," "him," and "his," I employ their suggested common-gender form, derived from the plural, namely, "tey," "tem," and "ter(s)."

[3] Shulamith Firestone, *The Dialectic of Sex: The Case for Feminist Revolution* (New York: Bantam Books, 1971).

[4] Ti-Grace Atkinson, "The Institution of Sexual Intercourse" and "Radical Feminism," in *Notes from the Second Year,* ed. S. Firestone (New York, 1970).

[5] As far as I know, this distinction was first made with respect to racial prejudice by Stokely Carmichael and Charles V. Hamilton in their book *Black Power: The Politics of Liberation in America* (New York: Vintage Books, 1967).

[6] This is suggested, for example, by the subtitle of Baker's paper (n. 1 above).

[7] Although the difference in reproductive capacity is what makes the physiological differences between the sexes important to us, the physiological distinction is normally taken as the primary criterion for determining the sex of an individual, and one who is unable to reproduce is not thereby described as sexless. Therefore, I call the distinction physiological rather than functional.

[8] Christine Garside's "Women and Persons" was the winning entry in "The Problem of Women" prize essay competition. It is published in *Mother Was Not a Person,* ed. Margret Andersen (Montreal: Content, 1972). My criticism of Garside's argument should in no way be taken, of course, as reflecting a lack of admiration for her work.

[9] Ibid., p. 196.

[10] Ibid., p. 202.

[11] Parts of this paper were read in response to mine at the Western Division meetings of the American Philosophical Association in April 1973. It is as yet unpublished, but copies can probably be obtained by writing to the author at Sir George Williams University in Montreal.

[12] Christine Garside, "True Sex-Polarity," p. 10 of the typescript.

[13] Ibid., pp. 10–11.

[14] For a discussion of some of the problems of investigating empirically whether there are innate psychological differences between the sexes, see my "On Female Nature," forth-

coming in *The Problem of Women,* incorporating prize essays on "The Problem of ♀," a competition sponsored by SUNY at Fredonia.

[15] *The Dialectic of Sex* (n. 3 above).

[16] The latter suggestion was made by Carolyn Korsmeyer of the State University of New York at Buffalo.

[17] I am using here my original definition of a feminist, namely, someone who believes in sexual equality.

[18] It has become fashionable to use the term "culture" very loosely to describe the special practices of a certain group within a larger society. A more accurate term might be "subculture," but in this discussion I shall follow the usage of the writers whose views I am discussing. Much of the characterization of male and female "culture" which follows is taken from the *Fourth World Manifesto,* by Barbara Burris, reprinted in *Notes from the Third Year* (Women's Liberation), edited by Anne Koedt and Shulamith Firestone (New York, 1971), pp. 102–19.

[19] This well-known passage from one of Freud's letters to his fiancée is quoted in *Masculine/ Feminine: Readings in Sexual Mythology and the Liberation of Women,* ed. Betty Roszak and Theodore Roszak (New York: Harper & Row, 1969).

[20] Simone de Beauvoir, *The Second Sex* (New York: Bantam Books, 1961), p. 686.

[21] Ibid., p. 687.

[22] For some of the following ideas I am indebted to my former colleague, Peter M. Schuller of Miami University, Ohio, who explains them in an unpublished paper entitled "Anti-nomic Elements in Higher Education."

[23] This seems to be an implication of Robert Paul Wolff's thesis in his *In Defense of Anarchism* (New York: Harper & Row, 1970).

[24] I was forced to this realization by argument with Marlene Fried.

[25] For a fuller discussion of this claim, see my "The Just State as a Round Square," *Dialogue* 11, no. 4 (December 1972): 580–83.

[26] These measures are among those suggested by Baker (n. 1 above).

Discussion Questions

1. Jaggar seems to equate sexual equality with a unisex society. Does she offer any argument for this position? How might her position be criticized?

2. Does Jaggar agree with Lucas on any matter of fact? On any principle? Where they disagree, who is right? Why?

3. How is Garside's position as described by Jaggar like and unlike Lucas's position? Does Jaggar's criticism of Garside apply to Lucas? How might Lucas reply to Jaggar's criticisms?

4. What are Jaggar's criticisms of the idea of specifically female rights? Are they justified? Why or why not?

5. What is Jaggar's criticism of the idea of female culture? Argue for or against this idea.

6. What are Jaggar's arguments against the idea that "it is desirable to preserve a social distinction between the sexes"? Are they successful? Why or why not?

A Two-Sexed Species

Elizabeth Wolgast

The idea that sex differences are or should be negligible is curious. Nor can it be explained just by looking to arguments about rights; its roots are deeper and more various. What makes us suppose that sex differences can be ignored? . . .

[Are sex differences and sexual nature] independent of culture[?] We can change our culture; and supposing we do, to what degree would our natures remain intractable? Margaret Mead demonstrates the wide variability of forms that relations of men and women can take. From the gentle, unassertive, child-nurturing Arapesh, to the noisy and assertive Iatmul, to the artistic Tchambuli—the contrasts between male and female virtues, roles, and personalities change radically. Among the Tchambuli, for instance, where sons were especially treasured and men freed from many practical concerns, "the minds of small males, teased, pampered, neglected and isolated, had a fitful fleeting quality, an inability to come to grips with anything." The small girls, on the other hand, were more alertly intelligent and enterprising. By contrast, the Mundugumor tribe, which is more egalitarian, raises children to be "independent, hostile, vigorous," producing boys and girls with similar personalities. Ah-ha, notes the egalitarian, sexual equality is possible after all! Not so clear:

> In such a society, women are handicapped by their womanly qualities. Pregnancy and nursing are hated and avoided if possible, and men detest their wives for being pregnant. . . . Women are masculinized to a point where every feminine feature is a drawback except their highly specific genital sexuality, . . . [even] to a point where any aspect of their personalities that might hold an echo of the feminine or maternal is a vulnerability and a liability.[1]

Precisely what one would expect. Sex egalitarianism leads to sexual uniformity and this means the suppression of whatever does not conform to some neutral or masculine norm. In a professedly egalitarian society like ours, one where pregnancy is also increasingly optional, a woman might conclude that it is best avoided. Yet this general form of sexual arrangement is clearly not viable.

With her observation that sexual roles are almost incredibly malleable Mead might be expected to support the assimilationist ideal and that of a more or less androgynous society. But she does not.

> A one-sex world would be an imperfect world, for it would be a world without a future. Only a denial of life itself makes it possible to deny the interdependence of the sexes. . . . We must think instead of how to live in a two-sex world so that each sex will benefit at every point from each expression of the presence of two sexes.[2]

The moral problems sex gives rise to need to be dealt with, she implies, but not . . . by abolishing sexuality and sexual distinctness. They need addressing within a two-sex framework.

Sex roles are malleable: that is not in dispute. The question is how to make decisions about altering them. What kinds of considerations should guide us? If we are committed to an egalitarian form of society, then our decisions will be guided by a vision where the roles of men and women will be indistinguishable. But such an arrangement may not find answering resonance in our nature—on the contrary, our nature may constitute an obstacle and something this vision has to strive against. If, on the other hand, we start with the assumption that some differences in roles will exist, and then ask how to balance them justly—what latitude is possible within them and where the community should provide support—then our options are wide and interesting. Such a starting point seems intuitively reasonable. As Midgley wrote, "we can vary enormously the forms [the roles of the sexes] take and our own individual part in them. We can no more get rid of them than we can grow wings and tusks."[3] . . .

The picture we get from Mead and Goodall is that of a species whose character is rather unclear. It is characterized on the one hand by the fatherly role of the male parent, but not consistently; it is characterized on the other by a tendency to promiscuity, but most noticeably among the young and among single males. Therefore it seems difficult to say anything very general about our nature except that for humans sexuality is a mighty concern and that responsible fatherhood is a tendency stronger for us than for other primates but less strong than it is for wolves.

Perhaps then it is most characteristic of humans that they feel divided, ambivalent, pulled in conflicting ways. That is the conclusion Mary Midgley comes to, and not only with regard to sex roles.

> We are fairly aggressive, yet we want company and depend on long-term enterprises. We love those around us and need their love, yet we want independence and need to wander. We are restlessly curious and meddling, yet long for permanence. Unlike many primates, we do have a tendency to pair-formation, but it is an incomplete one, and gives us a lot of trouble.[4]

We are unsettled and creatures of conflict. We have deep motivations going in opposite directions. For such creatures a commitment may be difficult.

> No *long-term* commitment is ever always easy and unforced. And no commitment involving more than one person ever suits all parties equally. Yet human nature certainly demands long-term enterprises. We are therefore bound to be frustrated if we cannot finish them, so commitment is necessary.[5]

Among our long-term enterprises is the rearing of children. But more than this, we bind ourselves in marriage because we *want* long attachments. We don't just accept them as the price of something else, sex or children, she argues.

> We want deep and lasting relationships. And because these are often difficult, we "bind ourselves" in all sorts of ways to go through with whatever we have started, even when it proves annoying. Marriage is simply one of these arrangements.[6]

The answer to why we have such an institution is, then, that we want it—not just something else to which it is the means. The desire for pair-formation among humans is not derivative from the desire for children but is strong on its own. Midgley says, "Pair-formation could never have entered anybody's head as a device deliberately designed to promote utility. . . . Individuals want to live in pairs before they have any children, and continue to do so when their children are gone."[7]

Other forms of conflict also go deep, Midgley believes.

> Let us consider the predicament of primitive man. He is not without natural inhibitions, but his inhibitions are weak. . . . He does horrible things and is filled with remorse afterwards. These conflicts are prerational; they . . . [fall] between two groups of . . . primitive motives. . . . They are not the result of thinking; more likely they are among the things that first made him think.[8]

Instead of one rudimentary conflict between reason and the animal self, a number of diverse conflicts pertain to human nature, and reason may be brought in to help deal with them. Even at best, this account suggests, resolutions will be temporary. The nature we live with is essentially divided.

Midgley's representation of human nature explains why psychology and morality should be intertwined. She writes: "Only a creature of this intermediate kind, with inhibitions that are weak *but genuine* would ever have been likely to develop a morality." We have inhibitions, but they are not as strong in motivating us as they are in other creatures; they need reinforcing. "Conceptual thought formalizes and extends what instinct started."[9] We reason because we need to, and we need to because we are ambivalent.

These four natural scientists [Mead, Midgley, Goodall, and Eibl-Eibesfeldt] hold different views about the character of the human species, and about its sexual and social character in particular. While Eibl-Eibesfeldt sees male humans as egoistic, needing special incentives to mate monogamously, the other three see humans as basically social, the need for pairing a deep one, however unreliable. But it is striking that all four agree in the perception that sex differences are important, not just in respect to the process of reproduction, but in a multitude of other ways. Nor does society play an incidental role in the development of sex differences. Rather it has a productive and essential part. From the mother chimpanzee, a young female learns how to care for her own young, and without that learning may not be an adequate mother. From other males, young males learn to copulate, something animals brought up in isolation may never learn to do.[10] With humans too there is learning connected with our adequacy as sexual beings. Mead goes further, claiming that society has credit for creating fathers of male humans, teaching them in this role which is then identified with our "higher" nature. Midgley sees culture as an essential part of our nature, needed to "complete" us, and not something that stands in contrast to what we are. Nor on her view can sex roles or sexual identity be separated from what we are. They are bound up with our motivation, our conflicts, and so our most fundamental character.

The roles of males and females in different species may be very stylized, and often the *point* of the role contrasts is far from clear. Among birds, for instance, there will be one species in which only females build nests, and another in which only males do, and another in which both cooperate. Within a species there is great uniformity, but among species there is very great variation. This difference seems clearly to show that part of the roles identified with sex are arbitrary. In part they are roles that creatures of either sex could perform as well as the other. Here is an argument for equality, for androgynous roles. One feminist writer, Jane English, characterizes sex roles:

> "Sex roles" and "gender traits" refer to the patterns of behavior which the two sexes are socialized, encouraged, or coerced into adopting, ranging from "sex-appropriate" personalities to interests and professions.[11]

Sex roles are imposed upon us by culture and education. Without them we would be more free and our lives richer in possibilities. Another feminist writer, Ann Ferguson, defends androgyny:

> I shall argue that male/female sex roles are neither inevitable results of "natural" biological differences between the sexes, nor socially desirable ways of socializing children in contemporary societies. In fact, the elimination of sex roles and the development of androgynous human beings is the most rational way to allow for the possibility of . . . love relations among equals, and . . . development of the widest possible range of intense and satisfying social relationships between men and women.[12]

Ferguson goes further, claiming that "human babies are bisexual and only *learn* a specific male or female identity by imitating and identifying with adult models."[13] Gender identity is entirely a creation of society, she seems to say; biological differences could be virtually dropped out.

Sex roles are not entirely the result of natural differences, and in many respects they are only indirectly related to reproduction. Furthermore, some of the characteristics of one sex role *could have* characterized the other. This is tantamount to saying that in some sense sex roles are largely arbitrary. But is this the same as saying they are largely indispensable? Does it mean that no reason exists against dispensing with them? That isn't obvious.

Consider that human infants need a great deal of care, and care of certain kinds. They also need education in a variety of things if they are to survive in this, or in any other, environment. Someone has to teach them, and it is reasonable to suppose that one parent or both should help to do it. Now, caring for and teaching children are roles, which is to say, these in turn need to be taught. To whom should they be taught? In view of the fact that mothers are the primary parents, bearing young with or without an acknowledged father, they surely need to learn something of child care, just as they should know something about pregnancy and childbirth. But then it does not follow that men should *not* also learn. If they did learn, moreover, their involvement would not exemplify an *absence* of roles. Parental roles *are needed*. Nor does it dispose of the underlying asymmetry of parenthood.

The attack against sex roles is commonly made in rather Rousseau-like terms—society corrupts and perverts man's nature, and would do better to leave us alone. But this objection to child-care roles is silly. A human who relied entirely on instinct in these matters would be taking grave risks and acting with unnecessary individual responsibility. Even young animals learn about the care of infants by observation; we can hardly do less. But this learning *is* the learning of a *role*. Such roles are beneficial and necessary.

The egalitarian protest is more plausibly made against the sex-differentiated aspect of parental roles. Why should *only* women learn child care, why not men too? One traditional answer is that, since women must learn it, men should be exempt. But of course this doesn't follow. If only women learn the role, their options to do other things will be severely limited, while if men learn it as well, their options will not be greatly impaired. A cooperative conjunction of child-caring roles may be an optimum solution for both men and women. While releasing women to pursue their careers, it may also improve men's lives in their roles as fathers, since in this way they become more familiar with the offspring they are formally encouraged to love and protect. All around, a sharing of child care may enrich the lives of both parents, and probably of children as well.[14]

To accept this solution is simply to accept that—since some sex roles can be changed—parenthood and its skills need not be left exclusively to women but should be taught to men as well. This shift, however, would not make the roles androgynous. Consider, if both men and women are taught about the delivery of a baby, and both are taught to "participate" in it, their roles will still be sex-differentiated. And similarly, there will be some sex-differentiation in parenthood. But there will be greater cooperation between parents on this score than is found in most Western societies, and that is an important improvement.

To train both men and women in parental roles is not to banish roles but to change and enrich them. Nor is it clear that we would be any happier with fewer and leaner roles. Midgley says that "social animals cannot live the life they are fitted for at all without their own form of society. The demand for it is as deeply inherent as the demand for one's own future safety."[15] She goes further:

> Forms and ceremonies are not idle. "Stereotypes" . . . are utterly necessary. And they are *not,* as people often unthinkingly suppose, merely means to an end, devices that any "intelligent" being would naturally hit on for reaching a few, simple, physical ends like food and shelter. In the first place, half of them are not means at all; they are ends in themselves. The joys of friendship and affection, and also of hatred and revenge, jokes, dancing, stories and the whole business of the arts, games and other play, disinterested curiosity, and the enjoyment of risk are natural *tastes,* things that make life worth living, not things that could possibly have been invented as a means to staying alive.[16]

She suggests that we *need* roles as we need a culture, though it is not a need connected with survival. We will not die without them. Nevertheless, games and dancing and story-telling and a great variety of things natural to all people involve roles. Why disparage them as a class?

Suppose the objection is narrowed so that it is directed simply against those social sex roles which are not connected with reproduction. These, it might be argued, are inherently pernicious for they serve to divide and separate the sexes, thus encouraging differences of status. If we cannot have a completely androgynous society (the argument would go), at least we could reduce the amount of difference between the sexes to its minimum. But it is not altogether clear that minimal sex roles would serve us well, and to Midgley's voice we can add Mead's:

> If society defines each sex as having inalienable and valuable qualities of its own but does not relate those qualities to the reproductive differences between the sexes, then each sex may be proud and strong, but some of the values that come from sex contrast will be lacking. If women are defined without reference to their maternity, men may find that their own masculinity seems inadequate, because its continuance into paternity will also lose definition.[17]

As we are born with sexual identity, we need its definition in social terms, and particularly we need recognition of its connection to parenthood and reproduction. For these matters, she seems to say, constitute a fair part of what life is *about*. This recognition means, however, the introduction of precisely the kind of sex roles that feminists object to. The nonfunctional and functional aspects need to be tied together, Mead proposes.

Reproduction is left out of the recommendation for androgyny. That is logical because androgyny is primarily concerned with relations between adult males and females. It is for such adults that "love relations among equals" and "development of the widest possible range of intense and satisfying relationships" are advocated. "Mere reproduction," like "mere biology," is irrelevant to this image of the good society. But for some people, important "love relations" will include those between parent and child, to which, in turn, "the widest possible range of intense relationships" is meaningless. There is a difference in life view or perspective involved here.

The most powerful argument on the side of androgyny and against sex roles is the egalitarian one. If sex roles interfere with equality, as Ferguson and English . . . believe, then, *if* equality is an important moral goal, this is good reason for saying that sex roles are bad, even though we like them and find them natural. If giving up games and story-telling and dancing were necessary in order to achieve a better society, we would at least have to give some thought to their eradication, and probably make a serious effort in that direction. Midgley writes: "We could, after all, quite plausibly say that friendship or sport or the arts threatened freedom; . . . [but] this would be a bad reason for abolishing them altogether."[18] One might answer that it depends on how serious the threat was. But we have seen that equality does not offer us a clear vision of society at all, much less of a good society. In the absence of a compelling reason against them, it seems reasonable to suppose that sex roles in some form or other are tolerable. What is needed is not their abolition or their amalgamation to a single androgynous role, but adjustments within them. In many respects adjustment is needed to make the roles more similar. For females to be stereotyped as unintelligent and illogical and unable to make serious commitments shows ignorance of the lives most women lead. It is literally false. To base role differences on these supposed differences is consequently unfair. But to say that grown women are generally somewhat easier with children than men, somewhat more expressive of feelings, more understanding of others' feelings, more demonstrative, and somewhat less competitive, is not clearly false. Nor are the consequences for sex roles clearly negligible. Some differences between the sexes, their nature, temperament, and roles, may actually be a nice thing.

The thesis that androgyny is a good model for human society depends on the assumption that males and females are, for all reasonable intents and purposes, alike. Differences between them, it is maintained, are chiefly due to culture and conditioning. If sex roles were abolished we would see the similarities stand sharp and clear, where now they are muddied by roles and stereotypes. Thus Jane English argues:

> Of course it may be true that there are some personality differences between the sexes in any case, regardless of social pressures . . . to conform. With the present evidence, however, since there is no stereotype-free society available to observe, we cannot establish scientifically whether such biological or innate differences exist.[19]

But there *are* studies establishing sex differences between infants that may account for some personality differences. For example, there is evidence that girl infants are more sensitive to touch at birth. From this difference it has been inferred that females "also have a greater reactivity to physical stimuli," and that this greater tactile sensitivity is "a necessary precondition for empathy and imagination."[20] The inferences seem exaggerated even if some difference is granted. Yet there are other differences less disputable, for instance, the greater maturity of females at birth and their earlier arrival at puberty. Then there is firm evidence that girls excel at verbal tasks at school, and evidence that their brain development is somewhat different from that of males.[21] Are these differences interrelated?[22] The subject is fascinating to physiologists and psychologists. What is sure is that sex differences exist from infancy which are not the result of conditioning.

Evaluating a vast array of studies, two psychologists, Eleanor E. Maccoby and C. N. Jacklin, disclaim the judgments that girls are more social than boys, more suggestible than boys, better at rote-learning and simple repetitive tasks; and that boys are more analytic, more affected by environment, and more motivated than girls. Among differences they find "well established," however, are: girls have greater verbal ability than boys; boys better visual-spatial ability and, as they mature, better mathematical ability than girls; and boys are more aggressive. Maccoby and Jacklin specifically disclaim the inference that socialization may be responsible for differences in intellectual abilities and in aggressiveness. The latter, "cross-culturally universal" and susceptible to change by sex hormone treatment, they argue, is clearly related to sex.[23]

There is evidence that concrete differences exist between the sexes besides the reproductive ones. What does this show? It shows first of all that society does not create all those differences that are not directly connected with reproduction. On the contrary; it suggests that we should allow for various differences between the sexes and not adopt single linear scales for distinguishing all individuals regardless of sex. It suggests that men and women of talent, for example, will not generally match on the same set of parameters, and therefore, if a single standard is assumed and if that should be drawn from a sample of males, the comparison with a sample of women may be invidious. It will produce a bias against women while it is defended as an "objective measure" of ability. One often hears that women candidates for important offices do not "measure up" to the standards met by males. Without awareness of the possible range of differences between the sexes, this linear approach to merit must be treated with suspicion.

The connection between nonreproductive psychological and physiological differences between the sexes and comfortable sex roles is obvious. If (as has been proved) males are more aggressive than females, then their roles ought to allow for that fact. To insist that they *not* be would involve repression. But exactly how will male roles allow aggression to be expressed? In fierce competition for success? In athletic feats? In military activity? In manipulation of powerful machines? Somewhere room should be made for its expression. Inasmuch as females will not so characteristically want to express aggression, this will amount to difference in sex roles. Such a male role will be created by culture, to be sure, but its roots are much deeper.

Reasoning from sex differences to sex roles is, however, more complicated than this suggests. Maccoby and Jacklin explain one aspect of the problem.

> It has been argued . . . that where a biological basis exists, it behooves societies to socialize children in such a way as to emphasize and exaggerate the difference. That is, since males are more aggressive, girls should be carefully trained in nonaggression throughout childhood; otherwise they will be doomed to failure and disappointment as adults in their encounters with men. . . .

The curious fact is, however, that social pressures to shape individuals toward their "natural" sex roles sometimes boomerang. Traits that may be functional for one aspect of a sex role may be dysfunctional for other aspects. A man who adopts the "machismo" image may gain prestige with his peers, or enhance his short-term attractiveness to women, at the expense of his effectiveness as a husband and father.[24]

The authors thus warn against justifying sex roles simply by reference to natural tendencies. The fabric of social relations may be upset rather than promoted by making too much of these. These authors are doubtful that fostering sex-typed behavior does serve to make for better men and women, and support the option of minimizing differences between the sexes. They conclude:

> In our view, social institutions and social practices are not merely reflections of the biologically inevitable. A variety of social institutions are viable within the framework set by biology. It is up to human beings to select those that foster the life styles they most value.[25]

This sounds very simple. But how do we describe the roles that would reflect the values we hold? Is the role of a warm and nurturing father a unisex role, identical with that of a warm and nurturing mother? If equality is also one of the values to be reflected, then we would be more comfortable if both roles were really one. Difficult questions of a conceptual sort remain, as well as questions about how to *combine* values in our choice of roles, and then how to express our support of them in institutions. But it does not seem impossible.

Identifying one set of abilities with one sex is in general pernicious. If one identifies nurturing with women, for example, then for a man to nurture others is to take a feminine role. Yet we highly value male ministers and teachers and counselors, and partly they are valued because their nurturing is somewhat different from that of women. The kind of nurturing given may be sex-differentiated, then, while nurturing is not. A similar problem arises for women. Vigorous, independent, adventurous, and creative activities as well as intellectual activity are often associated with a male role; but women have the same tendencies, talents, and desires, even though they may characteristically pursue them differently. In departing from a female stereotype do they show themselves less than female? Such rigid stereotyping is unnecessary and counter productive. In this conclusion one can hardly disagree with Maccoby and Jacklin.

On the other hand, to insist that the sexes be in every dimension similar seems to me also a kind of stereotyping—androgynous stereotyping—and like the exaggerated sex-differentiated roles, these androgynous roles too may be uncomfortable and constraining. With Midgley, I am inclined to support a "piecemeal" approach to the matter of choosing roles relating the sexes, so that in the process of making new options for both sexes, our enjoyment and interest in sexual differences should not be lost, our wonder at the talents and perspective of the other sex should not be dulled. And as a guiding principle, the protection and teaching of our children and our affectionate regard for them needs to be kept in sight.

If, as the present studies suggest, the sexes are different in dimensions not connected with reproduction, we have reason for concluding that women should make their own distinctive contribution to the culture and society. Such studies suggest that representation of women's perspective is needed, and so *women* are needed in all areas of thought and art and science that affect members of both sexes.

This argument gives support to affirmative action for women. Because women are under-represented in many professions and important categories of positions, while there is no question of women's talent or intelligence, they appear to be systematically excluded. Are the procedures and tests biased? That is difficult to answer without having women in a good position to judge—so the problem is self-perpetuating. But we may suspect that there will be some difference in interpretation of tests by men and women. How can such a problem be dealt with? It is not hard to see that quotas would be not only a justifiable but perhaps the only means to correct bias or assure that there is none.

Midgley, deploring the intense competitiveness of the Western world, our obsession "with success, with examinations, tests, and record-breaking," our "behaving as if life were not worth living except at the top of the dominance hierarchy," sees one avenue of change.

> The only thing that could make the change [of women at the top of the ladder instead on only men] important would be *if* females at the top, being rather less competitive by nature than males, could do something to bring about a saner climate. To get there and do this, however, they would have to compete without catching the competitive spirit.

And she adds, "This is a lot to expect."[26] Especially if the channels to the top work effectively to weed out the women who might help make such a change.

As a support of affirmative action for women, this argument is superior to an egalitarian one. For it says that *it makes a difference* whether top positions in various areas are held exclusively by males, or by males and females both; and given that there is some relevant difference in perspective, one should prefer a mixture. If, as Justice White said, the sexes are not "fungible" and their interaction is an important "imponderable," exactly the same argument that supports their representation on juries should support their representation on important councils and major positions of influence. Women should be involved in the full spectrum of decisions that affect men and women both. This seems only reasonable and fair.

Our inclination to think of humans as androgynous has many roots. One that lies deep in our thinking is the idea that each human is possessed of a higher part, a rational or spiritual part, which is unaffected by sexual identity. This is the idea of an androgynous soul. It leads us toward the conclusion, also deep, that *one* figure—the figure of Every-man—can represent all of us alike. His moral struggles and education in patience and forbearance can stand for those of everyone, in every age, men and women alike. If such a representation were possible, this would signify an overwhelming similarity in our lives and perspectives and the unimportance of our differences. The question is whether it is possible.

If we were talking about another species, say chimpanzees, we would have to distinguish some of the concerns of females from those of males. The female chimpanzees spend a great part of their adult lives caring for their young. Though they bear only every five years or so and thus have widely spaced offspring, each child is the object of countless hours of play and education and watchful care. It is also for the mother to oversee the early social life of her young, to tutor the young female as the offspring learns to handle an infant, to restrain the rambunctious and reckless young males. These concerns do not enter a grown male's perspective at all. Occasionally a male will discipline or play with a young chimp, but males have no responsibility in the child-rearing process. (It is difficult to use the term "father" of the adult males here, just as it is of the worker bee—not just because there is a question of their biological parenthood, but because there is no parental *role* for them.) With these differences, what kind of figure would "Everychimp" be? Would it rove freely or would it stay with the slow and distractable young? Would it challenge for dominance or would it be content with whatever hierarchy the others find acceptable? Would it be watchful over its children or would it ignore them? The image of Everychimp can surely not ignore all such differences. If they *were* ignored, many interesting and distinctive features of its perspective would be blurred or missing. There is no androgynous chimpanzee perspective.

Or consider the langurs. For most males, life is comprised of roaming in bands, hoping for the opportunity of mating with a female, using whatever deceit may work to elude and distract the watchful, dominant male. Were a male to become dominant, it would be his role to kill unweaned infants in the female band, then to mate, and then give fatherly protection to infants born thereafter. The female's life is altogether different. Upon the birth of an infant, her attention centers about it. Should a new male take over the troop, her concern is for the safety of her infant, and she will deceive the male if it is possible, hiding it or making him think it is his. What can we say of the "Everylangur" nature? Does it incline toward the practice of infanticide? Does it protect its young from that fate? Is it free and roving or communal? One needs to allow that different patterns exist, some exhibited by males, others by females. Nor does a single individual exhibit signs of conflict between these tendencies. The "Everylangur" figure cannot contain them both; then must it leave both out? And leave out all other features relating to sex and reproduction? It appears that such a representation would have to be androgynous—but in that case it can hardly represent this two-sexed species.

Humans are no doubt less polarized than these creatures. Still if there were a single human perspective, it too should be androgynous, leaving out all reference to sex and reproduction and the care of children, leaving out the roles of mothers as well as those of fathers. But then, what will be said of the clusters of young and mature individuals—the families—which are connected with human mating. Are they too supposed to be androgynous? What unites them? From the Everyman view, one cannot say.

The idea of an androgynous soul and that of the Everyman perspective serve the egalitarian well. They reinforce the idea that we are, in all important ways, alike. The taboo against sexual identity here is logical.

We have a moral commitment to the concept of a sexless human soul as the essential form of ourselves. Among its benefits is the implication that men and women are not of intrinsically different worth, that there is no difference in their moral status. But among its drawbacks is the way it deprives us of the ability to distinguish kinds of moral concerns, contrasting those that are characteristic of men with those characteristic of women. Given this state of things, either we have to seek a least common denominator to represent us—which in truth would not be a human representation at all—or we have to identify the concerns of both sexes with the concerns of one—not a propitious beginning for planning a just society. It is a conceptual dilemma.

Inasmuch as women and men have different connections to reproduction, some differences in attitude will be likely, no matter what freedom exists with respect to roles. And their moral concerns will differ some too, in emphasis if nothing else. Hear this complaint of the mother of Edward IV and Richard III, upon hearing news of Richard's latest attempt to get the throne:

> Accursed and unquiet wrangling days,
> How many of you have mine eyes beheld!
> My husband lost his life to get the crown;
> And often up and down my sons were toss'd,
> For me to joy and weep their gain and loss:
> And being seated, and domestic broils
> Clean over-blown, themselves, brother to brother, the conquerors,
> Make war upon themselves;
> Blood to blood, self against self: O, preposterous
> And frantic outrage, end thy damned spleen;
> Or let me die, to look on death no more![27]

Rather than see such events, she should have strangled Richard in her womb. The anguish expressed in such terms is unequivocally a mother's.

In his most recent work, Wasserstrom makes a defense of pluralism that harmonizes well with what I have said here. He writes:

> Part of the characteristic, white, male point of view consists in the belief that reasonably well-educated, well-intentioned white males possess the capacity to view both social and natural phenomena in a detached, objective, non-distorted fashion. [Often however] the view [they hold] is one that white males hold exclusively about themselves.[28]

This fact need not seem curious. If there is an Everyman view, then there is only one right human perspective. Why should a man not think it is his? And it is not surprising that white males, as Wasserstrom says,

> are quite ready and eager to acknowledge that others—members of various racial groups, or women—do look at the world, approach problems, define issues, etc., through particular, nonobjective points of view. But while this is something others do, it is not something that they do.[29]

On the contrary, they are confident that "they possess the capacity and the detachment to look at things fairly, comprehensively, and completely, in short, to view things as they really are." This need not be seen as sheer arrogance; it is partly the result of a conceptual framework.

The answer to such dictatorship of one perspective is the representation of others. Once we cease to stress similarities and equality, we can give some respect to pluralism, in particular to the points of view of *both* sexes. Wasserstrom adopts a pluralistic position when it comes to some institutions, such as universities. He says:

> If there are distinctive points of view that are typically connected with minority group membership, then the case for programs which make this identity relevant is in part the case for a useful and valuable type of intellectual pluralism which advances the pursuit of knowledge and the fair resolution of social issues.[30]

But the perspectives associated with women need not be represented merely in programs that are intellectual; nor is it reasonable to speak to women as constituting a "minority group membership." The pluralism that I argue for is much wider than whatever the "pursuit of knowledge" comprehends. It relates to social and moral and economic spheres as well. The pluralism I mean can be broadly stated by saying that the perspective of one sex cannot be relied on, in general, to represent the concerns of the other.

The kind of argument I have used to support women's rights is formed along the same lines as arguments for rights of the lame or blind or retarded. Does this imply that women are, qua women, handicapped human beings? That conclusion cannot be farther from my meaning. Nevertheless women are thought of as handicapped by some thinkers, for instance Ann Ferguson:

> The two biological disadvantages of women, relative male strength and the female role in biological reproduction, explain the persistence of the sexual division of labor and the sexual stereotypes based on this.[31]

This reminds me of Mill's remark that women are weak men, and Freud's view that women can be thought of as men without a phallus. All smack of an Everyman perspective that is identifiably male. The biological features of women differentiate them; but what makes their sexual features disadvantageous is a society that does not grant respect to people with these features.

Wasserstrom speaks of "nullifying" sex differences just as we "nullify" the disadvantages of being lame or blind.[32] But this too assumes that there is a sex standard from which any deviation is a handicap or disadvantage, just as there is a set of normal capabilities with respect to seeing and hearing and moving around; the good society will treat the handicap of sex like any other, attempting to compensate for it and so to "nullify" it.

But here is a wrong order of things. Being female is a disadvantage in a society that makes it one, in particular a society which, like the Mundugumor, disparages reproduction. Do we then set out to "nullify" the injury society thus produces, as if its production were unavoidable? Why not accept a different social form? Why not put egalitarian androgynous models aside and look to a social form fitting a species of two sexes, both having their own strengths, virtues, distinctive tendencies, and weakness, neither being fully assimilable to the other? That would give a right order to our priorities.

Notes

[1] Weininger, *Sex and Character,* authorized trans. (London: Heineman; New York: Putnam, 1906), 100.

[2] *Ibid.,* 368–369.

[3] Mary Midgley, *Beast and Man* (Ithaca, Cornell University Press, 1978), p. 326.

[4] Midgley, 282.

[5] *Ibid.,* 302.

[6] *Ibid.*

[7] *Ibid.,* 304.

[8] *Ibid.,* 40.

[9] *Ibid.,* 41.

[10] Harry F. Harlow, "Love in Infant Monkeys," *Scientific American,* 204 (June 1959).

[11]Jane English, an introductory essay on sex roles and gender in Mary Vetterling-Braggin, Frederick Ellston, and Jane English, eds., *Feminism and Philosophy* (Totowa, N.Y.: Littlefield, Adams, 1977), 39.

[12]Ferguson, "Androgyny as an Ideal for Human Development," in *Feminism and Philosophy,* 45.

[13]*Ibid.,* 61.

[14]This point is the thesis of Dorothy Dinnerstein's *The Mermaid and the Minotaur: Sexual Arrangements and the Human Malaise* (New York: Harper, 1976), though she argues the issue from the point of androgyny in parenthood rather than in terms of flexible parent roles.

[15]Midgley, 300.

[16]*Ibid.,* 298.

[17]Mead, *Male and Female* (New York: Morrow, 1975) p. 368.

[18]Midgley, 329.

[19]English, *Feminism and Philosophy,* 40–41.

[20]J. M. Bardwick, *Psychology of Women* (New York: Harper & Row, 1971), 102.

[21]Eleanor E. Maccoby, ed., *The Development of Sex Differences* (Stanford: Stanford University Press, 1966), 25–55.

[22]Debora P. Waber, "Sex Differences in Mental Abilities, Hemispheric Lateralization, and Rate of Physical Growth at Adolescence," *Developmental Psychology,* 13 (1977), 29–38; also D. P. Waber, "Sex Differences in Cognition: A Function of Maturation Rate?" *Science,* 192 (May 7, 1976), 572–573.

[23]Maccoby and Jacklin, *The Psychology of Sex Differences* (Stanford: Stanford University Press, 1974), 349–355, 360–363.

[24]Maccoby and Jacklin, 373–374.

[25]*Ibid.,* 374.

[26]Midgley, 330.

[27]William Shakespeare, *King Richard III,* Act II, sc. iv.

[28]Wasserstrom, *Philosophy and Social Issues: Five Studies* (Notre Dame, Ind.: University of Notre Dame Press, 1980), 57–58.

[29]*Ibid.,* 58.

[30]*Ibid.*

[31]*Ibid.,* 59–60.

[32]Wasserstrom, *Philosophy and Social Issues,* 36ff.

Discussion Questions

1. On what matters of fact does Wolgast disagree with Jaggar? In what ways, if any, do they disagree about principles? Where they disagree, who is right? Why?

2. Is Wolgast's position in any way similar to Lucas's? Would Haack's criticisms of Lucas apply to Wolgast? Why or why not?

3. What is Wolgast's position on sex roles? How might Jaggar criticize this position?

4. What are Wolgast's criticisms of androgyny? How is androgyny like or unlike the unisex ideal? Are Wolgast's criticisms successful? Why or why not?

5. How does Wolgast use anthropology and biology to support her argument? How might this line of argument be criticized?

6. How does Wolgast's view of the ideal society differ from Jaggar's? Argue in favor of one of these views and against the other.

7. Would Sayers be likely to find Wolgast's view or Jaggar's more congenial? Why?

Suggested Readings for Chapter Six

English, Jane. *Sex Equality*. Englewood Cliffs, N.J.: Prentice-Hall, 1977.

Jaggar, Alison, and Paula Rohenborg Struhl, eds. *Feminist Frameworks*. New York: McGraw-Hill, 1978.

PART III

NEW PROBLEMS, NEW CHALLENGES

In one sense there are no new problems in ethics. Broadly speaking, moral problems in every age are concerned with helping or harming others, with keeping or not keeping obligations, and so on. But in a narrower sense each century has its own new ethical problems as circumstances change and new knowledge is gained. For example, problems of fair treatment and reparation for past injuries arise. But never before in history have there been any laws quite like the present affirmative action laws, which try to balance past injustices to certain groups by giving present representatives of those groups preferential treatment. In past ages there have been problems concerning invasion of privacy, but the technology of the computer has added new dimensions to these problems; in past ages there have been problems concerning pornography, but modern communications techniques make these problems especially acute. And though some philosophers in the past have proclaimed respect for life or respect for animals, the present day concern with ecology and animal rights has few parallels in past ages.

In all of the problems mentioned there is a contrast between the attitudes of many, if not all, political liberals and the attitudes of many, if not all, political conservatives. The person who considers himself or herself a political liberal is likely to be in favor of affirmative action laws, against censorship of pornography, defensive of personal privacy, and supportive of environmental causes and animal welfare. Conservatives, on the other hand, are often critical of affirmative action laws and sometimes support censorship of pornography. While conservatives value privacy, they are more likely than liberals to be willing to sacrifice some privacy to achieve such goals as control of crime. Some conservatives are critical of what they see as the excesses of environmentalists, and many conservatives take the view that there are essential differences between animals and humans that cast serious doubt on the notion of animal rights.

Are there underlying reasons that account for the different attitudes of political liberals and conservatives? It seems clear that there are basic philosophical differences between political liberals and conservatives, but these are not the differences that are used in political rhetoric. Some individual liberals may be irresponsible spenders of public funds; some individual conservatives may lack compassion for the less fortunate. But most people on each side of this political division are probably men and women of good will who differ on such topics as human nature and the relation of individuals to society.

The conservative usually sees human nature as unchanging and perhaps unchangeable. Conservatives are especially sceptical of attempts to change long-standing human characteristics by laws and other government action; this explains their reservations about affirmative action laws. However, conservatives often hold that just as there is an unchanging human nature, so there is an unchanging moral law and that the laws of society should conform to this moral law. This view is often at the root of conservative objections to pornography and the willingness to sacrifice some degree of privacy for the sake of society. Conservatives often hold a hierarchical view of the world, which includes the view that human beings are naturally superior to animals and have the right to use animals and the environment for human purposes.

Political liberals, on the other hand, are often more confident that changes in laws and social arrangements can eventually change attitudes and behavior. They point out that long-standing practices such as slavery, which have in the past been defended as "natural," have been abolished as the result of changes in laws and social arrangements. Liberals are likely to defend changes in past social practices, such as busing for school integration, in the hope of changing attitudes and behavior. They have similar hopes for affirmative action laws.

Some liberals are sceptical about absolute moral values, and many liberals hold the view that society has no right to interfere in an individual's private life; thus liberals tend to condemn censorship even of hard-core pornography and defend privacy in other areas. Traditionally, liberalism has often been tied up with a confidence in progress, but at present liberals are increasingly sceptical about progress in the sense of continual economic expansion because of the environmental damage involved. At least some liberals hold that humans do not have the right to exploit animals and the natural environment, especially for luxuries and nonessentials.

It is important to see that popular versions of conservatism and liberalism often include ideas that are inconsistent or not thoroughly thought out. It is possible to start from principles thought of as conservative and reach many liberal conclusions, and vice versa. A person who has studied and thought about ethical systems and problems may reach conclusions that seem liberal or conservative, but it is hoped that these conclusions will be based on reason and not on political rhetoric or emotion.

7

Affirmative Action

The idea behind affirmative action or preferential hiring programs is that since certain groups have formerly been discriminated against in employment, the balance should be restored by giving them special consideration in hiring at the present time. Some supporters of affirmative action hold simply that members of formerly disadvantaged groups should be hired in preference to others only if they are as well qualified as the others. However, some supporters of affirmative action maintain that even less-qualified members of disadvantaged groups should be hired in preference to others who are better qualified.

One argument against affirmative action is the "two wrongs don't make a right" argument, which goes as follows: "If it was wrong then to hire whites instead of better-qualified blacks or men instead of better-qualified women, surely it is wrong now to hire blacks instead of better-qualified whites or women instead of better-qualified men. Two wrongs don't make a right; reverse discrimination is just as bad as the original discrimination."

What this argument ignores is the fact that past harms or benefits can create obligations in the present. If I steal from you I ought to make reparation; if I do you a favor you ought to repay me. It can be argued that reparations for past injuries take precedence over ordinary equal treatment. So a member of a disadvantaged group is not getting an unjust advantage in receiving preferential treatment in hiring; he or she is only being recompensed for past injuries.

However, this answer may be too simple. After all, it is not usually the person now receiving preferential treatment who was formerly discriminated against, but only someone belonging to a group to which this person belongs. Does the mere fact that I belong to a group that was formerly discriminated against entitle *me* to reparation? And even if the answer is yes, surely there must be some limitations to my entitlement to reparations. Almost everyone belongs to some group that has been discriminated against at some time and place.

Furthermore, what about the rights of those who are refused jobs because of preferential hiring of members of disadvantaged groups? Suppose that in Boston an Irish Catholic is not hired on a certain construction job because the contractor is giving preferential consideration for jobs to blacks, as the result of a government-mandated affirmative action program. The Irish Catholic might well argue that Irish and Catholics had often been discriminated against in Boston, and that people in power who denied jobs to blacks in the past were not very often Irish or Catholic. "Why should *I* pay for the sins of others," the Irish Catholic might ask, "when my ancestors were often exploited and discriminated against by the same power structure that exploited and discriminated against blacks?"

A good deal of the current debate over affirmative action concerns preferential hiring programs for women. Many of the papers in this chapter focus on such programs rather than on preferential hiring of racial minorities, but the same basic principles are involved. Judith Jarvis Thomson limits herself to preferential hiring of blacks or women in universities and is "concerned with cases in which several candidates present themselves for a job, in which the hiring officer finds, on examination, that all are equally qualified to hold that job, and he then straightway declares for the black, or for the woman, because he or she *is* a black or a woman." Thomson argues for preferential hiring on the grounds of reparations for past injuries and deals with objections to this argument that are similar to those raised in this introduction. Robert Simon replies to Thomson's paper, arguing that "even if her claim that compensation is due victims of social injustice is correct . . . it is questionable nevertheless whether preferential hiring is an acceptable method of distributing such compensation."

Lisa H. Newton criticizes what she characterizes as reverse discrimination on the grounds that it involves "a confusion fundamentally relevant to our understanding of the notion of the rule of law." The selection from Dorothy L. Sayers is not directly on the subject of affirmative action, but it raises some questions about women and work that are relevant to discussions of affirmative action. Finally, George Sher discusses the question of whether there are any temporal limits to compensation for past injustices, using that question to cast new light on a number of questions related to affirmative action.

Preferential Hiring

Judith Jarvis Thomson

Many people are inclined to think preferential hiring an obvious injustice. I should have said "feel" rather than "think": it seems to me the matter has not been carefully thought out and that what is in question, really, is a gut reaction.

I am going to deal with only a very limited range of preferential hirings: that is, I am concerned with cases in which several candidates present themselves for a job, in which the hiring officer finds, on examination, that all are equally qualified to hold that job, and he then straightway declares for the black, or for the woman, because he or she *is* a black or a woman. And I shall talk only of hiring decisions in the universities, partly because I am most familiar with them, partly because it is in the universities that the most vocal and articulate opposition to preferential hiring is now heard—not surprisingly, perhaps, since no one is more vocal and articulate than a university professor who feels deprived of his rights.

I suspect that some people may say, Oh well, in *that* kind of case it's all right; what we object to is preferring the less qualified to the better qualified. Or again, What we object to is refusing even to consider the qualifications of white males. I shall say nothing at all about these things. I think that the argument I shall give for saying that preferential hiring is not unjust in the cases I do concentrate on can also be appealed to to justify it outside that range of cases. But I won't draw any conclusions about cases outside it. Many people do have that gut reaction I mentioned against preferential hiring in *any* degree or form; and it seems to me worthwhile bringing out that there is good reason to think they are wrong to have it. Nothing I say will be in the slightest degree novel or original. It will, I hope, be enough to set the relevant issues out clearly.

I

But first, something should be said about qualifications.

I said I would consider only cases in which the several candidates who present themselves for the job are equally qualified to hold it; and there plainly are difficulties in the way of saying precisely how this is to be established, and even what is to be established. Strictly academic qualifications seem at a first glance to be relatively straight-forward: the hiring officer must see if the candidates have done equally well in courses (both courses they took, and any they taught), and if they are recommended equally strongly by their teachers, and if the work they submit for consideration is equally good. There is no denying that even these things are less easy to establish than first appears: for example, you may have a suspicion that Professor Smith is given to exaggeration, and that his "great student" is in fact less strong than Professor Jones's "good student"—but do you *know* that this is so? But there is a more serious difficulty still: as blacks and women have been saying, strictly academic indicators may themselves be skewed by prejudice. My impression is

From Judith Jarvis Thomson, "Preferential Hiring," *Philosophy and Public Affairs,* vol. 2, no. 4 (copyright © 1973 by Princeton University Press), pp. 364–384. Reprinted by permission of Princeton University Press.

that women, white and black, may possibly suffer more from this than black males. A black male who is discouraged or down-graded for being black is discouraged or down-graded out of dislike, repulsion, a desire to avoid contact; and I suspect that there are very few teachers nowadays who allow themselves to feel such things, or, if they do feel them, to act on them. A woman who is discouraged or down-graded for being a woman is not discouraged or down-graded out of dislike, but out of a conviction she is not serious, and I suspect that while there are very few teachers nowadays who allow themselves to feel that women generally are not serious, there are many who allow themselves to feel of the particular individual women students they confront that Ah, this one isn't serious, and in fact that one isn't either, nor is that other one—women generally are, of course, one thing, but these particular women, really they're just girls in search of husbands, are quite another. And I suspect that this will be far harder to root out. A teacher could not face himself in the mirror of a morning if he had down-graded anyone out of dislike; but a teacher can well face himself in the mirror if he down-grades someone out of a conviction that that person is not serious: after all, life is serious, and jobs and work, and who can take the unserious seriously? who pays attention to the dilettante? So the hiring officer must read very very carefully between the lines in the candidates' dossiers even to assess their strictly academic qualifications.

And then of course there are other qualifications besides the strictly academic ones. Is one of the candidates exceedingly disagreeable? A department is not merely a collection of individuals, but a working unit; and if anyone is going to disrupt that unit, and to make its work more difficult, then this counts against him—he may be as well qualified in strictly academic terms, but he is not as well qualified. Again, is one of the candidates incurably sloppy? Is he going to mess up his records, is he going to have to be nagged to get his grades in, and worse, is he going to lose students' papers? This too would count against him: keeping track of students' work, records, and grades, after all, is part of the job.

What seems to me to be questionable, however, is that a candidate's race or sex is itself a qualification. Many people who favor preferential hiring in the universities seem to think it is; in their view, if a group of candidates is equally well qualified in respect of those measures I have already indicated, then if one is of the right race (black) or of the right sex (female), then that being itself a qualification, it tips the balance, and that one is the best qualified. If so, then of course no issue of injustice, or indeed of any other impropriety, is raised if the hiring officer declares for that one of the candidates straightway.

Why does race or sex seem to many to be, itself, a qualification? There seem to be two claims in back of the view that it is. First, there is the claim that blacks learn better from a black, women from a woman. One hears this less often in respect of women; blacks, however, are often said to mistrust the whites who teach them, with the result that they simply do not learn as well, or progress as far, as they would if taught by blacks. Secondly, and this one hears in respect of women as well as blacks, what is wanted is *role models*. The proportion of black and women faculty members in the larger universities (particularly as one moves up the ladder of rank) is very much smaller than the proportion of blacks and women in the society at large—even, in the case of women, than the proportion of them among recipients of Ph.D. degrees from those very same universities. Black and women students suffer a constricting of ambition because of this. They need to see members of their race or sex who are accepted, successful professionals. They need concrete evidence that those of their race or sex *can* become accepted, successful professionals.

And perhaps it is thought that it is precisely by virtue of having a role model right in the classroom that blacks do learn better from a black, women from a woman.

Now it is obviously essential for a university to staff its classrooms with people who can teach, and so from whom its students can learn, and indeed learn as much and as well as possible—teaching, after all, is, if not the whole of the game, then anyway a very large part of it. So if the first claim is true, then race and sex *do* seem to be qualifications. It obviously would not follow that a university should continue to regard them as qualifications indefinitely; I suppose, however, that it would follow that it should regard them as qualifications at least until the proportion of blacks and women on the faculty matches the proportion of blacks and women among the students.

But in the first place, allowing this kind of consideration to have a bearing on a hiring decision might make for trouble of a kind that blacks and women would not be at all happy with. For suppose it could be made out that white males learn better from white males? (I once, years ago, had a student who said he really felt uncomfortable in a class taught by a woman, it was interfering with his work, and did I mind if he switched to another section?) I suppose we would feel that this was due to prejudice and that it was precisely to be discouraged, certainly not encouraged by establishing hiring ratios. I don't suppose it is true of white males generally that they learn better from white males; I am concerned only with the way in which we should take the fact, if it were a fact, that they did—and if it would be improper to take it to be reason to think being a white male is a qualification in a teacher, then how shall we take its analogue to be reason to think being black, or being a woman, is a qualification in a teacher?

And in the second place, I must confess that, speaking personally, I do not find the claim we are looking at borne out in experience; I do not think that as a student I learned any better, or any more, from the women who taught me than from the men, and I do not think that my own women students now learn any better or any more from me than they do from my male colleagues. Blacks, of course, may have, and may have had, very different experiences, and I don't presume to speak for them—or even for women generally. But my own experience being what it is, it seems to *me* that any defense of preferential hiring in the universities which takes this first claim as premise is so far not an entirely convincing one.

The second claim, however, does seem to me to be plainly true: black and women students do need role models; they do need concrete evidence that those of their race or sex can become accepted, successful professionals—plainly, you won't try to become what you don't believe you can become.

But do they need these role models right there in the classroom? Of course it might be argued that they do: that a black learns better from a black teacher, a woman from a woman teacher. But we have already looked at this. And if they are, though needed, not needed in the classroom, then is it the university's job to provide them?

For it must surely be granted that a college, or university, has not the responsibility—or perhaps, if it is supported out of public funds, even the right—to provide just *any* service to its students which it might be good for them, or even which they may need, to be provided with. Sports seem to me plainly a case in point. No doubt it is very good for students to be offered, and perhaps even required to become involved in, a certain amount of physical exercise; but I can see no reason whatever to think that universities should be expected to provide facilities for it, or taxpayers to pay for those facilities. I suspect others may disagree, but my own feeling is that it is the same with medical and psychiatric services: I am sure that at least some students need medical and psychiatric help, but I cannot see why it should be provided for them in the universities, at public expense.

So the further question which would have to be answered is this: granting that black and female students need black and female role models, why should the universities be expected to provide them within their faculties? In the case of publicly supported universities, why should taxpayers be expected to provide them?

I don't say these questions can't be answered. But I do think we need to come at them from a quite different direction. So I shall simply sidestep this ground for preferential hiring in the universities. The defense I give will not turn on anyone's supposing that of two otherwise equally well qualified candidates, one may be better qualified for the job by virtue, simply, of being of the right race or sex.

II

I mentioned several times in the preceding section the obvious fact that it is the taxpayers who support public universities. Not that private universities are wholly private: the public contributes to the support of most of them, for example by allowing them tax-free use of land, and of the dividends and capital gains on investments. But it will be the public universities in which the problem appears most starkly: as I shall suggest, it is the fact of public support that makes preferential hiring in the universities problematic.

For it seems to me that—other things being equal—there is no problem about preferential hiring in the case of a wholly private college or university, that is, one which receives no measure of public support at all, and which lives simply on tuition and (non-tax-deductible) contributions.

The principle here seems to me to be this: no perfect stranger has a right to be given a benefit which is yours to dispose of; no perfect stranger even has a right to be given an equal chance at getting a benefit which is yours to dispose of. You not only needn't give the benefit to the first perfect stranger who walks in and asks for it; you needn't even give him a chance at it, as, e.g., by tossing a coin.

I should stress that I am here talking about *benefits,* that is, things which people would like to have, which would perhaps not merely please them, but improve their lives, but which they don't actually *need.* (I suspect the same holds true of things people do actually need, but many would disagree, and as it is unnecessary to speak here of needs, I shall not discuss them.) If I have extra apples (they're mine: I grew them, on my own land, from my own trees), or extra money, or extra tickets to a series of lectures I am giving on How to Improve Your Life Through Philosophy, and am prepared to give them away, word of this may get around, and people may present themselves as candidate recipients. I do not have to give to the first, or to proceed by letting them all draw straws; if I really do own the things, I can give to whom I like, on any ground I please, and in so doing, I violate no one's *rights,* I treat no one *unjustly.* None of the candidate recipients has a right to the benefit, or even to a chance at it.

There are four caveats. (1) Some grounds for giving or refraining from giving are less respectable than others. Thus, I might give the apples to the first who asks for them simply because he is the first who asks for them. Or again, I might give the apples to the first who asks for them because he is black, and because I am black and feel an interest in and concern for blacks which I do not feel in and for whites. In either case, not merely do I do what it is within my rights to do, but more, my ground for giving them to that person is a not immoral ground for giving them to him. But I might instead give the apples to the sixth who asks, and this because the first five were black and I hate blacks, or because the first five were white and I hate whites. Here I do what I have a right to do (for the apples are *mine*), and I violate no one's rights in doing it, but my ground for disposing of the apples as I did was a bad one; and it might even, more strongly, be said that I ought not have disposed of the apples in the way I did. But it is important to note that it is perfectly consistent, on the one hand, that a man's ground for acting as he did was a bad one, and even that he ought not have done what he did, and, on the other hand, that he had a right to do what he did, that he violated no one's rights in doing it, and that no one can complain he was unjustly treated.

The second caveat (2) is that although I have a right to dispose of my apples as I wish, I have no right to harm, or gratuitously hurt or offend. Thus I am within my rights to refuse to give the apples to the first five because they are black (or because they are white); but I am not within my rights to say to them "I refuse to give you apples because you are black (or white) and because those who are black (or white) are inferior."

And (3) if word of my extra apples, and of my willingness to give them away, got around because I advertised, saying or implying First Come First Served Till Supply Runs Out, then I cannot refuse the first five because they are black, or white. By so advertising, I have *given* them a right to a chance at the apples. If they come in one at a time, I must give out apples in order, till the supply runs out; if they come in together and I have only four apples, then I must either cut up the apples, or give them each an equal chance, as, e.g., by having them draw straws.

And lastly (4), there may be people who would say that I don't really, or don't fully, own those apples, even though I grew them on my own land, from my own trees, and therefore that I don't have a right to give them away as I see fit. For after all, I don't own the police who protected my land while those apples were growing or the sunlight because of which they grew. Or again, wasn't it just a matter of luck for me that I was born with a green thumb?—and why should I profit from a competence that I didn't deserve to have, that I didn't earn? Or perhaps some other reason might be put forward for saying that I don't own those apples. I don't want to take this up here. It seems to me wrong, but I want to let it pass. If anyone thinks that I don't own the apples, or, more generally, that no one really or fully owns anything, he will regard what I shall say in the remainder of this section, in which I talk about what may be done with what is privately owned, as an idle academic exercise. I'll simply ask that anyone who does think this be patient: we will come to what is publicly owned later.

Now what was in question was a job, not apples; and it may be insisted that to give a man a job is not to give him a benefit, but rather something he needs. Well, I am sure that people do need jobs, that it does not fully satisfy people's needs to supply them only with food, shelter, and medical care. Indeed, I am sure that people need, not merely jobs, but jobs that interest them, and that they can therefore get satisfaction from the doing of. But on the other hand, I am not at all sure that any candidate for a job in a university needs a job in a university. One would very much like it if all graduate students who wish it could find jobs teaching in universities; it is in some measure a tragedy that a person should spend three or four years preparing for a career, and then find there is no job available, and that he has in consequence to take work which is less interesting than he had hoped and prepared for. But one thing seems plain: no one *needs* that work which would interest him most in all the whole world of work. Plenty of people have to make do with work they like less than other work—no economy is rich enough to provide everyone with the work he likes best of all—and I should think that this does not mean they lack something they *need*. We are all of us prepared to tax ourselves so that no one shall be in need; but I should imagine that we are not prepared to tax ourselves (to tax barbers, truck drivers, salesclerks, waitresses, and factory workers) in order that everyone who wants a university job, and is competent to fill it, shall have one made available to him.

All the same, if a university job is a benefit rather than something needed, it is anyway not a "pure" benefit (like an apple), but an "impure" one. To give a man a university job is to give him an opportunity to do work which is interesting and satisfying; but he will only *be* interested and satisfied if he actually does the work he is given an opportunity to do, and does it well.

What this should remind us of is that certain cases of preferential hiring might well be utterly irrational. Suppose we have an eating club and need a new chef; we have two applicants, a qualified French chef, and a Greek who happens to like to cook, though he doesn't do it very well. We are fools if we say to ourselves, "We like the Greeks and dislike the French, so let's hire the Greek." We simply won't eat as well as we could have, and eating, after all, was the point of the club. On the other hand, it's *our* club, and so *our* job. And who shall say it is not within a man's rights to dispose of what really is his in as foolish a way as he likes?

And there is no irrationality, of course, if one imagines that the two applicants are equally qualified French chefs, and one is a cousin of one of our members, the other a perfect stranger. Here if we declare directly for the cousin, we do not act irrationally, we violate no one's rights, and indeed do not have a morally bad ground for making the choice we make. It's not a morally splendid ground, but it isn't a morally bad one either.

Universities differ from eating clubs in one way which is important for present purposes: in an eating club, those who consume what the club serves are the members, and thus the owners of the club themselves—by contrast, if the university is wholly private, those who consume what it serves are not among the owners. This makes a difference: the owners of the university have a responsibility not merely to themselves (as the owners of an eating club do), but also to those who come to buy what it offers. It could, I suppose, make plain in its advertising that it is prepared to allow the owners' racial or religious or other preferences to outweigh academic qualifications in its teachers. But in the absence of that, it must, in light of what a university is normally expected to be and to aim at, provide the best teachers it can afford. It does not merely act irrationally, but indeed violates the rights of its student-customers if it does not.

On the other hand, this leaves it open to the university that in case of a choice between equally qualified candidates, it violates no one's rights if it declares for the black because he is black, or for the white because he is white. To the wholly *private* university, that is, for that is all I have so far been talking of. Other things being equal—that is, given it has not advertised the job in a manner which would entitle applicants to believe that all who are equally qualified will be given an equal chance at it, and given it does not gratuitously give offense to those whom it rejects—the university may choose as it pleases, and violates no one's rights in doing so. Though no doubt its grounds for choosing may be morally bad ones, and we may even wish to say, more strongly, that it ought not choose as it does.

What will have come out in the preceding is that the issue I am concerned with is a moral, and not a legal, one. My understanding is that the law does prevent an employer wholly in the private sector from choosing a white rather than a black on ground of that difference alone—though not from choosing a black rather than a white on ground of that difference alone. Now if, as many people say, legal rights (or perhaps, legal rights in a relatively just society) create moral rights, then even a moral investigation should take the law into account; and indeed, if I am not mistaken as to the law, it would have to be concluded that blacks (but not whites) do have rights of the kind I have been denying. I want to sidestep all this. My question can be re-put: would a private employer's choosing a white (or black) rather than a black (or white) on ground of that difference alone be a violation of anyone's rights if there were no law making it illegal. And the answer seems to me to be: it would not.

III

But hardly any college or university in America is purely private. As I said, most enjoy some public support, and the moral issues may be affected by the extent of the burden carried by the public. I shall concentrate on universities which are entirely publicly funded, such as state or city universities, and ignore the complications which might arise in case of partial private funding.

The special problem which arises here, as I see it, is this: where a community pays the bills, the community owns the university.

I said earlier that the members, who are therefore the owners, of a private eating club may declare for whichever chef they wish, even if the man they declare for is not as well qualified for the job as some other; in choosing amongst applicants, they are *not* choosing among fellow members of the club who is to get some benefit from the club. But now suppose, by contrast, that two of us who are members arrive at the same time, and there is only one available table. And suppose also that this has never happened before, and that the club has not voted on any policy for handling it when it does happen. What seems to me to be plain is this: the headwaiter cannot indulge in preferential seating, he cannot simply declare for one or the other of us on just any ground he pleases. He must randomize: as it might be, by tossing a coin.

Or again, suppose someone arrives at the dining room with a gift for the club: a large and very splendid apple tart. And suppose that this, too, has never happened before, and that the club has not voted on any policy for handling it when it does happen. What seems to me plain is this: the headwaiter cannot distribute that tart in just any manner and on any ground he pleases. If the tart won't keep till the next meeting and it's impossible to convene one now, he must divide the tart among us equally.

Consideration of these cases might suggest the following principle: every owner of a jointly owned property has a right to either an equal chance at, or an equal share in, any benefit which that property generates, and which is available for distribution among the owners—equal chance rather than equal share if the benefit is indivisible, or for some reason is better left undivided.

Now I have all along been taking it that the members of a club jointly own the club, and therefore jointly own whatever the club owns. It seems to me possible to view a community in the same way: to suppose that its members jointly own it, and therefore jointly own whatever it owns. If a community is properly viewed in this way, and if the principle I set out above is true, then every member of the community is a joint owner of whatever the community owns, and so in particular, a joint owner of its university; and therefore every member of the community has a right to an equal chance at, or equal share in, any benefit which the university generates, which is available for distribution amongst the owners. And that includes university jobs, if, as I argued, a university job is a benefit.

Alternatively, one might view a community as an imaginary Person: one might say that the members of that community are in some sense participants in that Person, but that they do not jointly own what the Person owns. One might in fact say the same of a club: that its members do not jointly own the club or anything which the club owns, but only in some sense participate in the Person which owns the things. And then the cases I mentioned might suggest an analogous principle: every "participant" in a Person (Community-Person, Club-Person) has a right to either an equal chance at, or an equal share in, any benefit which is generated by a property which that Person owns, which is available for distribution amongst the "participants."

On the other hand, if we accept any of this, we have to remember that there are cases in which a member may, without the slightest impropriety, be deprived of this equal chance or equal share. For it is plainly not required that the university's hiring officer decide who gets the available job by randomizing among *all* the community members, however well- or ill-qualified, who want it. The university's student-customers, after all, have rights too; and their rights to good teaching are surely more stringent than each member's right (if each has such a right) to an equal chance at the job. I think we do best to reserve the term "violation of a right" for cases in which a man is unjustly deprived of something he has a right to, and speak rather of "overriding a right" in cases in which, though a man is deprived of something he has a right to, it is not unjust to deprive him of it. So here the members' rights to an equal chance (if they have them) would be, not violated, but merely overridden.

It could of course be said that these principles hold only of benefits of a kind I pointed to earlier, and called "pure" benefits (such as apples and apple tarts), and that we should find some other, weaker, principle to cover "impure" benefits (such as jobs).

Or it could be said that a university job is not a benefit which is available for distribution among the community members—that although a university job is a benefit, it is, in light of the rights of the students, available for distribution only among those members of the community who are best qualified to hold it. And therefore that they alone have a right to an equal chance at it.

It is important to notice, however, that unless *some* such principle as I have set out is true of the publicly owned university, there is no real problem about preferential hiring in it. Unless the white male applicant who is turned away had a right that this should not be done, doing so is quite certainly not violating any of his rights. Perhaps being joint owner of the university (on the first model) or being joint participant in the Person which owns the university (on the second model) does not give him a right to an equal chance at the job; perhaps he is neither joint owner nor joint participant (some third model is preferable), and it is something else which gives him his right to an equal chance at the job. Or perhaps he hasn't a right to an equal chance at the job, but has instead some other right which is violated by declaring for the equally qualified black or woman straightway. It is here that it seems to me it emerges most clearly that opponents of preferential hiring are merely expressing a gut reaction against it: for they have not asked themselves precisely what right is in question, and what it issues from.

Perhaps there is lurking in the background some sense that everyone has a right to "equal treatment," and that it is this which is violated by preferential hiring. But what on earth right is this? Mary surely does not have to decide between Tom and Dick by toss of a coin, if what is in question is marrying. Nor even, as I said earlier, if what is in question is giving out apples, which she grew on her own land, on her own trees.

It could, of course, be argued that declaring for the black or woman straightway isn't a violation of the white male applicant's rights, but is all the same wrong, bad, something which ought not be done. As I said, it is perfectly consistent that one ought not do something which it is, nevertheless, no violation of anyone's rights to do. So perhaps opponents of preferential hiring might say that rights are not in question, and still argue against it on other grounds. I say they *might,* but I think they plainly do better not to. If the white male applicant has no rights which would be violated, and appointing the black or woman indirectly benefits other blacks or women (remember that need for role models), and thereby still more indirectly benefits us all (by widening the available pool of talent), then it is very hard to see how it could come out to be morally objectionable to declare for the black or woman straightway.

I think we should do the best we can for those who oppose preferential hiring: I think we should grant that the white male applicant has a right to an equal chance at the job, and see what happens for preferential hiring if we do. I shall simply leave open whether this right issues from considerations of the kind I drew attention to, and so also whether or not every member of the community, however well- or ill-qualified for the job, has the same right to an equal chance at it.

Now it is, I think, widely believed that we may, without injustice, refuse to grant a man what he has a right to only if *either* someone else has a conflicting and more stringent right, *or* there is some very great benefit to be obtained by doing so—perhaps that a disaster of some kind is thereby averted. If so, then there really is trouble for preferential hiring. For what more stringent right could be thought to override the right of the white male applicant for an equal chance? What great benefit obtained, what disaster averted, by declaring for the black or the woman straightway? I suggested that benefits are obtained, and they are not small ones. But are they large enough to override a right? If these questions cannot be satisfactorily answered, then it looks as if the hiring officer does act unjustly, and does violate the rights of the white males, if he declares for the black or woman straightway.

But in fact there are other ways in which a right may be overridden. Let's go back to that eating club again. Suppose that now it has happened that two of us arrive at the same time when there is only one available table, we think we had better decide on some policy for handling it when it happens. And suppose that we have of late had reason to be especially grateful to one of the members, whom I'll call Smith: Smith has done a series of very great favors for the club. It seems to me we might, out of gratitude to Smith, adopt the following policy: for the next six months, if two members arrive at the same time, and there is only one available table, then Smith gets in first, if he's one of the two: whereas if he's not, then the headwaiter shall toss a coin.

We might even vote that for the next year, if he wants apple tart, he gets more of it than the rest of us.

It seems to me that there would be no impropriety in our taking these actions—by which I mean to include that there would be no injustice in our taking them. Suppose another member, Jones, votes No. Suppose he says, "Look. I admit we all benefited from what Smith did for us. But still, I'm a member, and a member in as good standing as Smith is. So I have a right to an equal chance (and equal share), and I demand what I have a right to." I think we may rightly feel that Jones merely shows insensitivity: he does not adequately appreciate what Smith did for us. Jones, like all of us, has a right to an equal chance at such benefits as the club has available for distribution to the members; but there is no injustice in a majority's refusing to grant the members this equal chance, in the name of a debt of gratitude to Smith.

It is worth noticing an important difference between a debt of gratitude and debts owed to a creditor. Suppose the club had borrowed $1000 from Dickenson, and then was left as a legacy, a painting appraised at $1000. If the club has no other saleable assets, and if no member is willing to buy the painting, then I take it that justice would precisely require *not* randomizing among the members who is to get that painting, but would instead require our offering it to Dickenson. Jones could not complain that to offer it to Dickenson is to treat him, Jones, unjustly: Dickenson has a right to be paid back, and that right is more stringent than any member's right to an equal chance at the painting. Now Smith, by contrast, did not have a right to be given anything, he did not have a right to our adopting a policy of preferential seating in his favor. If we fail to do anything for Dickenson, we do him an injustice; if we fail to do anything for Smith, we do *him* no injustice—our failing is, not injustice, but ingratitude. There is no harm in speaking of debts of gratitude and in saying that they are owed to a benefactor, by analogy with debts owed to a creditor; but it is important to remember that a creditor has, and a benefactor does not have, a right to repayment.

To move now from clubs to more serious matters, suppose two candidates for a civil service job have equally good test scores, but that there is only one job available. We could decide between them by coin-tossing. But in fact we do allow for declaring for A straightway, where A is a veteran, and B is not.[1] It may be that B is a nonveteran through no fault of his own: perhaps he was refused induction for flat feet, or a heart murmur. That is, those things in virtue of which B is a nonveteran may be things which it was no more in his power to control or change than it is in anyone's power to control or change the color of his skin. Yet the fact is that B is not a veteran and A is. On the assumption that the veteran has served his country,[2] the country owes him something. And it seems plain that giving him preference is a not unjust way in which part of that debt of gratitude can be paid.

And now, finally, we should turn to those debts which are incurred by one who wrongs another. It is here we find what seems to me the most powerful argument for the conclusion that the preferential hiring of blacks and women is not unjust.

I obviously cannot claim any novelty for this argument: it's a very familiar one. Indeed, not merely is it familiar, but so are a battery of objections to it. It may be granted that if we have wronged A, we owe him something: we should make amends, we should compensate him for the wrong done him. It may even be granted that if we have wronged A, we must make amends, that justice requires it, and that a failure to make amends is not merely callousness, but injustice. But (a) are the young blacks and women who are amongst the current applicants for university jobs among the blacks and women who were wronged? To turn to particular cases, it might happen that the black applicant is middle class, son of professionals, and has had the very best in private schooling; or that the woman applicant is plainly the product of feminist upbringing and encouragement. Is it proper, much less required, that the black or woman be given preference over a white male who grew up in poverty, and has to make his own way and earn his encouragements? Again, (b), did we, the current members of the community, wrong any blacks or women? Lots of people once did; but then isn't it for them to do the compensating? That is, if they're still alive. For presumably nobody now alive owned any slaves, and perhaps nobody now alive voted against women's suffrage. And (c) what if the white male applicant for the job has never in any degree wronged any blacks or women? If so, *he* doesn't owe any debts to them, so why should *he* make amends to them?

These objections seem to me quite wrong-headed.

Obviously the situation for blacks and women is better than it was a hundred and fifty, fifty, twenty-five years ago. But it is absurd to suppose that the young blacks and women now of an age to apply for jobs have not been wronged. Large-scale, blatant, overt wrongs have presumably disappeared; but it is only within the last twenty-five years (perhaps the last ten years in the case of women) that it has become at all widely agreed in this country that blacks and women must be recognized as having, not merely this or that particular right normally recognized as belonging to white males, but all of the rights and respect which go with full membership in the community. Even young blacks and women have lived through down-grading for being black or female: they have not merely not been given that very equal chance at the benefits generated by what the community owns which is so firmly insisted on for white males, they have not until lately even been felt to have a right to it.

And even those who were not themselves down-graded for being black or female have suffered the consequences of the down-grading of other blacks and women: lack of self-confidence and lack of self-respect. For where a community accepts that a person's being black, or being a woman, are right and proper grounds for denying that person full membership in the community, it can hardly be supposed that any but the most extraordinarily independent black or woman will escape self-doubt. All but the most extraordinarily independent of them have had to work harder—if only against self-doubt—than all but the most deprived white males, in the competition for a place amongst the best qualified.

If any black or woman has been unjustly deprived of what he or she has a right to, then of course justice does call for making amends. But what of the blacks and women who haven't actually been deprived of what they have a right to, but only made to suffer the consequences of injustice to other blacks and women? *Perhaps* justice doesn't require making amends to them as well; but common decency certainly does. To fail, at the very least, to make what counts as public apology to all, and to take positive steps to show that it is sincerely meant, is, if not injustice, then anyway a fault at least as serious as ingratitude.

Opting for a policy of preferential hiring may of course mean that some black or woman is preferred to some white male who as a matter of fact has had a harder life than the black or woman. But so may opting for a policy of veterans' preference mean that a healthy, unscarred, middle class veteran is preferred to a poor, struggling, scarred non-veteran. Indeed, opting for a policy of settling who gets the job by having all equally qualified candidates draw straws may also mean that in a given case the candidate with the hardest life loses out. Opting for any policy other than hard-life preference may have this result.

I have no objection to anyone's arguing that it is precisely hard-life preference that we ought to opt for. If all, or anyway all of the equally qualified, have a right to an equal chance, then the argument would have to draw attention to something sufficiently powerful to override that right. But perhaps this could be done along the lines I followed in the case of blacks and women: perhaps it could be successfully argued that we have wronged those who have had hard lives, and therefore owe it to them to make amends. And then we should have in more extreme form a difficulty already present: how are these preferences to be ranked? shall we place the hard-lifers ahead of blacks? both ahead of women? and what about veterans? I leave these questions aside. My concern has been only to show that the white male applicant's right to an equal chance does not make it unjust to opt for a policy under which blacks and women are given preference. That a white male with a specially hard history may lose out under this policy cannot possibly be any objection to it, in the absence of a showing that hard-life preference is not unjust, and, more important, takes priority over preference for blacks and women.

Lastly, it should be stressed that to opt for such a policy is not to make the young white male applicants themselves make amends for any wrongs done to blacks and women. Under such a policy, no one is asked to give up a job which is already his; the job for which the white male competes isn't his, but is the community's, and it is the hiring officer who gives it to the black or woman in the community's name. Of course the white male is asked to give up his equal chance at the job. But that is not something he pays to the black or woman by way of making amends; it is something the community takes away from him in order that *it* may make amends.

Still, the community does impose a burden on him: it is able to make amends for its wrongs only by taking something away from him, something which, after all, we are supposing he has a right to. And why should *he* pay the cost of the community's amends-making?

If there were some appropriate way in which the community could make amends to its blacks and women, some way which did not require depriving anyone of anything he has a right to, then that would be the best course of action for it to take. Or if there were anyway some way in which the costs could be shared by everyone, and not imposed entirely on the young white male job applicants, then that would be, if not best, then anyway better than opting for a policy of preferential hiring. But in fact the nature of the wrongs done is such as to make jobs the best and most suitable form of compensation.

What blacks and women were denied was full membership in the community; and nothing can more appropriately make amends for that wrong than precisely what will make them feel they now finally have it. And that means jobs. Financial compensation (the cost of which could be shared equally) slips through the fingers; having a job, and discovering you do it well, yield—perhaps better than anything else—that very self-respect which blacks and women have had to do without.

But of course choosing this way of making amends means that the costs are imposed on the young white male applicants who are turned away. And so it should be noticed that it is not entirely inappropriate that those applicants should pay the costs. No doubt few, if any, have themselves, individually, done any wrongs to blacks and women. But they have profited from the wrongs the community did. Many may actually have been direct beneficiaries of policies which excluded or down-graded blacks and women—perhaps in school admissions, perhaps in access to financial aid, perhaps elsewhere; and even those who did not directly benefit in this way had, at any rate, the advantage in the competition which comes of confidence in one's full membership, and of one's rights being recognized as a matter of course.

Of course it isn't only the young white male applicant for a university job who has benefited from the exclusion of blacks and women: the older white male, now comfortably tenured, also benefited, and many defenders of preferential hiring feel that he should be asked to share the costs. Well, presumably we can't demand that he give up his job, or share it. But it seems to me in place to expect the occupants of comfortable professorial chairs to contribute in some way, to make some form of return to the young white male who bears the cost and is turned away. It will have been plain that I find the outcry now heard against preferential hiring in the universities objectionable; it would also be objectionable that those of us who are now securely situated should placidly defend it, with no more than a sigh of regret for the young white male who pays for it.

IV

One final word: "discrimination." I am inclined to think we so use it that if anyone is convicted of discriminating against blacks, women, white males, or what have you, then he is thereby convicted of acting unjustly. If so, and if I am right in thinking that preferential hiring in the restricted range of cases we have been looking at is *not* unjust, then we have two options: (a) we can simply reply that to opt for a policy of preferential hiring in those cases is not to opt for a policy of discriminating against white males, or (b) we can hope to get usage changed—e.g., by trying to get people to allow that there is discriminating against and discriminating against, and that some is unjust, but some is not.

Best of all, however, would be for that phrase to be avoided altogether. It's at best a blunt tool: there are all sorts of nice moral discriminations [*sic*] which one is unable to make while occupied with it. And that bluntness itself fits it to do harm: blacks and women are hardly likely to see through to what precisely is owed them while they are being accused of welcoming what is unjust.[3]

Notes

[1]To the best of my knowledge, the analogy between veterans' preference and the preferential hiring of blacks has been mentioned in print only by Edward T. Chase, in a Letter to the Editor, *Commentary,* February 1973.

[2]Many people would reject this assumption, or perhaps accept it only selectively, for veterans of this or that particular war. I ignore this. What interests me is what follows if we make the assumption—as, of course, many other people do, more, it seems, than do not.

[3]This essay is an expanded version of a talk given at the Conference on the Liberation of Female Persons, held at North Carolina State University at Raleigh, on March 26–28, 1973, under a grant from the S & H Foundation. I am indebted to James Thomson and the members of the Society for Ethical and Legal Philosophy for criticism of an earlier draft.

Discussion Questions

1. Suppose a woman and a black man were equally qualified candidates for a university job. In view of what Thomson says in this paper, which candidate should be preferred?

2. How might Thomson's principles be applied to a case where the black or woman was *less* qualified than the other candidate?

3. What problems does Thomson see about qualifications? Can you find any objections to the view she presents?

4. What relation does Thomson see between jobs and benefits? What principle does she invoke with regard to distributing benefits? Criticize this principle.

5. What important difference does Thomson see between public and private universities? How does Thomson use this distinction in her arguments? Find at least one objection to her line of argument here.

6. What objections does Thomson consider to her argument for preferential hiring as making amends? Does she answer these objections satisfactorily? Are there objections she does not consider?

Preferential Hiring: A Reply
to Judith Jarvis Thomson

Robert Simon

Judith Jarvis Thomson has recently [previous selection in this chapter] defended preferential hiring of women and black persons in universities.[1] She restricts her defense of the assignment of preference to only those cases where candidates from preferred groups and their white male competitors are equally qualified, although she suggests that her argument can be extended to cover cases where the qualifications are unequal as well. The argument in question is compensatory; it is because of pervasive patterns of unjust

From *Philosophy and Public Affairs*, vol. 3, no. 3. Copyright 1974 by Princeton University Press. Reprinted by permission of Princeton University Press.

discrimination against black persons and women that justice, or at least common decency, requires that amends be made.

While Thomson's analysis surely clarifies many of the issues at stake, I find it seriously incomplete. I will argue that even if her claim that compensation is due victims of social injustice is correct (as I think it is), it is questionable nevertheless whether preferential hiring is an acceptable method of distributing such compensation. This is so, even if, as Thomson argues, compensatory claims override the right of the white male applicant to equal consideration from the appointing officer. For implementation of preferential hiring policies may involve claims, perhaps even claims of right, other than the above right of the white male applicant. In the case of the claims I have in mind, the best that can be said is that where preferential hiring is concerned, they are arbitrarily ignored. If so, and if such claims are themselves warranted, then preferential hiring, while *perhaps* not unjust, is open to far more serious question than Thomson acknowledges.

I

A familiar objection to special treatment for blacks and women is that, if such a practice is justified, other victims of injustice or misfortune ought to receive special treatment too. While arguing that virtually all women and black persons have been harmed, either directly or indirectly, by discrimination, Thomson acknowledges that in any particular case, a white male may have been victimized to a greater extent than have the blacks or women with which he is competing. . . . However, she denies that other victims of injustice or misfortune ought automatically to have priority over blacks and women where distribution of compensation is concerned. Just as veterans receive preference with respect to employment in the civil service, as payment for the service they have performed for society, so can blacks and women legitimately be given preference in university hiring, in payment of the debt owed them. And just as the former policy can justify hiring a veteran who in fact had an easy time of it over a nonveteran who made great sacrifices for the public good, so too can the latter policy justify hiring a relatively undeprived member of a preferred group over a more disadvantaged member of a nonpreferred group.

But surely if the reason for giving a particular veteran preference is that he performed a service for his country, that same preference must be given to anyone who performed a similar service. Likewise, if the reason for giving preference to a black person or to a woman is that the recipient has been injured due to an unjust practice, then preference must be given to anyone who has been similarly injured. So, it appears, there can be no relevant *group* to which compensation ought to be made, other than that made up of and only of those who have been injured or victimized.[2] Although, as Thomson claims, all blacks and women may be members of that latter group, they deserve compensation *qua* victim and not *qua* black person or woman.

There are at least two possible replies that can be made to this sort of objection. First, it might be agreed that anyone injured in the same way as blacks or women ought to receive compensation. But then, "same way" is characterized so narrowly that it applies to no one except blacks and women. While there is nothing logically objectionable about such a reply, it may nevertheless be morally objectionable. For it implies that a nonblack male who has been terribly injured by a social injustice has less of a claim to compensation than a black or woman who has only been minimally injured. And this implication may be morally unacceptable.

A more plausible line of response may involve shifting our attention from compensation of individuals to collective compensation of groups.[3] Once this shift is made, it can be acknowledged that as individuals, some white males may have stronger compensatory claims than blacks or women. But as compensation is owed the group, it is group claims that must be weighed, not individual ones. And surely, at the group level, the claims of black persons and women to compensation are among the strongest there are.

Suppose we grant that certain groups, including those specified by Thomson, are owed collective compensation. What should be noted is that the conclusion of concern here—that preferential hiring policies are acceptable instruments for compensating groups—does not directly follow. To derive such a conclusion validly, one would have to provide additional premises specifying the relation between collective compensation to groups and distribution of that compensation to individual members. For it does not follow from the fact that some group members are compensated that the group is compensated. Thus, if through a computer error, every member of the American Philosophical Association was asked to pay additional taxes, then if the government provided compensation for this error, it would not follow that it had compensated the Association. Rather, it would have compensated each member *qua* individual. So what is required, where preferential hiring is concerned, are plausible premises showing how the preferential award of jobs to group members counts as collective compensation for the group.

Thomson provides no such additional premises. Moreover, there is good reason to think that if any such premises were provided, they would count against preferential hiring as an instrument of collective compensation. This is because although compensation is owed to the group, preferential hiring policies award compensation to an arbitrarily selected segment of the group; namely, those who have the ability and qualifications to be seriously considered for the jobs available. Surely, it is far more plausible to think that collective compensation ought to be equally available to all group members, or at least to all kinds of group members.[4] The claim that although compensation is owed collectively to a group, only a special sort of group member is eligible to receive it, while perhaps not incoherent, certainly ought to be rejected as arbitrary, at least in the absence of an argument to the contrary.

Accordingly, the proponent of preferential hiring faces the following dilemma. Either compensation is to be made on an individual basis, in which case the fact that one is black or a woman is irrelevant to whether one ought to receive special treatment, or it is made on a group basis, in which case it is far from clear that preferential hiring policies are acceptable compensatory instruments. Until this dilemma is resolved, assuming it can be resolved at all, the compensatory argument for preferential hiring is seriously incomplete at a crucial point.

II

Even if the above difficulty could be resolved, however, other problems remain. For example, once those entitled to compensatory benefits have been identified, questions arise concerning how satisfactorily preferential hiring policies honor such entitlements.

Consider, for example, a plausible principle of compensatory justice which might be called the Proportionality Principle (PP). According to the PP, the strength of one's compensatory claim, and the quantity of compensation one is entitled to is, *ceteris paribus,* proportional to the degree of injury suffered. A corollary of the PP is that equal injury gives rise to compensatory claims of equal strength. Thus, if X and Y were both injured to the same extent, and both deserve compensation for their injury, then, *ceteris paribus,* each has a compensatory claim of equal strength and each is entitled to equal compensation.

Now, it is extremely unlikely that a hiring program which gives preference to blacks and women will satisfy the PP because of the arbitrariness implicit in the search for candidates on the open market. Thus, three candidates, each members of previously victimized groups, may well wind up with highly disparate positions. One may secure employment in a prestigious department of a leading university while another may be hired by a university which hardly merits the name. The third might not be hired at all.

The point is that where the market place is used to distribute compensation, distribution will be by market principles, and hence only accidentally will be fitting in view of the injury suffered and compensation provided for others. While any compensation may be better than none, this would hardly appear to be a satisfactory way of making amends to the victimized.

"Compensation according to ability" or "compensation according to marketability" surely are dubious principles of compensatory justice. On the contrary, those with the strongest compensatory claims should be compensated first (and most). Where compensatory claims are equal, but not everybody can actually be compensated, some fair method of distribution should be employed, e.g., a lottery. Preferential hiring policies, then, to the extent that they violate the PP, *arbitrarily* discriminate in favor of some victims of past injustice and against others. The basis on which compensation is awarded is independent of the basis on which it is owed, and so distribution is determined by application of principles which are irrelevant from the point of view of compensatory justice.

Now, perhaps this is not enough to show that the use of preferential hiring as a compensatory instrument is unjust, or even unjustified. But perhaps it is enough to show that the case for the justice or justification of such a policy has not yet been made. Surely, we can say, at the very least, that a policy which discriminates in the arbitrary fashion discussed above is not a particularly satisfactory compensatory mechanism. If so, the direction in which considerations of compensatory justice and common decency point may be far less apparent than Thomson suggests.

III

So far, I have considered arbitrariness in the distribution of compensatory benefits by preferential hiring policies. However, arbitrariness involved in the assessment of costs is also of concern.

Thus, it is sometimes argued that preferential hiring policies place the burden of providing compensation on young white males who are just entering the job market. This is held to be unfair, because, first, there is no special reason for placing the burden on that particular group and, second, because many members of that group are not responsible for the injury done to blacks and women. In response to the first point, Thomson acknowledges that it seems to her "in place to expect the occupants of comfortable professorial chairs to contribute in some way, to make some form of return to the young white male who bears the cost. . . . " In response to the second point, Thomson concedes that few, if any, white male applicants to university positions individually have done any wrong to women or black persons. However, she continues, many have profited by the wrongs inflicted by others. So it is not unfitting that they be asked to make sacrifices now. . . .

However, it is far from clear, at least to me, that this reply is satisfactory. For even if the group which bears the cost is expanded to include full professors, why should that new group be singled out? The very same consideration that required the original expansion would seem to require a still wider one. Indeed, it would seem this point can be pressed until costs are assessed against society as a whole. This is exactly the position taken by Paul Taylor, who writes, "The obligation to offer such benefits to (the previously victimized) group . . . is an obligation that falls on society in general, not on any particular person. For it is the society in general that, through its established (discriminatory) social practice, brought upon itself the obligation."[5]

Perhaps, however, the claim that preferential hiring policies arbitrarily distribute burdens can be rebutted. For presumably the advocate of preferential hiring does not want to restrict such a practice to universities but rather would wish it to apply throughout society. If so, and *if* persons at the upper echelons are expected to share costs with young white male job applicants, then perhaps a case can be made that burdens are equitably distributed throughout society.

Even here, however, there are two points an opponent of preferential hiring can make. First, he can point out that burdens are not equitably distributed now. Consequently, to the extent that preferential policies are employed at present, then to that extent are burdens arbitrarily imposed now. Second, he can question the assumption that if someone gains from an unjust practice for which he is not responsible and even opposes, the gain is not really his and can be taken from him without injustice. This assumption is central to the compensatory argument for preferential hiring since if it is unacceptable, no justification remains for requiring "innocent bystanders" to provide compensation.

If X benefits at the expense of Y because of the operation of an unjust social institution, then is the benefit which accrues to X really deserved by Y? It seems to me that normally the answer will be affirmative. But it also seems to me that there is a significant class of cases where an affirmative response *may* not be justified. Suppose X himself is the victim of a similarly unjust social practice so that Z benefits at his expense. In such circumstances, it is questionable whether X ought to compensate Y, especially if X played no personal role in the formation of the unjust institutions at issue. Perhaps *both* X and Y ought to receive (different degrees of) compensation from Z.

If this point is sound, it becomes questionable whether *all* members of nonpreferred groups are equally liable (or even liable at all) for provision of compensation. It is especially questionable in the case where the individual from the nonpreferred group has been unjustly victimized to a far greater extent than the individual from the preferred group. Hence, even if it were true that all members of nonpreferred groups have profited from discrimination against members of preferred groups, it does not automatically follow that all are equally liable for providing compensation. Insofar as preferential hiring policies do not take this into account, they are open to the charge of arbitrariness in assessing the costs of compensation.

One more point seems to require mention here. If preferential hiring policies are expanded, as Thomson suggests, to cases where the candidates are not equally qualified, a further difficulty arises. To the extent that lowering quality lowers efficiency, members of victimized groups are likely to lose more than others. This may be particularly important in educational contexts. Students from such groups may have been exposed to poorer instruction than was made available to others. But they might have greater need for better instruction than, say, middle class students from affluent backgrounds.[6]

Suppose that members of previously discriminated against groups deserve special support in developing their capacities and talents. Then, it would seem that educational institutions charged with promoting such development have a corresponding obligation to develop those capacities and talents to the best of their ability. Presumably, this requires hiring the best available faculty and administration.

What we seem to have here is a conflict within the framework of compensatory justice itself. Even if preferential hiring is an acceptable method for distributing compensation, the compensation so distributed may decrease the beneficial effects of education. And this may adversely affect more members of the preferred groups than are helped by the preferential policy.[7]

IV

The argument of this paper is not directed against the view that victims of grave social injustice in America deserve compensation. On the contrary, a strong case can be made for providing such compensation.[8] Rather, I have tried to show that the case for using preferential hiring as a *means* of providing such compensation is incomplete at three crucial points:

(1) It is not clear to whom compensation should be made, groups or individuals. If the former, it has not been shown that preferential hiring compensates the group. If the latter, it has not been shown why membership in a group (other than that composed of, and only of, the victimized) is relevant to determining who should be compensated.

(2) It has not been shown that compensation should be awarded on grounds of marketability, grounds that certainly seem to be irrelevant from the compensatory point of view.

(3) It has not been shown that arbitrariness and inequity are or can be avoided in distributing the costs of preferential hiring policies of the sort in question.

If these charges have force, then whether or not preferential hiring can be justified on other grounds, the compensatory argument for such a practice is far more doubtful than Thomson's article suggests.[9]

Notes

[1] Judith Jarvis Thomson "Preferential Hiring," *Philosophy & Public Affairs* 2, no. 4 (Summer 1973): 364–384. . . .

[2] This point also has been argued for recently by J. L. Cowen, "Inverse Discrimination," *Analysis* 33, no. 1 (1972): 10–12.

[3] Such a position has been defended by Paul Taylor, in his "Reverse Discrimination and Compensatory Justice," *Analysis* 33, no. 4 (1973): 177–182.

[4] Taylor would apparently agree, *ibid.*: 180.

[5] *Ibid.*: 180. Parentheses are my own.

[6] At the time these arguments were first formulated, I unfortunately did not have access to Charles King's article "A Problem Concerning Discrimination" (presented to a symposium on reverse discrimination at the Eastern Division Meetings of the American Philosophical Association in 1972) in which a similar point is made. King also argues, although along lines somewhat different from my own, that preferential hiring policies distribute compensatory benefits arbitrarily.

[7]This will not apply as frequently as might be thought, however, if it is true that membership in a preferred group is itself an *educational* qualification. That this is so is sometimes argued on the grounds, for example, that women and black professors are necessary as "role models" for women and black students. Thomson, however, expresses doubts about arguments of this sort. . . . More important, if such arguments were strong, it would seem that a case could be made for hiring black and women professors on grounds of merit. That is, they should be hired because they can do the job better than others, not (only) because they are owed compensation. In any case, however, my argument in the text would still apply to those instances in which the candidate from the preferred group was not as qualified (in the broad sense of "qualified" in which membership in the preferred group is one qualification) as the candidates from nonpreferred groups.

[8]For a defense of the provision of monetary compensation or reparations, see Hugo Bedau, "Compensatory Justice and the Black Manifesto," *The Monist* 56, no. 1 (1972): 20–42.

[9]I am grateful to the American Council of Learned Societies and to Hamilton College for their support during the period the arguments set forth here were first formulated.

Discussion Questions

1. What is Simon's argument that blacks and women are not the relevant groups to which compensation should be made? Is the argument successful?

2. Simon argues that compensating individuals is not the same as compensating a group. How does he use this idea against Thomson? Criticize Simon's argument.

3. What dilemma does Simon pose for Thomson? How might Thomson reply?

Reverse Discrimination
as Unjustified

Lisa H. Newton

I have heard it argued that "simple justice" requires that we favor women and blacks in employment and educational opportunities, since women and blacks were "unjustly" excluded from such opportunities for so many years in the not so distant past. It is a strange argument, an example of a possible implication of a true proposition advanced to dispute the proposition itself, like an octopus absent-mindedly slicing off his head with a stray tentacle. A fatal confusion underlies this argument, a confusion fundamentally relevant to our understanding of the notion of the rule of law.

Reprinted from *Ethics*, Vol. 83, No. 4 (1973), 308–312. Copyright 1973 by The University of Chicago Press. Reprinted by permission of the publisher and author.

Two senses of justice and equality are involved in this confusion. The root notion of justice, progenitor of the other, is the one that Aristotle (*Nichomachean Ethics* 5.6; *Politics* 1. 2; 3.1) assumes to be the foundation and proper virtue of the political association. It is the condition which free men establish among themselves when they "share a common life in order that their association bring them self-sufficiency"—the regulation of their relationship by law, and the establishment, by law, of equality before the law. Rule of law is the name and pattern of this justice; its equality stands against the inequalities—of wealth, talent, etc.—otherwise obtaining among its participants, who by virtue of that equality are called "citizens." It is an achievement—complete, or, more frequently, partial—of certain people in certain concrete situations. It is fragile and easily disrupted by powerful individuals who discover that the blind equality of rule of law is inconvenient for their interests. Despite its obvious instability, Aristotle assumed that the establishment of justice in this sense, the creation of citizenship, was a permanent possibility for men and that the resultant association of citizens was the natural home of the species. At levels below the political association, this rule-governed equality is easily found; it is exemplified by any group of children agreeing together to play a game. At the level of the political association, the attainment of this justice is more difficult, simply because the stakes are so much higher for each participant. The equality of citizenship is not something that happens of its own accord, and without the expenditure of a fair amount of effort it will collapse into the rule of a powerful few over an apathetic many. But at least it has been achieved, at some times in some places; it is always worth trying to achieve, and eminently worth trying to maintain, wherever and to whatever degree it has been brought into being.

Aristotle's parochialism is notorious; he really did not imagine that persons other than Greeks could associate freely in justice, and the only form of association he had in mind was the Greek *polis*. With the decline of the *polis* and the shift in the center of political thought, his notion of justice underwent a sea change. To be exact, it ceased to represent a political type and became a moral ideal: the ideal of equality as we know it. This ideal demands that all men be included in citizenship—that one Law govern all equally, that all men regard all other men as fellow citizens, with the same guarantees, rights, and protections. Briefly, it demands that the circle of citizenship achieved by any group be extended to include the entire human race. Properly understood, its effect on our associations can be excellent: it congratulates us on our achievement of rule of law as a process of government but refuses to let us remain complacent until we have expanded the associations to include others within the ambit of the rules, as often and as far as possible. While one man is a slave, none of us may feel truly free. We are constantly prodded by this ideal to look for possible unjustifiable discrimination, for inequalities not absolutely required for the functioning of the society and advantageous to all. And after twenty centuries of pressure, not at all constant, from this ideal, it might be said that some progress has been made. To take the cases in point for this problem, we are now prepared to assert, as Aristotle would never have been, the equality of sexes and of persons of different colors. The ambit of American citizenship, once restricted to white males of property, has been extended to include all adult free men, then all adult males including ex-slaves, then all women. The process of acquisition of full citizenship was for these groups a sporadic trail of half-measures, even now not complete; the steps on the road to full equality are marked by legislation and judicial decisions which are only recently concluded and still often not enforced. But the fact that we can now discuss the possibility of favoring such groups in hiring shows that over the area that concerns us, at least, full equality is presupposed as a basis for discussion. To that extent, they are full citizens, fully protected by the law of the land.

It is important for my argument that the moral ideal of equality be recognized as logically distinct from the condition (or virtue) of justice in the political sense. Justice in this sense exists *among* a citizenry, irrespective of the number of the populace included in that citizenry. Further, the moral ideal is parasitic upon the political virtue, for "equality" is unspecified—it means nothing until we are told in what respect that equality is to be realized. In a political context, "equality" is specified as "equal rights"—equal access to the public realm, public goods and offices, equal treatment under the law—in brief, the equality of citizenship. If citizenship is not a possibility, political equality is unintelligible. The ideal emerges as a generalization of the real condition and refers back to that condition for its content.

Now, if justice (Aristotle's justice in the political sense) is equal treatment under law for all citizens, what is injustice? Clearly, injustice is the violation of that equality, discriminating for or against a group of citizens, favoring them with special immunities and privileges or depriving them of those guaranteed to the others. When the southern employer refuses to hire blacks in white-collar jobs, when Wall Street will only hire women as secretaries with new titles, when Mississippi high schools routinely flunk all black boys above ninth grade, we have examples of injustice, and we work to restore the equality of the public realm by ensuring that equal opportunity will be provided in such cases in the future. But of course, when the employers and the schools *favor* women and blacks, the same injustice is done. Just as the previous discrimination did, this reverse discrimination violates the public equality which defines citizenship and destroys the rule of law for the areas in which these favors are granted. To the extent that we adopt a program of discrimination, reverse or otherwise, justice in the political sense is destroyed, and none of us, specifically affected or not, is a citizen, a bearer of rights —we are all petitioners for favors. And to the same extent, the ideal of equality is under-mined, for it has content only where justice obtains, and by destroying justice we render the ideal meaningless. It is, then, an ironic paradox, if not a contradiction in terms, to assert that the ideal of equality justifies the violation of justice; it is as if one should argue, with William Buckley, that an ideal of humanity can justify the destruction of the human race.

Logically, the conclusion is simple enough: all discrimination is wrong prima facie because it violates justice, and that goes for reverse discrimination too. No violation of justice among the citizens may be justified (may overcome the prima facie objection) by appeal to the ideal of equality, for that ideal is logically dependent upon the notion of justice. Reverse discrimination, then, which attempts no other justification than an appeal to equality, is wrong. But let us try to make the conclusion more plausible by suggesting some of the implications of the suggested practice of reverse discrimination in employ-ment and education. My argument will be that the problems raised there are insoluble, not only in practice but in principle.

We may argue, if we like, about what "discrimination" consists of. Do I discriminate against blacks if I admit none to my school when none of the black applicants are qualified by the tests I always give? How far must I go to root out cultural bias from my application forms and tests before I can say that I have not discriminated against those of different cultures? Can I assume that women are not strong enough to be roughnecks on my oil rigs, or must I test them individually? But this controversy, the most popular and well-argued aspect of the issue, is not as fatal as two others which cannot be avoided: if we are regarding the blacks as a "minority" victimized by discrimination, what is a "minority"? And for any group—blacks, women, whatever—that has been discriminated against, what amount of reverse discrimination wipes out the initial discrimination? Let us grant as true that women and blacks were discriminated against, even where laws forbade such discrimination, and grant for the sake of argument that a history of discrimination must be wiped out by reverse discrimination. What follows?

First, are there other groups which have been discriminated against? For they should have the same right of restitution. What about American Indians, Chicanos, Appalachian Mountain whites, Puerto Ricans, Jews, Cajuns, and Orientals? And if these are to be included, the principle according to which we specify a "minority" is simply the criterion of "ethnic (sub) group," and we're stuck with every hyphenated American in the lower-middle class clamoring for special privileges for *his* group—and with equal justification. For be it noted, when we run down the Harvard roster, we find not only a scarcity of blacks (in comparison with the proportion in the population) but an even more striking scarcity of those second-, third-, and fourth-generation ethnics who make up the loudest voice of Middle America. Shouldn't they demand *their* share? And eventually, the WASPs will have to form their own lobby, for they too are a minority. The point is simply this: there is no "majority" in America who will not mind giving up just a bit of their rights to make room for a favored minority. There are only other minorities, each of which is discriminated against by the favoring. The initial injustice is then repeated dozens of times, and if each minority is granted the same right of restitution as the others, an entire area of rule governance is dissolved into a pushing and shoving match between self-interested groups. Each works to catch the public eye and political popularity by whatever means of advertising and power politics lend themselves to the effort, to capitalize as much as possible on temporary popularity until the restless mob picks another group to feel sorry for. Hardly an edifying spectacle, and in the long run no one can benefit: the pie is no larger—it's just that instead of setting up and enforcing rules for getting a piece, we've turned the contest into a free-for-all, requiring much more effort for no larger a reward. It would be in the interests of all the participants to reestablish an objective rule to govern the process, carefully enforced and the same for all.

Second, supposing that we do manage to agree in general that women and blacks (and all the others) have some right of restitution, some right to a privileged place in the structure of opportunities for a while, how will we know when that while is up? How much privilege is enough? When will the guilt be gone, the price paid, the balance restored? What recompense is right for centuries of exclusion? What criterion tells us when we are done? Our experience with the Civil Rights movement shows us that agreement on these terms cannot be presupposed: a process that appears to some to be going at a mad gallop into a black takeover appears to the rest of us to be at a standstill. Should a practice of reverse discrimination be adopted, we may safely predict that just as some of us begin to see "a satisfactory start toward righting the balance," others of us will see that we "have already gone too far in the other direction" and will suggest that the discrimination ought to be reversed again. And such disagreement is inevitable, for the point is that we could not *possibly* have any criteria for evaluating the kind of recompense we have in mind. The context presumed by any discussion of restitution is the context of rule of law: law sets the rights of men and simultaneously sets the method for remedying the violation of those rights. You may exact suffering from others and/or damage payments for yourself if and only if the others have violated your rights; the suffering you have endured is not sufficient reason for them to suffer. And remedial rights exist only where there is law: primary human rights are useful guides to legislation but cannot stand as reasons for awarding remedies for injuries sustained. But then, the context presupposed by any discussion of restitution is the context of preexistent full citizenship. No remedial rights could exist for the excluded; neither in law nor in logic does there exist a right to *sue* for a standing to sue.

From these two considerations, then, the difficulties with reverse discrimination become evident. Restitution for a disadvantaged group whose rights under the law have been violated is possible by legal means, but restitution for a disadvantaged group whose grievance is that there was no law to protect them simply is not. First, outside of the area of justice defined by the law, no sense can be made of "the group's rights," for no law recognizes that group or the individuals in it, qua members, as bearers of rights (hence *any* group can constitute itself as a disadvantaged minority in some sense and demand similar restitution). Second, outside of the area of protection of law, no sense can be made of the violation of rights (hence the amount of the recompense cannot be decided by any objective criterion). For both reasons, the practice of reverse discrimination undermines the foundation of the very ideal in whose name it is advocated; it destroys justice, law, equality, and citizenship itself, and replaces them with power struggles and popularity contests.

Discussion Questions

1. What is the importance of "rule-governed equality" for Newton's view? How does she believe reverse discrimination violates rule-governed equality? Criticize Newton's argument.

2. How does Newton distinguish between equality and justice? What objections can you see to her discussion on this point?

3. Is Newton's argument similar to the "two wrongs don't make a right" objection discussed in the introduction to this chapter? Does her discussion answer the objections to the "two wrongs . . . " argument?

4. What contradiction does Newton find in reverse discrimination? Criticize her argument.

5. Besides her principal argument, what other objections does Newton raise to reverse discrimination? How might Thomson answer her objections?

Women and Work

Dorothy L. Sayers

. . . When we hear that women have once more laid hands upon something which was previously a man's sole privilege, I think we have to ask ourselves: . . . Is it something useful, convenient, and suitable to a human being as such? Or is it merely something unnecessary to us, ugly, and adopted merely for the sake of collaring the other fellow's property? These jobs and professions, now. It is ridiculous to take on a man's job just in order to be able to say that "a woman has done it—yah!" The only decent reason for tackling any job is that it is *your* job, and *you* want to do it.

From Dorothy L. Sayers, *Are Women Human?* (William B. Eerdmans Publishing Co., 1980). Reprinted by permission of the publisher.

At this point, somebody is likely to say: "Yes, that is all very well. But it *is* the woman who is always trying to ape the man. She *is* the inferior being. You don't as a rule find the men trying to take the women's jobs away from them. They don't force their way into the household and turn women out of their rightful occupations."

Of course they do not. They have done it already.

Let us accept the idea that women should stick to their own jobs—the jobs they did so well in the good old days before they started talking about votes and women's rights. Let us return to the Middle Ages and ask what we should get then in return for certain political and educational privileges which we should have to abandon.

It is a formidable list of jobs: the whole of the spinning industry, the whole of the dyeing industry, the whole of the weaving industry. The whole catering industry and . . . the whole of the nation's brewing and distilling. All the preserving, pickling and bottling industry, all the bacon-curing. And (since in those days a man was often absent from home for months together on war or business) a very large share in the management of landed estates. Here are the women's jobs—and what has become of them? They are all being handled by men. It is all very well to say that woman's place is the home—but modern civilization has taken all these pleasant and profitable activities out of the home, where the women looked after them, and handed them over to big industry, to be directed and organized by men at the head of large factories. Even the dairy-maid in her simple bonnet has gone, to be replaced by a male mechanic in charge of a mechanical milking plant.

Now, it is very likely that men in big industries do these jobs better than the women did them at home. The fact remains that the home contains much less of interesting activity than it used to contain. What is more, the home has so shrunk to the size of a small flat that—even if we restrict woman's job to the bearing and rearing of families—there is no room for her to do even that. It is useless to urge the modern woman to have twelve children, like her grandmother. Where is she to put them when she has got them? And what modern man wants to be bothered with them? It is perfectly idiotic to take away women's traditional occupations and then complain because she looks for new ones. Every woman is a human being—one cannot repeat that too often—and a human being *must* have occupation, if he or she is not to become a nuisance to the world.

I am not complaining that the brewing and baking were taken over by the men. If they can brew and bake as well as women or better, then by all means let them do it. But they cannot have it both ways. If they are going to adopt the very sound principle that the job should be done by the person who does it best, then that rule must be applied universally. If the women make better office-workers than men, they must have the office work. If any individual woman is able to make a first-class lawyer, doctor, architect or engineer, then she must be allowed to try her hand at it. Once lay down the rule that the job comes first and you throw that job open to every individual, man or woman, fat or thin, tall or short, ugly or beautiful, who is able to do that job better than the rest of the world.

Now, it is frequently asserted that, with women, the job does not come first. What (people cry) are women doing with this liberty of theirs? What woman really prefers a job to a home and family? Very few, I admit. It is unfortunate that they should so often have to make the choice. A man does not, as a rule, have to choose. He gets both. In fact, if he wants the home and family, he usually has to take the job as well, if he can get it. Nevertheless, there have been women, such as Queen Elizabeth and Florence Nightingale, who had the choice, and chose the job and made a success of it. And there have been and are many men who have sacrificed their careers for women—sometimes, like Antony or Parnell, very disastrously. When it comes to a *choice,* then every man or woman has to choose as an individual human being, and, like a human being, take the consequences.

As human beings! I am always entertained—and also irritated—by the news-mongers who inform us, with a bright air of discovery, that they have questioned a number of female workers and been told by one and all that they are "sick of the office and would love to get out of it." In the name of God, what human being is *not,* from time to time, heartily sick of the office and would *not* love to get out of it? The time of female office-workers is daily wasted in sympathizing with disgruntled male colleagues who yearn to get out of the office. No human being likes work—not day in and day out. Work is notoriously a curse—and if women *liked* everlasting work they would not be human beings at all. *Being* human beings, they like work just as much and just as little as anybody else. They dislike perpetual washing and cooking just as much as perpetual typing and standing behind shop counters. Some of them prefer typing to scrubbing—but that does not mean that they are not, as human beings, entitled to damn and blast the typewriter when they feel that way. The number of men who daily damn and blast typewriters is incalculable; but that does not mean that they would be happier doing a little plain sewing. Nor would the women.

I have admitted that there are very few women who would put their job before every earthly consideration. I will go further and assert that there are very few men who would do it either. In fact, there is perhaps only one human being in a thousand who is passionately interested in his job for the job's sake. The difference is that if that one person in a thousand is a man, we say, simply, that he is passionately keen on his job; if she is a woman, we say she is a freak. . . .

Which brings us back to this question of what jobs, if any, are women's jobs. Few people would go so far as to say that all women are well fitted for all men's jobs. When people do say this, it is particularly exasperating. It is stupid to insist that there are as many female musicians and mathematicians as male—the facts are otherwise, and the most we can ask is that if a Dame Ethel Smyth or a Mary Somerville turns up, she shall be allowed to do her work without having aspersions cast either on her sex or her ability. What we ask is to be human individuals, however peculiar and unexpected. It is no good saying: "You are a little girl and therefore you ought to like dolls"; if the answer is, "But I don't," there is no more to be said. Few women happen to be natural born mechanics; but if there is one, it is useless to try and argue her into being something different. What we must *not* do is to argue that the occasional appearance of a female mechanical genius proves that all women would be mechanical geniuses if they were educated. They would not.

Discussion Questions

1. How do Sayers's points about women and work relate to affirmative action? Would Sayers be likely to support affirmative action programs? Why or why not?

2. What relevance does the takeover by men of industries once run by women have to debates about work and women? How could it be used as an argument for affirmative action? Could it be used as an argument *against* affirmative action? How?

3. Sayers answers the argument that "the job does not come first" for women by arguing that it does not come first with most men either. Is this an adequate answer? Why or why not?

4. Sayers says that "the most we can ask" is that women with the required talents be given access to jobs they can do, even if those jobs remain largely men's jobs. Do you agree that this is "the most we can ask"? Why or why not?

5. How is Sayers's position on women and work related to her general view of women in the selection from her work in Part II? Support or criticize her view.

Ancient Wrongs and Modern Rights

George Sher

It is widely acknowledged that persons may deserve compensation for the effects of wrong acts performed before they were born. It is such acts that are in question when we say that blacks deserve compensation because their forebears were originally brought to this country as slaves, or that American Indians deserve compensation for the unjust appropriation of their ancestors' land. But although some principle of compensation for the lasting effects of past wrongs seems appropriate, the proper temporal scope of that principle is not clear. We may award compensation for the effects of wrongs done as many as ten or twenty generations ago; but what of wrongs done a hundred generations ago? Or five hundred or a thousand? Are there any temporal limits at all to the wrong acts whose enduring effects may call for compensation? In the first section of this paper, I shall discuss several reasons for addressing these neglected questions. In subsequent sections, I shall discuss some possible ways of resolving them.

I

A natural initial reaction to questions about compensation for the effects of ancient wrongs is that these questions are, in the main, hopelessly unrealistic. In the case of blacks, Indians, and a few analogous groups, we may indeed have enough information to suggest that most current group members are worse off than they would be in the absence of some initial wrong. But if the wrong act was performed even longer ago, or if the persons currently suffering its effects do not belong to a coherent and easily identified group, then such information will *not* be available to us. There are surely some persons alive today who would be better off if the Spanish Inquisition had not taken place, or if the Jews had never been originally expelled from the land of Canaan. However, to discover who these persons are and how much better off they would be, we would have to draw on far more genealogical, causal, and counterfactual knowledge than anyone can reasonably be expected to possess. Because this information is not and never will be completely available, the question of who, if anyone, deserves compensation for the current effects of these wrongs will never be answered. But if so, why bother asking it?

This relaxed approach to compensation has the virtue of realism. The suggestion that we might arrive at a complete understanding of the effects of ancient wrongs is a

From *Philosophy and Public Affairs*, vol. 10, no. 1. Copyright © 1981 by Princeton University Press. Reprinted by permission of the publisher.

philosopher's fantasy and nothing more. Nevertheless, despite its appeal, I think we cannot rest content with a totally pragmatic dismissal of the issue of compensating for ancient wrongs. For one thing, even if compensatory justice is a partially unrealizable ideal, its theoretical limits will retain an intrinsic interest. For another, even if we cannot now ascertain which persons deserve compensation for the effects of ancient wrongs, the insight that such persons exist might itself suggest new obligations to us. In particular, if the victims of even the most ancient of wrongs can qualify for compensation, and if our current compensatory efforts are therefore aimed at only a small subset of those who deserve it, then we will at least be obligated to enlarge the subset by extending our knowledge of the effects of ancient wrongs as far as possible. Alternatively, the discovery that desert of compensation is not invariant with respect to temporal distance might force us to reduce our compensatory efforts in certain areas.

These considerations suggest that clarifying the theoretical status of ancient wrongs may dictate certain (rather marginal) changes in our actual compensatory policies. But there is also another, far more significant implication which such clarification might have. Given the vastness of historical injustice, and given the ramification of every event over time, it seems reasonable to assume that most or all current individuals have been both benefited and harmed by numerous ancient wrongs. For (just about) every current person *P*, there are likely to be some ancient wrongs which have benefited *P* but harmed others, and other ancient wrongs which have benefited others but harmed *P*. In light of this, neither the distribution of goods which actually prevails nor that which would prevail in the absence of all recent wrongs is likely to resemble the distribution which would prevail in the absence of all historical wrongs. But if so, and if the effects of ancient wrongs do call as strongly for compensation as the effects of recent ones, then it seems that neither compensating nor not compensating for the known effects of recent wrongs will be just. On the one hand, since the point of compensating for the effects of wrong acts is to restore a just distribution of goods among the affected parties, the injustice of the distribution that would prevail in the absence of recent wrongs will undermine our rationale for restoring it. However, on the other hand, even if that distribution is unjust, the distribution that actually prevails is no better; and so a failure to compensate for recent wrongs will be every bit as unpalatable. The only strategy that *is* just that of restoring the distribution that would have prevailed in the absence of all historical wrongs. But, as we have seen, we will never have the information to do this.

How to respond to this combination of pervasive injustice and indefeasible ignorance is a complicated and difficult question. One possible strategy is to argue that even if compensating for recent wrongs would not restore full justice, it would at least bring us substantially closer to a totally just distribution than we are now. A second alternative is to revise our account of the aim of compensating for recent wrongs—to say that the point of doing this is not to restore a fully just distribution among the affected parties, but rather only to nullify the effects of one particular set of injustices. A third is to accept Nozick's suggestion that we "view some patterned principles of distributive justice [e.g., egalitarianism or Rawls' difference principle] as rough rules of thumb meant to approximate the general results of applying the principle of rectification of injustice."[1] A fourth is to abandon hope of achieving justice by either compensating or not compensating, and simply start afresh by redistributing goods along egalitarian or Rawlsian lines. If their positions can be grounded in either of the latter ways, egalitarians and Rawlsians may hope to rebut the charge that they ignore such historical considerations as entitlement and desert.[2] But as interesting as these issues are, it would be premature for us to consider them further here. The choice among the suggested options arises only if ancient wrongs do call for compensation as strongly as recent ones; and so that claim must be investigated first. The discussion so far has been merely to establish the claim's importance. Having done that, we may now turn to the question of its truth.

II

Intuitively, the effects of ancient wrongs do not seem to call as strongly for compensation as the effects of recent ones. Indeed, the claim that persons deserve compensation even for the effects of wrongs done in biblical times appears to be a reductio of the ideal of compensatory justice. But we should be wary of intuitions of this sort. It is perfectly possible that they reflect only an awareness of the epistemological difficulty of establishing desert of compensation for ancient wrongs; and if they do, then all the problems limned above will remain untouched. To clarify the force of our intuitions, we must ask whether they can be traced to any deeper source in the notion of compensation itself. Is there anything *about* compensation which reduces the likelihood that ancient wrongs may call for it? More precisely, are there any necessary conditions for desert of compensation which become progressively harder to satisfy over time?

Prima facie, the answer to this question is clearly yes. On its standard interpretation, compensation is the restoration of a good or level of well-being which someone would have enjoyed if he had not been adversely affected by another's wrong act. To enjoy (almost) any good, a person must exist. Hence, it seems to be a necessary condition for X's deserving compensation for the effect of Y's doing A that X would have existed in A's absence. Where A is an act performed during X's lifetime, this requirement presents few problems. However, as A recedes into the past, it becomes progressively more likely that the effects of the non-performance of A will include X's non-existence. If X's currently low level of well-being is due to the defrauding of his great-grandfather in Europe, the very same fraudulent act which reduced X's great-grandfather to poverty may be what caused him to emigrate to America and so to meet X's great-grandmother. Because the prevalence of such stories increases as the relevant wrong act recedes into the past, the probability that the effects of the wrong act will call for compensation must decrease accordingly. And where the wrong act is an ancient one, that probability may approach zero.

This way of explaining our intuitions about ancient wrongs may at first seem quite compelling. But once we scrutinize it more closely, I think doubts must arise. If X cannot deserve compensation for the effects of A unless X would have existed in the absence of A, then not only ancient wrongs, but also the slave trade, the theft of the Indians' land, and many other acts whose effects are often deemed worthy of compensation will turn out to be largely non-compensable. As Lawrence Davis notes, "were we to project the 200 years of our country's history in a rectified movie, the cast of characters would surely differ significantly from the existing cast."[3] Moreover, even if we were to accept this conclusion, as Michael Levin has urged that we do,[4] further problems would remain. Even in the case of some wrong acts performed very shortly before their victims' existence (for example, acts of environmental pollution causing massive genetic damage), it seems reasonable to suppose that it is not the victim, but rather some other person, who would exist in the absence of the wrong act. And there are also cases in which wrong acts do not produce but rather preserve the lives of their victims, as when a kidnapping accidentally prevents a child from perishing in the fire that subsequently destroys his home. Since compensation may clearly be deserved in all such cases, it seems that the proposed necessary condition for deserving it will have to be rejected.

If we do wish to reject that necessary condition, there are at least two alternatives available to us. One is to alter our interpretation of the counterfactual presupposed by the standard account of compensation—to read that counterfactual as requiring not simply that X be better off in the closest possible world in which A is absent, but rather that X be better off in the closest possible world in which A is absent *and X exists*. A more drastic alternative, for which I have argued elsewhere, is to modify the standard view of compensation itself—to say that compensating X is not necessarily restoring X to the level of well-being which *he* would have occupied in the absence of A, but rather that it is restoring X to the level of well-being that some *related* person or group of persons would have occupied in the absence of A.[5] Although both suggestions obviously require further work,[6] it is clear that neither yields the unacceptable consequences of the simpler account. However, it is also true that neither implies that the probability of desert of compensation will decrease over time. Hence, the shift to either of them will call for a different explanation of our intuitions about compensation for ancient wrongs.

III

A more promising way of explaining these intuitions can be extracted from a recent article by David Lyons. In an important discussion of the American Indian claims to land,[7] Lyons argues that property rights are unlikely to be so stable as to persist intact through all sorts of social changes. Even on Nozick's extremely strong conception of property rights, the "Lockean Proviso" implies that such rights must give way when changing conditions bring it about that some individuals are made worse off by (originally legitimate) past acts of acquisition. In particular, this may happen when new arrivals are disadvantaged by their lack of access to established holdings. Because property rights do thus change over time, Lyons argues that today's Indians would probably not have a right to their ancestors' land even if it had *not* been illegitimately taken. Hence, restoring the land or its equivalent to them is unlikely to be warranted as compensation. But if this is true of America's Indians, then it must be true to an even greater degree of the victims of ancient wrongs. If property rights are so unstable, then rights held thousands of years ago would surely not have survived the world's drastic population growth, the industrial revolution, or other massive social changes. Hence, their violation in the distant past may appear to call for no compensation now.

Because wrongful harm and deprivation of property are so closely connected, this approach initially seems to offer a comprehensive solution to our problem. However, here again, a closer examination reveals difficulties. First, even if we grant Lyons' point that changing conditions can alter people's entitlements and that new arrivals may be entitled to fair shares of goods already held, it remains controversial to suppose that these fair shares must be equal ones. If the shares need not be equal, then the instability of property rights may well permit the preservation of substantial legitimate inequalities through both time and inheritance. Moreover, second, even if property rights do fade completely over time, there will still be many current persons whom ancient wrongs have in one way or another prevented from acquiring *new* property rights. Because these new rights would ex hypothesi not have been continuations of any earlier rights, they would not have been affected by the instability of those earlier rights. Hence, the persons who would have held them will apparently still deserve to be compensated. Finally, despite the close connection between property and well-being, there are surely many ways of being harmed which do not involve violations of property rights at all. As many writers on preferential treatment have suggested, a person can also be harmed by being deprived of self-respect, by being rendered less able to compete for opportunities when they arise, and in other related ways. Although these claims must be scrutinized with considerable care, at least some appear clearly true. Moreover, there is no reason to believe that the psychological effects of a wrong act are any less long-lived, or any less likely to be transmitted from generation to generation, than their economic counterparts. It is true that the psychological effects of wrong acts are often themselves the result of property violations; but the case for compensating for them does not appear to rest on this. Because it does not, that case seems compatible with any view of the stability of property rights.

IV

Given these difficulties, Lyons' insight about property does not itself resolve our problem. However, it suggests a further line of inquiry which may. We have seen that because property rights are not necessarily stable, we cannot assume that anyone who retains his property in a world without the initial wrong is entitled to all (or even any) of it in that world. A world in which that particular wrong is rectified may still be morally deficient in other respects. Because of this, the real question is not how much property the victim *does* have in the rectified world, but rather how much he *should* have in it. Moreover, to avoid arbitrariness, we must say something similar about persons whose losses do not involve property as well. If this is not generally recognized, it is probably because deleting the initial wrong act, which is properly only necessary for establishing what the victim should have had, is easily taken to be sufficient for it. But whatever the source of the oversight, the fact that the operative judgments about rectified worlds are themselves normative is a major complication in the theory of compensation; for normative judgments do not always transfer smoothly to the actual world. By spelling out the conditions under which they do not, we may hope finally to clarify the status of ancient wrongs.

Let us begin by considering a normative judgment which plainly does not carry over from a rectified world to our own. Suppose that X, a very promising student, has been discriminatorily barred from entering law school; and suppose further that although X knows he will be able to gain entry in another year, he becomes discouraged and so does not reapply. In a rectified world Wr which lacks the initial discrimination, X studies diligently and eventually becomes a prominent lawyer who enjoys great prestige and a high salary. In that world, we may suppose, X is fully entitled to these goods. However, in the actual world, Wa, the compensation to which X is entitled appears to fall far short of them or their equivalent. Hence, our normative judgment does not fully carry over from Wr to Wa.

Why does our normative judgment about Wr not fully carry over? In part, the answer to this question seems to lie in X's own contribution to the actual course of events. Given more perseverance, X could have avoided most of the effects of the initial wrong act; and this certainly seems relevant to what he should now have. However, quite apart from what X does or does not do in Wa, there is also another factor to consider here. Insofar as X's entitlements in Wr stem from what X does in law school and thereafter, they arise through a sequence of actions which X does not perform in Wr until well after the original wrong, and which he does not perform in Wa at all. These entitlements are not merely inherited by X in Wr, but rather are created anew by his actions in that world. But if X's actions in Wr are themselves the source of some of his entitlements in that world, then it will make little sense to suppose that those entitlements can exist in an alternative world (that is, the actual one) which lacks the generating actions. To say this would be to hold that what a person should have may be determined by certain actions which neither he nor anyone else has actually performed.[8] We are plainly unwilling to say things like this in other contexts (nobody would say that a person deserves to be punished simply because he would have committed a crime if given the opportunity),[9] and they seem to be no more supportable here.

In view of these considerations, it seems that the transferability of a person's entitlements from a rectified world to the actual one is limited by two distinct factors. It is limited first by the degree to which one's actual entitlements have been diminished by one's own omissions in this world, and second by the degree to which one's entitlements in a rectified world are generated anew by one's own actions there. In the case of X, this means that what transfers is not all of his entitlements in Wr, but at best his entitlement to the basic opportunity to *acquire* these entitlements—in this instance, the entitlement to (the value of) the lost opportunity to attend law school. Of course, the value of this opportunity is itself determined by the value of the further goods whose acquisition it makes possible. But the opportunity is clearly not worth as much as the goods themselves.

This reasoning, if sound, sheds considerable light on the general concept of compensation. But because the reasoning applies equally to compensation for ancient *and* recent wrongs, its connection with our special problem about ancient wrongs is not yet clear. To bring out this connection, we must explore its implications over time. So let us now suppose that not just X, but also X's son Z, has benefited from X's admission to law school in Wr. As a result of X's wealth and status, Z enjoys certain advantages in Wr that he does not enjoy in Wa. Assuming that X is fully entitled to his advantages in Wr, and assuming also that X only confers advantages upon Z in morally legitimate ways (whatever these are), it follows that Z too is fully entitled to his advantages in Wr. Under these circumstances, Z may well deserve some compensation in Wa. However, because Z's entitlement to his advantages in Wr stems directly from X's exercise of his own entitlements in that world, it would be anomalous to suppose that the former entitlements could transfer in greater proportion than the latter. Moreover, and crucially, given the principles already adduced, it seems that Z's entitlements in Wr will have to transfer to Wa in even *smaller* proportion than X's.

The reason for this diminution in transferability is easy to see. Just as the transferability of X's entitlements is limited by certain facts about X's omissions in Wa and X's actions in Wr, so too is the transferability of Z's entitlements limited by similar facts about Z's omissions in Wa and Z's actions in Wr. More specifically, the transferability of Z's entitlements is also limited by Z's own failure to make the most of his opportunities in Wa and by the degree to which Z's entitlements in Wr have arisen through his use of his own special opportunities there. Of course, the opportunities available to Z in Wr and Wa may be very different from the opportunity to attend law school; but this difference is hardly a relevant one. Whether Z's advantages in Wr and Wa take the form of wealth, political power, special skills or abilities, or simply self-confidence, the fact remains that they are, inter alia, potential opportunities for him to acquire further entitlements. Because of this, the way they contribute to his total entitlements in these worlds must continue to affect the degree to which his entitlements in Wr can transfer to Wa.

Once all of this is made clear, the outline of a general solution to our problem about ancient wrongs should begin to emerge. Because the transferability of Z's entitlements is diminished twice over by the contribution of actions performed in Wr and omitted in Wa, while that of X's entitlements is diminished only once by this contribution, it follows that Z is likely to deserve proportionately less compensation for the effects of the original wrong than X; and Z's offspring, if any, will deserve proportionately less compensation still. Moreover, since few original entitlements are preserved intact over succeeding generations (quite apart from any instability of property rights, the consumption of goods and the natural non-inheritability of many entitlements must each take a large toll), the progressive diminution in the transferability of entitlements from Wr to Wa must be absolute, not just proportional. But if the transferability of entitlements from rectified worlds does decrease with every generation, then over the course of very many generations, any such transferability can be expected to become vanishingly small. Where the initial wrong was done many hundreds of years ago, almost all of the difference between the victim's entitlements in the actual world and his entitlements in a rectified world can be expected to stem from the actions of various intervening agents in the two alternative worlds. Little or none of it will be the automatic effect of the initial wrong act itself. Since compensation is warranted only for disparities in entitlements which *are* the automatic effect of the initial wrong act, this means that there will be little or nothing left to compensate for.

V

This approach to the problem posed by ancient wrongs is not dissimilar to the one extracted from Lyons' discussion. Like Lyons, we have argued that a proper appreciation of the entitlements upon which claims to compensation are based suggest that these claims must fade with time. However, whereas Lyons argued that the entitlement to property itself fades with time, we have held instead that it is the transferability of that and other entitlements from rectified worlds to the actual one which becomes progressively weaker. By thus relocating the basic instability, we avoid the objections that the analysis of property rights is controversial, that some claims to compensation do not view the right to the lost property as continually held in a rectified world, and that other claims to compensation do not involve property at all. But although our account is not open to these objections, it may seem to invite others just as serious. More specifically, it may seem that our presupposition that entitlements are historically transmitted is itself controversial, that our distinction between newly generated and continuing entitlements is problematical, and that we have failed to account satisfactorily for the status of wrongs that are neither recent nor ancient. In this final section, I shall consider each of these objections in its turn.

The first objection, that the historical transmission of entitlements is as controversial as any analysis of property, is easily answered. Put briefly, the answer is that this presupposition *is* controversial, but that unlike any special view of property rights, it is internal to the very notion of compensation which generates our problem. If entitlements were never historically transmitted—if a person's entitlements at a given time were never derived from the prior entitlements of others—then someone like Z would not be entitled to any special advantages in Wr, and so would not deserve any compensation in Wa. Moreover, although it is less obvious, the same point holds even if Z is only minimally well off in Wr, but is extremely disadvantaged in Wa. It may seem, in that case, that Z's entitlements in Wr are independent of X's—that Z, like everyone else in Wr, is entitled to a certain decent minimum no matter what X was entitled to or did in the past. But even if this is so, it cannot form the basis for compensating Z for the effects of the initial wrong act; for if Z *is* absolutely entitled to such a minimum in Wr, then he will also be absolutely entitled to it in Wa, and so the original wrong act will drop out as irrelevant.

Given these considerations, some form of historical transmission of entitlements is plainly presupposed by any view permitting compensation for a variety of prenatal (and so a fortiori ancient) wrongs.[10] But just because of this, there may seem to be a problem with our central distinction between continuing and newly produced entitlements. This distinction appeared plausible enough when we first considered X's entitlements in Wr.

However, once we take seriously the fact that people can transmit, confer, and waive their entitlements, the distinction seems to blur. When a parent confers advantages upon his children by educating or bequeathing wealth to them, the entitlements acquired are both related to earlier ones *and* the product of new generating actions. Moreover, something similar may be said to hold even when someone merely retains his own entitlement to property; for he too is acting at least in the sense that he is refraining from transferring or waiving that entitlement. Because human actions and omissions are thus crucial in perpetuating so many entitlements, our premise that this role cancels transferability from rectified worlds may well appear too strong. Given this premise, it seems to follow that not only ancient wrongs, but also recent ones, such as systematic racial discrimination, and perhaps even fresh property crimes, are largely non-compensable.

These worries are serious ones, and would require careful consideration in any full account of compensation. Here, however, I shall only outline what I take to be the correct response to them. Put briefly, my response is that the transferability of entitlements from rectified worlds should be viewed as disrupted not by *all* intervening acts or omissions in those worlds, but rather only by those acts or omissions which alter previously established structures of entitlements. When an entitlement is already established in a rectified world and is naturally stable over a period of time, its retention during that period is totally explainable in terms of its initial acquisition. In this case, the entitlement need not be attributed to any further doings of the agent; and so those doings seem irrelevant to the entitlement's transferability to the actual world. Moreover, assuming the legitimacy of inheritance, something similar may well hold for advantages that are transmitted to one's offspring; for here again, the resulting entitlements can be viewed as natural continuations of initial ancestral acts of acquisition. Of course, the principle of the conservation of entitlements which underlies these remarks would require considerable elaboration to be fully convincing. But something like it does seem initially plausible; and anything along these lines will nicely preserve the conclusion that desert of compensation is not entirely momentary and evanescent.

A final difficulty remains. Our argument has been that desert of compensation fades gradually over time, and that ancient wrongs therefore call for no significant amounts of compensation. But even if this is correct, it does not dispose of the vast intermediate class of wrongs which are not ancient, but were still done one or more generations ago. Since the process we have described is gradual, our account suggests that such wrongs do call for some compensation, although not as much as comparable recent ones. But if this is so, then our account may seem at once too strong and too weak. The account may seem too strong because it will classify as intermediate even the wrongs done to blacks and Indians—wrongs which appear to be among our paradigms of full compensability. However, the account may also seem too weak, since it implies that very many partially compensable wrongs remain undiscovered, and that our problem of how to act justly in the face of incurable ignorance is therefore unresolved. Because any response to one aspect of this objection will only aggravate the other, the difficulty seems intractable.

But this dilemma is surely overdrawn. On the side of the claims of blacks and Indians, it may first be said that even if the initial wrongs to these persons do go back several centuries, the real source of their claims to compensation may lie elsewhere. As Lyons notes, the truly compensable wrong done to the Indians may be not the initial appropriation of their land, but rather the more recent acts of discrimination and neglect which grew out of this; and the same may hold, mutatis mutandis, for the truly compensable wrongs done to blacks.[11] Moreover, even if the compensable wrongs to blacks and Indians do go back a number of generations, they may be highly atypical of other wrongs of that period. We have seen that one reason that compensability fades over time is that victims neglect reasonable opportunities to acquire equivalent entitlements; and so if slavery or the appropriation of Indian lands have made it specially difficult for their victims to recoup their lost entitlements, then these wrongs may call for far more compensation than others of similar vintage. Here our earlier results provide a natural framework for further inquiry. Finally, even if these suggestions do not establish full compensability for blacks and Indians, they do at least promise very substantial compensation for them; and this is perhaps all that is needed to satisfy our intuitions on the matter.

The other horn of the dilemma, that this account leaves untouched our incurable ignorance about past compensable wrongs, is also overstated. The account does leave us unable to diagnose more than a small fraction of the past wrongs requiring compensation; but by itself, this only implies that we cannot right all of history's wrongs. The deeper worry, that in rectifying one injustice we may only be reverting to another, is at least mitigated by the fact that the most significant period of history from the standpoint of compensation is also the best known. Given this fact, the likelihood that our compensatory efforts will make things better rather than worse is greatly increased. If this solution is less precise than we might wish, it is perhaps the best that we have a right to expect.[12]

Notes

[1]Robert Nozick, *Anarchy, State, and Utopia* (New York: Basic Books, 1974), p. 231.

[2]For development of this charge as it pertains to entitlement, see Nozick, *Anarchy, State, and Utopia,* chap. 7. For discussion involving desert, see George Sher, "Effort, Ability, and Personal Desert," *Philosophy & Public Affairs* 8, no. 4 (Summer 1979): 361–376.

[3]Lawrence Davis, "Comments on Nozick's Entitlement Theory," *The Journal of Philosophy* 73, no. 21 (2 December, 1976): 842.

[4]Michael E. Levin, "Reverse Discrimination, Shackled Runners, and Personal Identity," *Philosophical Studies* 37, no. 2 (February 1980): 139–149.

[5]George Sher, "Compensation and Transworld Personal Identity," *The Monist* 62, no. 3 (July 1979): 378–391.

[6]Although I have presented them as alternatives, the two suggestions need not be viewed as mutually exclusive. Indeed, the most promising approach appears to be to combine them. The first suggestion appears the more natural in those cases where there are many close alternative worlds that lack the initial wrong act but contain the victim himself; while the second appears indispensable in those instances where the initial wrong is so intimately associated with the victim's existence that there is no such world.

[7]David Lyons, "The New Indian Claims and the Original Rights to Land," *Social Theory and Practice* 4, no. 3 (1977): 249–272.

[8]This point is discussed in a more limited context in George Sher, "Justifying Reverse Discrimination in Employment," *Philosophy & Public Affairs* 4, no. 2 (Winter 1975): 166 ff.

[9]For discussion, see Thomas Nagel, "Moral Luck," in his *Mortal Questions* (Cambridge: Cambridge University Press, 1979), pp. 24–38.

[10]Thus, compensation is in one sense a strongly conservative notion. One can consistently advocate redistributive measures on compensatory grounds or on non-historical consequentialist grounds; but not, I think, on both grounds together.

[11]Lyons, "The New Indian Claims," esp. pp. 268–271. See also Boris Bittker, *The Case for Black Reparations* (New York: Random House, 1973), chap. 2.

---

[12]I am grateful to Patricia Kitcher, Philip Kitcher, and Alan Wertheimer for their helpful comments and suggestions.

Discussion Questions

1. What is Sher's reply to the "pragmatic dismissal" of ancient wrongs? Can you find any objections to Sher's argument?
2. What is Sher's argument about the effect of deciding ancient wrongs deserve compensation? How could you reply to this argument?
3. What arguments does Sher consider in favor of the view that ancient wrongs do not call as strongly for compensation? How does he reply to these arguments? Are his replies successful?
4. How does Sher use the idea of alternate worlds in his arguments? How might this use of alternate worlds be criticized?
5. What is Sher's own view? What arguments does he give for it? Are these arguments successful?
6. What objections to his own view does Sher consider? Are his replies successful?

Suggested Readings for Chapter Seven

Blackstone, William and Robert Henlep, eds. *Social Justice and Preferential Treatment.* Athens: University of Georgia Press, 1971.

Cohen, Marshal, Thomas Nagel, and Thomas Scanlon, eds. *Equality and Preferential Treatment.* Princeton, N.J.: Princeton University Press, 1977.

English, Jane. *Sex Equality.* Engelwood Cliffs, N.J.: Prentice Hall, 1977.

Gross, Barry. *Reverse Discrimination.* Buffalo, N.Y.: Prometheus Books, 1977.

8

Pornography and Privacy

Two major issues arise with regard to pornography: Is the production and use of pornography right or wrong? Is the regulation of pornography by the state right or wrong? The two questions are independent. Even if pornography is not clearly wrong, the state may have a right to regulate it as it does other activities such as banking or moneylending, which are not wrong in themselves but may be open to abuses. Thus, since the right to privacy is often cited as an argument against state regulation of pornography, the issues of pornography and privacy have become intertwined and will be treated together in this chapter.

Pornography might be defined as writings or pictorial representations that are intended to stimulate or titillate sexual desire. It is an important fact that pornography cannot by its nature satisfy the desires it arouses. One possible view of pornography involves the principle that if the satisfaction of a desire is legitimate, the encouragement of the desire is legitimate. Thus because satisfying the desire to eat is, in general, legitimate, writings or pictures that arouse the desire to eat are also legitimate—even if they might accidentally do harm, for example, to a person on a diet for medical reasons. On the other hand, the desire to torture and kill innocent victims is not right, and therefore writings or pictures that stimulate the desire to do this are not legitimate.

Some defenders of pornography seem to use a form of this argument when they argue that since sexual activity is not in itself wrong, depictions of sexual activity that stimulate a desire for such activity are not wrong. However, to be consistent they must admit that if some sexual activity, such as rape, is wrong, depictions of that activity are wrong if they encourage the desire for it. (An interesting corollary of this position might be that it is wrong to depict legitimate activities, such as eating, in such a way as to *discourage* desire for that activity.)

A more frequently heard argument in favor of pornography is that it is never wrong to *describe* an activity, whether that activity is right or wrong. However, even if this is so it does not settle the question of whether encouraging desire for an activity is legitimate if that activity is wrong.

Opponents of pornography sometimes feel that certain sexual activities are wrong and that pornography is wrong because it stimulates desire for those forms of activity. However, if this is their major objection to pornography it seems that to be consistent they should have no objections to vivid and desire-stimulating depictions of forms of sexual activities that they deem right, such as sexual intimacies and intercourse between faithful, loving husbands and wives—especially if the primary audience were people in a position to engage in such approved forms of sexual activity without delay or hindrance.

Some opponents of pornography, however, argue that certain forms of activity, perfectly legitimate in themselves, ought not to be enjoyed vicariously through writings or pictures, but only enjoyed in reality. One argument sometimes used in this context is that the vacarious enjoyment of some activities actually impedes real-life enjoyment of those activities.

The issue of privacy is raised on both sides of the pornography issue. Opponents of pornography sometimes argue that sexual activities are private and that depiction of such activities violates the privacy of those depicted and encourages other invasions of privacy. On the other hand, defenders of pornography sometimes argue that prohibitions or even condemnations of pornography violate *their* right to enjoy such material in privacy. As to whether the state should regulate pornography, the claim is often made that freedom of speech and artistic expression is so valuable that no writings or pictorial representations should be forbidden, even if they stimulate desires for activities that are wrong.

This argument appears related to the argument that governments should not interfere with an individual's private activities unless there is a clear and present danger. Thus the state may punish you for yelling "Fire!" in a crowded theatre, but not for saying or writing that the theatre is a firetrap if no clear and present danger is caused by your statements. (Of course, the theatre owners are free to bring a civil suit against you.) Such arguments are sometimes broadly utilitarian ones: It is better on the whole if individuals are free to express unpopular ideas or depict activities offensive to some than if the state interferes to prevent such expression.

Claims to a right to privacy are a fairly recent phenomenon. Part of the problem in evaluating such claims is clarifying just what rights are being claimed and how they are related to more familiar claims to liberty from state interference.

In the selection "Is Pornography Beneficial?" G. L. Simons argues that pornography as such has social value, even aside from any subsidiary, literary, artistic, or scientific value particular pornographic works may have. In "Pornography and Respect for Women," Ann Garry introduces an argument increasingly influential among feminists: Pornography decreases respect for women and may encourage violence against them. (In some areas, for instance, feminist groups have demonstrated against videotape rental firms that rent pornographic tapes.) Lycurgis M. Starkey gives a religiously based view of sex in literature which applies to literary works which are not necessarily considered pornographic as well as to those which are.

In a paper on privacy, H. J. McCloskey argues that any right to privacy "must be a qualified, conditional right." Finally, Charles Fried attempts to show that "privacy provides the rational context for a number of our most significant ends."

Is Pornography Beneficial?

G. L. Simons

It is not sufficient, for the objectors' case, that they demonstrate that some harm has flowed from pornography. It would be extremely difficult to show that pornography has *never* had unfortunate consequences, but we should not make too much of this. Harm has flowed from religion, patriotism, alcohol and cigarettes without this fact impelling people to demand abolition. The harm, if established, has to be weighed against a variety of considerations before a decision can be reached as to the propriety of certain laws. Of the British Obscenity Laws the Arts Council Report comments[1] that "the harm would need to be both indisputable and very dire indeed before it could be judged to outweigh the evils and anomalies inherent in the Acts we have been asked to examine."

The onus therefore is upon the anti-pornographers to demonstrate not only that harm is caused by certain types of sexual material but that the harm is considerable: if the first is difficult the second is necessarily more so, and the attempts to date have not been impressive. It is even possible to argue that easily available pornography has a number of benefits. Many people will be familiar with the *catharsis* argument whereby pornography is said to cut down on delinquency by providing would-be criminals with substitute satisfactions. This is considered later, but we mention it here to indicate that access to pornography may be socially beneficial in certain instances and that where this is possible the requirement for anti-pornographers to *justify* their objections must be stressed.

The general conclusion[2] of the U.S. Commission was that no adequate proof had been provided that pornography was harmful to individual or society—"if a case is to be made out against 'pornography' [in 1970] it will have to be made on grounds other than demonstrated effects of a damaging personal or social nature." . . .

The heresy (to some ears) that pornography is harmless is compounded by the even greater impiety that it may be beneficial. Some of us are managing to adjust to the notion that pornography is unlikely to bring down the world in moral ruin, but the idea that it may actually do good is altogether another thing. When we read of Professor Emeritus E. T. Rasmussen, a pioneer of psychological studies in Denmark and a government adviser, saying that there is a possibility "that pornography can be beneficial," many of us are likely to have *mixed* reactions, to say the least. In fact this thesis can be argued in a number of ways.

The simplest approach is to remark that people enjoy it. This can be seen to be true whether we rely on personal testimony or the most respectable index of all in capitalist society—"preparedness to pay." The appeal that pornography has for many people is hardly in dispute, and in a more sober social climate that would be justification enough. Today we are not quite puritan enough to deny that *pleasure* has a worthwhile place in human life: not many of us object to our food being tasty or our clothes being attractive. It was not always like this. In sterner times it was *de rigueur* to prepare food without spices and to wear the plainest clothes. The cult of puritanism reached its apotheosis in the most fanatical asceticism, where it was fashionable for holy men to wander off into a convenient desert and neglect the body to the point of cultivating its lice as "pearls of God." In such a bizarre philosophy pleasure was not only condemned in its sexual manifestations but in all areas where the body could conceivably take satisfaction. These days we are able to countenance pleasure in most fields but in many instances still the case for *sexual* pleasure has to be argued.

Pleasure is not of course its own justification. If it clearly leads to serious malaise, early death, or the *dis*pleasure of others, then there is something to be said against it. But the serious consequences have to be demonstrated: it is not enough to condemn certain forms of pleasurable experience on the grounds of *possible* ill effect. With such an approach *any* human activity could be censured, and freedom would have no place. In short, if something is pleasurable and its bad effects are small or nonexistent then it is to be encouraged: opposition to such a creed should be recognized as an unwholesome antipathy to human potential. Pleasure is a good except where it is harmful (and where the harmfulness is *significant*). . . .

That pornography is enjoyable to many people is the first of the arguments in its favor. In any other field this would be argument enough. It is certainly sufficient to justify many activities that have—unlike a taste for pornography—demonstrably harmful consequences. Only in a sexually neurotic society could a tool for heightening sexual enjoyment be regarded as reprehensible and such as to warrant suppression by law. The position is well summarized[3] in the *first* of the Arts Council's twelve reasons for advocating the repeal of the Obscenity Publications Acts:

> It is not for the State to prohibit private citizens from choosing what they may or may not enjoy in literature or art unless there were incontrovertible evidence that the result would be injurious to society. There is no such evidence.

A further point is that availability of pornography may *aid*, rather than frustrate normal sexual development. Thus in 1966, for example, the New Jersey Committee for the Right to Read presented the findings of a survey conducted among nearly a thousand psychiatrists and psychologists of that state. Among the various personal statements included was the view that "sexually stimulating materials" might help particular people develop a normal sex drive.[4] In similar spirit, Dr. John Money writes[5] that pornography "may encourage normal sexual development and broadmindedness," a view that may not sound well to the anti-pornographers. And even in circumstances where possible dangers of pornography are pointed out conceivable good effects are sometimes acknowledged. In a paper issued[6] by The Danish Forensic Medicine Council it is pointed out that neurotic and sexually shy people may, by reading pornographic descriptions of normal sexual activity, be freed from some of their apprehension regarding sex and may thereby attain a freer and less frustrated attitude to the sexual side of life. . . .

One argument in favor of pornography is that it can serve as a substitute for actual sexual activity involving another person or other people. This argument has two parts, relating as it does to (1) people who fantasize over *socially acceptable* modes of sexual involvement and (2) people who fantasize over types of sexual activity that would be regarded as illegal or at least immoral. The first type relates to lonely and deprived people who for one reason or another have been unable to form "normal" sexual contacts with other people; the second type are instances of the much quoted *catharsis* argument.

One writer notes[7] that pornography can serve as a substitute for both the knowledge of which some people have been deprived and the pleasure in sexual experience which they have not enjoyed. One can well imagine men or women too inhibited to secure sexual satisfaction with other adults and where explicit sexual material can alleviate some of their misery. It is facile to remark that such people should seek psychiatric assistance or even "make an effort": the factors that prevent the forming of effective sexual liaisons are just as likely to inhibit any efforts to seek medical or other assistance. Pornography provides *sex by proxy,* and in such usage it can have a clear justification.

It is also possible to imagine circumstances in which men or women—for reasons of illness, travel or bereavement—are unable to seek sexual satisfaction with spouse or other loved one. Pornography can help here too. Again it is easy to suggest that a person abstain from sexual experience, or, if having *permanently* lost a spouse, seek out another partner. Needless to say such advice is often quite impractical—and the alternative to pornography may be prostitution or adultery. Montagu notes that pornography can serve the same purpose as "dirty jokes," allowing a person to discharge harmlessly repressed and unsatisfied sexual desires.

In this spirit, Mercier (1970) is quoted by the U.S. Commission:

> . . . it is in periods of sexual deprivation—to which the young and the old are far more subject than those in their prime—that males, at any rate, are likely to reap psychological benefit from pornography.

And also Kenneth Tynan (1970):

> For men on long journeys, geographically cut off from wives and mistresses, pornography can act as a portable memory, a welcome shortcut to remembered bliss, relieving tension without involving disloyalty.

It is difficult to see how anyone could object to the use of pornography in such circumstances, other than on the grounds of a morbid anti-sexuality.

The *catharsis argument* has long been put forward to suggest that availability of pornography will neutralize "aberrant" sexual tendencies and so reduce the incidence of sex crime or clearly immoral behavior in related fields. (Before evidence is put forward for this thesis it is worth remarking that it should not be necessary to demonstrate a *reduction* in sex crime to justify repeal of the Obscenity Laws. It should be quite sufficient to show that an *increase* in crime will not ensue following repeal. We may even argue that a small increase may be tolerable if other benefits from easy access to pornography could be shown: but it is no part of the present argument to put this latter contention.)

Many psychiatrists and psychologists have favored the catharsis argument. Chesser, for instance, sees[8] pornography as a form of voyeurism in which—as with sado-masochistic material—the desire to hurt is satisfied passively. If this is so and the analogy can be extended we have only to look at the character of the voyeur—generally furtive and clandestine—to realize that we have little to fear from the pornography addict. Where consumers are preoccupied with fantasy there is little danger to the rest of us. Karpman (1959), quoted by the U.S. Commission, notes that people reading "salacious literature" are less likely to become sexual offenders than those who do not since the reading often neutralizes "aberrant sexual interests." Similarly the Kronhausens have argued that "these 'unholy' instruments" may be a safety-valve for the sexual deviate and potential sex offender. And Cairns, Paul and Wishner (1962) have remarked that *obscene materials* provide a way of releasing strong sexual urges without doing harm to others.

It is easy to see the plausibility of this argument. The popularity of all forms of sexual literature—from the superficial, *sexless,* sentimentality of the popular women's magazine to the clearest "hard-core" porn—has demonstrated over the ages the perennial appetite that people have for fantasy. To an extent, a great extent with many single people and frustrated married ones, the fantasy constitutes an important part of the sex-life. The experience may be vicarious and sterile but it self-evidently fills a need for many individuals. If literature, as a *symbol* of reality, can so involve human sensitivities it is highly likely that when the sensitivities are *distorted* for one reason or another the same sublimatory function can occur: the "perverted" or potentially criminal mentality can gain satisfaction, as does the lonely unfortunate, in *sex by proxy*. If we wanted to force the potential sex criminal onto the streets in search of a human victim perhaps we would do well to deny him his sublimatory substitutes: deny him fantasy and he will be forced to go after the real thing. . . .

The importance of this possibility should be fully faced. If a causal connection *does* exist between availability of pornographic material and a *reduction* in the amount of sex crime—and the evidence is wholly consistent with this possibility rather than its converse—then people who deliberately restrict pornography by supporting repressive legislation are prime architects of sexual offenses against the individual. The anti-pornographers would do well to note that their anxieties may be driving them into a position the exact opposite of the one they explicitly maintain—their commitment to reduce the amount of sexual delinquency in society.

The most that the anti-pornographers can argue is that at present the evidence is inconclusive. . . . But if the inconclusive character of the data is once admitted then the case for repressive legislation falls at once. For in a *free* society, or one supposedly aiming after freedom, social phenomena are, like individuals, innocent until proven guilty—and an activity will be permitted unless there is clear evidence of its harmful consequences. This point was well put—in the specific connection with pornography—by Bertrand Russell, talking[9] when he was well over 90 to Rupert Crawshay-Williams.

After noting how people beg the question of causation in instances such as the Moors murders (where the murders and the reading of de Sade *may* have a common cause), Russell ("Bertie") said that on the whole he disapproved of sadistic pornography being available. But when Crawshay-Williams put the catharsis view, that such material might provide a harmless release for individuals who otherwise may be dangerous, Russell said at once—"Oh, well, if that's true, then I don't see that there is anything against sadistic pornography. In fact it should be encouraged. . . . " When it was stressed that there was no preponderating evidence either way Russell argued that we should fall back on an overriding principle—"in this case the principle of free speech."

Thus in the absence of evidence of harm we should be permissive. Any other view is totalitarian. . . .

If human enjoyment *per se* is not to be condemned then it is not too rash to say that we *know* pornography does good. We can easily produce our witnesses to testify to experiencing pleasure. If in the face of this—and no other favorable argument—we are unable to demonstrate a countervailing harm, then the case for easy availability of pornography is unassailable. If, in such circumstances, we find some people unconvinced, it is futile to seek out further empirical data. Once we commit ourselves to the notion that the evil nature of something is axiomatic we tacitly concede that evidence is largely irrelevant to our position. If pornography never fails to fill us with predictable loathing then statistics on crime, or measured statements by careful specialists, will not be useful: our reactions will stay the same. But in this event we would do well to reflect on what our emotions tell us of our own mentality. . . .

Notes

[1]The Obscenity Laws, André Deutsch, 1969, p. 33.

[2]The *Report of the Commission on Obscenity and Pornography*, Part Three, II, Bantam Books, 1970, p. 169.

[3]The Obscenity Laws, André Deutsch, 1969, p. 35.

[4]Quoted by Isadore Rubin, "What Should Parents Do About Pornography?" *Sex in the Adolescent Years*, Fontana, 1969, p. 202.

[5]John Money, contribution to "Is Pornography Harmful to Young Children?" *Sex in the Childhood Years*, Fontana, 1971, p. 181–5.

[6]Paper from The Danish Forensic Medicine Council to The Danish Penal Code Council, Published in The Penal Code Council Report on Penalty for Pornography, Report No. 435, Copenhagen, 1966, pp. 78–80, and as appendix to *The Obscenity Laws*, pp. 120–4.

[7]Ashley Montagu, "Is Pornography Harmful to Young Children?" *Sex in the Childhood Years*, Fontana, 1971, p. 182.

[8]Eustace Chesser, *The Human Aspects of Sexual Deviation*, Arrow Books, 1971, p. 39.

[9]Rupert Crawshay-Williams, *Russell Remembered*, Oxford University Press, 1970, p. 144.

Discussion Questions

1. Simon argues that pornography should not be forbidden unless it can be shown to cause considerable harm, and that no such harm is known to result from pornography. Criticize his argument.

2. Simon states that one beneficial outcome of pornography is enjoyment. He suggests that only a "cult of puritanism" should condemn pleasurable activity that causes no major harm. Argue for or against his position.

3. Simon suggests that pornography can be a *substitute* for sexual activity. Is there anything about the nature of pornography that makes this implausible?

4. Simon considers what he calls the "catharsis" argument: that pornography may discourage rather than encourage sex crimes. Support or criticize his arguments on this point.

5. Simon presents the principle that in a free society an activity should be permitted unless there is clear evidence of harmful consequences. Do you agree? Why or why not?

Pornography and Respect for Women

Ann Garry

Pornography, like rape, is a male invention, designed to dehumanize women, to reduce the female to an object of sexual access, not to free sensuality from moralistic or parental inhibition. . . . Pornography is the undiluted essence of anti-female propaganda.

Susan Brownmiller, *Against Our Will: Men, Women and Rape*[1]

It is often asserted that a distinguishing characteristic of sexually explicit material is the degrading and demeaning portrayal of the role and status of the human female. It has been argued that erotic materials describe the female as a mere sexual object to be exploited and manipulated sexually. . . . A recent survey shows that 41 percent of American males and 46 percent of the females believe that "sexual materials lead people to lose respect for women." . . . Recent experiments suggest that such fears are probably unwarranted.

Presidential Commission on
Obscenity and Pornography[2]

The kind of apparent conflict illustrated in these passages is easy to find in one's own thinking as well. For example, I have been inclined to think that pornography is innocuous and to dismiss "moral" arguments for censoring it because many such arguments rest on an assumption I do not share—that sex is an evil to be controlled. At the same time I believe that it is wrong to exploit or degrade human beings, particularly women and others who are especially susceptible. So if pornography degrades human beings, then even if I would oppose its censorship I surely cannot find it morally innocuous.

In an attempt to resolve this apparent conflict I discuss three questions: Does pornography degrade (or exploit or dehumanize) human beings? If so, does it degrade women in ways or to an extent that it does not degrade men? If so, must pornography degrade women, as Brownmiller thinks, or could genuinely innocuous, nonsexist pornography exist? Although much current pornography does degrade women, I will argue that it is possible to have nondegrading, nonsexist pornography. However, this possibility rests on our making certain fundamental changes in our conceptions of sex and sex roles. . . .

From *Social Theory and Practice*, vol. 4. Reprinted with permission of the publisher and the author.

I

The . . . argument I will consider [here] is that pornography is morally objectionable, not because it leads people to show disrespect for women, but because pornography itself exemplifies and recommends behavior that violates the moral principle to respect persons. The content of pornography is what one objects to. It treats women as mere sex objects "to be exploited and manipulated" and degrades the role and status of women. In order to evaluate this argument, I will first clarify what it would mean for pornography itself to treat someone as a sex object in a degrading manner. I will then deal with three issues central to the discussion of pornography and respect for women: how "losing respect" for a woman is connected with treating her as a sex object; what is wrong with treating someone as a sex object; and why it is worse to treat women rather than men as sex objects. I will argue that the current content of pornography sometimes violates the moral principle to respect persons. Then, in [the concluding part] of this paper, I will suggest that pornography need not violate this principle if certain fundamental changes were to occur in attitudes about sex.

To many people, including Brownmiller and some other feminists, it appears to be an obvious truth that pornography treats people, especially women, as sex objects in a degrading manner. And if we omit "in a degrading manner," the statement seems hard to dispute: How could pornography *not* treat people as sex objects?

First, is it permissible to say that either the content of pornography or pornography itself degrades people or treats people as sex objects? It is not difficult to find examples of degrading content in which women are treated as sex objects. Some pornographic films convey the message that all women really want to be raped, that their resisting struggle is not to be believed. By portraying women in this manner, the content of the movie degrades women. Degrading women is morally objectionable. While seeing the movie need not cause anyone to imitate the behavior shown, we can call the content degrading to women because of the character of the behavior and attitudes it recommends. The same kind of point can be made about films (or books or TV commercials) with other kinds of degrading, thus morally objectionable, content—for example, racist messages.

The next step in the argument is to infer that, because the content or message of pornography is morally objectionable, we can call pornography itself morally objectionable. Support for this step can be found in an analogy. If a person takes every opportunity to recommend that men rape women, we would think not only that his recommendation is immoral but that he is immoral too. In the case of pornography, the objection to making an inference from recommended behavior to the person who recommends is that we ascribe predicates such as "immoral" differently to people than to films or books. A film vehicle for an objectionable message is still an object independent of its message, its director, its producer, those who act in it, and those who respond to it. Hence one cannot make an unsupported inference from "the content of the film is morally objectionable" to "the film is morally objectionable." Because the central points in this paper do not depend on whether pornography itself (in addition to its content) is morally objectionable, I will not try to support this inference. (The question about the relation of content to the work itself is, of course, extremely interesting; but in part because I cannot decide which side of the argument is more persuasive, I will pass.[3]) Certainly one appropriate way to evaluate pornography is in terms of the moral features of its content. If a pornographic film exemplifies and recommends morally objectionable attitudes or behavior, then its content is morally objectionable.

Let us now turn to the first of our three questions about respect and sex objects: What is the connection between losing respect for a woman and treating her as a sex object? Some people who have lived through the era in which women were taught to worry about men "losing respect" for them if they engaged in sex in inappropriate circumstances find it troublesome (or at least amusing) that feminists—supposedly "liberated" women—are outraged at being treated as sex objects, either by pornography or in any other way. The apparent alignment between feminists and traditionally "proper" women need not surprise us when we look at it more closely.

The "respect" that men have traditionally believed they have for women—hence a respect they can lose—is not a general respect for persons as autonomous beings; nor is it respect that is earned because of one's personal merits or achievements. It is respect that is an outgrowth of the "double standard." Women are to be respected because they are more pure, delicate, and fragile than men, have more refined sensibilities, and so on. Because some women clearly do not have these qualities, thus do not deserve respect, women must be divided into two groups—the good ones on the pedestal and the bad ones who have fallen from it. One's mother, grandmother, Sunday School teacher, and usually one's wife are "good" women. The appropriate behavior by which to express respect for good women would be, for example, not swearing or telling dirty jokes in front of them, giving them seats on buses, and other "chivalrous" acts. This kind of "respect" for good women is the same sort that adolescent boys in the back seats of cars used to "promise" not to lose. Note that men define, display, and lose this kind of respect. If women lose respect for women, it is not typically a loss of respect for (other) women as a class but a loss of self-respect.

It has now become commonplace to acknowledge that, although a place on the pedestal might have advantages over a place in the "gutter" beneath it, a place on the pedestal is not at all equal to the place occupied by other people. (i.e., men). "Respect" for those on the pedestal was not respect for whole, full-fledged people but for a special class of inferior beings.

If a person makes two traditional assumptions—that (at least some) sex is dirty and that women fall into two classes, good and bad—it is easy to see how that person might think that pornography could lead people to lose respect for women or that pornography is itself disrespectful to women. Pornography describes or shows women engaging in activities inappropriate for good women to engage in—or at least inappropriate for them to be seen by strangers engaging in. If one sees these women as symbolic representatives of all women, then all women fall from grace with these women. This fall is possible, I believe, because the traditional "respect" that men have had for women is not genuine, whole-hearted respect for full-fledged human beings but half-hearted respect for lesser beings, some of whom they feel the need to glorify and purify.[4] It is easy to fall from a pedestal. Can we imagine 41 percent of men and 46 percent of women answering "yes" to the question, "Do movies showing men engaging in violent acts lead people to lose respect for men?"

Two interesting asymmetries appear. The first is that losing respect for men as a class (men with power, typically Anglo men) is more difficult than losing respect for women or ethnic minorities as a class. Anglo men whose behavior warrants disrespect are more likely to be seen as exceptional cases than are women or minorities (whose "transgressions" may be far less serious). Think of the following: women are temptresses; Blacks cheat the welfare system; Italians are gangsters; but the men of the Nixon administration are exceptions—Anglo men as a class did not lose respect because of Watergate and related scandals.

The second asymmetry concerns the active and passive roles of the sexes. Men are seen in the active role. If men lose respect for women because of something "evil" done by women (such as appearing in pornography), the fear is that men will then do harm to women—not that women will do harm to men. Whereas if women lose respect for male politicians because of Watergate, the fear is still that male politicians will do harm, not that women will do harm to male politicians. This asymmetry might be a result of one way in which our society thinks of sex as bad—as harm that men do to women (or to the person playing a female role, as in a homosexual rape). Robert Baker calls attention to this point in " 'Pricks' and 'Chicks': A Plea for 'Persons.' "[5] Our slang words for sexual intercourse— "fuck," "screw," or older words such as "take" or "have"—not only can mean harm but have traditionally taken a male subject and a female object. The active male screws (harms) the passive female. A "bad" woman only tempts men to hurt her further.

It is easy to understand why one's proper grandmother would not want men to see pornography or lose respect for women. But feminists reject these "proper" assumptions: good and bad classes of women do not exist; and sex is not dirty (though many people believe it is). Why then are feminists angry at the treatment of women as sex objects, and why are some feminists opposed to pornography?

The answer is that feminists as well as proper grandparents are concerned with respect. However, there are differences. A feminist's distinction between treating a woman as a full-fledged person and treating her as merely a sex object does not correspond to the good-bad woman distinction. In the latter distinction, "good" and "bad" are properties applicable to groups of women. In the feminist view, all women are full-fledged people—some, however, are treated as sex objects and perhaps think of themselves as sex objects. A further difference is that, although "bad" women correspond to those thought to deserve treatment as sex objects, good women have not corresponded to full-fledged people; only men have been full-fledged people. Given the feminist's distinction, she has no difficulty whatever in saying that pornography treats women as sex objects, not as full-fledged people. She can morally object to pornography or anything else that treats women as sex objects.

One might wonder whether any objection to treatment as a sex object implies that the person objecting still believes, deep down, that sex is dirty. I don't think so. Several other possibilities emerge. First, even if I believe intellectually and emotionally that sex is healthy, I might object to being treated *only* as a sex object. In the same spirit, I would object to being treated *only* as a maker of chocolate chip cookies or *only* as a tennis partner, because only one of my talents is being valued. Second, perhaps I feel that sex is healthy, but it is apparent to me that you think sex is dirty; so I don't want you to treat me as a sex object. Third, being treated as any kind of object, not just as a sex object, is unappealing. I would rather be a partner (sexual or otherwise) than an object. Fourth, and more plausible than the first three possibilities, is Robert Baker's view mentioned above. Both (i) our traditional double standard of sexual behavior for men and women and (ii) the linguistic evidence that we connect the concept of sex with the concept of harm point to what is wrong with treating women as sex objects. As I said earlier, "fuck" and "screw," in their traditional uses, have taken a male subject, a female object, and have had at least two meanings: harm and have sexual intercourse with. (In addition, a prick is a man who harms people ruthlessly; and a motherfucker is so low that he would do something very harmful to his own dear mother.)[6] Because in our culture we connect sex with harm that men do to women and because we think of the female role in sex as that of harmed object, we can see that to treat a woman as a sex object is automatically to treat her as less than fully human. To say this does not imply that no healthy sexual relationships exist; nor does it say anything about individual men's conscious intentions to degrade women by desiring them sexually (though no doubt some men have these intentions). It is merely to make a point about the concepts embodied in our language.

Psychoanalytic support for the connection between sex and harm comes from Robert J. Stoller. Stoller thinks that sexual excitement is linked with a wish to harm someone (and with at least a whisper of hostility). The key process of sexual excitement can be seen as dehumanization (fetishization) in fantasy of the desired person. He speculates that this is true in some degree of everyone, both men and women, with "normal" or "perverted" activities and fantasies.[7]

Thinking of sex objects as harmed objects enables us to explain some of the first three reasons why one wouldn't want to be treated as a sex object: (1) I may object to being treated only as a tennis partner, but being a tennis partner is not connected in our culture with being a harmed object; and (2) I may not think that sex is dirty and that I would be a harmed object; I may not know what your view is; but what bothers me is that this is the view embodied in our language and culture.

Awareness of the connection between sex and harm helps explain other interesting points. Women are angry about being treated as sex objects in situations or roles in which they do not intend to be regarded in that manner—for example, while serving on a committee or attending a discussion. It is not merely that a sexual role is inappropriate for the circumstances; it is thought to be a less fully human role than the one in which they intended to function.

Finally, the sex–harm connection makes clear why it is worse to treat women as sex objects than to treat men as sex objects and why some men have had difficulty understanding women's anger about the matter. It is more difficult for heterosexual men than for women to assume the role of "harmed object" in sex; for men have the self-concept of sexual agents, not of passive objects. This is also related to my earlier point concerning the difference in the solidity of respect for men and for women; respect for women is more fragile. Despite exceptions, it is generally harder for people to degrade men, either sexually or nonsexually, than to degrade women. Men and women have grown up with different patterns of self-respect and expectations regarding the extent to which they deserve and will receive respect or degradation. The man who doesn't understand why women do not want to be treated as sex objects (because he'd sure like to be) would not think of himself as being harmed by that treatment; a woman might.[8] Pornography, probably more than any other contemporary institution, succeeds in treating men as sex objects.

Having seen that the connection between sex and harm helps explain both what is wrong with treating someone as a sex object and why it is worse to treat a woman in this way. I want to use the sex–harm connection to try to resolve a dispute about pornography and women. Brownmiller's view, remember, was that pornography is "the undiluted essence of anti-female propaganda" whose purpose is to degrade women. Some people object to Brownmiller's view by saying that, since pornography treats both men and women as sex objects for the purpose of arousing the viewer, it is neither sexist, anti-female, nor designed to degrade women; it just happens that degrading of women arouses some men. How can this dispute be resolved?

Suppose we were to rate the content of all pornography from most morally objectionable to least morally objectionable. Among the most objectionable would be the most degrading—for example, "snuff" films and movies which recommend that men rape women, molest children and puppies, and treat nonmasochists very sadistically.

Next we would find a large amount of material (probably most pornography) not quite so blatantly offensive. With this material it is relevant to use the analysis of sex objects given above. As long as sex is connected with harm done to women, it will be very difficult not see pornography as degrading to women. We can agree with Brownmiller's opponent that pornography treats men as sex objects, too, but we maintain that this is only pseudoequality: such treatment is still more degrading to women.[9]

In addition, pornography often exemplifies the active/passive, harmer/harmed object roles in a very obvious way. Because pornography today is male-oriented and is supposed to make a profit, the content is designed to appeal to male fantasies. Judging from the content of the most popular legally available pornography, male fantasies still run along the lines of stereotypical sex roles—and, if Stoller is right, include elements of hostility. In much pornography the women's purpose is to cater to male desires, to service the man or men. Her own pleasure is rarely emphasized for its own sake, she is merely allowed a little heavy breathing, perhaps in order to show her dependence on the great male "lover" who produces her pleasure. In addition, women are clearly made into passive objects in still photographs showing only close-ups of their genitals. Even in movies marketed to appeal to heterosexual couples, such as *Behind the Green Door,* the woman is passive and undemanding (and in this case kidnapped and hypnotized as well). Although many kinds of specialty magazines and films are gauged for different sexual tastes, very little contemporary pornography goes against traditional sex roles. There is certainly no significant attempt to replace the harmer/harmed distinction with anything more positive and healthy. In some stag movies, of course, men are treated sadistically by women; but this is an attempt to turn the tables on degradation, not a positive improvement.

What would cases toward the least objectionable end of the spectrum be like? They would be increasingly less degrading and sexist. The genuinely nonobjectionable cases would be nonsexist and nondegrading; but commercial examples do not readily spring to mind.[10] The question is: Does or could any pornography have nonsexist, nondegrading content?

II

I want to start with the easier question: Is it possible for pornography to have nonsexist, morally acceptable content? Then I will consider whether any pornography of this sort currently exists.

Imagine the following situation, which exists only rarely today: Two fairly conventional people who love each other enjoy playing tennis and bridge together, cooking good food together, and having sex together. In all these activities they are free from hang-ups, guilt, and tendencies to dominate or objectify each other. These two people like to watch tennis matches and old romantic movies on TV, like to watch Julia Child cook, like to read the bridge column in the newspaper, and like to watch pornographic movies. Imagine further that this couple is not at all uncommon in society and that nonsexist pornography is as common as this kind of nonsexist sexual relationship. This situation sounds fine and healthy to me. I see no reason to think that an interest in pornography would disappear in these circumstances. People seem to enjoy watching others experience or do (especially do well) what they enjoy experiencing, doing, or wish they could do themselves. We do not morally object to people watching tennis on TV; why would we object to these hypothetical people watching pornography?

Can we go from the situation today to the situation just imagined? In much current pornography, people are treated in morally objectionable ways. In the scene just imagined, however, pornography would be nonsexist, nondegrading, morally acceptable. The key to making the change is to break the connection between sex and harm. If Stoller is right, this task may be impossible without changing the scenarios of our sexual lives—scenarios that we have been writing since early childhood. (Stoller does not indicate whether he thinks it possible for adults to rewrite their scenarios or for social change to bring about the possiblity of new scenarios in future generations.) But even if we believe that people can change their sexual scenarios, the sex–harm connection is deeply entrenched and has widespread implications. What is needed is a thorough change in people's deep-seated attitudes and feelings about sex roles in general, as well as about sex and roles in sex (sexual roles). Although I cannot even sketch a general outline of such changes here, changes in pornography should be part of a comprehensive program. Television, children's educational material, and nonpornographic movies and novels may be far better avenues for attempting to change attitudes; but one does not want to take the chance that pornography is working against one.

What can be done about pornography in particular? If one wanted to work within the current institutions, one's attempt to use pornography as a tool for the education of male pornography audiences would have to be fairly subtle at first; nonsexist pornography must become familiar enough to sell and be watched. One should realize too that any positive educational value that nonsexist pornography might have may well be as short-lived as most of the effects of pornography. But given these limitations, what could one do?

Two kinds of films must be considered. First is the short film with no plot or character development, just depicted sexual activity in which nonsexist pornography would treat men and women as equal sex partners.[11] The man would not control the circumstances in which the partners had sex or the choice of positions or acts; the woman's preference would be counted equally. There would be no suggestion of a power play or conquest on the man's part, no suggestion that "she likes it when I hurt her." Sexual intercourse would not be portrayed as primarily for the purpose of male ejaculation—his orgasm is not "the best part" of the movie. In addition, both the man and woman would express their enjoyment; the man need not be cool and detached.

The film with a plot provides even more opportunity for nonsexist education. Today's pornography often portrays the female characters as playthings even when not engaging in sexual activity. Nonsexist pornography could show women and men in roles equally valued by society, and sex equality would amount to more than possession of equally functional genitalia. Characters would customarily treat each other with respect and consideration, with no attempt to treat men or women brutally or thoughtlessly. The local Pussycat Theater showed a film written and directed by a woman *(The Passions of Carol)*, which exhibited a few of the features just mentioned. The main female character in it was the editor of a magazine parody of *Viva*. The fact that some of the characters treated each other very nicely, warmly, and tenderly did not detract from the pornographic features of the movie. This should not surprise us, for even in traditional male-oriented films, lesbian scenes usually exhibit tenderness and kindness.

Plots for nonsexist films could include women in traditionally male jobs (e.g., long-distance truckdriver) or in positions usually held in respect by pornography audiences. For example, a high-ranking female Army officer, treated with respect by men and women alike, could be shown not only in various sexual encounters with other people but also carrying out her job in a humane manner.[12] Or perhaps the main character could be a female urologist. She could interact with nurses and other medical personnel, diagnose illnesses brilliantly, and treat patients with great sympathy as well as have sex with them. When the Army officer or the urologist engage in sexual activities, they will treat their partners and be treated by them in some of the considerate ways described above.

In the circumstances we imagined at the beginning of [this part of the] paper, our nonsexist films could be appreciated in the proper spirit. Under these conditions the content of our new pornography would clearly be nonsexist and morally acceptable. But would the content of such a film be morally acceptable if shown to a typical pornography audience today? It might seem strange for us to change our moral evaluation of the content on the basis of a different audience, but an audience today is likely to see the "respected" urologist and Army officer as playthings or unusual prostitutes—even if our intention in showing the film is to counteract this view. The effect is that, although the content of the film seems morally acceptable and our intention in showing it is morally flawless, women are still degraded.[13] The fact that audience attitude is so important makes one wary of giving wholehearted approval to any pornography seen today.

The fact that good intentions and content are insufficient does not imply that one's efforts toward change would be entirely in vain. Of course, I could not deny that anyone who tries to change an institution from within faces serious difficulties. This is particularly evident when one is trying to change both pornography and a whole set of related attitudes, feelings, and institutions concerning sex and sex roles. But in conjunction with other attempts to change this set of attitudes, it seems preferable to try to change pornography instead of closing one's eyes in the hope that it will go away. For I suspect that pornography is here to stay.

Notes

[1](New York: Simon and Schuster, 1975), p. 394.

[2]*The Report of the Commission on Obscenity and Pornography* (Washington, D.C., 1970), p. 201.

[3]In order to help one determine which position one feels inclined to take, consider the following statement: It is morally objectionable to write, make, sell, act in, use, and enjoy pornography; in addition, the content of pornography is immoral; however, pornography itself is not morally objectionable. If this statement seems extremely problematic, then one might well be satisfied with the claim that pornography is degrading because its content is.

[4]Many feminists point this out. One of the most accessible references is Shulamith Firestone, *The Dialectic of Sex: The Case for the Feminist Revolution* (New York: Bantam, 1970), especially pp. 128–32.

[5]In Richard Wasserstrom, ed., *Today's Moral Problems* (New York: Macmillan, 1975), pp. 152–71; see pp. 167–71. Also in Robert Baker and Frederick Elliston, eds., *Philosophy and Sex* (Buffalo, N.Y.: Prometheus Books, 1975).

[6]Baker, in Wasserstrom, *Today's Moral Problems,* pp. 168–169.

[7]"Sexual Excitement," *Archives of General Psychiatry* 33(1976): 899–909, especially p. 903. The extent to which Stoller sees men and women in different positions with respect to harm and hostility is not clear. He often treats men and women alike, but in *Perversion: The Erotic Form of Hatred* (New York: Pantheon, 1975), pp. 89–91, he calls attention to differences between men and women especially regarding their responses to pornography and lack of understanding by men of women's sexuality. Given that Stoller finds hostility to be an essential element in male-oriented pornography and given that women have not responded readily to such pornography, one can speculate about the possibilities for women's sexuality: their hostility might follow a different scenario; they might not be as hostile, and so on.

[8]Men seem to be developing more sensitivity to being treated as sex objects. Many homosexual men have long understood the problem. As women become more sexually

aggressive, some heterosexual men I know are beginning to feel treated as sex objects. A man can feel that he is not being taken seriously if a woman looks lustfully at him while he is holding forth about the French judicial system or the failure of liberal politics. Some of his most important talents are not being properly valued.

[9]I don't agree with Brownmiller that the purpose of pornography is to dehumanize women, rather it is to arouse the audience. The differences between our views can be explained, in part, by the points from which we begin. She is writing about rape; her views about pornography grow out of her views about rape. I begin by thinking of pornography as merely depicted sexual activity, though I am well aware of the male hostility and contempt for women that it often expresses. That pornography degrades women and excites men is an illustration of this contempt.

[10]Virginia Wright Wexman uses the film *Group Marriage* (Stephanie Rothman, 1973) as an example of "more enlightened erotica." Wexman also asks the following questions in an attempt to point out sexism in pornographic films:

Does it [the film] portray rape as pleasurable to women? Does it consistently show females nude but present men fully clothed? Does it present women as childlike creatures whose sexual interests must be guided by knowing experienced men? Does it show sexually aggressive women as castrating viragos? Does it pretend that sex is exclusively the prerogative of women under twenty-five? Does it focus on the physical aspect of lovemaking rather than the emotional ones? Does it portray women as purely sexual beings? ("Sexism of X-rated Films," Chicago Sun-Times, 28 March 1976.)

[11]If it is a lesbian or male homosexual film, no one would play a caricatured male or female role. The reader has probably noticed that I have limited my discussion to heterosexual pornography, but there are many interesting analogies to be drawn with male homosexual pornography. Very little lesbian pornography exists, though lesbian scenes are commonly found in male-oriented pornography.

[12]One should note that behavior of this kind is still considered unacceptable by the military. A female officer resigned from the U.S. Navy recently rather than be court-martialed for having sex with several enlisted men whom she met in a class on interpersonal relations.

[13]The content may seem morally acceptable only if one disregards such questions as, "Should a doctor have sex with her patients during office hours?" More important is the propriety of evaluating content wholly apart from the attitudes and reactions of the audience; one might not find it strange to say that one film has morally unacceptable content when shown tonight at the Pussycat Theater but acceptable content when shown tomorrow at a feminist conference.

Discussion Questions

1. Garry argues that some pornography "violates the moral principle to respect persons." Should Simon recognize this as a kind of serious harm that might justify restricting pornography? Why or why not?

2. Garry holds that even if seeing a given movie need not cause anyone to imitate the behavior shown, the movie might be morally objectionable because of the character of the behavior and attitudes it recommends. Would this justify censoring the movie in question? Why or why not?

3. Garry considers but does not develop an argument that if the content or message of pornography is immoral then pornography is immoral. Criticize or support this argument.

4. What is Garry's argument with regard to respect for women? How might this argument be criticized?

5. What reasons does Garry give for thinking that it is always an evil to be treated as an object? Can you find any counterarguments to or arguments in support of this position?

6. What types of pornography would Garry not find objectionable? What objections could still be made to these types of pornography?

The Manly Art of Seduction

Lycurgis M. Starkey

The manly art of seduction—that suits James Bond to a tee. Only twice in thirteen novels does he fail to seduce the girl he fancies. "With most women his manner was a mixture of taciturnity and passion. The lengthy approaches to a seduction bored him almost as much as the subsequent mess of disentanglement."[1] Mr. Bond's primary concern is the passion of an animal function. But what's manly about corrupting or debauching the ladies—and what real man would have to hit and run? It would seem that Agent 007 can't face the music of responsible, adult male-female relationships.

Whether Bond be spoof or truth, let us say that Fleming's popular novels point to a world of sexual values entertained by many. The traveling salesman jokes and James Bond are in the same category—we may enjoy the story but the moral decay implied is not so funny. And where is the moral decay, you say? Well, examine the sexual assumptions in the Bond books, in the Kinsey report, in some of Billy Wilder's movies, in *Playboy's* play for profit.

The Kinsey reports of a few years back pointed to widespread sexual promiscuity in America. Kinsey reported 67 percent[2] of college men and 60 percent[3] of college women to have experienced premarital intercourse. Lower the educational level, and the percentage increased for the men according to his research. Fifty percent[4] of all women are not virgin at marriage, he claimed. On the basis of what he believed to be the widespread practice of promiscuity, Kinsey suggested a realignment of sexual values to cohere with public practice.[5] There have always been those of the "morality by nose count" school.

Billy Wilder's movies have overturned all the sexual mores, glorified promiscuity, glamorized prostitution, and elevated adultery to a virtue. Contrast Wilder's films such as "The Apartment" and "Irma La Douce" with the treatment of sexual deviation in Fellini's "La Dolce Vita." The saccharine sweet life of sexual dissipation is shown in this Italian film for the self-destructive delusion that it is.

Reprinted from Lycurgis M. Starkey, *James Bond's World of Values* (Nashville Abingdon Press, 1966). Reprinted by permission of the author.

Again *Playboy* magazine with its 300,000 plus circulation chiefly in the 18–30 age, single-male bracket trumpets sexual promiscuity and seduction of the innocent as the male ideal. Women are bunnies to be fondled, kept, used. The girl is no more than a playboy accessory. Sex is to be enjoyed wherever one can steal it without the encumbrance of responsibility or loyalty of any kind. If she wants to tie you up or talk about marriage, run, rogue-male, run.

"The Playboy Philosophy," which one army man described as a phony attempt to give academic status to a girlie magazine, seems to advocate free sexual relationships between adults as long as there is a measure of responsibility and no coercion. Again, Hefner seems to insist that the marriage bond be respected. But the cartoons, jokes, and advice to the lovelorn in *Playboy* completely contradict this. Adultery is as much good clean fun as fornication. Like James Bond, the subtle and at times not so subtle insistence is upon the seduction of the nude, bosomy female. One letter to the *Playboy* advisor in the July, 1965, issue reads:

> Nearly all the girls we date at our Midwestern college are fine where the physical aspects of love are concerned, but they lack the brain power necessary to make stimulating partners on other levels. Although we place a high value on sensual satisfaction we feel there should be a sound intellectual relationship as well. Any suggestions?

Playboy's answer:

> Since you'll never make your girls intellectual, . . . why don't you reverse your technique—and try *making* intellectual girls?

Another such letter in August of 1965 describes the guilt feelings of a young lad who had followed *Playboy's* advice. It seems he had removed a twenty-year-old girl's sexual reluctance (she had been raped at fourteen), had aroused her inner fire, and now the blaze was a runaway. He had turned the former prude into a profligate. Now she was "shacking up" with practically everybody on the campus and had gained a bad reputation. What could he do?

Playboy's answer:

> Don't blame yourself. You did Sue a favor by helping her overcome a serious emotional shock.

The overall tone of *Playboy* is clear; it promotes the "manly art of seduction."

In other words, these contemporary voices speak out for promiscuity. They would have us believe:

1. Every woman is waiting and wanting to be seduced.
2. Man is primarily an animal with a sexual drive, a drive which must be satisfied with anybody, any type, married or single.

I'm not sure whether these hot-blooded males and weak-kneed women are more to be pitied than censured or horselaughed into place. But certainly such a view of sexual relationships, of love and procreation, of human personality and potential, is warped and self-destructive, to say the least.

What about this assumption that all women are waiting and wanting to be seduced? Margaret Mead has suggested this to be a laughable period piece which belongs with mastodons, saber-tooth tigers, and pea-brain cave men pulling their women around by the hair. No self-respecting women in these days is going to be treated like a playboy accessory, a cardigan sweater to be put in mothballs and placed on the shelf when not in use. Sexuality is far more deeply rooted in human personality than that. Certainly this assumption is belittling to women, an assumption to be deplored by the liberated ladies of the mid-twentieth century. Such male profligacy in the ancient world went hand in hand with the inferior position of women who were little more than expendable mattresses for the male animal. It has often been said that one of Christianity's great contributions to western society has been the elevation of women and children to a place of dignity and reverence. This came part and parcel with a Christian sex ethic which gave women and children a personal importance alongside men. Women could not be treated as sexual chattels or easily put off by divorce. They had rights and privileges of their own. The unwanted children of illicit relations could not be tossed in the ditch to die of cold or hunger. They too had rights and privileges. Thank God for the progress. With the increase of birth control methods, of course, the risk of unwanted children is lessened, but the inferior attitude toward women and children characteristic of promiscuity prevails.

Sexual promiscuity also belittles the male. Here man is assumed to be an irrational creature of undisciplined drives, little more than a sexual animal with the hunger to copulate. Under the lens of common sense we see this as a far less than adequate view of many. Some have suggested that the male rogue, *Playboy*-Bond approach to women is really antisexual, perhaps homosexual in a latent way.[6] For when men want to use women only as bunnies and accessories, thus running away from responsible sexual involvement, there is something basically wrong. Psychoanalysis recognizes that promiscuous sexual behavior springs from a disturbed personality.

But maturity demands sexual behavior that is motivated by respect for persons, the other party as well as one's self.

In contrast to this pagan drift toward promiscuity, consider the biblical view of man. In Genesis 1:27–28, 31, we read:

> So God created man in his own image, in the image of God he created him; male and female he created them. And God blessed them, and God said to them, "Be fruitful and multiply. . . . " And God saw everything that he had made, and behold, it was very good.

The biblical view of man affirms that our sexual differences and drives are given by God. God has made us male and female so that we may find joyful fulfillment in sexual union and the procreation of children. As a part of God's creation sex is good. The sexual organs are as much a part of God's handiwork as the eyes and ears of man. As the God-given sexual drive is what relates us to other people and opens the door to community, it is one of God's greatest gifts. In this we rejoice. There's nothing wrong with the appreciation of handsome physical proportions in either a man or a woman. God made us to enjoy them. Sometimes the church has failed to rejoice in God's creation of the human body. You remember Michelangelo's glorious painting of the creation on the ceiling of the Sistine Chapel in the Vatican. All the figures are in the nude as God created them. But then the artist's papal patron thought this indecent. He required clothes be painted on. Pope Julius II had his due reward, however, when Michelangelo painted the last judgment at the end of the chapel. The artist painted him in hell! We should rejoice in God's gift of sexual drives and differences. The biblical view of sex rejects both prudery and asceticism. *But once we think of persons only as physical, or begin to think of exploiting their bodies without concern for the whole person, then we are in trouble.* Such exploitation is possible in a beauty contest as well as in a bedroom. Man has a way of misusing the good things of God's creation, of diverting sex from its intended course so that its misuse destroys community and harms the self. So on the other extreme the biblical view of man rejects pornography and libertinism.

The Christian sex ethic with a biblical base may be expressed by four "R's": reverence, relatedness, responsibility, and renewal.

I

God calls us to reverence in our sexual life. God made and loves every human being; Christ died to redeem every child of man; therefore every person, male and female, is sacred. In I Corinthians 3:16, we read:

> Do you not know that you are God's temple and that God's Spirit dwells in you? If any one destroys God's Temple, God will destroy him. For God's temple is holy, and that temple you are.

Every individual must be treated as an end rather than a means or an accessory to an end. Another person is not just a "thing," an "it," a sexual organ or function to be used quite apart from the rest of his personality. Even a prostitute tries to protect her own dignity. Though she sells a sexual function, she specifically refuses to get involved as a person. Thus she can feel she has not given her self to be used as an accessory to someone else's pleasure. She has only sold a "function," not her self. Whether she or anyone can ever succeed in separating the sexual function from the rest of her *self* is doubtful. But that she tries to, so as to see a certain difference in sold sex and the giving of her *self,* points to that certain reverence, dignity, self-acceptance for which we have been created.

Think about it. Don't you want to be treated as a person in your own right with feelings and needs of your own to be respected by others? Of course you do. Are you willing to treat your wife or husband this way, your date or fiancé? God calls us to see every human being as our "neighbor" and to love, to care, to reverence the neighbor. We are to be a Christ to our neighbor, said Luther, and that includes every potential sexual partner.

II

God calls us to relatedness in our sexual life. God created man and woman so that when they have sexual union they become one flesh:

> Therefore a man leaves his father and his mother and cleaves to his wife, and they become one flesh. (Genesis 2:24.)

"This means that sexual union brings about the joining of two existences, economically, spiritually, and psychologically—and not just the union of two bodies. To attempt the one without the other is dangerous to the entire relationship."[7] Sexual compatibility and satisfaction between a couple involves the blending of mind and attitude as well as bodily contact. Helmut Thielicke has indicated the very difference between male and female "readiness," for sexual relationship requires a concern for the other person in order to achieve one's own fulfillment. Physical compatibility requires spiritual compatibility. Animal copulation is merely an instinctual, physical functioning. Human sexual relationships require a mutual concern and communication.[8]

Also guilt feelings and previous bad experiences can sour the relationship one wants to be most meaningful and genuine. Thielicke insists there is a monogamous physical nature in a woman since "she is the one who receives, the one who gives herself and participates with her whole being." She is marked by the first man who "possesses" her—"a girl never forgets her first love," as the old saying goes. It is to the polygamous male's interest to guard the monogamous female's self so that the female can give herself unreservedly to the male who desires her fully and finally.[9]

For sexual experience to mean the most, there must be a willingness for each to relate to the other with all candor, care, and concern. This rules out promiscuity.

III

God calls us to responsibility in our sexual life. If love means anything, it means loyalty. Remember again, "A man leaves his father and his mother and cleaves to his wife. . . . " This word "cleave" is old English for adhere to, stick to. It means that a couple are glued together. In societies where marriages are arranged, the loyalty comes first and the love comes later. Romantic love in our society can be a very superficial basis for sexual union because it may lack loyalty. Genuine love, giving ourselves completely to another person and receiving his gift of self in return, requires trust and trustworthiness—cleaving to, glueing ourselves to another "for better for worse, for richer for poorer, in sickness and in health, to love and to cherish, till death us do part." How can we love someone for long whom we don't trust, someone who is unfaithful and dishonest with the deepest expression of our being? So a satisfying sexual union means we assume the responsibility for the feelings and affections of the other person, a responsibility for children which may result to the union, a responsibility toward the larger community—the protection of other couples, the protection of family property rights.

This is precisely why there are civil laws governing sexual union—to protect the wider community. And the marriage service of the churches frequently implies a responsibility to the community in the command, "If any man can show just cause why they may not lawfully be joined together, let him now speak, or else hereafter for ever hold his peace." Loyalty and community obligation can reduce the anxieties and insecurities which threaten a happy sexual union. The promiscuous male or female who trifles with the affections of others deserves to be publicly censured. He or she is a criminal threat to every other marriage and family on the block, and hence a threat to a stable society.

Of course there are always some whose indiscretions have gotten them into trouble. They are not to be condoned. For them there is, however, the unique Christian message of renewal.

IV

God calls us to renewal in our sexual life. God will help each of us to begin again. Once we have made our bed, we don't have to lie in it. Every man and woman and all our relationships which we misuse for selfish reasons can and must be renewed by the self-giving, all-bearing, never-failing love of God. Pure lust or even romantic love are quite inadequate for an abiding relationship. So we must be renewed by a richer, deeper, more responsible love such as God has addressed toward us in Jesus Christ. The scripture passage most frequently requested by couples to be read at the marriage service is the apostle Paul's hymn to Christlike love, the thirteenth chapter of I Corinthians. Hear this portion of it:

> Love is patient and kind; love is not jealous or boastful; it is not arrogant or rude. Love does not insist on its own way; it is not irritable or resentful; it does not rejoice at wrong, but rejoices in the right. Love bears all things, believes all things, hopes all things, endures all things.

As God has loved us in this way, so we can love others in this way with the help of his empowering presence within. As he forgives us, so we are enabled to forgive our marriage partner. As he bears all things and endures all things from us, so he can enable us to endure the temper tantrums and depressions of our spouse. Our lesser loves can take on the quality of his love defined in Jesus Christ. "Love one another," said Jesus, "even as I have loved you."

In the course of this chapter, I have insisted that the manly art of seduction is not manly at all. It is an escape from man's normal sexual role. Such sexual promiscuity belittles woman to the status of a mattress and belittles man to an irrational creature of appetites. Man's sexual appetite must be directed and disciplined by the greater drive for meaning in his life. Christianity provides a system and source for our life's meaning. It rejoices in the sexual differences and drives given us by God. It insists that these differences and drives must be handled with reverence, relatedness, responsibility, and renewal. And all this points toward chastity before marriage and fidelity afterward. This age-old consensus still stands as the best ethical standard for modern sexual behavior.

One of the characters in Richard Llewellyn's *None but the Lonely Heart* observed, "I was out walking one day and in the distance I saw an animal. I came up closer and saw it was a man. I came up closer still and saw it was my brother." Here is the transition from pagan promiscuity to responsible Christian concern. Our fellowman is not an animal. God calls upon us to look upon our fellows as brothers and treat male and female as members of the family of God.

Notes

1. *Casino Royale,* p. 120.
2. Kinsey, Pomeroy, and Martin, *Sexual Behavior in the Human Male* (Philadelphia: W. B. Saunders Co., 1948), p. 552.
3. Kinsey, Pomeroy, Martin, and Gebbard, *Sexual Behavior in the Human Female* (Philadelphia: W. B. Saunders Co., 1953), p. 293.
4. *Ibid.,* p. 287.
5. See chapters 10 and 13, *Sexual Behavior in the Human Male;* William Graham Cole, *Sex in Christianity and Psychoanalysis* (New York: Oxford University Press, 1955), pp. 288, 317; *Sex Habits of American Men,* ed. Deutsch (New York: Prentice-Hall, Inc., 1948), p. 176. See also chapter 8, *Sexual Behavior in the Human Female.*

[6]See James M. Wall, "James Bond: Hero of Death and Destruction," *The Christian Advocate,* July 15, 1965, pp. 11–12.

[7]William Graham Cole, *Sex in Christianity and Psychoanalysis* (New York: Oxford University Press, 1965), p. 297.

[8]Helmut Thielicke, *The Ethics of Sex* (New York: Harper and Row, 1964), p. 48.

[9]*Ibid.,* p. 84.

Discussion Questions

1. Starkey says that James Bond cannot face responsible adult male/female relationships. Is this true of other figures in popular literature or in movies? (Give an example if possible.) What does this show about morality in relation to these stories?

2. What is the relationship between the examples Starkey cites (R-rated films, *Playboy,* etc.) and pornography? How would some of the points made by Simons on the one hand and Gerry on the other hand apply to Starkey's examples?

3. What ideas does Starkey think are assumed by the films, books, and magazines he discusses? What are Starkey's objections to these ideas? Do you agree or disagree? Why?

4. What principles does Starkey apply to condemn movies, magazines, and books which encourages promiscuity? Could you agree with these principles if you did not share Starkey's religious beliefs? Why or why not?

Privacy and the Right to Privacy

H. J. McCloskey

The right to privacy is one of the rights most widely demanded today. Privacy has not always so been demanded. The reasons for the present concern for privacy are complex and obscure. They obviously relate both to the possibilities for very considerable enjoyment of privacy by the bulk of people living in affluent societies brought about by twentieth-century affluence, and to the development of very efficient methods of thoroughly and systematically invading this newly found privacy. However, interesting and important as it is as a socio-philosophical inquiry, the concern of this paper is not with why privacy has come to be so highly prized, but rather with whether it is rightly prized, and if so, when and why. This means that my concern will be with what privacy is, what is its domain, whether there is a right to privacy, and, if so, whether it is an ultimate, basic, albeit a *prima facie,* right, or simply a conditional right.

From *Philosophy,* vol. 55, 1980. Reprinted by permission of the Royal Institute of Philosophy.

A. What Is Privacy? To What Is the Right to Privacy a Right?

We demand recognition of our right to privacy, we complain when privacy is invaded, yet we encounter difficulties immediately [when] we seek to explain what we mean by privacy, what is the area, the content of privacy, what is outside that area, what constitutes a loss of privacy, a loss to which we have consented, a justified loss, an unjustified loss. This problem is more acute in respect of privacy than with the rights to life, liberty, equality of opportunity, and the like, even though with each of these there is a problem of conceptual clarification to be solved before the nature and the basis of the right can be determined. . . .

A clear, well-defined concept is to be realized only by way of a stipulative definition. However, it is possible to distinguish concepts distinct from privacy which have been confused with that of privacy, and thereby to make clearer the core notion of privacy. To look now at some of the more important attempts to characterize privacy.

1. Privacy as Consisting in Being Let Alone

There are many versions of this account, that of Warren and Brandeis, although linked with and suggestive of other, radically different accounts, being the most important. They wrote:

> These considerations lead to the conclusion that the protection afforded to thoughts, sentiments, and emotions, expressed through the medium of writing or of the arts, so far as it consists in preventing publication, is merely an instance of the enforcement of the more general right to be let alone. . . . The principle which protects personal writings and all other personal productions, not against theft and physical appropriation, but against publication in any form, is in reality not the principle of private property, but of inviolate personality.[1]

. . . M. L. Ernst and A. U. Schwartz in *The Right to Be Let Alone,* also write of privacy in the context of seclusion and solitude, observing:

> [Privacy consists in being] protected from intrusion upon himself, his home, his family, his relationships and communications with others, his property and his business affairs, including intrusion by spying, prying, watching and besetting and the unauthorized overhearing . . . of spoken words.[2]

This latter account moves towards the distinct account of privacy and the right to privacy in terms of control over and possession of the right of selective disclosure.

There is initial plausibility in the account of privacy as consisting in being let alone. If one is let alone, one's privacy would seem to be secure. Is this really so? I suggest that it all depends on what is meant by being let alone. If a tourist visiting a new country innocently spies on people from his liner, using binoculars to observe them gardening, entertaining friends in their gardens, getting drunk, he has, in an important sense, let them alone; yet he has invaded their privacy. On the other hand, if a person is shipwrecked on a lonely island and no one bothers about his fate, it is not clear that it is privacy that he is enjoying. Yet he is being let alone. Vague though this account is, it covers too much and things other than privacy in such a way that it will not do as a guide to what is involved in the right to privacy. To enjoy *seclusion* or *solitude* is usually, although not necessarily, to enjoy privacy. Yet they clearly are distinct things. It would be a mockery to guarantee a person his privacy by ensuring that he enjoys solitude on a remote island. Privacy is something that we can enjoy and wish to enjoy in society. It is not clear that it is meaningful outside of societies.

Some writers construe the intrusion of noise and obnoxious smells into one's home as invasions of privacy. Indeed, all nuisances which invade the home are seen as such. This would be the case if privacy consisted in being let alone. So too, to be assaulted, would be to suffer a loss of privacy. Against this, I suggest that that of which it would be reasonable to complain with the noise, smell, assault would be loss of enjoyment, harm, injury, but not a loss or invasion of privacy. To be hurt, to suffer loss of enjoyment and other goods, is not to suffer loss of privacy, unless one is to construe everything that harmfully affects one as involving a loss of privacy. On such a view, to be affected, either harmfully or beneficially, would be to lose privacy, unwillingly or willingly. Some seek to argue, more moderately, that it is only when such evils enter one's private domain, that one suffers a loss of privacy. It is not any unwanted smell, noise, etc., that invades one's privacy, but unwanted smells, noises, and nuisances that enter one's own private dwelling that do so. This is to move towards an account of privacy in part at least in terms of an area of privacy relating to one's person and personal domain. This kind of account will be examined later.

Liberty and being let alone are commonly equated. The negative concept of liberty is commonly explained in terms of being free from interference, in being let alone. Yet privacy, negative liberty, and being let alone, are clearly, evidently distinct. Not to let a person alone may be to deprive him only of his negative liberty, or it may simply be to interfere with him in other ways as by assaulting him or benefiting him in a way that is desired/undesired by him. In a secondary sense of leaving alone, to spy on a person is not to leave him alone; it is to invade his privacy. In a more basic, primary sense, to coerce a person into doing what he does not want to do is not to leave him alone; it is to invade his liberty, not his privacy. Here it may be replied that all loss of liberty is *ipso facto* a loss of privacy. Against this, it may easily be shown that privacy and liberty are conceptually distinct. Privacy can be totally invaded throughout the whole of a person's life, without his knowledge, without his liberty being in any way restricted, and without the person becoming any less a person *qua* person. By contrast, the greater the interference with a person's liberty, the more inclined we are to think of him as being rendered incapable of being a full person. Complete interference in the form of control of his thoughts, decisions, actions during the whole of his life, is incompatible with his remaining a person in the Kantian sense of person. Secondly, privacy and negative liberty may conflict. Part of the right to liberty is the right to observe, know, report, publish, free of interference. Consider the right to freedom to bird-watch. The ideal society for the lover of negative liberty as the sole political value would be one in which there is as little interference by way of coercion as possible, where the only coercion that is accepted is coercion against coercive interference. Yet members of such a community could invade the privacy of their fellows without interfering with their liberty, as by eavesdropping, person-watching as a hobby, and the like. These are not forms of interference in the sense relevant to negative liberty. Thirdly, the contrasts with negative liberty are interference and coercion; the contrasts with privacy are many, including some such as publicity, which are not contrasts with negative liberty. Similarly, the protections needed for the one may differ from those needed for the other.

2. Privacy as the Lack of Disclosure, and the Right to Privacy as the Right to Selective Disclosure

Privacy and the right to privacy have been explained in terms of knowledge of the self and its extensions, and the right to determine what is known about one's self. In this connection, in *Private Rights and the Freedom of the Individual* (Ditchley Foundation Paper 41), it is observed of a seminar conducted about privacy that:

> The word is easily used, but it was soon seen that it had different implications for different people. This made it much harder to define what precise rights should attach to it than to consider the general concept in relation to other factors. It was accepted that it concerned two main elements in the attitudes of the individuals or groups in their outlook on society. These were, first, the claim to be let alone and secondly, the claim by a holder of information to decide for himself what should be disclosed, at what time and to whom. . . .[3]

In terms of this general view that the right to privacy is the right of the individual to determine what is known or communicated about him, privacy, it would seem, would relate to all the facts relating to one's self and to what are parts and extensions of one's self. There are obvious problems here, problems relating to marking off the self and its real extensions from the non-self, and to showing, as against the ordinary, very inclusive claims to privacy that commonly embrace much more than this, that this is all that relates to privacy. These problems constitute no basic objection to the theory. However they do bear on the need for a detailed elaboration of it and of its practical implications.

A basic objection to this account is that it fails to attend to [some] important points . . . namely, that we can show lack of respect for our own privacy, that we can improperly forgo our own privacy. A person who bares his soul to all is commonly thought not to have a proper respect for his own privacy, he gives it up too readily, he lacks a decent reticence. This account implies that self-disclosure can involve neither invasions nor loss of privacy, and further, that habituation to invasions and loss of privacy that leads to acquiescence and even consent to such invasions causes them to become neither invasions nor losses of privacy. Yet part of that about which those concerned with privacy are concerned, is this phenomenon of people getting used to their privacy being invaded so that they come freely to accept this and no longer to demand a right to privacy, or to privacy in those areas that are regularly invaded. People today have freely accepted vast inroads into their privacy. They have accepted intelligence and other psychological and medical tests for their children, where the information obtained may now be stored in data banks; they accept questionnaires by schools, universities, employers, banks, creditors, and many others, with little or no protest. They demand that their newspapers report news based on invasions of privacy of those in the public eye, those before the courts, and those who suffer great misfortune or good fortune, and they seek to foster in those whose privacy is invaded the belief that they ought to consent to such invasions of their privacy. Clearly, there are considerable difficulties then in the way of explaining privacy in terms of selective disclosure. The relationships between consent and losses and invasions of privacy are multifarious and complex. Concern for privacy may dictate the protecting of people against their own consent. It may dictate the creating of conditions which free them from having to decide whether they are willing to give up privacy to secure some desired good.

3. Privacy as the Absence of Publicity

This kind of thinking about privacy in terms of selective disclosure has also led to the suggestion that privacy consists in the absence of publicity about one's person, one's affairs, and the like. Certainly, those concerned with privacy are concerned with and about unwanted publicity. Suzanne Uniacke in an unpublished paper argues that this is a view of privacy I espouse in "The Political Ideal of Privacy."[4] This was not my intention, even though I did write to the effect that publicity is the basic contrast with privacy. However this is so only in the very technical sense of publicity as openness to some other person. To lose one's privacy is for some information about one to become public in the sense of becoming known by one or more persons. It need not involve publicity in the sense of the publicizing of the information. The eavesdropper, the Peeping-Tom, and other pryers, deprive persons of privacy, whether or not they publicize what they learn. Indeed, what they may learn may be such as not to be for them communicable knowledge. Nonetheless, clearly, anyone concerned with privacy must be vigilant about publicity, as the more certain kinds of information are publicized, the greater is the loss of privacy.

4. Privacy and Secrecy

Privacy and secrecy are obviously distinct, so that to respect secrecy is not neccessarily to respect privacy, to force the divulging of what is secret, is not necessarily to invade privacy. Indeed, the whole logical grammar of expressions relating to secrecy is different from that of those relating to privacy. More importantly, secrecy may relate to things that have nothing to do with privacy. thus, after the sudden deaths of the directors, the chief clerk may be the only one to have the secret knowledge of the combination of the company's safe. Coercively to force him to reveal this knowledge—for example, by threatening dismissal—is not to invade his privacy. Similarly, it may be possible to show respect for all of a man's secret knowledge and yet to show no or scant respect for his privacy, for example, where he is a person who lacks a decent reserve or reticence.

5. Privacy as Exclusive Access

E. van den Haag in "On Privacy" gives a somewhat similar account:

> Privacy is the exclusive access of a person (or other legal entity) to a realm of his own. The right to privacy entitles one to exclude others from (a) watching, (b) utilizing, (c) invading (intruding upon, or in other ways affecting) his private realm.
>
> Privacy is the exclusive right to dispose of access to one's proper (private) domain.[5]

This leads van den Haag to suggest that privacy is best to be treated as a property right, the right to privacy being like a property right to dispose of access to one's proper (private) domain. This view is distinct from the seemingly similar view put by J. J. Thomson that so-called privacy rights are really a cluster of derivative rights, rights in many cases derivative from or analogous with property rights, but such as not to be *sui generis* privacy rights.[6]

Clearly, claims to exclusive access are claims to privacy only if the access is to something personal, something relating to privacy. This leads on to the problem of determining what is the personal, the private, that underlies this right to exclusive access.

In this it shares a common problem with the distinct view that privacy relates to selective disclosure. What is true and important in this account is its stress on access as something distinct from disclosure. Both appear to be involved in privacy. Thus, while it may be the case that a person does not know what are his inner motivations, and hence not be in a position to disclose or not disclose what they are, access to them by a state psychiatrist contrary to his wishes constitutes an invasion of privacy. What privacy dictates is that access to them be exclusively under that person's control. None the less various of the points made in respect of privacy explained in terms of selective disclosure relate also to privacy explained in terms of exclusive access. To respect the right of exclusive access by buying and thereby obtaining the consent of a person to access to his realm of the private is not necessarily to respect his privacy. He may confer on those from whom he is seeking credit the right to full access to all aspects of his life. Yet those who exercise this right show lack of respect for his privacy. Similarly, even though they buy right of access to what is private, scandal newspapers and their readers show scant respect for the privacy of those whose confessions they buy.

6. Respect for Privacy as Respect for Personal Autonomy

Various of the foregoing accounts seek to relate privacy and liberty, privacy and autonomy. Obviously, privacy and respect for privacy, autonomy and respect for autonomy, are related. Many breaches of the right to privacy will be breaches of the duty to respect autonomy; many will involve lack of regard for the wishes of others. However, the latter need not involve lack of respect for autonomy. Thus secret spying which is never discovered by the victim need involve no lack of respect for autonomy. Consider here the girl who, unknown to herself, has been spied on by a man she knows and whom she may or may not be willing to see her naked. Has her will been forced in either case, if the man never talks and if she never comes to know what he has done? It has been suggested here that such actions of invading privacy, even secret, unknown invasions, involve a forcing of the will, a loss of autonomy. The girl wishes to act free from observation. If spied upon, she is no longer free to opt for the unobserved action. Two replies are sufficient to meet this argument. Even if the girl hoped and desired that the man she loved would secretly observe her beauty, her lover who did so without her permission would be invading her privacy. There would however be no thwarting of her will. Further, many things other people do and do not do are counter to our wishes. To vote a sitting member out of office is to thwart his wishes. It is not to violate his autonomy, even less is it to invade his privacy. Such a view of autonomy would imply that only one being can enjoy autonomy and that all others would be at risk of becoming his slaves in order to respect his autonomy.

7. Privacy, Trust, Respect, Love, Friendship and Respect for Persons

C. Fried, . . . in *An Anatomy of Values: Problems of Personal and Social Choice,*[7] while not defining privacy and the right to privacy, seeks to bring out the area of privacy, what it involves, and its deep interrelation with other values, the values of respect, love, and friendship in particular. He seeks to base the right to privacy on the right to respect, and on the value and possibility of love and friendship, these being based on the morality of respect for persons, the right to privacy being seen as an aspect of the right to respect as a person. . . .

If construed as attempts to define privacy, such accounts would encounter various of the difficulties already noted in (5) and (6) above. However they are more plausibly and accurately to be construed as attempts to explain the importance of privacy and of how privacy relates to our basic values. However, as is evident from J. H. Reiman's very damaging critique of Rachels' and Fried's discussions, and of their implied very strange and debased accounts of love and friendship on the one hand and of the knowledge that is gained through such practical sciences as psychiatry, urology, sexology, on the other, the relationship is a subtle, complex one, one that is extremely difficult to unravel.[8]

8. Privacy as Being Lost by the Wrongful Appropriation or Exploitation of One's Personality, the Publicizing of One's Private Affairs with Which the Public Has No Legitimate Concern

S. H. Hofstadter and G. Horowitz offer an account which links with that given by van den Haag, one which explains the right to privacy as a special kind of property right. They write:

> It (the right to privacy) may be described broadly as the right against unwarranted appropriation or exploitation of one's personality; or the publicizing of one's private affairs with which the public has no legitimate concern; or the wrongful intrusion into one's private activities in such a manner as to outrage a person of ordinary sensibilities or cause him mental suffering, shame or humiliation.[9]

This kind of account of the right to privacy is essentially an attempt to mark off illegitimate invasions of privacy rather than to define and mark out the domain of privacy. It rests on more basic views concerning privacy itself. Greater clarity of thought is to be achieved by separating the questions of what privacy is, what is its domain, and what infringements of privacy are justifiable, what is unjustifiable. Such an account is also exposed to the difficulties to which all attempts to explain privacy rights as kinds of property rights are exposed, namely, that payment in full of the price demanded is still compatible with gross invasion of privacy, that compensation by way of payment of damages, no matter how great the payment, may be no more real compensation for lack of respect for privacy than is financial compensation for loss of sight or limbs.

9. Privacy Defined in Terms of Feelings Such as Mental Suffering, Shame, Embarrassment, Humiliation

An attempt may be made to define what is private, and hence what constitutes an invasion of privacy, along the lines suggested in the latter part of the statement in (8) above, namely, in terms of certain human feelings. Thus it is suggested that privacy relates to that which, when known or made public, outrages a person of ordinary sensibilities or causes him mental suffering, shame, or humiliation. This approach has the advantage or seeming advantage over others of explaining privacy in a way that takes note of the social relativity in respect of what is considered to be a matter of privacy. Thus, according to one's society and the period of the society, matters relating to sexual conduct, eating, drinking, ancestry, grief, and so on, may or may not be matters of privacy. . . . What are regarded as matters of privacy may change even within the one society. In our society, much that forty years ago was regarded as a matter of privacy—social background, salary, possessions, marital state if divorced, nature of illnesses, various sexual matters, facts about relatives and forebears—are not now so regarded. This is readily explicable if privacy is to be defined in terms of feelings, and the area of privacy in terms of matters which, if known and publicized, cause or would reasonably cause such feelings to be aroused. It has the further seeming advantage of relating offenses against privacy with offenses against decency, since the latter are socially relative, and this because they are defined in terms of acts which arouse feelings of embarrassment, shame, distress, indignation.

However there are very considerable difficulties in the way of such an account of privacy. Part of our objection to totalitarian regimes is that they render persons of ordinary sensibilities no longer outraged, hurt, shamed, or humiliated by invasions of privacy. The invasions become so frequent, so commonplace, the emotional reactions and hurts cease to follow. This is true even of the losses and invasions of privacy experienced in the armed services in war, in institutional life as in a public hospital, etc. Persons of ordinary sensibilities become used to all their affairs becoming known, to the most intimate details of their lives and thoughts becoming common knowledge and handled with insensitivity, so that before long only the hypersensitive are outraged, hurt, shamed, or humiliated. Clearly, any account of privacy and of what constitutes losses and invasions of privacy must explain life under Nazism, and life in institutions, the armed forces, and the like, as life with little privacy. It is true that any account of privacy, to be satisfactory, must offer a satisfactory explanation of the relativity of beliefs about what is the area of privacy, but it cannot make such relativity basic to privacy.

A further objection is that many things besides loss of privacy may cause the feelings identified with loss of privacy. Offensive and indecent conduct, as well as public imprudent, stupid, cowardly conduct may also cause such feelings. Further, people may have grandiose or obsessive ideas about the area of their privacy and include in it much that does not in fact relate to privacy. Thus they may believe, wrongly, that what relates to their forebears and relatives relates to their privacy, and feel embarrassment if it is discovered that they are murderers, lunatics, prostitutes, or menials. Imprudent, stupid, cowardly conduct of one's self, whether public or private, does relate to privacy, but this is not because of the feelings which publicity about it may arouse. On the other hand, the conduct, roles, etc., of other people, whether or not connected with one by blood or marriage do not relate to one's privacy. whatever publicity about them may cause one to feel, and this because facts about them are not facts about one's self. They are other people. The facts relate to their privacy if they are still alive.

10. Privacy as Relating to the Person, to the Personal, Personality, Inviolate Personality

Other accounts of privacy stress the person and the protection of the personal in the person. In one way or another, most of the foregoing accounts involve the relating of privacy to the self, to the person as a unique self, but not as a stressed aspect of the account. Thus P. A. Freund in "Privacy: One Concept or Many" in this context speaks of the protection of the interest of personality.[10] Warren and Brandeis in their influential ariticle stressed that the principle of respect for privacy is that of "inviolate personality." The private is seen to relate not to everything and anything about the individual but to him as a person and as a unique person.

Such an account of privacy in terms of access to, awareness and knowledge of a person's self, readily explains what is true in other accounts. Most people desire that in at least certain areas and respects, they not be known about or intruded upon; they desire to have some control over access to themselves and publicity concerning what relates to themselves as selves. This is the nature and the extent of the connection between privacy and autonomy. Not all losses of privacy are unwanted, and when not unwanted, we usually, although not always, decline to call them intrusions, invasions, violations of privacy. The entering into any human relationship involves some loss of privacy, some intrusions of others into what is, or is of, one's self. The closer, the more intimate the relationship, as in being a member of a family, a lover, a friend, the more freely and properly is privacy usually given up; it is given up none the less. Those so yielding up part of their privacy are opting for kinship, love, friendship, ahead of privacy. They may, as in love, marriage, the family, seek to create a larger self which becomes the focus of a new privacy.

Whether the acquisitive, proprietorial desires to control privacy which are so common in our society are natural, innate desires, or simply socially acquired desires, can be determined only by scientific research which, at this point of time, has not reached clear answers. If there are no innate, but only acquired, socially inculcated desires for privacy— or if the innate desires are easily eradicated—this will clearly affect the duties persons and states will have in respect of the privacy of others.

While it is true that people commonly feel indignation, shame, distress, and embarrassment when the private is intruded upon or made public, they may experience quite other feelings, pleasant feelings such as those of pride and joy, as when a private, secret act of heroism or altruism is revealed. This is because they see themselves as being inspected, exposed to judgment. Much of the relativity in respect of what causes these feeling responses in different communities and in different ages is due to different views being taken of the nature and content of the self and of what are extensions of the self. It is also true that different social conditions, moral and religious beliefs, make different things important to a person's person; they may even make him into a different self. Why publicity is seen to be so directly in conflict with privacy is also evident from this account. Given the Kantian view of the good life, it is easy to see why respect for privacy, respect for persons, and the personal virtues and values noted by Fried, are so intimately linked.

To fill out this account, it would be necessary to say more about what constitutes a person's unique self, as it is through it that we must fill out the content of privacy. This is no easy task, and is one that can simply be noted here. The person's unique self is a thinking, feeling, self-conscious being, typically aware of its self-identity. Its thoughts, feelings, and body are clearly its own, not someone else's. There is no problem at this point about the area of the private. The problem arises in respect of extensions of the self which come to be identified with the self. Persons come to see many products of their labor as extensions of themselves, and as entitled to the same privacy as they themselves—diaries, paintings, books. They come also to see their families as extensions, and with them, their possessions, and even anything they identify with themselves. Clearly, not all that is seen to be an extension of the self is such, and hence, not all that is thought to be in the area of privacy is really so. The test is, is it of the self or not of the self? However our thinking something to be of, or not of, the self can be relevant to although not determinant of whether or not it is so. To this extent there will be some scope to mold the area of the private. So too, if it is desirable that feelings such as embarrassment, shame, distress are to be associated with invasions of privacy— I do not believe that it is so—to that extent social and legal measures could be used to foster the arousal of these feelings by and only by genuine losses of privacy, or only by illegitimate losses of privacy.

B. Grounds of the Right to Privacy

Very many different types of arguments are advances in defense of a right to privacy. Many derive the right from some more basic right, seeking to show that some more basic right can be secured only if the right to privacy is respected. More commonly, the right to privacy is construed as one of the basic rights of men. Here it is contended either that there is something intrinsically valuable about privacy and its enjoyment such that persons thereby have a right to it, or that, unless persons enjoy privacy, they cannot be full persons, that in this respect, privacy is like liberty. Against the latter views, I shall argue that such claims lack empirical and metaphysical support, and that, when respect for privacy is morally obligatory, it is because privacy is involved in securing, attaining, enjoying other goods, respecting other, more basic rights, and hence, that in so far as there is a right to privacy, it is a derivative right, derived from concern for other values and rights, a conditional right, one that not simply may be overridden but one that ceases to be any sort of right at all, when respect for privacy is not dictated by concern for these other values and rights. This is to argue that it is not an intrinsic, *prima facie* right like the right to life, one which remains a real right even when it is legitimately overridden, and which may give rise to claims and duties when overridden. The following appear to be among the more important arguments for a right to privacy:

The Right to Respect for Privacy as Based on the Utility of Such Respect

The utility of respect for privacy has been defended by reference to utilitarian goods such as pleasure, happiness, self-development, and to non–utilitarian values including justice, honesty, respect for persons. The arguments in terms of the latter values which represent the enjoyment of privacy as not simply a means to, condition of, such values, but as intertwined with respect for them, may best be considered later. Our problem here is: is there a moral right to privacy? The utilitarian arguments are more typically stated as arguments for the legal protection of privacy, arguments for a legal right to privacy, and not as arguments for there being a moral right. Yet, clearly, it may be useful for the state to confer legal rights even where there are no corresponding moral rights. Is this so with privacy? Or can a moral right to privacy successfully be grounded on utilitarian considerations?

Quite clearly, invasions of privacy may cause great evils, and they may permit and lead on to other evils. One argument here parallels the utilitarian argument against indecent, offensive, conduct, claiming that the hurt caused by invasions of privacy is itself a reason for respecting and protecting privacy, and hence for acknowledging a moral and legal right to privacy. This is a very unsatisfactory argument, as unsatisfactory as is the argument for making indecent, offensive conduct criminal. In each case, the hurt suffered by the "victim" is one which ought to be borne for the sake of the greater good of liberty. Further, until it is clear beyond doubt that the hurt is caused not by socially inculcated feelings which can readily be changed by education and training, but by ineradicable innate feelings, there is no case provided by this argument for acknowledging either a moral or a legal right to privacy.

The more basic utilitarian argument is that invasions of privacy involve or lead on to other evils. The Peeping-Tom (but not the Peeping-Jane) may be a rapist and not simply a voyeur, the spy may be a blackmailer, the industrial spy a thief, the police and security agent may harass us, disrupt our private lives, ruin our careers, and the like. And all may significantly reduce our purely private enjoyment of our own. At best this is an argument for the legal protection of privacy, where there is a danger of such evils resulting from invasions of privacy. As already noted, there may be no ground for the protection of privacy against Peeping-Janes (unless their peeping is related to theft or some other evil). It is not an argument for a moral right to privacy. The legal right towards which this kind of argument is directed is a very limited one, and one derived from non-privacy rights, rights to bodily integrity, to life, to property, and to liberty.

In assessing the case for such a legal right to privacy, it is necessary to weigh the goods that are secured against the goods lost and the evils brought into being. Among the goods lost are those lost because the police have been unable to solve crimes, apprehend criminals, obtain evidence necessary for securing convictions; there are also those goods lost in respect of national security as in war, if security agents are prevented from invading the privacy of innocent and suspected persons alike. The price paid here is very high. More serious still are the evils involved in making such acts crimes. Morally innocent persons, voyeurs, and the like are rendered criminals, and hence to suffer all the evils of punishment and of becoming social misfits for life because ex-criminals. Innocent dependents will suffer. They are not all who are affected. All members of society are constrained in their action. Their liberty is gravely circumscribed. By so constraining people, other evils come into being, other goods are prevented. Such effects are already evident in the operation of the US laws relating to privacy. Liberty too is defended in terms of its utility. Mill's most famous arguments were along these lines. If they have any basis in truth, and I believe that they do have some basis, to that extent the limitation of liberty for the sake of privacy is at risk of the goods of liberty. Whatever be the truth here, it is clear that the calculus is not an easy one to work out, and further, that until it is clear that the calculus is in favour of protection of privacy, in each specific area, things should be left as they now are.

Privacy and Justice

An extension of this argument is that from justice, that if there were no protection of privacy, there would be grave injustices, and that respect for justice is vitally involved in respect for persons.

It is obviously true that great injustices are being perpetrated, and will in the future be made possible, by unrestricted invasions of privacy being permitted. This argument most commonly, but not only, arises in respect of data banks, and the use made of the information that is stored in them. Injustices result from misuse of true information, about a person's criminal record, health, employment record, credit-rating and its basis, and such like. Such information has been unjustly used by those who might be thought to have a right to it. It has also been passed on without cost to those who might be thought to have a right to it. It has also been passed on without cost to those who can have no claim to have it, newspapers, banks, retail stores. Indeed, whoever will pay a small fee seems to be able to obtain it. Not relevant to this particular argument, but relevant to the case for protection of privacy, is the consideration of the ways and means, often illegal, used to collect this information. Thus deserving, honorable citizens may be ruined because their files contain the information that they were convicted for stealing when aged twelve, or that they had treatment for a mental illness when aged twenty-five, or that they have changed jobs a number of times between the ages of thirty and forty.

This argument cannot be ignored. If privacy is to be protected against such evils, it may not be necessary to ban all invasions of privacy. However, those whose names are on file must have a right of access to the information so that, even if it is true, they may know what they have to combat. Secondly only relevant information should so be collected. Problems about what is relevant and what not are considerable, but guiding principles are possible. Thirdly, where information is obtained from a person under conditions of confidentiality, as by a bank in respect of a mortgage, that information should be confidential between those parties and not be available for the bank to pass on to other banks, agencies, newspapers. Breach of such confidentiality should be made a criminal offense, with punitive and/or civil damages where the person suffers significantly from the breach of confidentiality. This must hold equally of doctors, hospitals, government agencies such as social welfare departments, taxation, education.

Probably the greatest concern about data banks is that they store and propagate false facts about persons. The injury here is not one of injury to privacy, but that of libel, defamation, slander, with the consequent injustices. Because the owners of data banks demand and successfully achieve for themselves complete legal right to privacy in respect of their information and misinformation, it is difficult, for the ordinary person well-nigh impossible, to determine when such injuries are being perpetrated against him and by whom. Although no more an offense against privacy than is defamation as it ordinarily occurs, those concerned with privacy and the evils that occur as a result of its lack of protection must take note of this evil. Again, open access to such information by those concerned is an essential first step; again, rendering such lies, and the propagation of lies, crimes with punitive damages attached is an essential second step. The state should leave available also the present rights to damages via the laws relating to slander, defamation, and libel. Tough measures are essential in this area to stop on the one hand the high-handed, often irresponsible compilation and distribution of this material, and on the other hand, to prevent the distress, injustices, and even the ruination of lives that now occur.

Privacy as a Basic Need

Many argue that there is a need for privacy. Westin draws analogies with animals which are claimed to have a similar need for privacy. The need for privacy is variously explained as a need for an area of seclusion, of intimacy, of security from observation by others, an area in which one can let off steam, and the like. It is claimed that the need is one which, if not satisfied, leads to a stunted development as a human being and person, and such that we shall not be able to develop the delicate, sensitive feelings and relationships so vital to our development as persons.

This is an empirical, factual claim—or at least purports to be such—yet only the scantiest empirical support is offered by those who adopt this view. On the other hand, the observation of other societies, of how people have fared in prisons, concentration camps, institutions, does little to support this claim. Typically, if a need is not met, this results in ill-health and disorders. Societies have failed to respect privacy, as we understand privacy and in the senses in which privacy is claimed to be a need, without their members suffering from either physical or mental ill-health as a result. Consider here slaves in slave-owning societies, those who serve long sentences in prisons, those confined in concentration camps, those who live in very closely supervised totalitarian societies such as China, and those who live in small villages and whose lives are an open book to all others.

A related, more modest claim that we need privacy to develop the finer human feelings is more interesting. More will be said of this in connection with Fried's argument from respect for persons. Here it is sufficient to note that Bunyan's *Pilgrim's Progress* is only one of the best known of the very many sensitive creations of human imagination and feeling to be written in prison, and that it is indicative of the deep, delicate, sensitive feelings and relationships that develop in prisons and concentration camps. To this it may perhaps be replied that such feelings are merely carry-overs from personalities and characters which were developed in societies in which privacy has been respected, that Bunyan was a formed Bunyan before he entered prison. Further it is pressed as a fact that in communes in which the members have never known privacy, deeper human feelings do not develop. Communes are very special, ideologically based societies. It is hard to know what could be concluded from such claims if true. I suggest that the examples cited of modern totalitarian states and slave-owning societies tell against such atypical societies.

Privacy and Freedom

Arguments for privacy from freedom have been urged, even though to protect privacy is to restrict freedom. What is construed as an argument from freedom is that from the claim that the individual has a right to control of knowledge about himself. This is not an argument from freedom: not to have such exclusive control is not to lack freedom. To be granted such control is to be granted something distinct from and other than freedom. Another argument which relates privacy and liberty is to the effect that to invade privacy is to invade liberty—the person who is spied upon is unfree. He wishes to act under conditions free of observation and is unable to do so. A curious view of freedom is involved in this claim, it being suggested that any one doing what another person desires he not do is infringing his enjoyment of his liberty. Secret spying and prying need involve no curtailment of liberty, no coercion, no impeding or preventing of individuals realizing their wills, being masters of their destinies. However, it is true that often an invasion of privacy may also be an invasion of liberty as well as of other rights. Unrestricted bugging, phone-tapping, mail-reading, reading of thoughts, may well influence us to curtail our actions, but usually only as a result of our own free choice, and not because of coercion. More basically, others may gain the knowledge and power to manipulate us, to thwart our wishes, to frustrate our efforts, by invading our privacy. Concern is felt about the use of information gained by invasions of privacy via data banks in this connection.

I suggest that this argument points to a real problem. To protect liberty we need to restrict liberty, and this can be true in the area of privacy as it is in other areas. If there is a case for the legal protection of liberty, it extends that far to the legal protection of privacy. However, the issues here are complex and complicated. Each restriction of privacy for the sake of liberty must be weighed against the loss of liberty involved in the legal protection of privacy and in the light of the liberty that is protected. A blanket protection of privacy is not justified by this argument from liberty. Much liberty, more importantly, the liberty to inquire and to gain knowledge, more particularly about man and men, the liberty to engage in psychological, historical, biographical inquires, and to publish and to share with other scientists, historians, thinkers, the world, what one has discovered, is a basic liberty, one that is the very core of the structure of our liberal society. So to protect privacy that this liberty, and similar kinds of liberties, are curtailed or lost is to threaten the very life of our society as a liberal society.

Relevant to this, although a distinct point, is the consideration that the liberal society is an open society, the open society, in which truth is knowable, accessible, assessable; a society which gives maximum protection to privacy must of necessity be a closed society. A closed society is exposed to very many evils to which an open society is not exposed.

A lover of privacy may reply to all this that the areas of privacy which need protection for the sake of liberty can safely be marked off without seriously jeopardizing the freedom to inquire in the ways indicated here. This may be possible; if so, it needs to be shown to be so. I greatly doubt whether it can be done because one never knows in advance what piece of knowledge is going to be important. In any case, those concerned to defend privacy are unlikely to be content to restrict the protection of privacy along these lines.

Privacy as Dictated by Respect for Persons

Many different arguments have been suggested here. That of C. Fried proceeds by relating respect for persons, respect, love, friendship, and trust. Fried argues that love, friendship, and trust are possible only in societies in which persons enjoy and accord to others a significant amount of privacy. Fried seeks to combine this claim with an acknowledgment of the relativity of matters which are matters of privacy, these being such as may be determined by convention. While it appears to be the case that there is a close connection between privacy and respect for persons, respect, trust, love, and friendship, the details of Fried's argument are unconvincing. Trust is still possible in the absence of all privacy—it may not be any longer necessary, it may not be called upon, but it is still possible. Friendship and love involve a voluntary forgoing of privacy and may dictate the invasion of the privacy of the other. Both are possible without trust. Respect for privacy would seem to be dictated by respect for persons only in that persons commonly wish their privacy to be respected, hence insofar as we ignore such wishes, without good reason, to that extent we show lack of respect. If we have good reason to ignore a person's wishes, for example, if we suspect that he is concealing a tumor which is now operable but which will soon become inoperable and fatal, we are showing no lack of respect in intruding on his privacy in this matter. This suggests that it is not respect for privacy as such but respect for the wishes of persons that is dictated by respect for persons. Fried's discussion is much richer and fuller than these brief comments bring out. However, this brief discussion does suggest that not a great deal by way of a case for the legal protection of privacy follows from this kind of argument, the more so as it would be, not privacy, but what persons think to be matters of privacy that should be respected and protected.

Privacy as Valuable for Its Own Sake

Basic rights are those which are not derived from more basic rights, but relate to some ultimate value, good, or duty which is possessed of intrinsic value, worth, moral binding force. Nothing that emerged from our examination of the concept of privacy suggests that privacy relates to something of intrinsic worth or value. In this respect privacy differs from life of persons, from self-development of persons, from justice, and even from liberty, even though there is room for argument as to the source of the value of liberty, it seemingly not being intrinsic but due to liberty being an essential element and condition of being a person. Privacy relates to the lack of something. Its definition must be essentially negative. How can the absence of something have intrinsic value? Any value it has must relate to the absence of evils or to this absence being a condition of goods, or the like. What is valuable if anything in this area is valuable, is the state of mind or the existence of the person who enjoys privacy, not privacy in and for itself. Perhaps a better comparison here would be with pleasure or happiness. We have discovered nothing about privacy to suggest that it has intrinsic value in the way that pleasure and happiness do. And, in so far as the state of mind or existence of the person who enjoys privacy is valuable, it will be so because it contains goods such as pleasure and happiness.

If this contention that privacy has no intrinsic worth or value is sound—and to rebut it much more than has been done to date will be needed by so elucidating privacy that it is self-evidently of value—then there can be no basic moral right to privacy which parallels the traditionally recognized rights to life, self-development, moral integrity, liberty. Any right to privacy will be a derivative one from other rights and other goods. This means that it will be a conditional right, and not always a right. Whether or not it will be a derivative right, derivative from the rights to life, self-development, justice, moral integrity, and the like, will depend on practical considerations as to whether respect for privacy is necessary for the enjoyment of these rights. Sometimes it will be, and sometimes it will not be so involved. Thus again, any attempt to give blanket legal protection to a right to privacy as favored in the USA will be in danger of protecting what ought not to be protected, and of thereby unjustifiably restricting liberty, inquiry, and equally important, the realization of justice.

Besides being subject to qualifications by reference to its very basis, and to clashes with other rights (and this is where the public interest but not public curiosity may create a right to invade privacy), there are inbuilt limitations. It is evident that we can consent to forgo privacy, properly, as in marriage, friendship, and certain other social relationships, putting certain areas of our lives outside the sphere of privacy for certain other persons. Consent may however be improperly given and improperly accepted—improperly given as when a person betrays himself and his own privacy by selling his sordid confessions, improperly accepted in those cases, and in respect of many credit-worthiness inquiries and compilations of credit data-banks with the clients' co-operation. The issues here are complex and do not readily lend themselves to regulation by the state, especially by the use of the criminal law. Civil laws, the setting up of advisory bodies, the stating of guidelines concerning respect for privacy may help, but ultimately, the proper respecting of privacy must depend on the individual person's moral responsibility and integrity.

To Conclude

To be plausible, any account of privacy must explain privacy as something distinct from being let alone, solitude, secrecy, liberty, and such like, and as something *sui generis*. When so explained, privacy of itself does not provide grounds for believing men as men to possess a basic moral right to privacy. Any right to privacy must be based on other rights and goods. For this reason, and for reasons inherent in its nature, such a right must be a qualified, conditional right. Efficient, just protection of it, without injury to the enjoyment of other rights and goods, is fraught with difficulties. The law is a clumsy, insensitive instrument. If used to protect privacy in those areas where concern for other rights and values dictates the protection of privacy, the law must be made sensitive, and be used with the greatest of sensitivity and with an awareness of the values behind privacy which it is seeking to safeguard.

Notes

[1][Editor's note: S. D. Warner and L. D. Brandeis, "The Right to Privacy," in *Harvard Law Review* IV, no. 5 (December 1890–91), p. 206.]

[2]M. L. Ernst and A. U. Schwartz, *The Right to Be Let Alone* (New York: Macmillan & Co., 1962), 17.

[3]C. F. O. Clarke, *Private Rights and the Freedom of the Individual* (Enstone; The Ditchley Foundation, 1972), 8.

[4]H. J. McCloskey, "The Political Ideal of Privacy," *Philosophical Quarterly* 21, No. 85 (October 1971), 303–314.

[5]E. van den Haag, "On Privacy," *Nomos* XIII (1971), 149, 151.

[6]J. J. Thomson, "The Right to Privacy," *Philosophy and Public Affairs* 4, No. 4 (Summer 1975), 295–314.

[7]C. Fried, *An Anatomy of Values: Problems of Personal and Social Choice* (Cambridge: Harvard, 1970).

[8]J. H. Reiman, "Privacy, Intimacy and Personhood," *Philosophy and Public Affairs* 6, No. 1 (Fall 1976), 26–44, esp. 29–39.

[9]S. H. Hofstadter and G. Horowitz, *The Right To Privacy* (New York: Central Book Co., 1964), 7.

[10]P. A. Freund, "Privacy: One Concept or Many," *Nomos* XIII (1971), 182–198.

Discussion Questions

1. What difficulties does McCloskey find with the notion of privacy as "being let alone"? How might this notion of privacy be modified to meet his obligations?
2. How does McCloskey object to the definition of privacy as "right to selective disclosure"? Support or criticize his arguments.
3. What is the relation between consent and loss or invasion of privacy in your view? Defend your position with arguements.
4. Which definition of privacy considered by McCloskey do you find most plausible? Why?
5. Which argument for privacy considered by McCloskey do you find most convincing? Why? How might McCloskey's criticisms of this argument be answered?

Privacy: A Rational Context

Charles Fried

In this chapter I analyze the concept of privacy and attempt to show why it assumes such high significance in our system of values. There is a puzzle here, since we do not feel comfortable about asserting that privacy is intrinsically valuable, an end in itself—privacy

From Charles Fried, *An Anatomy of Values: Problems of Personal and Social Choice,* chap. IX. Cambridge, Mass.: Harvard University Press. Copyright © 1970 by the President and Fellows of Harvard College. Reprinted by permission of the author and the publishers.

is always for or in relation to something or someone. On the other hand, to view privacy as simply instrumental, as one way of getting other goods, seems unsatisfactory too. For we feel that there is a necessary quality, after all, to the importance we ascribe to privacy. This perplexity is displayed when we ask how privacy might be traded off against other values. We wish to ascribe to privacy more than an ordinary priority. My analysis attempts to show why we value privacy highly and why also we do not treat it as an end in itself. Briefly, my argument is that privacy provides the rational context for a number of our most significant ends, such as love, trust and friendship, respect and self-respect. Since it is a necessary element of those ends, it draws its significance from them. And yet since privacy is only an element of those ends, not the whole, we have not felt inclined to attribute to privacy ultimate significance. In general this analysis of privacy illustrates how the concepts in this essay can provide a rational account for deeply held moral values.

An Immodest Proposal: Electronic Monitoring

There are available today electronic devices to be worn on one's person which emit signals permitting one's exact location to be determined by a monitor some distance away. These devices are so small as to be entirely unobtrusive: other persons cannot tell that a subject is "wired," and even the subject himself—if he could forget the initial installation—need be no more aware of the device than of a small bandage. Moreover, existing technology can produce devices capable of monitoring not only a person's location, but other significant facts about him: his temperature, pulse rate, blood pressure, the alcoholic content of his blood, the sounds in his immediate environment—for example, what he says and what is said to him—and perhaps in the not too distant future even the pattern of his brain waves. The suggestion has been made, and is being actively investigated, that such devices might be employed in the surveillance of persons on probation or parole.

Probation leaves an offender at large in the community as an alternative to imprisonment, and parole is the release of an imprisoned person prior to the time that all justification for supervising him and limiting his liberty has expired. Typically, both probation and parole are granted subject to various restrictions. Most usually the probationer or parolee is not allowed to leave a prescribed area. Also common are restrictions on the kinds of places he may visit—bars, pool halls, brothels, and the like may be forbidden—the persons he may associate with, and the activities he may engage in. The most common restriction on activities is a prohibition on drinking, but sometimes probation and parole have been revoked for "immorality"—that is, intercourse with a person other than a spouse. There are also affirmative conditions, such as a requirement that the subject work regularly in an approved employment, maintain an approved residence, report regularly to correctional, social, or psychiatric personnel. Failure to abide by such conditions is thought to endanger the rehabilitation of the subject and to identify him as a poor risk.

Now the application of personal monitoring to probation and parole is obvious. Violations of any one of the conditions and restrictions could be uncovered immediately by devices using present technology or developments of it; by the same token, a wired subject assured of detection would be much more likely to obey. Although monitoring is admitted to be unusually intrusive, it is argued that this particular use of monitoring is entirely proper, since it justifies the release of persons who would otherwise remain in prison, and since surely there is little that is more intrusive and unprivate than a prison regime. Moreover, no one is obliged to submit to monitoring: an offender may decline and wait in prison until his sentence has expired or until he is judged a proper risk for parole even without monitoring. Proponents of monitoring suggest that seen in this way monitoring of offenders subject to supervision is no more offensive than the monitoring of an entirely voluntary basis of epileptics, diabetics, cardiac patients, and the like.

Much of the discussion about this and similar (though perhaps less futuristic) measures has proceeded in a fragmentary way to catalog the disadvantages they entail: the danger of the information falling into the wrong hands, the opportunity presented for harassment, the inevitable involvement of persons as to whom no basis for supervision exists, the use of the material monitored by the government for unauthorized purposes, the danger to political expression and association, and so on.

Such arguments are often sufficiently compelling, but situations may be envisaged where they are overridden. The monitoring case in some of its aspects is such a situation. And yet one often wants to say the invasion of privacy is wrong, intolerable, although each discrete objection can be met. The reason for this, I submit, is that privacy is much more than just a possible social technique for assuring this or that substantive interest. Such analyses of the value of privacy often lead to the conclusion that the various substantive interests may after all be protected as well by some other means, or that if they cannot be protected quite as well, still those other means will do, given the importance of our reasons for violating privacy. It is just because this instrumental analysis makes privacy so vulnerable that we feel impelled to assign to privacy some intrinsic significance. But to translate privacy to the level of an intrinsic value might seem more a way of cutting off analysis than of carrying it forward.

It is my thesis that privacy is not just one possible means among others to insure some other value, but that it is necessarily related to ends and relations of the most fundamental sort: respect, love, friendship, and trust. Privacy is not merely a good technique for furthering these fundamental relations; rather without privacy they are simply inconceivable. They require a context of privacy or the possibility of privacy for their existence. To make clear the necessity of privacy as a context for respect, love, friendship, and trust is to bring out also why a threat to privacy seems to threaten our very integrity as persons. To respect, love, trust, or feel affection for others and to regard ourselves as the objects of love, trust, and affection is at the heart of our notion of ourselves as persons among persons, and privacy is the necessary atmosphere for these attitudes and actions, as oxygen is for combustion.

Privacy and Personal Relations

Before going further, it is necessary to sharpen the intuitive concept of privacy. As a first approximation, privacy seems to be related to secrecy, to limiting the knowledge of others about oneself. This notion must be refined. It is not true, for instance, that the less that is known about us the more privacy we have. Privacy is not simply an absence of information about us in the minds of others; rather it is the control we have over information about ourselves.

To refer, for instance, to the privacy of a lonely man on a desert island would be to engage in irony. The person who enjoys privacy is able to grant or deny access to others. Even when one considers private situations into which outsiders could not possibly intrude, the context implies some alternative situation where the intrusion is possible. A man's house may be private, for instance, but that is because it is constructed—with doors, windows, window shades—to allow it to be made private and because the law entitles a man to exclude unauthorized persons. And even the remote vacation hideaway is private just because one resorts to it in order—in part—to preclude access to unauthorized persons.

Privacy, thus, is control over knowledge about oneself. But it is not simply control over the quality of information abroad; there are modulations in the quality of the knowledge as well. We may not mind that a person knows a general fact about us and yet feel our privacy invaded if he knows the details. For instance, a casual acquaintance may comfortably know that I am sick, but it would violate my privacy if he knew the nature of the illness. Or a good friend may know what particular illness I am suffering from, but it would violate my privacy if he were actually to witness my suffering from some symptom which he must know is associated with the disease.

Privacy in its dimension of control over information is an aspect of personal liberty. Acts derive their meaning partly from their social context—from how many people know about them and what the knowledge consists of. For instance, a reproof administered out of the hearing of third persons may be an act of kindness, but if administered in public it becomes cruel and degrading. Thus if a man cannot be sure that third persons are not listening—if his privacy is not secure—he is denied the freedom to do what he regards as an act of kindness.

Besides giving us control over the context in which we act, privacy has a more defensive role in protecting our liberty. We may wish to do or say things not forbidden by the restraints of morality but nevertheless unpopular or unconventional. If we thought that our every word and deed were public, fear of disapproval or more tangible retaliation might keep us from doing or saying things which we would do or say if we could be sure of keeping them to ourselves or within a circle of those who we know approve or tolerate our tastes.

These reasons support the familiar arguments for the right of privacy. Yet they leave privacy with less security than we feel it deserves; they leave it vulnerable to arguments that a particular invasion of privacy will secure to us other kinds of liberty which more than compensate for what is lost. To present privacy, then, only as an aspect of or an aid to general liberty is to miss some of its most significant differentiating features. The value of control over information about ourselves is more nearly absolute than that. For privacy is the necessary context for relationships which we would hardly be human if we had to do without—the relationships of love, friendship, and trust.

Love and friendship . . . involve the initial respect for the rights of others which morality requires of everyone. They further involve the voluntary and spontaneous relinquishment of something between friend and friend, lover and lover. The title to information about oneself conferred by privacy provides the necessary something. To be friends or lovers persons must be intimate to some degree with each other. Intimacy is the sharing of information about one's actions, beliefs, or emotions which one does not share with all, and which one has the right not to share with anyone. By conferring this right, privacy creates the moral capital which we spend in friendship and love.

The entitlements of privacy are not just one kind of entitlement among many which a lover can surrender to show his love. Love or friendship can be partially expressed by the gift of other rights—gifts of property or of service. But these gifts, without the intimacy of shared private imformation, cannot alone constitute love or friendship. The man who is generous with his possessions, but not with himself, can hardly be a friend, nor—and this more clearly shows the necessity of privacy for love—can the man who, voluntarily or involuntarily, shares everything about himself with the world indiscriminately.

Privacy is essential to friendship and love in another respect besides providing what I call moral capital. The rights of privacy are among those basic entitlements which men must respect in each other; and mutual respect is the minimal precondition for love and friendship.

Privacy also provides the means for modulating those degrees of friendship which fall short of love. Few persons have the emotional resources to be on the most intimate terms with all their friends. Privacy grants the control over information which enables us to maintain degrees of intimacy. Thus even between friends the restraints of privacy apply; since friendship implies a voluntary relinquishment of private information, one will not wish to know that his friend or lover has not chosen to share with him. The rupture of this balance by a third party—the state perhaps—thrusting information concerning one friend upon another might well destroy the limited degree of intimacy the two have achieved.

Finally, there is a more extreme case where privacy serves not to save something which will be "spent" on a friend, but to keep it from all the world. There are thoughts whose expression to a friend or lover would be a hostile act, though the entertaining of them is completely consistent with friendship or love. That is because these thoughts, prior to being given expression, are mere unratified possibilities for action. Only by expressing them do we adopt them, choose them as part of ourselves, and draw them into our relations with others. Now a sophisticated person knows that a friend or lover must entertain thoughts which if expressed would be wounding, and so—it might be objected—why should he attach any significance to their actual expression? In a sense the objection is well taken. If it were possible to give expression to these thoughts and yet make clear to ourselves and to others that we do not thereby ratify them, adopt them as our own, it might be that in some relations, at least, another could be allowed complete access to us. But this possibility is not a very likely one. Thus the most complete form of privacy is perhaps also the most basic, since it is necessary not only to our freedom to define our relations with others but also to our freedom to define ourselves. To be deprived of this control over what we do and who we are is the ultimate assault on liberty, personality, and self-respect.

Trust is the attitude of expectation that another will behave according to the constraints of morality. Insofar as trust is only instrumental to the more convenient conduct of life, its purposes could be as well served by cheap and efficient surveillance of the person upon whom one depends. One does not trust machines or animals; one takes the fullest economically feasible precautions against their going wrong. Often, however, we choose to trust people where it would be safer to take precautions—to watch them or require a bond from them. This must be because, as I have already argued, we value the relation of trust for its own sake. It is one of those relations, less inspiring than love or friendship but also less tiring, through which we express our humanity.

There can be no trust where there is no possibility of error. More specifically, man cannot know that he is trusted unless he has a right to act without constant surveillance so that he knows he can betray the trust. Privacy confers that essential right. And since, as I have argued, trust in its fullest sense is reciprocal, the man who cannot be trusted cannot himself trust or learn to trust. Without privacy and the possibility of error which it protects that aspect of his humanity is denied to him.

The Concrete Recognition of Privacy

In concrete situations and actual societies, control over information about oneself, like control over one's bodily security or property, can only be relative and qualified. As is true for property or bodily security, the control over privacy must be limited by the rights of others. And as in the cases of property and bodily security, so too with privacy, the more one ventures into the outside, the more one pursues one's other interests with the aid of, in competition with, or even in the presence of others, the more one must risk invasions. As with property and personal security, it is the business of legal and social institutions to define and protect the right of privacy which emerges intact from the hurly-burly of social interactions. Now it would be absurd to argue that these concrete definitions and protections, differing as they do from society to society, are or should be strict derivations from general principles, the only legitimate variables being differing empirical circumstances (such as differing technologies or climatic conditions). The delineation of standards must be left to a political and social process the results of which will accord with justice if two conditions are met: (1) the process itself is just, that is, the interests of all are fairly represented; and (2) the outcome of the process protects basic dignity and provides moral capital for personal relations in the form of absolute title to at least some information about oneself.

The particular areas of life which are protected by privacy will be conventional at least in part, not only because they are the products of political processes, but also because of one of the reasons we value privacy. Insofar as privacy is regarded as moral capital for relations of love, friendship, and trust, there are situations where what kinds of information one is entitled to keep to oneself is not of the first importance. The important thing is that there be *some* information which is protected. Convention may quite properly rule in determining the particular areas which are private.

Convention plays another more important role in fostering privacy and the respect and esteem which it protects; it designates certain areas, intrinsically no more private than other areas, as symbolic of the whole institution of privacy, and thus deserving of protection beyond their particular importance. This apparently exaggerated respect for conventionally protected areas compensates for the inevitable fact that privacy is gravely compromised in any concrete social system: it is compromised by the inevitably and utterly just exercise of rights by others, it is compromised by the questionable but politically sanctioned exercise of rights by others, it is compromised by conduct which society does not condone but which it is unable or unwilling to forbid, and it is compromised by plainly wrongful invasions and aggressions. In all this there is a real danger that privacy might be crushed altogether, or, what would be as bad, that any venture outside the most limited area of activity would mean risking an almost total compromise of privacy.

Given these threats to privacy in general, social systems have given symbolic importance to certain conventionally designated areas of privacy. Thus in our culture the excretory functions are so shielded that situations in which this privacy is violated are experienced as extremely distressing, as detracting from one's dignity and self-esteem. Yet there does not seem to be any reason connected with the principles of respect, esteem, and the like why this would have to be so, and one can imagine other cultures in which it was not so, but where the same symbolic privacy was attached to, say, eating and drinking. There are other more subtly modulated symbolic areas of privacy, some of which merge into what I call substantive privacy (that is, areas where privacy does protect substantial interests). The very complex norms of privacy about matters of sex and health are good examples.

An excellent, very different sort of example of a contingent, symbolic recognition of an area of privacy as an expression of respect for personal integrity is the privilege against self-incrimination and the associated doctrines denying officials the power to compel other kinds of information without some explicit warrant. By according the privilege as fully as it does, our society affirms the extreme value of the individual's control over information about himself. To be sure, prying into a man's personal affairs by asking questions of others or by observing him is not prevented. Rather it is the point of the privilege that a man cannot be forced to make public information about himself. Thereby his sense of control over what others know of him is significantly enhanced, even if other sources of the same information exist. Without his cooperation, the other sources are necessarily incomplete, since he himself is the only ineluctable witness to his own present life, public or private, internal or manifest. And information about himself which others have to give out is in one sense information over which he has already relinquished control.

The privilege is contingent and symbolic. It is part of a whole structure of rules by which there is created an institution of privacy sufficient to the sense of respect, trust, and intimacy. It is contingent in that it cannot, I believe, be shown that some particular set of rules is necessary to the existence of such an institution of privacy. It is symbolic because the exercise of the privilege provides a striking expression of society's willingness to accept constraints on the pursuit of valid, perhaps vital, interests in order to recognize the right of privacy and the respect for the individual that privacy entails. Conversely, a proceeding in which compulsion is brought to bear on an individual to force him to make revelations about himself provides a striking and dramatic instance of a denial of title to control information about oneself, to control the picture we would have others have of us. In this sense such a procedure quite rightly seems profoundly humiliating. Nevertheless it is not clear to me that a system is unjust which sometimes allows such an imposition.

In calling attention to the symbolic aspect of some areas of privacy I do not mean to minimize their importance. On the contrary, they are highly significant as expressions of respect for others in a general situation where much of what we do to each other may signify a lack of respect or at least presents no occasion for expressing respect. That this is so is shown not so much on the occasions where these symbolic constraints are observed, for they are part of our system of expectations, but where they are violated. Not only does a person feel his standing is gravely compromised by such symbolic violations, but also those who wish to degrade and humiliate others often choose just such symbolic aggressions and invasions on the assumed though conventional area of privacy.

The Concept of Privacy Applied to the Problem of Monitoring

Let us return now to the concrete problem of electronic monitoring to see whether the foregoing elucidation of the concept of privacy will help to establish on firmer ground the intuitive objection that monitoring is an intolerable violation of privacy. Let us consider the more intrusive forms of monitoring where not only location but conversations and perhaps other data are monitored.

Obviously such a system of monitoring drastically curtails or eliminates altogether the power to control information about oneself. But, it might be said, this is not a significant objection if we assumed the monitored data will go only to authorized persons—probation or parole officers—and cannot be prejudicial so long as the subject of the monitoring is not violating the conditions under which he is allowed to be at liberty. This retort misses the importance of privacy as a context for all kinds of relations, from the most intense to the most casual. For all of these may require a context of some degree of intimacy, and intimacy is made impossible by monitoring.

It is worth being more precise about this notion of intimacy. Monitoring obviously presents vast opportunities for malice and misunderstanding on the part of authorized personnel. For that reason the subject has reason to be constantly apprehensive and inhibited in what he does. There is always an unseen audience, which is the more threatening because of the possibility that one may forget about it and let down his guard, as one would not with a visible audience. Even assuming the benevolence and understanding of the official audience, there are serious consequences to the fact that no degree of true intimacy is possible for the subject. Privacy is not, as we have seen, just a defensive right. It forms the necessary context for the intimate relations of love and friendship which give our lives much of whatever affirmative value they have. In the role of citizen or fellow worker, one need reveal himself to no greater extent than is necessary to display the attributes of competence and morality appropriate to those roles. In order to be a friend or lover one must reveal far more of himself. Yet where any intimate revelation may be heard by monitoring officials, it loses the quality of exclusive intimacy required of a gesture of love or friendship. Thus monitoring, in depriving one of privacy, destroys the possibility of bestowing the gift of intimacy, and makes impossible the essential dimension of love and friendship.

Monitoring similarly undermines the subject's capacity to enter into relations of trust. As I analyzed trust, it required the possibility of error on the part of the person trusted. The negation of trust is constant surveillance—such as monitoring—which minimizes the possibility of undetected default. The monitored parolee is denied the sense of self-respect inherent in being trusted by the government which has released him. More important, monitoring prevents the parolee from entering into true *relations* of trust with persons in the outside world. An employer, unaware of the monitoring, who entrusts a sum of money to the parolee cannot thereby grant him the sense of responsibility and autonomy which an unmonitored person in the same position would have. The parolee, in a real—if special and ironical—sense, cannot be trusted.

Now let us consider the argument that however intrusive monitoring may seem, surely prison life is more so. In part, of course, this will be a matter of fact. It may be that a reasonably secure and well-run prison will allow prisoners occasions for conversation among themselves, with guards, or with visitors, which are quite private. Such a prison regime would in this respect be less intrusive than monitoring. Often prison regimes do not allow even this, and go far toward depriving a prisoner of any sense of privacy; if the cells have doors, these may be equipped with peepholes. But there is still an important difference between this kind of prison and monitoring: the prison environment is overtly, even punitively unprivate. The contexts for relations to others are obviously and drastically different from what they are on the "outside." This itself, it seems to me, protects the prisoner's human orientation where monitoring only assails it. If the prisoner has a reasonably developed capacity for love, trust, and friendship and has in fact experienced ties of this sort, he is likely to be strongly aware (at least for a time) that prison life is a drastically different context from the one in which he enjoyed those relations, and this awareness will militate against his confusing the kinds of relations that can obtain in a "total institution" like a prison with those of freer social settings on the outside.

Monitoring, by contrast, alters only in a subtle and unobtrusive way—though a significant one—the context for relations. The subject appears free to perform the same actions as others and to enter the same relations, but in fact an important element of autonomy, of control over one's environment, is missing: he cannot be private. A prisoner can adopt a stance of withdrawal, of hibernation as it were, and thus preserve his sense of privacy intact to a degree. A person subject to monitoring by virtue of being in a free environment, dealing with people who expect him to have certain responses, capacities, and dispositions, is forced to make at least a show of intimacy to the persons he works closely with, those who would be his friends, and so on. They expect these things of him, because he is assumed to have the capacity and disposition to enter into ordinary relations with them. Yet if he does—if, for instance, he enters into light banter with slight sexual overtones with the waitress at the diner where he eats regularly—he has been forced to violate his own integrity by revealing to his official monitors even so small an aspect of his private personality, the personality he wishes to reserve for persons toward whom he will make some gestures of intimacy and friendship. Theoretically, of course, a monitored parolee might adopt the same attitude of withdrawal that a prisoner does, but in fact that too would be a costly and degrading experience. He would be tempted, as in prison he would not be, to "give himself away" and to act like everyone else, since in every outward respect he seems like everyone else. Moreover, by withdrawing, the person subject to monitoring would risk seeming cold, unnatural, odd, inhuman, to the very people whose esteem and affection he craves. In prison the circumstances dictating a reserved and tentative facade are so apparent to all that adopting such a facade is no reflection on the prisoner's humanity.

The insidiousness of a technique which forces a man to betray himself in this humiliating way or else seem inhuman is compounded when one considers that the subject is also forced to betray others who may become intimate with him. Even persons in the overt oppressiveness of a prison do not labor under the burden of this double betrayal.

As against all of these considerations, there remains the argument that so long as monitoring depends on the consent of the subject, who feels it is preferable to prison, to close off this alternative in the name of a morality so intimately concerned with liberty is absurd. This argument may be decisive; I am not at all confident that the alternative of monitored release should be closed off. My analysis does show, I think, that it involves costs to the prisoner which are easily overlooked, that on inspection it is a less desirable alternative than might at first appear. Moreover, monitoring presents systematic dangers to potential subjects as a class. Its availability as a compromise between conditional release and continued imprisonment may lead officials who are in any doubt whether or not to trust a man on parole or probation to assuage their doubts by resorting to monitoring.

The seductions of monitored release disguise not only a cost to the subject but to society as well. The discussion of trust should make clear that unmonitored release is a very different experience from monitored release, and so the educational and rehabilitative effect of unmonitored release is also different. Unmonitored release affirms in a far more significant way the relations of trust between the convicted criminal and the society which he violated by his crime and which we should now be seeking to re-establish. But trust can only arise, as any parent knows, through the experience of being trusted.

Finally, it must be recognized that more limited monitoring—for instance where only the approximate location of the subject is revealed—lacks the offensive features of total monitoring and is obviously preferable to prison.

The Role of Law

This evaluation of the proposal for electronic monitoring has depended on the general theoretical framework of this whole essay. It is worth noting the kind of evaluation that framework has permitted. Rather than inviting a fragmentation of the proposal into various pleasant and unpleasant elements and comparing the "net utility" of the proposal with its alternatives, we have been able to evaluate the total situation created by the proposal in another way. We have been able to see it as a system in which certain actions and relations, the pursuit of certain ends, are possible or impossible. Certain systems of actions, ends, and relations are possible or impossible in different social contexts. Moreover, the social context itself is a system of actions and relations. The social contexts created by monitoring and its alternatives, liberty or imprisonment, are thus evaluated by their conformity to a model system in which are instantiated the principles of morality, justice, friendship, and love. Such a model, which is used as a standard, is of course partially unspecified in that there is perhaps an infinite number of specific systems which conform to those principles. Now actual systems, as we have seen, may vary in respect to how other ends—for example, beauty, knowledge—may be pursued in them, and they may be extremely deficient in allowing for the pursuit of such ends. But those who design, propose, and administer social systems are first of all bound to make them conform to the model of morality and injustice, for in so doing they express respect and even friendship—what might be called civic friendship—toward those implicated in the system. If designers and administrators fail to conform to this model, they fail to express that aspect of their humanity which makes them in turn fit subjects for the respect, friendship, and love of others.

●   ●   ●

Discussion Questions

1. Give arguments for or against the electronic monitoring discussed at the beginning of Fried's paper.
2. How does Fried's definition of privacy compare with those considered by McCloskey? Does Fried's definition escape McCloskey's criticisms? Why or why not?
3. What is Fried's major argument for privacy? Do you find it convincing? Why or why not?
4. McCloskey considers and criticizes Fried's arguments. How might Fried answer his criticisms?
5. How does Fried apply his defense of privacy to the electronic monitoring case? Support or criticize his arguments on this point.

Suggested Readings for Chapter Eight

Bier, William C. *Privacy: A Vanishing Value?* New York: Fordham University Press, 1980.

Dworkin, Andrea. *Pornography: Men Possessing Women.* New York: G. P. Putnam's, 1981.

Griffin, Susan. *Pornography and Silence.* New York: Harper & Row, 1981.

Simons, G. L. *Pornography without Prejudice.* London: Abelard-Schuman, Ltd., 1972.

9

Animal Rights and
Environmental Ethics

One way of viewing moral progress is to think of it as the gradual extension of rights and status to larger and larger groups. First, members of some dominant group are accorded full status and full rights; then these rights are gradually extended to minority groups. For example, in the United States at first only property-owning white males had full rights, but these were gradually extended to non-property-owning white males, to blacks, and other minorities, and eventually to women. No doubt this account is oversimple in some ways and applies more obviously to such things as voting rights than to other kinds of rights and statuses, but it does fit the historical facts.

Some philosophers now argue that the next step in moral progress is to extend rights and some status to animals and even in a sense to the natural environment. It is alleged, for example, that animals have a right to life and that it is wrong to kill them for food or other purposes. The destruction of the natural environment for human purposes is also condemned, though the term *rights* is less often used in this context.

Some of the rhetoric of the human liberation has been applied to animal liberation. Racism is a preference for one race at the expense of others, and sexism is a preference for one sex at the expense of the other; by extension, the term *speciesism* has been coined to indicate a preference for the human species at the expense of other species. The subtle inference of the use of such terms is that just as racism and sexism have been gradually admitted by many people to be morally wrong, so speciesism will eventually be seen as morally wrong.

However, many philosophers who find absurd the equation of, or even the comparison of, racism and speciesism are concerned with cruelty toward and in-humane treatment of animals. A good case can be made that a great deal of scientific experimentation with animals is both cruel and unnecessary. And the treatment of food animals in our crowded and competitive society would horrify many consumers of the food produced.

A person's attitude toward animal rights and ecological ethics is likely to be very much bound up with his or her whole world view. A religious world view often goes with a *hierarchical* view of the relations among human beings, animals, and nature. Humans are seen as created to love and serve God, while animals and nature are created by God to serve human needs. Such a world view gives a justification for the use of animals and the environment for human purposes. It is sometimes claimed that this kind of world view encourages us to exploit animals and the environment. However, a religious world view often includes the idea of stewardship—that humans are responsible for their use of animals and the environment to the Creator of all things.

Some nontheistic world views that are religious in a broad sense include ideas such as reverence for life or the unity of all nature; such views are likely to support the idea of animal rights and ecological ethics. However, such world views face a problem in that the "natural order" does not always seem to exhibit reverence for life or unity. Animals prey on other animals; natural forces like fire or drought can devastate the environment. An impersonal nature seems to give no moral directives or else contradictory directives.

A nonreligious world view for which humans are no more important or valuable than any other natural phenomena may seem to favor animal rights and ecological concern. However, if nature has no inherent purpose or meaning, presumably the only meanings or purposes in the world are those imposed on it by individual humans. And many individuals seem quite content to sacrifice animals or nature for human purposes.

In the papers in this section, Peter Singer makes a strong defense of animal rights both giving theoretical arguments and citing some disturbing facts about the inhumane treatment of animals. Philip Devine criticizes Singer's arguments and similar arguments. Emile Fackre discusses ecological issues from a religious point of view. Joel Feinberg extends the discussion to ecological concerns by considering what we owe to future generations in the way of not spoiling the environment. Finally, Richard De George discusses the relationship of a number of questions about the environment rights and future generations.

Animal Liberation

Peter Singer

I

We are familiar with Black Liberation, Gay Liberation, and a variety of other movements. With Women's Liberation some thought we had come to the end of the road. Discrimination on the basis of sex, it has been said, is the last form of discrimination that is universally accepted and practiced without pretense, even in those liberal circles which have long prided themselves on their freedom from racial discrimination. But one should always be wary of talking of "the last remaining form of discrimination." If we have learned anything from the liberation movements, we should have learned how difficult it is to be aware of the ways in which we discriminate until they are forcefully pointed out to us. A liberation movement demands an expansion of our moral horizons, so that practices that were previously regarded as natural and inevitable are now seen as intolerable.

Animals, Men and Morals is a manifesto for an Animal Liberation movement. The contributors to the book may not all see the issue this way. They are a varied group. Philosophers, ranging from professors to graduate students, make up the largest contingent. There are five of them, including the three editors, and there is also an extract from the unjustly neglected German philosopher with an English name, Leonard Nelson, who died in 1927. There are essays by two novelist/critics, Brigid Brophy and Maureen Duffy, and another by Muriel the Lady Dowding, widow of Dowding of Battle of Britain fame and the founder of "Beauty Without Cruelty," a movement that campaigns against the use of animals for furs and cosmetics. The other pieces are by a psychologist, a botanist, a sociologist, and Ruth Harrison, who is probably best described as a professional campaigner for animal welfare.

Whether or not these people, as individuals, would all agree that they are launching a liberation movement for animals, the book as a whole amounts to no less. It is a demand for a complete change in our attitudes to nonhumans. It is a demand that we cease to regard the exploitation of other species as natural and inevitable, and that, instead, we see it as a continuing moral outrage. Patrick Corbett, Professor of Philosophy at Sussex University, captures the spirit of the book in his closing words:

> . . . We require now to extend the great principles of liberty, equality and fraternity over the lives of animals. Let animal slavery join human slavery in the graveyard of the past.

The reader is likely to be skeptical. "Animal Liberation" sounds more like a parody of liberation movements than a serious objective. The reader may think: We support the claims of blacks and women for equality because blacks and women really are equal to whites and males—equal in intelligence and in abilities, capacity for leadership, rationality, and so on. Humans and nonhumans obviously are not equal in these respects. Since justice demands only that we treat equals equally, unequal treatment of humans and nonhumans cannot be an injustice.

This is a tempting reply, but a dangerous one. It commits the non-racist and non-sexist to a dogmatic belief that blacks and women really are just as intelligent, able, etc., as whites and males—and no more. Quite possibly this happens to be the case. Certainly attempts to prove that racial or sexual differences in these respects have a genetic origin have not been conclusive. But do we really want to stake our demand for equality on the assumption that there are no genetic differences of this kind between the different races or sexes? Surely the appropriate response to those who claim to have found evidence for such genetic differences is not to stick to the belief that there are no differences, whatever the evidence to the contrary; rather one should be clear that the claim to equality does not depend on IQ. Moral equality is distinct from factual equality. Otherwise it would be nonsense to talk of the equality of human beings, since humans, as individuals, obviously differ in intelligence and almost any ability one cares to name. If possessing greater intelligence does not entitle one human to exploit another, why should it entitle humans to exploit nonhumans?

Jeremy Bentham expressed the essential bias of equality in his famous formula: "Each to count for one and none for more than one." In other words, the interests of every being that has interests are to be taken into account and treated equally with the like interests of any other being. Other moral philosophers, before and after Bentham, have made the same point in different ways. Our concern for others must not depend on whether they possess certain characteristics, though just what that concern involves may, of course, vary according to such characteristics.

Bentham, incidentally, was well aware that the logic of the demand for racial equality did not stop at the equality of humans. He wrote:

> The day *may* come when the rest of the animal creation may acquire those rights which never could have been withholden from them but by the hand of tyranny. The French have already discovered that the blackness of the skin is no reason why a human being should be abandoned without redress to the caprice of a tormentor. It may one day come to be recognized that the number of the legs, the villosity of the skin, or the termination of the *os sacrum,* are reasons equally insufficient for abandoning a sensitive being to the same fate. What else is it that should trace the insuperable line? Is it the faculty of reason, or perhaps the faculty of discourse? But a full-grown horse or dog is beyond comparison a more rational, as well as a more conversable animal, than an infant of a day, or a week, or even a month, old. But suppose they were otherwise, what would it avail? The question is not, Can they *reason?* nor Can they *talk?* but, Can they *suffer?*[1]

Surely Bentham was right. If a being suffers, there can be no moral justification for refusing to take that suffering into consideration, and, indeed, to count it equally with the like suffering (if rough comparisons can be made) of any other being.

So the only question is: Do animals other than man suffer? Most people agree unhesitatingly that animals like cats and dogs can and do suffer, and this seems also to be assumed by those laws that prohibit wanton cruelty to such animals. Personally, I have no doubt at all about this and find it hard to take seriously the doubts that a few people apparently do have. The editors and contributors of *Animals, Men and Morals* seem to feel the same way, for although the question is raised more than once, doubts are quickly dismissed each time. Nevertheless, because this is such a fundamental point, it is worth asking what grounds we have for attributing suffering to other animals.

It is best to begin by asking what grounds any individual human has for supposing that other humans feel pain. Since pain is a state of consciousness, a "mental event," it can never be directly observed. No observations, whether behavioral signs such as writhing or screaming or physiological or neurological recordings, are observations of pain itself. Pain is something one feels, and one can only infer that others are feeling it from various external indications. The fact that only philosophers are ever skeptical about whether other humans feel pain shows that we regard such inference as justifiable in the case of humans.

Is there any reason why the same inference should be unjustifiable for other animals? Nearly all the external signs which lead us to infer pain in other humans can be seen in other species, especially "higher" animals such as mammals and birds. Behavioral signs—writhing, yelping, or other forms of calling, attempts to avoid the source of pain, and many others—are present. We know, too, that these animals are biologically similar in the relevant respects, having nervous systems like ours which can be observed to function as ours do.

So the grounds for inferring that these animals can feel pain are nearly as good as the grounds for inferring other humans do. Only nearly, for there is one behavioral sign that humans have but nonhumans, with the exception of one or two specially raised chimpanzees, do not have. This, of course, is a developed language. As the quotation from Bentham indicates, this has long been regarded as an important distinction between man and other animals. Other animals may communicate with each other, but not in the way we do. Following Chomsky, many people now mark this distinction by saying that only humans communicate in a form that is governed by rules of syntax. (For the purposes of this argument, linguists allow those chimpanzees who have learned a syntactic sign language to rank as honorary humans.) Nevertheless, as Bentham pointed out, this distinction is not relevant to the question of how animals ought to be treated, unless it can be linked to the issue of whether animals suffer.

This link may be attempted in two ways. First, there is a hazy line of philosophical thought, stemming perhaps from some doctrines associated with Wittgenstein, which maintains that we cannot meaningfully attribute states of consciousness to beings without language. I have not seen this argument made explicit in print, though I have come across it in conversation. This position seems to me very implausible, and I doubt that it would be held at all if it were not thought to be a consequence of a broader view of the significance of language. It may be that the use of a public, rule-governed language is a precondition of conceptual thought. It may even be, although personally I doubt it, that we cannot meaningfully speak of a creature having an intention unless that creature can use a language. But states like pain, surely, are more primitive than either of these, and seem to have nothing to do with language.

Indeed, as Jane Goodall points out in her study of chimpanzees, when it comes to the expression of feelings and emotions, humans tend to fall back on non-linguistic modes of communication which are often found among apes, such as a cheering pat on the back, an exuberant embrace, a clasp of hands, and so on.[2] Michael Peters makes a similar point in his contribution to *Animals, Men and Morals* when he notes that the basic signals we use to convey pain, fear, sexual arousal, and so on are not specific to our species. So there seems to be no reason at all to believe that a creature without language cannot suffer.

The second, and more easily appreciated way of linking language and the existence of pain is to say that the best evidence that we can have that another creature is in pain is when he tells us that he is. This is a distinct line of argument, for it is not being denied that a non-language-user conceivably could suffer, but only that we could know that he is suffering. Still, this line of argument seems to me to fail, and for reasons similar to those just given. "I am in pain" is not the best possible evidence that the speaker is in pain (he might be lying), and it is certainly not the only possible evidence. Behavioral signs and knowledge of the animal's biological similarity to ourselves together provide adequate evidence that animals do suffer. After all, we would not accept linguistic evidence if it contradicted the rest of the evidence. If a man was severely burned, and behaved as if he were in pain, writhing, groaning, being very careful not to let his burned skin touch anything, and so on, but later said he had not been in pain at all, we would be more likely to conclude that he was lying or suffering from amnesia than that he had not been in pain.

Even if there were stronger grounds for refusing to attribute pain to those who do not have a language, the consequences of this refusal might lead us to examine these grounds unusually critically. Human infants, as well as some adults, are unable to use language. Are we to deny that a year-old infant can suffer? If not, how can language be crucial? Of course, most parents can understand the responses of even very young infants better than they understand the responses of other animals, and sometimes infant responses can be understood in the light of later development.

This, however, is just a fact about the relative knowledge we have of our own species and other species, and most of this knowledge is simply derived from closer contact. Those who have studied the behavior of other animals soon learn to understand their responses at least as well as we understand those of an infant. (I am not just referring to Jane Goodall's and other well-known studies of apes. Consider, for example, the degree of understanding achieved by Tinbergen from watching herring gulls.)[3] Just as we can understand infant human behavior in the light of adult human behavior, so we can understand the behavior of other species in the light of our own behavior (and sometimes we can understand our own behavior better in the light of the behavior of other species).

The grounds we have for believing that other mammals and birds suffer are, then, closely analogous to the grounds we have for believing that other humans suffer. It remains to consider how far down the evolutionary scale this analogy holds. Obviously it becomes poorer when we get further away from man. To be more precise would require a detailed examination of all that we know about other forms of life. With fish, reptiles, and other vertebrates the analogy still seems strong, with molluscs like oysters it is much weaker. Insects are more difficult, and it may be that in our present state of knowledge we must be agnostic about whether they are capable of suffering.

If there is no moral justification for ignoring suffering when it occurs, and it does occur in other species, what are we to say of our attitudes toward these other species? Richard Ryder, one of the contributors to *Animals, Men and Morals*, uses the term "speciesism" to describe the belief that we are entitled to treat members of other species in a way in which it would be wrong to treat members of our own species. The term is not euphonious, but it neatly makes the analogy with racism. The non-racist would do well to bear the analogy in mind when he is inclined to defend human behavior toward nonhumans. "Shouldn't we worry about improving the lot of our own species before we concern ourselves with other species?" he may ask. If we substitute "race" for "species" we shall see that the question is better not asked. "Is a vegetarian diet nutritionally adequate?" resembles the slave-owner's claim that he and the whole economy of the South would be ruined without slave labor. There is even a parallel with skeptical doubts about whether animals suffer, for some defenders of slavery professed to doubt whether blacks really suffer in the way that whites do.

I do not want to give the impression, however, that the case for Animal Liberation is based on the analogy with racism and no more. On the contrary, *Animals, Men and Morals* describes the various ways in which humans exploit nonhumans, and several contributors consider the defenses that have been offered, including the defense of meat-eating mentioned in the last paragraph. Sometimes the rebuttals are scornfully dismissive, rather than carefully designed to convince the detached critic. This may be a fault, but it is a fault that is inevitable, given the kind of book this is. The issue is not one on which one can remain detached. As the editors state in their Introduction:

> Once the full force of moral assessment has been made explicit there can be no rational excuse left for killing animals, be they killed for food, science, or sheer personal indulgence. We have not assembled this book to provide the reader with yet another manual on how to make brutalities less brutal. Compromise, in the traditional sense of the term, is simple unthinking weakness when one considers the actual reasons for our crude relationships with the other animals.

The point is that on this issue there are few critics who are genuinely detached. People who eat pieces of slaughtered nonhumans every day find it hard to believe that they are doing wrong; and they also find it hard to imagine what else they could eat. So for those who do not place nonhumans beyond the pale of morality, there comes a stage when further argument seems pointless, a stage at which one can only accuse one's opponent of hypocrisy and reach for the sort of sociological account of our practices and the way we defend them that is attempted by David Wood in his contribution to this book. On the other hand, to those unconvinced by the arguments, and unable to accept that they are merely rationalizing their dietary preferences and their fear of being thought peculiar, such sociological explanations can only seem insultingly arrogant.

II

The logic of speciesism is most apparent in the practice of experimenting on nonhumans in order to benefit humans. This is because the issue is rarely obscured by allegations that nonhumans are so different from humans that we cannot know anything about whether they suffer. The defender of vivisection cannot use this argument because he needs to stress the similarities between man and other animals in order to justify the usefulness to the former of experiments on the latter. The researcher who makes rats choose between starvation and electric shock to see if they develop ulcers (they do) does so because he knows that the rat has a nervous system very similar to man's, and presumably feels an electric shock in a similar way.

Richard Ryder's restrained account of experiments on animals made me angrier with my fellow men than anything else in this book. Ryder, a clinical psychologist by profession, himself experimented on animals before he came to hold the view he puts forward in his essay. Experimenting on animals is now a large industry, both academic and commercial. In 1969, more than 5 million experiments were performed in Britain, the vast majority without anesthetic (though how many of these involved pain is not known). There are no accurate U.S. figures, since there is no federal law on the subject, and in many cases no state law either. Estimates vary from 20 million to 200 million. Ryder suggests that 80 million may be the best guess. We tend to think that this is all for vital medical research, but of course it is not. Huge numbers of animals are used in university departments from Forestry to Psychology, and even more are used for commercial purposes, to test whether cosmetics can cause skin damage, or shampoos eye damage, or to test food additives or laxatives or sleeping pills or anything else.

A standard test for foodstuffs is the "LD50." The object of this test is to find the dosage level at which 50 percent of the test animals will die. This means that nearly all of them will become very sick before finally succumbing or surviving. When the substance is a harmless one, it may be necessary to force huge doses down the animals, until in some cases sheer volume or concentration causes death.

Ryder gives a selection of experiments, taken from recent scientific journals. I will quote two, not for the sake of indulging in gory details, but in order to give an idea of what normal researchers think they may legitimately do to other species. The point is not that the individual researchers are cruel men, but that they are behaving in a way that is allowed by our speciesist attitudes. As Ryder points out, even if only 1 percent of the experiments involve severe pain, that is 50,000 experiments in Britain each year, or nearly 150 every day (and about fifteen times as many in the United States, if Ryder's guess is right). Here then are two experiments:

> O. S. Ray and R. J. Barrett of Pittsburg gave electric shocks to the feet of 1,042 mice. They then caused convulsions by giving more intense shocks through cup-shaped electrodes applied to the animals' eyes or through pressure spring clips attached to their ears. Unfortunately some of the mice who "successfully completed Day One training were found sick or dead prior to testing on Day Two." [*Journal of Comparative and Physiological Psychology*, 1969, vol. 67, pp. 110–116]

> At the National Institute for Medical Research, Mill Hill, London, W. Feldberg and S. L. Sherwood injected chemicals into the brains of cats—"with a number of widely different substances, recurrent patterns of reaction were obtained. Retching, vomiting, defecation, increased salivation and greatly accelerated respiration leading to panting were common features." . . .

> The injection into the brain of a large dose of Tubocuraine caused the cat to jump "from the table to the floor and then straight into its cage, where it started calling more and more noisily whilst moving about restlessly and jerkily . . . finally the cat fell with legs and neck flexed, jerking in rapid clonic movements, the condition being that of a major [epileptic] convulsion . . . within a few seconds the cat got up, ran for a few yards at high speed and fell in another fit. The whole process was repeated several times within the next ten minutes, during which the cat lost feces and foamed at the mouth."

> This animal finally died thirty-five minutes after the brain injection. [*Journal of Physiology*, 1954, vol. 123, pp. 148–167]

There is nothing secret about these experiments. One has only to open any recent volume of a learned journal, such as the *Journal of Comparative and Physiological Psychology*, to find full descriptions of experiments of this sort, together with the results obtained—results that are frequently trivial and obvious. The experiments are often supported by public funds.

It is a significant indication of the level of acceptability of these practices that, although these experiments are taking place at this moment on university campuses throughout the country, there has, so far as I know, not been the slightest protest from the student movement. Students have been rightly concerned that their universities should not discriminate on grounds of race or sex, and that they should not serve the purposes of the military or big business. Speciesism continues undisturbed, and many students participate in it. There may be a few qualms at first, but since everyone regards it as normal, and it may even be a required part of a course, the student soon becomes hardened and, dismissing his earlier feelings as "mere sentiment," comes to regard animals as statistics rather than sentient beings with interests that warrant consideration.

Argument about vivisection has often missed the point because it has been put in absolutist terms: Would the abolitionist be prepared to let thousands die if they could be saved by experimenting on a single animal? The way to reply to this purely hypothetical question is to pose another: Would the experimenter be prepared to experiment on a human orphan under six months old, if it were the only way to save many lives? (I say "orphan" to avoid the complication of parental feelings, although in doing so I am being overfair to the experimenter, since the nonhuman subjects of experiments are not orphans.) A negative answer to this question indicates that the experimenter's readiness to use nonhumans is simple discrimination, for adult apes, cats, mice, and other mammals are more conscious of what is happening to them, more self-directing, and, so far as we can tell, just as sensitive to pain as a human infant. There is no characteristic that human infants possess that adult mammals do not have to the same or a higher degree.

(It might be possible to hold that what makes it wrong to experiment on a human infant is that the infant will in time develop into more than the nonhuman, but one would then, to be consistent, have to oppose abortion, and perhaps contraception, too, for the fetus and the egg and sperm have the same potential as the infant. Moreover, one would still have no reason for experimenting on a nonhuman rather than a human with brain damage severe enough to make it impossible for him to rise above infant level.)

The experimenter, then, shows a bias for his own species whenever he carries out an experiment on a nonhuman for a purpose that he would not think justified him in using a human being at an equal or lower level of sentience, awareness, ability to be self-directing, etc. No one familiar with the kind of results yielded by these experiments can have the slightest doubt that if this bias were eliminated the number of experiments performed would be zero or very close to it.

III

If it is vivisection that shows the logic of speciesism most clearly, it is the use of other species for food that is at the heart of our attitudes toward them. Most of *Animals, Men and Morals* is an attack on meat-eating—an attack which is based solely on concern for nonhumans, without reference to arguments derived from considerations of ecology, macrobiotics, health, or religion.

The idea that nonhumans are utilities, means to our ends, pervades our thought. Even conservationists who are concerned about the slaughter of wild fowl but not about the vastly greater slaughter of chickens for our tables are thinking in this way—they are worried about what we would lose if there were less wildlife. Stanley Godlovitch, pursuing the Marxist idea that our thinking is formed by the activities we undertake in satisfying our needs, suggests that man's first classification of his environment was into Edibles and Inedibles. Most animals came into the first category, and there they have remained.

Man may always have killed other species for food, but he has never exploited them so ruthlessly as he does today. Farming has succumbed to business methods, the objective being to get the highest possible ratio of output (meat, eggs, milk) to input (fodder, labor costs, etc.). Ruth Harrison's essay "On Factory Farming" gives an account of some aspects of modern methods and of the unsuccessful British campaign for effective controls, a campaign which was sparked off by her *Animal Machines* (Stuart: London, 1964).

Her article is in no way a substitute for her earlier book. This is a pity since, as she says, "Farm produce is still associated with mental pictures of animals browsing in the fields, . . . of hens having a last forage before going to roost. . . . " Yet neither in her article nor elsewhere in *Animals, Men and Morals* is this false image replaced by a clear idea of the nature and extent of factory farming. We learn of this only indirectly, when we hear of the code of reform proposed by an advisory committee set up by the British government.

Among the proposals, which the government refused to implement on the grounds that they were too idealistic, were: "*Any animal should at least have room to turn around freely.*"

Factory farm animals need liberation in the most literal sense. Veal calves are kept in stalls five feet by two feet. They are usually slaughtered when about four months old and have been too big to turn in their stalls for at least a month. Intensive beef herds, kept in stalls only proportionately larger for much longer periods, account for a growing percentage of beef production. Sows are often similarly confined when pregnant, which, because of artificial methods of increasing fertility, can be most of the time. Animals confined in this way do not waste food by exercising, nor do they develop unpalatable muscle.

"*A dry bedded area should be provided for all stock.*" Intensively kept animals usually have to stand and sleep on slatted floors without straw, because this makes cleaning easier.

"*Palatable roughage must be readily available to all calves after one week of age.*" In order to produce the pale veal housewives are said to prefer, calves are fed on an all-liquid diet until slaughter, even though they are long past the age at which they would normally eat grass. They develop a craving for roughage, evidenced by attempts to gnaw wood from their stalls. (For the same reason, their diet is deficient in iron.)

"*Battery cages for poultry should be large enough for a bird to be able to stretch one wing at a time.*" Under current British practice, a cage for four or five laying hens has a floor area of twenty inches by eighteen inches, scarcely larger than a double page of the *New York Review of Books*. In this space, on a sloping wire floor (sloping so the eggs roll down, wire so the dung drops through) the birds live for a year or eighteen months while artificial lighting and temperature conditions combine with drugs in their food to squeeze the maximum number of eggs out of them. Table birds are also sometimes kept in cages. More often they are reared in sheds, no less crowded. Under these conditions all the birds' natural activities are frustrated, and they develop "vices" such as pecking each other to death. To prevent this, beaks are often cut off, and the sheds kept dark.

How many of those who support factory farming by buying its produce know anything about the way it is produced? How many have heard something about it, but are reluctant to check up for fear that it will make them uncomfortable? To non-speciesists, the typical consumer's mixture of ignorance, reluctance to find out the truth, and vague belief that nothing really bad could be allowed seems analogous to the attitudes of "decent Germans" to the death camps.

There are, of course, some defenders of factory farming. Their arguments are considered, though again rather sketchily, by John Harris. Among the most common: "Since they have never known anything else, they don't suffer." This argument will not be put by anyone who knows anything about animal behavior, since he will know that not all behavior has to be learned. Chickens attempt to stretch wings, walk around, scratch, and even dustbathe or build a nest, even though they have never lived under conditions that allowed these activities. Calves can suffer from maternal deprivation no matter at what age they were taken from their mothers. "We need these intensive methods to provide protein for a growing population." As ecologists and famine relief organizations know, we can produce far more protein per acre if we grow the right vegetable crop, soy beans for instance, than if we use the land to grow crops to be converted into protein by animals who use nearly 90 percent of the protein themselves, even when unable to exercise.

There will be many readers of this book who will agree that factory farming involves an unjustifiable degree of exploitation of sentient creatures and yet will want to say that there is nothing wrong with rearing animals for food, provided it is done "humanely." These people are saying, in effect, that although we should not cause animals to suffer, there is nothing wrong with killing them.

There are two possible replies to this view. One is to attempt to show that this combination of attitudes is absurd. Roslind Godlovitch takes this course in her essay, which is an examination of some common attitudes to animals. She argues that from the combination of "animal suffering is to be avoided" and "there is nothing wrong with killing animals" it follows that all animal life ought to be exterminated (since all sentient creatures will suffer to some degree at some point in their lives). Euthanasia is a contentious issue only because we place some value on living. If we did not, the least amount of suffering would justify it. Accordingly, if we deny that we have a duty to exterminate all animal life, we must concede that we are placing some value on animal life.

This argument seems to me valid, although one could still reply that the value of animal life is to be derived from the pleasures that life can have for them, so that, provided their lives have a balance of pleasure over pain, we are justified in rearing them. But this would imply that we ought to produce animals and let them live as pleasantly as possible, without suffering.

At this point, one can make the second of the two possible replies to the view that rearing and killing animals for food is all right so long as it is done humanely. This second reply is that so long as we think that a nonhuman may be killed simply so that a human can satisfy his taste for meat, we are still thinking of nonhumans as means rather than as ends in themselves. The factory farm is nothing more than the application of technology to this concept. Even traditional methods involve castration, the separation of mothers and their young, the breaking up of herds, branding or ear-punching, and of course transportation to the abattoirs and the final moments of terror when the animal smells blood and senses danger. If we were to try rearing animals so that they lived and died without suffering, we should find that to do so on anything like the scale of today's meat industry would be a sheer impossibility. Meat would become the prerogative of the rich.

I have been able to discuss only some of the contributions to this book, saying nothing about, for instance, the essays on killing for furs and for sport. Nor have I considered all the detailed questions that need to be asked once we start thinking about other species in the radically different way presented by this book. What, for instance, are we to do about genuine conflicts of interest like rats biting slum children? I am not sure of the answer, but the essential point is just that we *do* see this as a conflict of interests, that we recognize that rats have interests too. Then we may begin to think about other ways of resolving the conflict—perhaps by leaving out rat baits that sterilize the rats instead of killing them.

I have not discussed such problems because they are side issues compared with the exploitation of other species for food and for experimental purposes. On these central matters, I hope that I have said enough to show that this book, despite its flaws, is a challenge to every human to recognize his attitudes to nonhumans as a form of prejudice no less objectionable than racism or sexism. It is a challenge that demands not just a change of attitudes, but a change in our way of life, for it requires us to become vegetarians.

Can a purely moral demand of this kind succeed? The odds are certainly against it. The book holds out no inducements. It does not tell us that we will become healthier, or enjoy life more, if we cease exploiting animals. Animal Liberation will require greater altruism on the part of mankind than any other liberation movement, since animals are incapable of demanding it for themselves, or of protesting against their exploitation by votes, demonstrations, or bombs. Is man capable of such genuine altruism? Who knows? If this book does have a significant effect, however, it will be a vindication of all those who have believed that man has within himself the potential for more than cruelty and selfishness.

Notes

[1] *The Principles of Morals and Legislation,* ch. XVII, sec. 1, footnote to paragraph 4. (Italics in original.)

[2] Jane van Lawick-Goodall, *In the Shadow of Man* (Houghton Mifflin, 1971), p. 225.

[3] N. Tinbergen, *The Herring Gull's World* (Basic Books, 1961).

Discussion Questions

1. Singer argues that since humans are unequal in various respects we cannot argue for different treatment for animals on the grounds that they are not equal to humans. Criticize this argument.

2. Singer argues that "if a being suffers, there can be no moral justification for refusing to take that suffering into consideration, and, indeed, to count it equally with like suffering . . . of any other being." Does agreeing with the first part of the statement commit you to agreeing with the second? Why or why not?

3. Singer draws parallels between racism and speciesism. Are those parallels justified? Why or why not?

4. Do Singer's facts about the mistreatments of animals in scientific experiments and in food production support his main conclusion that animal rights can be equated with human rights? Why or why not?

5. Criticize or support Singer's arguments that human infants or retarded humans are less conscious, self-directing, and so on than full-grown animals.

Ecology and Theology

Gabriel Fackre

"Earth Sunday!" So read the flier from church headquarters that clergy received a few weeks before the April, 1970, teach-in. The national conscience had been stung awake to the ecological crisis. And now the churches were being urged to action.

From Ian G. Barbour, ed., *Western Man and Environmental Ethics* (Reading, Mass., Addison-Wesley Publishing Co., 1973). Reprinted by permission of the author.

The reaction to both the general interest in ecology and the church's new zeal for the environment is mixed. Those deeply caught up in the struggles for racial justice or peace wonder if the pollution fever is a diversionary tactic on the part of those in power. Others despair at the ecclesiastical trumpet call, for it seems once again that the church is the "tail light rather than the headlight."

Why should the church turn its attention to the environmental issue? There is, of course, the obvious reason that we have to do with the survival of the planet itself, if the somber prophecies of Ehrlich and Commoner are correct. But there are other reasons. One is this temptation to thrust the "crisis in Eden" forward to the exclusion of social anguishes that are as clamant as ever.[1] As partisans in the battles of the 60s—race, peace, poverty—we have a special responsibility to see that these do not get lost from view, and to lobby for full-orbed mission. Yet another reason for the church's urgent attention is the allegation by some of the most dedicated pollution crusaders that the debasing of the environment is traceable to an attitude toward nature rooted in the Judeo-Christian tradition itself. Thus Lynn White, whose comments appear in *The Environmental Handbook* used in conjunction with the teach-in, charges that the biblical mandate that man should have "dominion over" nature and "subdue the earth" lies back of Western society's exploitation of its natural resources.[2] In contrast to this "anthropocentric" view of the world, more than a few ecological activists recommend a nature-affirming reverence for all of life and look to the religions of the East to sustain it. In particular, the "counter culture," which sets itself against the technocracy and goes back to the land in primitive communes, experiments with native Indian and non-Western religious options.[3] See how these tendencies come together (with a few exceptions) in the Berkeley Ecological Revolutionary Organization's statement:

> It seems evident that there are throughout the world certain social and religious forces which have worked through history toward an ecologically and culturally enlightened state of affairs. Let these be encouraged: Gnostics, hip Marxists, Teilhard de Chardin Catholics, Druids, Taoists, Biologists, Witches, Yogins, Bhikkus, Quakers, Sufis, Tibetans, Zens, Shamans, Bushmen, American Indians, Polynesians, Anarchists, Alchemists . . . the list is long. All primitive cultures, all communal and ashram movements.[4]

There are no Jews or Protestants in that list. The Christians mentioned are a select group. The rest of us are the culprits.

If the charges are true, we have a massive job of reforming our teaching and ourselves. If they are not true, then we have an equally massive job of interpretation, to our own constituencies as well as to others. One way or the other, serious religious reflection on the environment is an absolute must. The ecological problem is a theological problem.

The Doctrine of Creation: Its Use and Abuse

An environmental theology, in the context of the pollution question, must confront head-on the allegations that the biblical doctrine of creation espouses an anthropocentricism which shows respect for man at the price of disrespect for the environment. Lynn White is indeed correct when he says that the biblical story places man above nature. Man is the crown of creation, made in the very image of God. This Old Testament premise is confirmed in the New Testament. God chooses to enter his world in the form of man: "the Word became flesh and dwelt among us." As Karl Barth has put it, "God did not become a stone or a star, or even an angel. He became man. Man, therefore, enjoys an unique status within creation. He is the 'apple of God's eye.'"

Embedded deeply in the cultures influenced by this conviction is the belief in human dignity, honored far better in its charters, of course, than in practice. But it is there. The life of a starving child takes precedence over a sacred cow. A tree is not worshipped but felled to provide shelter for a pioneer family. (Not only that, for a Joyce Kilmer or Martin Buber can commune with the tree as well, a dimension of Judeo-Christian sensitivity we shall subsequently explore.)

Nature, in this perspective, undergoes a "disenchantment," as it is described by Harvey Cox, following Max Weber.[5] This matter-of-fact relationship to the environment is grounded in the biblical idea of creation itself, specifically the doctrine of *creatio ex nihilo*. To affirm that God brings the world to be "out of nothing" means that the created order is not cut from the same cloth as deity, but rather "invented" by God. Tribal man, on the other hand, associates divinity so intimately with the natural world—all, or parts of it—that awe, incantation, imprecation, worship, become the ways of relating to it. The overagainstness of God and the world in the biblical teaching forbids the divinizing of anything finite. It therefore frees creation for use to the glory of God, and man is enjoined to steward it to that end. As Whitehead, Butterfield, and White himself have pointed out, the rise of science and technology in the West are directly related to this fundamental assumption.

But that is just the point, say the critics. This teaching encouraged the rape of Mother Earth. Standing alone, such a belief can do just that. That is what, in fact, happened with the rise of modern commerce and industrialization. The mechanization of nature in the Cartesian world view provided further ideological cover for the ruthless exploitation of natural resources. And now we are suffering the consequences. But the reason is that a society hellbent on profit and/or technological salvation tore loose from a larger context the assumption that nature was a thing only to be used (the Marxists are no better than the capitalists, for both ideologies were born in the womb of the technological revolution, accredited nature's despoliation, and continue to do so—this in spite of fugitive references in the early Marx to the dignity of nature). That larger context is the *full* biblical doctrine of creation, basic notes of which were censored in the era of feverish industrial expansion currently expressing itself in the phenomenon of "technocracy."

A group of contemporary writers with quite varying perspectives (Theodore Roszak, Robert Theobald, Jacques Ellul, Alvin Toffler, Paul Goodman, Kenneth Boulding) are sharpening our understanding of that complex of institutions, methodologies, cultural premises and passions that constitutes technocracy. In describing the character of this phenomenon it seems appropriate to speak of its "components."

1. The belief that the methods and momentum of science-technology can and will create a viable society.
2. "Econocentrism" (Toffler)—a confident faith in economic growth as the polestar of that society.
3. Present-orientation, the focus upon and drive toward immediate achievements, with little or no attention to the long-range effects of *now* activity.
4. The rule of elites—on the one hand, managerial generalists, and on the other, highly specialized "experts."
5. The lust for political, economic, and social power—a day-to-day "anthropocentrism" that finds easy the choice "between God and mammon."

It is this technocratic juggernaut that has rolled over the helpless in man and nature. Its victims include the young, the poor, the women, the black, brown, and red, and in less obvious ways the blue-collar white. Now in our time of ecological sensitivity we become aware that it has ravaged the air, the water, and the soil. And among the fabrics it has shredded are the tender things of human relationship and inner feeling.

Technocracy's steamroller has produced responses that run from the bizarre to the explosive. Chemical fantasy and neomystical reverie in the counter culture of the young represent both protest against and flight from the rational-empirical techniques whose fruits seem to be the hardware of war and blight. The quest for the community ruptured by the mechanisms and individualisms of technocracy casts about for the utopian commune or the togetherness of an encounter group. The ritual flaggery and super-patriotism of middle America are themselves distress signals of dehumanization. And for the lowest levels of the under class whose lives have been most seriously wounded there is always heroin, hooch, and holy rolling. Alongside these symptoms of anguish, there is the more aggressive feedback, the clenched fist and the midnight bomb of the terrorist.

To get beyond the first screams of pain and anger will involve building a strategy of ideas and actions that loosen the grip of technocracy on our future. It will mean taming technology, not disdaining it, and harnessing it to the purposes of personal, social, and environmental healing. It is the latter which here engages us, particularly the quest for a Christian interpretation of nature consistent with the biblical perspective and preparing the church for both the human and ecological struggles of the 70s.

The doctrine of creation out of nothing had a twin development. It served to refute, on the one hand, the divinizing and romanticizing of nature. But, on the other, it fought the degradation of nature. Strangely enough, one of the very movements in history approved by the Ecological Revolutionary Organization actually denigrated nature—Gnosticism. (It is probably the astrological interests of Gnosticism which prompted ERO to list it in the approved category of nature-affirming religions.) For that reason Gnosticism was attacked by patristic writers who fought for the significance of the finite, earthly terrain. Gnosticism, of course, was not a monolithic religious system, but rather the ideological atmosphere breathed by large segments of the ancient world. Variegated it was—but for all that, consistent in its estimate of the natural order. The world was second-class stuff. The earth was of inferior material, made either by a lieutenant deity, an emanation many times removed down the scale of being from the True God, or by a rebel "aeon" alienated from the source of all things. The purpose of religion was to extract from the mire of materiality the souls of men, helping them to escape from the burdens of their fleshly existence and its defiled visibilities into the realm of pure spirit.

Other ancient philosophical commitments also had their doubts about the importance of nature in the scheme of things. Modern ecologists bewail the denuding of Greece, the stripping away of the forests in the interest of building navies and engines of war. The rationalist tendencies of the Greek schools of thought gave little aid and comfort to Mother Earth. Goodness was located in reason, the purpose of which was to order the recalcitrant vitalities of life. God himself was conceived as Mind that gave form, and therefore significance, to a low-grade pre-existent stuff.

It was against this demeaning of the earth, in both the Gnostic and rationalistic temper of the times, that the fathers of the first centuries laid out the Christian doctrine of creation. The world was not the product of a lower divinity, an estranged emanation. Nor was it a pre-existent stuff of dubious parentage. "I believe in God the Father almighty, Maker of heaven and earth," read the early rule of faith that came to be the present Apostles' Creed. It asserted that the world was made by God himself. As such, it bore his stamp and enjoys a derived dignity. "God saw everything that he had made, and behold, it was very good." Or as someone put it, "God invented matter, therefore he must like it."

The Genesis affirmation of the earth is echoed in a thousand biblical passages that celebrate the intrinsic worth, beauty, and order of the natural environment. Thus the psalmist repeats a familiar refrain: "Thou [God] art clothed with honor and majesty, who coverest thyself with light as with a garment; who has stretched out the heavens as a tent, who hast laid the beams of they chambers on the waters, who makest the clouds thy chariot, who ridest on the wings of the wind" (*Psalm* 104:1–3). And the One who preaches the love of neighbor can also say, "Consider the lilies of the field, how they grow; they neither toil nor spin; yet I tell you, even Solomon in all his glory was not arrayed like one of these" (*Matt.* 6:28–29). The biblical love of neighbor extends to our neighbor the earth, as St. Francis so clearly understood.

To struggle to defend the dignity of man does not mean one has to denigrate the earth. In fact, one requires the other, as the very struggle against pollution demonstrates. What has given the environmental crisis its special urgency is the threat to the survival of man. Those who are most concerned about the welfare of man on earth will be those moved most passionately to restore a healthy environment.

Responsible Christian participation in that struggle requires, therefore, the rediscovery of the forgotten aspects of the doctrine of creation, the respect for and rapport with nature. One does not have to worship or romanticize nature in order to treat it as precious, any more than one has to worship or romanticize man in order to affirm his dignity. Both naturalists and humanists have propagated those theses. We have paid a heavy price for those kinds of absolutizations of the finite. The romantic naturalism of the Nazi era that deified blood and soil is a particularly demonic expression of the tendency. The Judeo-Christian tradition affirms, in the case of both man and nature, a *derived* dignity, and accords each a respect commensurate with its source in God. It is the *relationship* in which creation stands to its Creator that confers upon it value, not any presumed virtues or vitalities whose claims outrun the facts.

Man, Creator out of Something

The Genesis saga has yet more light to shed on ecological issues. Theologians of the secular have underscored the call to man to take responsibility for the future in the mandate to "name the animals" and "subdue the earth," the challenge to be co-creators with God. Again ecological critics of Christian tradition can find grist for their mills in what sounds like a thoughtless subservience of nature to man's machinations. And again they would be right if only one side of this passage's meaning were stressed. It is no accident that Harvey Cox has become a target of environmentalists, for he has stressed only one facet of the divine–human partnership.[6] There is another dimension to co-creatorship.

To take responsibility for "naming the animals" is to work with givens. Man does not do his creating *de novo;* he works over what he has inherited. He is not God, who creates out of nothing; he creates out of something already present. God is infinite, man is finite. And as such he works within the limits of a created order with its own pre-existing character. "While men, indeed, cannot make anything out of nothing but only out of matter already existing, yet God is in this point pre-eminently superior to man. That He Himself called into being the substance of His creation, when previously it had no existence."[7]

A related premise of co-creatorship is that man's mandate comes from a Source outside himself. His management of creation is not one of absolute control. Rather it is stewardship of the earth before a higher Claimant. To "have dominion over" means to hold in trusteeship. Man is called to tend the earth in responsibility to its Creator.

These convictions have profound implications for the ecological crisis. Because man creates within the framework of givens, he must honor the integrity of the pre-existing material. Responsible human creativity takes into account the balances and harmonies of the natural world. Man cannot do anything he wants, but has to abide by the rules of the game. Humility is, therefore, a virtue appropriate to his secondary role in creation. And that modesty is underscored by his trusteeship. He is accountable to Another.

Our present environmental plight is traceable to man's failure to acknowledge the limitations attendant to his subsidiary creatorship. He has acted as if he were the Creator, rather than a creator, in defiance of the givens and their Giver. In fact, he has played out the role of Adam in the Genesis saga, claiming prerogatives reserved to God alone. He has sought to create out of nothing, when he in fact can only create out of something, in harmony with the rhythm of the created order. For overreaching his finitude, he must suffer the consequences. In the Genesis story man is cast out of paradise and nature itself falls. Man's relation to nature becomes one of contest with creation. He is set against nature and nature responds in kind. Red in tooth and claw, spawning the terrors of earthquake, fire, flood, disease, and destruction, groaning "the whole creation has been in travail together until now." Sophisticated moderns smile at this ancient imagery, and dismiss it as an old wives' tale, or at best, as the anthropomorphism of a primitive society fearful of natural disaster. But the ecologically sensitive today recognize in this saga some very accurate reporting of the terrors that nature has in store for a technological society that tries to play God, ignoring the limitations placed on man's dominion. Existing in symbiotic relationship, nature does fall when man violates the built-in balances. And further, the earth takes its toll on man when such anthropocentrism runs riot, whether it be in the form of the London smog that killed four thousand people, or a Colorado earthquake provoked by army engineers who poured chemical wastes into deep wells, or the threat to the planet's oxygen supply by the DDT destruction of ocean plankton. It may well be that we shall rediscover the meaning of that line in the insurance policy which describes natural havoc as an "act of God." Such calamities as they happen in a society of indiscriminate human technology are just that, the delicate harmonies that sustain life in the cosmos fighting back against the thoughtless intrusions of man. Those exquisite networks of order and rhythm bear the imprint of deity itself. Whether we take a leaf from a Whiteheadian philosophy which sees these mutualities as the work of the divine vision and creativity, or from the biblical testimony itself which lies behind such an insight—that the divine nature, love, has left its mark on its creation in the order of nature—we know that man cannot violate cosmic interrelationships without suffering the consequences. Where profit and self-aggrandizement exploit nature, the "wrath of God," the anger of Mother Nature, manifests itself in the coming of the four horsemen themselves: plague, pestilence, famine, and death.

Creation's Companion Themes

While we have focused on the Christian doctrine of beginnings to provide a framework for an environmental theology, the dignity of nature is honored all around the circle of Christian teaching. For example, we might have spoken about sacramental theology which finds in bread, water, and wine a dignity that enables them to be vehicles of the divine life. Or we could have explored the doctrine of the incarnation that lies behind this sacramental affirmation of nature, and proved to be the most important bulwark of the early church against the gnosticisms that threatened to derogate the world of time and space, nature and man. We might also have examined the doctrine of the end, which works in tandem with the doctrine of the beginning in affirming the goodness of the whole created order, especially the key vision of shalom. Thus shalom is God's dream and promise for the fulfillment of his creation, the knitting together of all the brokenness in the cosmos, in the relations between man and man, a man and himself, man and nature, within nature, and between man-nature and God. At one or another time we have been sensitized to one or another of these rifts. Thus the peace movement with its shalom symbol has underscored the biblical vision of a time when men shall beat their swords into plow-shares. The human potential movement is currently exposing the sham in interpersonal relations and the deep psychic cleavages in selves, and working for the transformation of those spears into pruning hooks. It is time now to recover other elements in the biblical vision that have to do with the reconciliation of man and nature, and nature with itself—the child putting her hand over the asp's hole, the lying down of the wolf and the lamb, and the stilling of the sea's turbulence.

The eschatological horizon not only drives us to set up signposts in the present to a healed earth, but it charges us to keep the environmental crusade in company with other visionary movements. How can the child play with the snake if it must be forever in flight from the sword and the spear? The Christian vision is a big picture, a tapestry of many scenes, all interrelated. Its seers are multi-visionaries, neglecting no dimension of mission—race, peace, poverty, pollution. One of their particular mandates in a time of parochial crusades is to stretch the spectrum of the mono-visionary to its full range.

Theology and the Strategies of Environmental Mission

Theology and ecology are mated not only in ends but also means. Our basic premises about the nature and destiny of the cosmos shape the way we go about our environmental mission. Insights in the Christian faith do not provide blueprints, but they do offer guidelines for action.

Human Nature: Incurvature and Creatureliness

Man's self-regarding impulses overwhelm his unselfish ones. He is always looking out for Number One. In the code language of Christian tradition, man is a sinner. In Luther's language, each one of us is curved inward.

To take this "Christian realism" seriously is to expect that those whose manifest self-interest is at stake will be the most likely prospects as change agents in the pollution struggle. "Manifest" is an important qualification, for one's personal welfare may indeed be jeopardized, but one might not be aware of it. Those whose are in fact threatened, and whose social location or aroused sensitivity alerts them to the peril, may be our most aggressive prophets. Presupposed here as a secondary motif is another biblical premise about man—his finitude. He is immersed in the contingencies and vicissitudes of time and space. The self is not a free-floating balloon of mind or spirit, as it is portrayed in some other religious and philosophical options. Man is a creature of his time and place. His ability to perceive reality is conditioned by where he lives, how he feels, who he knows, and what he sees.

It is no accident that some of the most fervent pollution crusaders are the West Coast wealthy. From Sierra Club outdoorsmen to activist movie stars Eddie Albert and Arthur Godfrey, people who have the leisure to enjoy the horizons of the earth and the sky (see

Godfrey's comments on flying his plane over the country's smog blanket, Albert's account of the death of bird and animal life, or the Sierra Club's aggressive *Ecotactics* handbook[8]) are positioned sociologically and physically to feel the weight of the environmental crisis. Further, the peculiar combination of accelerating population and technology on a collision course with a vast and virginal nature, and a geographic vulnerability to massive catastrophe (the Santa Barbara oil catastrophe and the atmospheric dangers in Los Angeles) have a way of producing ecological revolutionaries.

Ideologues have no place for the affluent in their designs for social change, except to consign them to hell. A biblical perspective, on the other hand, takes creatureliness and sin seriously, and harnesses them to healing. Rich men have to breathe too. In the quest for their own survival, they may prove to be significant allies in the struggle for the earthly shalom of us all.

Some may, but others may not. Again an appreciation of sin and finitude gives us some programmatic clues. Where self-interest is crystallized into the inertia and short-range vision of immense collectivities, the life and breath of even the individuals who sit atop them become secondary to corporate aggrandizement. Given sin, power, particularly structural power, seeks to perpetuate itself and expand its orbit. From the "principalities and powers" of our time that pollute the air, water, and soil we can expect the charge that the ecological drive is exaggerated, that what is needed is education, that we must not do anything hastily, that it is the hippies and the Communists who are behind it all, that jobs will be lost if drastic action is taken, that the problem is really the individual polluter and not the corporation, that the people must bear the burden anyway by increasing the price of the product to pay for anti-pollution measures. One of these claims does deserve careful consideration—the loss of jobs—and we shall address ourselves to it. But this catalog of industrial argumentation is essentially a rhetorical smoke-screen and one that can be anticipated within a biblical framework. Sin regularly clothes itself in the garments of righteousness. The fog of pious rhetoric is calculated to obscure the smoke from the furnaces.

Given "immoral society,"[9] the expectation that vested interest will not divest itself of its poisons on its own initiative, then it is clear that the impulses for change must come from another direction. As other movements learned about the intransigence of collective power and organized to resist it—woman power, labor power, black power, student power—so an aroused citizenry must aggregate anti-pollution power to challenge the powers that be. In addition to frontal assaults by Nader's Raiders and the like, there must be a bringing to self-consciousness of those within the population who suffer the most from pollution. The citizen of the city, be he white collar, blue collar, black, or poor, pays a big price for his habitat and style of life. Middle American and minority groups may well find themselves aligned against the same entrenched interests since they suffer from the same urban maladies.

Human Nature: The Social Bundle

"God setteth the solitary in families," declares the psalmist. "The fathers have eaten sour grapes, and the children's teeth are set on edge," intones Jeremiah. We are all part of the interdependent bundle of life, affected by our contemporaries and predecessors, affecting our contemporaries and our successors. The ecological threat has underscored this mutuality among men as well as our interrelationship with nature. Thus the two airline passengers in adjacent seats, one smoking a cigarette and the other chewing gum. The latter offers the former his well-masticated wad. The former expresses shock, "Chew your used-up gum!" The reply: "Well, I'm smoking your cigarette!"

What is true in space is also true in time. The acids of worked-out mines in the northern tier of Pennsylvania seep into the water supply of succeeding generations in the lower regions.

A free-wheeling technocracy has for decades operated in azure isolation, without taking into account the disastrous effect on human life of its effluents. How many steelworkers I buried in a decade of ministry in Pittsburgh who died from silicosis and other lung disorders! Industry is no more free to go its way with such destruction than is the rugged individualist permitted to cry "Fire" in a crowded theater. To affirm human interdependence is to demand responsibility from those whose wastes contaminate other humans. Further, it is to insist that the costs of this self-control be borne by the offender and not the offended. The absorption of these expenses are but small reparations that can be paid for the lives and health lost by years of thoughtlessness.

Human Nature: The Tragic Options

All that has been said points to ecological action. The healing of a wounded environment is an imperative. Yet the mission cannot be executed in a vacuum. There are other crises. And there are circumstances when we are faced with tragic choices among legitimate ethical claimants. The reserve and sometimes suspicion of the human rights and peace movements about the pollution crusade is rooted in this ambiguity. Will passion for the environment draw attention from the struggles against other injustices?

Yet another dimension of this ambiguity was unfurled in the NBC white paper on the plight of a depressed Maine coastal town. Environmentalists were campaigning against a proposed seaport to berth giant cargo ships because of the pollution and destruction of a spot of natural beauty. Local workers and unemployed persons took offense at the affluent who were leading the drive because a new industry would have meant jobs for the poor.

In a world of competing claims, where there are no simple moral choices, it is necessary to establish priorities in particular situations based on what constitutes the maximum welfare both to those affected by the choices and to posterity. It is possible, therefore, that in a given context where justice for the poor and black are overwhelming needs, and a technology with as-yet-unconquered environmental hazards is required to implement that justice (a factory with its thousands of jobs and equal employment practices), the ecological values may have to take second place. Or, if it could be demonstrated that the urban poisons have such a malignant effect on these very same persons and the citizens of the region, then the tragic choice of long-term ecological life rather than short-term economic life must be made. Ideally, those struggling on both the ecological and economic fronts should band together and seek complementary solutions. But, until such alliances can be formed, and nonpollutant technology developed, we shall be faced with such ambiguous options and must be prepared to make tragic choices, in "fear and trembling" and in penitence.

The Birth of a New Style of Life

In, with, and under the press for social controls and institutional restructuring for environmental health, there must be a quest for a new commitment and style of life. The best laws in the world are useless if there is no will to enforce them. Just social structures can also be corrupted if those that inhabit them espouse inimical values.

The classic Christian virtue of neighbor love is no pious luxury in a society whose ethic of self-aggrandizement bears within it the seeds of self-destruction. When men exploit other men and nature in the interest of personal profit, we pull our own social and natural house down about our ears. Lust for private gain and its attendant ravages must be replaced by care for our neighbor the earth, and his neighbor, mankind. This means a transvaluation of some of the values considered so basic to "success" in our society. So vocal a barker of modern products as Arthur Godfrey has been moved to observe, "Prosperity means progress, means people—the more people, the more progress, the more prosperity. Too late we have seen that it also means more pollution, more filth, more death."[10] We must call into question the shibboleth that sustained another age with its seemingly limitless resources and reach: "Growth equals progress." We need new goals: "life," "the quality of life," "cooperation," "mutuality," and behind them all the neighbor love of the Jericho road.

New values mean a new mode of personal conduct. Virtues long scorned by an affluent society will have to be woven into the new style of life. For example, thrift and frugality. Instead of consuming rapaciously and throwing away thoughtlessly, we must conserve, recycle, be scrupulous in our acquisition. Thus, on the "Activists' Check List" of the Sierra Club, it is proposed that we not only put a brick in our toilet tank (the back!), question the value of electric carving knives, can openers, and tooth brushes, but use only biodegradable materials, and even "save six packs of empty one-way containers and ship them back to the board of directors of the company that manufactured the product."[11] Through it all, we ponder the sin of the United States consuming 40 percent of the world's food supply.

Parsimony extends to production as well as consumption. Since the population explosion is integrally related to the environmental catastrophe, self-control and frugality in life style will mean the limitation of family size. It may mean not only a norm of two children to attain ZPG [zero population growth], but also a willingness (in a time of women's liberation) for the male to choose a vasectomy after the limit is reached.

Learning to live with much less, the control of the obscene affluence of our age of glut will contribute to a fairer distribution of the world's goods. It may even prevent us from being smothered in our own wastes. And the habit of restraint might teach us as well some of the joys of self-abnegation about which the ascetic tradition has known for millennia.

Conclusion

"It is one minute to midnight on the ecological clock." Some wonder whether it will be the sounds of nuclear explosion or the silent spring that will end it all—the bang or the whimper. There can be another future. To the extent the Christian community has contributed to the bleak prospect rather than a promising one, we need a fresh penitence, a reformation of our bad theology, and zealous action toward shalom. We have good guidelines deep in our tradition. . . . Priestly custodians of that much misunderstood and ignored heritage [have] set the pace. One of them sent out an early warning signal at the outset of a burgeoning nineteenth-century technocracy:

> Generations have trod, have trod, have trod;
> And all is seared with trade; bleared, smeared with toil;
> And wears man's smudge and shares man's smell: the soil
> Is bare now, nor can foot feel, being shod.

> And for all this nature is never spent;
> There lives the dearest freshness deep down things.[12]

Notes

[1] See Frederick Elder, *Crisis in Eden* (Nashville: Abingdon Press, 1970)—one of the pioneering religious works in the current environmental crusade.

[2] White, "The Historical Roots of Our Ecologic Crisis," in *The Environmental Handbook,* ed. Garrett De Bell (New York: Ballantine Books, 1970).

[3] See Theodore Roszak, *The Making of a Counter Culture* (Garden City, New York: Doubleday, 1969). It is often forgotten that Judaism and Christianity are also religions of the East.

[4] *The Lancaster Independent Press,* 14 February, 1970. For a much more critical assessment of environmental conditions in societies influenced by religions of the Far East, see Yi-Fu Tuan, "Our Treatment of the Environment in Ideal and Actuality," *American Scientist,* May–June, 1970.

[5] *The Secular City* (New York: Macmillan, 1965), pp. 21–24.

[6] See Elder, *Crisis in Eden,* pp. 73–80.

[7] Irenaeus, *Against Heresies; Ante-Nicene Fathers,* I (Buffalo: Christian Literature Publishing Company, 1886), 370.

[8] Godfrey, "Crud Ho!" *Journal* (Division of Higher Education, United Church of Christ), April–May, 1970; Albert, "God Help Us, Man Won't," *Lancaster Independent Press,* 28 March, 1970; *Ecotactics,* the Sierra Club Handbook for Environmental Activists (New York: Pocket Books, 1970).

[9] See Reinhold Niebuhr's classic portrayal of collective egoism, *Moral Man and Immoral Society* (New York: Scribner's, 1932, 1937).

[10] "Crud Ho!" p. 5.

[11] *Ecotactics,* p. 255.

[12] Gerard Manley Hopkins, "God's Grandeur."

Discussion Questions

1. How does Fackre defend Christianity against accusations that it is guilty of encouraging anti-environmental attitudes? Do you find his defense convincing? Why or why not?

2. What does Fackre mean by "technocracy"? How does he criticize this view. Do you agree or disagree with his criticisms? Why?

3. In Fackre's view how should the doctrine of creation affect our attitude towards nature. Do you agree with his arguments on this point? Why or why not?

4. How does Fackre propose to balance ecological concerns and social welfare concerns? Criticize or defend his views on this point.

5. Could you agree with Fackre's views on ecology even if you did not share his religious beliefs? Why or why not?

The Moral Basis of Vegetarianism

Philip E. Devine

If someone abstains from meat-eating for reasons of taste or personal economics, no moral or philosophical question arises. But when a vegetarian attempts to persuade others that they, too, should adopt his diet, then what he says requires philosophical attention.[1] While a vegetarian might argue in any number of ways, this essay will be concerned only with the argument for a vegetarian diet resting on a moral objection to the rearing and killing of animals[2] for the human table. The vegetarian, in this sense, does not merely require us to change or justify our eating habits, but to reconsider our attitudes and behavior towards members of other species across a wide range of practices.

If it is wrong to kill animals for food, it is wrong *a fortiori* to kill them for sport, although one might well object to hunters who do not eat the food they have gathered without objecting to the ordinary slaughter of animals for the human table. Yet it could be wrong to kill animals for food, and still legitimate to use them in some forms of research, for instance in the attempt to discover a cure for cancer. The interest human beings have in avoiding deadly and painful diseases is far more exigent than their interest in enjoying a certain item of diet. This essay will avoid this complexity by focusing on the killing and rearing of animals for food.

I

There are two approaches a vegetarian might take in arguing that rearing and killing animals for food is morally offensive. He might argue that eating animals is morally bad because of the pain inflicted on animals in rearing and killing them to be eaten. Or he could object to the killing itself.

These two kinds of argument support rather different conclusions. A vegetarian of the first sort has no grounds for objecting to the eating of animals—molluscs for example—too rudimentary in their development to feel pain. Nor could he object to meat-eating if the slaughter were completely painless and the raising of animals at least as comfortable as life in the wild. Nor could he object to the painless killing of wild animals. Such a vegetarian will, however, object to the drinking of milk, since the production of milk requires a painful separation between cow and calf. He will also object to the eating of eggs laid by hens which did not have scope for normal activity. (He will not, however, object to the eating of fertile eggs as such.) To that extent, he will be not only a vegetarian, but also a vegan, one who abstains not only from meat but also from animal products.

One might of course defend the consumption of animal products, while opposing the eating of meat, on the ground that killing a steer, say, produces more suffering than separating a cow from her calf. The argument seems to me a chancy one, but an intermediate kind of vegetarian on this kind of ground does seem possible.

From *Philosophy* vol. 53, 1978. Reprinted by permission of Cambridge University Press.

In contrast, a vegetarian who has objections only to the killing of animals will object to all forms of meat, but he will not object to milk or eggs, so long as the eggs are not fertile. For such a vegetarian, a borderline case would be the consumption of animal products not, in the ordinary course of nature, produced by the animal; for instance the drinking of cattle blood as practiced by the Masai. Of course one could be a vegetarian on both grounds and object to anything either kind of vegetarian objects to.

There is an important difference between the two kinds of vegetarian in the casuistry of diet. For one who objects to the killing of animals, the moral question will be straightforward. A meat diet requires that animals be killed, and to demand that animals be killed—whether by buying meat from the butcher, ordering a meat dish in a restaurant, or accepting an invitation to dinner in the expectation that meat will be served—will be wrong if killing animals for food is wrong. But if what one objects to is animal pain, the moral situation is cloudier. One might argue that more pain is inflicted on animals on factory farms than is morally acceptable, while still holding that animals could be killed for food with a morally acceptable degree of pain if the imperative to do so were recognized. And so, unless there is a moral objection to consuming a product which has an injustice in its history, the eating of meat might be legitimate though the way animals are reared and killed is not.

The premise that it is in general wrong to benefit from another's wrongdoing cannot be accepted. A child conceived in rape is obliged neither to kill himself nor to lament his own existence. If we live in the United States, the land on which we live, and on which our bread is grown, is land unjustly taken from the Indians. And yet it is difficult to argue that we have an obligation to leave the country or abstain from all products grown here. A similar point can be made for the inhabitants of most other parts of the world. I am not defending indifference to the injustices taking place in one's world, only maintaining that while a person might have an obligation to protest against the injustices from which he benefits, he does not have an obligation to refuse to consume the products of injustice. There has been so much injustice in human history that untainted merchandise is not available.

Peter Singer offers two arguments to evade this point and link an objection to factory farming to a requirement that one observe a vegetarian diet. One of these contends that one ought to boycott animal products, as many Americans have boycotted lettuce and grapes, on account of the injustices involved in their production, whether or not one believes that animal products could in some way be justly produced. The second contends that by withdrawing economic support from the production of meat one can save some animals (although which animals one is saving one does not know).

The first of these arguments rests on a misunderstanding of the nature of boycotts. A boycott is not merely a personal gesture: it is a political weapon. Pre-eminently, it is the weapon of a group acting as a group, able to lift the boycott when the behavior complained of is improved or, as happened with the League of Nations boycott of Italy or Ethiopia, to abandon the boycott when the cause is thought hopeless. A necessarily permanent boycott, such as Singer says most vegetarians are engaged in, is a contradiction in terms. Singer could evade this reply by dropping the word "boycott" and replacing it with, say, "resistance." The basis of the asserted obligation to resist the painful rearing of domestic animals would still have to be explained, however, and the analogy of lettuce and grapes would no longer be available.

The economic support argument is more plausible, but is not free of difficulty. If the demand for meat lessens fewer animals may be killed or otherwise molested. On the other hand, this result is not the only possible one. The price of meat may fall, thus increasing demand and permitting the producers of meat to hold production steady. Producers of meat may attempt to recoup falling profits by turning to yet more intensive (and thus more painful) forms of meat production. And animals unwanted for the market are likely to be killed, not necessarily any more humanely than those which are killed to be eaten.

Perhaps these are nothing more than an example of the unexpected bad consequences which may follow from any good deed, however admirably motivated. (After all, the person one rescues from drowning may turn out to be a vicious killer.) Still, if the ethics of diet is to be assessed in utilitarian terms, such possible consequences will have to be taken into account, and the case for a vegetarian diet has been since Bentham closely tied to utilitarian forms of argument.

A rule-utilitarian or a utilitarian generalizer might use the following argument. The adoption of a moral rule forbidding the killing of animals for food would have good effects on the whole, including the reduction of the amount of animal suffering in the universe. Therefore, one ought to adopt such a rule and live in accordance with its requirements. In a word, one ought to abstain from meat.

But the difficulty with this kind of argument is that it represents the kind of ethical utopianism into which rule-utilitarians are likely to fall, their tendency to argue as if we were under an obligation to live as if we lived (now) in the best of all possible societies, something we are not only not obliged to do, but rather frequently obliged not to do. It is for this reason that many rule-utilitarians insist that the rules to be assessed by utilitarian arguments be rules having some conventional standing.

In sum, vegetarians on strictly moral grounds fall into two classes: those who object to the infliction of suffering on animals and those who object to killing them. And the results of adopting these divergent principles are further apart than Singer realizes. While a vegetarian of the second sort can appeal to a highly plausible moral principle to support the claim that one ought to abstain entirely from meat-eating, no such principle is available for a vegetarian of the first sort. It is possible in good conscience to consume meat and other animal products while regretting and even opposing the suffering imposed on animals in producing these items. Let us examine the credentials of each of the two kinds of vegetarian argument.

II

The first argument starts with the fact that animals are capable of suffering pain, and do in fact suffer pain in being reared and slaughtered for food. To this fact it adds the widely shared ethical premise that pain is an intrinsic evil. Since it seems self-evident that it is wrong to produce an intrinsic evil for no reason at all, it follows that it is wrong to produce pain, including animal pain, for no reason at all. In other words, to cause animal pain is *prima facie* wrong.

But of course no one defends inflicting pain on animals for no reason at all. Practices entailing pain for animals are defended by the benefits they produce for human beings. In particular, the practice of killing and rearing animals for food is justified as necessary to provide for human beings the kind of food that they want. The question at issue is whether this benefit is a sufficient justification for the rearing and killing of animals.

One way of trying to show that it is not a sufficient justification is to attempt a pleasure–pain calculus, and to argue that killing and rearing animals for food causes them more pain than it causes us pleasure, and that the practice is for that reason morally objectionable.[3] But, first, this criterion is not, from a utilitarian point of view, the strictly correct one. One has also to take into account the pain that stopping the consumption of meat will cause human beings, including the pain that will result from the economic disruption involved in the dismantling of the industries which produce meat for human consumption. And, second, it is by no means clear that it is *true* that animals suffer more pain in being killed and reared for food than human beings enjoy pleasure in eating their flesh. For what it is worth, Jeremy Bentham, whose insistence on the importance of animal sufferings is frequently quoted in the literature, specifically defended the eating of meat.[4] One could say that Bentham's judgements on this point were biased by his taste for meat. But, first, a taste for meat is not the only possible bias which may distort the calculation. There is also the desire to feel morally superior to one's fellow human beings, a desire which might well lead a vegetarian to exaggerate animal sufferings in order to blacken the character of his meat-eating associates. And, second, to talk of human biases here is unsatisfactory in a more radical respect. *Any* judgement of the degree of animal suffering will have to be anthropocentric in the sense that it is made by human (or other rational) beings and thus filtered through their personalities and institutions, even though no particular bias need be universally shared.

"Pain" and "suffering" are after all words in human language. The ascription of these experiences to ourselves and other human beings is part of a complex mode of human life, including the making of statements like "I am in pain" as well as inarticulate expressions of pain, the noticing of damage to the body, and various forms of care for those in distress. Now in the case of animals one crucial element is lacking—animals are permanently and by their nature[5] incapable of telling that they are in pain, as distinct from (say) moaning. That this is the case does not mean that we should, like Descartes, refuse to ascribe pain of any sort to non-human animals. But it may well justify ascribing to them pains of much less intensity than those we ascribe to human beings. And it is this that from a utilitarian standpoint should be the crucial issue.

It is not completely satisfactory to put this last point in terms of the intensity of the pain suffered. One might, it seems, equally well argue that human pain is *less* intense, since human beings are able to construct intellectual defenses, however inadequate, against their pains, whereas animals are not. If, however, one is going to try to do Benthamite ethics at all, one will have to be prepared to translate considerations more naturally expressed in other terms into those of intensity of pain and pleasure. Thus there seems to be no good reason for a Benthamite to resist transposing into lack of intensity a consideration more naturally expressed by saying that animal pain is conceptually defective.

The same point can be made in a different way. Pain involves elements both of emotion and sensation—both of distress and of a particular kind of feeling which characteristically (but not invariably) produces such distress.[6] Now it is the capacity for pain as a sensation which chiefly unites human beings with other animals. But a credible hedonist theory of the good cannot maintain that only painful sensation is bad, but must instead take as its intrinsic evil suffering and distress. And it is highly plausible to maintain that non-human animals—even supposing that they experience pain as a sensation as intensely as human beings do—experience far less suffering. It would, however, be more accurate to speak here, not of more or less intense sufferings, but of sufferings of greater or lesser conceptual richness. A cow may experience some distress at losing her calf, but it makes little sense to speak of her grief.

The vegetarian may reply that animals still suffer intensely enough to warrant his conclusions. And it is easy enough to describe the suffering of animals in vivid terms while deprecating the "trivial desires" of the human palate. But the question is whether such rhetoric is appropriate: whether for example it is appropriate to compare the sufferings of a cow separated from her calf with the feelings of a human mother in a similar situation, or the feelings of a dying fish with those of a dying human being. Everything seems to depend on how we perceive animals: if we see birds as winged people and cattle as our four-footed cousins, then we will be disposed to take their sufferings very seriously; if not, we will not be so disposed.

A second vegetarian strategy is simply to reject as immoral the balancing of animal pains against human pleasures. Thus John Harris's reply to the Benthamite defense of meat-eating is quite simply: "Those who use it are saying that they think more about their stomach than their morals, and so a moral argument will probably not affect them."[7] We can call this move the deontological stop.

Deontological stops are not uncommon in philosophical discussions of moral questions. Perhaps the best known is in G. E. M. Anscombe's outburst: "If anyone really thinks, *in advance,* that it is open to question whether such an action as procuring the judicial execution of the innocent should be excluded from consideration—I do not want to argue with him; he shows a corrupt mind."[8] And it may not be possible to avoid them without giving up the discussion of practical issues altogether or claiming, implausibly, that our arguments could have convinced Hitler or Stalin. But Anscombe could at least count on a certain aversion to judicial murder on the part of her audience. For a vegetarian to employ a deontological stop against those who defend the eating of meat would be to guarantee that vegetarian views will remain, and deserve to remain, the exclusive property of a sect.

A third vegetarian strategy is the formulation of a plausible non-utilitarian principle, which will justify the rejection of the Benthamite defense of meat-eating. One such principle has been formulated in the following terms by Tom Regan: "No practice which causes undeserved non-trivial pain can be justified solely on the ground of the amount of pleasure it brings about for others."[9] This principle is acceptable (I should hope) to nearly everyone when the pain in question is inflicted on human beings or persons. Whether it applies to pain inflicted on animals, however, is another matter altogether.

One indication that this principle should not be applied to pains inflicted on the animals is the word "undeserved." While it is not strictly speaking false to say that an animal experiences undeserved pain, such a statement is surely misleading. Non-human animals—and vegetarians insist on this point as much as anyone—are not moral agents and thus can neither deserve to suffer nor, in a significant sense, suffer undeservedly. (They may of course still suffer in ways they ought not to.) A wolf which eats a lamb and a female hamster which eats her young are not guilty: neither are they, in a significant sense, innocent. Considerations of retributive justice, whether they are thought to warrant the infliction of deserved suffering or only to forbid the infliction of undeserved suffering, are irrelevant to the treatment of animals.

Two qualifications need to be made if this point is to be made accurate. First, there are human beings who are, like animals, neither guilty nor innocent in the sense explained. Our reasons for treating them as innocents will be explored below. Second, there is a sense in which a pet dog, say, can be punished, and in such contexts it makes sense to speak of punishing an innocent dog unjustly. But these are contexts in which we treat animals, by a kind of special grace, somewhat as if they were human, and thus are irrelevant to the treatment of animals which are in no respect so treated.

Perhaps a slightly stronger principle—one which omits reference to undeserved pain—will advance the vegetarian's case more adequately. It seems plausible, to me at least, that punishment cannot be justified, even where it is deserved, on the ground that others will enjoy the satisfaction of their retributive instincts. Only the segregation of dangerous persons, the teaching of the members of society that the conduct in question is wrong, the prevention of private vengeance, the deterrence of other offenders or of future offenses by the same subject, and (maybe) the rehabilitation of the offender (not, I think, the demands of mere retribution) can justify the infliction of even deserved punishment. If so, then we can assert it as a principle that no practice which causes the infliction of non-trivial pain can be justified solely on the ground that it produces pleasure for others. Once again, however, we must confront the crucial question: does this principle apply only to pain inflicted on human beings, or does it also apply to pain inflicted on animals?

There seem to be essentially three kinds of objections to such measures as Swift's "modest proposal" to rear the children of the poor for the tables of the rich. One is that the pain inflicted on the children themselves, the resentment the poor will experience in thinking that their children are being eaten by the rich, and so on, would tip the utilitarian balance against such a proposal. Another is that it is just wrong to use human beings, including the children of the poor, in such a manner, because they are, in Kant's expression, possessed of a dignity which forbids their employment merely as means. A compromise accepts the Kantian approach, not on Kant's grounds, but because the acceptance of such an approach seems likely to produce the best possible balance of happiness over unhappiness.

But none of these arguments reaches the killing of animals for food. The problem of resentment does not arise in the animal case, and the Kantian maxim, except the contrary be proved, applies only to human beings or persons. Nor is it possible to get anything out of a rule-utilitarian argument—at least where the argument is not ethically utopian—which cannot be got out of the two approaches to morality which it is intended to reconcile. Thus while the principle which forbids the infliction of suffering on human beings, regardless of desert, to satisfy the desires of other human beings, is highly plausible, we do not have adequate grounds for extending it to animals.

A fourth approach is to attempt to extend our moral principles from human beings to animals by means of the principle of equality. As part of the public morality of our day, or of the morality of social movements such as that against racism, the principle of equality has been a principle of *human* equality. So the burden is on the vegetarian to make a persuasive case for its extension to non-human animals. If he fails to make it, the expression "speciesism" will be a parody or reduction to absurdity of attempts to further other causes by borrowing odium from the concept of racism,[10] and "animal liberation" a parody or reduction to absurdity of the mystique of the liberation movement.

Some ways of invoking the principle of equality turn out, upon closer examination, to be spurious. Joel Feinberg for instance argues that once it is granted that human and animal pain are "equally pain—pain in the same sense and the same degree," then it follows immediately that animal as much as human pain is an intrinsic evil.[11] The difficulty here is with the expression "equally pain." To say that X and Y are equally pain is but a somewhat unfortunate way of saying that X and Y are both cases of pain, or at best that they are both equally central non-disputed cases of the phenomenon. (Neither X or Y is arguably an itch, for example.) Nothing at all follows concerning the intensity of the two pains. Furthermore, it does not follow from the premise that two pains are equally intense that they are equally bad from a moral standpoint. The badness of a pain might be a function not only of its intensity but also of other considerations, for instance the nature of the sufferer.

An approach which seeks to block this kind of move invokes the principle of the equal consideration of all interests. As Singer formulates the principle, "the interests of every being affected by an action are to be taken into account and given the same weight as the like interests of any other being."[12] The crucial expression here is "like interests." One meaning to be given the expression is "interests of the same general kind." On this view, the principle of equal consideration means that animal pain is to be weighted equally with human pain of the same general sort, and this reading of the principle seems best adapted to support the vegetarian viewpoint. But this interpretation leads to absurdities. In order to show that this is so, I shall need to argue against Singer that sentience is not a necessary condition of the possession of interests, that plants for instance can have interests. But that plants can have interests seems to me obvious once the dogma that they cannot have them is questioned—weeds for instance can flourish, can need light or water, and so on quite independently of any human interest in their flourishing. But I take it as conceded that it would be perverse to treat the needs of plants as of equal moral importance as the needs of human beings, even when the need in question (for water, say) is of the same general kind.

On the other hand, one can read the principle of equal consideration of interests as a strict corollary of the same principle of utility, namely as holding that all pains and pleasures of the same intensity are to be taken as equally bad and good respectively. This seems to me an unfortunate way of using the expression "interest" since it does not make it possible to account for a sleeping person's interest in being allowed to awaken without ascribing interests in being conceived to the unbegotten. (Neither will suffer if the supposed interest is frustrated, and both will experience pleasure if the supposed interest is satisfied.) In other words, such an approach—I am suggesting perversely—reduces talk about the interests of persons (or other subjects) to talk about their pleasures and pains, to which the subjects themselves appear as mere causal preconditions.

The principle of equality in real-life moral discourse has meant something rather stronger than the bare principle of the equal consideration of all interests. At the minimum it has meant such things as universal suffrage and contested elections; at the maximum the abolition of all differences in wealth, power, and status. And there have been all sorts of arguments against even minimum equality in this sense which begins with the equal consideration of all interests. The general form of these arguments is given by the saying that the lower orders are children in need of a strong father. One might instance John Stuart Mill's defense of paternalism for the uncivilized, and more recently Robert Heilbroner's contention that poor nations require highly authoritarian, preferably Communist, "modernizing élites," since "modernization is a kind of cultural imperialism that is forced upon the masses."[13]

A final vegetarian strategy goes as follows. Granted, the vegetarian might say, that if we take our present tastes in food as immutable we get more pleasure out of eating meat (or would suffer more from abandoning the habit) than animals suffer pain by being killed and reared for our table. But our tastes in food are not immutable. If we come to adopt a vegetarian regimen, we will find that we enjoy a vegetarian diet as much as we enjoy a meat one, and the sum of happiness prevailing in the universe will thus be increased. Perhaps the recipes and so on which Singer appends to his book are not merely helps to virtuous and happy living, but essential parts of his argument.

The problem is how the vegetarian knows that his meat-eating associates would enjoy a vegetarian (or vegan) diet as much as one containing meat, or that they could successfully free themselves of their desire for this form of food. The question would seem altogether to be one of individual psychology. Moreover, the prospect of guilt-feelings experienced by backsliding vegetarians and of the harmful effects of repressing desires for meat (kinds of considerations utilitarians are ready enough to emphasize in other contexts) make the arguments from mutable habits an extremely unattractive one.

The sum of the matter is as follows. Either the vegetarian argues on utilitarian premises, or he tries to supplement or replace his utilitarianism with some plausible non-utilitarian principles implying the wrongfulness of rearing and killing animals for food. In the first case, there is no way around the suggestion, which many people appear to believe, that animal experience is so lacking in intensity that the pains of animals are overridden by the pleasures experienced by human beings. That the argument may appear cynical is no concern of the utilitarian, who is forced by his moral theory to admit the relevance of even the most cynical-seeming arguments. On the other hand, all the non-utilitarian principles which have been put forward turn out on inspection to have reference only to human beings. If they were to be abandoned, the practical result would be more likely to be that human beings would be treated as we now treat animals rather than animals as we now treat (or believe that we should treat) human beings.

III

At least such is the result of taking seriously only the pains suffered by animals in being reared and killed for food. Perhaps a different result will be reached by taking into account the value of the animals' existence.

One needs first to see whether this value is one that can be taken into account by a (hedonistic or near-hedonistic) utilitarian. One might say "Yes," on the ground that the value of the future existence of an animal can be cashed in terms of the animal's pleasures, or else in terms of the animal's present desire to go on living. But neither of these approaches is satisfactory.

To say that animal existence is valuable (only) because animal pleasure is valuable runs into the following problem. Continuing the existence of presently existing animals is not the only way of producing animal pleasure: one could also produce *new* animals who will experience the same or greater pleasures. Hence the vegetarian who took this sort of tack would have to meet the following argument. If we did not rear animals for food, they would not exist at all, and hence would not enjoy the pleasures that they do. And this is a kind of argument that vegetarians, I think quite rightly, emphatically reject.

Nor are animal desires an adequate way of grounding a claim that animal existence is valuable. One might contest the claim that an animal (or an animal sufficiently below man in its intelligence) desires to continue to live, since such animals are not conscious of themselves as continuing beings. But it is reasonable, I think, to ascribe something like a desire to continue to live to all animals which behave in ways designed to preserve themselves in existence.

The real problem lies in the fact that utilitarians have a very difficult time with desires, such as the desire to continue existing, whose frustration is not experienced by the subject of the desire. To give such desires an importance proportionate to their intensity would be to give an importance to the desires of the dead that most utilitarians would be extremely reluctant to grant. Few utilitarians would be prepared to withdraw proposals for non-traditional ways of life on the ground that by living in those ways we would be frustrating the desires of our ancestors.

Yet utilitarianism may be inadequate for animals in some of the same ways that it is inadequate for people. As Robert Nozick has observed, we should not conclude that an animal's existence is not important to it until we have a better idea of how our existence is important to us. And, as Roslind Godlovitch has observed, it seems absurd to kill a healthy animal "to prevent cruelty," but such killing seems to be what is required if we wish only to avoid animal pain and care nothing for animal existence.[14]

Animal shelters often seem to act on this assumption, for instance by destroying unwanted kittens; but one suspects that what is really at work here, as in the practice of spaying or neutering pets, is an interest of human beings in keeping down the pet population. *Prima facie,* it would seem that sexual (and in the case of a female animal, reproductive) satisfactions are more important in the life of an animal than they are in that of a human being. Likewise, quite arguably the existence of an animal is more important relative to its other interests than is the case with a human being, since animals lack the various ways that human beings have of transcending their own deaths.

But none of this establishes how important animal existence is when it conflicts with human desires. In rough terms, animal life may be lived at such a low level of intensity that its value provides no serious competition with human gastronomic interests. Nozick concludes that we should stop eating animals, but he does not provide anything like an argument for his conclusions (only some rather odd examples). And it is at first blush hard to see what such an argument would even look like.

One possible argument goes as follows. The moral case for vegetarianism is in any case not a hopeless one. And no one is under any obligation to eat meat, so that one does not, by becoming a vegetarian, violate any requirement of morality. In the circumstances, one ought to take the safer course and abstain from meat. Let us call this the "tutiorist argument."

Most people most of the time are not tutiorist. The thought that the Roman Catholic Church is just possibly right about contraception is not for most people a persuasive reason for giving up the practice, even though where reproduction is morally undesirable it could be avoided by simple abstinence. (No one is under any obligation, surely, to enjoy sexual intercourse or enter into a relationship in which participation in sexual intercourse is a duty to another.) But common opinion is perhaps specially unpersuasive in this kind of case, since a hostility to tutiorist arguments might be, after all, a result of the plain man's ordinary moral laziness.

There are, however, excellent reasons to reject tutiorism, except perhaps as part of the pursuit of (morally optional) ideals. There is, to begin, a certain moral value in keeping oneself cheerful. The harm done by those who spread their depression among their associates is if anything underestimated by moralists. And the danger that someone overburdened with moral claims will rebel against all moral requirements whatever has also to be taken into account.

There are, moreover, specific considerations of moral importance on the side of meat-eating. There are forms of human solidarity expressed by eating together, and the effect of food prohibitions will be to break up these forms, or at least to make them more difficult.

At another level, while priority arguments are notoriously slippery, it remains the case that the energies available for moral and social reform or revolution, including the reform of one's own habits, are not unlimited. And there is evidence among vegetarians of a turning away from human problems to the question of animal liberation. Singer for instance observes:

> All reasonable people want to prevent war, racial inequality, inflation, and unemployment; the problem is that we have been trying to prevent these things for years, and now we have to admit that we do not really know how to do it. By comparison, the reduction of the sufferings of non-human animals at the hands of humans will be relatively easy, once human beings set themselves to do it.[15]

But the only reason why the task of animal liberation might look easy is that it is so far from success.

More subtly, vegetarianism might actually interfere with the attempt to improve the lot of human beings. A radical moral position has its costs, since it makes it easier for one's opponents to dismiss one as an eccentric. So that someone who wishes to change society should not be in a hurry to accept every radical moral position that looks vaguely attractive.[16]

None of this would matter, perhaps, were the vegetarian clearly right in his central contentions. But since he is not, since what we have here is a question of balancing values of very different sorts in a way of whose outcome we can never be really confident, considerations of the above sort do seem to bear very heavily towards the rejection of the vegetarian moral position.

A second way of attempting to bridge the gap is the argument from moral progress. One way moral progress takes place is by extending the scope of moral concern from the tribe to the nation, from the nation to the world, and so on. And so we should take the next step and extend our moral concern to animals. Once having done so, we will be unable to justify eating meat any longer.

I am not sure that everyone accepts the characterization of moral progress just offered. Many seem to consider it progressive to withdraw moral concern from the human fetus. But perhaps this is not a true counter-example, and what is at stake when inhibitions on abortion are abandoned in the name of moral progress is an inherited prohibition whose reason is not understood versus a sharper concern for the welfare of the mother. Certainly many defenders of abortion prefer to think as little as possible about the fetus.

Setting this point to one side, there remains a paradox in the notion of moral progress. Moral progress consists, it would seem, in discovering what the requirements of morality are and learning to keep them. So that whether a given change in our opinions constitutes moral progress depends entirely on whether it constitutes movement towards, or away from, the correct moral opinions. Hence one cannot argue for a change in moral belief as progressive without first arguing that it is (at least) a movement towards moral truth, in other words without having already decided the crucial question at issue.

Perhaps the progressive argument could be made like this. To an unknown extent, the moral requirements binding upon us are a function of the contingencies of our society, including its conventions. If a society improves or degenerates, these requirements change—in the one case we have moral progress, in the other moral retreat. And the changes which would produce a duty to stop rearing and killing animals for food would be desirable ones. But, supposing this to be so, it is still the case that a possible and desirable future in which a change in our mode of life would become morally required does not of itself establish that such a change is morally required now. Thus the upshot of the discussion so far is that it is morally legitimate (at least in the present world) to rear and kill non-human animals for the human table.

IV

If someone asked what differences there are between him and a chicken, such that it is right to kill the chicken to feed him and wrong to kill him to feed the chicken, he is likely to be embarrassed, not because there are so few differences between him and the chicken, but because there are so many. The strength of the vegetarian case comes, not from any such direct challenge, but by means of a set of intermediate considerations. These are (1) the problem of the extraordinary animal, (2) the problem of the extraordinary human being, (3) the invasion of super-humans, and (4) the question of meritocracy.

(1) It seems that we should believe that intelligent creatures not of the human species are entitled to the same consideration as human beings are entitled to. Whether we imagine talking cats or visitors from other galaxies, even if the intelligent non-human turns out to be "a realization of the typical sci-fi monster—an argute fifteen-and-half-foot purple preying mantis oozing goo from every orifice,"[17] this conclusion would hold so long as we

were not carried away by emotions like racial prejudice. (Of course if such non-humans proved dangerous to human beings, we would protect people against them on the same principles on which we protect them against dangerous human beings.) But this kind of case is of little relevance to the question of vegetarianism, since by hypothesis the non-humans in question differ as greatly as we do from chickens in their intelligence and other capacities.

A case closer to home is the chimpanzee, whose linguistic capacities are a matter of recent discovery.[18] Now I for one am prepared to grant that it would be wrong to kill, maim, or inflict pain upon a chimpanzee except under circumstances where it would be right to do these things to human beings. The only doubtful case is chimpanzee euthanasia: it appears that there would be fewer objections to killing an incurably ill chimpanzee (of necessity without the chimpanzee's consent) than to the similar killing of an incurably ill human being. One could argue that even here the relevant ethical principles should be the same, but if they are not the reason is (religious arguments apart) that the care of chimpanzees is not entangled in the kinds of institutions in which the care of human beings is.

The changes this concession requires in human behavior are fairly small, since we do not typically eat chimpanzee flesh, and the cost of acquiring a chimpanzee protects it (or him) against the more brutal kinds of experiment. A more radical conclusion—one which would raise real problems for present human behavior—would be that chimpanzees are entitled to the same rights as human beings in the areas of liberty, dignity, privacy, and welfare. In any case, the very capacities which entitle the chimpanzee to be treated in some respects as human also distinguish it from the chicken.

(2) There are two kinds of extraordinary human beings of interest here: infants and imbeciles. The infant presently lacks the traits we invoke to justify treating human adults differently from adult animals. And yet most of us would be extremely reluctant to justify even painless infanticide, let alone the use of babies in cancer research or the killing of infants for food.

The answer lies in the infant's potential for adult humanity. While some philosophers have attempted to play havoc with the notion, most of them understand the claim that a (sprouting) acorn is a potential oak, or a caterpillar a potential butterfly. And it is importantly on account of their potential that we think it wrong to kill sleeping, reversibly comatose, or curably mad human adults. Even in the case of an awake adult, what killing him deprives him of is his potential for future human existence. His past human existence cannot be taken from him in any case. Finally, as Kevin Donaghy points out, if we choose intelligence as the trait distinguishing the human from the animal, we have chosen a trait which, like talent, pertains essentially to the possessor's potential (in this case for learning).

This line of reasoning has an unfashionable implication, namely that it is not possible to defend abortion on the ground that it does not involve the death of a human being or person. The fetus is, it seems, as much a potential adult human being as the infant. But no one interested enough in vegetarianism to consider a refutation has any reason to object to unfashionable conclusions. In any case, there is no cause for concern that we might by this argument be forced to disapprove of contraception, since before conception there exists no organism to be a potential adult human being or to be killed.[19]

The severely mentally retarded, on the other hand, lack, even as potential, the capacities we invoke to justify treating normal adult and infant human beings differently from animals. True, one might appeal to the notion of potentiality even here, and speak of the capacities an imbecile would have had, had he not suffered some unfortunate accident. But this appeal would not be persuasive since one can speak in this sense of the capacities of a corpse. And such appeals are irrelevant to those of the retarded who suffer from genetic defects. (If my genes had been different, I would have been a cat.) And yet we would not kill imbeciles, at least not for food, nor would we employ them in cancer research.

It seems necessary, in the light of this example, to invoke a distinction resisted by many, and distinguish between human beings and persons. Thus the imbecile (though not the infant) is, while a human being, not a person. And yet there may be good reasons for treating human beings who are not persons as if they were persons, that is to say for treating them in accordance with what is normal for the species, rather than their individual traits.

Singer regards this proposal as intolerable. He points out that it would be grossly unjust to reject qualified female applicants to medical school on the ground that women on the whole are more suited to raising children than to being doctors, even if this characteristic of women should turn out to be a result of their biological nature rather than of their cultural conditioning. Likewise, he argues, it is unjust to treat the severely mentally retarded according to what is normal for the species rather than according to their individual characteristics. But, in so arguing, Singer has turned the proposal around. There is a difference between denying some benefit to a person because of a class to which he belongs despite his individual characteristics and extending a benefit on such grounds where it is too bothersome, costly, or dangerous to provide individual treatment.

Suppose for example that, in recognition of women's special role in the rearing of children, we decide to grant women priority over men in questions of rescue ("Women and children first"). If this decision is just, then it is surely also just not to exclude from this benefit a barren woman or a woman who has decided never to have children. Again: there would be nothing unjust about an amnesty for draft refusers which included those who evaded the draft for purely selfish reasons (let us say they supported the war politically), should this prove a better course from an administrative or political point of view.

And one argument against distinguishing the severely retarded from other human beings, including those who, though retarded, are not *so* retarded as to lack the faculty of speech, is that to do so would be to create too large a risk of error, and too much cost in anxiety among the mildly retarded and their relatives. One thing the human/animal distinction provides is a clear line which is in nearly all cases very easy to apply. That is, I think, the point of John Rawls' remark that "it would be unwise to withhold justice [from the severely retarded] on [the] ground [that moral personality was lacking]. The risk to just institutions would be too great."[20]

One could claim that being treated as a person is not always a benefit, that it may prevent a creature from getting the merciful death commonly accorded to incurably ill animals. Assuming for the moment that the mercy-killing of animals is for the benefit of the animal itself and not to spare human beings what Hobbes would call the "pains of compassion," this contention turns out to make no difference to the argument. For it would not be wrong, surely, to allow an animal to linger if an important human interest could be served thereby, at least if measures, short of directly ending its life, were taken to relieve its suffering. And so to treat even an incurably ill sufferer from severe retardation as a person to avoid "risk to just institutions" is to treat him no worse than an animal might be treated.

Many will find a utilitarian defense of the severely retarded unattractive. It seems not merely permissible or prudent, but morally imperative, to treat the severely retarded so far as possible as fully human. And even if we should think that it is a morally less grave matter to kill a human being lacking the intelligence of a pig than to kill an adult or infant of normal intelligence, it would be hard to accept the conclusion that such killing would be a less grave matter than the killing of a pig.

I do not think there is anything objectionable about treating a creature differently, even as a matter of moral principle, just because he is a member of our own kind. Recall that it is not a question of treating an intelligent non-human as a mere brute but of treating a human being lacking in intelligence in some respects as if he were a rational being. The only ground for objecting to such treatment that I can see is the notion that the employment in ethics of biological concepts, such as that of the species, is somehow suspect.

There seem to be four reasons for such suspicion in the vegetarian literature. One is the analogy, embedded in the word "speciesism," between the species and such classifications as race and gender. Another is a general repugnance for the kinds of conclusions which are supported by biological arguments. Another is a peculiar understanding of the is–ought problem in theoretical ethics. Yet another represents the impact of Cartesian dualism on ethical discussion. None of these reasons turns out upon consideration to be persuasive.

In the first place, part of the case against racism is that racial categories are in a profound sense not biologically real, that physical differences, real enough in themselves, are seized upon by racist societies in essentially arbitrary fashion in order to support a certain social ordering. This is, I think, especially true in the United States, where a Negro may be more white than black in his genetic endowment.[21] Of course slavery would not be justified even if blacks and whites were literally of different species, but if the biological differences between races were large enough I doubt that we would have the objections we have to, say, segregated education.

Sexual differentiation is biologically real enough, but arguments about the role of gender in society prove on examination to be irrelevant to the present discussion. No one really holds that women are inferior beings who may be killed with impunity. The archetypal male chauvinist position is that a woman's place is in the home, a place which carries with it benefits, such as exemption from the draft, as well as liabilities. And while there are no doubt good reasons to abolish many of the social distinctions based on gender, it does not follow that they are as odious as ones based on race, or that a difference which has crucially to do with the production of new human beings (a humanly important enough matter, surely) ought never to be the basis of a legal or customary distinction.[22]

In the second place, it is easy enough to reject those arguments founded on biology that one objects to without rejecting the employment of all biological concepts in ethics. For instance, if someone holds that the poor should not be protected against exploitation, citing in his defense the Darwinian principle of the survival of the fittest, it suffices to point out that the fittest from a Darwinian point of view are those who survive to reproduce. Hence the affluent are not any fitter than the poor, and even if they were, securing one's survival through appealing to the sympathies of the affluent is as legitimate from a Darwinian standpoint as the quills of a porcupine.

In the third place, the is–ought problem is no more severe for ethical arguments from biological premises than for such arguments from any factual premises whatever. The doctrine cannot mean that no ethical conclusions can be drawn from the premise that someone has promised something, desires something, or is in pain. How then could it bar an ethical conclusion being drawn from the premise that someone is a member of our species?

Finally, the Cartesian doctrine that it is not I that am male, or have a cut finger, or am a member of the human species, but something closely associated with me (my body) seems to me just false, so that there is no need to consider ethical arguments founded on a Cartesian premise. And apart from metaphysical Cartesianism, the ethical Cartesianism which holds that only mental states have ultimate ethical import seems most implausible. (Vegetarians who hold this view are closer to their arch-enemy Descartes than they realize). The distinction between killing someone in his sleep (and thus painlessly) and just not reproducing seems to require that value be ascribed to the continuation of human life itself.

(3) If beings who were truly as superior in intelligence to us as we are to animals were to invade the Earth and start eating us, we might not be entitled to regard their behavior as morally offensive. To take the nearest analogy I can think of, many theists (including St. Paul—see Romans, viii, 20–22) have held that God in strict justice is entitled to do whatever He wishes with His creatures, except in so far as He may limit His sovereign discretion by promises graciously made. Of course we would not be bound to *like* being reared and killed for food, to co-operate with these beings in any way, or even not to resist their activity. The analogy with the Pauline God is not intended as exact.

The only one of these conclusions which poses problems is that concerning resistance. It would be wrong to kill another person to prevent him from doing something he had every right to do (as distinct from someone who was innocently threatening our lives—innocently because he was not at the time a moral agent). And since these beings by hypothesis have every right to rear us and kill us for food, it would be wrong, it seems, for us to kill them to prevent them from so doing.

We do not (or should not) blame an animal for killing a human being (or doing anything else) because an animal is not a moral agent. Now if these beings are really as superior to us as we are to animals, then we are not moral agents in their reckoning either. Having recourse to capital letters, we may say that in their Morality, which stands to our morality as our morality stands to whatever morality-like phenomena we may observe among the lower animals, we are not accounted Moral Agents, and hence are not to be blamed for killing them. Nor does our morality require us not to kill them, since it contains no provision for our relations to superior beings of this sort. Accordingly from no point of view will our resistance be blameworthy.

Conversely, if the beings do not have a Morality in the sense explained, or if the notion of a Morality does not make sense, then they will not be, contrary to hypothesis, as much superior to us as we are to non-human animals. If the notion of a Morality does not make sense, then we can draw a stronger conclusion: the moral difference between human and animal rests, not upon a *comparison* of intelligences, but upon the reaching or failure to reach a *threshold* of intelligence, beyond which there are no further gradations of moral status.

(4) The fourth problem takes its start from the following remark of Thomas Jefferson: "Because Sir Isaac Newton was superior to others in understanding, he was not therefore lord of the property or person of others."[23] A vegetarian will ask how we can accept such a doctrine, given that we appeal to the differences in intelligence between us and animals to justify our rearing and killing them for food.

Donaghy argues that it is the fact that human beings are above a certain threshold that justifies the moral dichotomy between human and animal, just as it is the fact that children are below a certain threshold of experience and maturity that warrants adult authority over children. But the crucial justification of adult authority (i.e., that it is for the benefit of children) is not present for human dominance over animals. And, second, it seems problematic to assert that all children should be subject to paternalistic authority while no adults should ever be subject to such authority, however childlike they may be in comparison to their fellows.

Another answer is that the difference between Newton and the rest of us is not great enough to justify his enslaving us, but is sufficient to justify his having other advantages over us. A society which rewards achievement is to an unknown extent rewarding those innate capacities (not intellect alone, of course) which make achievement possible. And one criticism which is frequently levelled against hierarchical societies—that they keep down those whose capacities are not linked with fortunate birth—would not apply to a society which, while eliminating caste differences due to birth, and minimizing differences of environment, rewarded high achievements with a status far superior to that of the majority.

Those, like Thomas Nagel,[24] who hold strongly anti-meritocratic views will have particular difficulty in avoiding vegetarian conclusions. After all, I no more deserved being born human than I deserved being born with my particular intellectual capacities. But even if some degree of meritocracy is accepted, still there are ways of rewarding achievement—multiple votes, the passing of effective political power to a meritocratic House of Lords—which seem unacceptable, in part at least because they offend our ideas of human equality.

The problem here is a highly general one. What sense can be made of the notion of human equality given the fact that human beings are in no quantifiable respect equal? Not only do human beings differ in such qualities as intelligence, strength, and personal attractiveness: they also differ in their susceptibility to pain, their capacity to enjoy pleasure, and their propensity to discern and resent injustice. And it would seem unjust to sacrifice Jones for the common good just because Jones is a happy-go-lucky character who is not likely to feel the injustice of his treatment very strongly. The ultimate difficulty lies in the peculiar, at least semi-religious, logic of the notion of human equality. There is no reason to suppose, however, that this difficulty supports vegetarian conclusions.

V

To reject the vegetarian argument is not to settle the question of the moral importance of animal interests. On the one hand, it is necessary to deal with the contention that it is mere sentimentalism to ascribe any moral importance to animal interests at all; on the other hand, it is possible to take any number of intermediate positions between vegetarianism and a conventional acceptance of the eating of animals (and their use for various other purposes).

Some might argue that while eating meat is in general acceptable, we are under an obligation to abstain from meat produced in particularly harsh ways: from veal perhaps, or from lobster or from *pâté de foie gras*. Others might argue that what is important is the level of the animal's evolutionary development, so that while it is acceptable to eat poultry one should abstain from the flesh of animals, or while it is acceptable to eat fish one should abstain from the flesh of warm-blooded animals.[25] Or one might distinguish according to the kinds of value which may justify the eating of meat: turkey dinners on holidays with the family might be thought legitimate, while a bachelor cooking for himself would be under an obligation to abstain from meat. And there are many who see nothing wrong with buying meat at a supermarket, while disapproving of hunting even when the resulting meat is eaten by the hunter's family. Finally, one might, without accepting vegetarian ideas oneself, still feel that vegetarians are entitled to the kind of respect frequently accorded to pacifists by those who do not share their convictions.

One thing is clear: these questions cannot be resolved by a utilitarian calculus. There are a few instances where the result of such a calculus is unambiguous (or rather where such a calculus does not seem to be necessary). It would be right to perform one relatively painless experiment on an animal if one could thereby get a cure for cancer, and it would be wrong to burn an animal to death to spare one person a moment's mild annoyance. But in most cases no such calculus will be possible, because the pains and pleasures involved will be too different in their nature.

The first question that needs to be asked is why animals have any moral importance at all. Two answers need to be considered: first, the utilitarian claim that pain *qua* pain is bad, whatever the nature of the being suffering it; and second the view, associated with the names of Aquinas and Kant, that animals have moral importance only insofar as what is done to them may affect human beings—that, in Kant's terms, duties to animals are indirect duties to human beings.[26]

Neither of these positions is satisfactory. On the one hand, no one convinced that ethics has essentially to do with relations among rational beings is going to be persuaded that there is no morally relevant difference between pains suffered by such beings and the pains suffered by irrational creatures. On the other hand, that someone disposed to be cruel to animals is likely also to be cruel to human beings is at best a plausible psychological speculation. Our readiness to believe it rests, I would suggest, on the moral ties we see between human and animal existence rather than the other way round. But for such perceived ties, it would be equally plausible to maintain that animals should serve as punching bags—as outlets, that is, for aggressive and sadistic impulses which might otherwise find their target in human beings.

I propose that the moral significance of the suffering, mutilation, and death of non-human animals rests on the following, which may be called *the overflow principle: Act towards that which, while not itself a person, is closely associated with personhood in a way coherent with an attitude of respect for persons.* So stated, the overflow principle is intended to express a strict requirement of morality, although the principle will no doubt have ramifications within the aspirational dimension of morality as well.

One might argue for the overflow principle in a rule-consequentialist fashion, arguing that the teaching of such a principle will be ultimately conducive to the happiness of persons. But equally, the overflow principle might be made plausible by being exhibited as part of a way of life having respect for persons at its center. In any case, the overflow principle would seem to be as well ensconced in the moral consciousness of the plain man as, say, the principle that gratitude is due to benefactors.

One application of the overflow principle is the principle of respect for the dead. Although a dead body is not a person, still the fact that it (so to speak) *was* a person means that it ought not to be treated like ordinary garbage. Alternatively, we may say that respect for persons overflows to the human body, which forms the visible aspect of the bulk of the persons with whom we are acquainted and which persists when the person ceases to exist in death. Another and more controversial application is that human sexuality, since it is concerned with the generation of new persons, has a moral significance greater than that possessed by, say, pinball. Yet another application is that members of the human species who are not persons, even by virtue of their potentiality, still ought to be treated, in some respects at least, as if they were persons. Finally, those who do not accept the argument from potentiality will have to rely on the overflow principle to generate any restraints whatever on our behavior towards the fetus, the infant, the curably or incurably mad, and even, it would seem, the deeply but reversibly unconscious (someone in dreamless sleep for example).

The application of the overflow principle to animals is as follows. Man is not only a rational being, but also an animal. More precisely, he is a rational animal, a being possessed of not only the attributes of thought and intention but also those of shape, size, health or disease, biological gender, and capacity for sensation. And while it is as rational beings that we are in the first place entitled to respect, the respect due to us as rational beings overflows to our animal nature, and to those creatures which, while "dissociated from us by their want of reason"[27] are nonetheless associated with us in sharing our animal capacities including the ability to suffer pain. If capacity for pain were the only feature of persons which entitled them to our consideration, then vegetarians would be right in attacking the person/animal distinction. But I see no reason to admit this premise.

This approach to animal suffering allows us to reach a happy compromise between the utilitarian and non-utilitarian approaches to the problem of cruelty to animals. Animal pain will be bad in itself, apart from any consequence of that pain to human beings, but the badness of that pain will derive from a moral principle whose ultimate reference is to persons. Thus the ethics proposed here is anthropocentric (or person-centred) though only mildly so.

But anthropocentricity of some sort cannot be avoided. Morality is a human phenomenon, and the moral words are words in human language. Inevitably, therefore, the question at issue will be what place animals are to have in the concerns of human beings. What is more: all morality will be in one sense egocentric, in that the moral question for me will always be what I shall do, in particular what place the interests of others shall have in my concerns, and in that the root of morality will be my conception of myself as a moral agent. This is as true for vegetarians as it is for anyone else.

Turning to questions of application, torment justified by nothing more than human sadistic enjoyment can be condemned on the ground that sadistic pleasure is not good and therefore does nothing to offset animal pain. Disputes will still exist concerning which kinds of enjoyment count as sadistic; whether hunting, for example, or bullfighting is condemned by this principle. But that sort of problem is not limited to contexts involving animals: I can imagine someone arguing that it is not good to enjoy satire. In any case, we have here a happy compromise between those who object to cruelty to animals because it hurts the animal and those who object to it because it degrades the torturer.

Where justifications other than sadistic enjoyment experienced by human beings are advanced, the problem gets considerably more difficult. This difficulty of application seems to be a general feature of instances of the overflow principle. Consider the wide range of sexual attitudes held by those who are not completely liberated in their outlook (although they may falsely believe that they are) or the wide range of views on abortion held among moderates on the issue. (Moderates for present purposes include those who, while holding that there should be no legal restrictions on the practice of abortion, still hope that women and/or physicians will nonetheless treat the question as a morally serious one.) A similar range of views will exist concerning the degree of attention to be paid to the interests of animals: indeed the vegetarian moral position might itself be interpreted as a position intermediate between conventional morality and a view which would object to the use of oxen as beasts of burden, demand that deer be protected against wolves, or insist that non-humans be provided with social services.

The upshot is that animal welfare is a cause which is bound to prove extremely frustrating to someone of reflective intelligence who is attracted to it. There will inevitably be an element of arbitrariness in the decision whether to justify or condemn a particular practice which injures animals in the interest of human beings. Nonetheless it would be a mistake to dismiss the issue of animal rights as peripheral to morality. As I hope I have shown, the problems that this issue raises are central and inescapable.

Notes

[1]Pride of place among contemporary philosophical vegetarians probably belongs to Peter Singer. Singer's contribution includes an article [first selection in this chapter] and a book (*New York Review*, 1975), both sharing the title "Animal Liberation."

Singer's essay started life as a review (in *The New York Review of Books*) of *Animals, Man and Morals*, Stanley and Roslind Godlovitch and John Harris (eds), (New York: Grove, n.d.). Another anthology is *Animal Rights and Human Obligations*, Peter Singer and Tom Regan (eds), (Englewood Cliffs, New Jersey: Prentice-Hall, 1976).

Also worthy of mention are Tom Regan, "The Moral Basis of Vegetarianism," *Canadian Journal of Philosophy* V, No. 2 (October, 1975) and the discussion in Robert Nozick, *Anarchy, State, and Utopia* (Oxford: Blackwell, n.d.), 35 ff. Stephen R. L. Clark, *The Moral Status of Animals* (Oxford, 1977), is of special interest as a Christian vegetarian, but does not contribute much to the vegetarian argument. See also A. M. MacIver, "Ethics and the Beetle," in *Ethics,* Judith J. Thomson and Gerald Dworkin (eds), (New York: Harper & Row, 1968).

Useful critical discussions include Kevin Donaghy, "Singer on Speciesism," *Philsophic Exchange* (Summer, 1974); Bonnie Steinbock, 'Speciesism and the Idea of Equality,' American Philosophical Association (Eastern Division), 1975 (published in *Philosophy*, April, 1978); and Ronald DeSousa's comments on Steinbock's paper.

I am also indebted to the following for criticisms and suggestions: Merritt Abrash, Albert Fiores, Roger Guttentag, James Hanink, John Koller, Joseph Ryshpan, and David Wieck.

I discuss the issues concerning the killing of human beings touched on in this paper in *The Ethics of Homicide* (Cornell University Press, 1978).

[2]One might object to the use of the word "animal" in this context, as concealing the fact that human beings are also a kind of animal. But while this objection has greater merit than most ideological objections to common usage, it would be pedantic to attempt a greater revolutionary purity than that achieved by the revolutionaries themselves.

[3]This is the criterion proposed by John Stuart Mill, *Collected Works*, X, J. M. Robson (ed.), (Toronto: 1969), 187.

[4]The relevant passage in Bentham is n. 330 to *An Introduction to the Principles of Morals and Legislation*. In *The Utilitarians* (Garden City, New York: Doubleday, 1961), 380–381.

[5]The phrase "permanently and by their nature" distinguishes animal pain from that of human infants for example.

[6]For an attempt to sort out these elements, see Roger Trigg, *Pain and Emotion* (Oxford: 1970).

[7]John Harris, "Killing for Food," *Animals, Men and Morals,* op. cit., n. 1, p. 99.

[8]G. E. M. Anscombe, "Modern Moral Philosophy," in Thomson and Dworkin (eds), op. cit., n. 1, 206–207.

[9]Regan, op. cit., n. 1, 199.

[10]The strategy embedded in the word "sexism" is already questionable. For a brilliant critique see Ann Dummett, "Racism and Sexism," *New Blackfriars,* 56 (1975).

[11]See the passage from "Human Duties and Animal Rights," an unpublished essay under copyright by the Humane Society of America, quoted in Regan, op. cit., n. 1, 187.

[12]*Animal Liberation,* op. cit., n. 1, 6.

[13]See his debate with Dennis Wrong in *A Dissenter's Guide to Foreign Policy,* Irving Howe (ed.), (Garden City, New York: Doubleday, 1968), Pt. III. The quotation is from Heilbroner's "Rebuttal," 274, n. 2.

[14]Roslind Godlovitch, "Animals and Morals," in *Animals, Men and Morals,* op. cit., n. 1.

[15]*Animal Liberation,* op. cit., n. 1, 245–246.

[16]This is the point of George Orwell's discussion (*The Road to Wigan Pier* (New York: 1958), pp. 173–175).

[17]Roger Wertheimer, "Philosophy on Humanity," in *Abortion,* Robert L. Perkins (ed.), (Cambridge, Massachusetts, 1974), 123.

[18]See for instance Peter Jenkins, "Ask No Questions," in *Animal Rights and Human Obligations,* op. cit., n. 1.

[19]The questions of abortion and contraception are raised in this context by Singer, "Animal Liberation," op. cit., n. 1, 172. (A vegetarian may of course also be an opponent of abortion; see Clark, op. cit., n. 1, esp. 74–76.)

[20]John Rawls, *A Theory of Justice* (Cambridge, Massachusetts: Harvard, 1972), 506.

[21]See Ashley Montagu, *Man's Most Dangerous Myth,* 4th ed. (Cleveland: 1964).

[22]For detailed discussion see J. R. Lucas, "Because You are a Woman," in [Chapter 6 of this volume].

[23]Letter to Henri Grégoire, 25 February 1809. Quoted in *Animal Liberation,* op. cit. n. 1, 7.

[24]Thomas Nagel, "Equal Treatment and Compensatory Discrimination," *Philosophy & Public Affairs,* 4 (1973), esp. 356–358 and 362–363.

[25]Singer draws the line further down the scale, arguing that while we should abstain from ordinary fish, we may eat oysters and other molluscs (but not octopus); *Animal Liberation,* op. cit., n. 1, 188.

[26]For Aquinas see *Summa Theologiae,* IIa, IIae, Q 64 a. I. and Ia IIae, Q 102 a. 6 and 8; also *Summa Contra Gentiles,* III, 112. For Kant see *Lectures on Ethics,* tr. Louis Infeld (New York: 1963), 239–241.

[27]Augustine, *City of God,* I, 20. Tr. Marcus Dodds (New York: Modern Library, 1950), 26.

Discussion Questions

1. Do Singer's arguments seem to be against killing animals or against causing pain to animals? How might Singer reply to Devine's arguments?

2. Which of the five arguments Devine considers in Section II of his paper seems to be the strongest? Support or criticize that argument.

3. Which of the arguments for the value of animal existence given in Section III of Devine's paper seems strongest? Are Devine's criticisms of that argument effective? Why or why not?

4. Do Devine's arguments on the difference between animals and humans effectively answer Singer's arguments on this point? Why or why not?

5. How convincing is Devine's "overflow principle"? How does this principle relate to some of the questions raised by Singer?

The Rights of Animals and Unborn Generations

Joel Feinberg

Every philosophical paper must begin with an unproved assumption. Mine is the assumption that there will still be a world five hundred years from now and that it will contain human beings who are very much like us. We have it within our power now, clearly, to affect the lives of these creatures for better or worse by contributing to the conservation or corruption of the environment in which they must live. I shall assume furthermore that it is psychologically possible for us to care about our remote descendants, that many of us in fact do care, and indeed that we ought to care. My main concern then will be to show that it makes sense to speak of the rights of unborn generations against us, and that given the moral judgment that we ought to conserve our environmental inheritance for them, and its grounds, we might well say that future generations *do* have rights correlative to our present duties toward them. Protecting our environment now is also a matter of elementary prudence, and insofar as we do it for the next generation already here in the persons of our children, it is a matter of love. But from the perspective of our remote descendants it is basically a matter of justice, of respect for their rights. My main concern here will be to examine the concept of a right to better understand how that can be.

The Problem

To have a right is to have a claim[1] *to* something and *against* someone, the recognition of which is called for by legal rules or, in the case of moral rights, by the principles of an enlightened conscience. In the familiar cases of rights, the claimant is a competent adult human being, and the claimee is an officeholder in an institution or else a private individual, in either case, another competent adult human being. Normal adult human beings, then, are obviously the sorts of beings of whom rights can meaningfully be predicated. Everyone would agree to that, even extreme misanthropes who deny that anyone in fact has rights. On the other hand, it is absurd to say that rocks can have rights, not because rocks are morally inferior things unworthy of rights (that statement makes no sense either), but because rocks belong to a category of entities of whom rights cannot be meaningfully predicated. That is not to say that there are no circumstances in which we ought to treat rocks carefully, but only that the rocks themselves cannot validly claim good treatment from us. In between the clear cases of rocks and normal human beings, however, is a spectrum of less obvious cases, including some bewildering borderline ones. Is it meaningful or conceptually possible to ascribe rights to our dead ancestors? to individual animals? to whole species of animals? to plants? to idiots and madmen? to fetuses? to generations yet unborn? Until we know how to settle these puzzling cases, we cannot claim fully to grasp the concept of a right, or to know the shape of its logical boundaries.

From *Philosophy & Environmental Crisis,* edited by William T. Blackstone, pp. 43–68. Copyright © 1974 by the University of Georgia Press. Reprinted with permission.

One way to approach these riddles is to turn one's attention first to the most familiar and unproblematic instances of rights, note their most salient characteristics, and then compare the borderline cases with them, measuring as closely as possible the points of similarity and difference. In the end, the way we classify the borderline cases may depend on whether we are more impressed with the similarities or the differences between them and the cases in which we have the most confidence.

It will be useful to consider the problem of individual animals first because their case is the one that has already been debated with the most thoroughness by philosophers so that the dialectic of claim and rejoinder has now unfolded to the point where disputants can get to the end game quickly and isolate the crucial point at issue. When we understand precisely what *is* at issue in the debate over animal rights, I think we will have the key to the solution of all the other riddles about rights.

Individual Animals

Almost all modern writers agree that we ought to be kind to animals, but that is quite another thing from holding that animals can claim kind treatment from us as their due. Statutes making cruelty to animals a crime are now very common, and these, of course, impose legal duties on people not to mistreat animals; but that still leaves open the question whether the animals, as beneficiaries of those duties, possess rights correlative to them. We may very well have duties *regarding* animals that are not at the same time duties *to* animals, just as we may have duties regarding rocks, or buildings, or lawns, that are not duties *to* the rocks, buildings, or lawns. Some legal writers have taken the still more extreme position that animals themselves are not even the directly intended beneficiaries of statutes prohibiting cruelty to animals. During the nineteenth century, for example, it was commonly said that such statutes were designed to protect human beings by preventing the growth of cruel habits that could later threaten human beings with harm too. Prof. Louis B. Schwartz finds the rationale of the cruelty-to-animals prohibition in its protection of animal lovers from affronts to their sensibilities. "It is not the mistreated dog who is the ultimate object of concern," he writes. "Our concern is for the feelings of other human beings, a large proportion of whom, although accustomed to the slaughter of animals for food, readily identify themselves with a tortured dog or horse and respond with great sensitivity to its sufferings."[2] This seems to me to be factitious. How much more natural it is to say with John Chipman Gray that the true purpose of cruelty-to-animals statutes is "to preserve the dumb brutes from suffering."[3] The very people whose sensibilities are invoked in the alternative explanation, a group that no doubt now includes most of us, are precisely those who would insist that the protection belongs primarily to the animals themselves, not merely to their own tender feelings. Indeed, it would be difficult even to account for the existence of such feelings in the absence of a belief that the animals deserve the protection in their own right and for their own sakes.

Even if we allow, as I think we must, that animals are the intended direct bene-ficiaries of legislation forbidding cruelty to animals, it does not follow directly that animals have legal rights, and Gray himself, for one,[4] refused to draw this further inference. Animals cannot have rights, he thought, for the same reason they cannot have duties, namely, that they are not genuine "moral agents." Now, it is relatively easy to see why animals cannot have duties, and this matter is largely beyond controversy. Animals cannot be "reasoned with" or instructed in their responsibilities; they are inflexible and unadapt-able to future contingencies; they are subject to fits of instinctive passion which they are incapable of repressing or controlling, postponing or sublimating. Hence, they cannot enter into contractual agreements, or make promises; they cannot be trusted; and they cannot (except within very narrow limits and for purposes of conditioning) be blamed for what would be called "moral failures" in a human being. They are therefore incapable of being moral subjects, of acting rightly or wrongly in the moral sense, of having, discharging, or breaching duties and obligations.

But what is there about the intellectual incompetence of animals (which admittedly disqualifies them for duties) that makes them logically unsuitable for rights? The most common reply to this question is that animals are incapable of *claiming* rights on their own. They cannot make motion, on their own, to courts to have their claims recognized or enforced; they cannot initiate, on their own, any kind of legal proceedings; nor are they capable of even understanding when their rights are being violated, of distinguishing harm from wrongful injury, and responding with indignation and an outraged sense of justice instead of mere anger or fear.

No one can deny any of these allegations, but to the claim that they are the grounds for disqualification of rights of animals, philosophers on the other side of this controversy have made convincing rejoinders. It is simply not true, says W. D. Lamont,[5] that the ability to understand what a right is and the ability to set legal machinery in motion by one's own initiative are necessary for the possession of rights. If that were the case, then neither human idiots nor wee babies would have any legal rights at all. Yet it is manifest that both of these classes of intellectual incompetents have legal rights recognized and easily enforced by the courts. Children and idiots start legal proceedings, not on their own direct initiative, but rather through the actions of proxies or attorneys who are empowered to speak in their names. If there is no conceptual absurdity in this situation, why should there be in the case where a proxy makes a claim on behalf of an animal? People commonly enough make wills leaving money to trustees for the care of animals. Is it not natural to speak of the animal's right to his inheritance in cases of this kind? If a trustee embezzles money from the animal's account,[6] a proxy speaking in the dumb brute's behalf presses the animal's claim, can he not be described as asserting the animals' *rights?* More exactly, the animal itself claims its rights through the vicarious actions of a human proxy speaking in its name and in its behalf. There appears to be no reason why we should require the animal to understand what is going on (so the argument concludes) as a condition for regarding it as a possessor of rights.

Some writers protest at this point that the legal relation between a principal and an agent cannot hold between animals and human beings. Between humans, the relation of agency can take two different forms, depending upon the degree of discretion granted to the agent, and there is a continuum of combinations between the extremes. On the one hand, there is the agent who is the mere "mouthpiece" of his principal. He is a "tool" in much the same sense as is a typewriter or telephone; he simply transmits the instructions of his principal. Human beings could hardly be the agents or representatives of animals in this sense, since the dumb brutes could no more use human "tools" than mechanical ones. On the other hand, an agent may be some sort of expert hired to exercise his professional judgment on behalf of, and in the name of, the principal. He may be given, within some limited area of expertise, complete independence to act as he deems best, binding his principal to all the beneficial or detrimental consequences. This is the role played by trustees, lawyers, and ghost-writers. This type of representation requires that the agent have great skill, but makes little or no demand upon the principal, who may leave everything to the judgment of his agent. Hence, there appears, at first, to be no reason why an animal cannot be a totally passive principal in this second kind of agency relationship.

There are still some important dissimilarities, however. In the typical instance of representation by an agent, even of the second, highly discretionary kind, the agent is hired by a principal who enters into an agreement or contract with him; the principal tells his agent that within certain carefully specified boundaries, "You may speak for me," subject always to the principal's approval, his right to give new directions, or to cancel the whole arrangement. No dog or cat could possibly do any of those things. Moreover, if it is the assigned task of the agent to defend the principal's rights, the principal may often decide to release his claimee, or to waive his own rights, and instruct his agent accordingly. Again, no mute cow or horse can do that. But although the possibility of hiring, agreeing, contracting, approving, directing, canceling, releasing, waiving, and instructing is present in the typical (all-human) case of agency representation, there appears to be no reason of a logical or conceptual kind why that *must* be so, and indeed there are some special examples involving human principals where it is not in fact so. I have in mind legal rules, for example, that require that a defendant be represented at his trial by an attorney, and impose a state-appointed attorney upon reluctant defendants, or upon those tried *in absentia,* whether they like it or not. Moreover, small children and mentally deficient and deranged adults are commonly represented by trustees and attorneys, even though they are incapable of granting their own consent to the representation, or of entering into contracts, of giving directions, or waiving their rights. It may be that it is unwise to permit agents to represent principals without the latters' knowledge or consent. If so, then no one should ever be permitted to speak for an animal, at least in a legally binding way. But that is quite another thing than saying that such representation is logically incoherent or conceptually incongruous—the contention that is at issue.

H. J. McCloskey,[7] I believe, accepts the argument up to this point, but he presents a new and different reason for denying that animals can have legal rights. The ability to make claims, whether directly or through a representative, he implies, is essential to the possession of rights. Animals obviously cannot press their claims on their own, and so if they have rights, these rights must be assertable by agents. Animals, however, cannot be represented, McCloskey contends, not for any of the reasons already discussed, but rather because representation, in the requisite sense, is always of interest, and animals (he says) are incapable of having interests.

Now, there is a very important insight expressed in the requirement that a being have interests if he is to be a logically proper subject of rights. This can be appreciated if we consider just why it is that mere things cannot have rights. Consider a very precious "mere thing"—a beautiful natural wilderness, or a complex and ornamental artifact, like the Taj Mahal. Such things ought to be cared for, because they would sink into decay if neglected, depriving some human beings, or perhaps even all human beings, of something of great value. Certain persons may even have as their own special job the care and protection of these valuable objects. But we are not tempted in these cases to speak of "thing-rights" correlative to custodial duties, because, try as we might, we cannot think of mere things as possessing interests of their own. Some people may have a duty to preserve, maintain, or improve the Taj Mahal, but they can hardly have a duty to help or hurt it, benefit or aid it, succor or relieve it. Custodians may protect it for the sake of a nation's pride and art lovers' fancy; but they don't keep it in good repair for "its own sake," or for "its own true welfare," or "well-being." A mere thing, however valuable to others, has no good of its own. The explanation of that fact, I suspect, consists in the fact that mere things have no conative life: no conscious wishes, desires, and hopes; or urges and impulses; or unconscious drives, aims, and goals; or latent tendencies, direction of growth, and natural fulfillments. Interests must be compounded somehow out of conations; hence mere things have no interests. *A fortiori,* they have no interests to be protected by legal or moral rules. Without interests a creature can have no "good" of its own, the achievement of which can be its due. Mere things are not loci of value in their own right, but rather their value consists entirely in their being objects of other beings' interests.

So far McCloskey is on solid ground, but one can quarrel with his denial that any animals but humans have interests. I should think that the trustee of funds willed to a dog or cat is more than a mere custodian of the animal he protects. Rather his job is to look out for the interests of the animal and make sure no one denies it its due. The animal itself is the beneficiary of his dutiful services. Many of the higher animals at least have appetites, conative urges, and rudimentary purposes, the integrated satisfaction of which constitutes their welfare or good. We can, of course, with consistency treat animals as mere pests and deny that they have any rights; for most animals, especially those of the lower orders, we have no choice but to do so. But it seems to me, nevertheless, that in general, animals *are* among the sorts of beings of whom rights can meaningfully be predicated and denied.

Now, if a person agrees with the conclusion of the argument thus far, that animals are the sorts of beings that *can* have rights, and further, if he accepts the moral judgment that we ought to be kind to animals, only one further premise is needed to yield the conclusion that some animals do in fact have rights. We must now ask ourselves for whose sake ought we to treat (some) animals with consideration and humaneness? If we conceive our duty to be one of obedience to authority, or to one's own conscience merely, or one of consideration for tender human sensibilities only, then we might still deny that animals have rights, even though we admit that they are the kinds of beings that *can* have rights. But if we hold not only that we ought to treat animals humanely but also that we should do so for the animals' own sake, that such treatment is something we owe animals as their due, something that can be claimed for them, something the withholding of which would be an injustice and a wrong, and not merely a harm, then it follows that we do ascribe rights to animals. I suspect that the moral judgments most of us make about animals do pass these phenomenological tests, so that most of us do believe that animals have rights, but are reluctant to say so because of the conceptual confusions about the notion of a right that I have attempted to dispel above.

Now we can extract from our discussion of animal rights a crucial principle for tentative use in the resolution of the other riddles about the applicability of the concept of a right, namely, that the sorts of beings who *can* have rights are precisely those who have (or can have) interests. I have come to this tentative conclusion for two reasons: (1) because a right holder must be capable of being represented and it is impossible to represent a being that has no interest, and (2) because a right holder must be capable of being a beneficiary in his own person, and a being without interests is a being that is incapable of being harmed or benefitted, having no good or "sake" of its own. Thus, a being without interests has no "behalf" to act in, and no "sake" to act for. My strategy now will be to apply the "interest principle," as we call it, to the other puzzles about rights, while being prepared to modify it where necessary (but as little as possible), in the hope of separating in a consistent and intuitively satisfactory fashion the beings who can have rights from those which cannot.

Vegetables

It is clear that we ought not to mistreat certain plants, and indeed there are rules and regulations imposing duties on persons not to misbehave in respect to certain members of the vegetable kingdom. It is forbidden, for example, to pick wildflowers in the mountainous tundra areas of national parks or to endanger trees by starting fires in dry forest areas. Members of Congress introduce bills designed, as they say, to "protect" rare redwood trees from commercial pillage. Given this background, it is surprising that no one[8] speaks of plants as having rights. Plants, after all, are not "mere things"; they are vital objects with inherited biological propensities determining their natural growth. Moreover, we do say that certain conditions are "good" or "bad" for plants, thereby suggesting that plants, unlike rocks, are capable of having a "good." (This is a case, however, where "what we say" should not be taken seriously: we also say that certain kinds of paint are good or bad for the internal walls of a house, and this does not commit us to a conception of walls as beings possessed of a good or welfare of their own.) Finally, we are capable of feeling a kind of affection for particular plants, though we rarely personalize them, as we do in the case of animals, by giving them proper names.

Still, all are agreed that plants are not the kinds of beings that can have rights. Plants are never plausibly understood to be the direct intended beneficiaries of rules designed to "protect" them. We wish to keep redwood groves in existence for the sake of human beings who can enjoy their serene beauty and for the sake of generations of human beings yet unborn. Trees are not the sorts of beings who have their "own sakes," despite the fact that they have biological propensities. Having no conscious wants or goals of their own, trees cannot know satisfaction or frustration, pleasure or pain. Hence, there is no possibility of kind or cruel treatment of trees. In these morally crucial respects, trees differ from the higher species of animals.

Yet trees are not mere things like rocks. They grow and develop according to the laws of their own nature. Aristotle and Aquinas both took trees to have their own "natural ends." Why then do I deny them the status of beings with interest of their own? The reason is that an interest, however the concept is finally to be analyzed, presupposes at least rudimentary cognitive equipment. Interests are compounded out of *desires* and *aims,* both of which presuppose something like *belief,* or cognitive awareness. . . .

Whole Species

The topic of whole species, whether of plants or animals, can be treated in much the same way as that of individual plants. A whole collection, as such, cannot have beliefs, expectations, wants, or desires, and can flourish or languish only in the human interest-related sense in which individual plants thrive and decay. Individual elephants can have interests, but the species elephant cannot. Even where individual elephants are not granted rights, human beings may have an interest—economic, scientific or sentimental—in keeping the species from dying out, and *that* interest may be protected in various ways by law. But that is quite another matter from recognizing a right to survival belonging to the species itself. Still, the preservation of a whole species may quite properly seem to be a morally more important matter than the preservation of an individual animal. Individual animals can have rights but it is implausible to ascribe to them a right to life on the human model. Nor do we normally have duties to keep individual animals alive or even to abstain from killing them provided we do it humanely and nonwantonly in the promotion of legitimate human interests. On the other hand, we do have duties to protect threatened species, not duties to the species themselves as such, but rather duties to future human beings, duties derived from our housekeeping role as temporary inhabitants of this planet. . . .

Future Generations

We have it in our power now to make the world a much less pleasant place for our descendants than the world we inherited from our ancestors. We can continue to proliferate in ever greater numbers, using up fertile soil at an even greater rate, dumping our wastes into rivers, lakes and oceans, cutting down our forests, and polluting the atmosphere with noxious gases. All thoughtful people agree that we ought not to do these things. Most would say we have a duty not to do these things, meaning not merely that conservation is morally required (as opposed to merely desirable) but also that it is something due our descendants, something to be done for their sakes. Surely we owe it to future generations to pass on a world that is not a used up garbage heap. Our remote descendants are not yet present to claim a livable world as their right, but there are plenty of proxies to speak now in their behalf. These spokesmen, far from being mere custodians, are genuine representatives of future interests.

Why then deny that the human beings of the future have rights which can be claimed against us now in their behalf? Some are inclined to deny them present rights out of a fear of falling into obscure metaphysics, by granting rights to remote and unidentifiable beings who are not yet even in existence. Our unborn great-great-grandchildren are in some sense "potential" persons, but they are far more remotely potential, it may seem, than fetuses. This, however, is not the real difficulty. Unborn generations are more remotely potential than fetuses in one sense, but not in another. A much greater period of time with a far greater number of causally necessary and important events must pass before their potentiality can be actualized, it is true; but our collective posterity is just as certain to come into existence "in the normal course of events" as is any given fetus now in its mother's womb. In that sense the existence of the distant human future is no more remotely potential than that of a particular child already on its way.

The real difficulty is not that we doubt whether our descendants will ever be actual, but rather that we don't know who they will be. It is not their temporal remoteness that troubles us so much as their indeterminacy—their present facelessness and namelessness. Five centuries from now men and women will be living where we live now. Any given one of them will have an interest in living space, fertile soil, fresh air, and the like, but that arbitrarily selected one has no other qualities we can presently envision very clearly. We don't even know who his parents, grandparents, or great-grandparents are, or even whether he is related to us. Still, whoever these human beings may turn out to be, and whatever they might reasonably be expected to be like, they will have interests that we can affect, for better or worse, right now. That much we can and do know about them. The identity of the owners of these interests is now necessarily obscure, but the fact of their interest-ownership is crystal clear, and that is all that is necessary to certify the coherence of present talk about their rights. We can tell, sometimes, that shadowy forms in the spatial distance belong to human beings, though we know not who or how many they are; and this imposes a duty on us not to throw bombs, for example, in their direction. In like manner, the vagueness of the human future does not weaken its claim on us in light of the nearly certain knowledge that it will, after all, be human.

Doubts about the existence of a right to be born transfer neatly to the question of a similar right to come into existence ascribed to future generations. The rights that future generations certainly have against us are contingent rights: the interests they are sure to have when they come into being (assuming of course that they will come into being) cry out for protection from invasions that can take place now. Yet there are no actual interests, presently existent, that future generations, presently nonexistent, have now. Hence, there is no actual interest that they have in simply coming into being, and I am at a loss to think of any other reason for claiming that they have a right to come into existence (though there may well be such a reason). Suppose then that all human beings at a given time voluntarily form a compact never again to produce children, thus leading within a few decades to the end of our species. This of course is a wildly improbable hypothetical example but a rather crucial one for the position I have been tentatively considering. And we can imagine, say, that the whole world is converted to a strange ascetic religion which absolutely requires sexual abstinence for everyone. Would this arrangement violate the rights of anyone? No one can complain on behalf of presently nonexistent future generations that their future interests which give them a contingent right of protection have been violated since they will never come into existence to be wronged. My inclination then is to conclude that the suicide of our species would be deplorable, lamentable, and a deeply moving tragedy, but that it would violate no one's rights. Indeed if, contrary to fact, all human beings could ever agree to such a thing, that very agreement would be a symptom of our species' biological unsuitability for survival anyway.

Conclusion

For several centuries now human beings have run roughshod over the lands of our planet, just as if the animals who do live there and the generations of humans who will live there had no claims on them whatever. Philosophers have not helped matters by arguing that animals and future generations are not the kinds of beings who can have rights now, that they don't presently qualify for membership, even "auxiliary membership," in our moral community. I have tried in this essay to dispel the conceptual confusions that make such conclusions possible. To acknowledge their rights is the very least we can do for members of endangered species (including our own). But that is something.

Notes

[1] I shall leave the concept of a claim unanalyzed here, but for a detailed discussion, see my "The Nature and Value of Rights," *Journal of Value Inquiry* 4 (Winter 1971): 263–277.

[2] Louis B. Schwartz, "Morals, Offenses and the Model Penal Code," *Columbia Law Review* 63 (1963): 673.

[3] John Chipman Gray, *The Nature and Sources of the Law,* 2d ed. (Boston: Beacon Press, 1963), p. 43.

[4] And W. D. Ross for another. See *The Right and The Good* (Oxford: Clarendon Press, 1930), app. 1, pp. 48–56.

[5] W. D. Lamont, *Principles of Moral Judgment,* (Oxford: Clarendon Press, 1946), pp. 83–85.

[6] Cf. H. J. McCloskey, "Rights," *Philosophical Quarterly* 15 (1965): 121, 124.

[7] Ibid.

[8] Outside of Samuel Butler's *Erewhon.*

Discussion Questions

1. What is Feinberg's definition of a right? What objections can you find to it? How might these objections be answered?

2. How does Feinberg relate the issue of animal rights to the issue of the rights of unborn generations? How might Singer on the one hand and Devine on the other criticize his arguments on this point?

3. How might Feinberg's reasons for denying rights to vegetables be applied to some animals? To some human beings? Why or why not?

4. How does Feinberg argue for the rights of future generations? Support or criticize his arguments?

5. What practical conclusions would follow from Feinberg's position—would it, for example, support Singer's view? Why or why not?

The Environment, Rights, and Future Generations

Richard T. De George

The rapid growth of technology has outstripped our moral intuitions, which are consequently unclear and contradictory on many environmental issues. As we try to handle new moral problems we stretch and strain traditional moral concepts and theories. We do not always do so successfully. The difficulties, I believe, become apparent as we attempt to deal with the moral dimension of the depletion of nonrenewable resources.

Consider the use of oil, presently our chief source of energy. The supply of oil is limited. Prudence demands that we not waste it. But who has a right to the oil or to its use? From one point of view the owners of the oil have a right to it. And we each have a right to the amount we are able to buy and use. From another point of view everyone has a right to oil, since it is a natural resource which should be used for the good of all. Americans, as we know, use a great deal more oil than most other people in the world. Is it moral of us to do so? Will our use preclude people in other parts of the world from having it available to them when they will need it for uses we presently take for granted? Will some unborn generations not have the oil they will probably need to live as we presently do?

These questions trouble many people. They have a vague sense of moral uneasiness, but their intuitions concerning the proper answers are not clear. They feel that they should not waste oil or fuel or energy. They feel that they should not keep their houses as cool in summer and as warm in winter as they used to. They feel that they should impose these

From K. E. Goodposter and K. M. Sayre (eds.), *Ethics and Problems of the 20th Century* (Notre Dame University Press, 1979). Reprinted by permission of the author.

conditions on their children. Yet they are not, simply on moral grounds, ready to give up too much in the way of comfort. Once forced to do so by economics, they will. But they are somewhat uneasy about their own attitude. Is it morally proper that affluent individuals or nations are able to live in greater comfort and will have to make fewer sacrifices than the less well-to-do, simply because they have more money?

My intuitions on the issue of energy and oil are in no way privileged. I do not know how much oil or energy I have a right to; nor can I say with any certainty how much those in underdeveloped countries presently have a right to, or how much should be saved for them, or how much should be saved for generations yet to come. Nor do I know clearly how to weigh the claims to oil of the people in underdeveloped countries vis-à-vis the future claims to oil of generations yet unborn. If all presently existing members of the human race used energy at the rate that the average American does, there would obviously be much less left for future generations. Does this mean that others in the world should not use as much oil as Americans; or that Americans should use less, so that those in other countries will be able to use more; or that people in less developed countries should not use more in order that future generations of Americans will be able to use as much as present-day Americans?

Though our intuitions are not very clear on these issues, there is some consensus that present people have moral obligations vis-à-vis future generations. Yet stating the grounds for even these obligations is not an easy task, and it is one that I do not think has been adequately accomplished. The attempt to state them in terms of rights has not been fruitful. And the utilitarian or consequentialist approach has fared no better. Lack of clarity about collective responsibility further magnifies the complexity of the problem.

In this paper I shall not be able to solve the question either of the proper use of oil or of the basis of our obligations to future generations. I shall attempt only to test the ability of some moral theories and language to express them adequately. I shall negatively show why some approaches are not fruitful lines to pursue. And positively I shall argue for some considerations which I think are applicable, though by themselves they are not adequate to solve the moral problems at issue.

Talk about rights has proliferated in recent years.[1] Moral feelings and concerns have been put in terms of rights in a great many areas. It does not fit in some of them. Thus for instance some people concerned with the environment have come to speak of the rights of nature, or the rights of trees, or the rights of a landscape.[2] The intent of people who use such language is easy enough to grasp. They are concerned about man's abuse of the environment, his wanton cutting of trees, or his despoiling the countryside. But those who wish to attribute rights to nature or trees or landscapes must come up with some way of interpreting the meaning of rights which makes their assertions plausible. The usual ways of unpacking rights in terms of justifiable moral claims, or in terms of interests, or in terms of freedom do not apply to nature or trees.[3] Yet failure to provide an interpretation which both grounds the purported rights of trees and relates them to the rights of humans, while accounting for the obvious differences between them, leads to confusion and precludes arriving at a satisfactory solution to the moral problems posed.

These attempts are nonetheless instructive. For rights can be ascribed and rights-talk can be used with respect to almost anything,[4] even if the claims involved cannot always be adequately defended. When we restrict our use of rights-talk to human beings, therefore, it should be clear that the question of whether people have rights is not a factual one comparable to the question of whether they have brains, or whether they usually have two arms or two legs. The question of whether future generations have rights is similarly not one simply of fact; and the answer is compounded because there is no consensus and little precedent. Thus simply looking at ordinary language, or simply unpacking the concepts of person or rights, will not yield a definitive answer. Since the question is not a factual one, it is to be solved in part by making a decision. It is possible to say that future generations have rights. But I shall argue that we avoid more problems if we maintain that, properly speaking, future generations do not presently have rights, than if we say they do.

Future generations by definition do not now exist. They cannot now, therefore, be the present bearer or subject of anything, including rights. Hence they cannot be said to have rights in the same sense that presently existing entities can be said to have them. This follows from the briefest analysis of the present tense form of the verb "to have." To claim that what does not now exist cannot now have rights in any strong sense does not deny that persons who previously existed had rights when they existed, or that persons who will exist can properly be said to have rights when they do exist, or that classes with at least one presently existing member can correctly be said to have rights now. Nor does it deny that presently existing persons can and sometimes do make rights claims for past or future persons. It emphasizes, however, that in ascribing rights to persons who do not exist it is the existing person who is expressing his interests or concerns.

Those who claim that present existence is not necessary for the proper ascription of present rights sometimes cite the legal treatment of wills as a counterexample. In this instance, they argue, the courts act as if the deceased continued to have rights, despite the fact that he no longer exists. But this is not the only way of construing wills or the actions of courts. If we consider those countries in which inheritance laws were suddenly changed so that all the property of a deceased went to the state rather than to the heirs named in a will, it would be more plausible to argue that the rights of a particular heir were violated rather than the rights of the deceased. Equally plausible construals can, I believe, be made for each of the other standard supposed counterexamples.[5]

Consider next the supposed present rights of some future individual. Before conception potential parents can and should take into account the obligations they will have in connection with caring for the children they might produce. They can and should consider the rights their children will have if they come into being. But since the children do not yet exist, we should properly say they do not now have rights. Among the rights they do not have (since they have none) is the right to come into existence. By not bringing them into existence we do not violate *that* right, and we can obviously prevent their having any other rights. Now if we attempt to speak otherwise, I suggest, we invite confusion. What sense would it make to say that some entity which was not conceived had a right to be conceived? We cannot sensibly or intelligibly answer the question of whose right was infringed when there is no bearer of the right.

A similar difficulty, and therefore a similar reason for not using rights-talk, arises in speaking of the rights of future generations, providing we mean by that term some generation no members of which have presently been conceived and so in no sense presently exist. Such future generations could at least in theory be prevented from coming into existence. If they were never produced it would be odd to say that their rights had been violated. For since they do not now exist they can have no right to exist or to be produced. Now, they have no present rights at all.

Nonetheless possible future entities can be said to have possible future rights. And future generations when they exist will have rights at that time. But the temptation to consider all rights as temporally on a par should be resisted. Moreover, the weight which should now be given to the rights claims which future individuals or future generations will have should be proportional to the likelihood that such individuals will exist, and by analogy with the case of parents the obligations should be borne by those individuals (and collectively by those groups) most responsible for bringing the individuals into existence.

Future persons do not, individually or as a class, presently have the right to existing resources. They differ from presently existing persons who in general have the right to the judicious use of the goods necessary for them to continue in existence. And if some of these goods, because of present rational demands, are used up, then it is a mistake to say that future persons or future generations have or will have a right to *those* goods and that we violate their rights by using them up. Future generations or future individuals or groups should correctly be said to have a right only to what is available when they come into existence, and hence when their possible future rights become actual and present.

Many people feel that this is incorrect and that future persons and generations have as much right as presently existing persons to what presently exists, for example, in the way of resources. A few considerations, however, should suffice to show that such a view is mistaken. The first consideration is conceptual. Only once a being exists does *it* have needs or wants or interests. It has a right only to the kind of treatment or to the goods available to it at the time of its conception. It cannot have a reasonable claim to what is not available. Consider this on an individual level. Suppose a couple are so constituted that if they have a child, the child will have some disease, for example, sickle-cell anemia. Suppose the woman conceives. Does the fetus or baby have a right not to have sickle-cell anemia? Before it was conceived there was no entity to have any rights. Once it is conceived, its genetic make-up is such as it is. It makes no sense to speak of *its* having the right not to have the genetic make-up it has, since the alternative is its not being. This does not mean that it does not have the right to treatment, that if genetic engineering is able to remedy its defect it does not have the right to such remedy, and so on. But it does mean that there is no *it* to have rights before conception and that once conceived it is the way it is. There is therefore no sense in speaking of the antecedent right for it not to be the way it is, though it may have a subsequent right to treatment. Similarly, prehistoric cave men had no right to electric lights or artificial lungs since they were not available in their times, and we have no right to enjoy the sight of extinct animals. To claim a right to what is not available and cannot be made available is to speak vacuously. Some future people, therefore, will have no right to the use of gas, or oil, or coal, if, when they come into existence, such goods no longer exist. If the goods in question are not available, *they* could not be produced with a right to them.

Second, suppose we attempt to speak otherwise. Suppose we assume that all future generations have the same right to oil as we do; and suppose that since it is a nonrenewable resource, it is used up—as it is likely to be—by some future generation. What of the next generation that follows it? Should we say that since that generation cannot be produced without violating its right to oil it has a right not to be produced? Surely not. Or should we say that if it is produced one of its rights is necessarily infringed, and that the right of all succeeding generations will similarly necessarily be infringed? It is possible to speak that way; but to do so is at least confusing and at worst undermines the whole concept of rights by making rights claims vacuous.

The third reason for not speaking of the rights of future generations as if their rights were present rights is that it leads to impossible demands on us. Suppose we consider oil once again. It is a nonrenewable resource and is limited in quantity. How many generations in the future are we to allow to have present claim to it? Obviously if we push the generations into the unlimited future and divide the oil deposits by the number of people, we each end up with the right to a gallon or a quart or a teaspoon or a thimble full. So we must construe the claim to refer to the practical use of oil. But this means that we inevitably preclude some future generation from having oil. And if all future generations have equal claim, then we necessarily violate the rights of some future generations. It is clear, then, that we do not wish to let unending future claims have equal weight with present claims.

The alternative, if we do not consistently treat future rights differently from the rights of presently existing persons, is arbitrarily to treat some rights, those of sufficiently distant generations, as less deserving of consideration than the same claims of generations closer to us. What I have been arguing is that our approach turns out to be less arbitrary and more consistent if we refuse to take even the first step in considering future rights as anything other than future, and if we do not confuse them or equate them with the rights of presently existing people.

To ascribe present rights to future generations is to fall into the trap of being improperly motivated to sacrifice the present to the future, on the grounds that there will possibly (or probably) be so innumerably many future generations, each of which has a presently equal right to what is now available, as to dwarf the rights of present people to existing goods. The trap can be avoided by maintaining that present existence is a necessary condition for the possession of a present right. To the extent that rights-talk tends to be nontemporal and future generations are considered to have present rights, such talk tends to confuse rather than clarify our obligations for the future, and the ground for such obligations. For this and similar reasons future generations should not be said to have present rights.

If the argument so far is correct, however, we have not solved a problem, but merely seen how not to approach it if we want a solution. That future generations do not have present rights does not mean that present people, individually and collectively, have no obligations to try to provide certain kinds of environment and to leave open as many possibilities as feasible for those who will probably come after them, consistent with satisfying their own rational needs and wants. How are we to describe this felt moral imperative?

If the language of rights will not do, a theory such as utilitarianism does not fare much better. Consider once again the problem of how much oil we can legitimately use and how much we are morally obliged to save for future generations. Let every person count for one and let us decide on the basis of what produces the greatest good for the greatest number of people. The task is difficult enough in dealing with micro-moral problems, though we have the history of human experience to help us solve with at least a certain amount of assurance many ordinary moral questions. We can be fairly sure that lying in general is wrong, as is murder, and theft, and perjury, and so on.

When we try to carry out the analysis with respect to nonrenewable resources, the question of how many future generations we are to count is one problem. We have already seen the difficulties it leads to. Second, we cannot know how long people will actually need oil. We cannot know when a substitute will be found. We therefore do not know how many generations to count and how many to discount. Third, generations of people lived long before oil was discovered and put to its present uses. As oil becomes less available, if no substitute is found people may have to go back to doing things the way they did before the discovery of oil. Will such a world be morally poorer than ours? On a utilitarian calculation the answer may well be negative. But we can plausibly argue that good is not maximized if we waste our resources and that more good will probably be done for more people if we stretch out our resources while providing for our own rational needs. The difficulty of course consists in specifying our rational and justifiable needs. Utilitarianism does not help us do this, nor does it help us decide between the somewhat greater good (however defined) or presently existing people versus the lesser good of more people in the future when the totals are equal. Therefore this approach, too, does not provide the key for determining the proper use of our nonrenewable resources.

There is another dimension to the problem, however, which I have ignored thus far and which it would be well to consider at least briefly. With respect to the use of oil and future generations I have spoken of "we" and "they" and have traded on our common understanding of the terms. Moral obligation and responsibility, however, have for the most part been discussed in individual terms. The notion of collective responsibility and collective obligation and other collectively applied moral terms are in need of clarification. The concept of collective responsibility, for instance, despite some of the work that has been done on it,[6] remains in many cases obscure.

One difficulty arises in attempting to allocate individual responsibility under conditions in which individual effort has no real effect by itself. Who is responsible for preserving the environment for our children and grandchildren? The answer may be all of us. But what is required of each of us individually is far from clear. How responsible for strip mining is a carpenter in New York City? How responsible for oil depletion is someone who drives to work in a car? Is he morally obliged to drive less or not at all or to buy and use a smaller car? What if smaller cars are not available or if he cannot afford to buy one or if none of his neighbors drive less or buy smaller cars? Is the collective responsibility to fall primarily on collective agencies—on corporations and government? But this collective responsibility must also be allocated to individuals. Does each person have a responsibility to preserve resources no matter what others do? Or is it a prima facie obligation which becomes a real obligation only when our action and the action of others will effect the results desired? Are we therefore individually freed of our responsibility when others do not do their share? Does collective failure to fulfill a collective moral obligation absolve an individual of his individual obligation to do what he should under the collective obligation on the grounds that his sacrifice without that of the others is inefficacious? My claim is not that these questions do not have answers but that they have not been sufficiently discussed and that until we get clear about the answers we are unlikely to feel the pressure of the moral obligations we may have or to be able to weigh them against the individual moral pressures we feel with respect, for instance, to supplying our children or our fellow citizens with as high a quality of life as we can.

Consider further the questions of resources in the light of populations. If the population of one country grows unchecked to the detriment of the people of that country and to the exhaustion of that country's resources, do the people of other countries have the obligation to keep alive the individuals produced by parents who had no regard for whether the children could be supported? Who is the "we" who should preserve resources, and for whom should they be preserved? If the people of one nation sacrifice, should it be the heirs of that nation's people who reap the rewards of such sacrifice, or should it be all people wherever they might be and whoever they are? On the one hand our intuitions tell us that no country can do everything for the whole world, that people have to help themselves, and that each country's primary responsibility is to its own people and their descendants. On the other hand we have the unrelieved plight of human misery and death, some of which could be alleviated if some peoples would share more of what they have. By what right do some use many times more in the way of natural resources than others, especially when it is not by merit but partially by luck that they have natural riches available to them that are not available in their own countries to other people?

I mentioned earlier that our moral intuitions were still inadequate to some of the moral problems which seem to be looming before us. Part of the reason is that we have no precedent on which to build. Another is that we have no adequate institutions and practices on a global scale with which to relate global moral problems. Morality is a social institution and moral obligations are often closely tied to particular social practices. The moral obligations of parents with respect to their children, for instance, are different in a society with a nuclear family in which parents have almost exclusive responsibility for the support and care of their children, and in a society in which all children are raised by the state, cared for in communal nurseries, state schools, and so on. Moral problems about the use of resources and the preservation of the environment transcend national boundaries. Yet we have no world institutions or practices adequate to help ground pertinent moral judgments.

National sovereignty may be an anachronism in an age of such interdependence. But while it remains it sets a real limit to certain kinds of moral obligations richer nations have to poorer ones. Within the boundaries of a given country transfer payments can be effected in a variety of ways and are justified within the system because they achieve their goals. Within the system one practice fits together with others. But on the global scale there is no system, there is little in the way of enforceable law, there is great diversity of political systems, and there is disagreement about moral claims. Transfer payments from rich to poor within a nation can be handled, as in the United States, through taxes agreed to by the legislature representing the people. Internationally there is no such system. The extrapolation from individual moral cases to parallel national or collective cases consequently frequently falters.

If my analysis so far is correct the new large moral questions which are impinging upon us cannot be solved all at once. It may be that the most we can do individually—and where possible collectively—is to work on clarifying the problems, to suggest solutions, to impel others to work toward them, to be willing to cooperate in transcending national boundaries, to give up national sovereignty, and so on.

I have been arguing that environmental problems have developed faster than our intuitions, theories, practices, and institutions, and that some attempts to stretch our theories to fit our vague intuitions have not been successful. Yet I do not wish to imply that we are at a total loss from a moral point of view with respect to environmental problems or that they are ultimately unsolvable. I shall briefly argue three points, the first of which, I believe, is relatively uncontroversial and requires little defense.

Consider a couple planning to have a baby. Before they conceive him they have an obligation to be reasonably sure that they can raise him properly, that he will have enough to eat, and that he will under ordinary circumstances have the opportunity to grow and develop. Parents who knowingly and willingly have children whom they know they and their society cannot care for, who they know will soon die of starvation or disease, do not, if my earlier analysis is correct, violate any purported antecedent rights of the child. But they certainly seem to produce suffering and misery which they could have avoided producing. We can plausibly argue that we individually have an obligation to provide the minimum goods of life necessary for those for whom we have a rather close responsibility. And collectively we have a similar responsibility for preserving the environment in such a way that it can provide the goods necessary for those who come after us—or for roughly fifty or a hundred years. To be uncontroversial, however, the claim must be restricted to those for whom we have a rather close responsibility. For the obligation of care is tied to the causal chain of reproduction. If the population of one country goes unchecked to the detriment of the people of that country, it is not clear that other countries have the obligation to keep alive the individuals so produced. It may be that richer countries have some obligations in this regard. But it is clear that the obligation of the members of a society to care for their own people is greater than the obligation to care for people of other societies.

My two other claims are more controversial and may seem to some mistaken; hence they deserve more comment. The first is that we do not owe to others, either outside our society or to those who will come after us, what we need to maintain a reasonable quality of life and dignity for the present members of our society; the second is that we do not owe others, either in other societies or those who will come after us, a better life than we ourselves are able to attain and enjoy. Present sacrifice for a better future for others may be a noble, altruistic goal. But it is not morally demanded and cannot be legitimately forced on those who do not wish to be noble, altruistic, or heroic.

Moral theorists have long argued that each human being, if the resources are available, deserves enough of the goods of life so that he can enjoy at least a minimal standard of living required for human dignity. My claim is consistent with that view. It allows room for the moral obligation of those who are well off to help bring those below the minimal standard of dignity up to that standard. How that is to be done within our own society is easier to determine than how that is to be effectively achieved on a global scale. But my claim denies that any generation or people have to fall below that level in order to help others rise above it. The argument for that is fairly straightforward.

Starting from the equality of all persons qua persons my good for me is as valuable as your good for you. Other things being equal your good is not better or more important than mine. Hence, again other things being equal, there is no reason why, given a choice, I should be morally obliged to choose your good over mine. Otherwise, by like reasoning you would have to choose my good over yours. Secondly, my claim is that other things being equal those who, where it is possible to avoid it, bring misery on themselves or on those close to them, are the ones who should bear the brunt of consequences of their actions. This is part of what it means to accept the moral responsibility for one's actions. Hence there are limits to the sacrifice which can be morally required of one people to help those less well off than they. One limit is that equality is not required; what is required is simply helping those below the minimal standard to rise up to it. Another limit is that those who are aided can legitimately be expected, as a condition of such aid, to take the means available to them to help themselves.

My second more controversial claim was that there is no moral imperative that requires each generation to sacrifice so that the next generation may be better off than it is. Parents do not owe their children better lives than they had. They may wish their children to have better lives; but they do not owe it to them. If there is to be a peak followed by a decline in the standard of living, and if such a peak is tied to the use of natural resources, then providing there is no profligate waste, there is no reason why the present rather than a future generation should enjoy that peak. For no greater good is served by any future group enjoying the peak, since when its turn comes, if enjoying the peak is improper for us, it will be improper for them also.

We do not owe future generations a better life than we enjoy nor do we owe them resources we need for ourselves. When dealing with renewable resources, other things being equal, they should not be used up faster than they can be replaced. When they are needed at a greater rate than they can be replaced, they raise the same problem raised by nonrenewable resources. We should use what we *need,* but we should keep our needs rational, avoid waste, and preserve the environment as best we can. How this is to be translated into the specific allocation of goods and resources is not to be determined a priori or by the fiat of government but by as many members of the society at large who are interested and aware and informed enough to help in the decision-making process. Part of that process must involve clarifying the moral dimensions of the use of resources and developing the moral theory to help us state consistently and evaluate our moral intuitions.

Up until relatively recent times it may have seemed that each generation was better off than the previous one, and that just as each successive generation had received a better lot than its predecessor, it had an obligation to continue the process. But we are now at the stage where our own efforts are frequently counterproductive. Our progress in transportation has led to pollution; our progress in pest control has led to new strains of insects resistant to our chemicals or has resulted in pollution of our food; our expansion of industry has taken its toll in our rivers and in the ocean; and so on. We are now faced with shortages of the type we used to experience only during war times. So we can argue that in some ways we are already over the peak and will all be forced to cut down on certain kinds of consumption. That our children have to bear our fate is no reason for reproach. What would be reprehensible on the individual levee is if we lived in luxury and allowed our children to exist at a subsistence level. It is appropriate that we help them to live as well as we, where that is possible. But we have no responsibility for helping them live better at great expense to ourselves. Nor does it make much sense to speak in those terms where overlapping generations are concerned.

What I have been maintaining is that we should be careful not to assume the burden of the future on some mistaken notion of the need to sacrifice the present to the future. The past appeal of the call to sacrifice the present to the future depended on the foreseeable future being increasingly better, and each generation both being better off than the previous one and worse off than the following in an unending chain. The realization that the goods of the earth are limited should mitigate somewhat that appeal. The earth will not in the foreseeable future be able to support limitless numbers of human beings at a high standard of living.

There is one last caveat that I should like to add, however. I have been arguing that we do not owe the future more than we have in the way of goods of the earth or in terms of standard of living. This does not mean that we do not owe them the benefit of what we have learned, that we should not preserve and pass on culture, knowledge, moral values— all increased to the extent possible. For standard of living is not the only good in life and quality of life should not be confused with quantity of goods. In fact, if we do soon suffer a decline in our standard of living either voluntarily by freely sacrificing for others or simply because we use up our resources before we find adequate substitutes, then what we should pass on to our children are the qualities of mind and spirit which will help them to cope with what they have, to live as fully as possible with what is available, and to value the quality of life rather than the quantity of goods they have.

My three claims are not a solution to the problems of limited resources or a full analysis of what we owe to future generations. They are a start which needs a fuller theory to ground it and a set of institutions to work within. But they do not constitute a call to selfishness. Enlightened self-interest may well benefit mankind as a whole more than unenlightened self-sacrifice, even if the latter could be sold to large segments of the world's population. For we have come to a point where, if we limit our use and abuse of the environment, it is in our self-interest to do so. The needs of the present and of already existing generations should take precedence over consideration of the needs of those who may exist at some far distant time. Perhaps all we can expect is that each generation look that far ahead.

The moral issues raised by environmental questions are in some ways truly new and test both our moral intuitions and concepts. Not all our moral values and intuitions are inapplicable. But we have much analytic work to do before we can fully and clearly state—much less solve—some of the problems which face us.

Notes

[1]See Rex Martin and James W. Nickel, "A Bibliography on the Nature and Foundations of Rights 1947–1977," *Political Theory* (forthcoming).

[2]See, for example, Aldo Leopold, *A Sand Country Almanac and Sketches Here and There* (New York: Oxford University Press, 1949); Christopher Stone, *Should Trees Have Standing?: Toward Legal Rights for Natural Objects* (Los Altos, Calif.: Kaufmann, 1974).

[3]H. L. A. Hart, "Are There Any Natural Rights?," *Philosophical Review* 64 (1955): 175–91 argues that the natural right of men to be free is basic; Joel Feinberg, "Duties, Rights and Claims," *American Philosophical Quarterly* 3 (1966): 137–44; David Lyons, "The Correlativity of Rights and Duties," *Nous* 4 (1970): 45–57.

[4]H. J. McCloskey, "Rights," *Philosophical Quarterly* 15 (1965): 115–27, raises the question of whether art objects can have rights. A number of philosophers have recently argued for the rights of animals: Andrew Linzey, *Animal Rights* (London: S. C. M. Press, 1976); Peter Singer, *Animal Liberation* (London: Jonathan Cape, 1976); on the other hand, see Joseph Margolis, "Animals Have No Rights and Are Not Equal to Humans," *Philosophic Exchange* 1 (1974): 119–23. See also M. and N. Golding, "Value Issues in Landmark Preservation," in K. E. and K. M. Sayre, *Ethics and Problems of the 20th Century* (Notre Dame University Press, 1979).

[5]Joel Feinberg, "The Rights of Animals and Unborn Generations" [preceding selection in this chapter], defends the opposite view.

[6]See Peter A. French, ed., *Individual and Collective Responsibility: Massacre at My Lai* (Cambridge, Mass.: Schenkman 1972); Joel Feinberg, "Collective Responsibility," *Journal of Philosophy* 45 (1968): 674–87; W. H. Walsh, "Pride, Shame and Responsibility," *The Philosophical Quarterly* 20 (1970): 1–13; D. E. Cooper, "Collective Responsibility" *Philosophy* 43 (1968): 258–68.

Discussion Questions

1. In what ways does De George think that "the rapid growth of technology has outstripped our moral intuitions"? What does this show about his general views of ethical theory?

2. What are De George's arguments against extending the concept of rights to future generations, animals, and the environment? Support or criticize his arguments.

3. What are De George's objections to a utilitarian solution to the problems he discusses? How might a utilitarian reply?

4. What difficulties does De George see concerning responsibility for use of natural resources? Support or criticize his arguments on this point.

5. De George claims that we do not owe to other nations or future generations that which we need for a reasonable quality of life. He also claims we do not owe them a better life than that which we have. Support or criticize his arguments on these points.

Suggested Readings for Chapter Nine

Goodpaster, K. E., and K. M. Sayke, eds. *Ethics and Problems of the 21st Century.* Notre Dame, Ind.: Notre Dame University Press, 1979.

Regan, Tom, and Peter Singer, eds. *Animal Rights and Human Obligations.* Englewood Cliffs, N.J.: Prentice-Hall, 1976.

Singer, Peter, *Animal Liberation.* New York: New York Review, 1975.

Stone, Christopher. *Should Trees Have Standing?* Los Altos, Calif.: Kaufman, 1974.